The Good Hotel Guide 2017

GREAT BRITAIN & IRELAND

Editors
M Astella
Adam Raphael
Nicola Davies

Editor in Chief
Caroline Raphael

THE GOOD HOTEL GUIDE LTD

The Good Hotel Guide Ltd

This edition first published in 2016 by
The Good Hotel Guide Ltd

Copyright © 2016 Adam and Caroline Raphael
Maps © 2016 David Perrott

Consulting editor: Desmond Balmer
Chief executive: Richard Fraiman

Contributing editors:
Rose Shepherd
Emma Grundy Haigh
Bonnie Friend
Catherine Charles
Claire Baranowski

Production: Hugh Allan
Managing editor: Alison Wormleighton
Designer: Lizzy Laczynska
Text editor: Daphne Trotter
Computer consultant: Vince Nacey
Website design: HeadChannel
Researcher: Cristina Recio-Corral

A CIP catalogue record for this book may be found in the British Library.

ISBN 978 0 9932484 1 2

Cover photograph: Hambleton Hall, Hambleton

Printed and bound in Spain by Graphy Cems

*'A good hotel is where
the guest comes first'*

Hilary Rubinstein, founding editor
(1926–2012)

A good hotel is where the guest comes first

Hilary Rubinstein, founding Editor

CONTENTS

CONTENTS

INTRODUCTION

The Good Hotel Guide was founded nearly 40 years ago to promote small, independent hotels; to shine a spotlight on the best (often family-owned and managed) spots where guests could be assured of a genuine welcome and more than a pinch of personality. Down country lanes, along riverside paths, on city squares, we have continued that tradition. This year, you'll find old favourites still going strong, plus many enticing new suggestions. We want to tell you about crab shacks and coastal views, about rambling farmhouses and rooftop Airstream trailers, about waking to the sight of the steam train on the horizon. Read on: you'll discover more than one throne loo, and lots of cream teas.

Another tradition we proudly uphold: our team of inspectors and dedicated readers, who report on the best hotels, inns and B&Bs with real character. Our editors rely on these reports to write the 414 main entries, and the 411 Shortlist ones, in the Guide. Previous César winners, provided they have maintained their high standards, retain their award. The Guide does not accept payment or hospitality for an entry, giving us the freedom to make an unbiased judgment.

Elsewhere, new traditions are falling into place. The Good Hotel Guide website, along with our social media efforts on Twitter and Facebook, continues to win fans and followers. This year, we're developing a new website, which we have redesigned to make more of a splash online. You'll find a more efficient search function, easier readability, and larger, more inviting photographs, which show you where you'll be putting your feet up, wandering in suntrap gardens or hunkering down by a log fire.

As before, most, but not all, of the hotels in this volume are represented on the Good Hotel Guide website. We ask our UK and Ireland hotels to pay a modest fee for their entry to appear online; if they choose not to pay, their listing remains, without the full content.

Don't forget that we also have plenty of ideas for great places to visit on the Continent and around the world. Go to our website to find out which of the nearly 500 Guide-approved hotels you'll be staying in the next time you strike out further afield.

M. Astella Saw and Adam Raphael
July 2016

HOW TO USE THE GOOD HOTEL GUIDE

MAIN ENTRY

The 414 main entries, which are given a full page each, are those we believe to be the best of their type in Great Britain and Ireland.

Colour bands identify country; London has its own section.

An index at the back lists hotels by county; another index lists them by hotel name.

Hotels are listed alphabetically under the name of the town or village.

This hotel is making its first appearance, is returning after an absence, or has been upgraded from the Shortlist.

The maps at the back of the book are divided into grids for easy reference. A small house indicates a main entry, a triangle a Shortlist one.

We try to indicate whether a hotel can accommodate wheelchair-users. It's always worth calling the hotel to check the details of wheelchair access.

We name readers who have endorsed a hotel; we do not name inspectors, readers who ask to remain anonymous, or those who have written a critical report.

The panel provides the contact details, number of bedrooms and facilities.

---

130 ENGLAND

CHADDESLEY CORBETT Worcestershire   Map 3:C5

BROCKENCOTE HALL   NEW

In a 'lovely' sweep of green, this lakeside country house hotel is 'just about perfect in every way', say regular Guide correspondents, whose enthusiasm earns it a full entry this year. 'The staff are helpful, friendly and professional, the ambience exudes comfort, and encourages total relaxation.' Fresh flower arrangements and traditional elements (oil paintings, gilt candlesticks, an oak-carved bar) give the place a refined feel; find a favourite spot to sit by the open fire. The gracious bedrooms, ranging in size, are individually decorated in country house style, with fine views over the estate. 'Housekeeping is excellent.' Dinner is an attraction, with chef Adam Brown's modern mix of local produce, wild plants and home-grown fruit – perhaps duck breast, spelt, broccoli, blackberry, confit gizzards. 'The food in the beautiful restaurant was stalled, inventive, and a joy to experience.' Informal meals – 'less complex, but full of flavour, and very good' – are taken in the bar. Pretty Chaddesley Corbett village, with its real ale pubs, is worth a visit; there's no small amount of rustic pork pies nearby. (Graham and Elizabeth Collingham)

25% DISCOUNT VOUCHERS

Chaddesley Corbett
DY10 4PY

T: 01562 777876
F: 01562 777872
E: info@brockencotehall.com
W: www.brockencotehall.com

BEDROOMS: 21. Some on ground floor, 1 suitable for disabled.
OPEN: all year.
FACILITIES: lift, hall, lounge bar, library, restaurant, function facilities, free Wi-Fi, in-room TV (Freeview), civil wedding licence, 72-acre grounds (gardens, lake, fishing, croquet, tennis).
BACKGROUND MUSIC: all day in public areas.
LOCATION: 5 miles SE of Kidderminster.
CHILDREN: all ages welcomed.
DOGS: not allowed.
CREDIT CARDS: Amex, MasterCard, Visa.
PRICES: B&B from £135, D,B&B from £225. Set dinner £45, à la carte £60.

www.goodhotelguide.com

This hotel has agreed to give Guide readers a 25% discount off its normal bed-and-breakfast rate for one night only, subject to availability. Terms and conditions apply.

We give the range of room or B&B prices for 2017, or the 2016 prices when we went to press. The price for dinner is for a set meal, or the average cost of three courses from an à la carte menu.

HOW TO USE THE GOOD HOTEL GUIDE

SHORTLIST ENTRY

The Shortlist includes untested new entries and places we think should be appropriate in areas where we have limited choice. It also includes some hotels about which we have not had recent reports. There are no photographs; many of the hotels have chosen to be included, with pictures, on our website.

In some cases we list the entry under the nearest town.

Many readers tell us they find background music irritating. We tell you if music is played and where you might encounter it.

These are abbreviated descriptions listing the essential facilities.

Dinner prices are either for a set menu or an estimate of the likely price of a three-course meal.

This hotel has agreed to give Guide readers a 25% discount off its normal bed-and-breakfast rate for one night only, subject to availability. Terms and conditions apply.

ENGLAND 575

(1 on ground floor). Per room B&B £110–£130 (2-night min. stay preferred at weekends). Closed Christmas Day, New Year.

TENBURY WELLS Worcestershire
Map 3:C5
THE TALBOT INN, Newnham Bridge, WR15 8JF. Tel 01584 781941, www.talbotinnnewnhambridge.co.uk. 'A super all-round stay.' Fields of growing hops surround this red-brick former coaching inn in the Teme valley; inside the 19th-century building, order a local real ale or cider in the hop-hung bar. At lunch and dinner, chef Jacob Vaughan cooks an 'excellent, varied' menu, perhaps 'an enjoyable sirloin steak with all the trimmings'. Long country walks leave you famished? Pop in for an 'early bird' supper before retiring to one of the 'modern, bright and immaculately kept' bedrooms. 'Ours, of a good size, had a super-king-size bed, soft linen and pillows, a flask of fresh milk for hot drinks. In the natural-stone bathroom: a walk-in shower and lovely, fluffy towels.' Barnaby Williams is the 'hard-working, ever-present' host; his staff are 'friendly' and 'efficient'. 3 dining areas (optional background music), snug, bar. Free Wi-Fi, in-room TV (Freeview). Small function facilities. Garden. Parking. Children (extra beds; £10 per night) and dogs (allowed in 3 rooms; £10 per night) welcomed. Off the A456, 4 miles from Tenbury Wells. 7 bedrooms. Per room B&B £70–£110. Dinner £30, three-course 'early bird' supper £15 (Mon–Fri). 2-night min. stay at weekends May–Sept. Closed 2–12 Jan.
25% DISCOUNT VOUCHERS

TETBURY Gloucestershire
Map 3:E5
THE ROYAL OAK, 1 Cirencester Road, GL8 8EY. Tel 01666 500021, www.theroyaloaktetbury.co.uk. Family-friendly, dog-friendly, all around fun and lively, Chris York and Kate Lewis's pub-with-rooms attracts locals and passers-by with its real ales, updated pub menu, and bright-and-breezy vibe. The jukebox gets the thumbs-up, too. The buzzy bar and raftered restaurant occupy the 18th-century stone inn – here, chef Richard Simms's cooking, including a noteworthy vegan menu, is inspired by the seasons and the 'superb' Cotswold producers. In the summer months, the informal atmosphere spills outside, when food is served from a vintage Airstream trailer on the terrace. Rustic bedrooms are in a separate building across the courtyard. Pick a top-floor room for the views across the valley; for more space, lounge in the Oak Lodge mezzanine suite, which has leather armchairs and a wood-burner. Bar, restaurant (closed Sun eve), private dining/meeting room. Free Wi-Fi, in-room TV (Freeview). Background music, monthly live music sessions. Large garden (boules pitch). Parking. Bike shed. Children (special menu; games; not after 8 pm in restaurant; beds £30 per night) and dogs (in ground-floor rooms; £10 per night) welcomed. 6 bedrooms (1 suitable for disabled). Per room B&B £85–£170. Dinner £25. 2-night min. bookings preferred. Closed 1–2 weeks Jan.
25% DISCOUNT VOUCHERS

THORNTON HOUGH Merseyside
Map 4:E2
MERE BROOK HOUSE, Thornton Common Road, Wirral, CH63 0LU. Tel 07713 189949, www.merebrookhouse.co.uk. On the edge

www.goodhotelguide.com

CÉSARS 2017

We give our César awards to the ten best hotels of the year. Named after César Ritz, the most celebrated of hoteliers, these are the Oscars of hotel-keeping.

☘ COUNTRY HOUSE HOTEL OF THE YEAR
Gravetye Manor, East Grinstead
In glorious grounds, this Elizabethan manor house maintains period charm with utter unpretentiousness. It is managed in a personal style by Andrew Thomason. Come hungry: the exquisite Michelin-starred dishes draw inspiration from the vast kitchen garden.

☘ CITY HOTEL OF THE YEAR
Brocco on the Park, Sheffield
A Scandi-chic interior and buzzy 'neighbourhood kitchen' make Tiina Carr's smart hotel a vibrant urban hub. The bedrooms are modern and modish; the food is adventurous – try the local wild nettle purée. A bonus? Borrowable bicycles for city exploration.

☘ INN OF THE YEAR
The Nobody Inn, Doddiscombsleigh
Sue Burdge's jolly village pub-with-rooms bursts with local flavour, good-humoured charm and no small number of malt whiskies. No cutting-edge style here; just character and good cheer.

☘ NEWCOMER OF THE YEAR
The Royal Oak, Swallowcliffe
Immaculately refurbished, this thatched-roof 19th-century inn has custom-designed furniture and well-chosen pieces throughout. Bedrooms are country fresh and country chic; downstairs, join the locals dropping in for sophisticated, satisfying pub classics.

☘ SEASIDE HOTEL OF THE YEAR
Hell Bay Hotel, Bryher
On the smallest of the inhabited Isles of Scilly, Robert Dorrien-Smith's family-friendly hotel stands in beautifully tended gardens, and has breezy, coastal bedrooms within. Sample seasonal modern dishes, or head to the convivial Crab Shack for straight-from-the-boat shellfish.

⚜ FAMILY HOTEL OF THE YEAR
The Blakeney Hotel, Blakeney
Traditional in the best of ways, the Stannard family's
quayside hotel is popular with multigenerational
groups, who praise the cheery staff and the tranquil
marshland views. Beaches are nearby – get ready to
shake the sand out of shoes big and small.

⚜ VALUE HOTEL OF THE YEAR
Battlesteads, Hexham
On the edge of the Northumberland national park,
Dee and Richard Slade run their personable pub, hotel
and restaurant along green lines. Imaginative, modern
dinners are superb; the dark-sky observatory is simply
stellar.

⚜ SCOTTISH HOTEL OF THE YEAR
The Cross at Kingussie, Kingussie
By the River Gynack, this restaurant-with-rooms
pleases with its modern Scottish meals and lively
atmosphere. Come on the overnight sleeper train
– the warm hospitality from hosts Celia and Derek
Kitchingman is a wonderful thing to wake to.

⚜ RESTAURANT-WITH-ROOMS OF THE YEAR
The Hardwick, Abergavenny
Provenance is everything at Stephen and Joanna Terry's
friendly restaurant-with-rooms. Dine on generous
portions of Wye valley produce bang on season, then
retire to a contemporary courtyard room – and curl up
in a Welsh wool blanket, of course.

⚜ WELSH GUEST HOUSE OF THE YEAR
Ael y Bryn, Eglwyswrw
Feel properly spoiled: from royal breakfasts to sociable
dinners, Robert Smith and Arwel Hughes, generous
hosts, have thought of everything a guest might need in
their comfortable, well-thought-out home – including
freshly baked Welsh cakes at teatime.

REPORT OF THE YEAR COMPETITION

Readers' contributions are the lifeblood of the Good Hotel Guide. Everyone who writes to us is a potential winner of the Report of the Year competition. Each year we single out the writers of the most helpful reports. They win a copy of the Good Hotel Guide and an invitation to our annual launch party in October. This year's ten winners are:

CHRISTOPHER BORN of Doncaster
ANGIE DAVIES of Steyning
DIANA GOODEY of South Brent
ROBERT GRIMLEY of Oxford
CHARLES MEDAWAR of London
ANGELA NEUSTATTER of London
FRANCES AND HUMPHREY NORRINGTON of Berkhamsted
JOHN SAUL of Bedford
MABEL TANNAHILL of Cardiff
SUSAN WILLMINGTON of London

JOIN THE GOOD HOTEL GUIDE READERS' CLUB

Send us a review of your favourite hotel.
As a member of the club, you will be entitled to:

1. A pre-publication discount offer
2. Personal advice on hotels
3. Advice if you are in dispute with a hotel
4. Monthly emailed Guide newsletter

The writers of the ten best reviews will each win a free copy of the Guide and an invitation to our launch party. And the winner of our monthly web competition will win a free night, dinner and breakfast for two at one of the Guide's top hotels.

Send your review via
our website: www.goodhotelguide.com
or email: editor@goodhotelguide.com
or fax: 020 7602 4182
or write to:
Good Hotel Guide
50 Addison Avenue
London W11 4QP
England

EDITOR'S CHOICE

A visit to a hotel should be a special occasion. Here are some of our favourite hotels in various categories. Turn to the full entry for the bigger picture.

RED LION INN
BABCARY
A hive of community activity, Clare and Charlie Garrard's creeper-covered Somerset inn looks the thatched-roof part: step in to find local ales, table skittles, tasty pub classics, a leather sofa by the wood-burning stove. Decorated with local artwork, modern bedrooms (two accommodate a family) are in a converted barn across the pretty garden. Sleep well, then wake to large bowls of coffee at breakfast.
Read more, page 81

THE GALLIVANT
CAMBER
There's 'a sense of fun' at Harry Cragoe's family-friendly restaurant-with-rooms across the road from the sea grass-fringed dunes at Camber Sands. Airy, newly refurbished bedrooms – some with a private deck, others opening on to the coastal garden – look to New England for inspiration. Plunder the Larder of Guilty Pleasure for popcorn and champagne, then relax in the massage hut after a day at the beach.
Read more, page 124.

FOREST SIDE
GRASMERE
Choose among the super-stylish, super-soothing bedrooms at Andrew Wildsmith's much-rejuvenated modern-rustic Victorian pile, in the Lake District spot which Wordsworth considered 'the loveliest'. Dinner – based on a forage-to-fork philosophy – is highly praised, with adventurous modern menus from chef Kevin Tickle. When night falls, settle in – you'll have a 'sumptuous' bed, organic toiletries and home-baked biscuits.
Read more, page 169.

THE PLOUGH
KELMSCOTT
The welcome is 'warm and informal' at this well-liked Cotswold village pub-with-rooms in a 'beguiling' position close to the River Thames. Winter brings log fires in the cosy bar and restaurant; in the summer, clink glasses and eat alfresco in the cottage-style garden – chef Matthew Read's 'delicious' lunches and dinners attract locals and visitors in equal measure. Bedrooms are shabby chic; breakfast isn't shabby at all.
Read more, page 189.

THE DEVONSHIRE ARMS
LONG SUTTON

On the green of a Somerset village, Philip Mepham's popular inn has a pleasingly updated interior, with framed prints, wine-coloured banquettes and open fires on cool days. Fill up with craft ales and a 'first-class' meal, then sleep in one of the tastefully decorated bedrooms. On a sunny morning, wake to soak up the warmth in the wisteria-ringed courtyard garden.
Read more, page 206.

GOLDSTONE HALL
MARKET DRAYTON

Informal and characterful, this family-run Georgian manor house stands in large grounds in Shropshire countryside. Bedrooms, including a family suite at the top of the house, are individually decorated and supplied with home-made cookies; an inviting log fire burns in the lounge in cold weather. Come hungry: the huge kitchen garden supplies the modern dinners and 'delicious' breakfasts.
Read more, page 219.

CHAPEL HOUSE
PENZANCE

Sue Stuart's 'utterly immaculate and inviting' guest house is a coolly contemporary update of a handsome Georgian building, and has a regularly changing gallery of local artwork. Sit in the harbour-view drawing room with one of the many books to borrow; upstairs, relax in a chic sea-facing bedroom. Communal Friday- and Saturday-night dinners are fresh, simple, wholly engaging.
Read more, page 260.

THE DIAL HOUSE
REEPHAM

Home-baked cake is part of the friendly greeting at Iain Wilson's style-conscious Norfolk hotel, where nearly everything is for sale. The red-brick building is discreet at first glance, but surprises abound in the eclectic bedrooms: an air of British India here, a soupçon of (glamorous) Parisian garret there. At lunch and dinner, tuck in to 'uncomplicated, tasty' modern meals.
Read more, page 270.

THE INN AT WEST END
WEST END

The bright, pretty bedrooms at Ann and Gerry Price's Surrey pub/restaurant-with-rooms are set on a courtyard garden, and have thoughtful details (including good local information) within. In the well-run, well-liked bar and restaurant, a community gathering place, sample chef Mark Baines's 'excellent' modern cooking – the award-winning wine list has plenty of quaffable options to accompany the meal.
Read more, page 321.

PENALLY ABBEY
PENALLY

'A happy place', Lucas and Melanie Boissevain's smartly refurbished hotel, in an 18th-century Gothic house (pictured), charms with its refined bedrooms, flower-filled sitting room and pretty terrace looking out to sea. Modern dinners are inspired by the seasons; breakfast is 'excellent'. Explore the history-rich grounds; further afield, seaside towns and the wild beaches of the Pembrokeshire coast await.
Read more, page 428.

THE PORTOBELLO
LONDON

Peter and Jessica Frankopan's quirky Victorian stuccoed mansion-turned-hotel has put its rock'n'roll days behind it, while remaining beguilingly eccentric. Wholly unique, rooms have drapes, gilded mirrors, in-room baths; some flamboyant rooms overlook one of Notting Hill's private gardens. You might think twice before leaping into bed – one four-poster is so high you need steps to climb up to it.
Read more, page 61

THE ROYAL CRESCENT HOTEL & SPA
BATH

In 1772, the most beautiful of Georgian crescents was enmeshed in scandal when the soprano and renowned beauty Elizabeth Linley, aged 18, eloped from it with playwright Richard Brinsley Sheridan. These days, enamoured couples come to rendezvous here. With an elegant drawing room, a library, a 'secret' walled garden and a fabulous spa, this hotel is endlessly seductive. Treat yourselves to a four-poster suite.
Read more, page 90.

BURGH ISLAND HOTEL
BIGBURY-ON-SEA

What could be more glamorous than a 1930s Art Deco hotel like a gleaming ocean liner on its own sea-lapped tidal island? Rooms are named after past guests, suave, sexy or sensational. Elegant Cunard recalls Nancy, muse of artists and poets; Coward celebrates Noël 'The Master' himself. Here, indeed, you'll find a room with a view, a place to bill and coo. At dinner don your best bib and tucker.
Read more, page 97.

LANGAR HALL
LANGAR

An avenue of lime trees leads to this apricot-washed house in the Vale of Belvoir. Mature gardens surround; inside the house, find paintings, antiques and a collection of inviting bedrooms. One room overlooks ancient yew trees; another has its own entrance via a short walk through the church garden; yet another, chandelier-bedecked, has in its bathroom a 19th-century porcelain bath 'nearly big enough to swim in'.
Read more, page 194.

THE OLD RAILWAY STATION
PETWORTH
Make tracks for this very pretty Victorian station, and check in at the ticket window for a journey back in time. The B&B taps into the romance of rail travel evoked in Anna Karenina and Brief Encounter. Eight rooms are in Pullman carriages with Edwardian fittings and furnishings; two in the main building are reached by a spiral staircase. Breakfast is served in the lofty waiting room and ticket office.
Read more, page 262.

CLIVEDEN HOUSE
TAPLOW
A veritable palace on the Thames, this Italianate mansion, built for a duke, was once home to William Waldorf Astor, who added the 18th-century French rococo panelling and a balustrade from the Villa Borghese in Rome. Beauty abounds within and without. The lavish Lady Astor suite has antiques, artwork and a private terrace; the still-lovely and more affordable Club Rooms are named after past guests – Rudyard Kipling among them.
Read more, page 303.

ARDANAISEIG
KILCHRENAN
William Burn, architect involved in such great stately homes as the Duke of Buccleuch's Bowhill, was working on a more intimate scale when he designed this Scottish baronial mansion on the banks of Loch Awe. Its owner, Bennie Gray, has filled it with antiques; a set designer styled the theatrical bedrooms. Dinner is served by candlelight. The views of loch and mountain are dreamy, the star-filled skies revelatory.
Read more, page 361.

GLIFFAES
CRICKHOWELL
Twin campaniles and rare specimen trees rise above the morning mist at Victorian 'Gwlydd Faes' (the dewy field), by the River Usk. Built for a clergyman nostalgic for Italy, it has been in the same family for three generations. Amid paintings and fresh flowers, room choices include ones with river or garden views; in one, sleep under a hand-sewn canopy, then wake to views across the pheasant-spotted grounds.
Read more, page 408.

BALLYVOLANE HOUSE
CASTLELYONS
A classic Georgian house here combines grandeur with a warm and welcoming ambience. Jenny and Justin Green's is a family home, albeit one filled with antiques and artwork. The bedrooms have original features, views of gardens, parkland, lakes and mountains, but true romantics choose to spend a night under canvas, in a bell tent made for two, complete with furniture and a tea-light chandelier.
Read more, page 454.

NEWFORGE HOUSE
MAGHERALIN
The bedrooms recall the maiden names of the six Mathers wives who lived in and cherished this creeper-draped Georgian country mansion. Choose Hanna if you fancy an antique four-poster bed, tall sash windows, an original fireplace in the bathroom. The house is filled with period furniture, paintings and family photographs; the grounds are resplendent with flowering shrubs. Breakfast eggs are from the happy hens in the orchard.
Read more, page 467.

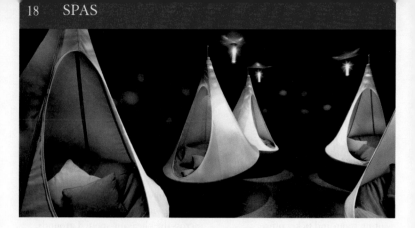

HARTWELL HOUSE
AYLESBURY

The exiled Louis XVIII's stately home-away-from-home refuge stands in idyllic parkland, just an hour's drive from London. Escape straight into the orangery-style spa, which has a mosaic-tiled swimming pool, steam room, sauna and whirlpool bath; the gym has all the latest equipment. For sustenance, choose among salads and light meals at the café/bar on a gallery overlooking the pool.
Read more, page 79.

THE ROYAL CRESCENT HOTEL & SPA
BATH

With wide views over the city where Georgian high society flocked to take the waters, this luxury hotel has added the new Bath House to its renovated spa. Purify, detoxify, be pummelled, massaged and soothed: there are relaxation and vitality pools, a Himalayan salt-infused sauna, a blossom steam room in which to inhale heady scents of eucalyptus and menthol. Outside, the spa garden is a green oasis.
Read more, page 90.

LIME WOOD
LYNDHURST

The great outdoors informs the spa experience at this ultra-stylish country house in the New Forest. Gaze out at the trees from the sauna; practise yoga or meditate in a rooftop herb garden; work out in the gym. There's an outdoor steaming hot pool, a mud house, a caldarium, single and double treatment rooms, a hydropool; after it all, opt for feel-good food in the Raw and Cured bar.
Read more, page 217.

THE SCARLET
MAWGAN PORTH

Under a thrift-planted roof, the spa at this luxury eco-hotel has Atlantic views, clifftop hot tubs and a chemical-free pool filtered by reeds. East meets West Country in the hushed treatment tents; other options include a hammam for scrubs and wraps, hanging canvas pods (pictured) for cocooning in, an outdoor barrel cedar sauna and a couples suite with a double bath.
Read more, page 224.

CHEWTON GLEN
NEW MILTON
Still one of the very best, this luxury spa piles on the specials: aromatherapy saunas, crystal steam rooms, drench showers, an outdoor whirlpool, a menu of organic treatments and more. Plus, overlooking the ozone-treated pool, the bar/lounge has smoothies, salads and plenty of healthy options besides. Need more oomph? Take a stroll or a jog around acres of New Forest woodland. Read more, page 236.

SEAHAM HALL
SEAHAM
An exotic underground walkway leads to the Serenity Spa at this 18th-century manor house, leaving the pressures of the world far behind. Find a pool with massage stations, a hammam with snail showers and a whirlpool bath, a black granite steam room, outdoor hot tubs, a fitness suite, plunge pools, a roof terrace and much more. Outside are landscaped gardens and the sea. Read more, page 285.

CLIVEDEN HOUSE
TAPLOW
Charles Barry's glorious Italianate mansion above the Thames stands in gardens with topiary, statuary, fountains and a four-acre parterre. It's all balm to the soul, but for the ultimate indulgence for body and mind, visit the Pavilion Spa behind the walled garden. Outdoor hot tubs and Britain's only listed (and most notorious) swimming pool are among the attractions. Try a volcanic hot-stone massage, or sign up for one of the signature treatments. Read more, page 303.

CALCOT MANOR
TETBURY
There's a rustic, back-to-nature feel at this spa in converted outbuildings in the grounds of a 14th-century farmhouse. At the centre is an open-air hot tub, with fragrant beds of lavender and a log fire. The facilities include a steam room, sauna and high-tech gym, with classes from power hoop to Pilates to Nia dance. Accompanied children are welcomed for an afternoon swim; a crèche is available at other times. Read more, page 306.

ISLE OF ERISKA HOTEL, SPA AND ISLAND
ERISKA
The island location of this Victorian baronial mansion-turned-luxury hotel lends a heightened sense of escape. Follow a path through the spa garden to the converted stables, where ingredients harvested on the island are used in facial and body treatments – salt and oil scrubs, mud envelopes, seaweed body wraps, hot-stone massages. Specialities include the Rasul Mud Experience – mineral mud, steam, a heated lounger and tropical rain shower. Read more, page 353.

BODYSGALLEN HALL AND SPA
LLANDUDNO
Beautiful Grade I listed Bodysgallen, in acres of parkland, houses a spa within a restored stone farmhouse, with a sunny, south-facing terrace. The mosaic-tiled swimming pool is a fine centrepiece, but worth attention, too, are the whirlpool spa bath, steam room, sauna and treatment rooms. Gym trainers, fitness assessments and personalised programmes are available to members. Read more, page 420.

THE CARY ARMS
BABBACOMBE

Effortless chic and a family-friendly feel mix at Lana de Savary's hotel, in 'fabulous' wooded seclusion on the cliff side overlooking the water. Most rooms have a balcony on which to sit and watch for dolphins – but book one of the new duplex beach-hut rooms and suites, set into the grassy slopes. Sample Lyme Bay lobster and line-caught seafood in the rustic dining rooms or on the sunny terrace, or take a picnic to the beach – buckets and shrimping nets provided. Read more, page 80.

THE WHITE HORSE
BRANCASTER STAITHE

With views stretching across the tidal salt marsh and sandy beach of the unspoilt north Norfolk coast, the Nye family's inn appeals especially to birdwatchers, walkers, cyclists and sailors. Book a table for Fran Hartshorne's 'excellent' meals, with local fish and shellfish, and mussels harvested at the bottom of the garden. Sleep well in New England-style bedrooms. 'Excellent' coastal walks begin from the garden's edge. Read more, page 111.

THE OLD COASTGUARD
MOUSEHOLE

A tropical garden slopes down to the harbour wall at the Inkin brothers' family-friendly hotel in a pretty fishing village. Guide readers like the 'young, buzzy atmosphere', and the sea-view bedrooms stocked with 'proper' tea and coffee, books and Cornish art. Daytime and night, chef Matt Smith cooks seasonal brasserie menus using freshly landed seafood. On a fine day, eat on the terrace looking out to St Clement's Island. Read more, page 231.

ROMNEY BAY HOUSE
NEW ROMNEY

'More like a home than a hotel', Clinton and Lisa Lovell's 1920s house, reached by a private road, stands between marshland and Littlestone's shingle beach. Some bedrooms have a view of the English Channel. Clinton Lovell cooks a 'superb' four-course, no-choice dinner, often including local shellfish and salt marsh lamb. One for walkers, birdwatchers and golfers. Read more, page 237.

DRIFTWOOD HOTEL
PORTSCATHO

There's 'an abundance of calm' at
Fiona and Paul Robinson's 'stylish but
informal' hotel, standing in beautifully
landscaped gardens with 'superb' views
of the Atlantic (pictured). Find a seat
on the sun terrace or in the cosy bar;
children have a games room for rainy
days. On Chris Eden's Michelin-starred
menus, fish and shellfish are cooked
with 'a lightness of touch'.
Read more, page 266.

IDLE ROCKS
ST MAWES

Vibrant coastal colours set the tone
at Karen and David Richards's smart
seaside hotel, perched 'truly on the
water'. Built in 1913, it recaptures the
leisure and luxury of its '30s heyday,
with Cornish cream teas on the terrace,
a brimming playroom for children, and
now a private cinema. Chef Guy Owen
cooks with ingredients locally farmed,
fished and foraged – in sunshine, try to
get a spot on the dining terrace.
Read more, page 282.

SOAR MILL COVE HOTEL
SOAR MILL COVE

Above a sandy cove, in an area of
outstanding natural beauty, stands Keith
Makepeace's family-friendly hotel.
There's plenty of diversion inside and
out: have a cream tea on the sun terrace,
play tennis, swim in a heated saltwater
pool or opt for an aromatherapy
massage in the spa. Each bedroom has
its own patio leading to the garden. At
lunch and dinner, Ian MacDonald cooks
with fresh local ingredients, including
much fish and shellfish. The coastal
park is close by.
Read more, page 291.

THE PIG ON THE BEACH
STUDLAND

A short stroll from sea and sand, the
fourth of Robin Hutson's Pig hotels is
'delightfully quirky'. Bedrooms have an
espresso machine, a 'larder' of snacks
and a view of sea, gardens or sheep-
grazed pastures. Two shepherd's huts
have been converted into treatment
rooms. In the conservatory dining
room, Andy Wright creates 'simple,
appetising' dishes using local, home-
grown and foraged ingredients.
Read more, page 297.

THE NARE
VERYAN-IN-ROSELAND

Toby Ashworth's family-friendly
hotel overlooks the sand and surf of
Gerrans Bay. Its decor and silver service
may seem old fashioned, but guests love
its timeless charm, from the balconied
bedrooms and sea-view restaurants
to the outdoor hot tub peering over
the beach. Ask about an outing on
the hotel's yacht – it's ideal for fishing
mackerel, exploring creeks or simply
bobbing along.
Read more, page 318.

THE WHITE HOUSE
HERM

You'll find neither telephone nor clock
in your room at this 'truly lovely' hotel
on a car-free island just half a mile wide,
where guests are encouraged to 'escape
the 21st century'. Step outside: there are
gardens, an outdoor swimming pool, a
croquet lawn, a tennis court. Most of the
bedrooms (including family rooms) face
west, for glorious views of the sunset.
Chef Karl Ginnever's daily-changing
menus include a catch of the day.
Read more, page 438.

FISCHER'S AT BASLOW HALL
BASLOW

A kitchen tasting bench at Max and Susan Fischer's Peak District Edwardian manor house gives guests a ringside seat to watch the culinary brigade at work. Most opt for the formal dining room, though, and dress up in expectation. Among Michelin-starred chef Rupert Rowley's 'outstanding' dishes: dry-aged Derbyshire beef sirloin and smoked short rib, wild salsify, onion purée; pan-fried John Dory, beetroot fondant, thyme velouté.
Read more, page 85.

ECKINGTON MANOR
ECKINGTON

Chefs Sue and Mark Stinchcombe's farm-to-fork philosophy informs their modern European menus, with such dishes as crab ravioli, daikon, Thai-spiced crab broth; Eckington Manor rib-eye of beef, braised shin, caramelised onion, wild mushrooms. Meanwhile, owner Judy Gardner brings designer chic to accommodation in manor house (pictured) and milking parlour. At the on-site cookery school, learn the tricks of the kitchen trade.
Read more, page 157.

MORSTON HALL
MORSTON

It's been a stellar rise for chef/patron Galton Blackiston, from selling home-baked 'Galton's Goodies' in Rye market, to owning and running this country house restaurant-with-rooms with his wife, Tracy. The Michelin-starred tasting menu might include such dishes as 'showcase of locally farmed rabbit'; confit loin of Norfolk horn lamb, pearl barley, swede purée. Sign up for one of the host's half-day demonstrations, to watch the master chef at work.
Read more, page 230.

THE NEPTUNE
OLD HUNSTANTON

A creeper-covered 18th-century coaching inn is a fine home for Jacki and Kevin Mangeolles's 'modern, elegant' restaurant-with-rooms. Here, the host, a Michelin-starred chef, cooks refined set menus – all praised for their 'execution and presentation'. Sample Norfolk quail, red pepper, couscous; brill fillet, potato gnocchi, broccoli purée, courgettes. A nine-course tasting menu feeds the hungriest gourmand.
Read more, page 248.

THE YORKE ARMS
RAMSGILL-IN-NIDDERDALE
There's 'real cheffery' at work in the Yorkshire Dales, at Frances and Bill Atkins's restaurant-with-rooms. The hostess is one of just six female Michelin-starred chefs in the UK; readers praise her 'divine' ways with top-quality ingredients. From her seasonal menu: saddle of venison, oxtail, puffed rice, sloe and cherry; herb-dusted halibut, scallop and shrimp, puntarella, truffled linguine.
Read more, page 268.

THE ALBANNACH
LOCHINVER
Self-taught chef/patrons Lesley Crosfield and Colin Craig are in their 26th year at this Highland restaurant-with-rooms. In the dining room, admire the mountain views before giving your full attention to their Michelin-starred cooking, perhaps roast Moray beef fillet, garden celeriac, baby turnip, amontillado; roast turbot, charred fennel, asparagus, black potatoes.
Read more, page 369.

THE PEAT INN
PEAT INN
There's an unhurried, welcoming ambience at Katherine and Geoffrey Smeddle's roadside restaurant-with-rooms, where the host has a Michelin star for his modern take on classical cooking techniques. Choose from such 'delicious and beautifully served' dishes as warm St Andrew's Bay lobster, caramelised onion tart; home-smoked monkfish, oyster mousse, marinated cucumber. Vegetarians might opt for heirloom beetroots, goat's curd, walnut brittle, apple and chilli purée.
Read more, page 373.

TYDDYN LLAN
LLANDRILLO
Susan Webb is the 'vibrant' hostess, and husband Bryan the Michelin-starred kitchen supremo at this Georgian stone-built former shooting lodge. The 'fabulous' daily-changing menu might include crubeens (stuffed pig's trotters), piccalilli, Wirral watercress salad; Cefnllan Farm duck breast, duck faggot, confit potato. From regular wine dinners to a children's selection, the whole is warm, inclusive and fun.
Read more, page 419.

LLYS MEDDYG
NEWPORT
Edward and Louise Sykes run their restaurant-with-rooms with a passion for things local. Eat in the rustic dining room, the flagstoned bar or, in summertime, the 'congenial' kitchen garden. You'll find 'punchily flavoured' dishes such as home-smoked salmon, pickled cucumber, pennywort; pan-fried cod, wild mushrooms, Solva crab jus. Hungering for more? Book a spot on one of the foraging, butchering, or smoking and curing courses.
Read more, page 427.

THE WHITEBROOK
WHITEBROOK
A 17th-century drovers' inn in the Wye valley lives again as Chris and Kirsty Harrod's stylish restaurant-with-rooms. Chris Harrod's Michelin-starred cooking presents diners with many 'firsts', from nasturtium tubers to flowers from the herbaceous border. In the 'atmospheric' restaurant, try hake with radish, sea aster and buttermilk; Ryeland lamb shoulder, kale, dragon spinach. It's all simply 'amazing'.
Read more, page 435.

THE MASTER BUILDER'S
BEAULIEU

Dogs get a masterful welcome at this affable hotel in a lovely setting by the river estuary. Pooch-friendly bedrooms come supplied with a dog bed, a bowl and a box of treats; a canines-only room-service menu includes rump steak and pork sausages with gravy. Coastal and countryside walks abound in the former shipbuilding hamlet and surrounding New Forest.

Read more, page 93.

OVERWATER HALL
IREBY

In a spread of gardens and woodland, this traditional hotel in the Lake District national park welcomes dogs and their owners in equal measure. The extensive grounds, including a woodland boardwalk, are ideal for doggy walks; further afield, set out on a scenic romp through the fells. Inside, dogs are welcomed in the bar and one of the lounges; a dog-sitting service allows for pet-free time.

Read more, page 188.

SUN INN
KIRKBY LONSDALE

The popular local pub and 'delightfully decorated' bedrooms please guests at this personable inn in a historic Cumbrian market town. Four-legged visitors have plenty to wag their tail about, too: a welcome pack with a towel, a bowl and treats; a map of dog walks; a log fire to curl up in front of. The restaurant has pooch-friendly eating areas – or ask about dog-walking and dog-sitting services for a couple of pet-free hours.

Read more, page 192.

MULLION COVE HOTEL
MULLION COVE

Time for walkies: the Grose family's clifftop hotel on the scenic Lizard Peninsula borders National Trust land just right for a ramble; the South West Coastal Path runs directly in front of the hotel. Take Fido on a scamper through heathland and grassland towards the beach; on your return, make use of the dedicated outdoor washing facilities before settling in to the pet-friendly sea view lounge. No extra charges for doggy guests in low season.

Read more, page 232.

THE PEAR TREE AT PURTON
PURTON

Anne Young's much-liked small hotel stands in a wild flower-strewn garden, with woodland, fields and Wiltshire countryside stretching out beyond. Canine friends are welcomed with chews, a bowl and a bottle of mineral water – plus a towel, in case they go paddling in the lily pond or wetlands. Travelling without your pup? The gardener's dogs, Smudge and Bramble, will happily fetch a stick or stone for you to toss.
Read more, page 267.

THE PEACOCK AT ROWSLEY
ROWSLEY

One for the independent hound – and its style-conscious owners – this modish 17th-century manor house stands in immaculate gardens that reach down to the River Derwent. Dogs aren't allowed in the bar or restaurant, but, outside mealtimes, they'll love a scamper in the grounds, or down the walking trails that wind through the moors and hills of the surrounding Peak District. Dog food and water bowls are provided.
Read more, page 276.

BRIARFIELDS
TITCHWELL

On the north Norfolk coast, this 'thoroughly enjoyable' hotel is a relaxed, congenial spot that extends a friendly greeting to four-legged friends. Dogs are welcomed in a number of bedrooms, with a blanket and snacks; owners may eat with their canine companions in the bar. A large terrace and sheltered courtyard are great for stretching legs, too.
Read more, page 308.

PRINCE HALL
TWO BRIDGES

Ringed by glorious Dartmoor wilderness, Chris Daly's country hotel has exceptional facilities for dogs: water bowls are provided; a bucket, sponge and towels are available for washing; there's also an enclosed, pet-friendly garden and a dog-friendly outdoor seating area. Treats are at hand, too, from bedroom to reception. For the pooch that's feeling under the weather, a visit from a dog healer may be arranged.
Read more, page 312.

HOLBECK GHYLL
WINDERMERE

It's a ruff life at Stephen and Lisa Leahy's Victorian hunting lodge in the Lake District. Dogs get their own welcome pack, while their owners are handed a list of dog-friendly walks from the hotel door. Splurge on the Very Important Canine package, put together by posh pet outfitters Mungo and Maud, which includes a dog bed, a blanket and a bowl, a toy and a bag of organic treats.
Read more, page 328.

TRIGONY HOUSE
THORNHILL

Jan and Adam Moore's cheerful country hotel is surrounded by rolling Dumfriesshire hills and farmland – all the better for a doggy romp. Exhaustively dog friendly – pooches are welcomed everywhere but the restaurant – the hotel has welcome packs, walking maps, gourmet treats, beds, towels and bowls for four-legged friends. Mornings, Fido won't even have to sit up and beg: lucky dogs find a sausage for breakfast.
Read more, page 390.

HAMBLETON HALL
HAMBLETON
Tim and Stefa Hart have created a 'haven of luxury' in their Victorian hunting lodge, where society hostess Eva Astley Cooper once entertained Noël Coward's set. Bedrooms overlook the gardens, which run down to Rutland Water; cosy lounges have fires, fresh flowers, magazines. The food is 'wonderful': modern, Michelin-starred dishes cooked by chef Aaron Patterson at dinner; newly laid eggs and freshly baked bread at breakfast.
Read more, page 174.

LEWTRENCHARD MANOR
LEWDOWN
'Uniformly excellent.' Dark panelling, stone fireplaces and leaded windows create a potent sense of history at this 'Jacobean' manor house (pictured) – largely a 19th-century creation – while owners Sue and James Murray encourage a 'very friendly' atmosphere. Choose among main-house or courtyard bedrooms overlooking parkland and hillside, woodland or gardens; all are individually styled. The modern dinners are 'impeccable'; breakfasts are 'copious'.
Read more, page 200.

ASKHAM HALL
PENRITH
'A hotel of character', Charles and Juno Lowther's Grade I listed Elizabethan mansion is furnished with eclectic pieces; paintings, well-worn rugs, family photos, log fires and crammed bookshelves create a homely feel. The best bedrooms, in a 14th-century pele tower, have views of fells and river. Come dinnertime, chef Richard Swale creates inventive menus using home-reared livestock, local game, produce from the kitchen garden.
Read more, page 257.

LORDS OF THE MANOR
UPPER SLAUGHTER
A portrait hanging on the first-floor landing at this plush, luxurious 17th-century house is of Ferdinando Tracy Travell, rector here from 1763; bring his Diary of a Cotswold Parson to read by the drawing-room fire. Bedrooms are a blend of traditional and contemporary furnishings, with 'splendid' views of verdant hills or lawns. Take afternoon tea in grand old English style, but leave room for Richard Picard-Edwards's 'spectacular' Michelin-starred cooking.
Read more, page 315.

GILPIN HOTEL AND LAKE HOUSE
WINDERMERE

From the home-made biscuits and fresh milk in the spacious bedrooms to the books, magazines and plump sofas in the lounge, the Cunliffe family's Edwardian country house is 'an absolute joy'. Seeking seclusion? Six bedrooms are in Lake House, half a mile away, with a private lake and spa. Dine in: Hrishikesh Desai's modern menus are 'superb'.

Read more, page 327.

JUDGES
YARM

A teddy bear, a goldfish in a bowl and a decanter of sherry await in the traditionally styled bedrooms at the Downs family's 'unstarchy' Victorian country house. (Choose well, and you might also find a four-poster bed or a spa bath.) Sample 'unusual' canapés before tucking in to a 'delicious' modern menu; next day, walk it off in 'lovely, manicured' parkland, where Saltergill Beck flows in the 36-acre grounds.

Read more, page 333.

ARDANAISEIG
KILCHRENAN

Antiques dealer Bennie Gray has filled his 19th-century baronial mansion with a joyous mix of grand and eccentric pieces – and 'a pleasingly old-fashioned air of country house grandeur'. Find oil paintings, statuary, mirrors and a grand piano in the public rooms; take in 'superb, romantic views' towards the peak of Ben Lui. Dinner is an elegant affair, with starched napery, candles, silverware, and chef Colin Cairns's fine cooking.

Read more, page 361.

THE LAKE
LLANGAMMARCH WELLS

In mid-Wales, Jean-Pierre Mifsud's 19th-century hunting and fishing lodge stands in extensive lawns that stretch down to a lake on the River Irfon. Inside, book a treatment at the spa before sitting down to bara brith at afternoon tea – taken on the patio, under the spreading chestnut tree, on fine days. Enjoy dinner: the modern Welsh dishes are 'first class'.

Read more, page 422.

HILTON PARK
CLONES

A mile-long avenue leads to this Georgian ancestral home, where Fred and Joanna Madden welcome visitors as cherished guests. The house is filled with oil paintings, curios and family memorabilia; some of the huge bedrooms have floor-to-ceiling windows overlooking parkland. In the evening, take a seat at the mahogany dinner table for a four-course, no-choice menu – and conversation of a high order.

Read more, page 457.

MARLFIELD HOUSE
GOREY

Thirty-six acres of parkland, with 'atmospheric' woodland walks, an ornamental lake and a rose garden, surround the Bowe family's Regency-style Victorian mansion. Step into the 'imposing' entrance hall, with its open fire and grand piano; beyond, there are antiques and paintings – much 'to fascinate the eye'. There's a choice of eating options: a 'tempting' dining-room menu or informal meals in The Duck.

Read more, page 461.

AUSTWICK HALL
AUSTWICK
Come in springtime to this historic manor house in the Yorkshire Dales, to find woodlands awash with snowdrops: owners Michael Pearson and Eric Culley have planted almost 50 varieties by the tens of thousands. Snowdrops are followed by wild daffodils and drifts of bluebells; elsewhere, there's a walled kitchen garden, a sculpture trail, a pergola resting on Tuscan columns, a lily pond and heather-thatched gazebo. Garden visits by arrangement.
Read more, page 77.

BARNSLEY HOUSE
BARNSLEY
Stay overnight at this 17th-century stone manor house to experience the stillness and the heightened scents of early morning that inspired Rosemary Verey. Doyenne of country house gardeners, Verey lived here and created the gardens in the 1950s. Emblematic of her style are the knot garden, clipped yews and laburnum walk. Wander freely, then enjoy fresh produce from the ornamental fruit and vegetable garden at dinner.
Read more, page 82.

LINDETH FELL
BOWNESS-ON-WINDERMERE
Widely regarded as the leading landscape architect of the Edwardian age, Thomas Mawson had the vision to harmonise buildings, plantings and the natural landscape. At this country house B&B overlooking Lake Windermere, take tea on Mawson's trademark terrace, keeping an eye out for deer. There are specimen trees, a private tarn and a croquet lawn, but it's all perhaps at its loveliest when the rhododendrons and azaleas are ablaze.
Read more, page 107.

GOLDSTONE HALL
MARKET DRAYTON
For 30 years, after arriving at this Georgian manor house, Helen Ward devoted herself to the gardens, reclaiming the wilderness, sowing and planting. Her 'extraordinary' kitchen garden is one of the largest at any hotel in the UK, with a herb walkway of a hundred or so varieties; along a double-tier herbaceous border, Ballerina roses dance in the breeze. The gardens are open periodically as part of the National Gardens Scheme.
Read more, page 219.

HOTEL ENDSLEIGH
MILTON ABBOT
In 108-acre grounds surrounding a Regency fishing lodge built for the Duke and Duchess of Bedford, Humphry Repton created a pastoral fantasy landscape (pictured) with the River Tamar running through. Wake to the beauty: dells, grottoes, streams, a waterfall, a rose and jasmine walkway, an arboretum of champion trees.
Read more, page 227.

MILLGATE HOUSE
RICHMOND
Austin Lynch and Tim Culkin's small walled garden, at their Georgian home off the town's main square, is 'full of interest'. Terraces lead down to the River Swale; paths thread through profusions of shrub roses, ferns and clematis. Ask for a bedroom with garden views, or simply sit on a rustic bench in one of the shady nooks, and breathe it all in.
Read more, page 272.

TALLAND BAY HOTEL
TALLAND-BY-LOOE
From the terrace of the O'Sullivans' clifftop hotel, gaze at the sea over subtropical gardens shaded by Monterey pines. There are some lovely plantings, and it's magical in the changing light, but there's further enchantment – especially for children – in the witty and wonderful statuary and figures throughout the grounds. You'll come across gauzy fairies, a goblin, a pig, perhaps a giant teapot – all quirky and endless fun.
Read more, page 302.

MIDDLETHORPE HALL & SPA
YORK
In the 1980s, Historic House Hotels set about restoring the gardens surrounding this William and Mary house, now in the care of the National Trust. A dovecote was rescued from ruin, a ha-ha repaired, a lake dug, a walled garden replanted. Tread the wide path through the rose garden, lined with lavender; in the spring garden, stroll under the shade of American red oaks, a line of beech trees, a cedar of Lebanon.
Read more, page 334.

THE GROVE
NARBERTH
Ancient oaks and towering beeches watch over Neil Kedward and Zoë Agar's friendly hotel, which stands in large, lush grounds on a hillside overlooking Pembrokeshire countryside. A network of paths winds through the grounds: stroll through the restored 17th-century walled garden, or ask for a tour of the organic kitchen garden, then picnic on the lawn, surrounded by seasonal flowers and wild blooms.
Read more, page 425.

BALLYVOLANE HOUSE
CASTLELYONS
The gardens at the Greens' historic country house were laid out in the early 1700s for the Pyne family by a cousin, Thomas Pennefeather. He came for a fortnight and stayed for 40 years, planting trees and creating walled and woodland gardens. Come in May, say the Greens, to see the formal gardens on the south side, when the tiered lawns are lined with magnolias in bloom.
Read more, page 454.

BELLE TOUT LIGHTHOUSE
EASTBOURNE

On a cloudless night, the starry sky seen from the lantern of this decommissioned lighthouse is something to behold. Belle Tout looms up in splendid isolation, a landscape of rolling pastures and heritage coastline stretching out all around. In the lighthouse tower, the Keeper's Loft has a small window looking towards Beachy Head's own lighthouse. Down below, Shiraz is a double-aspect room with views towards the Seven Sisters.
Read more, page 155.

THE HORN OF PLENTY
GULWORTHY

Book a room with a balcony at this Victorian mansion on the edge of Dartmoor bordering Cornwall. Best of all, perhaps, ask for one with floor-to-ceiling windows, and rest your eyes on the green vistas of the Tamar valley. The Victorian house was built for the Duke of Bedford's mine captain; on clear days, spot factory chimneys rising above the trees – a reminder of the once-thriving tin and copper mines that earn the valley World Heritage status.
Read more, page 172.

MULLION COVE HOTEL
MULLION COVE

'Brandy for the parson, baccy for the clerk…' Gaze from your window at this clifftop eyrie and recall tales of smugglers and sunken treasure ships in the waters below. A backdrop of craggy serpentinite rocks sets the scene for drama, from the working fishing harbour protected by two impressive walls, to Mullion Island, half a mile out and home to colonies of marine birds.
Read more, page 232.

EES WYKE COUNTRY HOUSE
NEAR SAWREY

Beatrix Potter was enchanted by the outlook from this Georgian country house overlooking Esthwaite Water, one of the smaller of the lakes in the Lake District national park. A watercolour she painted of the scene, in the V&A Museum, shows its timeless beauty. From the best bedrooms, look across to the Old Man of Coniston, the Langdale Pikes and Grizedale forest.
Read more, page 233.

DUNKERY BEACON COUNTRY HOUSE
WOOTTON COURTENAY

Try to spot wild Exmoor ponies amid the bracken, from this Edwardian hunting lodge; from the restaurant, take in views of the Coleridge Way, a trail in the footsteps of the Romantic poet, which skirts Dunkery Hill. At night, peer through the telescope at an unpolluted, star-spangled sky. Read more, page 331.

THE THREE CHIMNEYS AND THE HOUSE OVER-BY
DUNVEGAN

Eat, drink and be mesmerised at this Isle of Skye restaurant-with-rooms on the shores of Loch Dunvegan. The well-regarded restaurant looks out over the water, with the Outer Hebrides on the horizon; at breakfast-time, watch the lobster boats put out to sea. In The House Over-By, junior suites have loch views and French windows leading to gardens with a burn running through. Read more, page 350.

KYLESKU HOTEL
KYLESKU

In 'one of the wildest and most beautiful locations', this whitewashed inn stands between lochs Glencoul and Glendhu, within sound of the lapping water. The rugged landscape that surrounds (a designated UNESCO Global Geopark) is of grazing sheep, rushing burns and roaming red deer. Ask for a loch-facing room, but the views are all around. A bonus: take a boat trip to see Eas a' Chual Aluinn, Britain's highest waterfall. Read more, page 367.

KILCAMB LODGE
STRONTIAN

One of the oldest stone houses on the west coast of Scotland, this small hotel stands in 22 private acres bordering Loch Sunart (pictured) on the Ardnamurchan peninsula. Charter a boat to see whales and puffins, or simply stroll on the beach. With water on three sides, this is a playground for otters, pine martens and red squirrels, and a hunting ground for golden eagles. There's a wildlife hide, too, 20 minutes away. Read more, page 389.

BRYNIAU GOLAU
BALA

On the shores of Lake Bala, this Victorian guest house sits amid farmland in the foothills of the spectacular Snowdonia national park, looking out to the Arenig mountain. All the bedrooms have lovely lake views; the terrace is the ideal spot for a pre-dinner drink while the sun sets behind the slopes. Read more, page 402.

STELLA MARIS
BALLYCASTLE

There's drama and atmosphere in spades here, in a wild and empty landscape of deserted beaches, glacial loughs and grassy drumlins on the Wild Atlantic Way. In the midst of it all, this welcoming hotel, a Victorian coastguard headquarters, has uninterrupted ocean views across Bunatrahir Bay and the sea-stack of Downpatrick Head. Most bedrooms have a seaward outlook; the 100-foot-long conservatory calls for a sundowner. Read more, page 448.

APSLEY HOUSE
BATH

Built as a retreat – or love nest – for the Duke of Wellington, this house, decked with oil paintings and antiques, is a model of Georgian elegance. Model managers Miro Mikula and Kate Kowalczyk charm Guide readers. Pick a bedroom with a four-poster bed, a slipper bath or French doors on to the garden; most have great views over the city. Crisp white napkins at breakfast herald the feast to come.
Read more, page 88.

BLACKMORE FARM
CANNINGTON

Ann and Ian Dyer are welcoming hosts at their oak-beamed 15th-century manor house on a working farm in the lee of the Quantocks. Choose a bedroom in the main building or converted cider press – some have fascinating original features, nooks and crannies. Eat breakfast at a refectory table in the Great Hall; have a cream tea or home-made ice cream in the café after watching the cows being milked.
Read more, page 127.

TIMBERSTONE
CLEE STANTON

Draped in roses and wisteria, this extended stone cottage stands in gentle countryside just five and a half miles from foodie Ludlow. Natural hosts Tracey Baylis and Alex Read will put the kettle on the moment you arrive. There are beamed ceilings, oak floors, wood-burning stoves; a bedroom with French doors opens on to a balcony. Breakfast is rightly a source of pride; the hostess also cooks a communal dinner on request.
Read more, page 139.

OLD WHYLY
EAST HOATHLY

Sarah Burgoyne's very special Georgian manor house (pictured) stands in romantic gardens in a Wealden village, its country house-style bedrooms taking in lovely views. The vine-covered pergola is ideal for tea on a sunny day; more active sorts might enjoy the pool house or the tennis court in the orchard. The hostess, a Paris-trained chef, cooks breakfast using eggs from the house's hens; evenings, a three-course dinner may be served by candlelight.
Read more, page 153.

SWAN HOUSE
HASTINGS

Just behind the High Street in the Old Town, this timber-framed Tudor house is run as an elegant yet relaxed B&B by warm, welcoming host Brendan McDonagh. Come in to comfy sofas, an open fire and an honesty bar. Pleasing bedrooms mix charmingly wonky windows and sloping floors with contemporary styling. There are fresh flowers and linen napkins at breakfast – altogether 'a generally good mood'.
Read more, page 179.

2 BLACKBURNE TERRACE
LIVERPOOL

Glenn and Sarah Whitter have created a luxurious B&B in a Georgian town house in the city's cultural quarter. The rooms are a lovely mix of period and contemporary style, with original features, rich fabrics, antiques and artwork. Take tea in a drawing room with a marble fireplace; at breakfast, help yourself from a generous buffet and order a cooked dish to eat off fine china.
Read more, page 203.

JEAKE'S HOUSE
RYE

On a cobbled street in a town rich in literary associations, Jenny Hadfield's characterful 17th-century converted wool store was once home to American writer Conrad Aiken. Past low beams, open fires, dark panelling and a warren of passages, steep stairs lead to bedrooms named after men and women of letters. Breakfast is served in the galleried former Quaker meeting room – devilled kidneys, for example, or Rye rarebit.
Read more, page 278.

DALSHIAN HOUSE
PITLOCHRY

The name derives from 'dal sithean', meaning 'peaceful place', and it is peaceful indeed at Martin and Heather Walls's 18th-century house set in gardens and woodland. There are seven comfortable, individually styled bedrooms, plus a guests' lounge with a wood-burning stove, books and magazines. Praiseworthy breakfasts might include vanilla-scented pears, Stornoway black pudding, Dunkeld smoked salmon and potato scones.
Read more, page 375.

THE MANOR TOWN HOUSE
FISHGUARD

Order a cream tea on the terrace at Helen and Chris Sheldon's Georgian town house B&B. Below you, the fishing boats bob at sea and in the harbour that stood in for Llareggub in a film version of Under Milk Wood. Inside, the lounges, hung with work by Welsh artists, have plenty of books and an honesty bar; bedrooms are decked with antiques. Breakfast is big on local ingredients.
Read more, page 414.

THE QUAY HOUSE
CLIFDEN

Julia and Paddy Foyle have created an endlessly diverting B&B in four quayside houses filled with an exuberant mix of period furniture, paintings, ornaments and oddities. Twelve of the extraordinary bedrooms have a harbour view; some have a four-poster bed or a balcony. Sleep under a frilled canopy, a scallop-shell frieze, a zebra skin or a portrait of Napoleon, then breakfast royally in the conservatory.
Read more, page 455.

NEWBEGIN HOUSE
BEVERLEY
Paintings, photographs and fine furniture fill the rooms at Nuala and Walter Sweeney's 'remarkable' B&B, close to the centre of an old market town. Spacious bedrooms are well stocked with treats; there's wide choice at the 'superb' breakfast, including vegetarian options. No dinner is served, but the 'helpful' hosts have plenty of suggestions of restaurants nearby. A bonus: secure car parking and bicycle storage. Per room B&B £85.
Read more, page 96.

THE OLD RECTORY
BOSCASTLE
The essentials are just right at Sally and Chris Searle's Cornish countryside B&B: comfortable, cottage-style rooms; vases of garden blooms; a log fire on cool days; an organic kitchen garden providing ingredients for the home-grown breakfasts and convivial Victorian-greenhouse dinners. For the full rustic experience, help feed the rare-breed pigs and Jacob sheep in the surrounding fields. Per room B&B £70–£110.
Read more, page 104.

EIGHT CLARENDON CRESCENT
LEAMINGTON SPA
A five-minute stroll from the town centre, Christine and David Lawson run this elegant B&B in their Regency home. Gracious hosts, the Lawsons encourage guests to enjoy the house, from the spacious bedrooms to the sitting room decorated with antiques. Play the grand piano if the spirit moves, or step outside: the secluded garden and charming private dell are 'particular delights on a sunny day'. Per room B&B £85.
Read more, page 198.

THE SILVERTON
SHREWSBURY
Friendly staff and modern bedrooms attract visitors to Donna Miles and David Cheshire's restaurant-with-rooms across the river from the centre of the historic market town. Choose among the modern dishes in the restaurant (pre-theatre menus cater to guests heading to the Theatre Severn around the corner), then head upstairs to sleep in a 'super-comfy' bed. Per room B&B £75–£135.
Read more, page 289.

THE CARPENTER'S ARMS
STANTON WICK

A row of miners' cottages is now this popular inn, all low beams, exposed stone, leather armchairs and nooks to be cosy in. Come for dinner – Chris Dando's menu is 'imaginative yet unfussy' – then stay the night. Bedrooms are bright and modern, with a stylish contemporary bathroom; breakfast is served at table: hot toast, good coffee, a fruit platter, 'excellent' eggs. Room-only rates are available, too. Per room B&B £110–£120.
Read more, page 295.

THE MANOR COACH HOUSE
WORCESTER

Sylvia and Terry Smith's rural B&B is a 15-minute drive from the town centre and Worcester's cathedral. Modern bedrooms, set around a courtyard, each have their own access. Inside, find a tea tray, dressing gowns and toiletries. A duplex suite is ideal for a family. The host is 'rightly proud' of his breakfasts: a generous spread of fresh fruit and delicious yogurts; an expertly cooked hot breakfast. Per room B&B £85.
Read more, page 332.

BEALACH HOUSE
DUROR

'Completely isolated, but warm and cosy', Jim and Hilary McFadyen's modest guest house, on a rambling former shepherd's croft, is in a secluded spot at the end of a forestry track. There are home-made flapjacks to be had, and tea out of a quirky teapot; bring your own wine to the delicious, family-style dinners. A well-cooked breakfast makes for a fine awakening. Per room B&B £90–£110.
Read more, page 351.

GRASSHOPPERS
GLASGOW

There's a youthful vibe at this cool, modern hotel in an unbeatable city-centre location. Rooms may be compact, but they're cleverly laid out, with a shower 'pod' stocked with Scottish toiletries. Little treats keep things sweet, too: a tube of Smarties, home-made ice cream, a plate of cupcakes. A simple supper is available most evenings; local delis supply the breakfast buffet. Per room B&B £85–£125.
Read more, page 354.

CNAPAN
NEWPORT

In a pleasing coastal village, Judith and Michael Cooper's long-standing, family-run restaurant-with-rooms is liked for its relaxed atmosphere and tasty, unpretentious meals. Sip prosecco in the secluded garden before sitting down to dinner; afterwards, retire to one of the comfortable bedrooms hung with local artworks – each room is well supplied with books and plenty of local information. A self-catering cottage sleeps six. Per room B&B £95.
Read more, page 426.

SEA MIST HOUSE
CLIFDEN

Gossipy chickens might greet guests in the pretty garden of Sheila Griffin's Irish B&B. Inside, the 'lived-in' space has framed photographs, crockery collections, an inviting selection of books, and the perfect nook to read in. Comfortably large bedrooms have a supply of home-baked biscuits; breakfast, with thoughtful options for special diets (arranged in advance), is 'marvellous'. Per person B&B €40–€60.
Read more, page 456.

THE GRAZING GOAT
LONDON

Graze all day in the bar at this stylish yet relaxed pub-with-rooms among the smart independent shops of Portman Village, a refuge from teeming Oxford Street. After midday, head upstairs to the dining room (pictured). From house-cured meats and beer-battered fish and chips to such dishes as Trecorras Farm kid, beetroot gratin, spinach, raisin mustard jus, the food is imaginative, modern, beautifully judged and presented.
Read more, page 56.

BEECH HOUSE & OLIVE BRANCH
CLIPSHAM

Co-owner/chef Sean Hope cooks with palpable enthusiasm and the best ingredients he can source, at this popular village pub. Herbs from hedgerow and kitchen garden, vegetables from the Wolds and shellfish from Scotland all find their way on to short, seasonal menus. Try braised shoulder of lamb with sweet potato rösti and French-style peas, or opt for more familiar pub classics. Cookery demonstrations and masterclasses are a regular attraction.
Read more, page 140.

THE RED LION FREEHOUSE
EAST CHISENBURY

Guy Manning has a Michelin star for his cooking at the thatched village pub he runs with his wife, Brittany. From ketchup to cordial, everything possible is made on the premises. Eggs are from the Mannings' rescued hens; vegetables are local, home grown or foraged. Pork is from the owners' West Berkshire pigs. On appetising seasonal menus, expect such dishes as slow-cooked belly pork, Jersey royals, grelot onions, crackling.
Read more, page 151.

THE DEVONSHIRE ARMS
LONG SUTTON

Mingle with locals over pies and pints at Philip Mepham's pretty village inn, or sit in the restaurant overlooking church and village green – the excellent, unfussy country meals might include 'happy-making' duck pâté, chargrilled bread, pear and saffron chutney. When the sun comes out, the courtyard garden's the place to be: croquet, boules, garden Jenga – all best when accompanied by local ale or village cider.
Read more, page 206.

THE TALBOT INN
MELLS

Find pub cooking of a high order at this 15th-century coaching inn. Ingredients are super-local, with fish from day boats and everything possible made, cured or smoked on the premises. A regularly changing seasonal menu ranges from ham, egg and chips to red wine-braised ox cheek, pearl barley, pancetta, savoy cabbage. Weekends, a hearty charcoal grill menu is convivially served at shared tables.
Read more, page 226.

THE FEATHERED NEST
NETHER WESTCOTE

While beer drinkers imbibe cask-conditioned ales in the bar of Tony and Amanda Timmer's Cotswold pub, in the kitchen, chef Kuba Winkowski, a Raymond Blanc protégé, cooks delicious and visually 'stunning' dishes with locally sourced seasonal ingredients. Consider cod, mussels, squid-ink noodles, nasturtium, coconut; duck liver, morels, ravioli, wild garlic – this is pub grub for serious foodies.
Read more, page 234.

THE STAGG INN
TITLEY

Everything is perfectly pitched at this cosy, beamed pub – even the bar snacks are special (think home-made pickles with a three-cheese ploughman's). In the dining room, Steve Reynolds, co-owner and chef, showcases local ingredients in his seasonal menus – perhaps Herefordshire beef fillet, red wine sauce, smoked mash, parsnips, red cabbage. The Friday fish special might be turbot, warm potato salad, sorrel, samphire. Interesting vegetarian menus, too.
Read more, page 310.

THE GURNARD'S HEAD
ZENNOR

You'll find the Inkin brothers' signature mix of style, informality and traditional values at their mellow pub overlooking the Atlantic. From staff to suppliers, local is king. Max Wilson's short, appealing set menus might include foraged nettle and mint gazpacho; Newlyn crab; blonde ray wing, crushed potatoes, chard, samphire, brown shrimp butter. Children can have small portions or order from their own menu. Vegetarians are well served.
Read more, page 335.

THE BRIDGE INN AT RATHO
RATHO

The dining room overlooks the Union Canal at Graham and Rachel Bucknall's pub by the bridge in a conservation village. Ben Watson's menus range from haddock with hand-cut chips to charred fillet and braised flank of Borders beef with peppercorn jus; there's also local game in season. The Bucknalls raise their own saddleback pigs; vegetables and herbs for the kitchen are grown in the walled garden at nearby Ratho Hall.
Read more, page 383.

THE BELL AT SKENFRITH
SKENFRITH

In a postcard-worthy scene by the River Monnow, Richard Ireton and Sarah Hudson's whitewashed former coaching inn wins praise for warm hospitality. Chef Joseph Colman's menus run from 'refined' lunchtime pub classics, such as pork sausage, onion gravy, apple purée, long-stemmed broccoli, to a tempting dinner selection, perhaps including pan-seared rack of lamb, lamb croquette, fondant potato, currant jus.
Read more, page 433.

WOOLLEY GRANGE
BRADFORD-ON-AVON

In sprawling grounds that invite exploration, this Jacobean manor house in glorious Wiltshire countryside has a happy, relaxed atmosphere, where children and adults are pampered in equal measure. There are children's teas and family dinners; baby and toddler equipment come as standard. Beyond playrooms and pools, there are even 'mini-me' spa treatments using all-natural products.
Read more, page 108.

MOONFLEET MANOR
FLEET

A treat for young children, this Georgian manor house is exceedingly family friendly: find an Ofsted-registered crèche, three indoor swimming pools and an all-weather play zone. For families wanting to explore, the South West Coastal Path runs along the end of the garden. A ten-minute drive away through Dorset countryside, donkey rides, deckchairs and ice creams are for the taking at the seaside resort of Weymouth.
Read more, page 164.

FOWEY HALL
FOWEY

Mess about in boats – or on the trampoline, or in the swimming pool – at this family-focused Victorian mansion overlooking the Fowey estuary in Cornwall. Youngsters might like the chicken coop and bee hotel, or the kiddie cocktails at high tea; accompanying adults may escape to candlelit dinners, spa treatments and peaceful garden strolls. Heading to the water's edge? There are wellies, fishing nets, and buckets and spades to borrow.
Read more, page 166.

AUGILL CASTLE
KIRKBY STEPHEN

Warm, friendly and utterly unstuffy, Wendy and Simon Bennett's quirky Victorian castle is much liked by guests with children in tow. There are family rooms, communal dinners, afternoon teas (with lashings of jam), and a great expanse of garden to tumble about in; Cumbrian countryside surrounds. Fancy a quiet night? Ask about the 12-seat Art Deco cinema – popcorn optional.
Read more, page 193.

BEDRUTHAN HOTEL AND SPA
MAWGAN PORTH

Fun's the word at this bright, contemporary Cornish hotel in an unbeatable spot overlooking the beach. Choose between playgrounds and kites, indoor and outdoor swimming pools, tennis or a stop in the family spa. On weekends and during the school holidays, book the children (eight years and above) into the all-day youth club, then find a spot in the adults-only lounge and enjoy blissful silence. Read more, page 223.

TRESANTON
ST MAWES

There's a sophisticated but breezy air about Olga Polizzi's cliffside cluster of cottages, on the edge of a Cornish village overlooking Falmouth Bay. Young guests are made very welcome with a children's garden and Wendy house, a playroom and all-day children's teas; there's child-friendly activity all around – fishing, crabbing, sailing and much beachy diversion. Sleep in style: there are several family suites, including one with three bedrooms and a dining area. Read more, page 283.

THE COLONSAY
COLONSAY

Jane and Alex Howard's 18th-century inn, on the unspoilt Isle of Colonsay, is a laid-back, carefree place (particularly on live Scottish music nights). Unfussy bedrooms, including a suite for four, are simply furnished, but you'll be spending your time outside. Discover ancient hilltop forts, sprint along sandy beaches, spot dolphins and otters at sea, send the seagulls flying – then return in time for a family feast of local seafood. Read more, page 348.

TREFEDDIAN HOTEL
ABERDYFI

Between the Snowdonian mountains and the Cambrian coast, the Cave family's traditional hotel is a long-time favourite of multigenerational groups who praise the 'unfailingly cheerful' staff. Children have the run of indoor and outdoor play areas; beachgoers find buckets and spades to borrow. Evenings, switch on the baby-listening service and settle in to a five-course table d'hôte menu in the restaurant. Read more, page 397.

PORTH TOCYN HOTEL
ABERSOCH

Overlooking Cardigan Bay, the Fletcher-Brewer family's 'lovely, wacky' hotel is minutes from the beach. A congenial spot, the hotel has more-than-adequate facilities for young guests: a games room, a media snug, an outdoor swimming pool, high teas and family-time suppers (with home-made ice cream). Child-friendly adventure walks on the Wales Coastal Path are within easy reach. Children share their parents' bedroom free of charge. Read more, page 400.

LONGUEVILLE MANOR
ST SAVIOUR

With mini-croquet, nature trails and a swimming pool, the extensive grounds surrounding the Lewis family's luxury Jersey hotel are an exceptional play area for lucky children. Book interconnecting rooms stocked with fruit, board games and magazines, or splurge on the two-bedroom cottage, steps from the main building. Travelling with a baby? Pre-order baby food, wipes, nappies, potties and more, using the hotel's 'Little Needs' service. Read more, page 442.

BIGGIN HALL
BIGGIN-BY-HARTINGTON
Supplied with sandwiches, set off from James Moffett's popular, reasonably priced hotel to explore the Peak District and Britain's first designated national park. Walks start from or pass the door – embark on a gentle stroll, or take a hike up hill and down dale. Further afield, drive to nearby Alstonefield for a walk that takes in wooded Dovedale, 'Eagledale' in George Eliot's Adam Bede.
Read more, page 99.

TUDOR FARMHOUSE
CLEARWELL
There are walks in all directions, enchanting or challenging, from this farmhouse hotel in the Forest of Dean. Take a tour of the mine workings and caverns of Clearwell Caves, or follow the sculpture trail to see such installations as Grove of Silence, Iron Road and Cathedral of the Forest. Offa's Dyke Path and the Wye Valley Walk are nearby. Ask at reception for printed information or to order a packed lunch.
Read more, page 138.

PEN-Y-DYFFRYN
OSWESTRY
Pull on your hiking boots – you're in hill-walking country at this former rectory close to the Welsh border. Owners Miles and Audrey Hunter have plenty of route suggestions, from a half-hour constitutional or a 90-minute reservoir walk, to the Offa's Dyke long-distance path, which passes just a mile from the door. Climb to the top of Wales's highest waterfall, or just take a turn around adjoining woodland. Walking breaks are available.
Read more, page 251.

BOSKERRIS HOTEL
ST IVES
Set off on exhilarating walks along the South West Coastal Path from this chic seaside hotel. A five-mile National Trust clifftop route leads from Godrevy headland to the narrow inlet known as Hell's Mouth; another day, set off from Lelant on the St Michael's Way pilgrims' route towards St Michael's Mount (a European Cultural Route). Return, afterwards, for a cream tea on the terrace.
Read more, page 279.

HOWTOWN HOTEL
ULLSWATER
Ask for a picnic lunch from the kind hosts at this family-run hotel, then wander lonely as a cloud along the shore of the lake of Wordsworth's best-known poem – the Ullswater Way follows quiet roads and public rights of way around the lake. Got your sea legs? Take the steamer to Glenridding and walk back before the dinner gong sounds. More serious hikers head for the fells.
Read more, page 313.

DUNKERY BEACON COUNTRY HOUSE
WOOTTON COURTENAY
Exmoor rolls out before you at this Edwardian hunting lodge. Maps and advice are freely offered for a self-guided ramble, but guided walks are available, too. A circular three-mile National Trust route skirts Dunkery and takes you through Horner Wood; alternatively, follow the Coleridge Way in the footsteps of the Romantic poet, drawing inspiration, as he did, from the marvellous landscape.
Read more, page 331.

GLENFINNAN HOUSE HOTEL
GLENFINNAN
With views of Ben Nevis, and a loch at the bottom of the garden, this Victorian mansion is ringed by scenic walks. Visitors are drawn to the monument across the water, where Bonnie Prince Charlie raised his standard before the doomed '45 Jacobite Rebellion. Take a packed lunch for the fairly challenging way-marked route via woodland, heath and bog – it leads up above 'Concrete Bob' McAlpine's sublime viaduct and down to Glenfinnan Station.
Read more, page 355.

MOOR OF RANNOCH HOTEL
RANNOCH STATION
This remote hotel stands in the wide open spaces of Rannoch Moor, ideal country for the dedicated hiker and wildlife enthusiast. The owners enthusiastically share local knowledge. Drive or cycle to explore the Black Wood of Rannoch, an ancient Caledonian pine forest criss-crossed by paths, where you might spy deer, red squirrels, pine martens and capercaillies, or perhaps glimpse a wildcat.
Read more, page 382.

THE FELIN FACH GRIFFIN
FELIN FACH
The Inkin brothers' dining pub-with-rooms is situated between the Black Mountains and the Brecon Beacons in wonderful countryside for trekking or strolling. Serious walkers can take on the Beacons, perhaps with a hired guide or instructor, while the less ambulant cruise the bookshops of nearby Hay-on-Wye. Stoke up with a good Border breakfast before you go – and don't forget to ask for maps, guidebooks and first-hand advice.
Read more, page 413.

PEN-Y-GWRYD
NANT GWYNANT
In breathtaking scenery, it's all thrills and no frills for hill walkers at this family-run hotel at the foot of Snowdon, where the Everest team trained in 1953. Take a way-marked path to the picture-postcard village of Beddgelert, hoping to spot wild goats along the way; later, return for a dinner with plenty of ballast. At night, make the trek to a shared bathroom.
Read more, page 424.

THE ROOKERY
LONDON
Three adjoining Georgian town houses combine as one exceptional hotel near Smithfield Market and trendy Clerkenwell. Fires burn in marble fireplaces; rich rugs are spread on flagstone floors; silk curtains are draped at sash windows. There's something to catch the eye in every room: antiques, oil paintings, gilt-framed mirrors, ornate plastered ceilings. Sleep in an 18th-century carved oak or four-poster bed; breakfast comes to the door.
Read more, page 62.

THE ZETTER TOWNHOUSE MARYLEBONE
LONDON
'Every detail has been carefully thought out' at this deliciously designed town house hotel, which has been inspired by an imaginary yet larger-than-life 'wicked' uncle. Wonder at the collection of Chinese ceramics, architectural plaster mouldings and assorted bibelots in the seductive cocktail bar before heading to a spirited bedroom. A simple bar or room-service menu has 'perfect comfort food after an evening out'.
Read more, page 67.

THE QUEENSBERRY
BATH
The 'very good' cocktails here add to the pleasure of this 'excellent' hotel, in four Georgian town houses close to the city centre. Dine at its modern Olive Tree restaurant (popular with locals on a night out). Bedrooms are smart and contemporary; the L-shaped four-poster suite has an enormous bed and a double walk-through shower. A plus: valet parking in a busy city.
Read more, page 89.

ARTIST RESIDENCE BRIGHTON
BRIGHTON
On a wide Regency square, this town house hotel is all Bohemia and razzmatazz, with bold mixes of bare brick, murals, reclaimed materials and classic pieces. Some rooms are large, with views of the water, but size isn't everything: what the smallest bedrooms lack in space, they make up for in lively, artist-created decor and bespoke furniture. Plenty of animation, too: a café, a restaurant, a cocktail bar, a table-tennis room.
Read more, page 112.

NUMBER THIRTY EIGHT CLIFTON
BRISTOL

A relaxed boutique B&B, this Georgian merchant's house at the top of Clifton Downs has panoramic views over the city. The nine stylish bedrooms are painted in sophisticated hues; some have park views. Sit by the fire in the lounge with a cream tea or a cocktail, then dine at one of several recommended restaurants nearby. A breakfast of locally sourced ingredients includes good pastries and smoked salmon. Read more, page 114.

EDGAR HOUSE
CHESTER

Let the sound of rushing water lull you to sleep at this refurbished Georgian house on the historic city wall, overlooking the River Dee. The bedrooms are beautifully designed with glamorous wallpaper; one has French doors that open on to a private terrace. A fun touch: the 'amazing' John Myatt fakes – paintings by 'Monet', 'Vermeer', 'Turner', 'Dufy' – in the lounge and restaurant. Breakfast is 'truly excellent'. Read more, page 132.

KINGS HEAD HOTEL
CIRENCESTER

A medieval inn has been transformed into this fashionable hotel (pictured), popular with locals who come for the revitalised bar and buzzy, art-adorned restaurant. Bedrooms are generously proportioned, with even the cheapest rooms smartly supplied with a capsule coffee-maker and up-to-date gadgetry. Unwind from the daily grind in the vaulted spa – there are four treatment rooms for head-to-toe pampering. Read more, page 137.

SANDS HOTEL
MARGATE

Nick Conington's restored Victorian building on the seafront is 'impeccably maintained' and personably staffed; many of the sleek bedrooms have sea views. Local residents give the glass-fronted Bay restaurant 'a low-key buzz'. Sample modern dishes that draw on Kentish produce and the sea: the fish is 'very fresh – as you'd hope at the seaside'. The arty Old Town and new Turner Contemporary are nearby. Read more, page 218.

38 ST GILES
NORWICH

An upmarket B&B in the historic city centre, built in 1700, this was once home to the Lord Mayor of Norwich. After tea and freshly baked cakes, ascend the grand staircase to the spacious, tastefully designed bedrooms and suites, each with varnished floors, heritage shades, fresh flowers; a walk-in rain shower or a bath. Breakfast is a feast, with smartly laid tables, good, strong coffee, and home-made bread and preserves. Read more, page 246.

OLD PARSONAGE
OXFORD

With the atmosphere of a modern gentlemen's club, this luxury hotel occupies a 17th-century building at the heart of the city. A knotty old wisteria drapes the stone facade, but the interiors are bang up to date. 'Sleek' bedrooms and suites have a marble bathroom; the dapper restaurant serves classic British dishes all day. On the first floor, art, literature, culture and politics mingle in the very smart library. Read more, page 253.

THE LORD CREWE ARMS
BLANCHLAND

Comfy and cosy, this spruced-up
pub-with-rooms in the Pennine Moors
makes a charming backdrop for a
hearty, homespun wedding. Summer
celebrations might include a drinks
reception in the garden; in the winter
months, guests may toast the happy
couple with warmed apple cider, by a
fire. Chef Simon Hicks's contemporary
British fayre is garden fresh and
gloriously 'unfussy' – fitting for a
modern-rustic fête.
Read more, page 101.

LANGAR HALL
LANGAR

Host an informal wedding in this finely,
if eccentrically, decorated, apricot-hued
Georgian family home, which stands
in graceful grounds, half an hour from
Nottingham. Award-winning chef Gary
Booth caters for celebratory lunches,
teas and dinners. Book the whole house
for an overnight party and enjoy full use
of the country-style bedrooms – a special
one, with its own veranda, is in a chalet
on the croquet lawn.
Read more, page 194.

HOTEL ENDSLEIGH
MILTON ABBOT

Romance envelops the 'magical'
Dartmoor landscape surrounding this
Regency fishing lodge, now run as a
much-admired small hotel by Olga
Polizzi. Fill your pockets with confetti:
wedding ceremonies may take place
in the parterre garden or in the little,
fairytale-like Shell House – or ask for
a marquee to be set up on the lawn, to
accommodate a larger party.
Read more, page 227.

JESMOND DENE HOUSE
NEWCASTLE UPON TYNE

Close to the centre, Peter Candler's
Arts and Crafts mansion, in lovely
grounds, has a country house feel.
There's a choice of licenced function
rooms, to host ceremonies for ten (in the
intimate Apartment, with a secret roof
terrace) up to 120 (in the double-height,
wood-panelled, Gothic-windowed
Great Hall). After-hours, a rooftop
honeymoon suite awaits.
Read more, page 239.

THE ASSEMBLY HOUSE
NORWICH
High ceilings, chandeliers and gaze-upon-the-bride balconies at this Georgian building bring an air of grandeur to the city weddings that take place here. From the music room with its grand piano to the ballroom with private bar, a selection of rooms can accommodate varying sizes of party. Among the 'luxurious' bedrooms, the bridal suite has its own enclosed garden.
Read more, page 244.

THE COACH HOUSE AT MIDDLETON LODGE
RICHMOND
In beautiful Yorkshire countryside, this Georgian coach house is a fine setting for a wedding in any season. Pre-wedding barbecues may be held on the lawn in summer; in cooler months, sip winter Pimm's in front of the log fire before heading into the heated marquee. Younger guests are well catered for, too, with indoor and outdoor games.
Read more, page 271.

STAR CASTLE
ST MARY'S
For the starry-eyed, this characterful hotel, in a star-shaped 16th-century castle, is on the largest of the Isles of Scilly. Hold a civil ceremony in the sea-view lounge, the grapevine-hung conservatory or the castle dining room (in front of the original Elizabethan fireplace), then snack on canapés and champagne on the castle ramparts, with the sea stretching out below.
Read more, page 281.

BOATH HOUSE
AULDEARN
Religious, civil or humanist ceremonies may be held by the ornamental lake at this historic Regency house in 'delightful' mature grounds close to the Moray coast. Continue the celebrations over a meal cooked by Michelin-starred chef Charles Lockley – his Slow Food menus use organic produce from the kitchen garden.
Read more, page 340.

GREGANS CASTLE HOTEL
BALLYVAUGHAN
An otherworldly landscape steeped in romantic drama surrounds this chic 18th-century manor house on the edge of the Burren. Its 'splendid' views reach to Galway Bay. Exclusive-use parties can be arranged, with 'creative' dinners and late-night nibbles. Any one of the handsome suites (perhaps the one with a four-poster bed and private courtyard garden) is a magical place to begin married life.
Read more, page 451.

ROUNDWOOD HOUSE
MOUNTRATH
There's an air of nostalgic elegance at Paddy and Hannah Flynn's gracious Georgian country house, in parkland at the foot of the Slieve Bloom Mountains. Plan an alfresco ceremony with a sweetly retro feel for 16 to 60 guests – the garden, with its walls of ancient stone, is a picture-perfect setting. Book all the eclectically furnished bedrooms and make a house party of the event.
Read more, page 468.

Each of these hotels has
a tennis court (T) and/or
a swimming pool (S)

ENGLAND

Hartwell House,
  Aylesbury (T,S)

Park House,
  Bepton (T,S)

Burgh Island Hotel,
  Bigbury-on-Sea (T,S)

The Blakeney,
  Blakeney (S)

Woolley Grange,
  Bradford-on-Avon (S)

Dormy House,
  Broadway (S)

Hell Bay Hotel,
  Bryher (S)

Tor Cottage,
  Chillaton (S)

Corse Lawn House,
  Corse Lawn (T,S)

Dart Marina,
  Dartmouth (S)

Fingals,
  Dittisham (S)

Old Whyly,
  East Hoathly (T,S)

The Grand Hotel,
  Eastbourne (S)

Starborough Manor,
  Edenbridge (T,S)

Moonfleet Manor,
  Fleet (S)

Fowey Hall,
  Fowey (S)

Stock Hill House,
  Gillingham (T)

Hambleton Hall,
  Hambleton (T,S)

Congham Hall,
  King's Lynn (S)

Augill Castle,
  Kirkby Stephen (T)

The Feathers,
  Ledbury (S)

Lime Wood,
  Lyndhurst (S)

Bedruthan Hotel and Spa,
  Mawgan Porth (T,S)

The Scarlet,
  Mawgan Porth (S)

Budock Vean,
  Mawnan Smith (T,S)

Mullion Cove Hotel,
  Mullion Cove (S)

Hotel TerraVina,
  Netley Marsh (S)

Chewton Glen,
  New Milton (T,S)

The Old Rectory,
  Norwich (S)

Askham Hall,
  Penrith (S)

Star Castle,
  St Mary's (T,S)
Salcombe Harbour,
  Salcombe (S)
Seaham Hall,
  Seaham (S)
Soar Mill Cove Hotel,
  Soar Mill Cove (T,S)
Plumber Manor,
  Sturminster Newton (T)
Cliveden House,
  Taplow (T,S)
Calcot Manor,
  Tetbury (T,S)
The Nare,
  Veryan-in-Roseland (T,S)
Gilpin Hotel and Lake House,
  Windermere (S)
Holbeck Ghyll,
  Windermere (T)
Middlethorpe Hall,
  York (S)

SCOTLAND
Isle of Eriska Hotel,
  Spa and Island,
  Eriska (T,S)

WALES
Trefeddian,
  Aberdyfi (T,S)
Porth Tocyn,
  Abersoch (T,S)
Gliffaes,
  Crickhowell (T)
Bodysgallen Hall and Spa,
  Llandudno (T,S)
The Lake,
  Llangammarch Wells (T,S)
Hotel Portmeirion,
  Portmeirion (S)

CHANNEL ISLANDS
The White House,
  Herm (T,S)
The Atlantic Hotel,
  St Brelade (T,S)
Greenhills,
  St Peter (S)
Longueville Manor,
  St Saviour (T,S)

IRELAND
Rathsallagh House,
  Dunlavin (T)
Castle Leslie,
  Glaslough (T)
Marlfield House,
  Gorey (T)
Rosleague Manor,
  Letterfrack (T)
Currarevagh House,
  Oughterard (T)
Rathmullan House,
  Rathmullan (T,S)
Coopershill,
  Riverstown (T)
Ballymaloe House,
  Shanagarry (T,S)

Each of these hotels has at least one bedroom equipped for a visitor in a wheelchair. You should telephone to discuss individual requirements

LONDON
The Goring
The Rookery
The Zetter
The Zetter Townhouse
  Marylebone

ENGLAND
The Wentworth,
  Aldeburgh
Rothay Manor,
  Ambleside
Hartwell House,
  Aylesbury
Red Lion Inn,
  Babcary
Barnsley House,
  Barnsley
The Master Builder's,
  Beaulieu
Park House,
  Bepton
The Lord Crewe Arms,
  Blanchland
The Millstream,
  Bosham
Woolley Grange,
  Bradford-on-Avon
The White Horse,
  Brancaster Staithe
Brooks Guesthouse,
  Bristol
Dormy House,
  Broadway

Hell Bay Hotel,
  Bryher
Northcote Manor,
  Burrington
Pendragon Country
  House,
  Camelford
Brockencote Hall,
  Chaddesley Corbett
Crouchers,
  Chichester
Captain's Club Hotel,
  Christchurch
Kings Head Hotel,
  Cirencester
Beech House & Olive
  Branch,
  Clipsham
Clow Beck House,
  Croft-on-Tees
Dart Marina,
  Dartmouth
Dedham Hall,
  Dedham
The Red Lion Freehouse,
  East Chisenbury
The Grand Hotel,
  Eastbourne
Eckington Manor,
  Eckington
The Carpenters Arms,
  Felixkirk
Fowey Hall,
  Fowey

Forest Side,
  Grasmere
The Horn of Plenty,
  Gulworthy
Castle House,
  Hereford
Battlesteads,
  Hexham
Byfords,
  Holt
Congham Hall,
  King's Lynn
Northcote,
  Langho
Lewtrenchard Manor,
  Lewdown
The Clive,
  Ludlow
Lime Wood,
  Lyndhurst
Sands Hotel,
  Margate
Swinton Park,
  Masham
Bedruthan Hotel,
  Mawgan Porth
The Scarlet,
  Mawgan Porth
The Redesdale Arms,
  Moreton-in-Marsh
St Mary's Inn,
  Morpeth
Hotel TerraVina,
  Netley Marsh

Chewton Glen,
New Milton

Jesmond Dene House,
Newcastle upon Tyne

The Packhorse Inn,
Newmarket

Beechwood Hotel,
North Walsham

The Assembly House,
Norwich

Hart's Hotel,
Nottingham

Old Bank,
Oxford

Old Parsonage,
Oxford

Tebay Services Hotel,
Penrith

The Pig near Bath,
Pensford

The Black Swan,
Ravenstonedale

The Coach House at
Middleton Lodge,
Richmond

Idle Rocks,
St Mawes

Salcombe Harbour Hotel,
Salcombe

Seaham Hall,
Seaham

St Cuthbert's House,
Seahouses

Brocco on the Park,
Sheffield

The Silverton,
Shrewsbury

The Royal Oak,
Swallowcliffe

Briarfields,
Titchwell

Titchwell Manor,
Titchwell

Tuddenham Mill,
Tuddenham

The Nare,
Veryan-in-Roseland

The Inn at West End,
West End

Holbeck Ghyll,
Windermere

The Manor Coach House,
Worcester

Middlethorpe Hall,
York

SCOTLAND

Loch Melfort Hotel,
Arduaine

Boath House,
Auldearn

Dunvalanree in Carradale,
Carradale

Coul House,
Contin

The Three Chimneys and
The House Over-By,
Dunvegan

The Bonham,
Edinburgh

Isle of Eriska Hotel, Spa
and Island,
Eriska

Ballathie House,
Kinclaven

Kylesku Hotel,
Kylesku

Langass Lodge,
Locheport

Craigatin House,
Pitlochry

The Green Park,
Pitlochry

Viewfield House,
Portree

WALES

Harbourmaster Hotel,
Aberaeron

Trefeddian Hotel,
Aberdyfi

The Hardwick,
Abergavenny

The Bull,
Beaumaris

Gliffaes,
Crickhowell

Ynyshir Hall,
Eglwysfach

Penbontbren,
Glynarthen

Tyddyn Llan,
Llandrillo

Bodysgallen Hall and Spa,
Llandudno

The Lake,
Llangammarch Wells

Hotel Portmeirion,
Portmeirion

CHANNEL ISLANDS

Greenhills,
St Peter

IRELAND

The Mustard Seed at Echo
Lodge,
Ballingarry

Stella Maris,
Ballycastle

Seaview House,
Ballylickey

Gregans Castle Hotel,
Ballyvaughan

The Quay House,
Clifden

Castle Leslie,
Glaslough

Brook Lane Hotel,
Kenmare

No. 1 Pery Square,
Limerick

Sheedy's,
Lisdoonvarna

Rathmullan House,
Rathmullan

LONDON

The Tower of London and Tower Bridge

LONDON

Map 2:D4

ARTIST RESIDENCE

♔César award since 2016

Eclectic with a soupçon of romance, this 'quirky, characterful' hotel balances 'retro touches' with upcycled industrialism. Owners Charlotte and Justin Salisbury instil 'cheerful efficiency' at the stylishly restored former pub. Reception is a laptop in an alcove; stripped wooden flooring, vintage and bespoke furniture, and limited-edition prints characterise the variously sized bedrooms. 'The details were well thought through. Overlooking neighbouring houses, our small room had a metal-framed bed with good linen, well-positioned sockets (a necessity for technophiles), clever storage, excellent lighting; a fine rain shower in the bathroom. There was no noise at night.' Sit by the fire in the Club Room, pick up a paddle in the Ping-Pong Room, sip an art-inspired concoction in the 'youthful' cocktail bar. New chef Radek Nitkowski serves a weekly dinner menu in the popular Cambridge Street Kitchen. Breakfast, charged extra, is 'excellent value': freshly squeezed juice, leaf teas; banana pancakes, maple syrup; avocado, poached eggs, chilli on rye. Sister hotels are in Brighton (see entry) and Penzance (see Shortlist).

52 Cambridge Street
Pimlico
London
SW1V 4QQ

T: 020 7828 6684
E: london@artistresidence.co.uk
W: artistresidencelondon.co.uk

BEDROOMS: 10. 2 suites.
OPEN: all year except Christmas.
FACILITIES: bar, restaurant, Club Room, Ping-Pong Room, free Wi-Fi, in-room TV (Freeview), unsuitable for disabled.
BACKGROUND MUSIC: in public areas.
LOCATION: Pimlico, underground Pimlico.
CHILDREN: all ages welcomed.
DOGS: not allowed.
CREDIT CARDS: Amex, MasterCard, Visa.
PRICES: [2016] room £160–£380. Set breakfast £12.50, set dinner £35.

SEE ALSO SHORTLIST

LONDON

Map 2:D4

THE CAPITAL

♥ César award since 2008

'Old-fashioned hospitality and exceptional cuisine' come together at this 'intimate' luxury hotel. 'The team cultivates a strong relationship with each and every guest,' writes a Guide reader, himself no mean hotelier, in 2016. Launched by Scotsman David Levin 45 years ago on a quiet back street, this is one of London's last family-run hotels; daughter Kate Levin is general manager. Mount the stone steps and enter the flower- and painting-filled lobby to be greeted by one of the professional, long-standing staff. Head concierge Clive Smith, who has been here 25 years, has plenty of local information to share. From single rooms to spacious suites, each bedroom is elegantly styled with a mix of antique and modern English furnishings; all have a customisable minibar, and oversized bathrobes in a marble bathroom. At dinner, book a table in 'talented' chef Nathan Outlaw's Michelin-starred restaurant, where the menu specialises in 'exceptional' seafood, perhaps hake, mussels, cider and clotted cream sauce. Fancy a more informal meal? Pop into the bar, or sister hotel The Levin, next door (see entry). (Neil Kedward)

22–24 Basil Street
Knightsbridge
London
SW3 1AT

T: 020 7589 5171
F: 020 7225 0011
E: reservations@capitalhotel.co.uk
W: www.capitalhotel.co.uk

BEDROOMS: 49.
OPEN: all year.
FACILITIES: lift, sitting room, bar, restaurant, free Wi-Fi, in-room TV, access to nearby health club/spa, only restaurant suitable for disabled.
BACKGROUND MUSIC: none.
LOCATION: central, underground Knightsbridge, private car park.
CHILDREN: all ages welcomed.
DOGS: small dogs allowed, on request.
CREDIT CARDS: all major cards.
PRICES: [2016] room £280–£425. Continental breakfast £16, cooked breakfast £19.50. À la carte £55 (plus 12½% discretionary service charge).

SEE ALSO SHORTLIST

LONDON

Map 2:D4

DURRANTS

♛ César award since 2010

In an 'interesting' area with 'many individual shops and cafés', the Miller family's 'amiable' Georgian-fronted hotel is liked for its 'nicely old-fashioned' ambience and attention to detail. 'All the brass shines on the attractive entrance. With the union flag flying above, it makes a welcoming sight,' says a regular Guide reader this year. Inside, public rooms filled with antique furniture, paintings and prints 'give the hotel that special character'. Choose among the individually designed bedrooms, which vary in size and aspect. 'Down a pleasant, well-lit corridor, our fresh, refurbished room was fairly compact but attractive, with a well-designed bathroom. We'd requested a rear room on an upper floor to escape traffic noise; ours was quiet, with large windows that opened. We slept well.' Chef Cara Baird's modern British menu, perhaps with 'excellent' guineafowl ('and more vegetables, please!'), is taken in the wood-panelled dining room. In the morning, a 'tasty, well-presented' (and individually priced) breakfast is cooked to order; 'tea, butter and marmalade are served in a silver-plated pot, which adds style'. (Max Lickfold, and others)

26–32 George Street
Marylebone
London
W1H 5BJ

T: 020 7935 8131
F: 020 7487 3510
E: enquiries@durrantshotel.co.uk
W: www.durrantshotel.co.uk

BEDROOMS: 92. 7 on ground floor.
OPEN: all year, restaurant closed 25 Dec evening.
FACILITIES: lifts, bar, restaurant, lounge, function rooms, free Wi-Fi, in-room TV (Freeview).
BACKGROUND MUSIC: none.
LOCATION: off Oxford Street, underground Bond Street, Baker Street.
CHILDREN: all ages welcomed.
DOGS: allowed in George bar.
CREDIT CARDS: Amex, MasterCard, Visa.
PRICES: [2016] room from £195. Set dinner Mon–Fri £19.50–£21.50, Sun £27.50–£32.50, à la carte £55 (plus 12½% discretionary service charge).

SEE ALSO SHORTLIST

LONDON

Map 2:D4

THE GORING

♀César award since 1994

'It is without equal.' Busy city workers and Buckingham Palace tourists may throng the neighbourhood, but this 'conveniently located' luxury hotel is 'remarkably quiet and secluded from the urban bustle', say admirers in 2016, who were 'greeted with great courtesy'. 'You have the impression you're being invited into an elegant country house.' Today London's last remaining family-owned grand hotel, The Goring, its rooms full of 'beautiful flower arrangements', is 'immaculate'. Sophisticated bedrooms and suites, some overlooking the 'inviting' private garden, are tastefully styled. 'On a high floor, our superior room had two large double beds and an enormous bathroom. Remarkably, in the wardrobe hung a 19th-century doublet that once belonged to an officer of the Guards.' Chef Shay Cooper was awarded a Michelin star in 2015; book a table in the 'spacious, pleasantly light' restaurant for his refined dishes, perhaps roast halibut fillet, buttered crab, English peas, preserved lemon. Lighter fare may be taken in the bar, where 'everything's served with the same care'. (Ian and Crispina McDonald)

Beeston Place
Belgravia
London
SW1W 0JW

T: 020 7396 9000
F: 020 7834 4393
E: reception@thegoring.com
W: www.thegoring.com

BEDROOMS: 69. 2 suitable for disabled.
OPEN: all year.
FACILITIES: lifts, lounge, bar, restaurant, private dining rooms, free Wi-Fi, in-room TV (Sky), civil wedding licence, veranda, 1-acre private garden (croquet).
BACKGROUND MUSIC: none.
LOCATION: Belgravia, mews parking, underground Victoria.
CHILDREN: all ages welcomed (kids' welcome programme, little ones' library).
DOGS: not allowed.
CREDIT CARDS: all major cards.
PRICES: [2016] per room B&B from £420. Set dinner £56.50, à la carte £80.

SEE ALSO SHORTLIST

LONDON

Map 2:D4

THE GRAZING GOAT

There's more than a 'splendid' bacon and eggs at this 'youthful' pub-with-rooms in a 'hidden enclave' minutes from the flurry of Oxford Street. Its name recalls the time when goats grazed here on the Portman Estate. Pub guests can graze all day in the airy, stripped-down bar (open fireplaces, local ales, large French doors) – or, from midday, in the panelled first-floor dining room. Join the throng of locals, who come for the British bistro dishes – house-cured meats, daily fish specials, thoughtfully sourced produce. On the upper three floors ('quite a climb, but this keeps rooms insulated from pub noise'), spend the night in a 'simple, modern, beautifully furnished' bedroom. 'Ours looked over rooftops to a small mews. There were proper sash windows that you could open; noise wasn't a problem.' Thoughtful touches include high-end toiletries, cafetière coffee ('they gave me decaf when I asked for it'), a city map. Breakfast, charged extra, is 'excellent', with unusual options: coconut yogurt, honey, bee pollen; omelette, grilled crevettes, spring onion. The owners, the Cubitt House group, also run The Orange in Pimlico (see entry).

6 New Quebec Street
Marble Arch
London
W1H 7RQ

T: 020 7724 7243
E: reservations@thegrazinggoat.co.uk
W: www.thegrazinggoat.co.uk

BEDROOMS: 8.
OPEN: all year.
FACILITIES: bar, dining room, patio, free Wi-Fi, in-room TV, unsuitable for disabled.
BACKGROUND MUSIC: all day in bar.
LOCATION: central, underground Marble Arch.
CHILDREN: all ages welcomed.
DOGS: allowed in public rooms, not in bedrooms.
CREDIT CARDS: Amex, MasterCard, Visa.
PRICES: room from £210. Cooked breakfast from £7, à la carte £35.

SEE ALSO SHORTLIST

LONDON

HAZLITT'S

❦ César award since 2002

In raffish Soho, this 'stunningly original' boutique hotel occupies three Georgian houses. 'Friendly, efficient' staff open the door to reveal a lavish, intriguing collection of 'old architectural features, old furniture, old books and paintings – much to investigate and appreciate'. It was in one of the houses that the tempestuous 19th-century essayist William Hazlitt spent his dying days in poverty, drugged on opium. Today's guests will be exhilarated by the interiors, while Hazlitt would wonder at the high-tech lighting, air conditioning, modern plumbing and indulgent roll-top baths. Bedrooms and suites are astonishing. Sleep in the Duke of Monmouth suite – if you can bear to miss the rest of it, that is: there's much to discover, from the sitting room with a working fireplace to the private garden complete with sliding glass roof, to the life-sized eagle from whose mouth flows water to fill the marble bathtub. At breakfast, taken in the bedroom or the library, choose from bacon sandwiches, fresh fruit and yogurt, or a baker's basket of freshly baked croissants and pastries.

6 Frith Street
Soho Square
Soho
London
W1D 3JA

T: 020 7434 1771
F: 020 7439 1524
E: reservations@hazlitts.co.uk
W: www.hazlittshotel.com

BEDROOMS: 30. 2 on ground floor.
OPEN: all year.
FACILITIES: lift, library (honesty bar), meeting room, free Wi-Fi, in-room TV (Sky), unsuitable for disabled.
BACKGROUND MUSIC: none.
LOCATION: centre of Soho (front windows triple glazed, rear rooms quietest), underground Tottenham Court Road, Leicester Square.
CHILDREN: all ages welcomed.
DOGS: not allowed.
CREDIT CARDS: Amex, MasterCard, Visa.
PRICES: [2016] per room B&B from £288, D,B&B from £338. Limited room service menu.

SEE ALSO SHORTLIST

LONDON

THE LEVIN

Grand-hotel luxury mixes with small-scale intimacy at this 'immaculate' town house hotel, close to Hyde Park and the museums. It is owned by David Levin, who also owns the neighbouring Capital (see entry); the staff are 'superb' – 'interested, and interesting'. Pass the 'spectacular' light installation on the way to the smart, modern bedrooms, each with air conditioning, 'very good lighting', a marble bathroom with underfloor heating. Treats await: besides the chic teas and capsule coffee-maker, find a champagne minibar and a selection of books to borrow. Splurge on the spacious junior suite, its large windows looking down on the neighbourhood; especially good for a family, it has a large convertible sofa bed. In the informal basement bistro, try classics such as Cornish crab, coriander, chilli cake; confit duck leg, spring onions, mashed potatoes – then wash it down with a glass of something from the owner's wine estate in the Loire valley. Michelin-starred sister restaurant Outlaw's at The Capital is next door. Breakfast brings 'especially good croissants and pastries from the owner's bakery'. 'Mr Levin clearly sets high standards.'

28 Basil Street
Knightsbridge
London
SW3 1AS

T: 020 7589 6286
F: 020 7823 7826
E: reservations@thelevinhotel.co.uk
W: www.thelevinhotel.co.uk

BEDROOMS: 12.
OPEN: all year.
FACILITIES: lobby, library, honesty bar, The Metro bar/brasserie, free Wi-Fi, in-room TV, access to nearby health club/spa, unsuitable for disabled.
BACKGROUND MUSIC: 'calm' in restaurant.
LOCATION: central, underground Knightsbridge.
CHILDREN: all ages welcomed.
DOGS: allowed at extra cost.
CREDIT CARDS: all major cards.
PRICES: [2016] per room B&B (continental) £252–£515. À la carte £25.

SEE ALSO SHORTLIST

LONDON

NUMBER SIXTEEN

🏵 César award since 2011

Come 'home away from home', to this glamorous town house hotel 'conveniently' located on a quiet side street close to the museums and boutiques of South Kensington. Owned by Tim and Kit Kemp, it has striking interiors reminiscent of sister hotels in the Firmdale group. Here, find fresh flowers and a driftwood chandelier in the drawing room; bold artwork in the conservatory; an airy library for drinks and afternoon tea; a 'nice', tree-filled garden, ideal for a dish or two off the all-day brasserie-style menu. Staff are 'helpful and courteous'. Each bedroom, in Kit Kemp's fresh, individual style, has its own character. Pick one to suit – some standard rooms overlook the tranquil garden; more spacious deluxe rooms have a king-size bed and space to sit. All rooms have top-end bedlinen, fancy toiletries, a modern granite-and-oak bathroom. Travelling with children? They're made very welcome, with mini bathrobes, a book of London activities, DVDs and popcorn. (Ask for books or board games as the mood suits.) At breakfast, expect good choice: pancakes and maple syrup, avocado on rye, a 'doorstop' bacon sandwich.

16 Sumner Place
South Kensington
London
SW7 3EG

T: 020 7589 5232
E: sixteen@firmdale.com
W: www.firmdalehotels.com

BEDROOMS: 41. 1 on ground floor.
OPEN: all year.
FACILITIES: drawing room, library, conservatory, free Wi-Fi, in-room TV (Sky), civil wedding licence, garden.
BACKGROUND MUSIC: none.
LOCATION: Kensington, underground South Kensington.
CHILDREN: all ages welcomed.
DOGS: not allowed.
CREDIT CARDS: Amex, MasterCard, Visa.
PRICES: [2016] per room B&B single from £192, double from £312. À la carte £32.

SEE ALSO SHORTLIST

LONDON

Map 2:D4

THE ORANGE

Posh pub meets classy rooms-at-the-inn, at this 'beautifully proportioned' Georgian building in a conservation area of handsome stucco houses. Owned by the small Cubitt House group, it is a sister to The Grazing Goat at Marble Arch (see entry), with clear family resemblances in the stripped-down, limed-oak interiors and airy, high-ceilinged rooms. Step into the 'friendly, informal' ground-floor bar and 'bustling' restaurant – the sometimes-racing heart of the place – where coffee, drinks, pizzas and 'well-presented' modern dishes are served all day. 'There's always someone on duty to greet guests' with 'the warmest of welcomes'. On the upper floors, 'beautifully crafted' bedrooms, some compact, have a king-size bed with 'fine' linens, chic toiletries, a marble bathroom ('strong shower, decent fittings'), sash windows beneath which the city traffic faintly growls. At breakfast, order a bread basket with croissants, slices of sourdough, and sultana and fennel bread (though not the sticky Chelsea bun that originated at the 18th-century Bun House on the square). 'We enjoyed perfect scrambled eggs with delicious smoked bacon; good tea and coffee; freshly squeezed orange juice.'

37 Pimlico Road
Pimlico
London
SW1W 8NE

T: 020 7881 9844
E: reservations@theorange.co.uk
W: www.theorange.co.uk

BEDROOMS: 4.
OPEN: all year.
FACILITIES: restaurant, 2 bars, free Wi-Fi, in-room TV, unsuitable for disabled.
BACKGROUND MUSIC: in public areas.
LOCATION: Pimlico, underground Sloane Square.
CHILDREN: all ages welcomed (under-13s may share parents' room).
DOGS: not allowed.
CREDIT CARDS: Amex, MasterCard, Visa.
PRICES: per room B&B £205–£240. À la carte £35.

SEE ALSO SHORTLIST

LONDON

THE PORTOBELLO

Intrigued by the idea of an antique four-poster bed so high you need steps to get into it? Fascinated by the notion of a Victorian steampunk bath right in the bedroom? Look no further. The 'charming and quirky' Portobello may not be as rock'n'roll as when the likes of the Rolling Stones used to stay – it was taken over in 2014 by Peter and Jessica Frankopan, whose Curious Group of Hotels includes the Canal House, Amsterdam (see the Good Hotel Guide website) – but the original features and eccentricities remain. 'The result is a delight.' The manager is Douglas Cooper (no relation, we presume, to Alice Cooper, who kept snakes in the bath here); the staff are 'friendly' and 'helpful'. Overlooking communal gardens to the rear, the 19th-century stucco mansion has bedrooms ranging from 'tiny but beautifully coloured' attic singles to generously sized 'Exceptional' rooms. No two are remotely alike, but all have a coffee machine, minibar and apothecary-inspired bath products. Snacks are available all day; in the morning, sit down to a continental breakfast in the 'large, light' drawing room.

22 Stanley Gardens
Notting Hill
London
W11 2NG

T: 020 7727 2777
E: stay@portobellohotel.com
W: www.portobellohotel.com

BEDROOMS: 21.
OPEN: all year.
FACILITIES: lift, drawing room/breakfast room with honesty bar, free Wi-Fi, in-room TV, unsuitable for disabled.
BACKGROUND MUSIC: 'chill-out' in drawing room.
LOCATION: Notting Hill, underground Notting Hill Gate.
CHILDREN: not under 16.
DOGS: not allowed.
CREDIT CARDS: Amex, MasterCard, Visa.
PRICES: [2016] per room B&B (continental) from £195.

SEE ALSO SHORTLIST

LONDON

Map 2:D4

THE ROOKERY

Three's a charm: in a trio of elegantly refurbished town houses near buzzy Smithfield Market, Peter McKay and Douglas Blain's 'outstanding', 'friendly' small hotel has the rakish appeal of an 18th-century private gentlemen's club. 'A soothing space in a busy hub' of the city, it has painstakingly recreated Georgian interiors: rich colours and gilt-framed oil paintings on the walls; antiques and polished flagstone floors; open fires. Watch for the hotel cat curled up in an armchair in the conservatory/honesty bar downstairs. Bedrooms are sumptuous – find wood panelling, silk curtains or wooden shutters; fresh flowers; a carved oak or four-poster bed – while modern comforts haven't been forgotten: there are 'immaculate' bathrooms and 'solid soundproofing'. At dinner, head out to any of the well-regarded restaurants within strolling distance, or order from the small room-service menu. Breakfast may be delivered to the room at a pre-arranged time: perhaps freshly squeezed orange juice, a 'generous' pastry basket, fresh fruit and granola, or a bacon sandwich. Sister hotel Hazlitt's in Soho (see entry) has the same sophisticated air.

12 Peter's Lane
Cowcross Street
Smithfield
London
EC1M 6DS

T: 020 7336 0931
F: 020 7336 0932
E: reservations@rookery.co.uk
W: www.rookeryhotel.com

BEDROOMS: 33. 1 on ground floor, suitable for disabled.
OPEN: all year.
FACILITIES: drawing room, library, conservatory, meeting facilities, free Wi-Fi, in-room TV (Sky), small garden terrace.
BACKGROUND MUSIC: none.
LOCATION: Smithfield, underground Farringdon, Barbican.
CHILDREN: all ages welcomed.
DOGS: not allowed.
CREDIT CARDS: Amex, MasterCard, Visa.
PRICES: [2016] per room B&B from £258. À la carte (room service only) £28.

SEE ALSO SHORTLIST

LONDON

Map 2:D4

SAN DOMENICO HOUSE

Step through the doorway into the marble foyer of this red brick Victorian mansion, to be transported from 21st-century London. In 2005, Pugliese entrepreneur Marisa Melpignano bought the former Sloane Hotel and transformed it into a treasure trove. From the 'luxurious' and 'inviting' drawing room (open fire, fresh flowers) to the theatrical bedrooms, it's filled with European art and antiques – cherub clocks, lamps and vases, four-poster beds, gilt-framed mirrors and paintings, swags and statuary. Despite the 'pleasing' old-world setting, all rooms are kitted out with modern comforts: air conditioning, a marble bathroom, top-end linens, posh toiletries. A suite in the former master bedroom has a king-size bed with a towering draped bedhead, a walk-in wardrobe, a sitting area with a Victorian desk, and a private balcony. The 'charming' staff bring drinks and snacks to the room; high above the street, find a sunny roof terrace for afternoon tea. Take breakfast there, or in the breakfast room, with freshly squeezed orange juice, pastries, 'good coffee' (your hosts are Italian, after all). Sloane Square is just around the corner.

29–31 Draycott Place
Chelsea
London
SW3 2SH

T: 020 7581 5757
F: 020 7584 1348
E: info@sandomenicohouse.com
W: www.sandomenicohouse.com

BEDROOMS: 17.
OPEN: all year.
FACILITIES: lounge, breakfast room, roof terrace, free Wi-Fi, in-room TV (Freeview), unsuitable for disabled.
BACKGROUND MUSIC: varied in lounge and breakfast room.
LOCATION: Chelsea, underground Sloane Square.
CHILDREN: all ages welcomed.
DOGS: not allowed.
CREDIT CARDS: all major cards.
PRICES: [2016] room from £255 (excluding VAT). Breakfast from £15.

SEE ALSO SHORTLIST

LONDON

Map 2:D4

THE VICTORIA

Find 'good-value' rooms, gastropubby meals and jugs of seasonal, home-made pear lemonade at this family-friendly spot, a 'cheerful' pub-with-rooms in a leafy residential neighbourhood. Owned by restaurateur Greg Bellamy and TV chef Paul Merrett, it is known in the area for its 'imaginative' menus featuring locally sourced and foraged ingredients. In the conservatory restaurant, or on the terrace in good weather, sample modern dishes such as leek and nettle soup, roasted pine nuts, smoked oil; chargrilled chicken, bhel puri salad, paratha. A list of 25 wines by the glass is fine accompaniment. Children have their own menu with pesto pasta, burgers, a bowl of greens; there is a play area in the courtyard. In winter, partake of a light supper menu; come summertime, gather around evening barbecues until the sun goes down. Smart bedrooms (some compact) are comfortably equipped with a digital radio and flat-screen TV; a hospitality corner with an espresso machine, bottled water and home-baked cookies. Breakfast on a 'flowerpot' muffin or streaky bacon bap with an elderflower spritzer, then walk it off in glorious Richmond Park, minutes away.

10 West Temple Sheen
Mortlake
London
SW14 7RT

T: 020 8876 4238
E: bookings@thevictoria.net
W: www.thevictoria.net

BEDROOMS: 7. 3 on ground floor.
OPEN: all year, except 1 Jan.
FACILITIES: bar, lounge, restaurant, free Wi-Fi, in-room TV, garden, play area, unsuitable for disabled.
BACKGROUND MUSIC: in pub and dining room.
LOCATION: Mortlake (10 mins' walk) from Waterloo/Clapham Jct, car park.
CHILDREN: all ages welcomed.
DOGS: allowed in pub and garden.
CREDIT CARDS: MasterCard, Visa.
PRICES: [2016] per room B&B (continental) £135–£150. À la carte £33 (plus 12½% discretionary service charge).

SEE ALSO SHORTLIST

LONDON

Map 2:D4

THE ZETTER

A pink chandelier hangs in the lobby of this cool, contemporary hotel, in a modish neighbourhood where meatpackers and media folk walk the streets. 'The whole place is on good form,' say trusted Guide correspondents in 2016. 'The staff were exceptionally nice and skilled, going out of their way to make my parents happy; their room was in perfect condition.' The converted Victorian warehouse has bags of personality to spare: a clubby, light-filled workspace is open to locals and hotel guests; the atrium displays work by a regularly changing roster of modern artists. Food is available all day in the open-plan café/wine bar: morning coffees, light lunches and afternoon teas by day; small plates, sharing boards and a choice of tipples by night. (For more intriguing craft cocktails, visit The Zetter Townhouse across the square – see next entry.) All of the neat bedrooms have thoughtful touches: a hot-water bottle, Penguin paperbacks, top-end toiletries, mood lighting. Living the high life? Splurge on one of the rooftop studios, each with a private balcony, sun loungers and panoramic city views. (Bill Brewer)

25% DISCOUNT VOUCHERS

St John's Square
86–88 Clerkenwell Road
Clerkenwell
London
EC1M 5RJ

T: 020 7324 4444
E: info@thezetter.com
W: www.thezetter.com

BEDROOMS: 59. 2 suitable for disabled.
OPEN: all year.
FACILITIES: 2 lifts, café/wine room, function/meeting rooms, free Wi-Fi, in-room TV (Freeview, some with Smart TV).
BACKGROUND MUSIC: none.
LOCATION: Clerkenwell, NCP garage 5 mins' walk, underground Farringdon.
CHILDREN: all ages welcomed.
DOGS: only guide dogs allowed.
CREDIT CARDS: Amex, MasterCard, Visa.
PRICES: [2016] room from £185.

SEE ALSO SHORTLIST

LONDON

Map 2:D4

THE ZETTER TOWNHOUSE CLERKENWELL

♔ César award since 2012

Across the cobbled square from The Zetter (see previous entry) is its eccentric aunt, outwardly an 'elegant' Georgian town house, but inside resembling a riot in an antique shop. Walls are crowded with paintings and knick-knacks, shelves crammed with books and bibelots, all around is a quirky decadence. Admire examples of the taxidermist's art as you partake of a 'delightful' continental breakfast or supper snacks devised by chef Bruno Loubet – a mug of soup, sharing boards, 'Aunt Wilhelmina's "drop of sherry" trifle'. (A room-service menu is also available all day.) Evenings, mixologist Tony Conigliaro makes wicked cocktails in the 'stylish', 'atmospheric' lounge. Bedrooms are as quirky as you like – a four-poster bed has a union flag canopy; a bathtub is set in an alcove of gold – while all have amusing artwork, reclaimed and antique furniture, a raindance shower in the bathroom. They've all been thoughtfully kitted out, too, with a minibar and espresso machine, a selection of novels, still and sparkling water from the Zetter's own boreholes. (ML, and others)

49–50 St John's Square
Clerkenwell
London
EC1V 4JJ

T: 020 7324 4567
E: reservations@thezetter.com
W: www.thezettertownhouse.com

BEDROOMS: 13.
OPEN: all year.
FACILITIES: cocktail lounge, private dining room, games room, free Wi-Fi, in-room TV.
BACKGROUND MUSIC: none.
LOCATION: Clerkenwell, underground Farringdon.
CHILDREN: all ages welcomed.
DOGS: none.
CREDIT CARDS: Amex, MasterCard, Visa.
PRICES: [2016] room from £245.

SEE ALSO SHORTLIST

LONDON

Map 2:D4

THE ZETTER TOWNHOUSE NEW
MARYLEBONE

'A warm, inclusive atmosphere' reigns over
the Chinese ceramics, architectural plaster
mouldings and assorted ornaments in this
deliciously designed town house, a ten-minute
walk from Hyde Park. 'An interesting hotel
with character, it's as dotty as the Clerkenwell
version [see entry], but with a decidedly
masculine feel,' say Guide inspectors this year.
Past the 'discreet, club-like' entrance, find the
seductive cocktail bar: 'lots of comfortable
leather seating', 'low lighting, as is the fashion'.
Antique and reclaimed furniture and other
curios give the well-equipped bedrooms much
spirit. 'Our mews-facing superior room was
wonderfully quiet for London. Every detail had
been carefully thought out, from the brocade
curtains to the pieced-together map on the
bathroom wall.' A 'simple' menu, taken in
the room or in the bar, has 'reasonably priced'
nibbles and light meals. 'We enjoyed proper
shepherd's pie – perfect comfort food after
an evening out.' Breakfast in the cocktail bar
(charged extra) includes a continental buffet
with 'interesting cereals; excellent, fresh loaves;
freshly squeezed juices'.

28–30 Seymour Street
Marylebone
London
W1H 7JB

T: 020 7324 4544
E: reservations@thezetter.com
W: www.thezettertownhouse.com/
    marylebone

BEDROOMS: 24. 3 suitable for
disabled.
OPEN: all year.
FACILITIES: lift, cocktail lounge, free
Wi-Fi, in-room TV (Freeview).
BACKGROUND MUSIC: all day in
cocktail lounge.
LOCATION: central, underground
Marble Arch.
CHILDREN: all ages welcomed.
DOGS: not allowed.
CREDIT CARDS: Amex, MasterCard,
Visa.
PRICES: [2016] room from £215
(excluding VAT).

SEE ALSO SHORTLIST

ENGLAND

Glastonbury Tor, Somerset

ALDEBURGH Suffolk

THE WENTWORTH

Comfortingly timeless and traditional, this 'individual' family-run hotel in a Victorian building stands across the road from the shingle beach. It appeals to guests who enjoy its 'relaxed country-house feel' and the 'helpful, friendly, long-serving staff'. Michael Pritt, the owner, has been welcoming visitors, many of whom become regulars, for more than 40 years. 'What's their secret? The ability to make people feel rested and at ease, with no demands or rules,' says an admirer this year. Take things slowly, in 'large, comfy' public rooms; in fine weather, order tea on the terrace (don't miss the cake of the day). In the main hotel and Darfield House, across the road, 'the bedrooms vary, and suit one's needs exactly'. Many have sea views over Aldeburgh beach; pick a large room with a seating area. The tables are set with white linens and silverware at the candlelit dinner (open to, and sometimes 'extremely busy' with, non-residents), where the daily-changing menu of straightforward dishes has an 'excellent choice' of 'delicious' fish. 'Our vegetarian friend was very happy with the variety of food he could have.' (Simon Rodway, John and Margaret Speake, and others)

25% DISCOUNT VOUCHERS

Wentworth Road
Aldeburgh
IP15 5BD

T: 01728 452312
F: 01728 454343
E: stay@wentworth-aldeburgh.co.uk
W: www.wentworth-aldeburgh.com

BEDROOMS: 35. 7 in Darfield House opposite, 5 on ground floor, 1 suitable for disabled.
OPEN: all year.
FACILITIES: 2 lounges, bar, restaurant, private dining room, conference room, free Wi-Fi, in-room TV, 2 terrace gardens, shingle beach 200 yds, parking.
BACKGROUND MUSIC: none.
LOCATION: seafront, 5 mins' walk from centre.
CHILDREN: all ages welcomed.
DOGS: welcomed (£2 per dog per night), not allowed in restaurant.
CREDIT CARDS: all major cards.
PRICES: [2016] per room B&B £165–£295. Set dinner £26.50. 1-night bookings refused Sat.

SEE ALSO SHORTLIST

ALLERFORD Somerset

Map 1:B5

CROSS LANE HOUSE

NEW

Old and new cross paths at this popular restaurant-with-rooms occupying a beautifully restored medieval farmhouse leased from the National Trust. 'Dedicated hosts' Max Lawrence and Andrew Stinson are 'a mine of information and always at hand'. The setting is classic picture-book charm: in a village of thatched cottages, the house stands a short distance from a 500-year-old packhorse bridge. Inside, all has been done 'with excellent taste', the crooked floors, low ceilings, Victorian tiles and ancient panelled walls serving as a fine backdrop for the many modern touches the owners have implemented. (Look out for the Tudor brick romantically inscribed by a long-ago lover.) There are just four bedrooms – one a spacious two-bedroom suite – each thoughtfully equipped with a capsule coffee machine, Cornish-grown tea, a well-stocked complimentary minibar, posh toiletries. In the candlelit dining room, modern British menus feature Exmoor produce, perhaps wild mushroom risotto, wild asparagus, white truffle. Come summertime, eat in the ancient linhay across the cobbled courtyard. 'Breakfast had the lot.' (Ken and Mildred Edwards)

Allerford
TA24 8HW

т: 01643 863276
е: info@crosslanehouse.com
w: www.crosslanehouse.com

BEDROOMS: 4.
OPEN: Feb–Dec, open Christmas and New Year, restaurant closed Sun, Mon.
FACILITIES: lounge bar, restaurant, free Wi-Fi, in-room TV (Freeview), 1-acre garden (alfresco dining), unsuitable for disabled.
BACKGROUND MUSIC: in lounge and dining room in late afternoon and evening.
LOCATION: 4¼ miles W of Minehead.
CHILDREN: not under 16.
DOGS: allowed in bedroom (£8 per night), not in public rooms.
CREDIT CARDS: Amex, MasterCard, Visa.
PRICES: [2016] per room B&B from £150, D,B&B from £223. 2-night min. stay preferred.

AMBLESIDE Cumbria

Map 4: inset C2

NANNY BROW

Guests rave about the views at Sue and Peter Robinson's 'friendly' guest house. The home is surrounded by private woodland and landscaped gardens; its picture windows look across the Brathay valley to the Lakeland Fells beyond. The Robinsons have 'sympathetically' restored their pretty Arts and Crafts house (look out for characteristic flora and fauna motifs and the fine oak panelling). Each bedroom has its own style; some have an antique bed or original tiled fireplace; bathrooms are 'modern'. Rooms at the front of the house have the best views. Wind down with board games and magazines in the lounge; more active sorts might follow a woodland path or sign up for a guided walk in the fells. At teatime, enjoy sandwiches, buttered scones and home-made cakes, taken on the sun terrace in good weather. A light supper may be ordered in advance. The 'excellent' breakfast, served in the restored original dining room, is a feast: yogurts and fruit salads; locally smoked salmon; home-baked drop scones with maple syrup and berries; muesli, jams and marmalade, all home made. More reports, please.

Clappersgate
Ambleside
LA22 9NF

T: 01539 433232
E: unwind@nannybrow.co.uk
W: www.nannybrow.co.uk

BEDROOMS: 14. 2 in annexe, with own lounge.
OPEN: all year.
FACILITIES: lounge, bar, dining room, free Wi-Fi, in-room TV (Freeview), civil wedding licence, 6 acres of formal garden (sun terrace, croquet) and woodlands, unsuitable for disabled.
BACKGROUND MUSIC: 'low volume' in dining room and bar.
LOCATION: 1½ miles W of Ambleside.
CHILDREN: not under 12.
DOGS: not allowed.
CREDIT CARDS: Amex, MasterCard, Visa.
PRICES: per room B&B £130–£280. 1-night bookings refused weekends.

AMBLESIDE Cumbria

Map 4: inset C2

ROTHAY MANOR

In large, landscaped gardens a stroll from Lake Windermere, this 'friendly', traditional hotel, after 50 years in the same hands, has new owners, Jenna and James Shail. 'Everything has been spruced up,' say Guide inspectors in 2016. Many staff have stayed on from the old regime; Peter Sinclair (who in the evening 'took orders, served food and was ready to chat') remains as manager. Most of the bedrooms are in the Regency house; for more space, splurge on a suite in a bungalow in the grounds. 'Our pretty, charming room had a balcony overlooking the garden. There was a comfy bed, good storage, a small but efficient bathroom. Tea and biscuits were willingly brought to us on the lawn.' In the candlelit restaurant, Brandon Shepherd, the 'ambitious' new chef, cooks 'very fancy' dishes. 'We had a curious starter of heritage tomatoes with a mint sorbet; enjoyable turbot on green vegetables. Climbers would choke at the minute size of the starters and puddings, though.' Find leaf teas and a 'decent' buffet at breakfast; 'boring' toast is saved by 'delicious' marmalade.

Rothay Bridge
Ambleside
LA22 0EH

T: 015394 33605
F: 015397 33607
E: hotel@rothaymanor.co.uk
W: www.rothaymanor.co.uk

BEDROOMS: 19. 2 in bungalow in the grounds, 2 suitable for disabled.
OPEN: all year except 3 weeks Jan.
FACILITIES: lounge, drawing room, bar, 2 dining rooms, meeting/conference facilities, free Wi-Fi, in-room TV, 1-acre garden (croquet), free access to local leisure centre.
BACKGROUND MUSIC: all day in bar and restaurant.
LOCATION: ¼ mile SW of Ambleside.
CHILDREN: all ages welcomed.
DOGS: allowed in 4 rooms and drawing room, not in bar or restaurant.
CREDIT CARDS: MasterCard, Visa.
PRICES: per room B&B from £135, D,B&B from £211. À la carte £42.50. 1-night bookings often refused Sat.

AMPLEFORTH Yorkshire

Map 4:D4

SHALLOWDALE HOUSE

♜César award since 2005

Amid 'tranquillity and comfort', this 'immaculately kept' B&B is much liked by regulars who praise the 'superb' food, the 'delightful rooms' and the 'great kindness' of hosts Phillip Gill and Anton van der Horst. The hillside house stands amid flower-filled gardens; take in panoramic views of the Howardian hills from large picture windows in every room. Books and objets d'art fill the 'restful', traditionally furnished lounges – settle in here for tea and home-made cake every afternoon. In the 'spacious', 'thoughtfully equipped' bedrooms, binoculars are provided to spot the garden's resident robins. Bathrooms are stocked with 'fluffy' towels and 'nice' toiletries (a guest this year would have liked a more powerful shower). Give notice if you want to try Phillip Gill's 'eclectic' four-course dinner. 'In ten years of visiting Shallowdale, I have never had a dud course, let alone a dud meal.' At breakfast ('so generous you can skip lunch!') tuck in to dry-cured bacon and Whitby kippers; 'the freshly squeezed orange juice deserves a mention'. (Richard Creed, Andrew Warren, and others)

West End
Ampleforth
YO62 4DY

T: 01439 788325
E: stay@shallowdalehouse.co.uk
W: www.shallowdalehouse.co.uk

BEDROOMS: 3.
OPEN: all year except Christmas/ New Year, 'occasionally at other times'.
FACILITIES: drawing room, sitting room/library, dining room, free Wi-Fi, in-room TV (Freeview), 2½-acre gardens, unsuitable for disabled.
BACKGROUND MUSIC: none.
LOCATION: edge of village.
CHILDREN: not under 12.
DOGS: not allowed.
CREDIT CARDS: MasterCard, Visa.
PRICES: [2016] per room B&B £120– £145, D,B&B £205–£230. Set dinner £42.50 (min. 48 hours' notice). 1-night bookings occasionally refused weekends.

ARUNDEL Sussex

Map 2:E3

THE TOWN HOUSE

'Stuffiness is taboo' at Lee and Katie Williams's 'superb' restaurant-with-rooms. The fine Regency building has a prime position within the conservation area of this 'busy' historic market town; inside, Lee Williams's cooking is 'dazzling'. In the dining room, admire the impressive late Renaissance carved and gilded ceiling ('worth a visit in its own right'), then take in the delights on your plate: 'excellent', imaginative modern dishes might include corn-fed coquelette, roast beetroot, salsify; pan-fried fillet of stone bass, langoustine and pea risotto. Up 'steep' stairs (no lift; help with luggage is offered), bedrooms are individually styled. Luxuriate in the grand suite, whose private balcony overlooks Arundel Castle, or, if travelling with friends or family, check in to the top-floor suite, with two bedrooms, a shared shower room and rooftop views. There's plenty of diversion nearby to work off the hosts' full English breakfast: browse the antique shops in town; hire a motor boat for a trip on the Arun; visit the castle (ancient seat of the dukes of Norfolk) and the Victorian Gothic cathedral. (RC, and others)

25% DISCOUNT VOUCHERS

65 High Street
Arundel
BN18 9AJ

T: 01903 883847
E: enquiries@thetownhouse.co.uk
W: www.thetownhouse.co.uk

BEDROOMS: 5.
OPEN: all year except 25/26 Dec, 1 Jan, 2 weeks Easter, 2 weeks Oct, restaurant closed Sun/Mon.
FACILITIES: restaurant, free Wi-Fi, in-room TV (Freeview), unsuitable for disabled.
BACKGROUND MUSIC: 'easy listening' in restaurant.
LOCATION: top end of High Street.
CHILDREN: all ages welcomed.
DOGS: not allowed.
CREDIT CARDS: Diners, MasterCard, Visa.
PRICES: [2016] per room B&B £110–£150, D,B&B (midweek) £150–£190. Set dinner £25.50–£29.50. 1-night bookings refused weekends in high season.

ASHWATER Devon

BLAGDON MANOR

César award since 2006

Come 'home-away-from-home', to Liz and Steve Morey's 'faultless' restaurant-with-rooms in the heart of Devon countryside. 'We were greeted warmly by Liz and her three chocolate Labradors, who are great fun,' writes a returning guest. The 'quirky' building (parts of it date back to the 1600s) is 'smartly furnished' inside, and there are fresh flowers in the 'immaculate' public areas. Tastefully decorated bedrooms have views across the gardens to Dartmoor; guests appreciate the treats inside – hot drinks, biscuits, apples, sherry and toffees. 'Our room, Clawton, had a large bedroom and an adjoining sitting room. We even had two TVs and a good-quality radio; a deep claw-footed bath in the bathroom. We slept well in our huge, comfortable bed.' In the restaurant, sample Steve Morey's 'incredible' three-course dinners. 'The lemon sole tempura melted in the mouth; pan-fried Devon beef was so tender we had it on two evenings. The hosts catered for my gluten-free diet exceptionally well, even baking gluten-free bread containing various fruits.' 'Breakfast maintains the high standards.' (SH, F and IW)

25% DISCOUNT VOUCHERS

Ashwater
EX21 5DF

T: 01409 211224
E: stay@blagdon.com
w: www.blagdon.com

BEDROOMS: 6.
OPEN: all year except Christmas and New Year, restaurant closed Mon evenings and all day Tues.
FACILITIES: lounge, library, snug, bar, conservatory, restaurant, private dining room, free Wi-Fi in lounge, in-room TV (Freeview), 20-acre grounds (3-acre gardens, croquet, giant chess, gazebo, pond), unsuitable for disabled.
BACKGROUND MUSIC: none.
LOCATION: 8 miles NE of Launceston.
CHILDREN: not under 12.
DOGS: not allowed in restaurant.
CREDIT CARDS: MasterCard, Visa.
PRICES: per room B&B £155–£260. Set dinner £40.

AUSTWICK Yorkshire

Map 4:D3

AUSTWICK HALL

A galanthophile's paradise awaits in the woodland walks and sculpture-strewn trails at this B&B in the Dales. 'Lovingly' restored and run in a 'highly personal' manner, Michael Pearson and Eric Culley's is a manor house with history. Their 'obvious enthusiasm' and 'eclectic' taste are evident throughout, Guide inspectors say. Examine their vast collection of antiques and tribal and contemporary art – all of it 'mingles with style'. Arriving visitors are welcomed with tea and scones in the lounge. Make your way, afterwards, to bedrooms with garden views ('where the best entertainment is found'). 'Our cosy room had a very comfortable, beautifully draped four-poster bed, a good-sized wardrobe, plenty of seating; the en suite had a roll-top bath and walk-in shower – nice hot water.' Lazy mornings were made for the 'relaxed' breakfasts, served from 9 am. Help yourself to a buffet (fresh fruit, croissants, home-made jam); 'more substantial fare' includes locally dry-cured bacon and henhouse-fresh eggs. Ask for a picnic lunch and head to nearby Ingleborough Cave; the hosts have restaurant recommendations come evening ('torches are provided for the walk into the village').

Townhead Lane
Austwick
LA2 8BS

T: 01524 251794
E: austwickhall@austwick.org
W: www.austwickhall.co.uk

BEDROOMS: 4.
OPEN: all year.
FACILITIES: hall, drawing room, dining room, free Wi-Fi, in-room TV (Freeview), 14-acre gardens, hot tub, unsuitable for disabled.
BACKGROUND MUSIC: none.
LOCATION: edge of village.
CHILDREN: not under 16.
DOGS: not allowed.
CREDIT CARDS: MasterCard, Visa.
PRICES: per room B&B single £110–£140, double £125–£155 (rates lower Feb/Mar mid-week). 1-night bookings refused bank holiday weekends.

AUSTWICK Yorkshire

THE TRADDOCK

♥César award since 2014

'Warmth exudes' from the Reynolds family's 'happy', 'comfortable' small hotel: 'They obviously know exactly how to make the place tick.' This 'homey' spot has charm in spades, and 'lots of places to relax'; in 'snug' public areas, find a 'crackling' fire, board games, coffee-table books, 'well-stuffed armchairs'. Bedrooms vary in size and style; the best, in the newly converted Victorian loft, is a spacious open-plan suite with views across Burn Moor to the forest of Bowland beyond. 'Ours had a gilt wicker bedhead, brocade fabrics, a lovely Persian rug. The tea tray held a proper teapot, a cafetière and mugs, biscuits, fresh milk in a flask.' Yorkshire produce serves as inspiration in the restaurant, where John Pratt, a proponent of the Slow Food movement, cooks modern English dishes, perhaps brochette of local rabbit loin, pickled radish and cucumber salad. 'We loved the cheese menu, which gave details of both cheese and cheesemaker.' Breakfast is 'generous': tuck in to home-made preserves on 'thick toast'; an 'enormous' full English. Good walking from the door; guides, maps, packed lunches available. (SH, Julie Griffiths)

25% DISCOUNT VOUCHERS

Austwick
LA2 8BY

T: 01524 251224
F: 01524 251796
E: info@thetraddock.co.uk
W: www.thetraddock.co.uk

BEDROOMS: 12. 1 on ground floor.
OPEN: all year.
FACILITIES: 3 lounges, bar, 2 dining rooms, function facilities, free Wi-Fi, in-room TV (Freeview), 1½-acre grounds (sun deck), unsuitable for disabled.
BACKGROUND MUSIC: in public areas except 1 lounge.
LOCATION: 4 miles NW of Settle.
CHILDREN: all ages welcomed.
DOGS: allowed on lead in public rooms, not in dining rooms.
CREDIT CARDS: MasterCard, Visa.
PRICES: [2016] per room B&B £99–£245, D,B&B £164–£310. À la carte £32.50. 1-night bookings refused weekends in season.

AYLESBURY Buckinghamshire

Map 2:C3

HARTWELL HOUSE

César award since 1997

Wander through the 'extravagantly and sumptuously furnished' rooms at this stately mansion – it's not hard to imagine being a member of the court of Louis XVIII of France, who lived here, in exile, in the 19th century. Today, run by Historic House Hotels for the National Trust, it's a 'special', 'blissfully quiet' place to stay. 'It oozes history – we loved it,' say guests, including 'a keen historian', this year. The 'spectacular' building stands in 'incredible' grounds with a lake, a church and a Gothic tower; inside, 'super' bedrooms are decorated in period style. For a royal experience, book one of the lavish four-poster suites outfitted with antiques and fine paintings. 'Dine well' in the formal restaurant ('elegant in an old-fashioned way', with candles and floor-length tablecloths), where chef Daniel Richardson's seasonal menu uses 'beautifully fresh' fruit, vegetables and herbs from the garden and orchard. More casual dinners may be taken in the spa café on Friday and Saturday nights. Mornings, breakfast is 'fine': grilled Loch Fyne kippers, poached haddock, 'the best porridge we've tasted'.
(A and BB, Richard Morgan-Price, and others)

Oxford Road
Stone
Aylesbury
HP17 8NR

T: 01296 747444
E: info@hartwell-house.com
W: www.hartwell-house.com

BEDROOMS: 52. 16 in stable block, some on ground floor, 2 suitable for disabled.
OPEN: all year.
FACILITIES: lift, 4 drawing rooms, bar, 3 dining rooms, conference facilities, free Wi-Fi, in-room TV (Sky), civil wedding licence, spa (swimming pool, 8 by 16 metres), 94-acre grounds (gardens, parkland, tennis).
BACKGROUND MUSIC: pianist most Fri and Sat nights.
LOCATION: 2 miles W of Aylesbury.
CHILDREN: not under 6.
DOGS: allowed by arrangement in dedicated suites, guide dogs in main house, dining areas.
CREDIT CARDS: Amex, MasterCard, Visa.
PRICES: [2016] per room B&B from £200, D,B&B from £360. Set dinner £43–£59.

BABBACOMBE Devon

Map 1:D5

THE CARY ARMS

By a 'fabulously secluded' cove, Lana de Savary's chic hotel clings to wooded cliffs overlooking the beach. The approach involves a 'precipitous' descent by road; guests who are more seafarer than landlubber could arrive by yacht at the private quay. Seaside style comes in buckets (and shrimping nets) here; 'an appealing sense of domesticity' reigns. Arrive to a 'genuine welcome', then relax in the 'tastefully decorated' lounge (nautical prints, pot plants, a 'splendid' model yacht). It is thoughtfully supplied with board games, a 'well-stocked' library, 'binoculars to fully enjoy the view'. All but one of the 'attractive' bedrooms in the main house have a terrace or balcony, but you can get closer to the elements in one of the smart new duplex beach huts and suites set into the grassy slope overlooking the sea. Not quite unwound yet? Luxuriate in the new spa, with its glass-fronted plunge pool. Later, order a local ale in the beamed bar, then tuck in to chef Ben Kingdon's 'informal', 'beautifully cooked' dinners – 'seafood's a speciality'. In the morning, a splendid breakfast buffet is 'an uplifting start to the day'.

Beach Road
Babbacombe
TQ1 3LX

T: 01803 327110
F: 01803 323221
E: enquiries@caryarms.co.uk
W: www.caryarms.co.uk

BEDROOMS: 16. 2 on ground floor, 8 in beach huts.
OPEN: all year.
FACILITIES: lounge, bar, restaurant, conservatory, free Wi-Fi, in-room TV, civil wedding licence, spa (treatment rooms, plunge pool, mini-gym, steam room, sun deck), garden, terrace.
BACKGROUND MUSIC: all day in bar.
LOCATION: by beach, 2¼ miles N of Torquay harbour.
CHILDREN: all ages welcomed.
DOGS: allowed in some rooms, not in conservatory.
CREDIT CARDS: Amex, MasterCard, Visa.
PRICES: [2016] per room B&B from £195. À la carte £30. 1-night bookings sometimes refused.

BABCARY Somerset

Map 1:C6

RED LION INN   **NEW**

Wind down narrow lanes to arrive at this real-ale-serving, quiz-night-holding, Christmas-market-organising, summertime-pizza-serving pub-with-rooms, the thatched-roof heart of the hamlet. 'Fresh and tasteful', it enters the Guide this year thanks to inspectors who found it 'a hive of activity'. Owned by Clare and Charlie Garrard, the 'ancient' pub looks the part: dark flagstone floors; a burnished leather sofa by a wood-burning stove; newspapers, board games, table skittles. On chilly nights, a brazier is lit for guests who gather outside. Across the garden, modern bedrooms with 'excellent' facilities are in an 'immaculate' converted barn. 'Our elegant ground-floor room had comfortable beds, handsome table lamps, white slatted shutters; a well-lit wet room; a generous hospitality tray with home-made biscuits. The Wi-Fi didn't work (they provide a cable).' Settle into the 'spacious' dining room over a 'straightforward' daily-changing menu. 'We liked duck parfait with home-baked brioche toast; tasty slow-cooked pork belly with crackling.' 'The young staff are rather green – we stunned our waiter by asking for sherry – but they're very nice, and try hard to please.'

Babcary
TA11 7ED

T: 01458 223230
E: info@redlionbabcary.co.uk
W: www.redlionbabcary.co.uk

BEDROOMS: 6. All in converted barn, 1, on ground floor, suitable for disabled.
OPEN: all year.
FACILITIES: bar, dining room, breakfast room, meeting/function facilities, free Wi-Fi, in-room TV, garden (marquee).
BACKGROUND MUSIC: in public areas, regular live music nights.
LOCATION: 5 miles E of Somerton.
CHILDREN: all ages welcomed.
DOGS: allowed in bar only.
CREDIT CARDS: MasterCard, Visa.
PRICES: [2016] per room B&B single from £90, double £110–£120. À la carte £33.

BARNSLEY Gloucestershire

Map 3:E6

BARNSLEY HOUSE

Soak in the 'serenity' and 'romantic air' of this 'relaxed' 17th-century gabled stone manor house, once home to the garden designer Rosemary Verey. It was she who created the parterres and topiary, the laburnum walk and the ornamental fruit garden we see today; a winding path leads to the modern spa, outdoor hydrotherapy pool and 30-seat cinema. The luxury hotel is part of the Calcot Hotels group; there's 'a nice country house feel' throughout. Check in to bedrooms well equipped with aromatherapy products and magazines; bottled waters, hot drinks and biscuits. A 'lovely' junior suite in the main house was liked: 'flower prints on the walls; a comfy bed; a sitting room with a window seat; a garden view through a window like a porthole; the sound of birds singing'. Evenings, linger over a 'pleasant' meal in the restaurant, where Francesco Volgo's short menus reflect the abundance of seasonal, home-grown produce – pea and asparagus soup; roast carrots and purple sprouting broccoli with pork. 'We liked the flexibility of being able to dine at the Village Pub [see Shortlist] as an alternative.'

Barnsley
GL7 5EE

T: 01285 740000
F: 01285 740925
E: info@barnsleyhouse.com
W: www.barnsleyhouse.com

BEDROOMS: 18. 7 in stableyard, 4 in courtyard, 1 in cottage, 1 suitable for disabled.
OPEN: all year.
FACILITIES: 2 lounges, bar, restaurant, cinema, meeting room, free Wi-Fi, in-room TV (Sky, Freeview), civil wedding licence, terrace, 11-acre garden (spa, outdoor hydrotherapy pool).
BACKGROUND MUSIC: 'easy listening' in lounge and restaurant.
LOCATION: 5 miles NE of Cirencester.
CHILDREN: not under 14.
DOGS: allowed in stableyard rooms, not in grounds or public areas.
CREDIT CARDS: Amex, MasterCard, Visa.
PRICES: [2016] per room B&B £199–£310. À la carte £40. 1-night bookings sometimes refused.

SEE ALSO SHORTLIST

BARWICK Somerset

LITTLE BARWICK HOUSE

♀César award since 2002

'We could not have asked for better.' 'We have never been disappointed.' 'It seems to get better every time.' There is a chorus of praise this year for Tim and Emma Ford's restaurant-with-rooms in a Georgian dower house down 'a narrow road that could well have led to the Hobbits' Shire'. As Hobbits might, guests arrive to a 'sumptuous' afternoon tea. 'Smiling, efficient, informative, Emma sets the tone as front-of-house; Tim's cooking is of a consistently high standard.' After 'delicious' hors d'oeuvre in the 'well-appointed' lounge, taste 'well-balanced', 'excellently executed' dishes inspired by the seasons, perhaps an 'extraordinarily good' wild mushroom risotto. The 'unusually wide' selection of half bottles of wine makes a good accompaniment. Spend the night in 'comfy', 'clean', country-style bedrooms well equipped with cafetière coffee, fresh milk, home-made shortbread ('we didn't know what to do with the 13 scatter cushions'). Enjoy a leisurely morning after breakfast: 'The peaceful garden is part of the charm.' (Ron Greenman, Bryan and Mary Blaxall, Michael and Margaret Cross, Michael Gwinnell, WE Riddell)

25% DISCOUNT VOUCHERS

Rexes Hollow Lane
Barwick
BA22 9TD

T: 01935 423902
F: 01935 420908
E: reservations@barwick7.fsnet.co.uk
W: www.littlebarwickhouse.co.uk

BEDROOMS: 7. 1 for week-long let.
OPEN: all year except three weeks Jan, restaurant closed Sun night, Mon.
FACILITIES: 2 lounges, restaurant, conservatory, free Wi-Fi, in-room TV (Freeview), 3½-acre garden (terrace, paddock), unsuitable for disabled.
BACKGROUND MUSIC: none.
LOCATION: ¾ mile outside Yeovil.
CHILDREN: over-5s welcomed.
DOGS: allowed in bedrooms, only assistance dogs in restaurant.
CREDIT CARDS: MasterCard, Visa.
PRICES: [2016] per person B&B £60, D,B&B from £105. Set dinner £49.95. 1-night bookings sometimes refused.

BASLOW Derbyshire

Map 3:A6

THE CAVENDISH

 César award since 2002

Teatime brings 'some of the nicest, warm, home-baked scones' at this 'welcoming', 'beautifully kept', traditional hotel on the Chatsworth estate. It is owned by the Duke of Devonshire; Philip Joseph, the manager, 'runs it very well'. Across the oldest part of the hotel (the once-upon-a-time Peacock Inn) and the newer Devonshire wing, 'very attractive', refurbished bedrooms each has its own charm ('though I wish they'd make one with a walk-in shower'). All have 'welcoming touches': assorted hot drinks, biscuits, 'large, thick bathrobes'. Some rooms may have road noise. In the modern Gallery restaurant and the informal Garden Room, new chef Alan Hill's cooking is 'pretty faultless', as regular visitors discovered in 2016. 'Our Kitchen Table menu was well balanced and beautifully presented – delicious mushroom and wild garlic soup; wild sea bass timed to perfection; sweet, tender local lamb.' Cross the adjacent parkland to reach the stately home – or stay in and soak up the 'lovely' atmosphere. 'A morning cuppa sitting up in bed and looking across the estate doesn't get much better!' (Padi and John Howard, Beverley Adams, Susan Willmington)

Church Lane
Baslow
DE45 1SP

T: 01246 582311
F: 01246 582312
E: info@cavendish-hotel.net
W: www.cavendish-hotel.net

BEDROOMS: 24. 2 on ground floor.
OPEN: all year.
FACILITIES: lounge, bar, 2 restaurants, 2 private dining rooms, free Wi-Fi, in-room TV (Freeview), ½-acre grounds (putting), river fishing nearby.
BACKGROUND MUSIC: none.
LOCATION: on A619, in Chatsworth grounds, on edge of village.
CHILDREN: all ages welcomed.
DOGS: not allowed.
CREDIT CARDS: Amex, MasterCard, Visa.
PRICES: [2016] per room B&B from £244, D,B&B from £343. Set menus £49.50 (plus 5% service levy on all prices). 1-night bookings sometimes refused.

BASLOW Derbyshire

Map 3:A6

FISCHER'S AT BASLOW HALL

♦César award since 1998

'Outstanding' cooking brings guests up the winding, chestnut tree-lined drive to Susan and Max Fischer's Edwardian manor house. It stands in mature landscaped gardens 'delightful for a drink and a chat'. Come hungry: in the 'muted' dining room ('the expectation, largely observed, is that gentlemen will wear a jacket and, perhaps, a tie'), chef Rupert Rowley has a Michelin star for his modern menus. His dishes make remarkable use of British produce, home-grown vegetables, even honey from garden hives; in season, look out for foraged wild garlic and summer flowers on lunch and dinner dishes. Characteristic plates: quail tempura, toasted seeds; smoked beef rib, onion crust. Vegetarians are well catered for with an imaginative menu. Stay in country-style bedrooms, some more modern, others (perhaps with a half-tester bed or an original fireplace) rather traditional. 'Our excellent first-floor garden room had a private entrance. Inside: a settee, a comfortable chair, a nice, modern bathroom.' After a 'good' breakfast with 'plenty of choice', don't miss a wander round the lush kitchen garden. (Anthony Bradbury, and others)

Calver Road
Baslow
DE45 1RR

T: 01246 583259
E: reservations@fischers-baslow
   hall.co.uk
W: www.fischers-baslowhall.co.uk

BEDROOMS: 11. 5 in Garden House.
OPEN: all year except 25/26 and 24
and 31 Dec evening.
FACILITIES: lounge/bar, breakfast
room, 3 dining rooms, function
facilities, free Wi-Fi, in-room TV
(Freeview), civil wedding licence,
5-acre grounds, unsuitable for
disabled.
BACKGROUND MUSIC: none.
LOCATION: edge of village, 5 miles
NE of Bakewell.
CHILDREN: no under-8s in restaurant
in evening, no under-5s at lunch, all
ages welcomed at Sunday lunch.
DOGS: not allowed.
CREDIT CARDS: Amex, MasterCard,
Visa.
PRICES: [2016] per room B&B
£200–£270, D,B&B £320–£414. Set
dinners £55–£72. 1-night bookings
refused in Garden House June–Sept
weekends.

BASSENTHWAITE LAKE Cumbria

Map 4: inset C2

THE PHEASANT

The 'well-kept' gardens reach into woodland thick with rabbits and roe deer, while the 'remarkable' bar within the 17th-century coaching inn stocks over 70 malt whiskies. The whole is a 'lovely' country hotel, whose many fans think it 'a special place'. Come in to log fires, tufted armchairs, newspapers and afternoon teas; in the 200-year-old bar ('I'm not surprised it wins prizes'), rub shoulders with locals – and their dogs – who drop by for a chat. 'The young (mainly French) staff are friendly and hard-working.' Traditionally styled bedrooms are in the main house and garden lodge; each is supplied with a china tea service and a Roberts radio. 'Overlooking the garden, ours (Caldbeck) was delightful and spacious.' A guest this year thought dog-friendly lodge rooms didn't measure up to the more 'charming' main-house accommodation. Most evenings, there are two dinner options. 'The bistro is popular and fun; the restaurant is classy, with excellent food. We enjoyed both.' Twitchers, take note: through spring and summer, viewing points on the lake are ideal for spotting ospreys. (LW, Humphrey and Frances Norrington, and others)

Bassenthwaite Lake
CA13 9YE

T: 017687 76234
F: 017687 76002
E: info@the-pheasant.co.uk
W: www.the-pheasant.co.uk

BEDROOMS: 15. 2 on ground floor in lodge.
OPEN: all year except 25 Dec, restaurant closed Sun eve and Mon.
FACILITIES: 2 lounges, bar, bistro, restaurant, private dining room, free Wi-Fi, in-room TV (Freeview), 40-acre grounds, lake 200 yds (fishing), access to nearby spa, pool and treatment rooms, unsuitable for disabled.
BACKGROUND MUSIC: none.
LOCATION: 5 miles E of Cockermouth, ¼ mile off A66 to Keswick.
CHILDREN: not under 8 (£30 to share parents' room).
DOGS: allowed in 4 bedrooms (£10 charge) and public rooms.
CREDIT CARDS: MasterCard, Visa.
PRICES: [2016] per room B&B from £120. Set menu (restaurant) £35–£42.50, à la carte (bistro) £30. 1-night bookings sometimes refused.

BATH Somerset

ABBEY HOTEL   **NEW**

Slap bang in the centre, Christa and Ian Taylor's
'ambitious' city hotel has much to like: 'cheery'
staff, stylishly refurbished bedrooms, a 'lively'
bar and a 'smart', much-praised restaurant. 'It's
got flair to spare,' says a Guide inspector in 2016.
The Taylors have made many improvements
since taking over the once-outmoded hotel;
today, it's appreciably modern, its public areas
bright with 'varied, interesting art'. 'The staff
are an asset: upbeat, super-friendly, helpful.'
The hotel occupies a conversion of three
Georgian town houses; bedrooms are 'reached
via hallways and various flights of stairs'. 'My
standard room overlooking a quiet cobblestoned
lane had a comfy bed with excellent directional
bedside lights, glossy magazines, posh toiletries,
an iPad loaded with local information.'
Upgrading continues; in the meantime, ask for a
'properly "boutique"' refurbished room. 'Ours,
on the top floor, was spacious and spotless, with
lovely fixtures. A caveat: it faced the road, and
we could hear the Saturday-night revellers.'
Wake to an 'exemplary' breakfast in the 'jolly'
restaurant: 'restorative home-made smoothies',
'a fine buffet with pastries piled high'; 'pillowy
pancakes, local bacon'. (Susan Duffy, and others)

1 North Parade
Bath
BA1 1LF

T: 01225 461603
E: reception@abbeyhotelbath.co.uk
W: www.abbeyhotelbath.co.uk

BEDROOMS: 60.
OPEN: all year.
FACILITIES: lift, bar, restaurant,
private dining area, function
facilities, free Wi-Fi, in-room
TV, civil wedding licence, terrace
(alfresco meals and drinks).
BACKGROUND MUSIC: all day in bar.
LOCATION: central.
CHILDREN: all ages welcomed.
DOGS: allowed.
CREDIT CARDS: all major cards.
PRICES: [2016] per room B&B from
£190, D,B&B from £250. À la carte
£45. 1-night bookings sometimes
refused.

SEE ALSO SHORTLIST

BATH Somerset

Map 2:D1

APSLEY HOUSE

Original oil paintings, antiques and objets d'art fill this 'imposing' Georgian house, a 19th-century retreat built by the Duke of Wellington, rumour has it, for his mistress. Today it's a B&B owned by Claire and Nicholas Potts; little about it is clandestine or scandalous. 'Friendly, efficient and helpful', Miro Mikula and Kate Kowalczyk are the 'delightful' managers. Bedrooms are 'tastefully decorated'; 'most have views across Bath to the hills beyond'. 'Our room had a comfortable bed and a clean, modern bathroom with big bath towels. Niggles: basic tea, UHT milk.' Ring to discuss room choices before booking: visitors in 2016 liked their 'comfortable, well-proportioned' room, while another guest found her ground-floor accommodation overly snug. An 'excellent' breakfast (cereals, croissants, fresh fruit, etc) is taken in a room overlooking the 'attractive' garden; hot dishes, with sausages, bacon and eggs from a local farm, are cooked to order. The city centre is easily reached within a short bus ride or a five-minute drive ('adequate' parking at the B&B); keen walkers may appreciate the 30-minute stroll (uphill on the way back). (Ron Greenman, Suzanne Lyons, and others)

141 Newbridge Hill
Bath
BA1 3PT

T: 01225 336966
F: 01225 425462
E: claireypotts@btinternet.com
W: www.apsley-house.co.uk

BEDROOMS: 12. 1 on ground floor, plus 1 self-catering 2-bedroom apartment.
OPEN: all year except 24–26 Dec.
FACILITIES: drawing room, dining room, free Wi-Fi, in-room TV (BT, Freeview), ¼-acre garden, parking, unsuitable for disabled.
BACKGROUND MUSIC: Classic FM in drawing and dining rooms.
LOCATION: 1¼ miles W of city centre.
CHILDREN: all ages welcomed (under-2s free).
DOGS: not allowed.
CREDIT CARDS: Amex, MasterCard, Visa.
PRICES: [2016] per room B&B £99–£280. 1-night bookings refused Sat in peak season.

SEE ALSO SHORTLIST

BATH Somerset

THE QUEENSBERRY

'A near-faultless stay.' In a 'great' location – 'so easily reached from the centre, yet so quiet' – Laurence and Helen Beere's 'excellent' hotel continues to please guests with its 'personable, efficient' staff, 'delicious' food and 'generously sized' rooms. (The 'very good' cocktails help, too.) Pick one of the neat, modern bedrooms: they vary in size, from compact club rooms to junior suites with a seating area and space for a child's bed. Inspectors found a top-floor room 'quite hot (a fan was provided)', but they appreciated the 'abundant' storage space; the 'bright, well-designed' bathroom; the turn-down service. Take tea in the 'charming' garden; come evening, stay in for dinner: the Olive Tree restaurant, where chef Chris Cleghorn's modern dishes are 'presented with a great deal of care', 'rightly has a very good reputation locally'. 'We had beautifully cooked turbot preceded by a tasty, frothy amuse-bouche; delicious, warm bread rolls.' In the morning, skip the 'unfortunate' toast and go for a 'very good' kipper. 'The valet parking is a boon.' (Peter Jowitt, and others)

4–7 Russel Street
Bath
BA1 2QF

T: 01225 447928
F: 01225 446065
E: reservations@thequeensberry.co.uk
W: www.thequeensberry.co.uk

BEDROOMS: 29. Some on ground floor.
OPEN: all year, restaurant closed Mon/Tues lunch.
FACILITIES: lift, 2 drawing rooms, bar, restaurant, meeting room, free Wi-Fi, in-room TV (Freeview), 4 linked courtyard gardens, car-parking service, unsuitable for disabled.
BACKGROUND MUSIC: in restaurant and bar.
LOCATION: near Assembly Rooms.
CHILDREN: all ages welcomed.
DOGS: not allowed.
CREDIT CARDS: MasterCard, Visa.
PRICES: [2016] per room B&B £150–£445. À la carte £47. 1-night bookings sometimes refused.

SEE ALSO SHORTLIST

BATH Somerset

THE ROYAL CRESCENT HOTEL & SPA

Two elegantly converted town houses host this luxury hotel and atmospheric spa in a 'spectacular' location on the Georgian Royal Crescent, with its 'magical vista' across the city. Come in to grand, generously proportioned rooms filled with antiques, prints and paintings. In fine weather, take afternoon tea in the 'secret' walled garden – sweet Bath buns sit on a plate alongside scones and cinnamon butter. Sip a cocktail or a glass of in-house champagne in the smart bar before a fine dinner in the Dower House restaurant. Here, chef David Campbell cooks inventive modern dishes, perhaps slow-cooked duck egg, pea, wild garlic and mushroom broth, summer truffle; pork loin, honey-glazed belly and beignet, sage polenta, alliums. Vegetarians, rejoice: a sophisticated veggie menu is available. And so to bed. Take your pick among the 'stylish' bedrooms (some compact) and suites in the main house and refurbished outbuildings; some have a four-poster bed, others a conservatory sitting room with French doors leading to the garden. (Ask for a toy box, too, for young guests.) Next day, breakfast is 'delicious, varied, copious'.

16 Royal Crescent
Bath
BA1 2LS

T: 01225 823333
E: info@royalcrescent.co.uk
W: www.royalcrescent.co.uk

BEDROOMS: 45. 10 in Dower House, 14 in garden annexes, 8 on ground floor.
OPEN: all year.
FACILITIES: lift, bar, drawing room, sitting room, library, restaurant, function facilities, free Wi-Fi, in-room TV (Freeview), civil wedding licence, 1-acre garden, spa and bath house (12-metre 'relaxation' pool, gym, treatment rooms).
BACKGROUND MUSIC: in public areas.
LOCATION: ½ mile from city centre.
CHILDREN: all ages welcomed, no under-12s in spa.
DOGS: allowed in some bedrooms, not in public rooms.
CREDIT CARDS: Amex, MasterCard, Visa.
PRICES: [2016] per room B&B from £265. À la carte £65. 1-night bookings sometimes refused.

SEE ALSO SHORTLIST

BATH Somerset

Map 2:D1

TASBURGH HOUSE

Queen Victoria's photographer chose a 'gorgeous spot' on a hilltop for his red brick villa, with 'lovely views' of Bath in the distance. Today, the late Victorian house is run as a 'friendly', upmarket B&B by 'kind' hostess Susan Keeling and 'helpful, considerate' manager Grant Atkinson. Choose among 'luxurious-feeling' bedrooms, each named after a writer, with floral fabrics, comfy seating, a book or two by the wordsmith in question; some larger rooms are set up for a family. 'Our troop of four was put in two rooms opposite each other. The children were delighted – they thought theirs was better than ours. A sweet note in the room welcomed them by name, and gave the number to call if they needed us.' Breakfast in the 'pretty' conservatory is a fine way to wake, with fruits, meats, cheeses and 'fantastic' home-made muesli (though an 'odd' choice of piped music); cooked dishes cost extra. 'The lady serving couldn't have been nicer, and made it an enjoyable experience.' After, take 'a fun walk' down to the Kennet and Avon Canal, then a stroll into town.

Warminster Road
Bath
BA2 6SH

T: 01225 425096
E: stay@tasburghhouse.co.uk
W: www.tasburghhouse.co.uk

BEDROOMS: 14. 2, on ground floor, accessed off the garden terrace.
OPEN: all year except Christmas.
FACILITIES: drawing room, dining room, conservatory, free Wi-Fi, in-room TV (Freeview), terrace, 7-acre gardens and terracing (canal walks, mooring), unsuitable for disabled, free parking space for each room.
BACKGROUND MUSIC: in public areas.
LOCATION: ½ mile E of city centre.
CHILDREN: not under 6.
DOGS: not allowed.
CREDIT CARDS: Amex, MasterCard, Visa.
PRICES: [2016] per room B&B (continental) single from £95, double from £100. Cooked breakfast £5.50–£9.50. Set dinner for groups of 10 or more, by arrangement. 1-night bookings sometimes refused Sat.

SEE ALSO SHORTLIST

BEAMINSTER Dorset

Map 1:C6

BRIDGEHOUSE

'A nice welcome' and 'an excellent dinner' await at this 'very pleasant place', a stone-built former priests' house by the River Brit, deep in Thomas Hardy's Wessex. The owners, Joanna and Mark Donovan, 'make you feel welcome the moment you arrive'. Within, find cosy interiors seemingly unchanged since before Hardy's time – low ceilings, oak beams, inglenook fireplaces – all with 'plenty of modern comfort'. Choose from 'well-furnished', individually styled bedrooms in the 700-year-old main building and a converted coach house. Some are remarkably spacious; all have Italian linens, waffle bathrobes, high-end toiletries, a modern bathroom. The quietest rooms overlook the walled garden. Travelling with family? Two suites easily accommodate children. At dinner (Geraldine Gay has been promoted to head chef), tuck in to brasserie favourites with a twist, perhaps sweet potato and coconut beignets, tomato and coriander gazpacho, avocado-lime mayonnaise; braised ox cheek, horseradish mash, herb dumplings. At breakfast, breads and preserves are home made. 'A good base for west Dorset; strikingly attractive market towns and good walks are nearby.' (Mary Woods, and others)

25% DISCOUNT VOUCHERS

3 Prout Bridge
Beaminster
DT8 3AY

T: 01308 862200
F: 01308 863700
E: enquiries@bridge-house.co.uk
W: www.bridge-house.co.uk

BEDROOMS: 13. 4 in coach house, 4 on ground floor.
OPEN: all year.
FACILITIES: hall/reception, lounge, bar, sunroom/conservatory, restaurant, free Wi-Fi, in-room TV (Freeview), civil wedding licence, ¼-acre walled garden, terrace (alfresco dining), unsuitable for disabled.
BACKGROUND MUSIC: light jazz/classical in most public areas.
LOCATION: 100 yards from centre.
CHILDREN: all ages welcomed.
DOGS: allowed.
CREDIT CARDS: Amex, MasterCard, Visa.
PRICES: [2016] per room B&B £160–£230, D,B&B £230–£310. 1-night bookings refused weekends and bank holidays.

BEAULIEU Hampshire

Map 2:E2

THE MASTER BUILDER'S

'Unpretentious style' combines with 'a real feel of history' at this 'friendly' hotel (part of the Hillbrooke Hotels group) in a 'lovely setting' by the river estuary. Green slopes tumble down to the water, where boats were once built; Beaulieu is a riverside walk away. Within the 18th-century building, 'charming' public areas have a nautical air (pictures of boats and maritime heroes); in warm weather, find a seat on the lawn for a swig of real ale and informal meals (pizzas, sharing boards, seasonal salads) from the bar. The individually styled bedrooms are thoughtfully equipped with posh teas, cafetière coffee, biscuits, 'a wee bottle' of organic vodka. Superior rooms in the main house have the best views over the water; in newly refurbished rooms in the Henry Adams wing, the breezy decor brings the coastal ambience indoors. Fido won't have to sit up and beg for a fine welcome: dog-friendly rooms have a dog bed, bowl and treats, including a room-service menu. Dine in: Edward Cracknell's modern dishes, perhaps Lymington mackerel, Puy lentils, olives, salsa verde, are 'very good'.

Buckler's Hard
Beaulieu
SO42 7XB

T: 01590 616253
F: 01590 616297
E: enquiries@themasterbuilders.
   co.uk
W: www.themasterbuilders.co.uk

BEDROOMS: 27. 17 in Henry Adams wing, 1 suitable for disabled.
OPEN: all year.
FACILITIES: lounge, bar, restaurant, free Wi-Fi, in-room TV, civil wedding licence, ½-acre garden (alfresco dining).
BACKGROUND MUSIC: in bar and restaurant.
LOCATION: 6 miles NE of Lymington.
CHILDREN: all ages welcomed.
DOGS: allowed in 9 bedrooms, not in restaurant.
CREDIT CARDS: Amex, MasterCard, Visa.
PRICES: [2016] per room B&B £140, D,B&B £200. À la carte £35.

BEAULIEU Hampshire

Map 2:E2

MONTAGU ARMS

'Pretty much perfect for country lovers', this 'very special' hotel in the New Forest 'charms' with its 'relaxed' ambience and 'excellent' food. 'We enjoy the exceptional welcome and service, and sitting in the picturesque garden before dining in the restaurant.' Settle into the Victorian lounge, 'well-furnished' in traditional country house style (oak panelling, a log fire, a grandfather clock); find a spot in the conservatory for 'delicious' freshly baked scones with afternoon tea. In the Terrace restaurant overlooking the garden, chef Matthew Tomkinson's Michelin-starred dishes take inspiration from the kitchen garden. Sample modern dishes like 'lasagne' of slow-cooked oxtail, celeriac purée; escalope of turbot, sautéed wild mushrooms, braised pearl barley. Informal gatherings, over sophisticated versions of classic pub food, take place in Monty's Inn ('heaving on a sunny Sunday'). Individually styled bedrooms, overlooking the garden or Beaulieu Palace, may not be 'the latest in design', but are 'comfortable' and well equipped. In the morning, freshly brewed tea or coffee may be brought to the room for a very civilised wake-up. (MC)

Palace Lane
Beaulieu
SO42 7ZL

T: 01590 612324
F: 01590 612188
E: reservations@
    montaguarmshotel.co.uk
W: www.montaguarmshotel.co.uk

BEDROOMS: 22.
OPEN: all year, Terrace restaurant closed Mon, Tues lunch.
FACILITIES: lounge, conservatory, bar/brasserie, restaurant, free Wi-Fi, in-room TV (Freeview), civil wedding licence, garden, access to spa at nearby Careys Manor, unsuitable for disabled.
BACKGROUND MUSIC: in Monty's Inn.
LOCATION: village centre.
CHILDREN: all ages welcomed (under-3s stay free), no under-11s in restaurant.
DOGS: not allowed.
CREDIT CARDS: Amex, MasterCard, Visa.
PRICES: [2016] per room B&B from £219, D,B&B from £289. À la carte £28 (Monty's Inn), £75 (Terrace restaurant). 1-night bookings sometimes refused.

BEPTON Sussex

PARK HOUSE

'Top of its class', this 'wonderful', well-run country house hotel and spa beneath the South Downs wins praise from guests who appreciate the 'beautiful', 'well-maintained' grounds and the 'intimate', 'relaxed' atmosphere within. 'All the staff are excellent.' The drawing room has fresh flowers, paintings, an oriental carpet; an open fire burns in the cool months. In the dining room, chef Callum Keir puts his own spin on the classics, using local meat, and vegetables, herbs and soft fruit from the kitchen garden. Typical dishes: pork belly and loin, pickled cauliflower florets, snow peas; lamb cutlet, shoulder and mini-shepherd's pie, winter vegetables. In the main house, or in cottages in the grounds, sleep well in refined, amply furnished bedrooms decorated in pretty country house style (a sleek Apple TV is a nod to the modern day). Come morning, do justice to the full English breakfast, then work it off on the lawn tennis courts, in the open-air swimming pool, or on the putting green or six-hole golf course. Polo fans, take note: the hotel has a long history with the game; Cowdray Park is nearby. (Mary Woods, and others)

Bepton
GU29 0JB

T: 01730 819020
E: reservations@parkhousehotel.com
W: www.parkhousehotel.com

BEDROOMS: 21. 5 on ground floor, 1 suitable for disabled, 9 in cottages in grounds.
OPEN: all year, except 25/26 Dec.
FACILITIES: drawing room, bar, dining room, conservatory, function rooms, free Wi-Fi, in-room TV (Sky), civil wedding licence, 10-acre grounds, spa, indoor and outdoor swimming pools (both heated, 15 metres), tennis, pitch and putt.
BACKGROUND MUSIC: in dining room/conservatory.
LOCATION: village, 2½ miles SW of Midhurst.
CHILDREN: all ages welcomed.
DOGS: allowed in certain bedrooms (charge), not in public rooms.
CREDIT CARDS: Amex, MasterCard, Visa.
PRICES: [2016] per room B&B from £108, D,B&B from £173. Dinner £37.50. 1-night bookings refused weekends.

BEVERLEY Yorkshire

Map 4:D5

NEWBEGIN HOUSE

'Attentive and helpful' owners Walter and Nuala Sweeney run their 'lovely, welcoming home-away-from-home' in the centre of this attractive market town. B&B accommodation occupies part of the 'fine' Georgian house standing in a 'lived-in' walled garden ('remarkable, so close to the centre'); the rest of the building, in which three generations of the Sweeney family live, is 'full of life, with family members moving about, though not intrusively'. 'The house reflects the style and tastes of its owners – it's full of paintings, photos and fine furniture, some clearly antiques.' Put your feet up in 'spacious' bedrooms well stocked with hot drinks, sodas, fresh milk, biscuits and chocolates; each has a 'very comfortable' super-king-size bed, silent mini-fridge, up-to-date tech. 'Good, adjustable lighting, so unusual in most hotels, enabled easy reading.' The hosts have much 'useful information' about the town to share; ask for dinner recommendations nearby. Breakfast is 'superb': 'proper black pudding freshly prepared, beautiful fruit, decent toast and great coffee'. 'We were spoilt.' (J and TS, Sue and John Jenkinson)

10 Newbegin
Beverley
HU17 8EG

T: 01482 888880
E: wsweeney@wsweeney.karoo.
co.uk
W: www.newbeginhousebbbeverley.
co.uk

BEDROOMS: 3.
OPEN: all year except 'when we are on holiday'.
FACILITIES: sitting room, dining room, free Wi-Fi, in-room TV (Freeview), walled garden, unsuitable for disabled.
BACKGROUND MUSIC: none.
LOCATION: central.
CHILDREN: all ages welcomed.
DOGS: not allowed.
CREDIT CARDS: none accepted.
PRICES: [2016] per room B&B single £60, double £85. 1-night bookings sometimes refused.

BIGBURY-ON-SEA Devon

Map 1:D4

BURGH ISLAND HOTEL

César award since 2012

Arrive by sea tractor ('an experience in itself')
to fully appreciate this 'amazing' Grade II
listed hotel – an 'Art Deco tour de force', and a
dreamlike tribute to the now-faded glamour of
the 1930s. 'It's a complete one-off.' The setting,
on a tidal island at the end of Bigbury beach, is
'magical': 'What total pleasure, to walk round
the island with a gin and tonic as the sun set,
then to sit by the roaring fire in the Pilchard
Inn.' Pick among bedrooms individually
decorated with vintage finds in period style,
each given the name of one of the hotel's famous
– and infamous – guests (Josephine Baker and
Gertie Lawrence among them). 'A sofa set by
the window in our room made the most of the
amazing sea views.' Dinner is a ball – almost
literally. 'It's simply impossible to be overdressed
at Burgh Island,' the owners say; give in to the
spirit of the place, and show up in black tie or
evening gown. Chef Tim Hall's daily-changing
menus are 'very good'; in the morning, an
'outstanding' breakfast awaits. (AT)

Burgh Island
Bigbury-on-Sea
TQ7 4BG

T: 01548 810514
E: reception@burghisland.com
W: www.burghisland.com

BEDROOMS: 25. 1 suite in Beach
House, apartment above Pilchard
Inn.
OPEN: all year.
FACILITIES: lift, bar, restaurant,
ballroom, sun lounge, billiard
room, private dining room, spa,
free Wi-Fi, civil wedding licence,
17-acre grounds on 26-acre island
(30-metre natural sea swimming
pool), unsuitable for disabled.
BACKGROUND MUSIC: 1920s and 1930s
in bar, live music Wed, Sat with
dinner in ballroom.
LOCATION: 5 miles S of Modbury,
private garages on mainland.
CHILDREN: not under 5, no under-
13s at dinner.
DOGS: not allowed.
CREDIT CARDS: MasterCard.
PRICES: [2016] per room D,B&B from
£400. 1-night bookings refused Sat,
some bank holidays.

BIGBURY-ON-SEA Devon

THE HENLEY

💧César award since 2003

'What a wonderful hotel – more like a lovely home,' writes a visitor this year to this Edwardian holiday cottage with 'sea views to die for'. More praise: 'We were mightily impressed, our expectations exceeded.' Owners Martyn Scarterfield and his wife, Petra Lampe, serve up 'hospitality and fab food' in a 'truly delightful' situation overlooking the Avon estuary; their black Labrador, Caspar, is 'well beloved' by guests. Potted palms and Lloyd Loom chairs fill the public rooms; there are paintings, books and magazines, a wood-burning stove. Traditionally and amply furnished, bedrooms are equipped with binoculars to take in the 'inspiring' view. Guests gather at 7 pm for Martyn Scarterfield's three-course dinner, served in the conservatory. A typical dish: pan-fried John Dory, lemongrass-marinated prawns. 'Though limited in choice, dinner was splendid, and beautifully cooked.' (Vegetarians are well catered for, by prior arrangement.) Breakfast is 'super'. The sandy beach is approached by a private cliff path at the bottom of the terraced garden. Board the sea tractor to cross the causeway to Burgh Island. (Irene Kearney, Chris Savory, SR)

Folly Hill
Bigbury-on-Sea
TQ7 4AR

T: 01548 810240
F: 01548 810240
E: thehenleyhotel@btconnect.com
W: www.thehenleyhotel.co.uk

BEDROOMS: 5.
OPEN: Mar–end Oct.
FACILITIES: 2 lounges, bar, conservatory dining room, free Wi-Fi (in some areas), small garden (steps to beach, golf, sailing, fishing), Coastal Path nearby, unsuitable for disabled.
BACKGROUND MUSIC: jazz/classical in the evenings in lounge, dining room.
LOCATION: 5 miles S of Modbury.
CHILDREN: not under 12.
DOGS: not allowed in dining room.
CREDIT CARDS: Amex, MasterCard, Visa.
PRICES: [2016] per room B&B single £93, double £123–£155, D,B&B (2-night min.) single £120, double £182–£205. Set dinner £36. 1-night bookings sometimes refused weekends.

BIGGIN-BY-HARTINGTON Derbyshire

Map 3:B6

BIGGIN HALL

'Friendly', 'informal' and 'welcoming', James Moffett's 'characterful' hotel is well liked by walkers and dog owners, who come for the 'reasonable prices' and the 'marvellous Derbyshire Dales setting'. It's not to all tastes: some visitors find it too 'straightforward' – even 'scruffy' in parts. For fans, however, it's all part of the charm, from the 'delightful' piggy neighbours to the 'strange modern sculptures that made a good talking point at dinner'. 'I fully endorse this quirky hotel,' a regular Guide reader says in 2016. Simple, rustic bedrooms (some compact) are in the main house and varied outbuildings. 'Our room itself was quirky, with twin beds at right angles. It had a good modern bathroom; a raised area with comfortable seating up a few steps. The walk from the lodge to the main house was part of the pleasure.' Nibbles come with complimentary aperitifs before a 'delicious, well-prepared' country dinner, perhaps 'an excellent steak followed by treacle tart – bliss'. 'Each morning, they provided us with free sandwiches and drinks to take for our lunch – a wonderful touch.' (Simon Rodway, Anne Laurence Thackray, Christopher Born, and others)

Main Street
Biggin-by-Hartington
SK17 0DH

T: 01298 84451
E: enquiries@bigginhall.co.uk
W: www.bigginhall.co.uk

BEDROOMS: 21. 13 in annexes, some on ground floor.
OPEN: all year.
FACILITIES: sitting room, library, dining room, meeting room, free Wi-Fi (in sitting rooms, some bedrooms), in-room TV, civil wedding licence, 8-acre grounds (croquet), River Dove 1½ miles, unsuitable for disabled.
BACKGROUND MUSIC: none.
LOCATION: 8 miles N of Ashbourne.
CHILDREN: not under 12.
DOGS: allowed in courtyard and bothy bedrooms, not in public rooms.
CREDIT CARDS: MasterCard, Visa.
PRICES: [2016] per room B&B £70–£170, D,B&B £115–£215. Set dinner £25. 1-night bookings sometimes refused.

BLAKENEY Norfolk

❧ THE BLAKENEY HOTEL

César award: seaside hotel of the year

In a 'scenic' setting facing 'tranquil' marshland – 'a joy for painters' – the Stannard family's 'popular' traditional hotel attracts all generations of regular guests, who praise the 'remarkably high standards of service and amenities'. 'The greeting from the hands-on manager and cheerful staff starts each visit on a high note,' says a return visitor this year. Pick a bedroom to suit – each has its own character, with a balcony or patio, garden views or an estuary outlook. A 'quiet, restful' single room in the main house has 'a comfortable bed, lots of pillows, good lighting'; a ground-floor annexe room with a private patio, 'while convenient for anyone with mobility problems, needs a better designed bathroom'. Graze on snacks and sandwiches all day in the bar and lounges, but save room for dinner: 'The food is excellent and varied', perhaps 'particularly good' gravadlax; an 'excellent' chocolate torte. Breakfast wins acclaim. 'You've got to see it to believe it: wonderful home-made muesli; porridge with fresh strawberries; excellent fish, kedgeree, and bacon and eggs from the lengthy menu.' (Clive T Blackburn, MJ, Helen Anthony)

The Quay
Blakeney
NR25 7NE

T: 01263 740797
F: 01263 740795
E: enquiries@blakeneyhotel.co.uk
W: www.blakeneyhotel.co.uk

BEDROOMS: 63. 16 in Granary annexe opposite, some on ground floor.
OPEN: all year.
FACILITIES: lift, lounge, sun lounge, bar, restaurant, free Wi-Fi, in-room TV (Freeview), function facilities, heated indoor swimming pool (15 by 5 metres), steam room, sauna, mini-gym, games room, terrace, ¼-acre garden.
BACKGROUND MUSIC: none.
LOCATION: on quay.
CHILDREN: all ages welcomed.
DOGS: allowed in some bedrooms, not in public rooms.
CREDIT CARDS: all major cards.
PRICES: [2016] per person B&B £85–£165, D,B&B (2-night min.) £97–£193. À la carte £29. 1-night bookings sometimes refused weekends, bank holidays.

BLANCHLAND Co. Durham

THE LORD CREWE ARMS

♔César award since 2016

Contemporary country house meets 'cheerful' local pub at this 12th-century former abbot's lodge, in a 'beautiful' conservation village. The spirit of the place is immediately striking, say Guide inspectors this year. 'It blends effortlessly into the architecture and the ambience of the village'; 'the accent you hear and the mood created belong to the immediate area'. The main building – its thick stone walls and medieval vaulted bar, its 'maze of corridors' – 'reeks of history'; bedrooms, up the stairs, in adjacent cottages and in The Angel across the road, are modern and 'beautifully appointed'. 'Our first-floor Angel room had a restrained decor in tartan, greys and cream. It had a window seat, two chairs, very good storage, delicious home-made cookies; a great rain shower over the bath.' Eat in the Bishop's Dining Room: chef Simon Hicks's 'interesting', 'unfussy' dishes might include duck cooked on the open grill; a 'lovely' pea, lettuce and lovage soup. 'The tables were quite close together, encouraging chat between guests.' Calcot Manor, Tetbury (see entry), is under the same ownership. (DB, and others)

The Square
Blanchland
DH8 9SP

T: 01434 675469
E: enquiries@
   lordcrewearmsblanchland.co.uk
W: www.lordcrewearmsblanchland.
   co.uk

BEDROOMS: 21. 7 in adjacent cottages, 10 in The Angel across the road, some on ground floor, 1 suitable for disabled.
OPEN: all year.
FACILITIES: 3 lounges, restaurant, free Wi-Fi, in-room TV (Freeview), civil wedding licence, beer garden.
BACKGROUND MUSIC: none.
LOCATION: in village on the B6306, 9 miles S of Hexham.
CHILDREN: all ages welcomed.
DOGS: 'well-behaved dogs' allowed in some bedrooms, not in dining room.
CREDIT CARDS: MasterCard, Visa.
PRICES: [2016] per room B&B £164–£184. À la carte £30. 1-night bookings refused Fri/Sat Mar–Oct.

BLEDINGTON Oxfordshire

THE KING'S HEAD INN

Horse brasses hang above the stone fireplace, and old hunting prints decorate the walls of the beamed pub in this old stone inn on the village green. The whole, in a 16th-century cider house, is a picture of 'unspoilt rustic charm', from the 'informal' ambience and 'enthusiastic' staff to the country-cottage bedrooms. Locals (including 'a team of highly decorative Morris dancers', if you're lucky) prop up the low-ceilinged bar, all uneven flagstones, old settles, and wild flowers on wooden tables. In the dining room, find a daily-changing menu of 'updated favourites, with interesting modern touches', perhaps Upton smoked brown shrimps on toast; Windrush goat's cheese salad, walnuts, pickled beetroot. Tumble into one of the characterful bedrooms, afterwards, in the main building and across the courtyard – each has its own style, with a modern four-poster bed here, exposed beams there, generous doses of floral prints or tartan to tie it all together. Next day, find juices, granola and stewed fruit on the breakfast buffet; cooked dishes are prepared to order. Owners Archie and Nicola Orr-Ewing also manage The Swan Inn, Swinbrook (see entry).

The Green
Bledington
OX7 6XQ

T: 01608 658365
F: 01608 658902
E: info@kingsheadinn.net
W: www.thekingsheadinn.net

BEDROOMS: 12. 6 in annexe, some on ground floor.
OPEN: all year except 25/26 Dec.
FACILITIES: bar, restaurant, courtyard, free Wi-Fi, in-room TV, children's play area, unsuitable for disabled.
BACKGROUND MUSIC: none.
LOCATION: on village green.
CHILDREN: all ages welcomed.
DOGS: not allowed in bedrooms, restaurant.
CREDIT CARDS: MasterCard, Visa.
PRICES: [2016] per room B&B from £100. À la carte £28. 1-night bookings refused Sat.

BORROWDALE Cumbria

Map 4: inset C2

HAZEL BANK

✿César award since 2016

Gary and Donna MacRae have refurbished and revived this 1840s stone house, approached via a 'sweet little stone bridge' across a stream. When the MacRaes took it on in 2013, Hazel Bank had something of the 'shabby and forsaken' aspect described by novelist Hugh Walpole, a regular visitor, who used it as a backdrop for his Herries Chronicle. Today, the atmosphere is 'welcoming and relaxed'; the rural setting 'magical'. 'Gary obviously revels in his role as host.' Bedrooms are 'well equipped and comfortable', with sherry, home-made shortbread, fresh flowers; the 'practical' bathrooms have 'generous' toiletries. 'Cosy' evenings are spent by the open log fire in the 'pleasant' sitting room. Guests gather in the lounge at 7 pm for canapés; chef David Jackson's daily-changing four-course menu might include Herdwick lamb, crushed Charlotte potatoes, port pan gravy; Donna's sticky toffee pudding. Ask for a window seat and watch red squirrels and abundant birdlife in the four acres of garden. Plenty of choice at breakfast, including 'good' veggie options. 'Superb' walks begin at the front door; packed lunches and drying facilities are provided.

Rosthwaite
Borrowdale
CA12 5XB

T: 017687 77248
F: 017687 77373
E: info@hazelbankhotel.co.uk
W: www.hazelbankhotel.co.uk

BEDROOMS: 7. 1 on ground floor.
OPEN: all year except Jan, Christmas and New Year.
FACILITIES: lounge, dining room, drying room, free Wi-Fi, 4-acre grounds (croquet, woodland walks).
BACKGROUND MUSIC: none.
LOCATION: 6 miles S of Keswick on B5289 to Borrowdale.
CHILDREN: not under 15.
DOGS: not allowed.
CREDIT CARDS: MasterCard, Visa.
PRICES: [2016] per person B&B £55–£80, D,B&B £87–£112, single supplement £30. Set dinner £34. 1-night bookings sometimes refused.

SEE ALSO SHORTLIST

BOSCASTLE Cornwall

Map 1:C3

THE OLD RECTORY

The 'magical setting' in the Valency valley is the perfect spot for a whimsical tale. Thomas Hardy arrived here in 1870, to be met at the door by the rector's sister-in-law, Emma Gifford, his future first wife. If it's the romance of the story that draws guests to Sally and Chris Searle's B&B, it's the hospitality that inspires them to return. The 'beautifully restored' Victorian house has comfy sofas, log fires, fresh flowers; bedrooms decorated in cottage style. Choose Hardy's Room, and put your feet up in the antique carved bed. The Searles run their B&B along green lines: they keep an organic kitchen garden; a beehive buzzes with activity; ducks, hens and rare-breed pigs contribute to the 'home-grown breakfast'. 'The large garden, alive with birds and butterflies, is delightful'; ask the hosts for a tour – or a spare bee suit, if you're keen to look in the hive. Dinner (perhaps Cornish fish with freshly dug potatoes) may be served in the restored greenhouse, by arrangement. Then sink into sleep: breakfast is served till 10 am, if a lie-in appeals. (CS)

25% DISCOUNT VOUCHERS

St Juliot
Boscastle
PL35 0BT

T: 01840 250225
F: 01840 250225
E: sally@stjuliot.com
W: www.stjuliot.com

BEDROOMS: 4. 1 in stables (connected to house via conservatory).
OPEN: normally Feb–end Oct, 'but please check'.
FACILITIES: sitting room, breakfast room, conservatory, free Wi-Fi, in-room TV (Freeview), 3-acre garden (croquet lawn, 'lookout', walled kitchen garden), unsuitable for disabled.
BACKGROUND MUSIC: none.
LOCATION: 2 miles NE of Boscastle.
CHILDREN: not under 12.
DOGS: up to 2 allowed, only in stable room (£10 per stay).
CREDIT CARDS: MasterCard, Visa.
PRICES: [2016] per room B&B £70–£110. 2-course dinner (by arrangement; bring your own bottle) £17.50. 1-night bookings refused weekends and busy periods.

BOSHAM Sussex

Map 2:E3

THE MILLSTREAM

'The warmth of the welcome, the good food, the atmosphere and the unspoilt environs are hard to beat,' writes a regular Guide correspondent in 2016, of the Wild family's hotel in a 'charming' village near Chichester harbour. 'It gently hums with activity. We appreciated the enthusiastic welcome from the young staff: our bags were swept up and delivered to our room while we sat for a drink by the log fire.' The 'immaculate', extended 18th-century building is 'kept in pristine condition'; returnees, who like the 'traditional decor and ambience', consider it 'like an old friend'. Choose among 'comfortable' bedrooms, all 'well equipped' with dressing gowns and biscuits (but 'dreaded' captive hangers); the best have French doors leading to a private garden. Two 'quiet' suites are in a thatched garden cottage, reached via 'well-lit' paths and a bridge across the stream. In the evening, dine informally in Marwick's brasserie, or sample Neil Hiskey's modern dishes, perhaps fillet of bream, shellfish bisque, crab beignet, in the restaurant. 'The cooked breakfast is a treat.' 'I left feeling a lot better than when I arrived.' (Alec Frank, Michael Gwinnell, Robin Wright, Ian Marshall)

25% DISCOUNT VOUCHERS

Bosham Lane
Bosham, nr Chichester
PO18 8HL

T: 01243 573234
F: 01243 573459
E: info@millstreamhotel.com
W: www.millstreamhotel.com

BEDROOMS: 35. 2 in cottage, 7 on ground floor, 1 suitable for disabled.
OPEN: all year.
FACILITIES: lounge, bar, restaurant (pianist Sat eve), brasserie, conference room, free Wi-Fi, in-room TV (Freeview), civil wedding licence, 1¼-acre garden, Chichester Harbour 300 yards.
BACKGROUND MUSIC: all day in bar, lounge and restaurant.
LOCATION: 4 miles W of Chichester.
CHILDREN: all ages welcomed.
DOGS: not allowed.
CREDIT CARDS: MasterCard, Visa.
PRICES: [2016] per room B&B single from £79, double from £135, D,B&B from £174 (for two people, 2-night min. stay). À la carte £35. 1-night bookings refused Sat.

BOURTON-ON-THE-HILL Gloucestershire   Map 3:D6

THE HORSE AND GROOM

♡César award since 2012

There's local flavour aplenty at this 'cheerful' village pub-with-rooms: find copper jugs, horsey pictures, bunches of wild blooms, chalkboard menus and a throng of villagers and tourists, who come for the local real ales, craft ciders and 'imaginative' Cotswold-inspired cooking. Brothers Tom and Will Greenstock are manager and chef; together, they've 'worked tirelessly' to gather their legion of admirers. Find a table for an 'innovative', 'unpretentious' dinner, cooked with home-grown greens and, perhaps, handfuls of foraged blackberries or field mushrooms. A characteristic dish: griddled Cotswold Barnsley chop, braised white beans, rosemary aïoli. 'The young waiting staff are pleasant and knowledgeable.' Retire for the night to the 'well-equipped' bedrooms, each pleasing and modern. (Rooms at the back are quietest.) At breakfast, 'home-made croissants, buttery and gorgeous, are the pièce de résistance'. There's no guest lounge, but 'bedrooms are perfectly comfortable for sitting around in, and reading'; on warm days, the large garden is the place to be. (J and MB, Michael and Margaret Cross)

25% DISCOUNT VOUCHERS

Bourton-on-the-Hill
nr Moreton-in-Marsh
GL56 9AQ

T: 01386 700413
F: 01386 700413
E: greenstocks@horseandgroom.info
W: www.horseandgroom.info

BEDROOMS: 5.
OPEN: all year except Christmas/New Year, restaurant closed Sun eve except on bank holiday weekends.
FACILITIES: bar/restaurant, free Wi-Fi, in-room TV (Freeview), 1-acre garden, unsuitable for disabled.
BACKGROUND MUSIC: none.
LOCATION: village centre.
CHILDREN: all ages welcomed.
DOGS: not allowed.
CREDIT CARDS: MasterCard, Visa.
PRICES: [2016] per room B&B single £80, double £120–£170. À la carte £27. 1-night bookings refused weekends.

BOWNESS-ON-WINDERMERE Cumbria Map 4: inset C2

LINDETH FELL

♔César award since 2009

Family owned and family run, the Kennedys' 'excellent' luxury B&B is in an Edwardian country house overlooking Lake Windermere. Matriarch Diana Kennedy runs the place, while daughters Sheena and Joanna are manager and chef. 'They are lovely owners,' says a reader this year. The elegant public rooms have deep, comfy sofas; master bedrooms on the first floor are particularly spacious. In all bedrooms expect Egyptian cotton sheets, a decanter of sherry, a Roberts radio, fluffy towels and luxury toiletries. Afternoon tea, with warm scones and fresh cream, may be taken on the terrace in fine weather; in the evening, guests choosing to eat in may choose from a home-made soup of the day and a fine selection of platters (deep-fried sole goujons and potted Morecambe Bay shrimp on the fish platter; cheeses, grilled vegetables, and a white bean and basil dip for vegetarians). There is much choice at breakfast, including Finnan haddock and pan-fried haloumi; granola, yogurt and marmalade are all home made. Fitness-minded guests have complimentary access to local gym and pool facilities. (Peter Hutchinson)

25% DISCOUNT VOUCHERS

Lyth Valley Road
Bowness-on-Windermere
LA23 3JP

T: 01539 443286
F: 01539 447455
E: kennedy@lindethfell.co.uk
W: www.lindethfell.co.uk

BEDROOMS: 14. 1 on ground floor.
OPEN: all year except Christmas, Jan.
FACILITIES: 2 lounges, bar, dining room, free Wi-Fi, in-room TV (Freeview), 7-acre grounds (terrace, gardens, croquet, putting, bowls, tarn, fishing permits).
BACKGROUND MUSIC: classical music in dining room at breakfast, evenings in bar.
LOCATION: 1 mile S of Bowness on A5074.
CHILDREN: all ages welcomed.
DOGS: only assistance dogs allowed.
CREDIT CARDS: MasterCard, Visa.
PRICES: [2016] per person B&B £63–£120. 1-night bookings sometimes refused weekends, bank holidays.

SEE ALSO SHORTLIST

BRADFORD-ON-AVON Wiltshire

Map 2:D1

WOOLLEY GRANGE

Parents 'sleep like babies' at this 'fantastic' family-friendly hotel, in a Jacobean manor house in 'glorious' countryside. 'They've thought of absolutely everything to accommodate children and adults,' says an 'impressed' guest in 2016. Part of Nigel Chapman's Luxury Family Hotels group, the hotel has 'a happy, relaxed atmosphere'; there's 'character in spades', from the curio-filled public rooms to the 'beautiful' bedrooms and sprawling grounds – 'just wild enough, in parts' – that are 'ripe for exploration'. Long afternoons may be spent in playrooms and pools, picking through a garden maze, collecting eggs from the hens and ducks, peering at tadpoles in the ornamental pond; 'expert' childminders 'put parents' minds at ease'. 'We particularly liked the lovely extras: morning newsletters, hand-written notes to the children at breakfast, junior treatments in the spa.' Young guests eat well in The Orangery; once the kids are in bed, sit in the candlelit restaurant over Mark Bradbury's seasonal menus, the whole soothed by 'a contented murmur of adult conversation'. Breakfast brings pastries, fruit, thick yogurt from the buffet; cooked dishes are served at table. (ZH, and others)

Woolley Green
Bradford-on-Avon
BA15 1TX

T: 01225 864705
E: info@woolleygrangehotel.co.uk
W: www.woolleygrangehotel.co.uk

BEDROOMS: 25. 11 in annexes, 2 on ground floor, 1 suitable for disabled.
OPEN: all year.
FACILITIES: 2 drawing rooms, 2 restaurants, cinema, meeting rooms, free Wi-Fi, in-room TV (Freeview), crèche, spa, heated indoor and outdoor swimming pools (12 by 5 metres), civil wedding licence, 14-acre grounds (kitchen garden, children's play areas, fields).
BACKGROUND MUSIC: all day in restaurants.
LOCATION: 1 mile NE of Bradford-on-Avon.
CHILDREN: all ages welcomed.
DOGS: not allowed in restaurants.
CREDIT CARDS: Amex, MasterCard, Visa.
PRICES: [2016] per room B&B £120–£500, D,B&B £190–£570. À la carte £40. 1-night bookings sometimes refused weekends and bank holidays.

BRAITHWAITE Cumbria

Map 4: inset C2

THE COTTAGE IN THE WOOD

'We were not disappointed.' Beside Whinlatter Pass, Kath and Liam Berney extend the 'warmest welcome' to guests at their 'idyllic' restaurant-with-rooms. Take drinks on the terrace in warmer weather – the whitewashed 17th-century coaching inn has 'stunning views' towards Skiddaw – or retire to the sitting room, where a wood-burner, books and games await on rainy days. The 'clean, well-appointed' smaller Cottage bedrooms occupy the oldest part of the house, dating from 1654; the 'luxurious, generously proportioned' Garden Room has a private patio. 'The living area was divided by a wood-burning stove, creating separate cosy seating areas.' Eat well in the award-winning conservatory-style dining room, where chef Chris Archer 'cooks with flair', using 'lots of local produce: Herdwick hogget, brill from Whitehaven, the famous Waberthwaite sausage'. Each dish is paired with a complementing wine. (Try the vegetarian tasting menu, a tempting alternative.) Breakfast, with scrambled duck eggs and 'crispy' bacon, is 'great'. Walking and cycling trails from the door; a drying room for when you return. (HB, JP, Stephanie Thompson and Keith Sutton)

25% DISCOUNT VOUCHERS

Magic Hill
Whinlatter Forest
Braithwaite
CA12 5TW

T: 017687 78409
E: relax@thecottageinthewood.co.uk
W: www.thecottageinthewood.co.uk

BEDROOMS: 9. 1 in the garden with separate entrance.
OPEN: all year except Christmas, 2nd and 3rd week Jan, restaurant closed Mon.
FACILITIES: lounge, restaurant, free Wi-Fi, in-room TV (Freeview), drying room, secure bicycle storage, terraced garden, 2 acres of woodland, only restaurant suitable for disabled.
BACKGROUND MUSIC: none.
LOCATION: 5 miles NW of Keswick.
CHILDREN: not under 10.
DOGS: not allowed.
CREDIT CARDS: MasterCard, Visa.
PRICES: [2016] per room B&B from £88, D,B&B from £105. Set menu £50, tasting menu £65. 1-night bookings refused weekends.

BRAMPTON Cumbria

FARLAM HALL

♔ César award since 2001

'With a tradition of service that's second to none, this is one of the finest country house hotels – if not "the" finest – in England,' raves a regular Guide reader this year. In 'beautiful' grounds where 'magnificent mature trees' stand sentry, the Quinion family has welcomed guests to their creeper-clad sandstone retreat since 1975. Come in: 'It's like slipping into a pair of cosy slippers the moment you cross the doorstep.' The lounges have a Victorian feel, with original fireplaces, comfy sofas and objets d'art; settle in for morning coffee and biscuits. Bedrooms are large, traditional, eclectically furnished, with patterned wallpaper and a substantial bathroom. 'Dress smartly for dinner.' In the elegant dining room, its floor-to-ceiling windows overlooking garden and ornamental lake, Barry Quinion's 'excellent', short daily-changing menus ('no excessive portions') might include timbale of West Coast crab and avocado; loin of local lamb, roasted parsnips, rosemary, red onions. The area calls for days out – there are 'castles galore'; Hadrian's Wall is easily accessible. 'We had a fantastic stay.' (Chris Savory, EM Arnold, and others)

Hallbankgate
Brampton
CA8 2NG

T: 01697 746234
F: 01697 746683
E: farlam@farlamhall.co.uk
W: www.farlamhall.co.uk

BEDROOMS: 12. 1 in stables, 2 on ground floor.
OPEN: all year except 24–30 Dec, 3 weeks Jan.
FACILITIES: 2 lounges, restaurant, free Wi-Fi, in-room TV (Freeview), civil wedding licence, 6-acre grounds, unsuitable for disabled.
BACKGROUND MUSIC: none.
LOCATION: on A689, 2½ miles SE of Brampton (not in Farlam village).
CHILDREN: not under 5.
DOGS: allowed in bedrooms (not unattended), not in restaurant.
CREDIT CARDS: Amex, MasterCard, Visa.
PRICES: [2016] per person D,B&B £155–£185. Set dinner £49.50. 1-night bookings refused at New Year.

BRANCASTER STAITHE Norfolk

Map 2:A5

THE WHITE HORSE

♔César award since 2014

'Efficient, friendly' staff, 'well-appointed' rooms and 'splendid seafood meals' keep guests returning to the Nye family's 'charming', 'first-rate' inn on the north Norfolk coast. (The 'modern selection' of gins in the popular bar helps, too.) In the conservatory restaurant or on the terrace, chef Fran Hartshorne's cooking is 'excellent in quality and variety'. Her menu celebrates the local catch, with mussels harvested at the bottom of the garden, and fish and shellfish delivered to the door by the local fishermen – try the Cromer crab and Brancaster oysters. 'Very good, very comfortable' bedrooms in the main house and a garden annexe are outfitted in a cool New England-style decor. 'Our spacious room at the top had great views over the marshes. The bathroom, on a lower level, had a good shower; a generous amount of various toiletries. We particularly appreciated the quality coffee machine and fresh milk.' Another guest, in 2016: 'We happily watched avocets and oystercatchers from our large room.' 'Excellent coastal walks' are accessed via the path along the garden's edge. (Max Lickfold, Ivan and Veronica Allen, Peter Anderson)

Main Road
Brancaster Staithe
PE31 8BY

T: 01485 210262
F: 01485 210930
E: reception@whitehorsebrancaster.co.uk
W: www.whitehorsebrancaster.co.uk

BEDROOMS: 15. 8 on ground floor in annexe, 1 suitable for disabled.
OPEN: all year.
FACILITIES: 2 lounge areas, public bar, conservatory restaurant, dining room, free Wi-Fi, in-room TV (Freeview), ½-acre garden (covered sunken garden), harbour sailing.
BACKGROUND MUSIC: 'subtle' in restaurant.
LOCATION: centre of village just E of Brancaster.
CHILDREN: all ages welcomed.
DOGS: allowed in garden rooms (£10 per night) and bar.
CREDIT CARDS: MasterCard, Visa.
PRICES: [2016] per room B&B £100–£190, D,B&B (Sun–Thurs only, except bank holidays and school holidays) £150–£190. À la carte £29.

BRIGHTON Sussex

Map 2:E4

ARTIST RESIDENCE BRIGHTON

NEW

Charlotte and Justin Salisbury have created a 'laid-back, bohemian' town house hotel with 'jazzy' rooms, 'young, friendly, efficient' staff and 'a range of fun art'. 'It's perfect for the untraditional, un-conservative guest,' say inspectors in 2016. The decor combines rustic and eclectic elements throughout; there are rattan chairs and parlour games in the lounge. Wilder bedrooms have murals painted by local and international artists. 'Our fourth-floor room had an eye-catching Yellow Submarine-style mural; a comfy double bed; a compact but well-thought-out bathroom. Nice touches: a travel-trunk-turned-wardrobe, a pink TV, posh teabags, bright Anglepoise bedside lights. In the morning, we woke to a view of the sea.' Come nightfall, quaff 'delicious' cocktails in the bar, then mix with locals and tourists in the 'arty' restaurant, choosing from a selection of freewheeling seasonal tasting menus. Sample dishes: cuttlefish, wild garlic, crispy cockles, radish; hake, chicken wing, parsnip, cornflake. The Salisburys also run an Artist Residence in London (see entry) and one in Penzance (see Shortlist).

33 Regency Square
Brighton
BN1 2GG

T: 01273 324302
E: brighton@artistresidence.co.uk
W: www.artistresidence.co.uk

BEDROOMS: 23.
OPEN: all year, restaurant closed Sun eve, Mon, Christmas–New Year.
FACILITIES: lift, lounge, café, restaurant, ping pong/meeting room, free Wi-Fi, in-room TV (Freeview), unsuitable for disabled.
BACKGROUND MUSIC: in public areas.
LOCATION: town centre.
CHILDREN: not under 16.
DOGS: not allowed.
CREDIT CARDS: Amex, MasterCard, Visa.
PRICES: [2016] per room B&B £90–£300. 1-night bookings refused weekends.

SEE ALSO SHORTLIST

BRISTOL

Map 1:B6

BROOKS GUESTHOUSE

A 'good-value' option in 'a great, central location', Carla and Andrew Brooks's 'friendly' contemporary B&B is 'perfect for tourists and businesspeople', say Guide inspectors in 2016, who enjoyed 'another impressive stay'. The neat, modern bedrooms (including a triple) are supplied with hot chocolate, biscuits, a retro chair and a lambswool throw, but novelty and a spark of adventure lie in the ingenious, custom-built Airstream trailers on the AstroTurfed roof. 'Our beautifully sleek 20-foot Airstream camper van was comfortably done up, with a good-sized double bed, and two small singles for the kids. We had thick duvets, a good, strong shower, lots of fluffy towels; great lighting. We'd been advised about weekend noise; in the event, it was gorgeously quiet all night, though the seagulls were pretty noisy in the morning.' (Light sleepers should ask for more tranquil rooms overlooking the Mediterranean-style courtyard.) In the 'spacious, congenial' open-plan kitchen, breakfast is 'excellent': fruit compote, home-made granola, 'lovely' jams, 'great' cooked options, 'all served quickly and efficiently'. Rushing off? Ask for a bacon roll or smoked salmon bagel to take away.

Exchange Avenue
St Nicholas Market
Bristol
BS1 1UB

T: 0117 930 0066
F: 0117 929 9489
E: info@brooksguesthousebristol.com
W: www.brooksguesthousebristol.com

BEDROOMS: 27. 4 in Airstream caravans on roof, 1 on ground floor suitable for disabled.
OPEN: all year except 23–27 Dec.
FACILITIES: lounge/breakfast room, free Wi-Fi, in-room TV (Freeview), courtyard garden.
BACKGROUND MUSIC: contemporary in lounge and breakfast area.
LOCATION: central, next to St Nicholas Market.
CHILDREN: all ages welcomed.
DOGS: not allowed.
CREDIT CARDS: MasterCard, Visa.
PRICES: [2016] per room B&B from £99.

BRISTOL

Map 1:B6

NUMBER THIRTY EIGHT CLIFTON

♔César award since 2013

Regular guests praise the 'impeccable' service and 'well-appointed' rooms at Adam Dorrien-Smith's relaxed, modern B&B, in an 'excellent' location at the top of Clifton Downs. The refurbished Georgian town house is hung with vibrant original artwork; up the stairs, masculine bedrooms 'well decorated' in soothing heritage shades look across the city's rooftops. (Rooms at the back are quietest.) 'Our room was large and extremely clean, with views over the parkland opposite.' Living the high life? Book one of the two loft suites, which stretch over the length of the building, and have a bathtub big enough for two. The house is unstaffed after 8 pm, but 'it was easy to walk to the many restaurants on Whiteladies Road for dinner; the B&B provides a useful list'. Breakfast is 'excellent': served in the dining room or bedroom (for no extra charge), the menu includes granola, 'super-fresh' croissants, 'plenty of fresh fruit'; several cooked options. Limited parking permits available. Convenient for a stop-over on the way to or from the West. 'Highly recommended.' (John Patterson)

38 Upper Belgrave Road
Clifton
Bristol
BS8 2XN

T: 0117 946 6905
E: info@number38clifton.com
W: www.number38clifton.com

BEDROOMS: 9.
OPEN: all year.
FACILITIES: lounge, breakfast room, free Wi-Fi, in-room TV (Freeview), terrace, unsuitable for disabled.
BACKGROUND MUSIC: in public areas.
LOCATION: 2½ miles from city centre.
CHILDREN: not under 12.
DOGS: only guide dogs allowed.
CREDIT CARDS: all major cards.
PRICES: [2016] per room B&B £115–£235.

BROADWAY Worcestershire

Map 3:D6

THE BROADWAY HOTEL

'Pleasing' public rooms, 'helpful' staff, an 'attractive' garden and a 'central position' by the green make this Broadway character a show-stealer. The 16th-century stone house, part of the small Cotswolds Inns and Hotels group, 'has a lot going for it'. Take cocktails, local ales and light meals in the racing-themed bar; in the 'cool' modern restaurant, try British brasserie dishes, perhaps roast halibut, Jerusalem artichokes, burnt aubergine purée (though guests in 2016 thought portions could have been larger). Follow 'rambling corridors' ('a single journey can go down stairs as well as up them') to the individually styled bedrooms, some overlooking the 'pleasant' back garden. Otherwise comfortable, 'small to adequately sized' rooms suffer from being 'overburdened' by scatter cushions and other accessories, several guests have found. Visitors who like to live large might prefer the newly refurbished, one-bedroom Bumblebee Cottage a short stroll away. 'We enjoyed breakfast': bloomer bread, home-made Drambuie marmalade, Cotswold honeycomb; 'a good choice of well-prepared food'. (Tom and Sarah Mann, B and MB, and others)

The Green
Broadway
WR12 7AA

T: 01386 852401
F: 01386 853879
E: info@broadwayhotel.info
W: www.cotswold-inns-hotels.
   co.uk/broadway

BEDROOMS: 19. 1 on ground floor, 1-bed cottage a 2-min. walk away.
OPEN: all year.
FACILITIES: sitting room, bar, brasserie, free Wi-Fi, in-room TV (Freeview), garden.
BACKGROUND MUSIC: in brasserie.
LOCATION: village centre.
CHILDREN: all ages welcomed.
DOGS: allowed.
CREDIT CARDS: Amex, MasterCard, Visa.
PRICES: [2016] per room B&B £170–£240, D,B&B £234–£304. À la carte £38.

BROADWAY Worcestershire

Map 3:D6

DORMY HOUSE

Large vases of flowers, a well-stocked fruit bowl at reception, a tray of mix-it-yourself cordials and mineral water by a sofa – the details set the scene at the Sorensen family's upmarket countryside retreat, built around a 'lovely' refurbished farmhouse. 'The facilities are fantastic; the staff are friendly and eager to help. We felt well taken care of.' 'Tasteful, pleasingly decorated' Scandi-chic bedrooms are in the main house and annexes in the grounds; one, in a cottage, has a small courtyard and an outdoor hot tub. 'Our suite was an ideal family room with a separate sitting room, where the children slept on the pull-out sofa bed. There were current magazines, a good hospitality tray with fancy teas, a regularly replenished jar of biscuits.' At dinner, 'eat well' in the 'relaxed, rustic' Potting Shed, or in the 'civilised' Garden Room overlooking the 'neat' lawn. 'We started with warm breads and soft seaweed butter; particularly good was an exquisite fillet of cod in an intriguing yarrow chasseur sauce.' In the morning, feast anew: breakfast is 'memorable'. (Olivier le Mire, and others)

Willersey Hill
Broadway
WR12 7LF

T: 01386 852711
E: reservations@dormyhouse.co.uk
w: dormyhouse.co.uk

BEDROOMS: 38. 8 in Danish Court, 5 in Lavender Lodge, 2 suitable for disabled.
OPEN: all year.
FACILITIES: 4 lounges, Garden Room and Potting Shed restaurants, free Wi-Fi, in-room TV, civil wedding licence (for pagoda in garden), gardens, spa (16-metre indoor swimming pool, gym, treatment rooms).
BACKGROUND MUSIC: 'laid-back' in public areas.
LOCATION: 1½ miles E of Broadway.
CHILDREN: all ages welcomed.
DOGS: allowed in 4 bedrooms, lounges, not allowed in restaurants.
CREDIT CARDS: Amex, MasterCard, Visa.
PRICES: [2016] B&B from £255, D,B&B from £325. Set menu (Garden Room) £45, à la carte (Potting Shed) £34. 1-night bookings sometimes refused.

BROADWAY Worcestershire

Map 3:D6

RUSSELL'S

♔César award since 2006

Andrew and Gaynor Riley's 'excellent' restaurant-with-rooms is 'unhesitatingly recommended' by Guide readers who praise the 'exceptional' food, the 'rather special' rooms, and the staff 'who take the trouble to please'. The honey-stone building is the former showroom of Arts and Crafts designer Gordon Russell; careful restoration has achieved a contemporary, stylish feel, with huge fireplaces, exposed beams, stone walls. Individually designed bedrooms vary in size. 'Our two rooms were clean and excellently furnished. Room 4, which looks up the grassy climb to Broadway Tower, is a favourite, despite its sloping ceilings endangering the unwary. We were untroubled by traffic noise on the High Street.' In the 'busy' dining room, tuck in to Neil Clarke's much-praised modern British menu (including, perhaps, smoked pigeon breast, rhubarb crumble, fennel salad). Overnight guests may escape the activity of the popular restaurant in a residents' lounge, and use the honesty bar on the landing. A 'comprehensive' breakfast is 'cooked well (some diced fruit would have been welcomed)'. (T and SM, and others)

25% DISCOUNT VOUCHERS

The Green
20 High Street
Broadway
WR12 7DT

T: 01386 853555
F: 01386 853964
E: info@russellsofbroadway.co.uk
W: www.russellsofbroadway.co.uk

BEDROOMS: 7. 3 in adjoining building, 2 on ground floor.
OPEN: all year, restaurant closed Sun night and bank holiday Monday.
FACILITIES: residents' lounge, bar, restaurant, private dining room, free Wi-Fi, in-room TV (Freeview), patio (heating, meal service), unsuitable for disabled.
BACKGROUND MUSIC: in restaurant.
LOCATION: village centre.
CHILDREN: all ages welcomed (under-2s free).
DOGS: allowed in 2 bedrooms, public rooms.
CREDIT CARDS: Amex, MasterCard, Visa.
PRICES: [2016] per room B&B £120–£300. Set menus £14–£22, à la carte £45. 1-night bookings refused weekends.

BROCKENHURST Hampshire

Map 2:E2

THE PIG

Make merry at this convivial, creeper-covered country house standing in gardens with abundant 'space for gambolling'. Inside, expect a jolly mish-mash of oil portraits, boar's heads, wellies to borrow. 'This quirkiness isn't at the expense of comfort, however – there are plenty of comfortable places to relax.' Accommodation is in the main house, lodges and a cabin in the grounds, and the refurbished stable block next to the walled garden ('fragrant with all manner of herbs'). 'The bedrooms mix the high-tech with distressed genteel, but the essentials are both modern and of high quality – a large, comfortable bed; an espresso coffee machine in a cupboard with the tea-making equipment; an effective and generously sized power shower.' The 'inspired' cooking wins praise (though guests this year found the Bath pig chap – half a pig's jaw – 'radical'). 'There is a rustic assortment of furnishings in the conservatory restaurant, but the food is much more sophisticated than that – an imaginative range of choice, all superbly cooked, both at dinner and at breakfast.' Sister hotels are in Pensford, Southampton and Studland (see entries). (Robert Grimley, and others)

Beaulieu Road
Brockenhurst
SO42 7QL

T: 01590 622354
E: info@thepighotel.com
W: www.thepighotel.com

BEDROOMS: 31. 10 in stable block (100 yds), some on ground floor, 2 lodges and a cabin in the garden.
OPEN: all year.
FACILITIES: lounge, library, bar, restaurant, free Wi-Fi, in-room TV (Freeview), civil wedding licence, Potting Shed spa, kitchen garden, 6-acre grounds.
BACKGROUND MUSIC: in public areas.
LOCATION: 1 mile E of Brockenhurst village.
CHILDREN: all ages welcomed.
DOGS: not allowed.
CREDIT CARDS: MasterCard, Visa.
PRICES: [2016] room £155–£425. Breakfast £10–£15, à la carte £35. 1-night bookings refused weekends, Christmas, New Year.

SEE ALSO SHORTLIST

BRUTON Somerset

AT THE CHAPEL

Follow the smell of freshly baked bread into Catherine Butler and Ahmed Sidki's unusual restaurant-with-rooms: 'a great first impression'. Original stained-glass windows are a reminder of the building's origins as a congregational chapel; today, the 'stylishly' converted structure, its walls hung with modern art, houses a bakery, café and wine shop catering to locals and visitors (themselves 'decidedly stylish, too'). The heart of the place is the 'splendid' dining room in the original high-ceilinged chapel, filled with light and hubbub. Tables are laid with linen napkins; there are comfortable seats by the bar. In fine weather, eat outside, on the jasmine-scented terrace. Chef Dan Starnes serves food all day, perhaps 'vast' pizzas cooked in a wood-fired oven, or Mediterranean-inspired dishes like cauliflower arancini, wild garlic; Portland crab linguini. Stay the night in cool, calm, contemporary bedrooms, each with a marble bathroom; the best room opens on to a private walled garden. 'Delicious' freshly baked croissants are left outside the rooms for breakfast (Somerset butter and home-made jam are in the fridge); cooked dishes, charged extra, await downstairs.

High Street
Bruton
BA10 0AE

T: 01749 814070
E: mail@atthechapel.co.uk
W: www.atthechapel.co.uk

BEDROOMS: 8. 1 on ground floor.
OPEN: all year.
FACILITIES: club room, restaurant, free Wi-Fi, in-room smart TV, terrace, bakery, wine store, unsuitable for disabled.
BACKGROUND MUSIC: none.
LOCATION: 7 miles SE of Shepton Mallet.
CHILDREN: all ages welcomed.
DOGS: not allowed.
CREDIT CARDS: Amex, MasterCard, Visa.
PRICES: [2016] per room B&B (continental) £125–£250. À la carte £30–£50. 1-night bookings refused weekends.

BRYHER Isles of Scilly

Map 1: inset C1

🏵 HELL BAY HOTEL

César award: seaside hotel of the year

The rocky coastline may have been hell for sailors, but a short hop by propeller plane and boat brings you to the smallest of the inhabited Scilly Isles, something more like heaven. 'We loved the whole experience,' writes a reader in 2016, of a visit to Robert Dorrien-Smith's hotel overlooking the Atlantic. 'The young staff were utterly charming'; 'all our transfers were brilliantly organised'. Bedrooms have a breezy, coastal feel. 'Our top-floor Boathouse room had lovely views from the good-sized balcony. The large sitting area had two comfortable armchairs; brilliantly thought-out storage lined a corridor; a mini-kitchen behind cupboard doors had cafetière coffee, fresh milk and bottled water.' A short walk through 'beautifully tended' gardens leads to the restaurant. 'Dinner was always a treat, though we would've liked more shellfish. Breakfasts were excellent; a very interesting buffet.' Another option: visit the hotel's convivial, informal Crab Shack, where just three seafood dishes are served communally. 'Such fun, really different – one of the highlights of our trip.' The hotel's collection of Cornish art is 'unrivalled'. (Barbara Watkinson)

Bryher
TR23 0PR

T: 01720 422947
F: 01720 423004
E: contactus@hellbay.co.uk
W: www.hellbay.co.uk

BEDROOMS: 25 suites. In 5 buildings, some on ground floor, 1 suitable for disabled.
OPEN: early Mar–late Oct.
FACILITIES: lounge, games room, bar, 2 dining rooms, free Wi-Fi, in-room TV, gym, sauna, large grounds (heated swimming pool, 15 by 10 metres, children's playground, par-3 golf course), beach 75 yds.
BACKGROUND MUSIC: none.
LOCATION: W coast of island, boat from Tresco (reached by boat/helicopter from mainland) or St Mary's.
CHILDREN: all ages welcomed (high tea at 5.30 pm).
DOGS: allowed (£12 a night charge), not in public rooms.
CREDIT CARDS: MasterCard, Visa.
PRICES: [2016] per person B&B £85–£310, D,B&B £125–£350. Set dinner £45, evening bar menu à la carte £17.

BUDE Cornwall

THE BEACH

Take in 'lovely sea views' at Susie and Will Daniel's stylish hotel, whose lively bar and restaurant overlook the popular, family-friendly beach. The bedrooms are individually decorated in a breezy, New England style; the best have a private terrace or Juliet balcony overlooking the water. A nice touch: find fresh milk in the fridge; a capsule coffee machine in superior rooms. Sunset cocktails were made for drinking in the bar or on the wide terrace. In the restaurant, ask for a table by the floor-to-ceiling windows – all the better to soak in the seaside atmosphere while tucking into chef Joe Simmonds's modern dishes, perhaps spiced monkfish tail, monk cheek fritter, chorizo and red pepper tarte fine; herb-crusted lamb loin, truffled mash, pea and broad bean fricassée. In the morning, ease into the day with yogurts, muffins, fresh fruit salads; a selection of breakfast smoothies. The attractions of Summerleaze Beach are a sand-skip away: surfing (and surfers); shore walks; a seawater tidal pool at the base of the cliffs. More reports, please.

25% DISCOUNT VOUCHERS

Summerleaze Crescent
Bude
EX23 8HJ

T: 01288 389800
F: 01288 389820
E: enquiries@thebeachatbude.co.uk
W: www.thebeachatbude.co.uk

BEDROOMS: 16. 1 on ground floor.
OPEN: all year except Christmas.
FACILITIES: lift, 2 bars, restaurant, free Wi-Fi, in-room TV (Freeview), terrace, unsuitable for disabled.
BACKGROUND MUSIC: all day in public areas.
LOCATION: above Summerleaze beach.
CHILDREN: all ages welcomed.
DOGS: not allowed.
CREDIT CARDS: Amex, MasterCard, Visa.
PRICES: [2016] per room B&B £140–£250, D,B&B £197–£307. À la carte £28.50.

BURRINGTON Devon

NORTHCOTE MANOR

Surrounded by ancient fruit orchards and mature woodlands, quiet pathways and open lawns, Jean-Pierre Mifsud's 18th-century manor house in the Taw valley is 'a very special place', say Guide readers this year. 'An oasis of calm and tranquillity', it's just the spot for guests in search of 'comfort and relaxation'. The manor once belonged to Henry VIII; the history of the estate from its monastic days is told in murals on drawing room and dining room walls (with a certain artistic licence – spot the king and his croquet mallet). Choose among spacious bedrooms and suites, each individually styled, all with fresh fruit, mints and home-made shortbread. Victorian-inspired King's Nympton has a four-poster bed, the Manor suite a mirrored canopy and a marble-finish bath. In the restaurant, chef/manager Richie Herkes's seasonal menus – including, perhaps, slow-cooked pork belly, apple and black pudding gateau, honey-roasted parsnip purée – are praised for their 'balance of ingredients and flavour'. 'The tasting menu is not to be missed – the best we've had.' The Lake, Llangammarch Wells, Wales (see entry), is under the same ownership. (Mary Coles)

Burrington
EX37 9LZ

T: 01769 560501
F: 01769 560770
E: rest@northcotemanor.co.uk
W: www.northcotemanor.co.uk

BEDROOMS: 16. 5 in extension, 1 suitable for disabled.
OPEN: all year.
FACILITIES: 2 lounges, bar, 2 restaurants, free Wi-Fi, in-room TV (Freeview), civil wedding licence, 20-acre grounds.
BACKGROUND MUSIC: classical in public areas after midday.
LOCATION: 3 miles S of Umberleigh.
CHILDREN: all ages welcomed, no under-9s in restaurant in evening (early teas for children).
DOGS: allowed in some bedrooms, not in one lounge or restaurant.
CREDIT CARDS: Amex, MasterCard, Visa.
PRICES: B&B per room £170–£280, D,B&B £260–£340. Set dinner £45, gourmet menu £90 (incl. wines).

BURTON BRADSTOCK Dorset

Map 1:D6

THE SEASIDE BOARDING HOUSE

For those who like to be beside the seaside, this style-conscious hotel 'has much to recommend it'. Its informal 'charm and friendliness' attract admirers; its 'stunning' position, on a cliff above Chesil Bay, mollifies even the staunchest detractors. 'It is excellent in every way,' a regular Guide reader tells us in 2016. Mary-Lou Sturridge and Tony Mackintosh, both formerly of London's Groucho Club, are the owners; they have brought metropolitan gloss (and, some say, a city-slicker 'self-consciousness') to the beach retreat. While some guests like the 'obliging', laid-back atmosphere, others, visiting in cooler months, have commented on an off-season sluggishness. Still, 'everything is done in good taste'. 'Elegant, unfussy' bedrooms overlook coast or countryside; the best have 'wide sea views'; each has 'shelves of interesting books' (TV upon request). 'Excellent' meals (from a 'limited' menu) use freshly landed seafood; take afternoon tea, sundowners and nightcaps in the bar. At breakfast, choose from a small buffet of muesli, yogurt and juice before tucking into a locally smoked kipper and 'good' scrambled eggs. (John Walton, and others)

Cliff Road
Burton Bradstock
DT6 4RB

T: 01308 897 205
E: info@theseasideboardinghouse.com
W: theseasideboardinghouse.com

BEDROOMS: 8.
OPEN: all year.
FACILITIES: bar, restaurant, library, function facilities, free Wi-Fi, civil wedding licence, unsuitable for disabled.
BACKGROUND MUSIC: in bar.
LOCATION: ½ mile from village centre; 3½ miles SE of Bridport.
CHILDREN: all ages welcomed (1 family room).
DOGS: allowed in 2 bedrooms, bar; not in restaurant.
CREDIT CARDS: Amex, MasterCard, Visa.
PRICES: [2016] per room B&B £180–£235. À la carte £35. 1-night bookings sometimes refused.

CAMBER Sussex

THE GALLIVANT   **NEW**

'Jolly' dinners and a 'bright, friendly' atmosphere come together at Harry Cragoe's carefree restaurant-with-rooms, across the road from the high dunes of Camber Sands. 'There's a good spirit and sense of fun about the place,' say Guide inspectors in 2016. The motel-style timber building has 'an appealing weathered look' and New England-inspired bedrooms (some compact, many refurbished this year). 'Ours – freshly painted white, with a comfy double bed, good bedside lamps and an odd collection of books – had French doors on to a decked area with outdoor seating. With the doors open, the bedroom filled with birdsong. Quibbles: no wardrobe – just hooks with wooden hangers; no waste bin; no room to make tea.' A complimentary cake or two is set out at teatime, but you should keep room for an 'exceptional' dinner, perhaps 'a generous amuse-bouche of tasty mackerel pâté'; 'well-cooked' Dover sole; a 'delicious' ginger parfait dessert. Served till a 'guest-friendly' 10 am, breakfast includes 'endless' Bloody Marys. 'We liked the little Kilner jars of fruit compote, yogurt and toasted seeds; buttery, deep-orange scrambled eggs came on toast from home-baked bread.'

New Lydd Road
Camber
TN31 7RB

T: 01797 225057
F: 01797 227003
E: enquiries@thegallivant.co.uk
W: www.thegallivant.co.uk

BEDROOMS: 20. All on ground floor.
OPEN: all year.
FACILITIES: bar, restaurant, free Wi-Fi, in-room TV, wedding/function facilities, terrace, garden (beach massage hut).
BACKGROUND MUSIC: in restaurant and on terrace.
LOCATION: 3¾ miles SE of Rye.
CHILDREN: all ages welcomed, no under-8s in restaurant after 7 pm.
DOGS: allowed in some bedrooms (1 dog per room), by arrangement.
CREDIT CARDS: Amex, MasterCard, Visa.
PRICES: [2016] per room B&B from £95, D,B&B from £165. Set 'gourmet' menu £55, à la carte £36. 2-night min. stay at weekends.

CAMBRIDGE Cambridgeshire

Map 2:B4

DUKE HOUSE

Guests this year continue to endorse Liz and Rob Cameron's 'conveniently located' city-centre B&B. 'It is a great place to stay,' said one visitor. 'A delightful and refreshing choice,' said another. The Camerons, 'generous', 'hospitable' hosts, have smartly refurbished their Victorian house, once the student home of the Duke of Gloucester. Newspapers, guides and books are available in the 'pleasant' sitting room; a fridge and honesty bar on the first-floor landing are 'a good idea'. Bedrooms are praised. 'Our room, up two small flights of stairs, had a tiny sitting room that opened on to a small but very comfortable and tastefully decorated bedroom; French windows led to a private decking area.' Another guest liked her 'attractive, quiet', top-floor room in the building next door. 'There was good bedside lighting; we slept well in our large, luxurious bed.' Breakfast, with a 'marvellous selection' of home-made compotes and jams, is 'first rate'. 'There was an abundance of fresh fruits, yogurts and wonderful breads; excellent grilled bacon and baked tomatoes. We enjoyed the soft operatic background music.' 'Well placed for transport links.' (Jackie Tunstall-Pedoe, MG)

1 Victoria Street
Cambridge
CB1 1JP

T: 01223 314773
E: info@dukehousecambridge.co.uk
W: www.dukehousecambridge.co.uk

BEDROOMS: 5. 1 in adjacent cottage, plus self-catering apartment.
OPEN: all year.
FACILITIES: sitting room, breakfast room with courtyard, balcony, free Wi-Fi, in-room TV (Freeview), limited parking (by arrangement), unsuitable for disabled.
BACKGROUND MUSIC: classical in breakfast room.
LOCATION: city centre.
CHILDREN: babies, and over-10s welcomed.
DOGS: not allowed.
CREDIT CARDS: Diners, MasterCard, Visa.
PRICES: [2016] per room B&B £130–£195. 1-night bookings sometimes refused.

SEE ALSO SHORTLIST

CAMELFORD Cornwall

Map 1:C3

PENDRAGON COUNTRY HOUSE

'Enthusiastic', 'wonderfully hospitable' hosts Nigel and Sharon Reed welcome guests with a drink and a snack at their small guest house standing in 'beautiful' countryside. 'Tasteful', 'characterful' bedrooms in the former Victorian rectory have many 'individual touches': look out for the 1920s roll-top bath, the Cornish tin ceiling, and the many interesting antiques throughout the house. Each bedroom is equipped with cafetière coffee, speciality teas and a home-made treat; help yourself to fresh milk in a communal fridge on the landing. At a leisurely dinner in the 'large, light' dining room, Nigel Reed's home-cooked menu of the day might include slow-roasted belly of Cornish pork, crushed new potatoes, steamed vegetables. Need a special meal? With advance notice, the chef is happy to provide. 'Excellent' breakfasts, with home-baked bread, home-made jams and 'a full English without the usual grease', 'set you up for the day'. The Reeds run their guest house along green lines; plug in your electric car at their charging stations while you spend the night. There are coastal walks 'within easy reach'. (Gordon Evans, Michael Crick, Mandy Woodrow)

25% DISCOUNT VOUCHERS

Old Vicarage Hill
Davidstow
Camelford
PL32 9XR

T: 01840 261131
E: enquiries@pendragoncountry house.com
W: www.pendragoncountryhouse. com

BEDROOMS: 7. 1 on ground floor suitable for disabled.
OPEN: all year except Christmas, restaurant closed Sun eve.
FACILITIES: sitting room, bar, orangery breakfast/dining room, games room, free Wi-Fi, in-room TV (Freeview), civil wedding licence, 1½-acre grounds.
BACKGROUND MUSIC: none.
LOCATION: 3½ miles NE of Camelford.
CHILDREN: all ages welcomed.
DOGS: allowed in 1 bedroom, sitting room (£5 per night).
CREDIT CARDS: all major cards.
PRICES: [2016] per room B&B single £60, double £95–£140, D,B&B £143–£188. Set menu £24–£35.

CANNINGTON Somerset

Map 1:B5

BLACKMORE FARM

'I cannot fault this B&B in any way,' writes a first-time visitor in 2016. Children, medievalists, and guests seeking 'good, old-fashioned hospitality' appreciate Ann and Ian Dyer's 'fantastic' 15th-century manor house and working farm at the foot of the Quantock hills. 'I was looked after by the hosts and made to feel very welcome.' Enter under thick wisteria into the impressive Great Hall, with its large inglenook fireplace and long oak refectory table (a communal breakfast is taken here). The Dyers have embraced the house's history, retaining many architectural features: stone archways, medieval garderobes, cob-and-lime-plaster walls. Bedrooms are scattered across the main building and converted outbuildings. 'My large bedroom was amazing: great views, excellent bathroom, fresh milk for tea.' Inquisitive children might want to explore the nooks and crannies of the 'quirky' rooms, run free in the gardens and watch the cows being milked. Less active ones may appreciate the books and board games in the sitting room. 'Breakfast in front of the log fire was perfect.' Lunch, and Blackmore ice cream, can be had at the café. (Michael Eldridge)

25% DISCOUNT VOUCHERS

Blackmore Lane
Cannington
TA5 2NE

T: 01278 653442
E: dyerfarm@aol.com
W: www.blackmorefarm.co.uk

BEDROOMS: 10. 6 on ground floor in annexes, 1 in grounds.
OPEN: all year.
FACILITIES: lounge/TV room, hall/breakfast room, free Wi-Fi, in-room TV (Freeview), 1-acre garden (stream, coarse fishing), farm shop.
BACKGROUND MUSIC: none.
LOCATION: 3 miles NW of Bridgwater.
CHILDREN: all ages welcomed.
DOGS: not allowed.
CREDIT CARDS: Diners, MasterCard, Visa.
PRICES: [2016] per person B&B £60. 1-night bookings refused bank holiday weekends.

CARLISLE Cumbria

WILLOWBECK LODGE

'Light, modern' rooms and a 'friendly welcome'
bring guests to this refreshing, alpine-style
guest house run by Liz and John McGrillis.
Son Andrew joins the family affair, as chef.
Take in the view: the glass-fronted, cathedral-
ceilinged living and dining rooms look across
manicured lawns to the duck pond and mature
weeping willows beyond. A log fire burns in
the lounge; pick a book from the packed floor-
to-ceiling bookcases, and settle in. 'Spacious'
dormer bedrooms, all with views of the pond
and gardens, are 'superbly furnished' in a fresh,
country style, and have underfloor heating;
hospitality trays include chocolates and biscuits.
Relax with a complimentary aperitif before
sitting down to the three-course dinner (served
Monday to Thursday), perhaps with a 'posh,
boozy pâté'; gingered chicken, noodles. Fini's
Kitchen, the café, serves an à la carte dinner on
Friday and Saturday. In the morning, wake to
'proper bread, butter, marmalade' at breakfast,
with hot dishes cooked to order. Convenient for
the M6; the Solway Wetlands, RSPB reserve and
south-west Scotland are within easy access. More
reports, please.

Lambley Bank
Scotby
Carlisle
CA4 8BX

T: 01228 513607
F: 01228 501053
E: info@willowbeck-lodge.com
W: www.willowbeck-lodge.com

BEDROOMS: 4.
OPEN: all year except 23 Dec–3 Jan,
restaurant closed Sun.
FACILITIES: lounge, bar, restaurant,
free Wi-Fi, in-room TV (Now,
Freeview), 1½-acre garden (stream,
pond), unsuitable for disabled.
BACKGROUND MUSIC: in public areas.
LOCATION: 2½ miles E of Carlisle.
CHILDREN: babies and toddlers, and
over-12s.
DOGS: not allowed.
CREDIT CARDS: MasterCard, Visa.
PRICES: [2016] per room B&B
£100–£140. Set dinner £25.

CARTMEL Cumbria

Map 4: inset C2

AYNSOME MANOR

♦César award since 1998

When John Remington, vicar of Cartmel, entertained the Duke of Devonshire at this 17th-century stone manor in 1842, he built the fine dining room in his honour (visitors still admire its panelling, bay windows and ornate moulded ceiling today). Owners Christopher and Andrea Varley might not go to quite such lengths, but guests still love what they do. 'Our favourite place to eat out in Cartmel,' writes a local fan. 'Proper food; lovely atmosphere. Chris is such a welcoming host.' Old-fashioned in the best sense, the house has log fires, deep armchairs, gorgeous views, and 'space to keep to oneself' when privacy is desired. In the main house and the converted stable across the courtyard, bedrooms are traditional and well appointed. At a convivial dinner ('There were 12 other guests, and they really talked at mealtimes, compared to other hotels where whispering is normal'), Gordon Topp cooks a daily-changing menu, perhaps with 'generous' portions of guineafowl and leek terrine, apricot and sultana chutney; roast Cumbrian beef sirloin. 'In a quiet part of the South Lakes, away from the tourist crowds.' (Judy Rawlins, and others)

25% DISCOUNT VOUCHERS

Aynsome Lane
Cartmel
nr Grange-over-Sands
LA11 6HH

T: 01539 536653
F: 01539 536016
E: aynsomemanor@btconnect.com
W: www.aynsomemanorhotel.co.uk

BEDROOMS: 12. 2 in cottage (with lounge) across courtyard.
OPEN: all year except 23–27 Dec, 2–30 Jan, lunch served Sun only, Sun dinner for residents only.
FACILITIES: 2 lounges, bar, dining room, free Wi-Fi, in-room TV (Freeview), ½-acre garden, unsuitable for disabled.
BACKGROUND MUSIC: none.
LOCATION: ¾ mile N of village.
CHILDREN: all ages welcomed, no under-5s in dining room in evening.
DOGS: allowed (£5.50 a night), not in public rooms.
CREDIT CARDS: Amex, MasterCard, Visa.
PRICES: [2016] per room B&B £95–£150, D,B&B £162–£195. Set dinner £30. 1-night bookings occasionally refused weekends.

CHADDESLEY CORBETT Worcestershire   Map 3:C5

BROCKENCOTE HALL   **NEW**

In a 'lovely' sweep of green, this lakeside country house hotel is 'just about perfect in every way', say regular Guide correspondents, whose enthusiasm earns it a full entry this year. 'The staff are helpful, friendly and professional; the ambience exudes comfort, and encourages total relaxation.' Fresh flower arrangements and traditional elements (oil paintings, gilt candlesticks, an oak-carved bar) give the place a refined feel; find a favourite spot to sit by the open fire. The gracious bedrooms, ranging in size, are individually decorated in country house style, with fine views over the estate. 'Housekeeping is excellent.' Dinner is an attraction, with chef Adam Brown's modern mix of local produce, wild plants and home-grown fruit – perhaps duck breast, spelt, broccoli, blackberry, confit gizzards. 'The food in the beautiful restaurant was skilled, inventive, and a joy to experience.' Informal meals – 'less complex, but full of flavour, and very good' – are taken in the bar. Pretty Chaddesley Corbett village, with its real ale pubs, is worth a visit; there's no small amount of rustic pork pies nearby. (Graham and Elizabeth Collingham)

25% DISCOUNT VOUCHERS

Chaddesley Corbett
DY10 4PY

T: 01562 777876
F: 01562 777872
E: info@brockencotehall.com
W: www.brockencotehall.com

BEDROOMS: 21. Some on ground floor, 1 suitable for disabled.
OPEN: all year.
FACILITIES: lift, hall, lounge bar, library, restaurant, function facilities, free Wi-Fi, in-room TV (Freeview), civil wedding licence, 72-acre grounds (gardens, lake, fishing, croquet, tennis).
BACKGROUND MUSIC: all day in public areas.
LOCATION: 3 miles SE of Kidderminster.
CHILDREN: all ages welcomed.
DOGS: not allowed.
CREDIT CARDS: Amex, MasterCard, Visa.
PRICES: B&B from £135, D,B&B from £225. Set dinner £45, à la carte £60.

CHAGFORD Devon

Map 1:C4

PARFORD WELL

In a wooded valley close to open moorland, and within the Dartmoor national park, Tim Daniel runs his traditional B&B with much attention to detail. A discreet but attentive host, he has plenty of suggestions for walkers, day-trippers and all-round seekers of the country life. The house stands in a pretty walled garden with neat lawns, and blooms in season; inside, guests are welcomed with tea and home-made cake. Settle in: sit by the wood-burning stove, take your pick of books and board games. At night, sleep soundly in a 'very comfortable' bedroom. Two of the rooms have an en suite bathroom; the third has a private bathroom across the landing. A 'superb' breakfast is served around a communal table in the elegant dining room (guests desiring more privacy may eat at a table for two in a small side room). No dinner is served, but the pub opposite has local craft beers and food; there are restaurants in Chagford village, just a mile away (torches provided for night-time adventurers). 'Wonderful walks' straight from the door. More reports, please.

Sandy Park
Chagford
TQ13 8JW

T: 01647 433353
E: tim@parfordwell.co.uk
W: www.parfordwell.co.uk

BEDROOMS: 3. 1 with its own bathroom across the landing.
OPEN: all year.
FACILITIES: sitting room, 2 breakfast rooms, free Wi-Fi, ½-acre garden, unsuitable for disabled.
BACKGROUND MUSIC: none.
LOCATION: in hamlet 1 mile N of Chagford.
CHILDREN: not under 8.
DOGS: not allowed.
CREDIT CARDS: none.
PRICES: per room B&B £90–£110. 1-night bookings sometimes refused weekends in season.

CHESTER Cheshire

Map 3:A4

EDGAR HOUSE

NEW

Tim Mills and Michael Stephen's 'highly
enjoyable' small hotel is 'refreshingly different',
say Guide inspectors in 2016 – and not just for
the honesty bar secreted in an old telephone
kiosk. The 19th-century villa stands by the River
Dee; the city is reached via an easy stroll. (The
car park, where guests are allocated named
spaces, is 'a real bonus for drivers'.) 'From
check-in to check-out, the staff were friendly,
enthusiastic, unpretentious.' Most nights in the
smart dining room, order from a short menu of
modern dishes, perhaps 'tasty' beef carpaccio,
radishes, asparagus; grilled lobster, 'perfectly
cooked' new potatoes. Four of the 'beautifully
designed' bedrooms overlook the river. 'Our
stunning junior suite had chandeliers and
soaring beams; clever lighting; an impressive
copper bath. The good-sized bed had top-
quality bedding. Nice touches: fancy teas, little
treats of intense chocolate and fruit cubes. The
incessant sound of the weir was wonderful,
somehow. We slept well.' In the morning, wake
to a 'truly excellent' breakfast overlooking the
'pretty' garden: 'delicious' granola-fruit-and-
yogurt cups; 'perfectly poached' eggs; 'superb'
home-made hollandaise.

22 City Walls
Chester
CH1 1SB

T: 01244 347007
F: 01244 310147
E: hello@edgarhouse.co.uk
W: www.edgarhouse.co.uk

BEDROOMS: 7.
OPEN: all year, restaurant closed
Mon except bank holidays.
FACILITIES: garden lounge, mini-
cinema, restaurant, free Wi-Fi,
in-room TV, terrace, riverside
garden (alfresco meals), unsuitable
for disabled.
BACKGROUND MUSIC: Classic FM in
lounge.
LOCATION: central, on the river.
CHILDREN: not under 14.
DOGS: not allowed.
CREDIT CARDS: MasterCard, Visa.
PRICES: [2016] per room B&B £199–
£259, D,B&B £270–£329. À la carte
£35. 1-night bookings sometimes
refused in some bedrooms at
weekends.

SEE ALSO SHORTLIST

CHETTLE Dorset

CASTLEMAN

❧ César award since 2004

Something of the French country house permeates this former dower house turned restaurant-with-rooms: perhaps the 'gorgeous, unspoilt' setting, the 'air of faded gentility', the 'thoughtful, laid-back' staff or the 'real personality' of owners Barbara Garnsworthy and brother Brendan. 'Brilliantly' looked after 'as individuals', guests find their delight in the 'first-class' menus, the 'spot-on' service, the 'away-from-it-all' atmosphere. Most of the bedrooms are 'spacious, with a wonderful outlook', though 'careful selection' is advised. Trace architectural fashions in the building's period additions and expansions: one drawing room has Regency plasterwork, the other a Jacobean fireplace; ornate carved woodwork decorates ceiling, doors and shutters. In the 'delightful' dining room, Barbara Garnsworthy and Richard Morris's 'first-rate' cooking, 'promptly' served, often draws 'a full house for dinner'. Consider roast partridge, bacon, redcurrant jelly; pan-fried sea bass fillet, cobnut pesto. It is 'very good value'. Breakfast has home-baked bread, 'wonderful' plum jam, 'the finest scrambled eggs'. (AF, and others)

25% DISCOUNT VOUCHERS

Chettle
DT11 8DB

T: 01258 830096
F: 01258 830051
E: enquiry@castlemanhotel.co.uk
W: www.castlemanhotel.co.uk

BEDROOMS: 8. 1 family room.
OPEN: Mar–Jan, except 25/26, 31 Dec, restaurant closed midday except Sun.
FACILITIES: 2 drawing rooms, bar, restaurant, free Wi-Fi, in-room TV (Freeview), 2-acre grounds (stables for visiting horses), riding, fishing, shooting, cycling nearby, only restaurant suitable for disabled.
BACKGROUND MUSIC: none.
LOCATION: village, 1 mile off A354 Salisbury–Blandford, hotel signposted.
CHILDREN: all ages welcomed.
DOGS: not allowed.
CREDIT CARDS: MasterCard, Visa.
PRICES: [2016] per room B&B £100–£115, D,B&B (midweek only) £125–£145. À la carte £30.

CHICHESTER Sussex

Map 2:E3

CROUCHERS

NEW

'Everything is praiseworthy' at Lloyd van
Rooyen and Gavin Wilson's much-extended
hotel between buzzy Chichester and the beaches
of West Wittering. It earns a full entry thanks
to trusted Guide readers who were 'bowled
over' in 2016. Most of the 'elegant', 'spotless'
bedrooms are in converted outbuildings
around the restaurant. 'Ours, with a private
patio, overlooked a large field. There was
good lighting, plenty of storage, a well-stocked
hospitality tray. The four-poster bed had stacks
of pillows and cushions; the bathroom had lots
of towels and good-quality goodies. The main
road out front is fairly busy during the day,
but all was silent at night.' 'Well-spaced' tables
are 'smartly laid' at dinner, where chef Craig
Mustard's 'interesting, varied' menu is 'obviously
popular with local diners'. 'We enjoyed crispy
pork belly with pickled vegetables; fried soft-
shell crab with a cucumber sorbet; delicious
guineafowl.' Lighter meals, perhaps over
a cocktail or two, may be taken in the bar.
Wake to birdsong, then head to breakfast:
'good' coffee; eggs Benedict with an 'excellent'
hollandaise; a 'superbly dense' cherry compote.
(Francine and Ian Walsh)

Birdham Road
Chichester
PO20 7EH

T: 01243 784995
E: enquiries@crouchershotel.co.uk
W: www.crouchershotel.co.uk

BEDROOMS: 26. 23 in converted coach
house, barn and stables, 10 with
patio, 2 suitable for disabled.
OPEN: all year.
FACILITIES: lounge, bar, restaurant,
free Wi-Fi, in-room TV, civil
wedding licence/function facilities,
courtyard, 2-acre garden.
BACKGROUND MUSIC: in public areas.
LOCATION: 3 miles S of town centre.
CHILDREN: all ages welcomed.
DOGS: allowed in some bedrooms,
bar, not in restaurant.
CREDIT CARDS: Amex, MasterCard,
Visa.
PRICES: [2016] per room B&B from
£135, D,B&B from £187. À la carte
£25.50.

SEE ALSO SHORTLIST

CHILLATON Devon

TOR COTTAGE

Turn down a wooded track and keep going ('you'll think you've gone too far, but it's a little bit further'): at the end is a rustic B&B where sparkling wine, home-made truffles and Maureen Rowlatt's 'charming' hospitality await. Individually decorated bedrooms are in the main house and in converted outbuildings (a craftsman's workshop, an ancient cart house, a modest cottage) in the gardens; hammocks hang by the stream. Indulgent seclusion is the name of the game: each garden room has its own log fire, private terrace (some stream-side) or private conservatory. Set away, New England-style Laughing Waters is reached by a woodland walk; summer visitors will want to take advantage of its barbecue area. There are no evening meals, but platters of sandwiches, Cornish pasties, pudding, cheeses and chutney can be arranged; several restaurants and pubs are within easy driving distance. Breakfast, taken on the terrace or in the conservatory, has a copious selection of fruit, home-made muesli; cooked dishes include vegetarian options. The extensive grounds burst with flowers and wildlife; ideal for getting lost. (S and CR)

Chillaton
PL16 0JE

T: 01822 860248
F: 01822 860126
E: info@torcottage.co.uk
W: www.torcottage.co.uk

BEDROOMS: 5. 4 in garden.
OPEN: Feb–mid-Dec.
FACILITIES: sitting room, large conservatory, free Wi-Fi in conservatory, in-room TV (Freeview), 28-acre grounds (2-acre garden, heated outdoor swimming pool (14 by 5 metres, May–Sept), barbecue, stream, bridleway, walks), river (fishing ½ mile), unsuitable for disabled.
BACKGROUND MUSIC: none.
LOCATION: ½ mile S of Chillaton.
CHILDREN: not under 14.
DOGS: no dogs allowed.
CREDIT CARDS: MasterCard, Visa.
PRICES: [2016] per room B&B (min. 2 nights) £150–£155.

CHRISTCHURCH Dorset

Map 2:E2

CAPTAIN'S CLUB HOTEL

On the edge of the River Stour, the smooth metal-and-glass lines of this 'stylish', 'welcoming' bankside hotel call to mind a docked ocean liner. Step aboard: the interiors are 'modern but with character', judicious accents give colour. Don't expect portholes in the 'very comfortable' bedrooms, however: each has floor-to-ceiling windows with 'interesting' river views. The rooms vary in size; family suites are designed for open-plan living, with separate quarters for smaller shipmates. 'Ours had plenty of space for lounging around in.' In the brasserie, chef Andrew Gault's 'unfussy' modern menu leans towards seafood: try dishes such as fillet of sea trout, ratatouille, parsley mash potato. An all-day menu of light meals and snacks is available in the sleek bar/lounge. Take time for drinks on the riverside terrace – it's 'delightful when the sun shines' – or hire the hotel's yacht for a day's sailing on the Solent. 'The decking by the river seemed busy all day with visitors and lots of locals.' Morning brings an 'especially good' breakfast, with 'extensive' choice: crushed avocado on toast; apple-sultana porridge; waffles, fresh berries, maple syrup. (LW)

Wick Ferry
Christchurch
BH23 1HU

T: 01202 475111
F: 01202 490111
E: enquiries@captainsclubhotel.com
W: www.captainsclubhotel.com

BEDROOMS: 29. 2 suitable for disabled.
OPEN: all year.
FACILITIES: lifts, lounge, open-plan bar, restaurant, function facilities, free Wi-Fi, in-room TV (Sky, Freeview), civil wedding licence, terrace, spa (hydrotherapy pool, sauna, treatments).
BACKGROUND MUSIC: in public areas, live pianist some evenings.
LOCATION: 5 mins from Christchurch.
CHILDREN: all ages welcomed.
DOGS: allowed in suites, on terrace.
CREDIT CARDS: MasterCard, Visa.
PRICES: [2016] per room B&B from £269. Set dinner £30. 1-night bookings normally refused Sat.

CIRENCESTER Gloucestershire

Map 3:E5

KINGS HEAD HOTEL

Mark and Alison Booth spent a king's ransom to transform this medieval inn on the market square from staid to 'state of the art'. The facade is Victorian, while a Roman mosaic displayed in reception reveals the antiquity of the site. But the bedrooms all have modern comforts: an espresso machine; a fridge with mineral water and fresh milk; a TV with a built-in Apple computer. Each has been individually styled – some have exposed beams and brickwork, others an original fireplace; one, on the first floor, has a four-poster bed and a 'vast' copper bath beside it. Book ahead for dinner in the 'popular' restaurant, where 'a serendipitous collection of prints, photos and artwork adorns the walls'. The 'outstanding' modern English menu has 'limited' but interesting choice, perhaps 'well-judged portions' of seared saddle of venison, braised haunch, game jus; halibut, coastal herbs, steamed clams, Nantaise sauce. At breakfast, there's freshly squeezed orange juice, mini jars of marmalade, 'succulent' bacon, 'very tasty' Gloucester Old Spot sausages. 'We were offered warm milk for tea – a definite plus.' Limited parking can be a problem.

24 Market Place
Cirencester
GL7 2NR

T: 01285 700900
E: info@kingshead-hotel.co.uk
W: kingshead-hotel.co.uk

BEDROOMS: 45. 1 suitable for disabled.
OPEN: all year.
FACILITIES: lifts, lounge, bar, restaurant, private dining rooms, meeting rooms, spa (treatments, steam room, sauna), free Wi-Fi, civil wedding licence, rooftop garden.
BACKGROUND MUSIC: various in public areas.
LOCATION: town centre.
CHILDREN: all ages welcomed.
DOGS: allowed by prior arrangement (charge), not in restaurant.
CREDIT CARDS: Amex, MasterCard, Visa.
PRICES: [2016] per room B&B £165–£285, D,B&B from £235. À la carte £35. 1-night bookings sometimes refused.

CLEARWELL Gloucestershire
Map 3:D4

TUDOR FARMHOUSE

'Lovely' bedrooms, 'triumphant' dinners and a 'genuine welcome' come together at Hari and Colin Fell's relaxed hotel on a former working farm in the Forest of Dean. Stylish rooms (some recently refurbished) are divided between the main house and two airy, converted outbuildings: expect exposed beams, wool blankets with matching cushions, arty black-and-white photos; on the tea tray, a capsule coffee machine, fresh milk and home-made shortbread. The farm and kitchen garden provide most of the ingredients for the restaurant, where new chef Rob Cox's '20-mile menu', using super-local produce, might include Longhorn beef rump, braised feather blade, watercress, wild mushrooms. (The philosophy gamely informs the drinks list, too, with Tintern wines, Monmouthshire cider, and beers from local breweries.) Sample local honey and home-made marmalade at breakfast, along with 'excellent' cooked dishes. Ask for a picnic and strap on those hiking boots, afterwards: the hotel is set in acres of wild flower-rich ancient grassland; Offa's Dyke Path is a stroll away. Foraging courses, in search of wimberries or wild strawberries, may be arranged. (MC)

High Street
Clearwell
GL16 8JS

T: 01594 833046
F: 01594 837093
E: info@tudorfarmhousehotel.co.uk
W: www.tudorfarmhousehotel.co.uk

BEDROOMS: 20. 8 on ground floor, 9 in barn, 7 in cider house.
OPEN: all year.
FACILITIES: lounge, bar, restaurant, free Wi-Fi, in-room TV (Freeview), 14-acre grounds, unsuitable for disabled.
BACKGROUND MUSIC: 'discreet' in restaurant and lounge at lunch and dinner.
LOCATION: 7 miles SE of Monmouth.
CHILDREN: all ages welcomed.
DOGS: not allowed.
CREDIT CARDS: Amex, MasterCard, Visa.
PRICES: [2016] per room B&B £100–£230, D,B&B £170–£300. À la carte £30–£45. Min. 2-night stay at weekends.

CLEE STANTON Shropshire

TIMBERSTONE

'It was a total joy to return,' write readers this year on their fourth visit to Tracey Baylis and Alex Read's B&B in a rural hamlet. 'Their attention to detail is outstanding. They sensed that we preferred cups and saucers to mugs, and guess what…?' The extended stone cottage has an open-plan lounge/dining room with a wood-burning stove; glass doors open on to the terrace. Guests relax in bedrooms equipped with a king-size bed, and a well-stocked tea tray with coffee, teas, infusions and shortbread. Each room is different: the Oak room, in the heart of the house, has a sofa bed to accommodate a family; Clay has a balcony with views of garden and countryside. Tracey Baylis, who has worked for Michelin-starred chef Shaun Hill, cooks 'delicious' dinners for appreciative visitors. Using local, home-grown and organic ingredients, her traditional dishes might include baked mushrooms, Shropshire blue cheese; duck breast, red wine, blackcurrant. In the morning, a generous breakfast is served, with home-made bread and preserves; 'a large choice' of cooked dishes. The gastronomic mecca of Ludlow is five and a half miles away. (David Bartley)

25% DISCOUNT VOUCHERS

Lackstone Lane
Clee Stanton
SY8 3EL

T: 01584 823519
E: timberstone1@hotmail.com
W: www.timberstoneludlow.co.uk

BEDROOMS: 4. Plus summer house retreat in summer.
OPEN: all year.
FACILITIES: lounge/dining room, conservatory, free Wi-Fi, in-room TV (Freeview), ½-acre garden, treatment room, unsuitable for disabled.
BACKGROUND MUSIC: none.
LOCATION: 5½ miles NE of Ludlow.
CHILDREN: all ages welcomed.
DOGS: allowed by arrangement, not in public rooms.
CREDIT CARDS: MasterCard, Visa.
PRICES: per room B&B £98. Set menus £20–£25.

CLIPSHAM Rutland

BEECH HOUSE & OLIVE BRANCH

César award since 2012

'A quiet oasis,' writes a regular Guide reader this year, of Sean Hope and Ben Jones's well-liked village pub/restaurant-with-rooms. Get ready for the buzz at mealtimes, though: 'The food was excellent – no wonder the restaurant was full.' Sean Hope wins acclaim for his cooking, which makes good use of local and home-grown ingredients. 'We found the menu a little short (vegetarians might struggle) but very enticing.' Try grilled cutlet and braised shoulder of lamb, sweet potato rösti, French-style peas. 'Leave room for the mini-desserts – gorgeous little mouthfuls of sticky toffee pudding or chocolate mousse.' In fine weather, eat under the pergola in the 'beautiful' garden. Accommodation is in 'welcoming, restful' Beech House, across the road. 'Our large room was prettily furnished, with wide views. The bed was very comfortable, the hospitality tray well stocked, the bathroom large.' A plea to designers: 'We prefer a toilet with a door.' Come morning, a 'very good' breakfast is served in 'a beautifully restored old barn'. 'The full English will set you up for the day.' (Mary Hewson)

Main Street
Clipsham
LE15 7SH

T: 01780 410355
F: 01780 410000
E: beechhouse@theolivebranchpub.com
W: www.theolivebranchpub.com

BEDROOMS: 6. 2 on ground floor, family room (also suitable for disabled) in annexe.
OPEN: all year, pub closed evening 25 Dec/1 Jan.
FACILITIES: pub, dining room, breakfast room, free Wi-Fi, in-room TV (Freeview), small terrace, garden.
BACKGROUND MUSIC: classical/jazz in pub.
LOCATION: in village 7 miles NW of Stamford.
CHILDREN: all ages welcomed (children's menu).
DOGS: allowed in ground-floor bedrooms and bar.
CREDIT CARDS: MasterCard, Visa.
PRICES: [2016] per room B&B £115–£195, D,B&B £200–£250. Set dinner £32.50, à la carte £32.50.

CORSE LAWN Gloucestershire

CORSE LAWN HOUSE   NEW

'I love it as a place to get away from the business of everyday life.' Experience traditional hospitality at the Hine family's 'graceful' Queen Anne house in the Severn valley. It earns a main entry thanks to its 'rustic ambience' and 'old-fashioned values': 'crumbly scones taken by the fire; no piped music'; 'it avoids lots of "Do not" signs'. 'We liked the feel of a visit to a country cousin,' say Guide inspectors. Gilles Champier, the 'helpful, long-serving' manager, is 'always about' ('but not effusive: don't expect small talk'). 'The hosts understand how to make you welcome in an easy, unfussy way.' Bedrooms are 'relaxing and quiet'. 'Our good-value, spacious room had armchairs, a sofa, a comfortable bed with quality sheets and blankets; a modern, well-lit bathroom. There was leaf tea in a tin; a good information pack showed local walks.' Book ahead for dinner in the popular salmon-pink restaurant or the less formal bistro ('busy on a Saturday night'). 'Food is very tasty without being "arty-farty".' In the morning, 'Gilles takes orders and serves breakfast at table: good orange juice, delicious marmalade.'

25% DISCOUNT VOUCHERS

Corse Lawn
GL19 4LZ

T: 01452 780771
F: 01452 780840
E: enquiries@corselawn.com
W: www.corselawn.com

BEDROOMS: 18. 5 on ground floor.
OPEN: all year except 24–26 Dec.
FACILITIES: 2 drawing rooms, snug bar, restaurant, bistro, private dining/meeting rooms, free Wi-Fi, in-room TV (Sky, BT, Freeview), civil wedding licence, 12-acre grounds (croquet, tennis, covered heated swimming pool, 20 by 10 metres).
BACKGROUND MUSIC: none.
LOCATION: 5 miles SW of Tewkesbury on B4211.
CHILDREN: all ages welcomed.
DOGS: on lead in public rooms.
CREDIT CARDS: Amex, MasterCard, Visa.
PRICES: [2016] per room B&B from £170, D,B&B from £215. Set dinner (restaurant) £33.50, (bistro) £22.50, à la carte £35.

COWAN BRIDGE Lancashire

Map 4: inset D2

HIPPING HALL

♔ César award since 2008

'Well-appointed' bedrooms, a 'gem' of a restaurant and 'exceptionally helpful' staff combine at this 'very comfortable' countryside hotel. The 18th-century house has been 'sympathetically' refurbished by owner/manager Andrew Wildsmith; an 'unstuffy atmosphere' reigns, say trusted Guide contributors in 2016. 'Comfortable' bedrooms are furnished in a modern country style; a spacious attic suite, up narrow steps, has beams and a low window seat. The old stables were converted into five suites this year. In the 15th-century banqueting hall, savour Oliver Martin's 'vibrant' modern dishes, perhaps wild sea bass, shrimp butter, salt-baked celeriac. 'We enjoyed great flavours. While the limited dinner menu doesn't change daily, you can choose, à la carte style, from the tasting menu. The only negative? We felt the music didn't create the right ambience.' In the morning, a 'generous' breakfast is fuel for walks from the door ('no need to drive'). 'Ideally located' for the Yorkshire Dales and the southern Lake District. Andrew Wildsmith also owns Forest Side, Grasmere (see entry). (John Patterson, D and KW)

Cowan Bridge
LA6 2JJ

T: 01524 271187
E: info@hippinghall.com
W: www.hippinghall.com

BEDROOMS: 15. 3 in cottages, 5 in converted stables.
OPEN: all year.
FACILITIES: lounge, orangery, restaurant, 'chef's kitchen', wedding/function facilities, free Wi-Fi in lounge only, in-room TV (Freeview), civil wedding licence, 4-acre garden, unsuitable for disabled.
BACKGROUND MUSIC: in lounge, restaurant.
LOCATION: 2 miles SE of Kirkby Lonsdale, on A65.
CHILDREN: not under 12.
DOGS: allowed in 2 bedrooms and orangery.
CREDIT CARDS: MasterCard, Visa.
PRICES: [2016] per room B&B £169–£419, D,B&B £100 added per couple. À la carte £55.

CROFT-ON-TEES Yorkshire

Map 4:C4

CLOW BECK HOUSE

🔱 César award since 2007

'Standards are as high as they ever were' at David and Heather Armstrong's farmhouse hotel and restaurant, says a returning guest this year. The homely atmosphere is a draw. 'David and Heather go out of their way to oblige every request.' 'Stunning' gardens surround the building; inside, relax in the 'bright and comfortable' lounge, which has a piano and plenty of books. 'Large' bedrooms, some with 'flamboyant' touches, have a 'firm' double bed and 'every extra – lovely toiletries, home-made biscuits, chocolates/sweets and a fridge for milk, bottled water, etc'. Pre-dinner drinks and canapés are served in the lounge before visitors sit down to David Armstrong's 'very tasty' dinners. The 'well-cooked', 'farmhouse-style' dishes, served in 'manageable' portions, might include home-made pâté; rack of Yorkshire lamb, blackcurrant and port gravy. Vegetarians are well catered for with their own menu. Guests wake up to an 'extremely good' breakfast. 'It really sets you up for the day. The apricot and nut toast was wonderful with their apricot preserve.' Riverside walks are easily accessible. (Christine Hodgkin)

Monk End Farm
Croft-On-Tees
DL2 2SP

T: 01325 721075
F: 01325 720419
E: david@clowbeckhouse.co.uk
W: www.clowbeckhouse.co.uk

BEDROOMS: 13. 12 in garden buildings, 1 suitable for disabled.
OPEN: all year except Christmas and New Year.
FACILITIES: lounge, restaurant, free Wi-Fi, in-room TV (Freeview), small conference facilities, 2-acre grounds in 100-acre farm.
BACKGROUND MUSIC: classical, 'easy listening' in restaurant at mealtimes.
LOCATION: 3 miles SE of Darlington.
CHILDREN: all ages welcomed (child's bed £25, cot £20).
DOGS: not allowed.
CREDIT CARDS: Amex, MasterCard, Visa.
PRICES: per room B&B single £90, double £145. À la carte £37.

DARTMOUTH Devon

Map 1:D4

DART MARINA

'It gets better every time,' reports a devotee this year, after a sixth visit to Richard Seton's super-smart hotel and luxury spa on the River Dart – and no wonder. New Zealander Seton has spent millions updating, refurbishing and adding new bedrooms. Choose one of the 'immaculately clean' rooms, each with soothing, muted decor, binoculars, a coffee machine and fresh milk ('what a joy!'). In the bathroom, find high-end toiletries, and 'lovely, fluffy' towels and bathrobes. Newly remodelled superior rooms with a 'large' balcony are 'contemporary, and look fabulous'. In the dining room, Peter Alcroft uses fresh seafood and locally reared meat in such dishes as sea bass fillet, confit fennel, black olives; confit duck leg and breast, haricot bean cassoulet. A guest this year commented on a too-languid dinner, but staff are otherwise found 'enthusiastic', 'friendly', 'attentive'. At breakfast there are home-baked croissants, fresh fruit salad, smoked salmon with buttery scrambled eggs. Have it on your balcony and watch the boats, and the steam train across the water. In August, take a ringside seat for the regatta. (Ian Malone, Mary Woods, and others)

Sandquay Road
Dartmouth
TQ6 9PH

T: 01803 832580
E: pauld@dartmarinahotel.com
W: www.dartmarina.com

BEDROOMS: 49. 4 on ground floor, 1 suitable for disabled, plus 4 apartments.
OPEN: all year.
FACILITIES: lounge/bar, restaurant, free Wi-Fi, in-room TV (Freeview), riverfront terrace, small garden with seating, spa (heated indoor swimming pool, 8 by 4 metres, gym).
BACKGROUND MUSIC: in restaurant and lounge/bar during the day.
LOCATION: on waterfront.
CHILDREN: all ages welcomed.
DOGS: allowed in ground-floor rooms (£10 per stay), not in restaurant.
CREDIT CARDS: MasterCard, Visa.
PRICES: [2016] per room B&B double £180–£440, D,B&B £250–£510. À la carte £38. 1-night bookings usually refused Sat.

SEE ALSO SHORTLIST

DARTMOUTH Devon

Map 1:D4

NONSUCH HOUSE

🏅César award since 2000

'Caring, friendly' hosts Penny and Kit Noble run their homely guest house in a former sea captain's home, in a 'stunning location' overlooking the Dart estuary. 'Every bedroom looks down to the town, Dartmouth Castle and the river,' say appreciative guests on their 'third wonderful visit'. While away the day on the terrace, watching the Squib boats or paddle steamer on the water; in cool weather, an open fire makes the sitting room a cosy retreat. Four nights a week, Kit Noble cooks an 'excellent' three- or four-course dinner using local produce and home-grown vegetables (guests are asked in advance about likes and dislikes). Bring your own drinks – the hosts are happy to provide nibbles for aperitifs. Afterwards, retire to your spacious, individually decorated bedroom before waking to a 'great' breakfast: freshly squeezed juices; smoked fish; home-made muesli, jams, bread and fruit compotes. Heading out for the day? Ask for a picnic lunch, ideal for walks on the Coastal Path nearby. The Nobles are enthusiastic hosts and readily advise on car-free itineraries: boat trips, fishing excursions, river walks, adventures in secret coves. (CA)

Church Hill
Kingswear
Dartmouth
TQ6 0BX

T: 01803 752829
E: enquiries@nonsuch-house.co.uk
W: www.nonsuch-house.co.uk

BEDROOMS: 4.
OPEN: all year except Christmas, 2 weeks Jan, dining room closed midday, evening Tues/Wed/Sat.
FACILITIES: lounge, dining room/conservatory, free Wi-Fi, in-room TV (Freeview), ¼-acre garden (sun terrace), rock beach 300 yds (sailing nearby), membership of local gym and spa, unsuitable for disabled.
BACKGROUND MUSIC: none.
LOCATION: 5 mins' walk from ferry to Dartmouth.
CHILDREN: not under 12.
DOGS: not allowed.
CREDIT CARDS: MasterCard, Visa.
PRICES: [2016] per person (if sharing) B&B £67.50–£90, D,B&B £107–£129.50. Dinner £39.50. 1-night bookings usually refused weekends.

SEE ALSO SHORTLIST

DEDHAM Essex

DEDHAM HALL & FOUNTAIN HOUSE RESTAURANT

Jim and Wendy Sarton's 15th-century, timber-framed, wisteria-festooned manor house is popular with artists, who come for residential painting courses held from February to November; Dedham Vale, beloved by John Constable, invites exploration all year round. Informal, unusual and – like great artists – sometimes temperamental, this won't be everyone's cup of tea. Fans like the 'wonderfully quiet' situation and the folksy, familiar feel. The atmosphere is that of a large, well-loved and lived-in home, where visitors sink into squishy sofas, and the works of past course students hang on the walls. Plus, it's 'excellent value', says an enthusiastic guest in 2016. The bedrooms, some in converted barns, are spacious and eclectically furnished; each has views of the mature gardens. True to the spirit of the place, dinner is straightforward ('none of this itsy-bitsy nouvelle cuisine'); tuck in to 'generous' portions of roast sea bass or sirloin steak. Breakfast is 'beautifully cooked', even in the darkest hour: 'We had to leave very early in the morning, and they even prepared breakfast for us at 5.30 am!' (Michael Crick, and others)

25% DISCOUNT VOUCHERS

Brook Street
Dedham
CO7 6AD

T: 01206 323027
E: sarton@dedhamhall.co.uk
W: www.dedhamhall.co.uk

BEDROOMS: 20. 16 in annexe, some on ground floor, suitable for disabled.
OPEN: all year except Christmas–New Year.
FACILITIES: 2 lounges, bar, dining room, restaurant, studio, free Wi-Fi, in-room TV, 6-acre grounds (pond, gardens).
BACKGROUND MUSIC: none.
LOCATION: end of village High Street (set back from road).
CHILDREN: all ages welcomed.
DOGS: not allowed.
CREDIT CARDS: MasterCard, Visa.
PRICES: per person B&B £55–£75, D,B&B £85–£105. À la carte £30.

DEDHAM Essex

THE SUN INN

A butter-yellow, timber-framed inn in a medieval cloth-workers' village, this 'friendly', 'charming' pub-with-rooms is run by owner Piers Baker. Check in at the beamed bar (order a guest ale or a cup of fancy tea to go with your room key); relax by the wood-burner in the oak-panelled lounge (sofas, books, prints). On fine days, find a shady spot in the large garden. The individually decorated bedrooms (five refurbished in 2016) are 'beautifully styled' with 'quality furnishings', and well supplied with a Roberts radio, digital TV, posh toiletries. 'Ours was large, with a comfortable bed and good lighting. The bathroom, of a good size, had everything we needed.' In the restaurant, sit down to chef Jack Levine's 'really good' Italian-influenced menu, whose daily variations use local vegetables, rare breed meat, fish from the day boats at Mersea. Consider skate, hazelnuts, razor clams; lamb faggots, red wine sauce, polenta. Veggie options and Sunday roasts are equally appealing. Breakfast brings local juices, omelettes, porridge 'however you like it'; a full English is good fuel for boating on the Stour. (SP, and others)

25% DISCOUNT VOUCHERS

High Street
Dedham
CO7 6DF

T: 01206 323351
E: office@thesuninndedham.com
W: www.thesuninndedham.com

BEDROOMS: 7. 2 across the terrace, approached by Elizabethan staircase.
OPEN: all year except 25/26 Dec.
FACILITIES: lounge, bar, dining rooms, free Wi-Fi, in-room TV (Freeview), 1-acre garden (covered terrace, children's play area, garden bar), unsuitable for disabled.
BACKGROUND MUSIC: all day in public areas.
LOCATION: village centre.
CHILDREN: all ages welcomed.
DOGS: allowed by special arrangement.
CREDIT CARDS: Amex, MasterCard, Visa.
PRICES: [2016] per room B&B £145, D,B&B £190. À la carte £27.50.

DITTISHAM Devon

FINGALS

'The combination of boho chic with a fine regard for comfort, and proprietors who behave like friends, is perfect.' A family favourite, this farmhouse B&B in a secluded valley 'seduces' guests with its 'abundant character and general bonhomie'. 'Ebullient, efficient' Richard and Sheila Johnston 'welcome all with a generous spirit' to their 'relaxed', 'artistically extended' 17th-century house. 'It's slightly haphazard, and may be rough around the edges, but its magic lies in having a quirky space where everyone can chat, get involved, and just be,' say Guide inspectors in 2016. Mingle in the picture-lined lounge and 'convivial' bar; relax by the mural-decorated pool. Bedrooms and self-catering suites are 'individually styled', with English wallpaper, antiques, original art. 'Imaginative' dinners are bi-weekly, or by arrangement ('timings relaxed'); an 'ample tea' is available for children. 'Sheila is the queen of desserts': chocolate truffle torte, crème brûlée, crumble with cream. Fortunately, 'there are plenty of outdoor activities to balance this indulgence': walks from the door, bicycles to borrow, games. (Angela Neustatter, RM)

Old Coombe Manor Farm
Dittisham
TQ6 0JA

T: 01803 722398
E: info@fingals.co.uk
W: www.fingals.co.uk

BEDROOMS: 4. 1 in separate building by stream, plus 8 self-catering rooms available as B&B off-season.
OPEN: Easter–New Year, self-catering only at Christmas, restaurant closed mid-week unless by arrangement.
FACILITIES: dining room, honesty bar, sitting room, games room, free Wi-Fi, in-room TV (Freeview), indoor swimming pool (8 by 4 metres), 2-acre garden, grass tennis court, unsuitable for disabled.
BACKGROUND MUSIC: classical in bar and breakfast room.
LOCATION: in hamlet, 7 miles N of Dartmouth.
CHILDREN: all ages welcomed.
DOGS: allowed in bedrooms, not in public rooms.
CREDIT CARDS: Amex, MasterCard, Visa.
PRICES: [2016] per room B&B £110–£225. Set dinner £36.

DODDISCOMBSLEIGH Devon

Map 1:C4

⚜ THE NOBODY INN

César award: inn of the year

'What a fab place,' say Guide inspectors in 2016, who arrived on a jolly quiz night at Sue Burdge's 'wonderful' village pub-with-rooms. The 'lovely' old building – with its blackened beams, antiques and inglenook fireplace – is reached down a convolution of country lanes. Inside, bedrooms are accessed through the bar ('very trusting, with all those wonderful whiskies on display!') and up 'quite steep stairs'. 'The rooms are delightful – a lovely place to rest on arrival, and return to after a scrumptious dinner. Ours, glamorous and elegant, had a supremely comfy bed and plenty of magazines. A decanter of amontillado had been set out to welcome us.' Book in for dinner: 'The fabulous food makes this place a destination in its own right.' Among the 'attractively presented' dishes: 'sensational home-smoked salmon; an excellent potato-and-leek veggie pie, with a jug of yummy tarragon sauce; perfect rhubarb crumble'. ('A good selection of draft cider suits the high-class pub food well.') Make your choice the night before for a 'stupendous' breakfast. 'Can you give a César for devilled kidneys?' (Humphrey and Frances Norrington, and others)

Doddiscombsleigh
EX6 7PS

T: 01647 252394
F: 01647 252978
E: info@nobodyinn.co.uk
W: www.nobodyinn.co.uk

BEDROOMS: 5.
OPEN: all year except 1 Jan.
FACILITIES: 2 bars, restaurant, free Wi-Fi (may be patchy), in-room TV (Freeview), garden, patio, parking, unsuitable for disabled.
BACKGROUND MUSIC: none.
LOCATION: in village 6 miles SW of Exeter.
CHILDREN: not under 5 for overnight stays, not under 14 in 1 bar.
DOGS: not allowed.
CREDIT CARDS: MasterCard, Visa.
PRICES: [2016] per room B&B £75–£105. À la carte £26.

DUNSTER Somerset

THE LUTTRELL ARMS HOTEL

NEW

'A proper, old-fashioned coaching inn done right', Anne and Nigel Way's 15th-century stone-built building has history in its vaulted ceilings, medieval carvings and minstrels' gallery – look out for the old bread oven in one of the ancient fireplaces. It enters the Guide this year thanks to trusted correspondents, themselves hoteliers, who found a 'well-managed' spot, a 'very nice' restaurant and 'fun, helpful' staff. Hobnob with locals in the convivial bar areas ('popular with shooting parties and dog owners'); in good weather, find a seat under parasols in the garden. In the smart restaurant, modern meals might include slow-roasted local pork belly, sweet potato crisps, cauliflower purée. Spend the night in one of the individually styled bedrooms: some have a private terrace and garden access; others have views over historic Yarn Market. 'Clean, warm and lovely, our spacious four-poster room had a good view of the town. There was a tiny bit of noise from the bar, until late – but not too late! – guests went to bed. In the morning, a friendly local lady served a pleasant, well-organised breakfast.' (Richard Morgan-Price)

32–36 High Street
Exmoor National Park
Dunster
TA24 6SG

T: 01643 821555
F: 01643 821567
E: enquiry@luttrellarms.co.uk
W: www.luttrellarms.co.uk

BEDROOMS: 28. Some on ground floor.
OPEN: all year.
FACILITIES: lounge, bar, restaurant, function rooms, free Wi-Fi, in-room TV, civil wedding licence, courtyard, garden (alfresco dining), only public areas suitable for disabled.
BACKGROUND MUSIC: none.
LOCATION: village centre, 3½ miles SE of Minehead.
CHILDREN: all ages welcomed.
DOGS: allowed in most bedrooms, bar, not in restaurant (£10–£20 per night charge).
CREDIT CARDS: MasterCard, Visa.
PRICES: [2016] per room B&B £130–£190, D,B&B £210–£265. 2-night min. stay on weekends.

EAST CHISENBURY Wiltshire

Map 2:D2

THE RED LION FREEHOUSE

There is 'much to recommend' at Guy and Brittany Manning's thatched village pub, say trusted readers this year. With 'smiling service' and 'excellent' cooking, it is 'everything you could wish for'. In the restaurant, chef/patron Guy Manning has a Michelin star for his modern pub dishes, which make liberal use of home-grown and locally foraged produce. (The owners have their own chickens and pigs, and a kitchen garden in the grounds.) 'I had the tenderest sous-vide venison ever tasted; the citrus and cheesecake mousse-topped sablé was sensational.' In the Troutbeck guest house across the road, 'sleekly modern' bedrooms have a private deck overlooking the River Avon. 'We enjoyed watching the ducks whizz by on the current, from our comfortable bed in the Benjamin. The freestanding bath was a delight, with a view over fields and stream.' In-room snacks include 'delicious' cookies; guests also appreciate thoughtful extras ('even painkillers, in a discreet bag at the bedside'). Breakfast is taken seriously (though some find the background music unfortunate). 'The French toast was like eating a cloud – so light and melt-in-the-mouth.' (Tessa Stuart, and others)

East Chisenbury
SN9 6AQ

T: 01980 671124
E: troutbeck@redlionfreehouse.com
W: www.redlionfreehouse.com

BEDROOMS: 5. On ground floor, in adjacent building, 1 suitable for disabled.
OPEN: all year.
FACILITIES: pub/restaurant, private dining room, free Wi-Fi, in-room TV (Freeview), 1-acre garden.
BACKGROUND MUSIC: in pub/restaurant.
LOCATION: in village, 6 miles S of Pewsey.
CHILDREN: all ages accepted (under-2s free; children 2–10 £25 per night).
DOGS: allowed in pub, 1 bedroom (not unattended).
CREDIT CARDS: Amex, MasterCard, Visa.
PRICES: per room B&B from £130, D,B&B from £170. À la carte £42.

EAST GRINSTEAD Sussex   Map 2:D4

⚜GRAVETYE MANOR

César award: country house hotel of the year

'Classy, comfortable and tasteful, the house has kept its period character without being "old hat"; the rooms are elegantly furnished without being pretentious,' say trusted Guide correspondents in 2016, of this 'special' country house hotel. The Elizabethan manor house, former home of the lauded Victorian gardener William Robinson, stands in 'impeccably maintained' grounds. Inside, the lounges have 'huge' log fires, 'plenty of chairs and settees', freshly cut garden flowers. Andrew Thomason, the managing director, is 'much in evidence'. 'Housekeeping standards are high' in the 'sizeable' upstairs bedrooms. 'A lot of thought has gone into anticipating guests' needs. Our kettle was refilled during turn-down; a copy of the Radio Times was left open at the right page, with the TV remote control on top of it. All much appreciated.' In the dining rooms, chef George Blogg's 'delicious' Michelin-starred dishes draw inspiration from the vast kitchen garden. 'We enjoyed an exquisite parsnip mousse, beautifully tender duck, an excellent chocolate tart suitably offset by a sharp fruit sorbet.' (Francine and Ian Walsh, Bill Bennett)

25% DISCOUNT VOUCHERS

Vowels Lane
East Grinstead
RH19 4LJ

T: 01342 810567
F: 01342 810080
E: info@gravetyemanor.co.uk
W: www.gravetyemanor.co.uk

BEDROOMS: 17.
OPEN: all year.
FACILITIES: 2 lounges, bar, restaurant, 2 private dining rooms, free Wi-Fi, in-room TV, civil wedding licence, 1,000-acre grounds (woodland, ornamental and kitchen gardens, meadow, orchard, lake, croquet lawn, glasshouses), only restaurant suitable for disabled.
BACKGROUND MUSIC: none.
LOCATION: 4 miles SW of East Grinstead.
CHILDREN: not under 7.
DOGS: not allowed.
CREDIT CARDS: Amex, MasterCard, Visa.
PRICES: [2016] per room B&B £260–£995, D,B&B from £405. Set dinner £40, tasting menu £75–£85, à la carte £67.50. 1-night bookings sometimes refused weekends.

EAST HOATHLY Sussex

Map 2:E4

OLD WHYLY

Sarah Burgoyne's 'beautiful' Grade II listed Georgian manor house in a Wealden village is filled with antiques and oil paintings, and surrounded by flower-filled gardens, 'glorious' in all seasons. The four spacious bedrooms are done in country house style, with Irish linens and woollen blankets. Two are en suite, two have a private bathroom. At 7 pm, gather with fellow guests for drinks before a three-course dinner in the candlelit dining room or on the terrace under a vine-covered pergola. The hostess, who trained as a cook in Paris, uses home-grown and local produce in her much-praised dishes, perhaps Southdown lamb, creamed peas, leeks, bacon; 'intense' wild blackberry jelly. 'Her breakfasts are the best': the honey is from the beehives in the orchard, the eggs from the hens and ducks that range around outside. Racquets and balls are provided for a game on the tennis court; in summer, while away the afternoon in the wisteria-draped pool house. Book for Glyndebourne – a ten-minute drive away – and order one of the hostess's 'delicious' picnic hampers. (T and CT)

London Road
East Hoathly
BN8 6EL

T: 01825 840216
E: stay@oldwhyly.co.uk
W: www.oldwhyly.co.uk

BEDROOMS: 4.
OPEN: all year.
FACILITIES: drawing room, dining room, free Wi-Fi, in-room TV (Freeview), 4-acre garden, heated outdoor swimming pool (14 by 7 metres), tennis, unsuitable for disabled.
BACKGROUND MUSIC: none.
LOCATION: 1 mile N of village.
CHILDREN: all ages welcomed.
DOGS: not unattended in bedroom; not in dining room.
CREDIT CARDS: none.
PRICES: [2016] per room B&B £98–£145. Set dinner £35, Glyndebourne hamper £38 per person. 1-night bookings sometimes refused weekends in high season.

EAST LAVANT Sussex

THE ROYAL OAK

The scene gets to the rustic heart of village life: in Sarah and Charles Ullmann's 'popular, stylish' early-19th-century inn, find oak beams, flint walls, leather armchairs, fresh flowers and, on cold days, a blazing fire. The atmosphere is 'warm and cosy', the staff are 'attentive'. Village residents haunt the place to drink the locally brewed ales, walkers following the old Chichester-to-Midhurst railway line drop by. Up the stairs and in nearby cottages, smart bedrooms are 'comfortable', and 'well equipped' with books and games; two-bedroom cottages, complete with chocolates, milk and biscuits, are perfect for a family. Eat super-local in the adjacent 'busy' restaurant: Fran Joyce, the new chef, uses fish from the coast 20 minutes away ('please ask what's come in'), and game from local herdsmen. Try the bouillabaisse of fresh fish fillets on a mussel, squid and tomato base. On fine days make the most of seating on the terrace and in the garden. As the sun rises over the moors, savour a full Sussex breakfast – fuel for exploring the South Downs national park. More reports, please.

Pook Lane
East Lavant
PO18 0AX

T: 01243 527434
E: info@royaloakeastlavant.co.uk
W: www.royaloakeastlavant.co.uk

BEDROOMS: 10. Some in cottages.
OPEN: all year.
FACILITIES: bar/restaurant, free Wi-Fi, in-room TV (Freeview), terraces (alfresco meals), residents' garden, unsuitable for disabled.
BACKGROUND MUSIC: jazz/pop in restaurant.
LOCATION: 2 miles N of Chichester.
CHILDREN: all ages welcomed.
DOGS: allowed in bar, not in restaurant or bedrooms.
CREDIT CARDS: Amex, MasterCard, Visa.
PRICES: [2016] per room B&B £95–£295. À la carte £35. 1-night bookings refused weekends, bank holidays.

EASTBOURNE Sussex

Map 2:E4

BELLE TOUT LIGHTHOUSE

On a 'remote' cliff-top at Beachy Head, surrounded by 'dramatic landscape', this decommissioned lighthouse hosts an 'original', 'characterful' B&B. Guide inspectors visiting in 2016 were impressed by 'the extraordinary light' and 'the generous spirit with which the place is run'. The Keeper's Loft, with a ladder to climb to bed, is the only bedroom in the lighthouse; others are in a squat extension. 'Our bright, spacious room had a comfortable king-size bed, a small wardrobe, a shower room with soft towels on a heated rail. At night, it was utterly quiet, and very dark.' In the late afternoon, guests gather for drinks in the 'positively cosy' lounge (fresh flowers, a grandfather clock, a working fire, leather sofas) – 'a clever way to make newcomers feel at home'. 'Paul, one of the managers, poured us generous glasses of wine. He obviously loves the lighthouse and speaks easily of it.' In the morning, breakfast tables are 'nicely laid with white linens'; 'good' coffee is brought to the table; a daily special is cooked to order. 'They knew we don't eat meat, and had gone to the trouble of getting veggie sausages.' 'We loved it.'

Beachy Head Road
Eastbourne
BN20 0AE

T: 01323 423185
E: info@belletout.co.uk
W: www.belletout.co.uk

BEDROOMS: 6.
OPEN: all year, except Christmas/ New Year.
FACILITIES: 2 lounges, breakfast room, free Wi-Fi (in some rooms and some public areas), in-room TV (Freeview), terrace, garden, unsuitable for disabled.
BACKGROUND MUSIC: none.
LOCATION: 3 miles W of Eastbourne.
CHILDREN: not under 15.
DOGS: not allowed.
CREDIT CARDS: MasterCard, Visa.
PRICES: [2016] per room B&B £155–£230. Min. 2-night stay, 1-night bookings only accepted 7–10 days in advance.

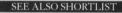

SEE ALSO SHORTLIST

EASTBOURNE Sussex

Map 2:E4

THE GRAND HOTEL

Beloved for its 'wonderfully old-fashioned' aura, this 'majestic', 'splendidly luxurious' Victorian hotel exults on the seafront, basking in the praise of ardent fans who have long lobbied for a full entry in the Guide. Its 'superb' public rooms, including sea-facing lounges with 'the sun streaming in through big windows', are 'happily plentiful and welcoming'. 'Admirable staff are efficient, smiling, helpful.' Book ahead for the 'ceremony' of afternoon tea in the 'very special' Palm Court ('It had echoes of Albert Sandler, but I preferred to think of Debussy finishing La Mer here'). Bedrooms have 'every conceivable comfort'; the best have 'sea views you could never tire of'. 'Our spacious junior suite was admirable in every way – a comfortable bed, armchairs and sofa, an excellent bathroom, everything in good nick – and nicely sunny in the late afternoon.' Men are requested to wear a jacket or collared shirt for dinner in the Mirabelle ('atmospheric, with impeccable service') and Garden restaurants. 'Very good' breakfasts have 'freshly squeezed juices and perfect kippers'. Popular for weddings and conferences. (Edward Mirzoeff, BMF and ADF, and others)

King Edwards Parade
Eastbourne
BN21 4EQ

T: 01323 412345
F: 01323 412233
E: enquiries@grandeastbourne.com
W: www.grandeastbourne.com

BEDROOMS: 152. 1 suitable for disabled.
OPEN: all year, Mirabelle restaurant closed Sun, Mon, first 2 weeks Jan.
FACILITIES: 5 lounges, bar, 2 restaurants, function/meeting facilities, free Wi-Fi, in-room TV (Freeview), civil wedding licence, terrace, spa/health club (indoor and outdoor pools), 2-acre garden.
BACKGROUND MUSIC: in restaurants, live music at weekends.
LOCATION: seafront, 1 mile from town centre.
CHILDREN: all ages welcomed.
DOGS: allowed ('strictly controlled') in bedrooms, not in public rooms.
CREDIT CARDS: all major cards.
PRICES: [2016] per room B&B £190–£250, D,B&B £270–£330. Set dinners £43.50 (Mirabelle), £40 (Garden), à la carte £55.

SEE ALSO SHORTLIST

ECKINGTON Worcestershire

Map 3:D5

ECKINGTON MANOR

25% DISCOUNT VOUCHERS

Mod cons in a milking parlour, designer chic in a cider mill – along with a working farm, well-regarded restaurant and cookery school, Judy Gardner's 'comfortably rural' set-up has much to please. Guests enjoy the 'tranquil' setting, among pastures grazed by Angus and Highland cattle and Lleyn sheep, but this is 'a foodie place at heart', where 'every table in the dining room was full' when Guide inspectors visited. Chefs Sue and Mark Stinchcombe's farm-to-fork philosophy informs the 'delicious' canapés and 'refined' menus, perhaps Birlingham asparagus, truffle mayonnaise, hazelnuts, cured pork; stone bass, wild garlic gnocchi. Well fed, head over (via a path 'prettily lit with candles and lanterns') to modern rustic bedrooms in converted outbuildings and the 17th-century Lower End House. 'Ours, accessed through a stylish lounge, was beautifully beamed, with a low door frame and a slightly sloping floor. A comfortable room, it had a super-king-size bed, crisp bedlinen, good towelling robes and slippers.' 'Before leaving the next morning, we were given directions for a lovely circular walk along the river, and offered a complimentary drink on our return.'

Hammock Road
Eckington
WR10 3BJ

T: 01386 751600
F: 01386 751362
E: info@eckingtonmanor.co.uk
W: www.eckingtonmanor.co.uk

BEDROOMS: 17. All in courtyard annexes, 1 suitable for disabled.
OPEN: all year except 24/25 Dec, restaurant closed Sun, Mon.
FACILITIES: lift, 3 reception rooms, restaurant, function rooms, free Wi-Fi, in-room TV (Freeview), civil wedding licence, cookery school, 260-acre grounds (lawns, herb garden, orchard, working farm).
BACKGROUND MUSIC: none.
LOCATION: 4 miles SW of Pershore.
CHILDREN: not under 8.
DOGS: allowed in some bedrooms, not in public rooms.
CREDIT CARDS: Amex, MasterCard, Visa.
PRICES: per room B&B £95–£249, D,B&B from £145. Set menus £32–£38.

EDENBRIDGE Kent

Map 2:D4

STARBOROUGH MANOR

'Brilliantly placed' for exploiting a wealth of Kentish history, this 18th-century Gothic folly was rescued by the Mathiases and transformed into a 'comfortable home' and 'informal' B&B, where 'friendly, chatty' Lynn Mathias welcomes visitors with tea and a baked treat fresh from her Aga. 'Immaculate, tastefully decorated' guest quarters occupy former servants' rooms with a separate side entrance. Bedrooms have a comfortable super-king-size bed, a 'comprehensive' tea tray; 'fluffy towels and quality toiletries' in the well-equipped bathroom. Two-bedroom Blue Room is a spacious family suite. Keep children entertained with games, toys and a train set in the first-floor TV room; nose through DVDs, videos, heaps of books. A second sitting room acts as a study. The 'generous' breakfast is taken communally in the 'spectacular' kitchen, or a walled courtyard in clement weather: sample varied yogurts, home-made granola, baked plums in cinnamon; blueberry pancakes with maple syrup. Bring your tennis kit for a match on the court; in summer months, cool off in the outdoor pool.

Moor Lane
Marsh Green
Edenbridge
TN8 5QY

T: 01732 862152
E: lynn@starboroughmanor.co.uk
w: www.starboroughmanor.co.uk

BEDROOMS: 4.
OPEN: all year.
FACILITIES: 2 sitting rooms, dining room, free Wi-Fi, in-room TV (Freeview), 4-acre gardens in 13-acre grounds (parkland, tennis, heated outdoor swimming pool in season), unsuitable for disabled.
BACKGROUND MUSIC: none.
LOCATION: 1½ miles W of Edenbridge.
CHILDREN: all ages welcomed.
DOGS: not allowed.
CREDIT CARDS: MasterCard, Visa.
PRICES: [2016] per room B&B single £90–£100, double £140. 1-night bookings usually refused weekends in summer.

SEE ALSO SHORTLIST

EMSWORTH Hampshire

Map 2:E3

36 ON THE QUAY

♀ César award since 2011

'A foodie destination', Karen and Ramon
Farthing's restaurant-with-rooms occupies a
17th-century inn on Chichester Harbour, with
shimmering views of the sea and tidal lagoon.
After 20 years at the helm, the Farthings now
work in partnership with Gary and Martina
Pearce, who are chef and manager – 'to give a
new edge' to the enterprise. 'They couldn't have
looked after us better,' visitors said. Bedrooms
are 'comfortable' and 'spotlessly clean' (a couple
are 'fairly compact'), but the 'impeccably
appointed' restaurant, popular with locals, is the
big draw. Here, the limited-choice, weekly-
changing menus of 'superbly presented' dishes
might include 'a tender aged beef sirloin with
well-balanced accompaniments, a great fusion of
flavours and a lovely, rich sauce'. Opt for a wine
flight to pair with the tasting menu of unusual
combinations (perhaps poached hake fillet,
salt and vinegar gel, potato foam). 'The food
didn't disappoint.' In the morning, tuck in to a
continental breakfast: cereals, pastries, 'lovely'
yogurt, 'good' toast and jams ('packet orange
juice and tinned peaches were the only niggles').
'A great experience.' (MC, IM)

47 South Street
Emsworth
PO10 7EG

T: 01243 375592
E: info@36onthequay.co.uk
W: www.36onthequay.co.uk

BEDROOMS: 4.
OPEN: all year except 24–26 Dec,
first 2 weeks Jan, restaurant closed
Sun/Mon.
FACILITIES: bar area, restaurant, free
Wi-Fi, in-room TV (Freeview),
small terrace, limited parking, only
restaurant suitable for disabled.
BACKGROUND MUSIC: none.
LOCATION: on harbour.
CHILDREN: all ages welcomed.
DOGS: not allowed.
CREDIT CARDS: Amex, MasterCard,
Visa.
PRICES: per room B&B £100–£200.
Set dinner £57.95.

ERMINGTON Devon

Map 1:D4

PLANTATION HOUSE

First impressions don't deceive at Richard Hendey's 'very special' hotel, in the countryside near Dartmoor and the Devon coast. Public rooms in the former Georgian rectory are filled with modern artwork and artefacts, tropical plants and 'artistically arranged' flowers from the garden. 'Richard is the ideal host; his friendly informality is delightful.' The whole is 'relaxing and comfortable'. Check in to bedrooms stocked with 'lovely' treats: home-made cake, tea and coffee, fresh fruit, biscuits and more garden blooms. Each bedroom has its own style, with feature lamps and some dramatic decor; sit in an armchair positioned for the best views over the surrounding countryside. Richard Hendey shares cooking duties with John Raines; their 'first-class' multi-course dinners might include roast rack, braised shoulder and crackling of local lamb, toasted barley risotto. 'We appreciated the option – very useful as we stayed for several days – of a lighter dinner culled from the set menu.' The extensive breakfast has home-made bread and marmalade, 'excellent' fresh fruit salads with Greek yogurt, good cooked options. (R and RI, and others)

Totnes Road
Ivybridge
Ermington
PL21 9NS

T: 01548 831100
E: info@plantationhousehotel.co.uk
W: www.plantationhousehotel.co.uk

BEDROOMS: 8.
OPEN: all year, restaurant closed midday, some Sunday evenings.
FACILITIES: lounge/bar, 2 dining rooms, free Wi-Fi, in-room TV (Freeview), terrace, garden, unsuitable for disabled.
BACKGROUND MUSIC: classical/easy jazz in public rooms, 'whenever required'.
LOCATION: 10 miles E of Plymouth.
CHILDREN: all ages welcomed.
DOGS: allowed in 1 bedroom only.
CREDIT CARDS: Amex, MasterCard, Visa.
PRICES: [2016] per room B&B £110–£230, D,B&B £190–£410. Set dinner £39.50. 1-night bookings sometimes refused.

EXFORD Somerset

THE CROWN HOTEL

Traditional hospitality and an unpretentious atmosphere draw guests to Sara Whittaker's modest 17th-century coaching inn, in Exmoor national park. In the popular pub, a hub of village life, pewter tankards hang from the bar; sit here for a real ale, or by the log fire burning in the stone fireplace, and get your fill of local gossip. 'It's amazing what you can find out when ear'oling the chatter at the bar: chasing a stag one day provided an hour-long discussion for one evening's entertainment.' In the restaurant, 'the food is plentiful and perfectly fine: good mussels and spicy prawns; a proper beef and ale pie – no dessert or starter needed!' Simple bedrooms are 'comfortable and quiet', with a king-size bed (though some rooms may be 'showing signs of wear and tear'). Look out for local small-batch whortleberry jam at breakfast. A fine base from which to explore the green valleys and heather-clad moorland of this 'lovely' part of the country; trail riders following the Coleridge Bridle Way can stable their horses at the inn. (P and KR, Peter Anderson)

Exford
TA24 7PP

T: 01643 831554
E: info@crownhotelexmoor.co.uk
W: www.crownhotelexmoor.co.uk

BEDROOMS: 16.
OPEN: all year.
FACILITIES: lounge, residents' bar, public bar, restaurant, meeting room, free Wi-Fi in lounge, in-room TV, 3-acre grounds (trout stream, water garden, terrace garden), stabling, unsuitable for disabled.
BACKGROUND MUSIC: in bar and restaurant in evening.
LOCATION: on village green.
CHILDREN: all ages welcomed.
DOGS: allowed, not in restaurant.
CREDIT CARDS: MasterCard, Visa.
PRICES: [2016] per room B&B £155–£179. À la carte £27.50.

FAVERSHAM Kent

Map 2:D5

READ'S

César award since 2005

Travellers who stop at this Georgian manor house on the way to Dover or the Channel Tunnel might be tempted to go no further. On the outskirts of a historic market town, Rona and David Pitchford's restaurant-with-rooms stands in its own grounds shaded by mature trees, with a walled kitchen garden. Rona Pitchford is a welcoming hostess, while her husband cooks seasonal fare featuring local produce and home-grown vegetables and leaves. At dinner, dishes are listed alongside foodie quotes: white asparagus, new season wild morel, poached egg comes with a hint of GK Chesterton; pan-fried halibut, crushed new potatoes, cep purée, confit lemon champagne is sauced with AA Milne. ('How long does getting thin take?' Pooh asked anxiously.) Bedrooms are individually styled, with a big bed, paintings, drapes, swags, antiques and expensive toiletries; guests may help themselves to the honesty bar and communal pantry well stocked with home-made biscuits and treats. Dinner, and the much-praised breakfast, may be worked off the next day at the seaside at Whitstable, just eight miles away.

Macknade Manor
Canterbury Road
Faversham
ME13 8XE

T: 01795 535344
F: 01795 591200
E: enquiries@reads.com
W: www.reads.com

BEDROOMS: 6.
OPEN: all year except Christmas, 1st week Jan, 2 weeks Sept, restaurant closed Sun/Mon.
FACILITIES: sitting room/bar, restaurant, private dining room, free Wi-Fi, in-room TV (Freeview), civil wedding licence, 4-acre garden (terrace, outdoor dining), only restaurant suitable for disabled.
BACKGROUND MUSIC: none.
LOCATION: ½ mile SE of Faversham.
CHILDREN: all ages welcomed.
DOGS: not allowed in public rooms.
CREDIT CARDS: all major cards.
PRICES: [2016] per room B&B single £140–£195, double £180–£210, D,B&B single £185–£250, double £290–£320. Set dinner £60.

FELIXKIRK Yorkshire

Map 4:C4

THE CARPENTERS ARMS

With 'friendly' staff and 'good, ultra-modern accommodation', this pub-with-rooms 'demonstrates a wish to make guests both comfortable and happy'. Owned by the small Provenance Inns group, the inn sits in a 'quiet' village overlooking the Vale of York. Inside, find open fires and old beams, tartan armchairs and rustic wooden furnishings, local beers and hand-pulled ales. Bedrooms are in the main building and around a 'well-tended' courtyard garden (each has its own patio). Outdoorsy guests should ask for a room with a drying cupboard – 'a boon after a wet day out'. 'We enjoyed our spacious garden room. A tip: it's worth requesting one with a fireplace.' Bistro-style dinners prioritise produce from local suppliers, including straight-from-the-earth vegetables from the owners' Mount St John potager round the corner; drink well, from an 'original and interesting' wine list. Wake to 'cheerful' service at breakfast; despite packaged juice and average toast, scrambled eggs and smoked salmon are 'particularly good'. 'Superb' mid-week offers. The Durham Ox, Crayke (see Shortlist entry), is under the same ownership. (Lorna Appiah, David and Kate Wooff)

Felixkirk
YO7 2DP

T: 01845 537369
E: enquiries@
   thecarpentersarmsfelixkirk.com
W: www.
   thecarpentersarmsfelixkirk.com

BEDROOMS: 10. 8 in garden annexe, 1 suitable for disabled.
OPEN: all year.
FACILITIES: bar/sitting area, 2 dining rooms, free Wi-Fi, in-room TV, terrace (alfresco meals), garden.
BACKGROUND MUSIC: 'easy listening' in public areas.
LOCATION: in village 3 miles NE of Thirsk.
CHILDREN: all ages welcomed.
DOGS: welcomed in certain bedrooms, bar and some dining areas.
CREDIT CARDS: Amex, MasterCard, Visa.
PRICES: [2016] per room B&B £120–£185. À la carte £28.

FLEET Dorset

MOONFLEET MANOR

With swimming pools, family films, play
facilities, a crèche and an early-morning
breakfast club, the kids are all right at
this Georgian manor house in 'beautiful'
countryside. 'It's a treat for families with young
children,' say Guide readers in 2016, 'though
we wouldn't call it "luxury".' 'Moonfleet really
is geared for kids,' writes another, with just a
hint of the curmudgeon. 'There are early teas
for children alone, and high teas for the whole
family. Mercifully children are not allowed at
dinner.' Find potted plants, hunting trophies
and open fires in the public areas. 'Spacious,
comfortable' bedrooms come in all shapes and
sizes to suit. 'Ours had an elegant, modern,
Edwardian-style bathroom, but no shower other
than a hand-held one.' Dinner is 'excellent,
with plenty of choice' (pastas, salads, sharing
platters and more ambitious dishes), and staff
are 'friendly and courteous', though guests
this year found ordering chaotic. A grouse:
'"Discretionary" gratuities are automatically
added to every bill.' Mornings, wake to a 'good'
breakfast: a buffet with juice, cereals, 'delicious'
jams; 'very good' cooked options. (Jane Bradley,
and others)

Fleet Road
Fleet
DT3 4ED

T: 01305 786948
F: 01305 774395
E: info@moonfleetmanorhotel.co.uk
W: www.moonfleetmanorhotel.co.uk

BEDROOMS: 36. 6 in annexes, 3 on
ground floor.
OPEN: all year.
FACILITIES: 2 lounges, family snug,
restaurant, indoor playroom, crèche,
cinema room, free Wi-Fi, in-room
TV, civil wedding licence, indoor
swimming pools, terrace, 15-acre
garden (play areas).
BACKGROUND MUSIC: contemporary
in restaurant.
LOCATION: 7 miles W of Weymouth.
CHILDREN: all ages welcomed.
DOGS: allowed in bedrooms (£10
charge per day), not in public
rooms.
CREDIT CARDS: Amex, MasterCard,
Visa.
PRICES: [2016] per room B&B from
£120, D,B&B from £190. À la carte
£40. 1-night bookings sometimes
refused.

FLETCHING Sussex

Map 2:E4

THE GRIFFIN INN

'Clearly a popular place', the Pullan family's 16th-century coaching inn is well liked for its village atmosphere and the 'friendly welcome' extended to locals and tourists. Beams, mounted antlers, country prints and open fires give it a rustic feel: sit in the 'busy, relaxed' pub over a local real ale or an option off the interesting pub menu (perhaps twice-cooked short rib of beef, bubble and squeak, claret jus). Each of the 'country-style' bedrooms is different. Some have sloping floors, one a 400-year-old fireplace, yet another a 'comfortable', 'shabby-chic' bed. Rooms in the coach house annexe are quietest. Guests this year urge careful discussion before booking: a small room in the main house, reached via 'narrow' stairs, was thought 'tiny'; a 'spacious' four-poster room in the coach house was much preferred. In the beamed restaurant, tables are set with white linens for dinner; modern European dishes might include confit pheasant croquettes, sweet pickled figs, micro herbs. In warmer months, parasols spring up in the large garden, its vista stretching over the South Downs; cocktails and barbecues hit the summer spot.

25% DISCOUNT VOUCHERS

High Street
Fletching
TN22 3SS

T: 01825 722890
E: info@thegriffininn.co.uk
W: www.thegriffininn.co.uk

BEDROOMS: 13. 4 in coach house, 5 in Griffin House next door, 4 on ground floor.
OPEN: all year except 25 Dec.
FACILITIES: 2 lounge bars (1 with TV), restaurant, free Wi-Fi, in-room TV (Freeview), gun room, terrace, 4-acre garden.
BACKGROUND MUSIC: none.
LOCATION: 3 miles NW of Uckfield.
CHILDREN: all ages welcomed.
DOGS: allowed, not in restaurant.
CREDIT CARDS: Amex, MasterCard, Visa.
PRICES: [2016] per room B&B £85–£155. À la carte £25. 1-night bookings refused bank holidays.

FOWEY Cornwall

Map 1:D3

FOWEY HALL

⚜ César award since 2015

What could be more perfect for a child-friendly hotel than the house that was Kenneth Graham's model for Toad Hall, overlooking an estuary for messing about in boats? Part of the small Luxury Family Hotels group, this Victorian revivalist baroque mansion, plus helipad, 'ticks all the boxes', says our mole, a trusted Guide correspondent. 'It's a well-managed place with well-trained staff and high standards. And we applaud the way they cater for families.' Bedrooms in the main house, garden wing and coach house mix contemporary comfort with antique pieces. 'Ours, upstairs in the old mansion, was warm and welcoming, with all the comforts, including a super bathroom, and a pretty view across the garden to the harbour.' Pick and mix from the panoply of family-friendly options and activities: collect eggs from the hens, walk Bramble, the dog, bounce on a trampoline, take bucket and spade to the beach. Children's meals are served all day, while, at grown-up dinner, modern dishes please (perhaps confit and smoked duck terrine; Cornish catch of the day). 'Our evening meal couldn't have been nicer.' (Abigail Kirkby-Harris)

Hanson Drive
Fowey
PL23 1ET

T: 01726 833866
E: info@foweyhallhotel.co.uk
W: www.foweyhallhotel.co.uk

BEDROOMS: 36. 8 in coach house, some on ground floor, 2 suitable for disabled.
OPEN: all year.
FACILITIES: 2 lounges, library/snug, 2 restaurants, free Wi-Fi, in-room TV (Freeview), crèche, games rooms, civil wedding licence, spa, 12-metre indoor swimming pool, 7-acre grounds (trampoline, zip wire).
BACKGROUND MUSIC: 'easy listening' in restaurants.
LOCATION: ½ mile from town centre.
CHILDREN: all ages welcomed.
DOGS: allowed in main house bedrooms (£15), not in restaurant.
CREDIT CARDS: Amex, MasterCard, Visa.
PRICES: [2016] per room B&B £190–£750. Set dinner £30–£40, à la carte £39. 1-night bookings refused weekends.

SEE ALSO SHORTLIST

GATESHEAD Tyne and Wear

Map 4:B4

ESLINGTON VILLA

'Pleasant', 'attentive' staff encourage guests to make themselves at home in Nick and Melanie Tulip's country hotel. The Victorian building stands in large, carefully tended gardens; inside, find paintings, photographs and antiques in the traditionally decorated lounge. Individually styled bedrooms vary considerably: pick from a modern seaside look; youthful colour schemes; peaceful, neutral shades. A spacious two-bedroom apartment under the eaves is available for short lets. Sharing platters are available all afternoon; come sundown on a fine day, the terrace is 'ideal for alfresco drinks'. In the dining room and conservatory, tuck in to chef Jamie Walsh's modern British dishes, perhaps ham knuckle press, home-made pease pudding, toasted peanuts; slow-cooked duck, confit potato, plum pickle. Occasional wine-tasting dinners match themed wines (from Bordeaux, Sicily or the Duero) to four-course dinners. Reach the sights of Gateshead easily: the Baltic Centre for Contemporary Art is a 15-minute drive away. Well-located for travellers to and from Newcastle; despite the A1 being nearby, 'the gardens mean the place feels quite rural'. More reports, please.

25% DISCOUNT VOUCHERS

8 Station Road
Low Fell
Gateshead
NE9 6DR

T: 01914 876017
F: 01914 200667
E: home@eslingtonvilla.co.uk
W: www.eslingtonvilla.co.uk

BEDROOMS: 18. 3, on ground floor, in annexe.
OPEN: all year except 25/26 Dec.
FACILITIES: lounge/bar, conservatory, restaurant, private dining room, conference/function facilities, free Wi-Fi, in-room TV (Freeview), 2-acre garden (patio).
BACKGROUND MUSIC: in public rooms.
LOCATION: 2 miles S of town centre, off A1.
CHILDREN: all ages welcomed (under-12s free of charge in parents' room).
DOGS: not allowed.
CREDIT CARDS: all major cards.
PRICES: [2016] per room B&B £79.50–£125, D,B&B £105–£175. Set dinner £24.50–£28.50.

GILLINGHAM Dorset

Map 2:D1

STOCK HILL HOUSE

Combine 'excellent' accommodation and a 'friendly' atmosphere for a 'relaxing' stay at Nita and Peter Hauser's late Victorian mansion. The Hausers have owned and run their traditional country hotel for more than 30 years, attracting many regular guests. Bedrooms are located in the main building and the former coach house; most overlook the landscaped gardens. Each is individually decorated (a cheerful country look here, a grand four-poster bed there); all have antiques to complement the period style. The expansive grounds invite a ramble – watch out for local birdlife. Weary explorers of the Dorset countryside return to home-made cake and a freshly brewed pot of tea in the afternoon; come nightfall, make your dinner choices over canapés in the lounge. Peter Hauser's 'exceptional' daily-changing menu of Austrian-inspired dishes reflects his homeland while making good use of local game and meat, and vegetables from the kitchen garden. In the morning, substantial breakfasts are served on crisply laid tables in an elegant room. Await a full English or a fish dish; toast is enjoyed with home-made jams and marmalade. 'We had a memorable stay.' (APPF)

Stock Hill
Gillingham
SP8 5NR

T: 01747 823626
F: 01747 825628
E: reception@stockhillhouse.co.uk
W: www.stockhillhouse.co.uk

BEDROOMS: 9. 2 on ground floor, in coach house.
OPEN: all year.
FACILITIES: 2 lounges, restaurant, breakfast/private dining room, free Wi-Fi (in reception), in-room TV (Freeview), 10-acre grounds (tennis, croquet, small lake, kitchen garden), unsuitable for disabled.
BACKGROUND MUSIC: none.
LOCATION: 1 mile W of Gillingham.
CHILDREN: all ages of 'well-behaved' children welcomed.
DOGS: not allowed.
CREDIT CARDS: MasterCard, Visa.
PRICES: [2016] per room D,B&B single from £175, double £255–£325.

GRASMERE Cumbria

Map 4: inset C2

FOREST SIDE

NEW

A log fire still burns in the original Victorian fireplace of this one-time walkers' hostel, but virtually everything else about the 'beautifully renovated', 'comfortably furnished' mansion is bright with a 'fabulous' new modern-rustic style, and a 'superb' team of staff to boot. Andrew Wildsmith, who owns Hipping Hall, Cowan Bridge (see entry), has created a 'top-of-the-market' hotel in the 'perfect Lake District location', say Guide readers in 2016. Choose among 'relaxing' bedrooms, some snug, others large enough to have a separate seating area; one of the best has a balcony overlooking the 'stunning' gardens and the fells beyond. Each has a 'sumptuous' bed, organic toiletries, home-baked biscuits. In the airy restaurant, chef Kevin Tickle furthers a forage-to-fork philosophy, with 'absolutely beautiful' modern menus mixing the finds of local orchards and wild-fruit hedges with produce from the hotel's extensive walled garden. Hyper-local dishes might include Cumbrian plaice, conifer, mussels, wispy leeks. Vegetarians are 'exceedingly well catered for'. Next day, soak in – and sample – the surroundings on a guided foraging walk. (Robert Nichol)

Keswick Road
Grasmere
LA22 9RN

T: 015394 35250
E: info@forestside.com
W: www.theforestside.com

BEDROOMS: 20. 1 suitable for disabled.
OPEN: all year.
FACILITIES: lounges, bar, restaurant, free Wi-Fi, in-room TV, terrace, garden.
BACKGROUND MUSIC: in public areas.
LOCATION: outskirts of village.
CHILDREN: all ages welcomed.
DOGS: allowed in some bedrooms (£20 per dog per stay).
CREDIT CARDS: MasterCard, Visa.
PRICES: [2016] per room B&B single from £159, double from £209. Set dinners £50–£75.

GRASMERE Cumbria

Map 4: inset C2

THE GRASMERE HOTEL

Wordsworth's Grasmere, with its 'multitude of small shops, galleries and cafés', is a magnet for literary sightseers, yet this 'lovely' Victorian country house is a 'haven of peace'. 'It's like staying at a friend's country house.' Owners Rob van der Palen and Anton Renac are 'hands-on' hoteliers; their staff are 'friendly and attentive'. Arrive to offers of tea and Grasmere gingerbread, then head to 'modern, spotless' bedrooms named after the Lake poets and other local luminaries. 'Small but well equipped', Wordsworth is on the ground floor, with French doors on to the garden; De Quincey's bathroom, with its heated stone floor, proved 'a joy'. The 'comfortable' lounge looks out to the garden, where the lawn runs down to the River Rothay. Sample 'excellent' canapés ('different every evening') with drinks before dinner. In the formal dining room ('perfect service and timing'), Anton Renac serves modern European dishes like roast guineafowl, pancetta, prunes. 'Dinner is a highlight – perfectly cooked and presented.' Breakfast wins praise, too, for both meaty and vegetarian selections, and home-baked bread. (J and DA, Michael Schofield)

Broadgate
Grasmere
LA22 9TA

T: 015394 35277
E: info@grasmerehotel.co.uk
W: www.grasmerehotel.co.uk

BEDROOMS: 11.
OPEN: all year except 31 Dec–26 Jan.
FACILITIES: lounge, restaurant, free Wi-Fi, in-room TV (Freeview), ½-acre garden, unsuitable for disabled.
BACKGROUND MUSIC: in lounge and restaurant during mealtimes.
LOCATION: in village.
CHILDREN: not under 10.
DOGS: 1 small to medium dog allowed, by arrangement, in some bedrooms (£10 per stay), not in public rooms.
CREDIT CARDS: MasterCard, Visa.
PRICES: per person B&B £59–£74, D,B&B £83–£98. Set dinner £21 residents, £30 non-residents. 2-night min. stay normally required (check for 1-night availability), Sat night reservations must include dinner.

GRASMERE Cumbria

Map 4: inset C2

OAK BANK

In an unassuming village in the Lake District (best known, perhaps, for its gingerbread and its Wordsworth connection), Glynis and Simon Wood's 'friendly', 'good-value' family-run hotel houses a remarkable restaurant offering 'imaginative' dishes with a local flavour. 'We couldn't have asked for better,' writes a Guide reader in 2016. Sample a local beer in the mature garden, or sink into a chair by the lounge fire with Dorothy Wordsworth's Home at Grasmere. 'The service is attentive without being obtrusive.' At dinner, the 'creative' modern dishes might include pan-seared wood pigeon, roast celeriac, pickled mushroom, dashi broth. 'Little extras like the home-baked breads and the canapés are a lovely bonus.' 'We were the only diners one night, and the chef asked what we liked.' Check into individually designed bedrooms, all with sherry and home-made biscuits. 'Our quiet second-floor room was warm on a cold day.' The 'varied' breakfast menu includes Scotch pancakes and omelettes, 'always piping hot' (though 'we would've liked better bread'). 'We've booked to return in a fortnight.' (Lorraine Burns, Donald Reid, and others)

Broadgate
Grasmere
LA22 9TA

T: 015394 35217
F: 015394 35685
E: info@lakedistricthotel.co.uk
W: www.lakedistricthotel.co.uk

BEDROOMS: 13. 1 on ground floor.
OPEN: all year except 18–26 Dec, 2–19 Jan.
FACILITIES: lounge, bar, restaurant, conservatory dining room, free Wi-Fi, in-room TV (Freeview or FreeSat), ½-acre garden, unsuitable for disabled.
BACKGROUND MUSIC: classical at breakfast, 'easy listening'/R&B at dinner in dining rooms.
LOCATION: just outside village centre.
CHILDREN: not under 10 in public rooms after 6 pm.
DOGS: allowed in 3 bedrooms, front lounge.
CREDIT CARDS: MasterCard, Visa.
PRICES: per person B&B £35–£87.50, D,B&B £63.50–£116. Set dinner £41.50, tasting menu £62.50. 1-night bookings usually refused weekends.

GULWORTHY Devon

Map 1:D4

THE HORN OF PLENTY

Guests exult over the 'spectacular' views from this 'comfortable' 19th-century manor house in a 'wonderful' location overlooking the wooded Tamar valley. The hotel is owned by Julie Leivers and Damien Pease, who encourage a 'friendly' atmosphere, with 'excellent staff who are always keen to help'. Take your pick of 'well-equipped' bedrooms in the main house (high-ceilinged, with original features) and in a converted coach house ('spacious', contemporary) a minute's walk away. 'It's worth paying extra for a room with a balcony overlooking the valley.' In the conservatory dining room, chef Scott Paton's 'exquisite' modern dishes accompany the stunning views. Consider Vulscombe goat's cheese, beetroot, elderflower, gingerbread; John Dory, lobster, heritage carrot. 'The food is excellent, but very nouvelle, with small, pretty portions. More vegetables, please!' Come breakfast time, find a buffet with cereals, yogurts, dried fruit and pastries; complimentary glasses of prosecco are a nice touch. 'I asked for more fruit in the morning, and they delivered brilliantly.' The Tamar valley trails are reached through the hotel's gardens and orchard. (Peter Anderson)

Gulworthy
PL19 8JD

T: 01822 832528
F: 01822 834390
E: enquiries@thehornofplenty.
co.uk
W: www.thehornofplenty.co.uk

BEDROOMS: 16. 10 in Coach House (20 yds), 7 on ground floor, 1 suitable for disabled.
OPEN: all year.
FACILITIES: bar, library, drawing room, restaurant, free Wi-Fi, in-room TV (Freeview), civil wedding licence, 5-acre grounds.
BACKGROUND MUSIC: in restaurant and drawing room 'when it's quiet'.
LOCATION: 3 miles SW of Tavistock.
CHILDREN: all ages welcomed.
DOGS: allowed by prior arrangement in designated Coach House rooms, not in public rooms.
CREDIT CARDS: MasterCard, Visa.
PRICES: [2016] per room B&B from £110, D,B&B from £190. Set dinner £49.50, tasting menu £65.

HALNAKER Sussex

Map 2:E3

THE OLD STORE

In a pretty village in the South Downs national park, 'thoughtful' hosts Heather and Patrick Birchenough greet B&B guests with tea and 'a firm handshake'. Guide inspectors in 2016 arrived to 'the pleasant smell of baking – and the delicious result: individual chocolate cakes and lovely slices of fruit-and-nut bread'. 'It might be a modest operation, but the things that really matter are there: an excellent bed, a wonderful shower, a great breakfast, efficient, accommodating hosts.' The small lounge is 'clean and dutifully maintained'; a 'well-stocked' bookshelf invites browsing. Homely bedrooms have a 'nicely equipped' hospitality tray and 'a bible of local information'. 'Our room was snug, but comfortable enough: a gorgeous bed, decent storage, soft bedside lighting, a good selection of tea (but instant coffee); locally made smellies in the well-equipped bathroom. Poor Wi-Fi, though.' In the morning, a 'nice' buffet in the 'bright' breakfast room includes 'tasty' fresh-pressed apple juice and 'possibly the nicest muesli in England'. 'I'd asked for a vegan breakfast, and Heather whipped up delightful cranberry and hazelnut risotto cakes – full of flavour and very filling.'

Stane Street
Halnaker
PO18 0QL

T: 01243 531977
F: 01243 531977
E: theoldstore4@aol.com
W: www.theoldstoreguesthouse.co.uk

BEDROOMS: 7. 1 on ground floor.
OPEN: Mar–Dec.
FACILITIES: lounge, breakfast room, free Wi-Fi, in-room TV, ¼-acre garden with seating.
BACKGROUND MUSIC: none.
LOCATION: 4 miles NE of Chichester.
CHILDREN: all ages welcomed.
DOGS: not allowed.
CREDIT CARDS: MasterCard, Visa.
PRICES: per person B&B £40–£60 (higher for Goodwood 'Festival of Speed' and 'Revival' meetings). 1-night bookings refused weekends, sometimes other nights in high season.

HAMBLETON Rutland

Map 2:B3

HAMBLETON HALL

♢César award since 1985

Arrive, as did Guide readers this year, 'in perfect time for sitting on the terrace and being wonderfully spoilt'. 'Almost impossible to fault', Tim and Stefa Hart's 'classy' country house hotel overlooking Rutland Water is a long-time favourite: the staff are 'warm and genuine', the food is 'a joy'. 'It is the standard by which we've come to judge the other establishments we stay at and eat in.' The 19th-century hunting lodge is 'a haven of luxury': step into 'elegant' public rooms with 'inviting sofas, generous flower arrangements, an array of magazines'; in good weather, explore the 'beautiful' gardens. 'Impeccable' bedrooms, some 'old fashioned', are a picture of cultivated country charm (sprinklings of toile de Jouy, spreads of chintz); some have a 'truly spectacular' view over the garden. 'The turn-down service is meticulous.' Michelin-starred chef Aaron Patterson continues to win acclaim for his 'wonderful' modern dishes. Hart's Hotel, Nottingham (see entry) is under the same ownership. (Caroline Faircliff, Susan Willmington, Roderic Rennison, Francine and Ian Walsh)

Oakham
Hambleton
LE15 8TH

T: 01572 756991
E: hotel@hambleton.co.uk
W: www.hambletonhall.com

BEDROOMS: 17. 2-bedroomed suite in cottage.
OPEN: all year.
FACILITIES: lift, hall, drawing room, bar, restaurant, 2 private dining rooms, free Wi-Fi, in-room TV, civil wedding licence, 17-acre grounds (tennis, swimming pool (heated May–Sept), croquet, vegetable garden).
BACKGROUND MUSIC: none.
LOCATION: 3 miles SE of Oakham, Rutland.
CHILDREN: all ages welcomed, only children 'of a grown-up age' in restaurant in evening.
DOGS: allowed in bedrooms (not unattended), not in public rooms.
CREDIT CARDS: all major cards.
PRICES: [2016] per room B&B from £270, D,B&B from £406. Set dinner £68, à la carte £68. 1-night bookings normally refused weekends.

HAROME Yorkshire

Map 4:D4

THE STAR INN

There's a 'congenial' ambience at this 14th-century inn on the edge of the North York Moors, the whole bolstered by intriguing modern meals and unabashedly rustic elements – stuffed birds, antlers, 'a stag's head of some size'. The Michelin-starred restaurant, run by chef/patron Andrew Pern, attracts gourmands in search of the taste-of-the-countryside dishes – try carpaccio of malt whisky barrel-smoked fallow deer, house-pickled walnuts, haggis bonbon, foraged berries; garden beetroot tarte Tatin, roasted crones, buttered curly kale, black truffle. In former farm buildings across the way, beams and quirky features abound in the characterful bedrooms: one has a rope-slung bed, another, tartan-walled, has a piano. Two rooms joined by a hallway work well as a family suite. 'Mine had a central snooker table; antique reproduction furnishings; biscuits, chocolate bars, magazines and books. A useful guide included details of expeditions and walks.' Take drinks on the terrace in fine weather, or retreat into the residents' lounge: 'candles created an intimate light on a winter's night'. 'Outstanding' breakfasts, with 'robust coffee right for stirring one into life', are 'not to be missed'. (RG)

High Street
Harome
YO62 5JE

T: 01439 770397
E: reservations@
   thestarinnatharome.co.uk
W: www.thestaratharome.co.uk

BEDROOMS: 9. All in Cross House Lodge opposite, 3 on ground floor.
OPEN: all year, restaurant closed midday Mon.
FACILITIES: lounge, restaurant, The Wheelhouse private dining room, free Wi-Fi, in-room TV (Freeview), civil wedding licence, terrace, 2-acre garden, unsuitable for disabled.
BACKGROUND MUSIC: 'gentle jazz' in lounge and dining room.
LOCATION: village centre.
CHILDREN: all ages welcomed.
DOGS: not allowed.
CREDIT CARDS: MasterCard, Visa.
PRICES: [2016] per room B&B £150–£260. Set menus £20–£25, à la carte £45.

HARWICH Essex

THE PIER AT HARWICH

In a 'great position' on the quayside of this pretty, historic port town, Paul Milsom's 'excellent' hotel comprises two handsome buildings – a 'striking' blue-and-white 19th-century palazzo-style former waiting room for ferry passengers, and a 17th-century pub. It underwent considerable redevelopment in 2016. A slick brasserie on the first floor now serves food all day, with alfresco meals on the extended balcony; snacks and light bites can be taken in the ground-floor bar. Access has been improved, too: a four-person lift now whizzes guests to bedrooms on the top floor. The individually decorated rooms, all 'rich colours', 'sophisticated' furnishings and original artwork, remain. 'Our good-sized, double-aspect corner bedroom had a settee and (hooray!) Anglepoise bedside lights.' Sea-lovers, ask for a room at the front for panoramic views of Old Harwich's heritage Ha'Penny Pier. (The sound-sensitive might want to discuss room choices before booking: some guests this year had 'a good night's sleep', while others were bothered by noise from the 'busy' harbour.) The Mayflower Museum is nearby. 'Great breakfasts.' (Richard Bright, John and Fay Waters)

25% DISCOUNT VOUCHERS

The Quay
Harwich
CO12 3HH

T: 01255 241212
F: 01255 551922
E: pier@milsomhotels.com
W: www.milsomhotels.com

BEDROOMS: 14. 7 in annexe, 1 on ground floor.
OPEN: all year.
FACILITIES: lift, bar, lounge (in annexe), restaurant, private dining room, free Wi-Fi, in-room TV (Sky, BT, Freeview), civil wedding licence, balcony (alfresco meals), small front terrace.
BACKGROUND MUSIC: none.
LOCATION: on quay, in old town.
CHILDREN: all ages welcomed.
DOGS: allowed in bedrooms, bar.
CREDIT CARDS: all major cards.
PRICES: [2016] per room B&B from £125, D,B&B from £110 per person. À la carte £35.

HASTINGS Sussex

BLACK ROCK HOUSE

'Helpful', 'talented', 'a terrific host', Yuliya Vereshchuk 'fully deserves high praise' for her 'delightful' B&B, guests say. The 'handsome' Victorian house is on a 'quiet' residential street on a hill above the town. It's a 'relaxing' place to stay, with 'immaculate' rooms and a calm, modern decor (wooden floors, white walls, an 'elegant' staircase). 'In the comfortable lounge, the open fire was lit for us each evening.' Sit here, and browse through the 'interesting' selection of paperback novels and books of local history. Bedrooms are thoughtfully stocked with home-made biscuits, cafetière coffee, a carafe of filtered water; there's fresh milk in the fridge, and a torch in the bedside drawer. 'We enjoyed having two bedrooms in the Westview suite; more seating would have been nice.' The tables are 'beautifully' laid with 'proper' napkins at breakfast. Tuck in to the buffet spread, including home-made granola and muesli, fresh fruit and fruit compote; freshly squeezed fruit juice, 'chunky' toast and home-made preserves are served at the table; cooked dishes are 'excellent'. (MG, and others)

25% DISCOUNT VOUCHERS

10 Stanley Road
Hastings
TN34 1UE

T: 01424 438448
E: enquiries@black-rock-hastings.
co.uk
W: www.hastingsaccommodation.
com

BEDROOMS: 5.
OPEN: all year.
FACILITIES: lounge, breakfast room, free Wi-Fi, in-room TV (Freeview), patio, unsuitable for disabled.
BACKGROUND MUSIC: in lounge and breakfast room.
LOCATION: central.
CHILDREN: not under 10.
DOGS: not allowed.
CREDIT CARDS: Amex, MasterCard, Visa.
PRICES: [2016] per person B&B single £90–£95, double £125–£140. 1-night bookings refused bank holidays, weekends.

SEE ALSO SHORTLIST

HASTINGS Sussex

Map 2:E5

THE OLD RECTORY NEW

'Welcoming, generous, on top of its game – it's altogether delightful.' From the hand-woven rugs designed by a local artisan to the home-baked bread and home-cured bacon at breakfast, much is super-local at this 'stylishly quirky', 'beautifully refurbished' B&B on the edge of the Old Town, say trusted Guide readers in 2016. 'Dynamic and friendly, with a can-do attitude', Tracey-Anne Cook and Helen Styles manage the house for Lionel Copley, who also co-owns Swan House, nearby (see next entry). The 'beautiful' lounges are all light, grandeur and tall vases of fresh flowers. In the distinctively styled bedrooms, admire the trompe l'oeil touches and vintage furnishings. 'Our room had sumptuous curtains, a roll-top bath, the most comfortable bed we've ever slept in; home-made rocky road and a book of local recommendations. Although the house is on a main(ish) road, it was completely quiet at night.' Wake to 'a breakfast of quality', with much that has been home made or locally procured. 'On a lovely spring day, we ate with the doors open to the impeccably maintained garden.' (Anna and Bill Brewer)

25% DISCOUNT VOUCHERS

Harold Road
Hastings
TN35 5ND

T: 01424 422410
E: info@theoldrectoryhastings.
co.uk
W: www.theoldrectoryhastings.
co.uk

BEDROOMS: 8.
OPEN: all year except 1 week at Christmas, 2 weeks Jan.
FACILITIES: 2 lounges (honesty bar), breakfast room, free Wi-Fi, local telephone calls, in-room TV (Freeview), civil wedding licence, walled garden, unsuitable for disabled.
BACKGROUND MUSIC: in breakfast room and main lounge.
LOCATION: outskirts of Old Town, limited parking.
CHILDREN: not under 10.
DOGS: not allowed.
CREDIT CARDS: Amex, MasterCard, Visa.
PRICES: per room B&B £90–£165. 1-night bookings refused most weekends.

SEE ALSO SHORTLIST

HASTINGS Sussex

Map 2:E5

SWAN HOUSE

The 'lovely, warm atmosphere' at Lionel Copley and Brendan McDonagh's elegant B&B puts guests in 'a good mood', say Guide inspectors in 2016. Most days, the door of the Tudor cottage might be opened by 'Harriet – young, very friendly, no shoes; this is a relaxed place'. Enter into the open-plan breakfast room and lounge (books, inglenook fireplace, linen-covered sofas); all but one of the 'pleasing' bedrooms are upstairs. 'Our beamed room, its floors gently sloping, overlooked St Clement's church. It had a window seat, an antique mirror-fronted wardrobe, blueberry flapjacks in a jar. There was crisp linen on the bed; good lamps, tumblers and two flasks of water. Absolutely quiet at night.' The host, 'welcoming and likeable', has plenty of suggestions for dinner (The Crown, a five-minute walk away, is 'exceptionally good'). Breakfast is served at tables laid with 'little bowls of jam and marmalade, butter, linen napkins, a small vase of flowers'. 'Brendan brought a cafetière of coffee and glass bowls of Greek yogurt; orange juice was freshly squeezed, the scrambled eggs very good.' Permits are provided for car parks a short walk away.

25% DISCOUNT VOUCHERS

1 Hill Street
Hastings
TN34 3HU

T: 01424 430014
E: res@swanhousehastings.co.uk
W: www.swanhousehastings.co.uk

BEDROOMS: 4. 1 on ground floor.
OPEN: all year except 24–26 Dec.
FACILITIES: lounge/breakfast room, free Wi-Fi, in-room TV, patio garden, unsuitable for disabled.
BACKGROUND MUSIC: none.
LOCATION: in old town, near seafront.
CHILDREN: not under 5.
DOGS: not allowed.
CREDIT CARDS: all major cards.
PRICES: per room B&B £120–£150. 1-night bookings refused weekends.

SEE ALSO SHORTLIST

HATCH BEAUCHAMP Somerset

Map 1:C6

FROG STREET FARMHOUSE

A 'friendly' welcome awaits at Louise and David Farrance's 'peaceful' B&B, in a 15th-century farmhouse along a country lane. 'We enjoyed tea and cake in the lovingly tended garden when we arrived.' The lounge has a traditional beamed ceiling and stone floor (uneven in places, with various steps and changes of level); in the winter, relax in a leather armchair in front of the log fire. Each of the country-style bedrooms is different. The characterful Willow room has exposed beams; the Snug (in fact, 'roomy and extremely comfortable') has a private entrance and a log fire. 'We stayed in the Orchard Suite, which had a spacious double bedroom and two armchairs; a shared lobby led to a second bedroom and a bathroom with a freestanding roll-top bath.' Book ahead for 'a simple supper' prepared by the hosts; bring your own holiday tipple (no corkage charged; ice bucket and glasses provided). 'Excellent' breakfasts with local bacon and sausages, home-made bread and preserves, and eggs from the Farrances' free-range hens provide fuel for exploring the Devon and Somerset coasts or Exmoor national park, all within easy reach. (Michael Gwinnell, Mary and Rodney Milne-Day)

Hatch Beauchamp
TA3 6AF

T: 01823 481883
E: frogstreet@hotmail.com
W: www.frogstreet.co.uk

BEDROOMS: 4. 1 with private entrance.
OPEN: all year except Dec.
FACILITIES: 1 lounge, dining room, free Wi-Fi, in-room TV (Sky), 150-acre grounds (½-acre garden, farmland), unsuitable for disabled.
BACKGROUND MUSIC: none.
LOCATION: 6 miles SE of Taunton.
CHILDREN: all ages welcomed in family suite.
DOGS: not allowed.
CREDIT CARDS: all major cards (charges may apply).
PRICES: per person B&B from £40.50. 1-night bookings refused weekends May–Sept.

HATHERSAGE Derbyshire

THE GEORGE HOTEL

Charlotte Brontë wrote much of Jane Eyre at the vicarage of this Peak District village, where Eric Marsh owns and runs a former coaching inn. Reader, we hear praise of him. 'He has created a happy ship.' The building is 17th-century, much updated. 'In ambience and architecture, it has most of the characteristics of a bustling inn, with numerous and helpful front-of-house staff,' say regular Guide correspondents this year. 'Our spacious, pleasant bedroom had two comfortable armchairs and adequate storage; bottles of mineral water were replenished regularly, facecloths changed daily. The bathroom was clean and inviting, but the bath had awkwardly high sides – grab rails would have helped.' Tealights are lit at dinner in the 'cosy' restaurant, where chef Helen Prince receives kudos for her modern Derbyshire dishes, perhaps 'generous' portions of 'tender' pigeon breast in pastry or 'very sweet and moist' rack of lamb. One guest wrote of 'unnecessary flourishes', however, and wished for more variety on the menu over a three-night stay. In the morning, find home-made bread and marmalade; choices of fish and egg dishes. (John and Padi Howard, and others)

25% DISCOUNT VOUCHERS

Main Road
Hathersage
S32 1BB

T: 01433 650436
F: 01433 650099
E: info@george-hotel.net
W: www.george-hotel.net

BEDROOMS: 24.
OPEN: all year.
FACILITIES: lounge/bar, restaurant, 2 function rooms, free Wi-Fi, in-room TV, civil wedding licence, courtyard, only restaurant suitable for disabled.
BACKGROUND MUSIC: light jazz in restaurant.
LOCATION: in village centre, parking.
CHILDREN: all ages welcomed.
DOGS: not allowed.
CREDIT CARDS: Amex, MasterCard, Visa.
PRICES: [2016] per room B&B single £105–£174, double £139–£198. Set dinner £36.95 (5% 'service levy' charged on all goods and services, for distribution directly to staff). 1-night bookings sometimes refused.

HEREFORD Herefordshire

Map 3:D4

CASTLE HOUSE

By the remains of the medieval castle moat, this 'excellent', 'welcoming' hotel 'would be difficult to better', says a trusted Guide correspondent this year. The Grade II listed Regency villa, its wrought iron balcony thick with flowers in season, is run by local farmer David Watkins and his son, George, with the help of 'plenty of cheerful, intelligent, helpful' staff. 'We couldn't have been more comfortable.' Choose between bedrooms in the main house, traditionally decorated with antique pieces, or more modern rooms in Number 25, a Georgian town house down the street. 'Our town house suite had furniture and fittings of the highest quality, with a large sofa, a small but charming conservatory with comfortable chairs, and a private garden with outdoor seating.' Informal meals are served in the bistro; book ahead for chef Claire Nicholls's 'good' modern dishes in the Castle restaurant. Using meat and vegetables from the owner's farm, seasonally-changing menus might include fillet of Hereford beef, squash, pickled shallots, braised shin. The cathedral is a stroll away; the River Wye across the green. (Lord Cormack)

Castle Street
Hereford
HR1 2NW

T: 01432 356321
E: info@castlehse.co.uk
W: www.castlehse.co.uk

BEDROOMS: 24. 8 in town house (a short walk away), some on ground floor, 1 suitable for disabled.
OPEN: all year.
FACILITIES: lift, lounge, bar/bistro, restaurant, free Wi-Fi, in-room TV (Freeview, Sky Sports), civil wedding licence, terrace, garden.
BACKGROUND MUSIC: light jazz in public areas.
LOCATION: central.
CHILDREN: all ages welcomed.
DOGS: not allowed.
CREDIT CARDS: Amex, MasterCard, Visa.
PRICES: [2016] per room B&B from £150, D,B&B from £195. À la carte £40, tasting menu £50. 1-night bookings sometimes refused.

HEXHAM Northumberland

⚜BATTLESTEADS

César award: value hotel of the year

A 'very special place in a very beautiful part of the world', this informal hotel and restaurant is run by Dee and Richard Slade with one eye on planet Earth and another on the stars. Eco-friendly touches include carbon-neutral heating and hot water systems; a dark-sky observatory is highly recommended. 'The owners have made a historic coaching inn into a characterful modern pub and hotel with invariably friendly, helpful and efficient staff,' say fans in 2016. Bedrooms are individually styled: five timber lodges have a spa bath and a separate sitting area. 'Our large, very comfortable luxury double room was like a junior suite; high-quality touches included the cafetière that came with a generous sachet of fresh coffee.' Chef Edward Shilton's cooking is 'superb'. 'The marvellous tasting menu comes with matching wines; a wild mushroom and truffle soup had a concentrated flavour; the imaginative beetroot "semifreddo" starter was unusual and delicious. The chef was much in evidence, and keen to chat.' An 'inspirational and enthusiastic' guided tour of the stars, with 'plenty of pairs of binoculars', is 'well worth booking'. (Pauline and Stephen Glover)

Wark-on-Tyne
nr Hexham
NE48 3LS

T: 01434 230209
F: 01434 230039
E: info@battlesteads.com
W: www.battlesteads.com

BEDROOMS: 22. 4 on ground floor, 5 in lodge, 2 suitable for disabled.
OPEN: all year except 25 Dec.
FACILITIES: bar, dining room, function facilities, drying room, free Wi-Fi, in-room TV (Freeview), civil wedding licence, 2-acre grounds (walled garden, kitchen garden, dark sky observatory).
BACKGROUND MUSIC: none.
LOCATION: 12 miles N of Hexham.
CHILDREN: all ages welcomed.
DOGS: allowed in public rooms, by arrangement in some bedrooms (£10).
CREDIT CARDS: Amex, MasterCard, Visa.
PRICES: per room B&B from £115, D,B&B from £160. À la carte £27.50.

SEE ALSO SHORTLIST

HOLT Norfolk

BYFORDS

A free-and-easy sort of place, with 'no bossy notes or house rules', Clair and Iain Wilson's 'all-day café, store and posh B&B' occupies the oldest house in a Georgian market town. Inspectors in 2016 were 'warmly welcomed': 'On checking in, we were offered free tea and cake in the café.' Guests on foot enter through the deli; bedrooms, some snug, are in the back. 'On the first floor, our well-lit standard room overlooking the car park was quiet, with a comfortable king-size bed, leather armchairs, an antique writing desk. Small but adequate, the bathroom had fresh lilies, fluffy towels, aromatherapy-style toiletries. A welcome touch: a "tipple menu" of aperitifs can be brought to the room without a service charge.' In the 'rustic' restaurant, candlelit at night, the 'inexpensive' food – pizza, fish stew, penne with boar ragout – can be 'hit or miss', though breakfast is 'good': newspapers, a buffet with fruit salad, yogurt, 'excellent' home-made croissants and pastries; 'whatever hot dishes you like, say splendid eggs hollandaise, from the café menu'. Pack a picnic from the deli: the north Norfolk coast awaits. Iain Wilson's Dial House, Reepham (see entry), enters the Guide this year.

1–3 Shirehall Plain
Holt
NR25 6BG

T: 01263 711400
E: queries@byfords.org.uk
W: www.byfords.org.uk

BEDROOMS: 16. 1 suitable for disabled.
OPEN: all year.
FACILITIES: 5 internal eating areas, free Wi-Fi, in-room TV (Sky), deli.
BACKGROUND MUSIC: in restaurant.
LOCATION: central, private secure parking.
CHILDREN: all ages welcomed.
DOGS: not allowed.
CREDIT CARDS: Amex, MasterCard, Visa.
PRICES: per room B&B from £155, D,B&B from £195. À la carte £25.

HOPE Derbyshire

UNDERLEIGH HOUSE

Walkers and countryside explorers find a warm welcome at Vivienne and Philip Taylor's B&B, in a scenic spot within the Peak District national park. The 19th-century cottage and barn is all rustic charm: there are flagstone floors and beamed ceilings; a wood-burner crackles in the lounge in cool weather. Three of the four traditionally decorated bedrooms have a private lounge; all have views of the garden and surrounding countryside. Twitchers, in particular, might appreciate the garden suite, from which guests may best watch the nuthatches and woodpeckers who visit the nearby feeders. Feeling green? Eco-minded hosts, the Taylors have plenty of ideas for a car-free holiday, such as walks from the front door, or bicycle rentals from the local cycle shop. Guidebooks are available to borrow. The award-winning breakfast, taken at a long communal table, is 'quite a ceremony'. A taste of the Peak District, it might include traditional Derbyshire oatcakes, bacon and sausages from the local butcher; home-made compotes and preserves made, perhaps, from locally grown blackcurrants or damsons. The hosts offer to meet guests who arrive by train. (JM)

Lose Hill Lane
off Edale Road
Hope
S33 6AF

T: 01433 621372
F: 01433 621324
E: info@underleighhouse.co.uk
W: www.underleighhouse.co.uk

BEDROOMS: 4. 3 suites with a private lounge.
OPEN: all year except mid-Dec to mid-Feb.
FACILITIES: lounge, breakfast room, free Wi-Fi, in-room TV (Freeview), ¼-acre garden, unsuitable for disabled.
BACKGROUND MUSIC: none.
LOCATION: 1 mile N of Hope.
CHILDREN: not under 12.
DOGS: not allowed in public rooms, allowed in 1 bedroom by prior arrangement.
CREDIT CARDS: MasterCard, Visa (both 1.75% surcharge).
PRICES: per room B&B £95–£125. 1-night bookings refused Fri/Sat, bank holidays.

SEE ALSO SHORTLIST

HOUGH-ON-THE-HILL Lincolnshire   Map 2:A3

THE BROWNLOW ARMS

'A fantastic surprise. More in the style of a micro country house than a rustic hang-out, this inn has been made over with impeccable taste. It oozes character.' Trusted readers were bowled over this year by Paul and Lorraine Willoughby's 17th-century sandstone inn, in a 'quiet and picturesque' hamlet. 'Paul welcomed us and escorted us to our room; Lorraine, smiling and warm, is totally delightful.' Bedrooms are in the main building and a barn conversion a few yards away. 'Our room was enchanting: comfortable and well lit, with all the touches that contribute to making a pleasant stay, from the electric blanket to the tray by the entrance for dirty shoes.' A 'joyful' log fire burns in the 'atmospheric' bar; in the 'smart' dining room, 'inspiring' chef Ruaraidh Bealby's cooking is 'first class'. 'Every course we ate was imaginative, well balanced and generous; the service was prompt and well timed.' Breakfast is praised: 'quality cereals, good fresh fruit salad, any juice you fancy'; 'perfectly cooked scrambled eggs with a generous portion of smoked salmon'; 'the tastiest bacon'. (Francine and Ian Walsh)

High Road
Grantham
Hough-on-the-Hill
NG32 2AZ

T: 01400 250234
F: 01400 250234
E: armsinn@yahoo.co.uk
W: www.thebrownlowarms.com

BEDROOMS: 5. 1 on ground floor in barn conversion.
OPEN: all year except 25/26 Dec, 1 Jan, restaurant closed Sun evening, Mon, Tues midday.
FACILITIES: bar, 3 restaurants, free Wi-Fi, unsuitable for disabled.
BACKGROUND MUSIC: in public areas.
LOCATION: rural, 2 miles E of town centre.
CHILDREN: not under 8.
DOGS: not allowed.
CREDIT CARDS: MasterCard, Visa.
PRICES: per room B&B single £70, double £110. À la carte £50.

HUNTINGDON Cambridgeshire

THE OLD BRIDGE

'Lively, comfortable, informal, stylish – at the top of its game.' There's a 'very special atmosphere' at John and Julia Hoskins's ivy-smothered Georgian town house, by the medieval bridge over the Great Ouse to Godmanchester. 'We greatly enjoyed the buzz that the hotel has from its popularity with locals.' Staff have an 'efficient', 'can-do' attitude. 'We were struck by John's friendliness and warmth.' Have a drink and a chat in the 'cosy' lounge and bar areas; later, relax in one of the 'plush' bedrooms decorated with a 'tasteful' mix of traditional and bold modern furnishings. Rooms facing the busy road system are triple glazed. 'Our inviting room, with a view over the river, was quiet and comfortable.' In the airy, 'atmospheric' terrace restaurant, tuck in to Jack Woolner's 'simple yet well-executed' British dishes, perhaps turbot, prawn ravioli, samphire, lobster bisque. Lighter food is served all day, in the bar and lounge, or alfresco on the terrace. Breakfast is 'equally impressive'. John Hoskins, a Master of Wine, runs a wine shop on the premises, with daily tastings. (A and BB)

1 High Street
Huntingdon
PE29 3TQ

T: 01480 424300
F: 01480 411017
E: office@huntsbridge.co.uk
W: www.huntsbridge.com

BEDROOMS: 24. 2 on ground floor.
OPEN: all year.
FACILITIES: lounge, bar, restaurant, private dining room, wine shop, business centre, free Wi-Fi, in-room TV (Freeview), civil wedding licence, 1-acre grounds (terrace, garden), river (fishing, jetty, boat trips), parking, unsuitable for disabled.
BACKGROUND MUSIC: none except in wine shop.
LOCATION: 500 yds from town centre, station 10 mins' walk.
CHILDREN: all ages welcomed.
DOGS: allowed in two bedrooms, lounge and bar, not in restaurant.
CREDIT CARDS: MasterCard, Visa.
PRICES: [2016] per room B&B from £125, D,B&B from £195. À la carte £34.

IREBY Cumbria

OVERWATER HALL

♜César award since 2015

'A fine example of a Good Hotel', this 18th-century house has been run as a 'friendly' hotel by Stephen Bore and Angela and Adrian Hyde since 1992. It continues to win lavish praise from readers who come for the 'attentive' staff, 'superb' dinners and 'relaxed, lived-in feel'. 'We enjoyed a warm welcome from Angela, who is the perfect hostess. The attention to detail, with many individual touches, sets this hotel apart.' The interior bursts with a wealth of stripes and florals; on cool days, a log fire burns in the drawing room. 'Very comfortable' bedrooms have fresh flowers, fresh milk; a good bathroom. Local produce and 'expert flavour combinations' feature in the restaurant, perhaps trio of Cumbrian lamb, dauphinoise potatoes, redcurrant jus; Goosnargh duck breast, butternut squash fondue, smoked duck croquette. 'It is a fine dining experience for hearty appetites after days out in this lovely area.' Breakfast has locally smoked kippers and home-made preserves. Dogs are spoiled with a 'good doggie welcome' and the run of the grounds, including a woodland boardwalk. (Mary Coles, David Boehm, James Banks)

25% DISCOUNT VOUCHERS

Ireby
CA7 1HH

T: 017687 76566
F: 017687 76921
E: welcome@overwaterhall.co.uk
W: www.overwaterhall.co.uk

BEDROOMS: 11. 1 on ground floor.
OPEN: all year, except first 2 weeks Jan.
FACILITIES: drawing room, lounge, bar area, restaurant, free Wi-Fi, in-room TV (Freeview), civil wedding licence, 18-acre grounds, Overwater tarn 1 mile.
BACKGROUND MUSIC: light instrumental in restaurant in evening.
LOCATION: 2 miles NE of Bassenthwaite Lake.
CHILDREN: all ages welcomed, not under 5 in restaurant (high tea at 5.30 pm).
DOGS: allowed except in main lounge, restaurant.
CREDIT CARDS: MasterCard, Visa.
PRICES: [2016] per person B&B £60–£135 (£50 single supplement). Set dinner £48. 1-night bookings refused Sat.

KELMSCOTT Oxfordshire

Map 3:E6

THE PLOUGH   **NEW**

The setting is 'wonderful', the welcome 'informal and warm'. In a 'beguiling' spot close to the River Thames, Guide inspectors in 2016 were won over by this 'popular' village pub-with-rooms. Chef/patron Sebastian Snow owns the refurbished 17th-century pub with his wife, Lana; 'chatty, charming' Tileri Charles-Jones is manager. Hobnob with locals (and their dogs) in the garden or the convivial, stone-walled bar, then tuck in to Matthew Read's 'delicious' dinners. 'We enjoyed a flavourful lamb and kidney pie in perfect shortcrust; nicely presented pan-fried sea trout; a fine rhubarb brûlée.' Afterwards, lay your head in a 'shabby chic' bedroom upstairs. 'Ours, with a large, comfortable bed and good linens, overlooked the front garden. The room was cool in January, but a portable radiator, swiftly proffered, made it much cosier.' Pub noise is inescapable; ask for one of the quietest rooms, or 'join in, and enjoy it!' Breakfast on 'nice croissants and locally sourced preserves'; an 'excellent' cooked option with 'crispy' bacon and sausages from the village farm. Kelmscott Manor, with its 'unrivalled collection of William Morris's work and possessions', is down the lane.

Kelmscott
GL7 3HG

T: 01367 253543
E: info@theploughinnkelmscott.com
W: www.theploughinnkelmscott.com

BEDROOMS: 8.
OPEN: all year except 25 Dec, restaurant closed Mon eve.
FACILITIES: bar, restaurant, private dining room, free Wi-Fi, in-room TV (Freeview), garden (alfresco drinks and meals), unsuitable for disabled.
BACKGROUND MUSIC: none.
LOCATION: 3 miles E of Lechlade.
CHILDREN: all ages welcomed.
DOGS: allowed in public rooms, not in bedrooms.
CREDIT CARDS: MasterCard, Visa.
PRICES: [2016] per room B&B £90–£130. Set dinner (6 pm–7 pm) £24, à la carte £30.

KING'S LYNN Norfolk

Map 2:A4

BANK HOUSE

Glance up at the statue of Charles I as you pass through the wrought iron gateway to this popular Georgian town house hotel on the quayside. 'Lynn Regis' was a Royalist town, besieged by Cromwell, later assaulted by 1960s wrecking balls. Despite this, many beautiful buildings survive, including this former bank, today a 'busy', 'imaginatively decorated' hotel with 'helpful, welcoming' staff and a 'relaxed' environment. Its owners, Anthony and Jeannette Goodrich, also own the Rose and Crown, Snettisham (see Shortlist entry). Choose among bedrooms decked out with modern paintings and antique furniture – each has its own style, and all are well stocked with books, magazines and home-made biscuits. 'Our comfortable room overlooking the estuary was one of the largest we'd ever stayed in; the memorable bathroom had a freestanding claw-footed bath.' Food is served all day in the 'sympathetically updated' dining rooms, in the courtyard and on the riverside terrace. Sit down to 'excellent' British brasserie dishes – perhaps roast pollack, pommes mousseline, oyster mushrooms, cockles – or simply sip an evening cocktail watching a 'glorious' summer sunset over the Ouse.

King's Staithe Square
King's Lynn
PE30 1RD

T: 01553 660492
E: info@thebankhouse.co.uk
W: www.thebankhouse.co.uk

BEDROOMS: 12.
OPEN: all year.
FACILITIES: bar, 3 dining rooms, vaulted cellars for private parties, free Wi-Fi, in-room TV (Freeview), riverside terrace, courtyard, unsuitable for disabled.
BACKGROUND MUSIC: 'mellow jazz' in public areas ('but can be turned down or off').
LOCATION: central.
CHILDREN: all ages welcomed.
DOGS: allowed in bar and on terrace, not in bedrooms.
CREDIT CARDS: Amex, MasterCard, Visa.
PRICES: [2016] per room B&B single £85–£120, double £115–£220, D,B&B double £170–£275. Pre-theatre dinner £15–£20, à la carte £28.

KING'S LYNN Norfolk

Map 2:A4

CONGHAM HALL

Wander in the herb garden here, and breathe in the aromas of 400 varieties, planted by a former owner of this 'lovely' Georgian country house hotel. Set in pretty gardens and horse-grazed parkland, the house, today owned by Nicholas Dickinson, is 'charming', with a 'spacious' lounge and library, an 'understated' decor, and 'lots of sitting areas, both indoors and out'. 'We took tea and scones in the sun, on a terrace facing green fields and ancient trees. In the orchard, trees laden with fruit, and fallen apples everywhere.' Bedrooms in the main house are traditionally furnished, and have a 'good, unfussy' bathroom; those in the garden, each with a private patio, are more contemporary. All have a capsule coffee machine, and a fridge with fresh milk and bottled water. Travelling with family? Ask for a pair of interconnecting rooms. The kitchen garden is harvested daily for the fresh greens used in chef Nick Claxton-Webb's modern menus, perhaps Brie and roasted tomato tart, watercress, cured shallot salad; pan-roasted fillet of rainbow trout, baby gem, cocotte potatoes. 'We were very satisfied.' (Roger Viner)

Lynn Road
Grimston
King's Lynn
PE32 1AH

T: 01485 600250
F: 01485 601191
E: info@conghamhallhotel.co.uk
W: www.conghamhallhotel.co.uk

BEDROOMS: 26. 11 garden rooms, 1 suitable for disabled.
OPEN: all year.
FACILITIES: sitting room, bar, library, restaurant, free Wi-Fi, in-room TV (Freeview), civil wedding licence, conference facilities, terrace, spa, 12-metre swimming pool, 30-acre grounds, herb garden.
BACKGROUND MUSIC: 'mellow' in bar and restaurant.
LOCATION: 6 miles E of King's Lynn.
CHILDREN: all ages welcomed.
DOGS: allowed in some bedrooms, bar.
CREDIT CARDS: MasterCard, Visa.
PRICES: [2016] per room D,B&B £219–£349, room only (Mon–Thurs) £135–£260. À la carte £40. 1-night bookings sometimes refused.

KIRKBY LONSDALE Cumbria

Map 4: inset C2

SUN INN

In a historic market town just right for a potter, Lucy and Mark Fuller's 17th-century inn pleases dogs ('and their well-behaved owners') with its personable atmosphere. 'Because it's small, you can tell that the staff put in that extra care.' Downstairs, find log fires and leather chesterfields in the popular local pub; on the upper levels, 'delightfully decorated' bedrooms, some with beams and thick stone walls, mix contemporary style and handmade furniture. The character of the old building is charmingly present: one room has a doorway just five feet high. 'I couldn't hear a sound from the bar and restaurant downstairs.' Order a local real ale in the pub, then sample chef Sam Carter's three-course dinner, perhaps including suckling pig, red chicory, black pudding; beef shin, celeriac, creamed potatoes. 'Fantastic' breakfasts are ideal for a day's exploring the town, and the countryside further afield. A buffet holds juices, home-made granola, and bread and croissants from the town bakery; cooked options include local sausages. Rainy day? Ask to borrow boots and a mac for a riverside walk, with a view painted by Turner.

6 Market Street
Kirkby Lonsdale
LA6 2AU

T: 015242 71965
E: email@sun-inn.info
W: www.sun-inn.info

BEDROOMS: 11.
OPEN: all year except Christmas Day, restaurant closed Mon lunch.
FACILITIES: bar, restaurant, free Wi-Fi, in-room TV (Freeview, Internet TV in some rooms), unsuitable for disabled.
BACKGROUND MUSIC: all day in bar.
LOCATION: town centre.
CHILDREN: all ages welcomed.
DOGS: allowed (separate dog-friendly area in restaurant).
CREDIT CARDS: MasterCard, Visa.
PRICES: [2016] per room B&B £114–£189, D,B&B £176–£257. À la carte £34. 1-night bookings refused Sat.

KIRKBY STEPHEN Cumbria

AUGILL CASTLE

César award since 2016

With 'no rules – just plenty of warm, friendly staff, and wonderful food and service', Wendy and Simon Bennett's Victorian fantasy castle continues to win rave reviews. 'The magic of the castle lies in its owners. They're passionate about it, and rightly so.' In 'lovely' grounds, the hotel has 'a feeling of indulgence, without any ceremony – you're made to feel at home'. There are 'warm fires', a 'relaxing' lounge with a grand piano and music books, a cinema complete with popcorn; four nights a week, a dinner menu, 'sensibly limited in choice', is 'attractively served' and communally – some say rowdily – eaten. (Platters of local meats and cheeses are served on other nights.) 'We all made friends over dinner.' Choose among eclectic bedrooms, each more characterful than the other (though a guest this year thought housekeeping could be stepped up). 'Ours was beautifully decorated in period style, with a huge four-poster bed and an open fire; books and a chesterfield armchair in an anteroom; our very own turrets.' 'Breakfast is a nicely laid-back start to the day.' (Kris Didymus, Mike Long, and others)

25% DISCOUNT VOUCHERS

Leacett Lane
Brough
Kirkby Stephen
CA17 4DE

T: 01768 341937
E: office@stayinacastle.com
W: www.stayinacastle.com

BEDROOMS: 15. 2 on ground floor, 7 in stableyard conversion.
OPEN: all year, dinner served Mon/Wed/Fri/Sat depending on demand; cold platters on other nights, children's high tea every day.
FACILITIES: hall, drawing room, library (honesty bar), music (sitting) room, conservatory bar, dining room, cinema, free Wi-Fi, in-room TV (Freeview), civil wedding licence, 20-acre grounds (landscaped garden, tennis).
BACKGROUND MUSIC: none.
LOCATION: 3 miles NE of Kirkby Stephen.
CHILDREN: all ages welcomed.
DOGS: allowed in 2 bedrooms.
CREDIT CARDS: all major cards.
PRICES: [2016] per room B&B £160–£200. Set dinner £20–£25. 1-night bookings sometimes refused weekends.

LANGAR Nottinghamshire

LANGAR HALL

♀ César award since 2000

'High standards are faultlessly maintained' at
this somewhat eccentric, wholly likeable hotel
in the Vale of Belvoir. It was run with much
spirit by Imogen Skirving, the well-loved
chatelaine, until her sudden death in 2016; an
'enthusiastic young team' upholds her traditions.
Within the apricot-coloured house – bought
by the late owner's great-grandmother in 1860
– guests are greeted with 'thoughtfulness' and
'consideration'. 'The staff are attentive but never
intrusive.' Public rooms and bedrooms are 'well
furnished in a restrained country house style',
with fine paintings and antiques. 'The bedrooms
are individual, and contain some surprises.
Cartland has a step in the middle of the floor,
which can be a minor hazard for nocturnal
expeditions.' Take afternoon tea in the brightly
decorated garden room (while the children
play on the swings and trampoline outside); at
dinner, enjoy 'reliable' dishes – perhaps Langar
lamb, heritage baby beetroot, goat's curd – along
with an 'extensive' wine list. 'Game is excellent;
twice-baked cheese soufflé is equally good at
either end of the meal.' (Peter Jowitt)

Church Lane
Langar
NG13 9HG

T: 01949 860559
F: 01949 861045
E: info@langarhall.co.uk
W: www.langarhall.com

BEDROOMS: 12. 1 on ground floor,
1 in garden chalet.
OPEN: all year.
FACILITIES: sitting room, study,
library, bar, garden room,
restaurant, free Wi-Fi, in-room TV
(Freeview), civil wedding licence,
30-acre grounds (gardens, children's
play area), unsuitable for disabled.
BACKGROUND MUSIC: none.
LOCATION: 12 miles SE of
Nottingham.
CHILDREN: all ages welcomed, by
arrangement.
DOGS: small dogs on a lead
allowed by arrangement, not
unaccompanied.
CREDIT CARDS: MasterCard, Visa.
PRICES: [2016] per room B&B single
£100–£160, double £125–£225,
D,B&B rates available Sun, Mon
nights. Set dinner (Fri, Sat) £49.50,
other nights £25, à la carte £50.

LANGHO Lancashire

Map 4:D3

NORTHCOTE

Plush and 'convivial', this luxury hotel on the edge of the 'stunning' Ribble valley is 'an old favourite of local residents'. Settle in: newspapers are 'thoughtfully provided' for reading by the fire in the 'comfortable' public rooms; the seductive bar has a fine list of cocktails. Food is at the heart of the operation. In the Michelin-starred restaurant, chef/patron Nigel Haworth and Lisa Goodwin-Allen cook 'outstanding' modern dishes (including accomplished vegetarian menus) using organic produce from the kitchen garden. Try salt-baked celeriac, mushroom cigar, orchard apples; charcoal roast Herdwick lamb, spinach, pistachio crumble, Sicilian lemon marmalade. Stay the night in individually designed bedrooms in the 19th-century manor house or a garden lodge; the best have a private terrace. 'Our spacious room overlooked garden and countryside. We had a comfortable bed; plenty of storage and reading material.' In the morning, 'orders are taken for breakfast': freshly squeezed juices, home-made jam, home-baked bread; a 'comprehensive' list of cooked dishes, including Lancashire cheese soufflé. On the North West motorway network; ideally located for trips to and from Scotland.

Northcote Road
Langho
BB6 8BE

T: 01254 240555
F: 01254 246568
E: reception@northcote.com
W: www.northcote.com

BEDROOMS: 26. 8 in garden lodge, 8 on ground floor, 2 suitable for disabled.
OPEN: all year.
FACILITIES: lift, 2 lounges, cocktail bar, restaurant, private dining/meeting room, free Wi-Fi, in-room TV (Sky), civil wedding licence, 3-acre garden.
BACKGROUND MUSIC: in bar in evening.
LOCATION: 5½ miles N of Blackburn, on A59.
CHILDREN: all ages welcomed.
DOGS: not allowed.
CREDIT CARDS: Amex, MasterCard, Visa.
PRICES: [2016] per room B&B from £260, D,B&B from £325. Set dinner £68, tasting menu £88.

LASTINGHAM Yorkshire

Map 4:C4

LASTINGHAM GRANGE

César award since 1991

On the edge of the North York Moors, where the road merges into a bridle path, this 'excellent' traditional country hotel is run by the hospitable Wood family – brothers Bertie and Tom and their mother, Jane. Visitors remark on the 'outstanding' service. The 'old-fashioned' decor might not be for everyone, but fans say it is all part of the charm. Bedecked in floral prints, 'spotlessly clean and comfortable' bedrooms in the 17th-century farmhouse have extras such as a flask of cold milk provided every evening. Afternoon tea with warm scones, butter, jam and cream is served every day in the lounge or on the terrace overlooking the garden. In the evening, tuck in to hearty country fare. Chefs Paul Cattaneo and Sandra Thurlow cook a daily-changing menu; typical dishes might include poached fillet of halibut, Pernod hollandaise; roast duckling, sage and onion stuffing. Discover a good selection of Yorkshire cheeses, too, perhaps Monks Folly or a Swaledale Old Peculier. Full Yorkshire breakfasts in the morning are just right for 'superb walking on to the moors, straight from the hotel door'. (VF)

25% DISCOUNT VOUCHERS

High Street
Lastingham
YO62 6TH

T: 01751 417345
F: 01751 417358
E: reservations@lastinghamgrange.com
W: www.lastinghamgrange.com

BEDROOMS: 11. Plus self-catering cottage in village.
OPEN: Mar–end Nov.
FACILITIES: hall, lounge, dining room, laundry facilities, free Wi-Fi, in-room TV (Freeview), 10-acre grounds (terrace, garden, orchard, croquet, boules), unsuitable for disabled.
BACKGROUND MUSIC: none.
LOCATION: 5 miles NE of Kirkbymoorside.
CHILDREN: all ages welcomed (adventure playground, special meals), children under 12 stay free of charge if sharing parents' room; cots and extra beds provided.
DOGS: not allowed in dining room or unattended in bedrooms.
CREDIT CARDS: all major cards.
PRICES: [2016] per room B&B £210, D,B&B £275. Set dinner from £42.

LAVENHAM Suffolk

Map 2:C5

THE GREAT HOUSE

♥ César award since 2009

Behind a Georgian facade at the medieval heart of this 'incredibly beautiful' village sits a smart restaurant-with-rooms whose 'well-deserved reputation' for 'magnificent' modern French food draws fans. It is more than 30 years since Martine and Régis Crépy came from France to learn English, fell in love with Lavenham and bought this 14th-century timber-frame house. Today, 'welcoming', long-serving manager Thierry Pennec leads a team of 'professional and attentive' staff. 'The atmosphere is excellent: formal but also very friendly.' There is no lounge; up 'steep' stairs with a rope handrail, most of the characterful bedrooms have their own sitting area. Individually decorated, they have a platter of fruit and a decanter of sherry. Despite the 'low lighting for readers', in all there is 'an aura of comfort'. In the restaurant, Régis Crépy and Enrique Bilbault cook a seasonal menu, perhaps wild halibut, rhubarb gel, baby spinach fondue. A guest in 2016 wished for larger portions. 'Breakfast cost extra, but was enhanced by a wide selection of breads, meats, cheeses, eggs, yogurt and fruit.' (David Grant, and others)

Market Place
Lavenham
CO10 9QZ

T: 01787 247431
E: info@greathouse.co.uk
W: www.greathouse.co.uk

BEDROOMS: 5.
OPEN: Feb–Dec, except 2 weeks in summer, restaurant closed Sun night, Mon, Tues midday.
FACILITIES: lounge/bar, restaurant, free Wi-Fi, in-room TV (BT, Freeview), patio dining area, ½-acre garden, unsuitable for disabled.
BACKGROUND MUSIC: 'easy listening' in restaurant.
LOCATION: town centre. Free public car park.
CHILDREN: all ages welcomed.
DOGS: not allowed.
CREDIT CARDS: Amex, MasterCard, Visa.
PRICES: [2016] room £99–£215, continental buffet breakfast £12, plus £5 for cooked breakfast. Set dinner £36.50, à la carte £52 (Sat only). 1-night bookings sometimes refused Sat.

SEE ALSO SHORTLIST

LEAMINGTON SPA Warwickshire

Map 2:B2

EIGHT CLARENDON CRESCENT

'Gracious hospitality' awaits at Christine and David Lawson's 'good-value' B&B, in a 'peaceful' Regency villa near the town centre. 'The lively owners delight in sharing their space – you're treated as a house guest in a private home. No rules here; Christine encouraged us to enjoy the house,' say Guide inspectors in 2016. Beyond the discreet entrance ('no signage, just the number 8'), the house 'might not be totally immaculate, but all is comfortable, elegant, homely'. 'Beautifully furnished' rooms are filled with antiques, paintings and prints; guests are welcome to play the grand piano in the 'massive' sitting room. 'The secluded gardens and beautiful private dell at the back are particular delights on a sunny day.' 'Our spacious bedroom, up a wide staircase, had a standard double bed, two comfy upholstered chairs, a dressing table, a small TV. The bathroom lacked style but worked well, with a hot, powerful shower. Despite the creaky floorboards, we slept well.' Mornings, come down to a 'good (though fairly limited)' communal breakfast: muesli, yogurt, fruit, 'generous' glasses of juice; a full English with 'eggs any which way'.

8 Clarendon Crescent
Leamington Spa
CV32 5NR

T: 01926 429840
F: 01926 424641
E: lawson@lawson71.fsnet.co.uk
W: www.eightclarendoncrescent.
co.uk

BEDROOMS: 4.
OPEN: all year except Christmas–New Year, Easter, occasional holidays.
FACILITIES: drawing room, breakfast room, free Wi-Fi, in-room TV, ¾-acre garden (private dell), unsuitable for disabled.
BACKGROUND MUSIC: none.
LOCATION: close to centre.
CHILDREN: all ages welcomed, by arrangement.
DOGS: not allowed.
CREDIT CARDS: none.
PRICES: per room B&B single £50, double £85.

LEDBURY Herefordshire

Map 3:D5

THE FEATHERS

With ancient foundations, this black-and-white-timbered Tudor pile, on the High Street of a medieval town, has been run as an inn since at least 1564. Breathe in the past: owner David Elliston has preserved the charm of the 'lovely old building' in its thick beams, wattle-and-daub walls, 'quirky' staircase and creaky original floorboards, though not at the expense of modern comfort – the bathrooms were upgraded this year. Check in to the individually designed bedrooms – they are 'very good', guests say. In the oldest part of the inn, 'comfortable, clean' rooms have exposed beams and original 17th-century wall paintings; the newer, high-ceilinged Dancing Rooms (originally built in the 1850s) are bright and attractively furnished. In Quills restaurant, chef Suzie Isaacs serves an 'excellent' modern British menu, perhaps wild mushroom risotto cakes, winter-vegetable ragout; boar fillet, bubble and squeak, Madeira jus. Fuggles brasserie is a popular lunch spot with 'excellent' coffee. Embrace warmer weather with drinks in the walled garden. Breakfast has a 'good choice', 'cheerfully served'. Hotel guests enjoy free access to the spa. (DH, and others)

25% DISCOUNT VOUCHERS

High Street
Ledbury
HR8 1DS

T: 01531 635266
F: 01531 638955
E: enquiries@feathers-ledbury.co.uk
W: www.feathers-ledbury.co.uk

BEDROOMS: 22. 1 suite in cottage, also self-catering apartments.
OPEN: all year.
FACILITIES: lounge, bar, brasserie, restaurant, free Wi-Fi, in-room TV (Sky, Freeview), function facilities, spa (heated 10-metre swimming pool, whirlpool, gym), civil wedding licence, courtyard garden (fountain, alfresco eating), unsuitable for disabled.
BACKGROUND MUSIC: none.
LOCATION: town centre, parking.
CHILDREN: all ages welcomed.
DOGS: allowed in bedrooms and public areas, only guide dogs in restaurant and brasserie.
CREDIT CARDS: all major cards.
PRICES: [2016] per room B&B £155–£240, D,B&B £175–£270. À la carte £30.

LEWDOWN Devon

LEWTRENCHARD MANOR

Admirers of Sue and James Murray's 'characterful', 'beautiful old manor' continue to sing its praises. 'It is uniformly excellent, with high standards of hotel-keeping, comfort and service,' says a guest this year. 'Welcoming and hospitable', the Murrays 'create a very friendly atmosphere'; 'they are always on hand to give advice and answer any questions'. Once home to the Duke of Albemarle, 'the hotel is full of history, including lots of antiques, portraits and books'. Individually decorated bedrooms (an oversized sleigh bed in one, a roll-top bath in another; glossy magazines throughout) overlook parkland and hillside, woodland or gardens. At aperitif o'clock, nibble on canapés by the log fire in the bar – 'the owner served our drinks himself, chatting amicably' – before sitting down to an 'impeccable' dinner. Chef Matthew Peryer wins acclaim for his modern dishes, perhaps citrus-roasted pollack, home-grown parsley root, steamed mussels and clams. Fruit compotes, yogurt, freshly squeezed juice and 'copious' amounts of smoked salmon are served at table at breakfast; 'a great basket of various breads and freshly baked pastries just for the two of us'. (Richard Batson)

Lewdown
EX20 4PN

T: 01566 783222
F: 01566 783332
E: info@lewtrenchard.co.uk
W: www.lewtrenchard.co.uk

BEDROOMS: 14. 1 in folly, 4 with separate entrance, 1 suitable for disabled.
OPEN: all year.
FACILITIES: lounge, bar, library, restaurant, function facilities, free Wi-Fi, in-room TV (Freeview), civil wedding licence, 12-acre garden.
BACKGROUND MUSIC: none.
LOCATION: rural, 10 miles N of Tavistock.
CHILDREN: not under 8 at dinner.
DOGS: allowed in bedrooms (not unattended), not in restaurant.
CREDIT CARDS: Amex, MasterCard, Visa.
PRICES: [2016] per room B&B from £155, D,B&B from £245. Set dinner £49.50; 5-course tasting menu £69. 1-night bookings sometimes refused.

LICHFIELD Staffordshire

Map 2:A2

NETHERSTOWE HOUSE

Follow the 'dense, tree-lined' drive to find Ben Heathcote's 'excellent' small hotel 'well hidden' in a walled garden – guests are impressed by the peace and quiet. Formerly a watermill, the 19th-century building today has 'comfortable' sitting areas, 'eclectic in style but generally pleasing'. (Acceptance of the decor is eclectic as well: another guest said it 'verges on the camp'.) There's plenty of choice of accommodation. Bedrooms in the main house are individually styled; the 'spacious' penthouse in the eaves has exposed beams and skylights, and a freestanding bath in the bathroom. 'Well-appointed' modern apartments, ideal for a family, are in the courtyard. In 2016, seven 'petite' bedrooms were added in an adjacent lodge. In the evening, tables are set with white linens and napkins in the smart restaurant. Try chef Stephen Garland's modern British dishes, perhaps twice-baked cheese soufflé, cheddar gougère, pickled onion and cheese tuile; rump of Derbyshire lamb, leg croquette, sweet potato and rosemary. After something heartier? Informal steakhouse meals are taken in the cellar brasserie. 'The menu for cooked items at breakfast was the longest we've seen.' (Suzanne Lyons, and others)

25% DISCOUNT VOUCHERS

Netherstowe Lane
Lichfield
WS13 6AY

T: 01543 254270
F: 01543 419998
E: info@netherstowehouse.com
W: www.netherstowehouse.com

BEDROOMS: 16. 7 rooms in adjacent lodge, 5 on ground floor, plus 8 serviced apartments in annexe.
OPEN: all year, restaurant closed Sun dinner.
FACILITIES: 2 lounges, bar, 2 dining rooms, private dining room, free Wi-Fi, in-room TV (Freeview), gymnasium, 1-acre grounds, unsuitable for disabled.
BACKGROUND MUSIC: in public rooms.
LOCATION: 1 mile N of city centre.
CHILDREN: not under 12 overnight in hotel, but all ages welcomed in serviced apartments.
DOGS: not allowed.
CREDIT CARDS: Amex, MasterCard, Visa.
PRICES: [2016] per room B&B £89–£195, D,B&B £169–£215. Set menu £34–£40.

SEE ALSO SHORTLIST

LIFTON Devon

Map 1:C3

THE ARUNDELL ARMS

ᘓCésar award since 2006

You don't have to be into field sports to love this 'very nice' sporting hotel, but it helps. It is 55 years since Gerald and Anne Fox-Edwards bought the characterful former coaching inn and renowned fishing school. Today run by Adam and Tina Fox-Edwards, it has comfortable, 'unfussy' bedrooms equipped with tea- and coffee-making facilities, home-made biscuits, fleecy towels and posh toiletries. Four annexe rooms are in Church Cottage, once the village tailor's shop. In the main dining room, long-serving chef Steve Pidgeon cooks modern dishes based on seasonal West Country ingredients. Characteristic dishes: pan-fried turbot, Brixham scallops, saffron potatoes; fillet of Aylesbury duck, English rhubarb, baby vegetables. For a more informal meal, tuck in to imaginative pub fare while rubbing shoulders with locals in the popular bar. Be a good sport: the hotel has exclusive rights to 20 miles of river bank; ghillies David Pilkington and Alexander Jones are on hand to instruct novices with rod and line. An 18th-century cockfighting pit in the garden houses a rod and tackle shop. Shooting and deer stalking are also on offer.

25% DISCOUNT VOUCHERS

Fore Street
Lifton
PL16 0AA

T: 01566 784666
F: 01566 784494
E: reservations@arundellarms.com
W: www.arundellarms.com

BEDROOMS: 27. 4 on ground floor, 4 in Church Cottage opposite.
OPEN: all year.
FACILITIES: lounge, bar, village pub, restaurant, brasserie, private dining rooms, conference rooms, free Wi-Fi, in-room TV (Freeview), skittle alley, civil wedding licence, 1-acre garden (lake), 20 miles fishing rights on River Tamar and tributaries, unsuitable for disabled.
BACKGROUND MUSIC: none.
LOCATION: 3 miles E of Launceston.
CHILDREN: all ages welcomed.
DOGS: welcomed, not allowed in restaurant.
CREDIT CARDS: Amex, MasterCard, Visa.
PRICES: [2016] per person B&B from £98, D,B&B from £140. Set dinner from £25, à la carte £35.

LIVERPOOL Merseyside

Map 4:E2

2 BLACKBURNE TERRACE NEW

Behind a row of lime trees on a calm cobbled drive, there's style (and home-made sweets) aplenty at Glenn and Sarah Whitter's 'excellent' upmarket B&B. In a discreet Georgian town house, it is within walking distance of theatres, restaurants and the two cathedrals. 'The owners welcomed us warmly and gave us a tour of the house and all aspects of our room. Sloe gin and macaroons were waiting for us.' Lush modern bedrooms, individually designed, have original artwork and polished antiques. 'All are done to a high standard', with theatrical touches (here a deep-button velvet sofa or silk drapes, there a marble bathroom and an elegant slipper bath); all have 'top-quality' soaps and perfume. In the design-magazine-worthy drawing room, find 'an excellent range of local history books alongside an interesting collection of Irish literature'. In summer, take advantage of the quiet walled garden. At breakfast, taken communally at a large table set with silver cutlery, porcelain and crystal, 'an enormous buffet' awaits (croissants, pastries, natural yogurts, jars of cereals); choose from 'a wide range' of cooked dishes. (Donald Reid)

2 Blackburne Terrace
Liverpool
L8 7PJ

T: 0151 708 5474
E: info@2bbt.co.uk
W: www.2blackburneterrace.com

BEDROOMS: 4.
OPEN: all year.
FACILITIES: drawing room, dining room, free Wi-Fi, in-room TV, walled garden, unsuitable for disabled.
BACKGROUND MUSIC: none.
LOCATION: city centre.
CHILDREN: not under 10.
DOGS: not allowed.
CREDIT CARDS: Visa.
PRICES: [2016] per room B&B from £160.

SEE ALSO SHORTLIST

LODSWORTH Sussex

Map 2:E3

THE HALFWAY BRIDGE

Country pub meets boutique guest house at this brick-built 17th-century coaching inn within the South Downs national park. Owners Sam and Janet Bakose have refurbished it with style. Locals come for the heartening pub, all wooden floors, exposed brick walls, log fires, newspapers and real ales. Visitors from further away stay in beamed bedrooms in converted stables, where rustic decor combines with contemporary flourish and thoughtful touches (locally produced organic toiletries, fresh milk, a cafetière with a house blend of ground coffee). Soak in the peace of the countryside: despite the proximity of the A272, rooms are quiet, with views of garden and woods (watch out for deer). In the dining rooms, 'enthusiastic', smartly dressed staff provide 'first-class' service. Try chef Luke Gale's sophisticated modern pub food, perhaps Moroccan-style haloumi and butternut squash kebabs; pan-fried fillet of sea trout, leek and chive crushed potatoes, crisp seaweed. Breakfast is served till 10.30 am ('very civilised'); the 'wide range' of cooked dishes includes 'naughty' fried bread. Popular with walkers on the South Downs. More reports, please.

Lodsworth
GU28 9BP

T: 01798 861281
E: enquiries@halfwaybridge.co.uk
W: www.halfwaybridge.co.uk

BEDROOMS: 7. In converted barns.
OPEN: all year.
FACILITIES: bar, restaurant, free Wi-Fi, in-room TV (Freeview), small beer garden, unsuitable for disabled.
BACKGROUND MUSIC: 'quiet' in bar and restaurant.
LOCATION: 3 miles W of Petworth, on A272.
CHILDREN: all ages welcomed.
DOGS: allowed in bar, not in bedrooms.
CREDIT CARDS: Amex, MasterCard, Visa.
PRICES: [2016] per room B&B £140–£230. À la carte £32. 1-night bookings may be refused weekends.

LONG MELFORD Suffolk

LONG MELFORD SWAN `NEW`

'Intimate and stylish', this 'informal' restaurant-with-rooms, part of the family-run Stuart Inns group, enters the Guide on the recommendation of inspectors in 2016, who like the 'friendly, accommodating' spirit of the place. 'They pride themselves on being part of the community': the 'tastefully furnished' restaurant ('lots of local artwork') is a 'buzzy' local destination. 'Our excellent dinner included a likeable "soupe aux truffes"; we loved the seared Scottish hake.' 'Boutiquey' bedrooms (some up stairs 'a little tricky to climb') are in the main stone-built building and in Melford House next door. (No staff remain overnight.) 'Our room – newly refurbished, with a comfortable super-king-size bed – was decorated more like a home than a hotel room, with lots of lovely details, though no sitting area. In the immaculately furnished bathroom: large, fluffy towels; lovely English bath products; no robes, which would've been nice. One gripe: the fire-exit light above the door [only in main-house rooms] could disturb sleep.' Mornings, a 'very good' breakfast includes a 'delightfully nutty' granola. 'We particularly liked the smashed avocado and crispy egg on toast.'

Hall Street
Long Melford
CO10 9JQ

T: 01787 464545
E: info@longmelfordswan.co.uk
W: www.longmelfordswan.co.uk

BEDROOMS: 6. 4 in adjacent Melford House, 2 on ground floor.
OPEN: all year.
FACILITIES: bar, restaurant, free Wi-Fi, in-room TV, garden.
BACKGROUND MUSIC: all day in public areas.
LOCATION: village centre.
CHILDREN: all ages welcomed.
DOGS: allowed in bar only.
CREDIT CARDS: Amex, MasterCard, Visa.
PRICES: [2016] per room B&B single £90–£125, double £135–£175, D,B&B (based on double occupancy) £204–£244.

LONG SUTTON Somerset

Map 1:C6

THE DEVONSHIRE ARMS `NEW`

'Thoroughly recommended', Philip Mepham's 'pretty' inn on the village green enters the Guide this year thanks to praise from regular correspondents who applaud the 'friendly, efficient' staff, 'comfortable' rooms and 'generous' portions of 'excellent' country meals. The former hunting lodge has been smartly decorated: framed prints, deep-red leather banquettes, fresh flowers, open fires; a clubby restaurant, all wood floors and gentlemanly panelling. Locals enjoy the craft ales and daily newspapers at the bar; the quick-witted or swift-footed might get one of the armchairs by the fireplace. On fine days, the courtyard garden's the place, with croquet, boules, garden Jenga. Eat in: the food is 'first class', perhaps 'wonderfully tender (and fat free!)' lamb shoulder; 'happy-making' duck pâté and roast wood pigeon. Retire, afterwards, to a tastefully decorated bedroom (larger ones can accommodate a child's bed). 'We slept well in our good-sized room, with a comfy four-poster bed, and two armchairs by the large window overlooking the village green. Adequate storage space; a freestanding bath and walk-in shower in the big bathroom.' (Peter Anderson)

Long Sutton
TA10 9LP

T: 01458 241271
E: info@thedevonshirearms.com
W: www.thedevonshirearms.com

BEDROOMS: 9. 2, on ground floor, in annexe behind main building.
OPEN: all year except 25/26 Dec.
FACILITIES: open-plan bar and restaurant, private dining room, free Wi-Fi, in-room TV (Freeview), courtyard, garden (croquet lawn), only public areas suitable for disabled.
BACKGROUND MUSIC: in bar.
LOCATION: by the village green.
CHILDREN: all ages welcomed.
DOGS: allowed in bar only.
CREDIT CARDS: MasterCard, Visa.
PRICES: per room B&B from £100, D,B&B from £165. À la carte £28.50. 1-night bookings sometimes refused weekends.

LONGHORSLEY Northumberland

Map 4:B3

THISTLEYHAUGH FARM

César award since 2011

Get back to the land at Enid Nelless's 'beautiful', rustic B&B close to the banks of the River Coquet. The Nelless family have farmed locally for three generations; the creeper-clad Georgian farmhouse stands in a 'peaceful' spot on the family's 720-acre organic livestock farm. (Remote, too – bring a good map.) Pictures and antiques adorn the pretty, traditionally furnished bedrooms; extra touches include fresh milk and home-baked biscuits. After a day's romping in the countryside ('take time to admire the sheep'), help yourself to a glass of sherry in the lounge before sitting down to a hearty roast, perhaps of Thistleyhaugh lamb shoulder, at 7 pm. Cooked by the hostess and her daughter-in-law, Zoë, the communal dinner with 'interesting' fellow guests can be 'great fun' – a fine accompaniment to the 'excellent hospitality and cooking'. At breakfast, fresh fruit, cereals and yogurt are followed by cooked dishes including a full English and Craster kippers. A good base for exploring the gardens at Alnwick and Howick Hall; the coast is half an hour away. (M Arnold, Gwyn Morgan)

25% DISCOUNT VOUCHERS

Longhorsley
NE65 8RG

T: 01665 570629
E: thistleyhaugh@hotmail.com
W: www.thistleyhaugh.co.uk

BEDROOMS: 5.
OPEN: all year except Christmas/ New Year, Jan, dining room closed Sat eve.
FACILITIES: 2 lounges, garden room, dining room, free Wi-Fi, in-room TV (Freeview), ¼-acre garden (summer house), fishing, shooting, golf, riding nearby, unsuitable for disabled.
BACKGROUND MUSIC: none.
LOCATION: 10 miles N of Morpeth, W of A697.
CHILDREN: all ages welcomed.
DOGS: not allowed (kennels nearby).
CREDIT CARDS: MasterCard, Visa.
PRICES: per person B&B £50, D,B&B £75.

LOOE Cornwall

Map

THE BEACH HOUSE

Take in the panorama over tea and home-made cake in the garden room whatever time you arrive: from sunrise to sunset, the views at this 'ideally located' seafront B&B are spectacular. Rosie and David Reeve are the 'superb' hosts. Individually decorated, the 'spotlessly clean' bedrooms draw the view inside with a beachy palette (sea blue, sandstone, sunset orange), cushioned handmade bamboo chairs, original seascapes. Three bedrooms are sea-facing; two have garden access. Ground-floor Whitsand has bay windows with sea views, a furnished patio. All rooms have an en suite bathroom; tea- and coffee-making facilities, a fridge with fresh milk, bottled Cornish water 'regularly replenished'. Breakfast is 'delightful': pick and mix from a comprehensive buffet of fresh fruit, home-made muffins and yogurt; from the kitchen, choose French toast, smoked salmon or Cornish sausages. Ask for recommended restaurants in nearby Looe; the Reeves also have advice to share on energetic day-trips to Polperro (the South West Coastal Path runs past the front gate). Beachcombers should take the steps down to the sandy beach to investigate the rock pools. More reports, please.

Marine Drive
Hannafore
Looe
PL13 2DH

T: 01503 262598
F: 01503 262298
E: enquiries@thebeachhouselooe
   .co.uk
W: www.thebeachhouselooe.co.uk

BEDROOMS: 5.
OPEN: all year except 23–25 Dec.
FACILITIES: garden room, breakfast room, free Wi-Fi, terrace, ½-acre garden, beach opposite, unsuitable for disabled.
BACKGROUND MUSIC: classical radio in dining room.
LOCATION: ½ mile from centre.
CHILDREN: children over 16 welcomed.
DOGS: not allowed.
CREDIT CARDS: MasterCard, Visa.
PRICES: [2016] per room B&B £85–£135. 1-night bookings refused weekends, high season.

LOOE Cornwall

Map 1:D3

TRELASKE HOTEL & RESTAURANT

NEW

'A feeling of tranquillity' prevails at Hazel Billington and Ross Lewin's 'exceptional' small hotel in a quiet spot between two historic fishing ports – 'just what you need when you're trying to get away from the city'. 'We were impressed by Hazel's warm welcome and Ross's cooking,' say Guide readers in 2016. Many agree, and 'most who come to stay, return'. 'Spacious' bedrooms have a balcony or patio; throughout, 'the attention to detail is second to none'. 'Our garden room had huge picture windows with lovely views of the grounds and the fields beyond.' Come dinnertime, Ross Lewin – 'a genius in the kitchen' – plans his Mediterranean-inspired menus around the catch of the day, perhaps Looe lemon sole, crushed new potatoes, chives. 'It's always a joy to read the ever-changing menu; fish lovers can have a different fish dish every evening.' In the morning, sample 'the best breakfast we've ever had'; lucky guests might be able to save a taste for later. 'We've taken home their home-made spiced muesli and home-baked rosemary and sea salt loaf.' (Yvonne Waite, and others)

Polperro Road
Looe
PL13 2JS

T: 01503 262159
E: info@trelaske.co.uk
W: www.trelaske.co.uk

BEDROOMS: 7. 4 garden rooms, on ground floor, in adjacent building.
OPEN: all year except Christmas/New Year, Jan, Feb.
FACILITIES: 2 lounges, bar/conservatory, free Wi-Fi (in main house), in-room TV (Freeview), function facilities, terrace (summer barbecues), 4-acre grounds, unsuitable for disabled.
BACKGROUND MUSIC: in lounge bar and restaurant during breakfast and dinner.
LOCATION: 2 miles W of Looe, 3 miles NE of Polperro.
CHILDREN: all ages welcomed (no under-4s in restaurant).
DOGS: allowed in 2 bedrooms (£7.50 per night), not in public rooms.
CREDIT CARDS: Amex, MasterCard, Visa.
PRICES: [2016] per room B&B £120, D,B&B £180. Set dinner £27.50–£33.50.

LORTON Cumbria

NEW HOUSE FARM

'People go to the Lakes for beauty, peace and solitude. New House Farm has all of this in abundance.' Close to Wordsworth's birthplace, Hazel Thompson's 'beautifully restored' Grade II listed 17th-century farmhouse marries the romance of tradition with the comfort of modern amenities. While the vast, fells-flanked setting is expansive, the house is warm and cosseting, with oak beams, flagged floors, an open stone fireplace. Check in to bedrooms individually decorated with rich red fabrics and dark wood furniture. The Stable Room has a king-size four-poster bed and uninterrupted views towards Fellbarrow and Low Fell; the Old Dairy has quirky tapestries, a Victorian bathroom with a slipper bath. Book the hot tub in the 'wonderful' gardens with views of the fells. At dinner, the hostess cooks traditional English dishes, perhaps local poached salmon, pesto sauce; ginger pudding, butterscotch sauce. Start the day with croissants 'straight from the Aga'. A reliable Cumbrian base: stop in the market town of Cockermouth on your way to St Bees, where the Coast to Coast Walk begins. More reports, please.

Lorton
CA13 9UU

T: 07841 159818
E: hazel@newhouse-farm.co.uk
W: www.newhouse-farm.com

BEDROOMS: 5. 1 in stable, 1 in Old Dairy.
OPEN: all year.
FACILITIES: 3 lounges, dining room, free Wi-Fi in main house, civil wedding licence, 17-acre grounds (garden, hot tub, streams, woods, field, lake and river, safe bathing 2 miles), unsuitable for disabled.
BACKGROUND MUSIC: none.
LOCATION: on B5289, 2 miles S of Lorton.
CHILDREN: not under 6.
DOGS: 'clean and dry' dogs allowed in bedrooms (£20 charge per night), not in public rooms.
CREDIT CARDS: MasterCard, Visa.
PRICES: [2016] per room B&B from £120.

LOUTH Lincolnshire

THE OLD RECTORY AT STEWTON

'Charming' owners Alan and Linda Palmer run their 'excellent-value' B&B in an early Victorian former rectory, 'with an attention to detail that is second to none'. 'The location is perfect – at the end of a country lane, yet close to the beautiful Georgian town.' Bedrooms may be old-fashioned, but they're 'clean and comfortable', and stocked with biscuits, bottled water, filter coffee and a selection of teas. Travelling with children? A suite with a sofa bed and a private sitting room can accommodate a family. At breakfast, tuck in to Lincolnshire sausages, smoked haddock, kippers, local eggs any way. Relax in the traditionally decorated sitting room (fresh flowers, books, leather sofas), or head out into the peaceful surroundings. The large, mature gardens, regularly visited by finches, pheasants, squirrels and the odd heron, are just right for a late-morning potter; the Lincolnshire Wolds, ideal for a ramble, are on the doorstep; the wild coast is just a few miles away. Cyclists and walkers are welcomed, and may use the drying facilities. (Stephen Murfitt, and others)

Stewton
Louth
LN11 8SF

T: 01507 328063
E: alanjpalmer100@aol.com
W: www.louthbedandbreakfast.
   co.uk

BEDROOMS: 3.
OPEN: all year except Christmas–New Year.
FACILITIES: sitting room, breakfast room, conservatory, free Wi-Fi, in-room TV (Freeview), 3-acre garden, unsuitable for disabled.
BACKGROUND MUSIC: none.
LOCATION: in the countryside, 2½ miles SE of Louth.
CHILDREN: all ages welcomed.
DOGS: allowed (£10 charge, owners provide bedding and food).
CREDIT CARDS: MasterCard, Visa.
PRICES: [2016] per room B&B £75–£85.

LOWER BOCKHAMPTON Dorset

Map 1:D6

YALBURY COTTAGE

♛ César award since 2015

'Comfortable' cottage-style bedrooms, 'first-class' food, 'friendly, efficient, helpful' staff and a 'cosy' atmosphere combine to form one 'lovely little hotel', say 'delighted' guests. Ariane and Jamie Jones run their restaurant-with-rooms in their 18th-century family home at the heart of Thomas Hardy country (the name recalls Yalbury Wood in Under the Greenwood Tree). Book ahead for a seat in the popular restaurant: Jamie Jones's 'delicious, beautifully presented' dishes – 'the chef has an eye for a picture' – attract much attention. 'We enjoyed a delicious fillet of aged beef with horseradish croquette potatoes; the Dorset plaice fillet came with creamy saffron mash.' Each of the simply decorated bedrooms looks out over the garden or surrounding countryside. 'Our spacious room under the thatch had a good-sized bathroom with a monsoon shower over the bath.' A guest this year wished for more efficient heating. Rise and shine with 'delicious home-made chunky marmalade, freshly squeezed juices, and a good country breakfast with thick bacon, herby sausages and little vine tomatoes'. (Peter Anderson, CJ, Gwyn Morgan)

25% DISCOUNT VOUCHERS

Lower Bockhampton
DT2 8PZ

T: 01305 262382
E: enquiries@yalburycottage.com
W: www.yalburycottage.com

BEDROOMS: 8. 6 on ground floor.
OPEN: all year except 23 Dec–20 Jan.
FACILITIES: lounge, restaurant, free Wi-Fi (in bedrooms), in-room TV (Freeview), garden with outdoor seating, unsuitable for disabled.
BACKGROUND MUSIC: 'easy listening' in lounge from 6 pm.
LOCATION: 2 miles E of Dorchester.
CHILDREN: all ages welcomed, no under-12s in restaurant after 8 pm.
DOGS: not in restaurant.
CREDIT CARDS: MasterCard, Visa.
PRICES: per room B&B single £75–£85, double £99–£120, D,B&B single £99–£115, double £160–£180. À la carte £37.50.

LUDLOW Shropshire

Map 3:C4

THE CLIVE
NEW

'It never fails to impress,' say regular readers this year, about this 'excellent-value' restaurant-with-rooms. Besides the 'friendly, efficient' staff and 'comfortable' bedrooms, 'the food is very good'. No wonder: part of the Oakly Park Estate of vast farmland, the 18th-century farmhouse neighbours the Ludlow Food Centre, that larger-than-life larder of local produce, treats and delicacies. Popular locally, the smart restaurant uses much seasonal produce and estate-reared meat. 'We had scallops with risotto; lamb; individual beef Wellingtons; a generous portion of apple crumble – all excellent.' A bar menu of light bites and comfort food satisfies diners looking for more informal meals. Stay in a modern bedroom in one of the converted barns around the neat courtyard – each is thoughtfully stocked with leaf teas, cafetière coffee, bathrobes and slippers. 'Our first-floor room wasn't the most spacious, but was perfectly adequate. Plenty of storage space in the big bathroom; a powerful shower over the bath.' In the morning, breakfast awaits in sister café, the Ludlow Kitchen, steps away: freshly baked breads, award-winning preserves, custom-blended coffee. (Peter Anderson)

Bromfield
Ludlow
SY8 2JR

T: 01584 856565
E: reservations@theclive.co.uk
W: www.theclive.co.uk

BEDROOMS: 15. All in adjoining annexes, some on ground floor, 1 suitable for disabled.
OPEN: all year except 24–26, 31 Dec.
FACILITIES: bar, restaurant, free Wi-Fi, in-room TV, conference room, courtyard.
BACKGROUND MUSIC: in public areas.
LOCATION: 4 miles NW of Ludlow.
CHILDREN: all ages welcomed.
DOGS: allowed in 1 bedroom, bar, not in restaurant.
CREDIT CARDS: all major cards.
PRICES: [2016] per room B&B £112.50–£172.50, D,B&B £162.50–£222.50. À la carte £28.

SEE ALSO SHORTLIST

LUDLOW Shropshire

Map 3:C4

OLD DOWNTON LODGE

'A stunning place for a special stay', Willem and Pippa Vlok's 'tranquil' restaurant-with-rooms in rolling countryside is praised for its 'exceptional staff', 'warm welcome' and 'fabulous food'. 'A lot of thought has gone into the design,' Guide inspectors say. Bedrooms are spread across a cluster of 'well-converted' farm buildings set around a courtyard garden. 'Up a short flight of stairs, our rustic room had high-tech touches (automatic lighting on the stairs, etc). It had a soaring ceiling, exposed stone walls, a super-king-size bed with tasteful fabrics.' Across the gardens, step into the 'stunning' lounge/bar before sitting down to chef Karl Martin's daily-changing five- or seven-course tasting menus. 'Dinner is quite something: delicate, with wonderful flavours; a flight of tasting wines if desired.' In the morning, enjoy a 'wholesome' breakfast with home-made marmalade, 'good portions' of smoked salmon and scrambled eggs. Walks abound, for afterwards. Take in the 'panoramic vistas peppered with sheep and lambs'; Leintwardine village is three miles away, across 'gently invigorating terrain'. (James Vincent, Roger McKechnie)

25% DISCOUNT VOUCHERS

Downton on the Rock
Ludlow
SY8 2HU

T: 01568 771826
E: bookings@olddowntonlodge.
   com
W: www.olddowntonlodge.com

BEDROOMS: 10. In buildings around courtyard.
OPEN: all year, except Christmas, restaurant closed Sun, Mon.
FACILITIES: sitting room, dining room, museum/function room, free Wi-Fi in public areas, in-room TV (Freeview), civil wedding licence, ½-acre courtyard, unsuitable for disabled.
BACKGROUND MUSIC: soft classical in sitting room and dining room.
LOCATION: 6 miles W of Ludlow.
CHILDREN: not under 12.
DOGS: allowed in some bedrooms by prior arrangement.
CREDIT CARDS: MasterCard, Visa.
PRICES: [2016] per room B&B £125, D,B&B £180. Tasting menus £40–£50.

SEE ALSO SHORTLIST

LURGASHALL Sussex

Map 2:E3

THE BARN AT ROUNDHURST

Set on a 'neat and tidy' organic farm within the South Downs national park, Moya and Richard Connell's 'beautifully decorated' B&B is a peaceful spot. Guide inspectors, who were 'pleasantly' welcomed with tea and home-made shortbread, found an 'impressive' 17th-century barn – the heart of the operation – and 'relaxing' bedrooms set around a 'secluded' courtyard. Enter the 'enormous, soaring' space to find modern art, magazines, plenty of 'comfy' seating; up a winding staircase, there are board games, DVDs, a library, an honesty bar. Bedrooms, each with its own patio, have been thoughtfully designed: 'the lighting is intimate; the twin-strength mirror is good for make-up; the desk has useful sockets for laptops'. Four nights a week, stay in for a four-course set dinner, perhaps with beef from the farm, wild mushrooms, pommes Anna. (Cold platters are available on other evenings.) Breakfast is a 'perfect' way to wake: bread, jams and muffins are home made; honey is local; early risers can collect eggs from the resident hens. 'Wonderful walks with exquisite views' all around – ask for a picnic before heading off.

25% DISCOUNT VOUCHERS

Lower Roundhurst Farm
Jobson's Lane
Lurgashall
GU27 3BY

T: 01428 642535
E: bookings@thebarnatroundhurst.com
W: thebarnatroundhurst.com

BEDROOMS: 6.
OPEN: all year.
FACILITIES: open-plan lounge/dining area, library/bar, free Wi-Fi, in-room TV (Freeview), small garden on 250-acre farm.
BACKGROUND MUSIC: mixed in lounge.
LOCATION: 2 miles S of Haslemere, Surrey.
CHILDREN: all ages welcomed.
DOGS: not allowed.
CREDIT CARDS: all major cards.
PRICES: [2016] per room B&B £150–£200. Set menu £40.

LYMINGTON Hampshire

BRITANNIA HOUSE

Step inside this 'quirky' B&B, infused with host Tobias 'Tobi' Feilke's personality: a collection of hats and a suit of armour stand ready to greet guests. Further in, find 'a warm and homely environment'. The first-floor sitting room, with views of Solent and marina, has comfy sofas, books, magazines, fresh flowers. Bedrooms, some in a newer building opposite, are lavishly styled with antiques, gilded mirrors, drapes, paintings. Each is individually decorated: the gold-and-black Britannia suite has a large bathroom; a courtyard suite, hand painted in eau de nil, overlooks 'lush' evergreens. 'Certainly not bland or impersonal, our delightful room had high-quality bedlinen and towels.' Head out to explore – the B&B is but a stroll to the quay and harbour; the New Forest is a five-minute drive away. An 'enthusiastic' host, Tobi Feilke has plenty of advice to offer on local restaurants and places of interest. In the morning, mingle with fellow guests around the communal breakfast table in the bright, farmhouse-style kitchen, while tucking in to fresh fruits, yogurts, leaf teas, cafetière coffee; an 'exceptional' cooked breakfast straight from the stove. (Jane and Dave Wainwright, and others)

25% DISCOUNT VOUCHERS

Station Street
Lymington
SO41 3BA

T: 01590 672091
E: enquiries@britannia-house.com
W: www.britannia-house.com

BEDROOMS: 5. 2 on ground floor.
OPEN: all year.
FACILITIES: lounge, kitchen/breakfast room, free Wi-Fi, in-room TV (Freeview), courtyard garden, parking, unsuitable for disabled.
BACKGROUND MUSIC: none.
LOCATION: 2 mins' walk from High Street/quayside, close to station.
CHILDREN: not under 8.
DOGS: not allowed.
CREDIT CARDS: MasterCard, Visa.
PRICES: [2016] per room B&B £90–£119. 1-night bookings refused weekends.

LYNDHURST Hampshire

Map 2:E2

LIME WOOD

'Stunning', super-hip yet utterly serene, this country house hotel and spa in the heart of the New Forest is a sophisticated, rustic playground for the stylish set. The Regency manor house and its collection of lodges and cottages stand in extensive grounds adjoining forest and parkland. Strike a vriksasana pose in the rooftop herb garden, jog around the gardens with a personal trainer, lie back for Ayurvedic and holistic therapies in the spa, learn tricks of the culinary trade in the new cooking school. All is 'relaxed' yet 'professional'; 'extremely friendly' staff ensure 'a lack of airs and graces'. The bedrooms, in calm-inducing colours, have been designed for countryside cocooning. Pick a main-house room overlooking woodland, or go deep: forest cottages for families and larger groups blend into their surroundings. With chefs Angela Hartnett and Luke Holder, the Italian-inflected food is 'superb': tortellini, nduja, buttered cock crab at dinner; omelettes with garden herbs in the morning. Children are made very welcome: bikes and trikes are available to borrow, family foraging courses are like a forest treasure hunt. (John Walton, and others)

Beaulieu Road
Lyndhurst
SO43 7FZ

T: 02380 287177
F: 02380 287199
E: info@limewood.co.uk
W: www.limewoodhotel.co.uk

BEDROOMS: 32. 5 on ground floor, 2 suitable for disabled, 16 in pavilions and cottages in the grounds.
OPEN: all year.
FACILITIES: lifts, 2 bars, 3 lounges, 2 restaurants, private dining rooms, free Wi-Fi, in-room TV (Freeview), civil wedding licence, spa (16-metre swimming pool), 14-acre gardens (outdoor hot pool), cookery school.
BACKGROUND MUSIC: all day in public areas.
LOCATION: in New Forest, 12 miles SW of Southampton.
CHILDREN: all ages welcomed.
DOGS: allowed in outside bedrooms, not in main house.
CREDIT CARDS: MasterCard, Visa.
PRICES: room from £330. Breakfast £16.50–£25, à la carte £65. 1-night bookings refused most weekends, bank holidays.

MARGATE Kent

Map 2:D5

SANDS HOTEL

'Sympathetically and stylishly refurbished', Nick Conington's Victorian seafront hotel is 'on top of its game', say Guide readers in 2016. 'The hotel has been impeccably maintained. Its young staff seem invested in the place, demonstrating effortless people skills and showing genuine interest in guests.' Local residents, who come for the 'striking', 'contemporary' restaurant and bar, give it 'a low-key buzz' (though one guest on a birthday celebration found herself 'stuffed cheek by jowl' among other partygoers). Head upstairs to 'peaceful, airy' bedrooms ('with flamboyant touches'); many have 'marvellous' views over the bay. 'Our smaller double room had plenty of space. The luxurious bathroom had a lovely hot power shower, and plump bathrobes and towels. At turn-down, herbal teabags were a nice touch.' 'Tasty, skilfully cooked' dinners have 'very fresh' fish – 'as you'd hope at the seaside' – and, oh, 'that' view: 'We loved looking out over the sea and the illuminated harbour.' Breakfast is 'a treat': an 'exceptionally fine selection of fresh fruit'; 'nice' porridge; 'the best black pudding I've sampled in recent years'. (Sara Hollowell, Anna and Bill Brewer)

16 Marine Drive
Margate
CT9 1DH

T: 01843 228228
E: info@sandshotelmargate.co.uk
W: www.sandshotelmargate.co.uk

BEDROOMS: 20. 1 suitable for disabled.
OPEN: all year.
FACILITIES: lift, bar, restaurant, free Wi-Fi, in-room TV, civil wedding licence, roof terrace, ice cream parlour.
BACKGROUND MUSIC: varied, in public areas.
LOCATION: town centre.
CHILDREN: all ages welcomed (family rooms, children's menus).
DOGS: not allowed.
CREDIT CARDS: MasterCard, Visa.
PRICES: [2016] per room B&B £120–£200. À la carte £32.

SEE ALSO SHORTLIST

MARKET DRAYTON Shropshire

Map 3:B5

GOLDSTONE HALL **NEW**

'Intimate and informal, this characterful, family-run Georgian manor house fits the bill for quiet weekends away,' say Guide inspectors in 2016. In 'lovely, well-kept grounds, with an extraordinary kitchen garden', the 'uniformly brilliant' hotel was founded by Helen Ward over 30 years ago. Today, son John Cushing is at the helm; 'his daughter Victoria, chatty and hospitable, clearly enjoys people'. 'We were greeted at the door with a welcoming smile (no check-in desk – a nice touch).' The 'inviting' lounges have sofas, leather chairs, 'a roaring log fire'; tables are 'nicely spaced' in the restaurant, where 'beautifully presented' modern meals use trugfuls of home-grown vegetables and fruit. 'A local cheese platter rounded it off.' Smart bedrooms, including a top-floor family suite, are kitted out with fresh milk and home-made cookies. 'Our tastefully furnished room had a small sitting area; a deep bath in the bathroom; a delightful view of the grounds. We could've slept for days in the super-comfy bed.' Do wake: breakfast is 'delicious': 'home-baked bread; a nice buffet; perfectly poached eggs; excellent home-made veggie sausages with tasty Staffordshire oatcakes'. (Peter Iles, and others)

Goldstone Road
Market Drayton
TF9 2NA

T: 01630 661202
F: 01630 661585
E: enquiries@goldstonehall.com
W: www.goldstonehall.com

BEDROOMS: 12.
OPEN: all year except Christmas.
FACILITIES: bar, lounge, drawing room, dining room, orangery, free Wi-Fi, in-room TV (Sky), function facilities, civil wedding licence, 5 acres of grounds (walled garden, kitchen garden), unsuitable for disabled.
BACKGROUND MUSIC: in bar and dining room.
LOCATION: 5 miles S of Market Drayton.
CHILDREN: all ages welcomed (toys and dressing gowns provided).
DOGS: not allowed.
CREDIT CARDS: MasterCard, Visa.
PRICES: per room B&B single £90–£110, double £150–£180, D,B&B single £135–£155, double £230–£260. Set dinner £45.

MARTINHOE Devon

Map 1:B4

HEDDON'S GATE HOTEL [NEW]

'Utterly peaceful', with 'fabulous views' of
the hidden Heddon valley, Mark and Pat
Cowell's 'unpretentious' hotel 'brings back
the feel of country living'. 'Under these
new owners, it's exceeded the qualities that
originally earned it a place in the Guide,' writes
a regular correspondent, whose compelling
recommendation wins it a renewed full entry.
Inspectors in 2016 were 'warmly welcomed'
by the 'enthusiastic, hands-on' host. 'Mark
gave us a tour of the house, and insisted on
carrying our bags. Our large, bright room, in
the newly redecorated wing, had a comfortable
bed and crisp linen; plentiful hot water in the
bathroom. We watched the deer in the woods
from dual-aspect windows.' Mobile and Wi-Fi
signals aren't the strongest: 'Best to forget the
digital world and just relax.' After a day's
'spectacular' walking, sit down to an 'enjoyable'
dinner, perhaps 'tasty grilled asparagus with a
poached egg and Parmesan crisp; well-cooked
plaice, local new potatoes'. Breakfast brings
'lovely, runny' scrambled eggs, 'first-class'
smoked salmon, freshly squeezed orange juice.
'A welcome revival.' (Sue and Mark Foster, E
Whatley, and others)

25% DISCOUNT VOUCHERS

Martinhoe
EX31 4PZ

T: 01598 763481
E: stay@heddonsgatehotel.co.uk
W: www.heddonsgatehotel.co.uk

BEDROOMS: 11.
OPEN: 12 Feb–13 Nov, group
bookings over Christmas and New
Year.
FACILITIES: lounge, bar, TV room,
library, breakfast/dining room,
free Wi-Fi in public areas, in-room
TV (Freeview), terrace, 2½-acre
grounds, unsuitable for disabled.
No mobile phone signal; guests may
use the landline free of charge.
BACKGROUND MUSIC: none.
LOCATION: 6 miles W of Lynton.
CHILDREN: all ages welcomed.
DOGS: allowed in bedrooms (not
unattended), not in dining room.
CREDIT CARDS: Amex, MasterCard,
Visa.
PRICES: [2016] per room B&B
£110–£150, D,B&B £140–£180. Set
dinner £27.

MARTINHOE Devon

Map 1:B4

THE OLD RECTORY HOTEL

César award since 2014

'Huw Rees and Sam Prosser, two perfectionists, have created a great place where every guest feels very welcome,' say visitors this year, of this 'beautiful' hotel close to the Exmoor coast. More accolades: 'It's a well-planned operation, with everything fine tuned to offer the best service. Sam, as front-of-house, is attentive; the staff are all friendly.' Fans like the 'intimate country house atmosphere' – many return annually to find old friends. Check in to 'warm, delightful' bedrooms; beds are 'very comfortable'; extras include cafetière coffee and a digital radio. 'We had our best sleep for years.' At dinner, Huw Rees's 'homely, well-cooked', 'reasonably priced' dishes use locally sourced meats, fish and seafood, perhaps Ilfracombe crab, lime and avocado cocktail; fillet of Red Ruby Devon beef, chateaubriand sauce. In the morning, tuck in to an 'excellent' breakfast (local apple juice, home-made marmalade, fruit smoothies) before heading out to explore: National Trust land surrounds. Plan well: 'Hugh's cakes, at the complimentary afternoon tea, are worth returning early for!' (Shirley and Brian Johns, Mary Coles, Roger Down)

25% DISCOUNT VOUCHERS

Berry's Ground Lane
Martinhoe
EX31 4QT

T: 01598 763368
E: reception@oldrectoryhotel.co.uk
W: www.oldrectoryhotel.co.uk

BEDROOMS: 11. 2 on ground floor, 3 in coach house.
OPEN: Mar–end Oct.
FACILITIES: 2 lounges, orangery, dining room, free Wi-Fi, in-room TV (Freeview), 3-acre grounds.
BACKGROUND MUSIC: 'very quiet jazz' in dining room 'so it doesn't feel like a hushed morgue'.
LOCATION: 4 miles W of Lynton.
CHILDREN: not under 14.
DOGS: not allowed.
CREDIT CARDS: Amex, MasterCard, Visa.
PRICES: per room B&B from £180, D,B&B from £205. À la carte £29.95.

MASHAM Yorkshire

Map 4:D4

SWINTON PARK

♀César award since 2011

'The first sight of the hotel is superb': preening in sweeping grounds with parkland, lakes, a herd of fallow deer and an impressive walled garden, this mock-Gothic castle recreates an 'authentic stately-home experience' for its guests. The ancestral seat of the Earl of Swinton, the luxury hotel is part of the vast Swinton Estate, which unfurls from the River Ure towards the moorland dales. Mark and Felicity Cunliffe-Lister run it in a 'warm', 'unfussy' style. There are antiques, oriental carpets, family portraits and complimentary refreshments in the public rooms; children will find much to like in the ready supply of toys, kites, bikes and games. Upstairs, bedrooms have 'everything we could ever need' – including help-yourself bottles of sloe gin. Choose well: the best rooms are lavishly decorated, with views stretching over the park. In the evening, dinner in the gold-ceilinged dining room is 'exquisite'. Inspired by the fruit, vegetables and herbs grown in the garden, chef Simon Crannage's menus might include salt-baked celeriac, rhubarb, egg, lovage; Masham lamb rump, artichoke, wild garlic. More reports, please.

Masham
HG4 4JH

T: 01765 680900
F: 01765 680901
E: reservations@swintonpark.com
W: www.swintonpark.com

BEDROOMS: 31. 4 suitable for disabled.
OPEN: all year, restaurant closed midday Mon–Fri.
FACILITIES: lift, 3 lounges, library, bar, restaurant, free Wi-Fi, in-room TV (Freeview), banqueting hall, spa, games rooms, civil wedding licence, 200-acre grounds (many activities).
BACKGROUND MUSIC: classical in evening in bar and dining room.
LOCATION: 1 mile SW of Masham.
CHILDREN: all ages welcomed.
DOGS: allowed (not unattended) in bedrooms, not in public rooms.
CREDIT CARDS: MasterCard, Visa.
PRICES: [2016] per room B&B from £195, D,B&B from £285. Set dinner £58, tasting menu £70. 1-night bookings often refused Sat.

MAWGAN PORTH Cornwall

BEDRUTHAN HOTEL AND SPA

César award since 2012

In an 'excellent' spot overlooking the beach, this post-war fun palace is 'a winning choice for families with young children', says a recent guest. 'They really do seem to have thought of everything.' In fact, with its spa, cocktail bar, indoor and outdoor swimming pools, tennis courts, pottery studio, art gallery, theatre, art and design fairs, playgrounds and kites, it has something for everyone. It's child friendly, dog friendly, all-round people friendly, with 'pleasant, helpful' staff and a 'relaxing' vibe that draws visitors back year after year. Sisters Emma Stratton, Deborah Wakefield and Rebecca Whittington are the owners. The style is bright and modern, with Scandinavian decor, lots of floor-to-ceiling windows and a sun terrace. Ask for a sea view in the 'spotless' bedrooms; watch the sunset from the fish-focused Herring restaurant. Pizzas, sharing plates and simpler fare are served in the Wild Café. 'We liked their flexibility in letting us arrive in the morning and use the facilities, even if our rooms weren't ready.' Child-free sister hotel The Scarlet (see next entry) is ideal for 'a more sophisticated stay'. (Diana Goodey)

Mawgan Porth
TR8 4BU

T: 01637 860860
F: 01637 860714
E: stay@bedruthan.com
W: www.bedruthan.com

BEDROOMS: 101. 1 suitable for disabled, apartment suites in separate block.
OPEN: all year except 2–27 Jan.
FACILITIES: lift, 2 lounges, bar, restaurant, café, free Wi-Fi, in-room TV (Freeview), poolside snack bar, ballroom, 4 children's clubs, spa (indoor swimming pool, sensory garden), civil wedding licence, 5-acre grounds (heated swimming pools, tennis, playing field).
BACKGROUND MUSIC: 'laid-back' in restaurant, café and bar.
LOCATION: 4 miles NE of Newquay.
CHILDREN: all ages welcomed.
DOGS: allowed in some bedrooms, some public areas.
CREDIT CARDS: MasterCard, Visa.
PRICES: [2016] per room B&B from £139, D,B&B from £179. À la carte £30. 1-night bookings sometimes refused.

MAWGAN PORTH Cornwall

Map 1:D2

THE SCARLET

An eco-friendly, low-tech ethos meets indulgent, high-spec style at this adults-only hotel in 'a superb situation overlooking a classic Cornish bay'. 'The ultra-modern design is intriguing and attractive; the staff are charming and efficient; the food is very good,' says a Guide reader this year. It is the grown-up sibling of family-friendly Bedruthan Hotel and Spa (see previous entry). From the airy reception lounge to the five levels of bedrooms, glass walls bring the wild Atlantic almost indoors (guests are encouraged to turn off their portable devices in public areas, to better take in the surroundings). 'Our spacious, comfortable room, on the lowest floor, opened on to the grassy slope leading to the beach. A spectacular clifftop walk begins almost immediately. The only caveat: the toilet, in a small wet room behind frosted glass, had no real privacy.' (The cool, contemporary feel might not suit all tastes: a guest in 2016 thought his room 'stark'.) Chill out with any of the 'New Age-type therapies and activities' on offer – 'though there's no pressure to avail oneself of them' – then sit down to a modern menu while watching the waves wash in. (David Lodge, and others)

25% DISCOUNT VOUCHERS

Tredragon Road
Mawgan Porth
TR8 4DQ

T: 01637 861800
F: 01637 861801
E: stay@scarlethotel.co.uk
W: www.scarlethotel.co.uk

BEDROOMS: 37. 2 suitable for disabled.
OPEN: all year except 2–27 Jan.
FACILITIES: lift, lobby, bar, lounge, library with pool table, restaurant, free Wi-Fi, in-room TV (Freeview), civil wedding licence, spa (indoor swimming pool, 4 by 15 metres, steam room, hammam, treatment room), natural outdoor swimming pool (40 sq metres), seaweed baths, terrace, meadow garden.
BACKGROUND MUSIC: all day in bar and restaurant.
LOCATION: 4 miles NE of Newquay.
CHILDREN: not under 16.
DOGS: allowed in selected bedrooms, some public areas.
CREDIT CARDS: MasterCard, Visa.
PRICES: [2016] per room B&B from £210, D,B&B from £280. Set dinner £44.50. 1-night bookings refused Fri/Sat.

MAWNAN SMITH Cornwall

Map 1:E2

BUDOCK VEAN

Guests express great fondness for Martin Barlow's 'super' hotel, an 18th-century manor house with a gently 'old-fashioned' atmosphere, where visitors are encouraged to dress up for dinner. 'While it initially seems a touch staid (perhaps the jacket-and-tie rule should be relaxed to encourage the youngsters to come), it grows on you,' says a reader this year. Roundly praised is the 'slick' service: 'There are always staff on hand.' Choose from 'well-appointed' traditional or modern bedrooms, each 'spotlessly clean'. 'Our spacious, refurbished room had everything we needed, including robes and slippers.' There's much to see and do: stroll to Helford Passage through the hotel grounds; sit next to the 'welcoming' open fire by the heated pool; sail down an 'idyllic' stretch of the water. 'Our highlight was a terrific Helford river cruise in the hotel's small boat. Roger, the skipper, is a mine of information.' Come dinnertime, sit down to Darren Kelly's daily-changing four-course menu of modern dishes, including 'plenty of fish', in the formal restaurant. 'A very good pianist entertained us each night.' (Anthony Bradbury, Suzanne Lyons)

Helford Passage
Mawnan Smith
TR11 5LG

T: 01326 252100
F: 01326 250892
E: relax@budockvean.co.uk
W: www.budockvean.co.uk

BEDROOMS: 57. Plus 4 self-catering cottages.
OPEN: all year except 2–20 Jan.
FACILITIES: lift, 4 lounges, cocktail bar, conservatory, Golf bar (Sky Sports), restaurant, snooker room, free Wi-Fi, in-room TV (Freeview), civil wedding licence, 65-acre grounds (covered heated swimming pool, 15 by 7 metres), spa, 9-hole golf course, tennis.
BACKGROUND MUSIC: 'gentle' live piano or guitar music in evening in restaurant.
LOCATION: 6 miles SW of Falmouth.
CHILDREN: all ages welcomed, no under-6s in dining room after 7 pm.
DOGS: allowed in most bedrooms, not in public rooms.
CREDIT CARDS: MasterCard, Visa.
PRICES: [2016] per person B&B £73–£141, D,B&B £88–£156. Set dinner £41.

MELLS Somerset

THE TALBOT INN

♕César award since 2015

Amid the coaching prints and framed vintage maps, there's a 'fantastically friendly' atmosphere at this popular pub-with-rooms. With flagstone floors, mismatched furnishings and a cobbled courtyard, the 15th-century coaching inn 'cheerfully' assumes its role as village pub (Sunday movie nights are attended by locals and visitors). At dinner, choose between 'well-priced' pub dishes and 'more sophisticated' options, such as trout and prawn salad, nigella yogurt, beetroot. 'We liked the simplicity of the table – its good glasses and tea towel-style napkins.' Come on a weekend for the convivial grill dinner, when a whole suckling pig might be spit-roasted over an open fire. Fed well, stay the night in 'simple, modern' bedrooms (most up 'steep' stairs – help with luggage offered), each with 'pristine' bedlinen, a vintage Welsh blanket, 'all-natural smellies' and the latest tech. In the morning, find 'creamy' yogurt, home-made jam, 'wonderful' bacon at breakfast; toast your own slices from a home-baked loaf. The Beckford Arms, Tisbury (see entry), is under the same ownership. (John C Walton, and others)

Selwood Street
Mells
BA11 3PN

T: 01373 812254
E: info@talbotinn.com
W: www.talbotinn.com

BEDROOMS: 8. 1 on ground floor.
OPEN: all year except 25 Dec.
FACILITIES: bar, restaurant, snug, map room, grill room, private dining rooms, free Wi-Fi, in-room Smart TV, courtyard, garden.
BACKGROUND MUSIC: in public areas.
LOCATION: in village.
CHILDREN: all ages welcomed.
DOGS: allowed in 1 bedroom, dining areas.
CREDIT CARDS: MasterCard, Visa.
PRICES: [2016] per room B&B £100–£160. À la carte £30.

MILTON ABBOT Devon

Map 1:D3

HOTEL ENDSLEIGH

César award since 2016

A Regency fishing lodge built for Georgiana, Duchess of Bedford, stands in a 'magical' landscape of grottoes and follies created by Humphry Repton, on the banks of the Tamar. 'I confess I never [was] so well pleased myself,' exclaimed the Duke, when he saw Repton's plans; our readers agree: 'A walk around the beautiful grounds makes one feel so good to be alive.' Within the cottage orné, Olga Polizzi contrasts rustic simplicity with antiques, hand-painted wallpaper and modern artwork. There are blazing fires, fresh flowers, a library thick with books; 'at night, myriad small candles burn in the public areas'. Many of the 'charming' bedrooms have views over the gardens (though a guest this year yearned, more simply, for a pair of bedroom slippers); for more space, splurge on a new suite in the converted stables, with a sitting room, and a kitchen dresser for preparing coffee and tea. Come dinnertime, sit down to Jose Graziosi's 'good', 'reasonably priced' modern European dishes, perhaps hare arancino, Parmesan; partridge pithivier, pancetta, wild mushrooms. 'A memorable experience.' (Ann Reynolds, and others)

Milton Abbot
PL19 0PQ

T: 01822 870000
F: 01822 870578
E: mail@hotelendsleigh.com
W: www.hotelendsleigh.com

BEDROOMS: 18. 1 on ground floor, 2 in stables, 1 in lodge (1 mile from main house).
OPEN: all year.
FACILITIES: drawing room, library, card room, bar, 2 dining rooms, free Wi-Fi, in-room TV (Freeview), civil wedding licence, terraces, 108-acre estate (fishing, ghillie available).
BACKGROUND MUSIC: none.
LOCATION: 7 miles NW of Tavistock.
CHILDREN: all ages welcomed (children's menu, baby-listening, games).
DOGS: allowed, not in restaurant, or 'near afternoon tea table'.
CREDIT CARDS: Amex, MasterCard, Visa.
PRICES: [2016] per room B&B £190–£425, D,B&B £255–£490. Set dinner £44. 1-night bookings refused weekends.

MORETON-IN-MARSH Gloucestershire

Map 3:D6

THE REDESDALE ARMS

'Friendly' staff, 'comfortable' rooms and 'excellent' food draw visitors to this 17th-century coaching inn 'with a modern twist'. Robert Smith is the 'hands-on' owner/manager. Pick a traditionally furnished bedroom in the 'charming' stone building, or a more up-to-date one in the refurbished stable block; expect extras such as cookies and a decanter of sherry in all of them (though 'a luggage rack would be welcome'). 'My large superior room in the extension was well furnished in a contemporary style; the shower room was clean and modern.' Discuss bedroom choices before booking: some guests this year thought their annexe room sombre; others found in-room amenities lacking. Dine on chef James Hitchman's 'satisfying' dishes, served in the restaurants, on the garden terrace or by the log fire in the bar. Local game and Cotswold meat (perhaps Cotswold ale and honey-glazed pork belly, boulangère potatoes, hogs pudding) are highlights. In the morning, help yourself to hot and cold breakfast buffets; smoked haddock, kippers and porridge are cooked to order. (MG, Ian Marshall, and others)

High Street
Moreton-in-Marsh
GL56 0AW

T: 01608 650308
F: 01608 654055
E: info@redesdalearms.com
W: www.redesdalearms.com

BEDROOMS: 32. 26 in annexe across courtyard, 1 suitable for disabled.
OPEN: all year.
FACILITIES: 3 lounge bars, 2 restaurants, heated open dining area, free Wi-Fi, in-room TV (Freeview).
BACKGROUND MUSIC: in all public areas.
LOCATION: town centre.
CHILDREN: all ages welcomed.
DOGS: not allowed.
CREDIT CARDS: Amex, MasterCard, Visa.
PRICES: [2016] per room B&B from £140, D,B&B from £180. À la carte £32. 1-night bookings refused Sat Apr–Oct.

SEE ALSO SHORTLIST

MORPETH Northumberland

ST MARY'S INN

There's a 'jovial, relaxed' feel at this modern pub-with-rooms, say Guide inspectors after an 'excellent' stay. The 'cleverly' renovated former hospital building is in an unlikely setting, on the edge of a new housing estate. Inside, 'a lot of time has been spent to make it interesting and very different'. Bedrooms are individually styled with a mix of modern furnishings and antique pieces – a Victorian wardrobe here, an Edwardian desk there. 'Ours was uncluttered, clean and bright, with a well-lit bathroom and a generous supply of toiletries.' Mingle with locals in the 'heaving' bar; try a pint of the pub's own locally brewed St Mary's Ale. In the restaurant, choose from classic pub grub or local specialities with a modern twist, perhaps roast chicken, carrot, cardamom, black truffle. Breakfast is served in a high-ceilinged room 'flooded with light': a buffet has 'excellent' juice, 'very good' croissants and pains au chocolat; pick from 'interesting' cooked dishes – grilled Craster kippers, perhaps, or salt beef hash, fried duck egg. Jesmond Dene House, Newcastle upon Tyne (see entry), is under the same ownership.

St Mary's Lane
St Mary's Park
Morpeth
NE61 6BL

T: 01670 293293
E: hello@stmarysinn.co.uk
W: www.stmarysinn.co.uk

BEDROOMS: 11. 1 suitable for disabled.
OPEN: all year.
FACILITIES: 4 bar areas, dining room, private dining rooms, free Wi-Fi, in-room TV (Freeview).
BACKGROUND MUSIC: 'easy listening' in bar and dining areas.
LOCATION: 2½ miles W of Stannington.
CHILDREN: all ages welcomed.
DOGS: allowed in 1 bedroom, bar, not in restaurant.
CREDIT CARDS: Amex, MasterCard, Visa.
PRICES: [2016] per room B&B from £110. À la carte £29.50.

MORSTON Norfolk

Map 2:A5

MORSTON HALL

♦ César award since 2010

'The surroundings are idyllic and the food is perfect' at Tracy and Galton Blackiston's 'great' restaurant-with-rooms, say regular Guide readers this year. The 17th-century country house stands in well-tended gardens in a coastal village; inside, expect a 'friendly' welcome from the hosts and staff members – 'exceptional, sunshiny people'. The 'superb', 'well-paced' seven-course dinner is the main attraction, with Galton Blackiston's 'excellent', inventive dishes changing according to the season. 'The Michelin star is well earned, but it would be nice to have a lighter option than the full menu.' Stay over in well-equipped bedrooms in the main house and in a pavilion in the grounds. 'Our spacious room in the main building had all the amenities one expects, including a capsule coffee machine; there were soft, fluffy towels in the well-heated bathroom.' Come morning, a 'very good' breakfast is served at table: grapefruit slices, muesli, a choice of egg dishes. 'I don't normally have a cooked breakfast, but the fried eggs and bacon were so delicious, I couldn't resist.' 'So good we've booked to return.' (Yvonne and Eric Kirk, Shirley Johns, Wolfgang Stroebe)

The Street
Morston
NR25 7AA

T: 01263 741041
F: 01263 740419
E: reception@morstonhall.com
W: www.morstonhall.com

BEDROOMS: 13. 6 in garden pavilion on ground floor.
OPEN: all year except Christmas, Jan.
FACILITIES: lounge, orangery, conservatory, restaurant, free Wi-Fi, in-room TV (Freeview), 3-acre garden (pond, croquet).
BACKGROUND MUSIC: none.
LOCATION: 2 miles W of Blakeney.
CHILDREN: all ages welcomed.
DOGS: allowed in bedrooms (£10 per night, free in kennels), not in public rooms.
CREDIT CARDS: Amex, MasterCard, Visa.
PRICES: [2016] per person D,B&B £175–£200. Set dinner £68, Sunday lunch £38.

MOUSEHOLE Cornwall

Map 1:E1

THE OLD COASTGUARD

In an old fishing village, a 'friendly' welcome and the 'young, buzzy atmosphere' attract visitors to this personable Victorian hotel overlooking the sea. 'It's a well-run spot with no flashy bits, just the things you need: good people, good rooms, a great vibe (ideal for single travellers, like me),' said a returning guest in 2016. 'Elegant and relaxed', the hotel is owned by brothers Charles and Edmund Inkin, whose other properties – The Gurnard's Head, Zennor, and The Felin Fach Griffin, Felin Fach (see entries) – have also won much praise. Pick from 'fantastic', seaside-simple bedrooms overlooking the water; all rooms have books, Cornish art, a Roberts radio, all-natural bath products, 'proper' coffee and local tea. 'We loved gazing out to sea as we sipped our morning coffee.' Come dinnertime, devour Matt Smith's bistro-style dishes, including appetising veggie options and 'the most delicious crab starter'. A handy stop-over for travellers to or from the Isles of Scilly. 'We had an early start to catch the Scillonian; the staff helpfully set out an excellent continental breakfast.' (Barbara Watkinson, Michael Eldridge, Ellin Osmond)

25% DISCOUNT VOUCHERS

The Parade
Mousehole
TR19 6PR

T: 01736 731222
E: bookings@oldcoastguardhotel.
   co.uk
W: www.oldcoastguardhotel.co.uk

BEDROOMS: 14.
OPEN: all year except 24/25 Dec.
FACILITIES: bar, sun terrace, restaurant, free Wi-Fi, sea-facing garden with path to beach, unsuitable for disabled.
BACKGROUND MUSIC: Radio 4 at breakfast, selected music at other mealtimes.
LOCATION: 2-min. walk from village, 3 miles S of Newlyn.
CHILDREN: all ages welcomed, under-5s stay free.
DOGS: welcomed (treats, towels, dog bowls), not allowed in dining room.
CREDIT CARDS: MasterCard, Visa.
PRICES: [2016] per room B&B £135–£225, D,B&B £187.50–£277.50. Set dinner £18.50–£23.50, à la carte £23.50.

MULLION COVE Cornwall

MULLION COVE HOTEL

Steps from the Coastal Path, with 'wonderful views' over cove and historic harbour, this 'friendly', 'welcoming' clifftop hotel has been run by the 'very nice' Grose family for ten years. The emphatic white building retains echoes of its elegant Edwardian heyday. 'I was slightly worried that it might be too homely, but I was wrong. It was well maintained – a lovely place to stay,' says a Guide reader in 2016. Order a Cornish cream tea and soak in the surroundings; enormous windows in three spacious lounges let the outside in. The bedrooms are muted in style – all the better, in premium rooms, to appreciate the watery vista. 'We liked our sea-view room, with its comfy bed and excellent bathroom.' Another guest: 'Our triple-aspect room had the most glorious views.' In the restaurant, Paul Stephens, the new chef, makes the most of locally landed fish and shellfish on his 'good' daily-changing menus. Dogs are welcomed with more than a pat on the head – they receive treats, and entry into the pet-friendly lounge. Put on your walking shoes: 'National Trust land stretches out to the south, and walks are easy, in dramatic scenery.' (Diana Goodey, Peter Govier)

25% DISCOUNT VOUCHERS

Cliff Road
Mullion Cove
TR12 7EP

T: 01326 240328
F: 01326 240998
E: enquiries@mullion-cove.co.uk
W: www.mullion-cove.co.uk

BEDROOMS: 30. Some on ground floor.
OPEN: all year.
FACILITIES: lift, 3 lounges, bar, restaurant, free Wi-Fi, in-room TV (Freeview), 1-acre garden, 10-metre heated outdoor swimming pool, unsuitable for disabled.
BACKGROUND MUSIC: none.
LOCATION: on edge of village.
CHILDREN: all ages welcomed, no under-7s in restaurant in evening.
DOGS: allowed in some bedrooms, 1 lounge.
CREDIT CARDS: Amex, MasterCard, Visa.
PRICES: [2016] per room B&B from £90, D,B&B from £146. Set dinner £35, à la carte £29.

NEAR SAWREY Cumbria

Map 4: inset C2

EES WYKE COUNTRY HOUSE

Set against a backdrop of mature trees, this 'lovely' white-painted Georgian house was called Lakefield when Beatrix Potter first spent a summer here in 1896. She sketched fungi and painted the view we share today, of Esthwaite Water. For the past 14 years, Richard and Margaret Lee have been 'hospitable', 'charming' owners whose guest house has 'much to admire' (not least the host's 'dry sense of humour'). 'It is excellent, with first-class food, wonderful views and a pleasant country house atmosphere,' says a Guide reader on his eighth visit. Another frequenter writes: 'We've stayed here many times and, unbelievably, the food improves each time. Margaret and Richard make you very comfortable.' Ask for one of the refurbished bedrooms: pretty and traditionally furnished, each is 'immaculate', with a modern bathroom. In the evening, sample Richard Lee's five-course, daily-changing menu of seasonal English dishes, perhaps breast of duckling, ginger and honey sauce; Yorkshire rhubarb and ginger crumble. Breakfast is 'a treat', with freshly baked croissants, freshly squeezed juices, local sausages, kipper or smoked haddock. (Eileen and George Goodbody, Ken Smart, and others)

Near Sawrey
LA22 0JZ

T: 015394 36393
E: mail@eeswyke.co.uk
W: www.eeswyke.co.uk

BEDROOMS: 8. 1 on ground floor.
OPEN: all year, except Christmas.
FACILITIES: 2 lounges, restaurant, free Wi-Fi, in-room TV (Freeview), veranda, ½-acre garden, unsuitable for disabled.
BACKGROUND MUSIC: none.
LOCATION: edge of village 2½ miles SE of Hawkshead on B5285.
CHILDREN: not under 12.
DOGS: not allowed.
CREDIT CARDS: MasterCard, Visa.
PRICES: [2016] per room B&B £90–£145, D,B&B £168–£232. Set dinner £43.50. 1-night bookings sometimes refused.

NETHER WESTCOTE Oxfordshire

Map 3:D6

THE FEATHERED NEST

♔ César award since 2013

In a 'delightful' 300-year-old Cotswold malthouse, Tony and Amanda Timmer continue to receive feathers in their cap. 'A truly amazing hotel/restaurant/pub – call it what you will, it scores highly in each category.' Mingle with locals in the pub (flagstone floors, sofas, log fire, cask-conditioned ales), then head into the 'pretty' dining room to savour the 'excellent' cooking of Raymond Blanc protégé Kuba Winkowski. 'The chef deserves much wider recognition for his wonderful dishes. My stand-out dish was a plate of lobster so beautifully arranged that it could have been a work of art. The flavours were stunning.' Up the stairs, modern, country-style bedrooms are 'thoughtfully equipped' with fresh flowers, books and magazines. 'Spacious and comfortable, our room, Cuckoo's Den, looked over the garden and rolling country. The bathroom had an efficient walk-in shower, and a roll-top bath under the eaves (not easily accessible for a tall person).' After a 'tasty' breakfast, stroll through 'meadows filled with wild flowers, orchids and all manner of butterflies'. (John Holland, and others)

Chipping Norton
Nether Westcote
OX7 6SD

T: 01993 833030
F: 01993 833031
E: info@thefeatherednestinn.co.uk
W: www.thefeatherednestinn.co.uk

BEDROOMS: 4.
OPEN: all year except 25 Dec, restaurant closed Mon except bank holidays.
FACILITIES: 2 bars, small lounge, dining room, free Wi-Fi, in-room TV (Freeview), civil wedding licence, 45-acre grounds, unsuitable for disabled.
BACKGROUND MUSIC: jazz in bar and restaurant.
LOCATION: in hamlet 5 miles S of Stow-on-the-Wold.
CHILDREN: not under 12 overnight.
DOGS: allowed in bar, not in bedrooms.
CREDIT CARDS: Amex, MasterCard, Visa.
PRICES: [2016] per room B&B £195–£250. À la carte £60. 1-night bookings refused weekends.

NETLEY MARSH Hampshire

Map 2:E2

HOTEL TERRAVINA

♔César award since 2009

When a world-class sommelier and a former hotel inspector open their own restaurant-with-rooms, expectations are high. 'Consistently excellent', Gérard and Nina Basset's Victorian villa in the New Forest does not disappoint. 'It uplifts the spirits with its warm welcome and its sunny, modern decor in Mediterranean colours.' Wine devotees find much to like: an open cellar provides inspiration; regular tastings and wine dinners are held. Ask for a tour of the vaulted basement cellars. The Napa Valley–inspired restaurant is the right place for food and wine pairings. In the open kitchen, chef Gavin Barnes serves seasonal menus using local, often organic, ingredients. A characteristic dish: slow-roasted veal shin, confit shallots, savoy cabbage, truffle potato purée. Vegan and vegetarian options are genuinely creative: consider wild mushroom pithivier, roast celeriac, cèpes, broad beans. Afterwards, stay over in smart, 'attractively furnished' bedrooms well equipped with fresh milk, a capsule coffee machine, organic toiletries. ('Quirky, too: several have a bath in the bedroom.') Three on the ground floor have a patio garden; four have their own roof terrace.

174 Woodlands Road
Woodlands
Netley Marsh
SO40 7GL

T: 02380 293784
F: 02380 293627
E: info@hotelterravina.co.uk
W: www.hotelterravina.co.uk

BEDROOMS: 11. 3 on ground floor, 1 suitable for disabled.
OPEN: all year.
FACILITIES: bar, lounge, restaurant, private dining room, free Wi-Fi, in-room TV (Sky, Freeview), civil wedding licence, 1½-acre grounds (small heated outdoor swimming pool).
BACKGROUND MUSIC: none.
LOCATION: NW of Southampton, 2 miles W of Totton.
CHILDREN: all ages welcomed.
DOGS: not allowed.
CREDIT CARDS: Amex, MasterCard, Visa.
PRICES: [2016] per room B&B £165–£265, D,B&B £215–£255. À la carte £45. 2-night bookings preferred at weekends.

NEW MILTON Hampshire

CHEWTON GLEN

There's a 'great atmosphere' at this privately owned country house spa hotel (Relais & Châteaux), unstintingly luxurious yet completely family friendly. Fifty years strong – with a commemorative book to prove it – it continues to innovate (a purpose-built cookery school and restaurant complex are next on the agenda). 'The attention to detail is excellent,' enthuses a reader in 2016. If the sky's the limit, book a tree-house suite, built on stilts in a secluded forest setting – each suite has floor-to-ceiling windows, a wood-burning stove, a whirlpool tub, a kitchenette, and a breakfast hamper delivered to the door. In the main house, even the cheapest rooms are large, traditionally and lavishly furnished, 'absolutely pristine, relaxing and very comfy', says a guest, for whom the whole experience was 'unreal'. Come hungry: 'delicious', sophisticated meals are served in the conservatory dining rooms, perhaps Wiltshire venison saddle, parsley root, sloe gin; line-caught sea bass, mussels, monk's beard. The estate is on the edge of the New Forest, a stroll from the sea – make your way through 'beautiful' grounds for 'lovely' walks along the beach. (Aminah Gianfrancesco, Sarah Heineman)

Christchurch Road
New Milton
BH25 6QS

T: 01425 275341
F: 01425 272310
E: reservations@chewtonglen.com
W: www.chewtonglen.com

BEDROOMS: 70. 14 on ground floor, 12 tree-house suites in grounds, 1 suitable for disabled.
OPEN: all year.
FACILITIES: 3 lounges, bar, restaurant, function rooms, free Wi-Fi, in-room TV (Sky), civil wedding licence, spa, indoor 17-metre swimming pool, 130-acre grounds (outdoor 15-metre heated swimming pool, tennis centre, par-3 golf course).
BACKGROUND MUSIC: 'subtle' in public areas.
LOCATION: on S edge of New Forest.
CHILDREN: all ages welcomed.
DOGS: allowed in tree-house suites only, not in public rooms.
CREDIT CARDS: Amex, MasterCard, Visa.
PRICES: [2016] per room £325–£1,595. Breakfast £26, à la carte £70. 1-night bookings refused weekends.

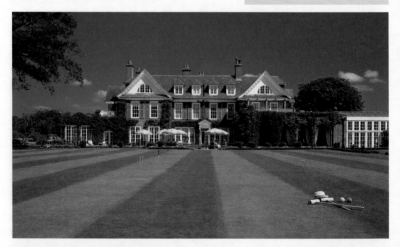

NEW ROMNEY Kent

Map 2:E5

ROMNEY BAY HOUSE

♔César award since 2012

Clinton and Lisa Lovell's 1920s mansion has a 'stunning, unique location' between Littlestone's shingle beach and miles of wild marshland scattered with ancient churches. The house was built for the American actress and gossip columnist Hedda Hopper, by Clough Williams-Ellis, architect of the Italianate village at Portmeirion, Wales (see entry). Hopper planned a kind of English Le Touquet; it never happened, and the area remains unspoilt, evocative, other-worldly. The hotel bedrooms, two with a four-poster bed, feel homey, with pictures and knick-knacks; all have tea- and coffee-making facilities, mineral water and bathrobes. Ask for one with views over the water. In the first-floor lounge, browse the collection of games and cookery books; train the telescope on France. Have a drink from the honesty bar before sampling Clinton Lovell's 'superb' four-course set dinners (including, perhaps, Romney Bay scallops; local marsh lamb) in the conservatory dining room. In the morning, breakfast on muesli, yogurt, fresh and poached fruit; hot dishes are cooked to order. The beach is steps away. (MB, and others)

25% DISCOUNT VOUCHERS

Coast Road
Littlestone
New Romney
TN28 8QY

T: 01797 364747
E: romneybayhouse@aol.co.uk
W: www.romneybayhousehotel.co.uk

BEDROOMS: 10.
OPEN: all year except 2 weeks Christmas, dining room closed midday, Sun/Mon/Thurs evenings.
FACILITIES: 2 lounges, bar, conservatory, dining room, free Wi-Fi, in-room TV (Freeview), small function facilities, 1-acre garden, unsuitable for disabled.
BACKGROUND MUSIC: none.
LOCATION: 1½ miles from New Romney.
CHILDREN: not under 14.
DOGS: not allowed.
CREDIT CARDS: Amex, MasterCard, Visa.
PRICES: per room B&B £95–£164. Set dinner £47.50. 1-night advance bookings refused weekends.

NEWBIGGIN-ON-LUNE Cumbria

Map 4:C3

BROWNBER HALL

Beyond the stone balustrade that encloses the terrace of this substantial Victorian house, the views over sheep-grazed pastures reach towards the Howgill fells and the North Pennines. Pass between imposing gate piers to approach Hilary and Andrew Woodward's Grade II listed building; inside, the atmosphere is warm and homey. Pick a book from the 'wide selection' on the shelves, pour a drink from the honesty bar, curl up in one of the winged armchairs in the lounge. 'On a wet and stormy winter evening, the wood-burning stove and efficient central heating kept us warm.' The traditionally styled bedrooms come in various shapes and sizes, including a family room under the eaves; all are clean and comfortable, with far-reaching views. The Black Swan, Ravenstonedale (see entry), is a popular choice for dinner; the Woodwards can arrange transport. 'Ample' breakfasts have 'good' toast, Cumbrian produce, and, for the lucky, glimpses of red squirrels in the garden. Ask for guidance on local walks: the B&B is on the Coast to Coast and Dales High Way routes, with walks accessible directly from the door. More reports, please.

Newbiggin-on-Lune
CA17 4NX

T: 015396 23208
E: enquiries@brownberhall.co.uk
W: www.brownberhall.co.uk

BEDROOMS: 10.
OPEN: Apr–Sept.
FACILITIES: lounge (honesty bar), breakfast room, free Wi-Fi, in-room TV (Freeview), terrace, garden, unsuitable for disabled.
BACKGROUND MUSIC: soft folk/ classical during breakfast.
LOCATION: 5 miles W of Kirkby Stephen.
CHILDREN: over-12s welcomed.
DOGS: allowed (numbers are limited).
CREDIT CARDS: MasterCard, Visa.
PRICES: [2016] per room B&B single £35–£55, double £70–£90. 1-night bookings refused bank holiday weekends.

NEWCASTLE UPON TYNE Tyne and Wear   Map 4:B4

JESMOND DENE HOUSE

🏆 César award since 2013

There is a country house feel to Peter Candler's 'friendly', 'surprisingly peaceful' Tudor-style mansion in a wooded valley just five minutes by car from the city centre. Standing in 'lovely' grounds, the listed building is an eclectic mix of historical architectural detail: admire the Jacobean panelling here, the florid William de Morgan tiles there. Cherry-pick from individually designed, 'beautifully appointed', modern bedrooms, many with an individual feature – a private terrace, perhaps, or a window seat. All have freshly ground coffee, fresh milk, glossy magazines. Friends or family might book larger rooms with a shared lobby. 'Our annexe room had a lovely garden – compliments to the gardener. One gripe? Poor lighting. But the staff brought a lamp when we mentioned it.' The 'vast' afternoon teas are popular with locals and walk-in visitors; in the evening, chef Michael Penaluna's modern British dinners are no less of a treat. The 'extraordinarily varied' breakfast is worth waking up for: besides freshly squeezed juices and 'excellent' home-baked croissants, try Caster kippers with seaweed butter. 'Good walks down to the dene.' (SH, and others)

Jesmond Dene Road
Newcastle upon Tyne
NE2 2EY

T: 0191 212 3000
F: 0191 212 3001
E: info@jesmonddenehouse.co.uk
W: www.jesmonddenehouse.co.uk

BEDROOMS: 40. 8 in adjacent annexe, 2 suitable for disabled.
OPEN: all year.
FACILITIES: lift, lounge, cocktail bar, billiard room, restaurant, conference/function facilities, terrace, free Wi-Fi, in-room TV (Sky), civil wedding licence, 2-acre garden.
BACKGROUND MUSIC: 'easy listening' in public areas and restaurant at mealtimes.
LOCATION: 2 miles from city centre.
CHILDREN: all ages welcomed.
DOGS: not allowed.
CREDIT CARDS: Amex, MasterCard, Visa.
PRICES: [2016] per room B&B from £140, D,B&B from £200. À la carte £45, set dinner £19.50–£23.50, tasting menu £70.

NEWMARKET Suffolk

Map 2:B4

THE PACKHORSE INN

In an 'attractive' rural village close to the Newmarket racecourse, jockey for a room at this 'smartly renovated' inn beside the medieval bridge. 'Modern, fresh and characterful', it's run by the chef, Chris Lee, and his wife, Hayley, for Philip Turner's small Chestnut Inns group. 'The place looks terrific,' say Guide readers in 2016: there are stripped floorboards and heritage shades; a fire burns in the double-aspect fireplace between bar and dining room. Staff are 'friendly and helpful'. In the restaurant ('subdued lighting; nicely laid tables'), ingredients from local suppliers are prioritised in the 'excellent, unusual' dishes. Try cauliflower velouté, grilled mackerel, apple; loin of Suffolk venison, boulangère potato, blackberries. Afterwards, head to 'uncluttered', 'appealing' bedrooms in the main house or former coach house. 'Our large room, Primrose, was well designed, with a comfortable king-size bed and limed-wood wardrobe; a spacious bath and shower in the bathroom. A pity the beautiful brass bedside lights were useless for reading.' Wake to a 'good' breakfast: scrambled eggs and smoked salmon, pots of jam, 'real bread for toast'. (John and Elspeth Gibbon, and others)

Bridge Street
Moulton
Newmarket
CB8 8SP

T: 01638 751818
E: info@thepackhorseinn.com
W: www.thepackhorseinn.com

BEDROOMS: 8. 4 on ground floor in coach house suitable for disabled.
OPEN: all year.
FACILITIES: bar/restaurant, function room, free Wi-Fi, in-room TV, courtyard.
BACKGROUND MUSIC: in public rooms.
LOCATION: opposite village green.
CHILDREN: all ages welcomed.
DOGS: allowed in courtyard rooms (£10 a night).
CREDIT CARDS: MasterCard, Visa.
PRICES: [2016] per room B&B from £85. À la carte £34.

SEE ALSO SHORTLIST

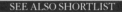

NEWTON ABBOT Devon

THE ROCK INN

'If there were an award for Upholding Traditional Values, The Rock Inn would be a clear winner,' Guide inspectors say. The 'charming' 19th-century inn, all thick stone walls and creaky floorboards, has been owned and run by the Graves family since 1983 – 'long enough to know what guests want'. 'Our first visit was nearly 30 years ago and it remains as good as ever,' writes a regular Guide correspondent in 2016. 'The food is always good, the staff are always efficient and friendly, the atmosphere is always pleasant.' Find books, board games, maps and guides in the 'lovely' public rooms; country-style bedrooms have antique pieces and a Bakelite phone. 'Our pretty room was warm and cosy, if small – but it had everything, including nice views across the valley. While we were at dinner, the room was tidied, the curtains drawn, and the bed turned down.' Chef Mark Tribble's 'seriously good food' is popular with locals; his 'unusual, delicious' dishes might include pan-roasted lamb rump, spiced carrot purée. Come morning, orders – perhaps for a 'wonderful' kipper – are 'swiftly delivered' at breakfast. (Diana Goodey, and others)

Haytor Vale
Newton Abbot
TQ13 9XP

T: 01364 661305
F: 01364 661242
E: info@rock-inn.co.uk
W: www.rock-inn.co.uk

BEDROOMS: 9.
OPEN: all year except 25/26 Dec.
FACILITIES: bar, 4 dining rooms, free Wi-Fi, in-room TV (Freeview), ¼-acre garden, unsuitable for disabled.
BACKGROUND MUSIC: none.
LOCATION: 3 miles W of Bovey Tracey.
CHILDREN: all ages welcomed.
DOGS: allowed in some bedrooms, bar, 1 dining room.
CREDIT CARDS: Diners, MasterCard, Visa.
PRICES: [2016] per room B&B from £100, D,B&B from £160. Set dinner £24.95. 1-night bookings sometimes refused.

NORTH WALSHAM Norfolk

Map 2:A6

BEECHWOOD HOTEL

A 'friendly' place, this 'traditional, comfortable' hotel has undergone a seamless transition under new owners Hugh and Emma Asher, assure Guide inspectors in 2016. 'It's held steady: standards are good; everything has been provided for the guests' comfort; it's obviously well liked by traditionalists and locals.' Each bedroom is different: some have large Georgian windows, others have French doors leading to 'rather wonderful' gardens. 'Our large room had a dark wood super-king-size four-poster bed, a dark wood table, a dark wood suitcase rest. The well-equipped bathroom had a roomy walk-in shower and a Mae West-style roll-top bath with claw feet. Flexible bedside reading lights were a nice touch, as were chocolates placed on our pillows at turn-down.' Book ahead for chef Steven Norgate's 'tasty' meals in the 'packed' restaurant, perhaps scallops, cauliflower purée, Parma ham crisp; Aylsham lamb canon, rosemary crumble; 'many exciting puddings'. In the morning, wake to 'nicely laid' tables at breakfast. 'There was a lovely starter buffet with great natural yogurt, freshly squeezed juices, a platter of fresh fruit; cooked dishes had a good choice, including a veggie option.'

25% DISCOUNT VOUCHERS

20 Cromer Road
North Walsham
NR28 0HD

T: 01692 403231
F: 01692 407284
E: info@beechwood-hotel.co.uk
W: www.beechwood-hotel.co.uk

BEDROOMS: 18. Some on ground floor, 1 suitable for disabled.
OPEN: all year except Christmas, restaurant closed midday Mon and Tues.
FACILITIES: 2 lounges, bar, restaurant, free Wi-Fi, in-room TV (Freeview), 100-metre garden (croquet).
BACKGROUND MUSIC: all day in public rooms.
LOCATION: near town centre.
CHILDREN: all ages welcomed.
DOGS: allowed, not in restaurant.
CREDIT CARDS: all major cards.
PRICES: [2016] per room B&B single £70–£90, double £100–£175. Set dinner £40. 1-night bookings sometimes refused.

NORTHLEACH Gloucestershire

Map 3:D6

THE WHEATSHEAF

Like coachmen and travellers of yore, visitors today head for this 'youthful, buzzy' pub-with-rooms, a smart conversion of an old coaching inn, in a Cotswold market town. Come in: there are varnished wooden floors, a handsome line of leather banquettes, an inviting cocktail list; 'lots of snugs and cubbyholes make it special'. Join the local crowd over regional beers and an 'extensive' wine list in the convivial bar. In the dining rooms, sample chef Ethan Rodgers's 'tasty' rustic dishes, perhaps carpaccio of orange, fennel, pine nuts; ox cheek, rib and oyster pie, roasted beets. Rest in 'very good' bedrooms, each different, with a 'comfortable' bed, 'large' shower, 'nice complimentary snacks, and bathroom bits and pieces'. Staff will 'happily' bring tea or coffee to the room, on request. Next day, breakfast on pastries, fancy teas, banana and oat smoothies; cooked dishes, charged extra, include pancakes, eggs with soldiers, a full English with beef-dripping toast. Fisherfolk, get your rods ready: trout fishing is available on a private beat on the River Coln nearby. More reports, please.

West End
Northleach
GL54 3EZ

T: 01451 860244
E: reservations@
cotswoldswheatsheaf.com
W: www.cotswoldswheatsheaf.com

BEDROOMS: 14. 3 on ground floor, 2 in annexe.
OPEN: all year.
FACILITIES: sitting room, snug, bar, dining room, 2 private dining rooms, free Wi-Fi, in-room TV (Sky), 1-acre garden (Wendy house, treatment room), unsuitable for disabled.
BACKGROUND MUSIC: all day in public areas.
LOCATION: town centre.
CHILDREN: all ages welcomed.
DOGS: allowed in 3 bedrooms, on lead in restaurant.
CREDIT CARDS: Amex, MasterCard, Visa.
PRICES: [2016] per room B&B (continental) from £120. À la carte £33.

NORWICH Norfolk

Map 2:B5

THE ASSEMBLY HOUSE **NEW**

The ornate rooms at this listed 18th-century mansion have seen grand balls, concerts, travelling circus acts and general merry-making over their many years; in 2016, the landmark venue added 'luxurious, tasteful' accommodation to the mix. 'Ideally situated', the red brick building is in a 'quiet' cul-de-sac next to the Theatre Royal; Guide inspectors this year praised the 'considerable investment in guests' comfort'. Past the 'impressive' reception hall, super-stylish bedrooms in an older house (six with their own garden) are reached via a modern extension. 'Our large room was appealingly decorated with a glass chandelier, countryside prints, a collection of polished brass cooking moulds. All the mod cons were there – espresso machine, stylish TV, adjustable reading lights; fruit, biscuits and umbrellas were available in a communal area.' Take an elegant afternoon tea with the locals, but skip the 'bland' early supper of 'standard fare' – the city's restaurants and cafés are on the doorstep. At breakfast find freshly squeezed orange juice, leaf tea, 'very fine' coffee served by the cup; a 'naughtily creamy' omelette Arnold Bennett with 'first-rate' smoked haddock.

Theatre Street
Norwich
NR2 1RQ

T: 01603 626402
E: admin@assemblyhousenorwich.co.uk
W: www.assemblyhousenorwich.co.uk

BEDROOMS: 11. All in St Mary's House extension, 6 with private garden, 2 suitable for disabled.
OPEN: all year except 1 week Jan.
FACILITIES: entrance hall, dining room, private dining and function rooms, civil wedding licence, free Wi-Fi, in-room TV.
BACKGROUND MUSIC: in dining room.
LOCATION: central, car park permits for pay-and-display.
CHILDREN: all ages welcomed.
DOGS: not allowed.
CREDIT CARDS: Amex, MasterCard, Visa.
PRICES: [2016] per room B&B £180–£240. Early supper £16–£20.

SEE ALSO SHORTLIST

NORWICH Norfolk

Map 2:B5

THE OLD RECTORY

'Kind, helpful' owners, 'well-presented' meals and 'peaceful, relaxing' rooms create 'exactly the cosseted, home-away-from-home experience that is the hallmark of a proper hotel', say contented guests this year, of Sally and Chris Entwistle's creeper-swathed Georgian rectory close to the city centre. The Entwistles are caring hosts who 'carefully' consider their guests' needs. 'Chris's driving directions were perfect on a dark, wet evening.' Pick from smart, traditionally furnished bedrooms in the main building and Victorian coach house. 'Our large, airy room at the top of the house had two armchairs, a good desk; double glazing kept traffic noise to an acceptable level. I had the best sleep I've had in many months.' Chef James Perry's 'excellent' dinners are served by candlelight. A typical dish: baked halibut, saffron, pea and brown shrimp risotto. Breakfast is 'superb': home-made jams, a 'beautifully presented' platter of 'perfectly ripe' fruit, hot dishes cooked to order – the whole served by 'two ladies who were great fun'. 'A good base for Norwich – a bus goes directly into the city'; the Broads are easily reached. (Susan and John Jenkinson, and others)

25% DISCOUNT VOUCHERS

103 Yarmouth Road
Thorpe St Andrew
Norwich
NR7 0HF

T: 01603 700772
E: enquiries@oldrectorynorwich.com
W: www.oldrectorynorwich.com

BEDROOMS: 8. 3 in coach house.
OPEN: all year except Christmas/New Year, restaurant closed Sun and Mon except bank holiday weekends when open Sun.
FACILITIES: drawing room, conservatory, dining room, free Wi-Fi, in-room TV (Freeview), 1-acre garden, unheated swimming pool, unsuitable for disabled.
BACKGROUND MUSIC: classical/jazz at dinner.
LOCATION: 2 miles E of Norwich.
CHILDREN: all ages welcomed.
DOGS: only assistance dogs allowed.
CREDIT CARDS: Amex, MasterCard, Visa.
PRICES: [2016] per room B&B £100–£185, D,B&B (min. 2 nights) £125–£235. Set dinner £30–£35.

SEE ALSO SHORTLIST

NORWICH Norfolk

Map 2:B5

38 ST GILES

In an 'excellent' central location, this upmarket B&B, all fresh flowers and polished floors, has new owners, father-and-son team Dennis and George Bacon. 'Good standards – and really good chocolate brownies – are being maintained,' say Guide inspectors in 2016. 'We were enthusiastically received. George carried our bags; he noticed our wet towels and swimming kit, offered to dry them for us, and duly returned them in the evening, warm and fluffy.' Past a 'sweet, neat' sitting room, most of the eclectically designed bedrooms are up a grand staircase. 'We were upgraded to a spacious, first-floor suite: original stripped-and-stained wood floors, panelled walls, gold damask curtains, a king-size bed and leather chesterfield sofa bed. The small bathroom was very good, with a walk-in shower; there was a separate loo with washbasin, old-fashioned style.' Breakfast is 'especially good, with interesting choices'. Wake to 'good' coffee, 'delicious' yogurt with honey and fresh berries, home-made bread and preserves. 'Excellent eggs Benedict came with a fresh hollandaise.' Private parking, 'slightly awkward to find', is nearby. (Susan Willmington)

38 St Giles Street
Norwich
NR2 1LL

T: 01603 662944
E: 38stgiles@gmail.com
W: www.38stgiles.co.uk

BEDROOMS: 7. 1 on ground floor.
OPEN: all year except Christmas.
FACILITIES: breakfast room, free Wi-Fi, in-room TV (Freeview), private parking by prior booking (3 spaces, £15 a day).
BACKGROUND MUSIC: Radio 3 at breakfast.
LOCATION: central.
CHILDREN: all ages welcomed.
DOGS: not allowed.
CREDIT CARDS: MasterCard, Visa.
PRICES: [2016] per room B&B £120–£245.

SEE ALSO SHORTLIST

NOTTINGHAM Nottinghamshire

Map 2:A3

HART'S HOTEL

♛ César award since 2007

On the ramparts of Nottingham's medieval castle, this modern, purpose-built hotel has a princely view over the whole city. 'Unreservedly recommended' by returning guests, it is owned by Tim Hart (who also owns Hambleton Hall, Hambleton, see entry). The contemporary bedrooms are 'small but well equipped', with a work area, flat-screen TV with DVD-player, fresh milk in the fridge; garden rooms have French doors leading to a terrace with outdoor seating. The Park bar received a facelift this year: new carpets, seating, decor and blinds. Hart's Restaurant, next door, has also been enlarged and redecorated, the seating updated. Chef Dan Burridge's daily-changing menus now include all-day snacks. At dinner, try a Rutland Pippin (cold ham hock pie, apple, Stilton); Hereford beef sirloin, breaded bone marrow, watercress and game crisps, quince soufflé. Breakfast, served in the bedroom or the bar, has fresh fruit and juice and locally produced yogurt, Melton Mowbray sausages and bacon, breads from Tim Hart's Hambleton Bakery in nearby Rutland. There is a small gym; in-room spa treatments are available.

25% DISCOUNT VOUCHERS

Standard Hill
Park Row
Nottingham
NG1 6GN

T: 0115 988 1900
F: 0115 947 7600
E: reception@hartsnottingham.co.uk
W: www.hartsnottingham.co.uk

BEDROOMS: 32. 2 suitable for disabled.
OPEN: all year, restaurant closed 1 Jan.
FACILITIES: lift, reception/lobby, bar, restaurant (30 yds), free Wi-Fi, in-room TV (Sky, Freeview), conference/banqueting facilities, small exercise room, civil wedding licence, courtyard, private garden, private car park with CCTV.
BACKGROUND MUSIC: in bar.
LOCATION: city centre.
CHILDREN: all ages welcomed.
DOGS: not allowed in public rooms, or unattended in bedrooms.
CREDIT CARDS: Amex, MasterCard, Visa.
PRICES: [2016] room £134–£274. Breakfast £9–£14, set dinner £28, à la carte £34.

OLD HUNSTANTON Norfolk

Map 2:A5

THE NEPTUNE

A one-time store for seized contraband, this creeper-covered former 18th-century coaching inn is today a 'modern, elegant' restaurant-with-rooms: wicker chairs sit on stripped wood floors; crisp linens cover the tables; a cool seascape hangs above an open fire. The name is nautical, and 'Hun'ston' beach is a stroll away, but local meat shares equal billing with fresh fish on chef/patron Kevin Mangeolles's refined menus. He holds a Michelin star for such dishes as pollack with wild garlic, artichoke, leeks, Pink Fir Apple potatoes; Creeder duck breast, veal sweetbreads, red cabbage. 'Dinner was excellent, both in execution and presentation,' writes a reader this year. There's praise, too, for the 'professional and friendly' service, with Jacki Mangeolles front-of-house. Accommodation is simple but stylish, with treats including an espresso machine, fresh milk and home-made biscuits. 'Our spotless bedroom and bathroom, though small, were well fitted-out.' In the morning, a 'superb' breakfast includes home-made croissants and jams, 'well-cooked' hot dishes, 'very good coffee'. 'Hands-on hosts, Kevin and Jacki deserve the obvious number of regulars who keep coming back.'

85 Old Hunstanton Road
Old Hunstanton
PE36 6HZ

T: 01485 532122
E: reservations@theneptune.co.uk
W: www.theneptune.co.uk

BEDROOMS: 5. Plus self-catering cottage.
OPEN: all year, except 26 Dec, 3 weeks Jan, 1 week May, 1 week Nov, Mon.
FACILITIES: residents' lounge, bar, restaurant, free Wi-Fi, in-room TV (Freeview), unsuitable for disabled.
BACKGROUND MUSIC: in restaurant in evening.
LOCATION: village centre, on A149.
CHILDREN: not under 10.
DOGS: not allowed.
CREDIT CARDS: Amex, MasterCard, Visa.
PRICES: per room B&B £155–£180, D,B&B £260–£285. Set menus £57–£75. 1-night bookings sometimes refused weekends.

OLDSTEAD Yorkshire

Map 4:D4

THE BLACK SWAN AT OLDSTEAD

♢César award since 2014

What's cooking at the Banks family's restaurant-with-rooms in a quiet corner of the North York Moors national park? 'Memorable' meals, 'very cosy' rooms, and service that's 'second to none', says a Guide reader in 2016. 'Hands-on' owners Tom and Ann Banks bought the old village pub ten years ago to save it from closing; in the years since, their younger son, Tommy, has earned a Michelin star for his innovative cooking. Elder son James is the manager. Regularly changing menus, served in the 'rustic but sophisticated' dining room, use much produce from the extensive kitchen gardens. A characteristic dish: aged Galloway beef, smoked bone marrow, wild garlic capers. Vegetarians have their own menu. Original cocktails might include one made from the fir trees in the woods nearby. A short stroll from the restaurant (umbrellas provided), bedrooms are in a quiet annexe and a refurbished Georgian house with a garden; they are simply decorated in homely, country style, with 'well-chosen' antiques. Wake up to 'proper' orange juice, home-made jams, 'excellent' cafetière coffee. (Flora Marriott)

Oldstead
YO61 4BL

T: 01347 868387
E: enquiries@blackswanoldstead.co.uk
W: www.blackswanoldstead.co.uk

BEDROOMS: 8. 4, on ground floor, in annexe; 4 in Ashberry House, 50 m away.
OPEN: all year except Christmas.
FACILITIES: bar, restaurant, private dining room, free Wi-Fi, in-room TV (Freeview), garden, 2½-acre kitchen garden and orchard.
BACKGROUND MUSIC: in restaurant.
LOCATION: in village 7 miles E of Thirsk.
CHILDREN: no under-10s in restaurant, only over-18s to stay.
DOGS: not allowed.
CREDIT CARDS: MasterCard, Visa.
PRICES: [2016] per room D,B&B £200–£450. Set dinner £60, tasting menu £85.

ORFORD Suffolk

Map 2:C6

THE CROWN AND CASTLE

🔱 César award since 2013

'It is warm, comfortable and without fuss.'
'You're always made to feel you're genuinely
wanted.' 'We felt at home, and so did the
dog.' 'We wanted it to be perfect, and it was.'
The accolades keep coming, for this popular
restaurant-with-rooms in a 'lovely area' close
to the River Alde. Owned by Ruth and David
Watson and Tim Sunderland, it is 'the best
kind of welcoming hotel'. 'The service is second
to none'; staff are 'smiling and interested'.
Take your pick of 'tasteful' bedrooms. 'Our
spacious room in the main house overlooked
the estuary; the equally large bathroom had all
the extras one needs. Home-made chocolate-
orange biscuits were to die for.' Two terrace
rooms sharing a lobby are ideal for a family. 'We
enjoyed the afternoon sun on our patio facing
Orford Castle.' In the restaurant, Charlene
Gavazzi cooks 'magical' Italian-inspired dishes.
The lively atmosphere isn't accidental – 'Ruth
Watson's ban on the use of electronic devices
in the dining room is a welcome one (although
she makes an exception for Kindle readers for
lone diners!)'. (Susan Chait, CL Hodgkin, Susan
Willmington, Michael Gwinnell)

Market Hill
Orford
IP12 2LJ

T: 01394 450205
E: info@crownandcastle.co.uk
W: www.crownandcastle.co.uk

BEDROOMS: 21. 10 (all on ground
floor) in garden, 2 (on ground floor)
in terrace, 1 in courtyard, 1 suite in
stable block.
OPEN: all year.
FACILITIES: lounge/bar, restaurant,
private dining room, free Wi-Fi,
in-room TV (Freeview), ¼-acre
garden.
BACKGROUND MUSIC: none.
LOCATION: market square, about
100 yds from the castle.
CHILDREN: not under 8 in restaurant
in evening or overnight in hotel; all
ages welcomed at lunch.
DOGS: allowed in 5 garden rooms, at
'doggie table' in restaurant, limited
number in bar.
CREDIT CARDS: MasterCard, Visa.
PRICES: [2016] per room B&B from
£130, D,B&B from £200. À la carte
£35. 1-night bookings refused
Fri/Sat.

OSWESTRY Shropshire

Map 3:B4

PEN-Y-DYFFRYN

❦ César award since 2003

In a 'gorgeous' setting, 'blending into the hillside' just yards from the Welsh border, Miles and Audrey Hunter have run their 'lovely' small hotel for nearly 30 years. 'It's the sort of place that attracts – and retains – loyal returning guests.' Visitors praise the 'charming', 'helpful', 'friendly' staff and the 'superb' food. The 19th-century stone rectory is surrounded by a 'beautifully kept' garden; inside, newspapers, books, notes about local walks and a bowl of fruit are on hand in the 'comfortable' lounges. New arrivals are welcomed with cream tea on the terrace. Bedrooms vary in style and facilities. 'We were pleasantly surprised by our airy, nicely decorated Coach House bedroom, which had great views and a whirlpool bath.' 'We slept soundly in our enormous bed.' (One caveat: bedlinen and bedside lighting 'could be improved'.) 'Perfect canapés, imaginative starters and beautifully presented main courses' – perhaps 'delicious' pan-fried scallops – please restaurant diners. 'Tasty, well-cooked' breakfasts are worth waking up for. (Carol Heaton, Mary Hewson, Steven Hur, F and IW)

25% DISCOUNT VOUCHERS

Rhydycroesau
Oswestry
SY10 7JD

T: 01691 653700
E: miles.hunter@virgin.net
W: www.peny.co.uk

BEDROOMS: 12. 4, each with patio, in Coach House, 1 on ground floor.
OPEN: all year except Christmas.
FACILITIES: 2 lounges, bar, restaurant, free Wi-Fi, in-room TV (Sky), 5-acre grounds (summer house, dog-walking area), unsuitable for disabled.
BACKGROUND MUSIC: in evening in bar and restaurant.
LOCATION: 3 miles W of Oswestry.
CHILDREN: not under 3.
DOGS: allowed in some bedrooms, not in public rooms after 6 pm.
CREDIT CARDS: MasterCard, Visa.
PRICES: [2016] per person B&B from £68, D,B&B from £97. Set dinner £41. 1-night bookings refused Sat.

OXFORD Oxfordshire

Map 2:C2

OLD BANK

♖ Cesar award since 2011

'Standards remain reassuringly high' at Jeremy Mogford's 'well-run', 'very pleasant' hotel, in a 'perfect' location steps from the Bodleian Library. ('Alas, prices are even higher – my one gripe.') 2016 saw extensive refurbishment: public areas have been refreshed; a sleek bar in white onyx now serves snacks and classic cocktails; the well-planted garden terrace has been extended for even more alfresco diners. The 'outstanding feature'? 'The friendliness and helpfulness of the staff.' Choose among smart bedrooms varying in size and aspect: front rooms have the best views, rear ones are quietest. All have flowers, bottled water, bathrobes, 'heavenly' toiletries. 'Our room was lovely, spacious, with a well-appointed bathroom.' The modern art divides opinion: one guest this year found the collection 'odd'; another 'liked it all'. Food is served all day in the popular restaurant: perhaps 'well-cooked' steaks at dinner; 'good choice', including 'enjoyable' buttermilk blueberry pancakes, at breakfast. 'The restaurant was frantically busy, but our waitress maintained a smile.' (Sara Hollowell, Elspeth and John Gibbon, Robert Cooper)

92–94 High Street
Oxford
OX1 4BJ

T: 01865 799599
E: reception@oldbank-hotel.co.uk
W: www.oldbank-hotel.co.uk

BEDROOMS: 42. 1 suitable for disabled.
OPEN: all year.
FACILITIES: lift, residents' library/bar, bar, dining terrace, 2 meeting/private dining rooms, free Wi-Fi, in-room TV, small garden.
BACKGROUND MUSIC: none.
LOCATION: central, car park.
CHILDREN: all ages welcomed.
DOGS: not allowed.
CREDIT CARDS: Amex, MasterCard, Visa.
PRICES: [2016] room £175–£355. Breakfast (full English) £15, (continental) £13.50, à la carte £35 (plus 12½% discretionary service charge).

SEE ALSO SHORTLIST

OXFORD Oxfordshire

Map 2:C2

OLD PARSONAGE

With 'excellent food and comfortable rooms', Jeremy Mogford's luxury hotel 'never disappoints', writes a trusted Guide correspondent, a regular guest, in 2016. 'Friendly', responsive staff are praised: 'Having told them I was bringing a car, I arrived to find a named space reserved for me.' The hotel maintains the 'intimate' atmosphere of a modern gentlemen's club; the well-considered library, its sliding doors opening on to a terrace, is 'a particular joy'. 'I could spend days there, just reading and enjoying the attractive decor.' Sleek bedrooms are 'nicely furnished' and 'very well equipped'; a bedside booklet of short stories (each a winner of the owner's Mogford Prize for Food and Drink Writing) is 'a special touch'. 'Our room was blissfully quiet, once the sport of campanology ceased at the nearby church.' Evenings, dine on chef Michael Wright's seasonal classics, perhaps lemon sole, roasted fennel, samphire. (One guest thought portions could have been more generous.) Breakfast on crab and avocado on toast, then join one of the daily walking tours, or hop on a free hotel bike to explore the historic city. (Victoria Maltby, Peter Jowitt)

1 Banbury Road
Oxford
OX2 6NN

T: 01865 310210
E: reception@oldparsonage-hotel.co.uk
W: www.oldparsonage-hotel.co.uk

BEDROOMS: 35. 10 on ground floor, 2 suitable for disabled.
OPEN: all year.
FACILITIES: lounge, library, bar/restaurant, free Wi-Fi, in-room TV (Freeview), civil wedding licence, terrace, 2 small gardens.
BACKGROUND MUSIC: 'light' in restaurant at dinner.
LOCATION: NE end of St Giles, small car park.
CHILDREN: all ages welcomed.
DOGS: not allowed.
CREDIT CARDS: Amex, MasterCard, Visa.
PRICES: [2016] per room B&B from £225, D,B&B from £285. Set dinner £45, à la carte £35 (plus 12½% discretionary service charge). 1-night bookings refused Sat during peak periods.

SEE ALSO SHORTLIST

PADSTOW Cornwall

PADSTOW TOWNHOUSE   **NEW**

Midnight pantry raids never felt so decadent as
they do at this indulgent B&B, in an art-filled,
candle-scented, hugely refurbished Georgian
town house marked by a polished front door.
It is owned by chef Paul Ainsworth and his
wife, Emma, who run two restaurants in town,
including the Michelin-starred Paul Ainsworth
at No. 6. 'The attention to detail is astonishing.'
Each bedroom – really a suite with a lounge/
dining area – seems more 'luxurious' and
'cocooning' than the other: vintage furnishings
mix with state-of-the-art audio-visual systems;
plush fabrics sweep along super-king-size beds;
there are well-stocked minibars, oversized rain
showers, custom-created toiletries, a claw-
footed slipper bath. That pantry? It's filled
with champagne, locally made juices and sodas,
home-baked cakes and pastries. Evenings,
take a stroll – or ask for a ride in the electric
car – to any of the town's restaurants; return
to find biscuits and a flask of snooze-inducing
hot chocolate. A five-minute promenade the
next morning brings you to breakfast at sister
restaurant Rojano's on the Square. Explore:
picnic baskets, walking boots and vintage-style
bicycles are all available to borrow.

16–18 High Street
Padstow
PL28 8BB

T: 01841 550950
E: stay@padstowtownhouse.co.uk
W: www.padstowtownhouse.co.uk

BEDROOMS: 6. 2 on ground floor.
OPEN: all year except 24–26 Dec.
FACILITIES: honesty pantry, free
Wi-Fi, in-room smart TV, electric
car for guest transport, unsuitable
for disabled.
BACKGROUND MUSIC: in public areas.
LOCATION: in old town, 5 mins' walk
from harbour.
CHILDREN: not under 16.
DOGS: not allowed.
CREDIT CARDS: MasterCard, Visa.
PRICES: [2016] per suite B&B
£280–£380.

PADSTOW Cornwall

THE SEAFOOD RESTAURANT

Rick and Jill Stein's original venture, a small seafood bistro with red-checked tablecloths, is now a 'first-division' restaurant-with-rooms, a short walk from the centre of this busy fishing port. 'We understand why the restaurant is a top tourist choice: it's spectacular,' say Guide inspectors. 'The room is surrounded by banquettes and modern art, with a large, zinc-topped bar in the centre; the staff are well trained, observant, proactive. An extensive menu included delicious crisp-smoked mackerel, Cornish crab with a wakame-cucumber salad, enjoyable pan-fried monkfish with garlic and fennel. A soufflé dessert was light as a feather.' Sleep in one of the seaside-inspired bedrooms afterwards – the best have a private roof terrace overlooking the estuary. 'Ours had an entire wall lined with books, including old editions of the Poldark saga. The large bed had lots of pillows, a generous duvet; the bathroom was exceptional, with luxurious goodies, deep-pile towels and a freestanding bath for a gorgeous soak (shame the walk-in shower was a bit feeble).' In the morning, rise and shine with 'strong cafetière coffee; a fine buffet; a copious crab omelette'.

Riverside
Padstow
PL28 8BY

T: 01841 532700
E: reservations@rickstein.com
W: www.rickstein.
com/stay/the-seafood-restaurant/

BEDROOMS: 16.
OPEN: all year except Christmas.
FACILITIES: wheelchair-accessible lift, lounge, reading room, restaurant, free Wi-Fi, in-room TV (Freeview).
BACKGROUND MUSIC: in restaurant.
LOCATION: town centre.
CHILDREN: all ages welcomed, not under 3 in restaurant.
DOGS: allowed in some bedrooms.
CREDIT CARDS: Diners, MasterCard, Visa.
PRICES: [2016] per room B&B £154–£285, D,B&B £237–£335. À la carte £55. 1-night bookings refused Sat.

THE PAINSWICK NEW

An 'easy informality' fills this 'fun' hotel, in an 'unspoilt' Cotswold village in the green Slad valley. The newest in the Calcot Hotels group, it enters the Guide thanks to inspectors who found it 'a happy place, with attentive staff'. 'A grand job,' agree trusted correspondents. 'Steep' steps lead to the front door; within, find 'casual yet stylish' public areas decorated with 'fine' modern art. Stake a spot in the 'glamorous' cocktail bar or 'delightful' lounges; take a sunshiny lunch on the terrace, with 'a wonderful view of the valley'. Bedrooms are done with 'great attention to detail': a 'comfortable' bed, 'ample' storage, a 'well-equipped' bathroom with organic toiletries and waffle bathrobes, 'up-to-date glossies – a nice touch'. 'We slept with the windows open; it was quiet as quiet overnight.' Dine on Michael Bedford's 'imaginative' modern dishes, perhaps rack of lamb 'served pink on a crisp pastry base', in the high-ceilinged restaurant. In the morning, a pick-'n'-mix breakfast (charged extra) has 'everything you might wish from an excellent buffet'; the 'wide-ranging' cooked menu includes 'good' scrambled eggs. (Pat and Jeremy Temple, and others)

Kemps Lane
Painswick
GL6 6YB

T: 01452 813688
E: enquiries@thepainswick.co.uk
W: www.thepainswick.co.uk

BEDROOMS: 16. 7 in garden wing, 4 in chapel wing.
OPEN: all year.
FACILITIES: bar, lounge, restaurant, games room, private dining room, free Wi-Fi, in-room TV (Sky, Freeview), civil wedding licence, terrace, beauty treatment rooms, ¾-acre garden, unsuitable for disabled.
BACKGROUND MUSIC: all day in public areas.
LOCATION: in village 5 miles NE of Stroud.
CHILDREN: all ages welcomed.
DOGS: allowed in some garden rooms, on terrace, in lounge (£15 per night).
CREDIT CARDS: Amex, MasterCard, Visa.
PRICES: [2016] room from £119. Continental breakfast £8, cooked dishes £6–£12, à la carte dinner £38. 1-night bookings refused weekends.

PENRITH Cumbria

ASKHAM HALL

Homey and faintly bohemian, the Lowther family's Grade I listed Elizabethan mansion is surrounded by terraces, topiary and lawns. Guests approach the house, which was built around a 14th-century pele tower, through a stone gateway; inside, Charles and Juno Lowther have redecorated with a mix of antique and contemporary, ethnic and English furnishings. It is 'a hotel of character', say pleased visitors. Three reception rooms are filled with books, paintings, family photographs. Staff are 'friendly and efficient'. The 'pretty' bedrooms are individually decorated; the best, in the pele tower, have an antique bath and views of the gardens, fells and the River Lowther. In the restaurant, chef Richard Swale makes abundant use of produce from the kitchen garden, the Lowther estate and local suppliers, then gives his 'seriously good' dishes an exotic twist. A typical dinner menu might include guineafowl, ramson; hoggart loin, spiced lentils, mibuna, goat's cheese. A converted barn houses a café with a wood-fired pizza oven; animal trails around the gardens introduce younger guests to shorthorn cattle, boer goats and ducks.

25% DISCOUNT VOUCHERS

Askham Hall
Askham
Penrith
CA10 2PF

T: 01931 712350
E: enquiries@askhamhall.co.uk
W: www.askhamhall.co.uk

BEDROOMS: 15.
OPEN: All year except Christmas, 2 Jan–mid-Feb, restaurant closed Sun.
FACILITIES: drawing room, library, billiard room, 3 dining rooms, free Wi-Fi, in-room TV (Freeview), civil wedding licence, 12-acre grounds, spa, 10 by 5 metre heated outdoor swimming pool (Apr–Oct), only restaurant suitable for disabled.
BACKGROUND MUSIC: in reception rooms in evening.
LOCATION: 10 mins from Penrith and junction 40 on M6.
CHILDREN: all ages welcomed.
DOGS: allowed in bedrooms (£15 charge per stay), public rooms except in restaurant.
CREDIT CARDS: all major cards.
PRICES: [2016] per room B&B £150–£320. Set dinner £50, tasting menu £65.

PENRITH Cumbria

TEBAY SERVICES HOTEL   NEW

'What a great find!' In a peaceful rural spot 'conveniently' close to the M6, this 'out-of-the-ordinary' motorway hotel (formerly the Westmorland) is upgraded to a full entry, thanks to trusted Guide correspondents whose stay in 2016 'exceeded expectations'. 'Maybe it's stigmatised by association with motorway service stations – if only they were all like this! – but the Tebay does it all so well, with such passion, that it deserves a promotion from the back of the book. The restaurant, the lounge and, above all, the staff are bright and interesting. Plus, overlooking the fells, it's far enough from the road that traffic noise is at a minimum.' The hotel is owned by the Dunning family, whose nearby farm supplies the restaurant's 'short but interesting' menu of rustic British dishes (the 'first-class' steaks are worth a try). 'Comfortable' – 'if slightly spartan' – bedrooms have home-made shortbread, cafetière coffee, locally made organic toiletries. 'A wonderful bed ensured a good night.' 'All the stops were pulled out at breakfast: home-made marmalade; exotic compotes; enough smoked salmon to see me through 'til teatime.' (Stephen Page, Richard Barrett)

nr Orton
Penrith
CA10 3SB

T: 01539 624351
E: reservations@tebayserviceshotel.com
W: www.tebayserviceshotel.com

BEDROOMS: 51. 1 suitable for disabled.
OPEN: all year except Christmas.
FACILITIES: lounge, bar, mezzanine, restaurant, free Wi-Fi, in-room TV, function/conference facilities, farm shop.
BACKGROUND MUSIC: none.
LOCATION: 2½ miles SW of Orton.
CHILDREN: all ages welcomed (family rooms).
DOGS: allowed in some bedrooms (£10 per dog), not in public rooms.
CREDIT CARDS: Amex, MasterCard, Visa.
PRICES: [2016] per room B&B from £89. À la carte £30.

PENSFORD Somerset

Map 2:D1

THE PIG NEAR BATH

Hospitality wizard Robin Hutson, who launched the Hotel du Vin chain, has since moved on to Pig husbandry. He began at Brockenhurst (see entry); at Hunstrete House, he has turned this 'glorious' Georgian manor in the Mendips into the third of (so far) five Pig hotels. A highly professional operation, it is nonetheless 'fresh and appealing' – heaps of fun, guests agree. The house is all stripped floorboards, open fires, 'slouchy' leather settees and potted herbs; gilt-framed portraits hang in the panelled drawing room; vegetable crates stack high in the conservatory dining room. Shabby chic bedrooms in the main house, coach house and garden cottages are equipped with a Roberts radio, a capsule coffee machine, a snack-filled larder; 'generously sized bathroom goodies'. Eat well: using plenty of produce from the kitchen garden and Victorian greenhouses, chef Kamil Oseka's 'uncomplicated' dinners might include slow-cooked crispy pig cheek, piccalilli and wild chive dressing; 'Kentucky' fried wild rabbit, carrot purée. At breakfast (charged extra), sample everything from the 'comprehensive' buffet; hot dishes, including 'a very fine kipper', are cooked to order.

Hunstrete House
Pensford
BS39 4NS

T: 01761 490490
E: info@thepighotel.com
W: www.thepighotel.com

BEDROOMS: 29. 5 in gardens, some on ground floor, 1 suitable for disabled.
OPEN: all year.
FACILITIES: 2 lounges, bar, restaurant, snug, private dining room, free Wi-Fi, in-room TV (Freeview), civil wedding licence, treatment room, kitchen garden, wild flower meadow, deer park.
BACKGROUND MUSIC: all day in public areas.
LOCATION: 7 miles SW of Bath.
CHILDREN: all ages welcomed.
DOGS: not allowed.
CREDIT CARDS: MasterCard, Visa.
PRICES: [2016] room £155–£300. Breakfast £10–£15, à la carte £35. 1-night bookings refused weekends, Christmas/New Year.

PENZANCE Cornwall

Map 1:E1

CHAPEL HOUSE

NEW

Be buoyed by the 'coastal lightness' at Sue Stuart's personable guest house, in a 'lovely' location close to the harbour wall. 'Immaculate and inviting, it's the sort of place you revel in enjoying,' say Guide inspectors in 2016. The 18th-century house has been 'beautifully' decorated: white-painted floorboards, a mix of antique and 'interesting' contemporary pieces, fresh flowers, 'comfy' sofas, a changing gallery of local artwork; a 'chic', 'uncluttered' feel throughout. 'Every window frames a picturesque aspect – the harbour, the coastline, the adjacent church tower.' 'Spacious' bedrooms on the upper floors have 'fine sea views'; three rooms at the top share a landing with books and games – ideal for a family. On Friday and Saturday evenings, stay in for a communal dinner in the 'gorgeous' open-plan kitchen/dining area: over complimentary aperitifs, the 'caring, hands-on' hostess cooks 'fresh, simple' meals, perhaps pan-fried brill, Cornish early potatoes, samphire. In summer, take breakfast in the 'pretty' garden – the west Cornwall option of sizzled cod roe, smoked bacon and a poached egg makes a fine partner to the 'splendid harbour views'.

Chapel Street
Penzance
TR18 4AQ

T: 01736 362024
E: hello@chapelhousepz.co.uk
W: www.chapelhousepz.co.uk

BEDROOMS: 6.
OPEN: all year except 'a few weeks' Jan.
FACILITIES: drawing room, open-plan kitchen/dining area, free Wi-Fi, in-room TV (Freeview), function facilities, terrace, garden, unsuitable for disabled.
BACKGROUND MUSIC: none.
LOCATION: town centre.
CHILDREN: all ages welcomed.
DOGS: 'well-behaved dogs' allowed, not on beds or furniture.
CREDIT CARDS: MasterCard, Visa.
PRICES: [2016] per room B&B £150. Set dinner £22.

SEE ALSO SHORTLIST

PETERSFIELD Hampshire

JSW

'We were seriously impressed,' write trusted correspondents this year of Jake Saul Watkins's 'well-regarded' restaurant-with-rooms. The 17th-century coaching inn has four doubles upstairs (no need to hold back on the wine, from a list of 900 bottles): 'spacious and immaculately maintained', they are 'quiet, peaceful, light and comfortable'. Still, the star attraction is the 'imaginative' food, served in the 'contemporary' dining room. 'Everything felt on good form – the restaurant deserves its Michelin credentials. Each dish was exquisitely executed; the waiting staff were well trained and professional.' ('We would have liked a lounge for a pre-dinner drink and a study of the menu, however.') Sample textures of lamb, salt-baked turnips, shepherd's pie sauce; 'suckling pig with – "a mite idiosyncratically" – what it eats'. Vegetarians may enjoy a sophisticated menu (perhaps open ravioli, leeks, fermented mushrooms, quail's egg). Breakfast, 'a straightforward continental', is delivered to the bedroom: freshly squeezed juice, home-baked bread, home-made lemon curd and preserves, 'quality' croissants and pastries from Paris. (Anna and Bill Brewer, Bryan and Mary Blaxall)

20 Dragon Street
Petersfield
GU31 4JJ

T: 01730 262030
E: jsw.restaurant@btconnect.com
W: www.jswrestaurant.com

BEDROOMS: 4.
OPEN: all year except New Year, 2 weeks Jan, 2 weeks Apr, 2 weeks Sept, restaurant closed Sun evening–Wed lunch.
FACILITIES: restaurant, free Wi-Fi, courtyard, unsuitable for disabled.
BACKGROUND MUSIC: none.
LOCATION: town centre.
CHILDREN: all ages welcomed but 'good behaviour a requirement'.
DOGS: not allowed.
CREDIT CARDS: Amex, MasterCard, Visa.
PRICES: [2016] per room D,B&B £195–£360. Tasting menus £45–£80, à la carte £50. 1-night bookings sometimes refused.

PETWORTH Sussex

THE OLD RAILWAY STATION

Train buffs make tracks for this 'quirky' B&B, occupying a handsomely restored timber-built late Victorian station and four refurbished Pullman carriages on the disused railway line. Gudmund Olafsson and Catherine Stormont, the 'helpful, informative' owners, have rebuilt and redecorated with colonial flair: check in at the old parcels office, then take afternoon tea in the former waiting room, now a smart lounge with pink panelled walls, vintage industrial lamps, intriguing objets d'art, leather armchairs, and black-and-white photographs of the train line's heyday. Two bedrooms are in the station building, one reached via a cast iron spiral staircase. Dreaming of riding on the Orient Express? Sleep, instead, in one of eight snug bedrooms in the stationary carriages. 'Clean and comfortable', they have Edwardian mahogany fittings and a proper bathroom. No dinner is served, but a local pub is a two-minute walk away. In the morning, sit down to a 'wonderful' breakfast in the lounge; in good weather, perch on the terrace overlooking a screen of trees – the blast of train whistles has been replaced by birdsong. (Barry Nichols)

Station Road
Petworth
GU28 0JF

T: 01798 342346
F: 01798 343033
E: info@old-station.co.uk
W: www.old-station.co.uk

BEDROOMS: 10. 8 in Pullman carriages.
OPEN: all year except 23–26 Dec.
FACILITIES: lounge/bar/breakfast room, free Wi-Fi, in-room TV (Freeview), platform/terrace, 2-acre garden, unsuitable for disabled.
BACKGROUND MUSIC: 'soft '20s, '30s, '40s music' at breakfast.
LOCATION: 1½ miles S of Petworth.
CHILDREN: not under 10.
DOGS: not allowed.
CREDIT CARDS: Amex, MasterCard, Visa.
PRICES: [2016] per room B&B £100–£198.

PICKERING Yorkshire

Map 4:D4

THE WHITE SWAN

Guide readers express much affection for the Buchanan family's 'delightful, traditional' 16th-century coaching house, its flower baskets brimming against an unassuming stone facade. 'In its modest way, it's lovely,' say guests this year. The staff are 'excellent' – 'not a hint of the obsequious, just naturally friendly people working happily as a team'. A beamed lounge occupies the Bothy (sofas, wood-burner, magazines); just ask for toys, board games and crayons for children. Choose between traditionally styled bedrooms in the main building, and more modern rooms in the converted stables. 'Airy, spacious, well appointed, the new rooms are a delight. We had a splendid bathroom (nice bathrobes, too) and our own little patio.' In the 'cosy' restaurant, Darren Clemmit serves a 'short, simple' menu of 'honest food in Yorkshire portions' – all 'fresh and beautifully cooked'. When day breaks, an 'excellent' breakfast awaits: 'good bacon, first-rate kippers and – our acid test – a worthy poached egg'. 'A good centre for coast and country': mountain bike trails, bridleways and miles of moorland are all on the doorstep. (Josephine and Tony Green, JB, MM)

Market Place
Pickering
YO18 7AA

T: 01751 472288
F: 01751 475554
E: welcome@white-swan.co.uk
W: www.white-swan.co.uk

BEDROOMS: 21. 9 in annexe.
OPEN: all year.
FACILITIES: lounge, bar, restaurant, private dining room, conference/meeting facilities, free Wi-Fi, in-room TV (Freeview), small terrace (alfresco meals), 1½-acre grounds, unsuitable for disabled.
BACKGROUND MUSIC: none.
LOCATION: central.
CHILDREN: all ages welcomed.
DOGS: allowed in bedrooms (not unattended), not in restaurant (owners may dine with dogs in snug).
CREDIT CARDS: Amex, MasterCard, Visa.
PRICES: per room B&B £149–£189, D,B&B £209–£249. À la carte £38. 1-night bookings sometimes refused.

PICKHILL Yorkshire

Map 4:C4

THE NAGS HEAD

Surrounded by verdant countryside with ample opportunity for rambles, this former coaching inn has been run by Janet and Edward Boynton for more than 40 of its 200 years. It is an 'unpretentious' place, say admirers with affection; 'genial and affable', the Boyntons are 'hard-working, hands-on' hosts. The 'classic' pub is 'old-fashioned in the nicest sense, all stained beams and brasses'; the library theme ('a huge bookcase crammed with books') creates a homey atmosphere. A 'terrific' menu, displayed on blackboards, is 'promptly and attractively served', perhaps including 'a flavoursome salad with delicate balsamic dressing; a seafood pancake, characterised by beautifully smoked haddock'. Home-made bread rolls are served warm, with 'proper' butter. Need advice on drinks? 'The owner clearly knows his wine.' Up 'steep' stairs, retire to one of the 'simple', 'basic' bedrooms – they're 'excellent value, if a little dated'. 'We slept well – even with the windows open, it was quiet.' The cooked options at breakfast are of 'excellent' quality; there is also a rudimentary buffet. Easy access to the A1(M), 'though the motorway is out of sight and sound'. (RG, and others)

25% DISCOUNT VOUCHERS

Pickhill
YO7 4JG

T: 01845 567391
F: 01845 567212
E: enquiries@nagsheadpickhill.co.uk
W: www.nagsheadpickhill.co.uk

BEDROOMS: 7.
OPEN: all year except 24/25 Dec.
FACILITIES: lounge, bar, restaurant, free Wi-Fi, in-room TV (Freeview), unsuitable for disabled.
BACKGROUND MUSIC: in lounge, bar and restaurant.
LOCATION: 5 miles SE of Leeming.
CHILDREN: all ages welcomed.
DOGS: allowed in 2 bedrooms (not unattended), not in public areas.
CREDIT CARDS: Amex, MasterCard, Visa.
PRICES: [2016] per room B&B single from £60, double from £80. À la carte £25.

PORLOCK Somerset

THE OAKS

'Excellent' hosts Tim and Anne Riley are the heart of this small hotel, in a village on the Exmoor coast. The Rileys have owned and run their hotel for more than 30 years; fans applaud the sense of tradition in the Edwardian house, its rooms filled with books, paintings, tufted armchairs, floral fabrics and period furniture. Arrive to tea and home-baked cake, then relax in spacious bedrooms with views of the sea, the village or the hills. Later, mingle with fellow guests over aperitifs in the lounge. At dinner, Anne Riley cooks traditional English dishes that feature local game and seasonal vegetables. Her four-course, daily-changing menu might include chilled melon, dry cider jelly; roast fillet of Exmoor venison, port wine, redcurrant. The chocolates that follow are home made. Walk off the meal along coastal footpaths or woodland bridleways the next day (ask the hosts for their favourite routes). Longing to feel the wind in your hair? The Rileys are classic car enthusiasts; hire their MGB Roadster convertible and take to the open road. (M and JP)

Porlock
TA24 8ES

T: 01643 862265
F: 01643 863131
E: info@oakshotel.co.uk
W: www.oakshotel.co.uk

BEDROOMS: 7.
OPEN: Easter–Oct.
FACILITIES: 2 lounges, bar, restaurant, free Wi-Fi, in-room TV (Freeview), 1-acre garden, pebble beach 1 mile, unsuitable for disabled.
BACKGROUND MUSIC: none.
LOCATION: edge of village.
CHILDREN: not under 8.
DOGS: not allowed.
CREDIT CARDS: MasterCard, Visa.
PRICES: [2016] per room D,B&B £245.

PORTSCATHO Cornwall

Map 1:E2

DRIFTWOOD HOTEL

🏵César award since 2010

'A poetic setting of beach and sea and garden.'
An 'abundance of calm' settles upon this smart
hotel, thanks to the 'very hands-on' owners,
Paul and Fiona Robinson, and their well-trained
staff. 'The owners went away towards the end
of our stay, but the hotel continued to run like
clockwork,' visitors this year said. Chill out
in the 'beautifully landscaped' garden ('lots of
seating hidden in nooks and behind hedges')
and the art-filled sitting room; 'the blue-and-
white decor lends itself to a stylish but informal
atmosphere'. Bedrooms have a 'comfortable'
bed, a 'spotless' bathroom; some have a private
deck with 'superb' sea views. A family suite
under low eaves can be made up with cots and
children's books. Chef Chris Eden uses 'clever
combinations' of interesting ingredients in his
Michelin-starred dishes; everything is cooked
with 'a lightness of touch'. A characteristic
dish: roast cod, St Austell mussels, kale crisps,
sea purslane. 'Plentiful' breakfasts are a treat:
pastries, fruit salad, 'just-one-more-spoonful'
granola; a good choice of hot dishes. (John
Patterson, M and TS-P, and others)

Rosevine
Portscatho
TR2 5EW

T: 01872 580644
E: info@driftwoodhotel.co.uk
W: www.driftwoodhotel.co.uk

BEDROOMS: 15. 4 accessed via
courtyard, 2 in cabin (2 mins' walk).
OPEN: 3 Feb–3 Dec.
FACILITIES: bar, restaurant, drawing
room, snug, children's games room,
free Wi-Fi, in-room TV (Freeview),
7-acre grounds (terraced gardens,
private beach, safe bathing),
unsuitable for disabled.
BACKGROUND MUSIC: all day in
restaurant and bar.
LOCATION: N side of Portscatho.
CHILDREN: all ages welcomed, no
under-7s in restaurant in evening
(early supper provided).
DOGS: not allowed.
CREDIT CARDS: Amex, MasterCard,
Visa.
PRICES: [2016] per room B&B
£190–£285, D,B&B £245–£305.
Tasting menus £70–£100, à la carte
£60. 1-night bookings refused
weekends.

PURTON Wiltshire

Map 3:E5

THE PEAR TREE AT PURTON

César award since 2015

A 'lovely' country welcome awaits at Anne Young's 'outstanding' small hotel. Standing in a 'very special' garden filled with 'a treasure trove of wild flowers', the 'delightful' 16th-century vicarage is 'an exceptional place – like a home away from home, or staying with good friends'. 'Pleasantly quirky, it barely feels like a hotel.' Alix Baldwin, the owner's daughter, manages a team of 'superbly trained' staff – 'they seem hand-picked for smiliness, quality and efficiency'. Choose between characterful vicarage rooms in the older part of the building or more spacious executive rooms; all come stocked with fresh fruit and home-made shortbread. In the 'peaceful' conservatory restaurant, Adam Conduit's 'imaginative' modern English menu mixes surprising elements, perhaps hake fillet, barley risotto, Cornish salami, cockle vinaigrette. Try the house wine, Cuvée Alix, from the hotel's own vineyard. Plenty of walks to be had in the 'extensive' grounds; dogs are welcomed with treats, a blanket and a basket. (Brian and Gwen Thomas, Josie Mayers, Charles Medawar, Andrew Warren)

25% DISCOUNT VOUCHERS

Church End
Purton
SN5 4ED

T: 01793 772100
F: 01793 772369
E: stay@peartreepurton.co.uk
W: www.peartreepurton.co.uk

BEDROOMS: 17. 6 on ground floor.
OPEN: all year except 25/26 Dec.
FACILITIES: lounge/bar, library, restaurant, free Wi-Fi, in-room TV (Freeview), function/conference facilities, civil wedding licence, 7½-acre grounds (vineyard, croquet, pond, jogging route).
BACKGROUND MUSIC: none.
LOCATION: 5 miles NW of Swindon.
CHILDREN: all ages welcomed.
DOGS: allowed, not unattended in bedrooms, not in restaurant.
CREDIT CARDS: Amex, MasterCard, Visa.
PRICES: [2016] per room B&B £110–£151, D,B&B £165–£220. À la carte £38.

RAMSGILL-IN-NIDDERDALE Yorkshire   Map 4:D3

THE YORKE ARMS

🏆 César award since 2000

A winning combination of 'first-class hospitality', 'divine' one-Michelin-star cooking and an 'unbeatable' location in the Yorkshire Dales draws visitors to Frances and Bill Atkins's 'friendly' restaurant-with-rooms. 'Things aren't static here. Little tweaks are continually made to add to the comfort and charm of the place,' say returnees in 2016. Sample 'delicious complimentary nibbles' by the log fire, while Bill Atkins ('charm personified') is on hand to recommend the specials of the day. Cooked by Frances Atkins, the 'superb' menu uses seasonal ingredients from the kitchen garden and surrounding moorland. 'There is real cheffery here!' Bedrooms have 'everything you'd expect of a luxury hotel', including magazines and 'delicious' biscuits. 'Accessed via a maze of corridors and a short stretch of wrought-iron balcony, our courtyard room turned out to be a substantial suite, faultlessly decorated. Generous wardrobes separated the bedroom area from a cosy sitting room. On a stormy night, it was immensely pleasant to be in.' 'Not cheap, but worth every penny.' (Francine and Ian Walsh)

25% DISCOUNT VOUCHERS

Ramsgill-in-Nidderdale
nr Harrogate
HG3 5RL

T: 01423 755243
F: 01423 755330
E: enquiries@yorke-arms.co.uk
W: www.yorke-arms.co.uk

BEDROOMS: 16. 4 in courtyard, 2 in Ghyll Cottage in the village.
OPEN: all year except 25 Dec, closed Sun and Mon.
FACILITIES: lounge, bar, 2 dining rooms, free Wi-Fi in drawing room and some bedrooms, in-room TV (Freeview), function facilities, 2-acre grounds.
BACKGROUND MUSIC: classical in dining rooms.
LOCATION: centre of village.
CHILDREN: not under 12.
DOGS: allowed by arrangement in 1 bedroom and cottage, and in bar area.
CREDIT CARDS: Amex, MasterCard, Visa.
PRICES: [2016] per room D,B&B £345–£430. Tasting menu £85, à la carte £65.

RAVENSTONEDALE Cumbria

Map 4:C3

THE BLACK SWAN

♥ César award since 2013

'Quite excellent', Louise Dinnes's 'friendly' country pub-with-rooms attracts regular visitors with its 'unstuffy, warm and welcoming' atmosphere, and 'remarkably good value for money'. We were sorry to mark the death of Alan Dinnes, the much-loved innkeeper, in 2016. Visitors and locals throng the stone-walled pub for its local ales and chatter; the wood-panelled lounge, with a log fire, is a cosy spot. 'We were impressed with everything.' Enjoy 'excellent, plentiful' dishes such as pork tenderloin, black pudding, mustard mash, savoy cabbage; in fine weather, sit among the chickens in the garden running down to the stream. Country-style bedrooms are individually decorated; some, with external access, are ideal for dog owners. 'Our large, ground-floor room overlooking a small courtyard was well maintained, though there was a slight "doggy" smell on the first night. We liked the good towels and toiletries in the bathroom.' After an 'adequate' breakfast, set out on one of the many walks from the door – maps and booklets provided. An 'excellent' stop for travellers to and from Scotland. (Gwyn Morgan, TL, Susan Willmington)

25% DISCOUNT VOUCHERS

Ravenstonedale
CA17 4NG

T: 015396 23204
F: 015396 23204
E: enquiries@blackswanhotel.com
W: www.blackswanhotel.com

BEDROOMS: 16. 5 in annexe, 2 on ground floor suitable for disabled.
OPEN: all year.
FACILITIES: bar, lounge, 2 dining rooms, free Wi-Fi, in-room TV (Freeview), beer garden in wooded grounds, tennis and golf in village.
BACKGROUND MUSIC: 'easy listening' in public areas, all day.
LOCATION: in village 5 miles SW of Kirkby Stephen.
CHILDREN: all ages welcomed.
DOGS: allowed in 4 ground-floor bedrooms, not in restaurant.
CREDIT CARDS: Amex, MasterCard, Visa.
PRICES: [2016] per room B&B single from £75, double from £85.
À la carte £25.

REEPHAM Norfolk

THE DIAL HOUSE   **NEW**

'Discreet' at first glance, this 'handsome' red brick building, in an 'appealing' small town, hosts grand surprises in its 'eclectic', 'faultlessly decorated' bedrooms. 'A living antique experience in a beautiful Georgian house', Iain Wilson's hotel is 'a cornucopia of delightful furnishings and curios – and practically everything is for sale!' The unusual venture includes a restaurant, interiors store and 'impressive' residential development – rather a contrast with the owner's deli/B&B at Byfords, Holt (see entry). Guide inspectors in 2016 were extended a 'friendly' greeting and an offer of 'delicious home-baked cake'. 'Everything was beautifully presented – leaf tea, a lovely teapot, pretty china.' Inspired by the Grand Tour, bedrooms are different as can be. 'Our stunning Natural History room had a huge bed, an antique desk, a superb TV-audio set-up, interesting books, a record-player; a private terrace; a marble bathroom. A spacious lobby housed vinyl LPs, honesty decanters, biscuits.' In the restaurant, locals come for the 'uncomplicated, tasty' food: 'excellent' mussel and leek chowder or a Thai pork burger at dinner; an 'inviting' buffet at breakfast.

Market Place
Reepham
NR10 4JJ

T: 01603 879900
E: info@thedialhouse.org.uk
W: www.thedialhouse.org.uk

BEDROOMS: 8.
OPEN: all year.
FACILITIES: lounge, restaurant, private dining rooms, free Wi-Fi, in-room TV (Sky), terrace, unsuitable for disabled.
BACKGROUND MUSIC: jazz at dinner.
LOCATION: on main square.
CHILDREN: all ages welcomed.
DOGS: allowed on terrace only.
CREDIT CARDS: all major cards.
PRICES: [2016] per room B&B £155–£190, D,B&B £195–£230. À la carte £28.

RICHMOND Yorkshire

Map 4:C3

THE COACH HOUSE AT MIDDLETON LODGE

🏆 César award since 2016

Minutes from the A1(M) at Scotch Corner, on a 'huge estate in beautiful countryside', James Allison's 'exciting', 'very chic' restaurant-with-rooms is approached by a tree-lined drive. Expert travellers found it 'thoroughly enjoyable'. Bedrooms are in the 'sensitively restored' Georgian coach house and outbuildings around a courtyard; for an extra rustic touch, choose a garden room with a small private terrace and seating amid seasonal flowers. In each bedroom, expect well-considered amenities: glossy magazines; an espresso machine, a minibar with bottled water, fruit juice and crisps; cotton robes and 'excellent' toiletries. 'Our double-height tack room was amazing, with a huge bed, three-seat sofa, and wood-burning stove with a basket of logs.' Cross the courtyard to the 'attractive' restaurant and bar, where Gareth Rayner cooks such 'fine and interesting' modern dishes as halibut, mussels, smoked oil, wild leeks. (There are menus for children, vegans, vegetarians.) The astute service receives 'bonus points'. In the morning, sample 'several Yorkshire specialities' at breakfast. (P and JT)

Kneeton Lane
Middleton Tyas
Richmond
DL10 6NJ

T: 01325 377 977
F: 01325 377 065
E: info@middletonlodge.co.uk
W: www.middletonlodge.co.uk

BEDROOMS: 14. 5 in coach house, 3 in hayloft, 1 in tack room, 1 suitable for disabled, plus 5 in farmhouse, a short walk away.
OPEN: all year except Christmas, closed Mon/Tues.
FACILITIES: bar, restaurant, free Wi-Fi, in-room TV, civil wedding licence, treatment rooms, garden, kitchen garden in 200-acre grounds.
BACKGROUND MUSIC: 'relaxed' in public areas.
LOCATION: 1 mile N of village, E of Scotch Corner.
CHILDREN: all ages welcomed.
DOGS: not allowed.
CREDIT CARDS: Amex, MasterCard, Visa.
PRICES: [2016] per room B&B £165–£220. À la carte £40.

SEE ALSO SHORTLIST

RICHMOND Yorkshire

Map

MILLGATE HOUSE

César award since 2011

Expect 'a warm welcome' at this 'lovely', characterful B&B in a 'peaceful' market town on the edge of the Yorkshire Dales. 'Slightly eccentric (in a good way!)', Austin Lynch and Tim Culkin are 'wonderful' hosts 'with a passion for Georgian interiors'. The 'beautiful' Georgian town house is filled with 'gorgeous' antique furniture, paintings, ornaments and objets d'art, from the 'elegant' drawing room to the 'stylish, comfortable', book-filled bedrooms. Much has been preserved – look out for the period fireplace and wig room in the King bedroom dating back to 1720. Outside is as inviting as in: leading down to the River Swale, the award-winning terraced garden – 'full of interest' – is ideal for quiet contemplation. 'Even on a drab autumn day, the garden was inspiring.' Breakfast is 'superb' – 'the best I've eaten, anywhere'. In the light-filled dining room (oriental carpets, mahogany tables, pristine china), help yourself to an 'outstanding array' of local produce, fresh fruit, 'a wide range of interesting cereals'; the cooked dishes receive much praise. (Lynn and Rodger Middleton, and others)

Richmond
DL10 4JN

T: 01748 823571
E: oztim@millgatehouse.demon.co.uk
W: www.millgatehouse.com

BEDROOMS: 4.
OPEN: all year.
FACILITIES: hall, drawing room, dining room, free Wi-Fi, in-room TV, 1/3-acre garden, unsuitable for disabled.
BACKGROUND MUSIC: none.
LOCATION: town centre.
CHILDREN: all ages welcomed, 'depending on the children'.
DOGS: not in public rooms, or unattended in bedrooms.
CREDIT CARDS: none.
PRICES: per room B&B £125–£165

SEE ALSO SHORTLIST

RICHMOND-UPON-THAMES Surrey

Map 2:D3

BINGHAM

Come twilight, this chic riverside hotel/restaurant glows over the Thames. 'Close enough to London to get all the benefits of the city, but far enough away to be tranquil', it is owned by mother-and-daughter team Ruth and Samantha Trinder, who transformed two Grade II listed 18th-century houses into a refined, modern space with 'sumptuous' interiors. Take tea or sip cocktails under the glass chandelier in the 'magnificent' bar/lounge; in the evening, book a spot for chef Andrew Cole's unpretentious modern meals, well supplied by produce from the potager. In warm months, French doors in the plush restaurant open on to a balcony for alfresco dining. Later, retire to one of the Art Deco-inspired bedrooms – ask for one with a view over the river. Need help unwinding? Book an in-room holistic treatment from eco-friendly sister company Bhuti, up the street. In the morning, a buffet holds thick yogurt, fruit compotes, cereals, pastries; hot dishes are cooked to order. On a lazy Sunday, linger over lunch (now served till late) or borrow one of the hotel's Pashley bicycles – Richmond Park is minutes away.

61–63 Petersham Road
Richmond-upon-Thames
TW10 6UT

T: 020 8940 0902
E: info@thebingham.co.uk
W: www.thebingham.co.uk

BEDROOMS: 15.
OPEN: all year, restaurant closed Sun evening.
FACILITIES: bar, restaurant, function room, free Wi-Fi, in-room TV, civil wedding licence, terrace, garden, unsuitable for disabled.
BACKGROUND MUSIC: in lounge bar and restaurant.
LOCATION: ½ mile S of centre.
CHILDREN: all ages welcomed.
DOGS: not allowed.
CREDIT CARDS: all major cards.
PRICES: [2016] room from £130. Set dinner £17–£20, tasting menu £55, à la carte £40, continental breakfast buffet £12.50 (plus 12½% discretionary service charge).

ROMALDKIRK Co. Durham

Map 4:C3

THE ROSE AND CROWN

With 'exceptional' food, 'exemplary' housekeeping and 'staff who are a real pleasure to be among', this 'delightful' creeper-clad coaching inn again finds favour among Guide readers. 'It is a place where one feels completely at ease,' say guests this year of Thomas and Cheryl Robinson's 18th-century inn on the village green. 'We were welcomed with an excellent afternoon tea and scones in the lounge', a cosy spot with comfy sofas, books and magazines. Bedrooms are in the main house, in a single-storey courtyard building, and around the corner in 17th-century Monk's Cottage, which has its own lounge and honesty bar. A suite overlooking the green, 'although not huge, was comfortable and certainly more than adequate'; an annexe room was 'first class'. Meals are served in the oak-panelled dining room and the rustic bar (pews, copper pans, a stone fireplace). Chef Dave Hunter's 'excellent' updated English dishes might include roast loin of lamb, sautéed potato, artichoke, beetroot. 'Breakfast was all we could have wished for.' The Robinsons also own Headlam Hall, Darlington (see Shortlist). (Alwyn and Thelma Ellis, Ken Smart)

Barnard Castle
Romaldkirk
DL12 9EB

T: 01833 650213
E: hotel@rose-and-crown.co.uk
W: www.rose-and-crown.co.uk

BEDROOMS: 14. 2 in Monk's Cottage, 5 in rear courtyard, some on ground floor.
OPEN: all year except 23–28 Dec.
FACILITIES: 2 lounges, bar, Crown Room (bar meals), restaurant, free Wi-Fi, in-room TV (Freeview), boot room; fishing, grouse shooting, birdwatching nearby.
BACKGROUND MUSIC: in restaurant.
LOCATION: village centre, 6 miles W of Barnard Castle.
CHILDREN: all ages welcomed.
DOGS: allowed.
CREDIT CARDS: Amex, MasterCard, Visa.
PRICES: [2016] per room B&B £115–£180. À la carte £35.

ROSS-ON-WYE Herefordshire

Map 3:D5

WILTON COURT

25% DISCOUNT VOUCHERS

History is baked into the walls at Helen and Roger Wynn's 'good-value' restaurant-with-rooms, in an Elizabethan magistrates' court on the banks of the River Wye. The 16th-century building retains many original features (stone mullion windows, ancient wood beams, fireplaces) – a characterful backdrop to the personal collection of objets d'art on display. In 'a great position' on the river bank, the old courthouse is 'close enough to walk easily into town, but far out enough to be very quiet'. Bedrooms are individually decorated with flowers boldly blooming on striking wallpaper; all look over the river or the garden. 'Our large room had a big, comfortable bed, and a splendid view over the river and the old stone bridge. The compact modern bathroom had plenty of storage space; a good shower,' said regular Guide contributors in 2016. Eat in: served in the conservatory restaurant, chef Rachael Williams's classic-with-a-twist dinners use seasonal Herefordshire ingredients, perhaps venison 'enhanced by good red cabbage and excellent, garlicky dauphinoise potatoes'. 'We will return.' (Peter Anderson, and others)

Wilton Lane
Ross-on-Wye
HR9 6AQ

T: 01989 562569
F: 01989 768460
E: info@wiltoncourthotel.com
W: www.wiltoncourthotel.com

BEDROOMS: 11. 1 on ground floor.
OPEN: all year except first 2 weeks Jan.
FACILITIES: library, bar, restaurant, private dining room, free Wi-Fi, in-room TV (Freeview), ½-acre grounds, only restaurant suitable for disabled.
BACKGROUND MUSIC: in restaurant at mealtimes.
LOCATION: ½ mile from centre.
CHILDREN: all ages welcomed.
DOGS: allowed (£10 per stay), not in restaurant.
CREDIT CARDS: Amex, MasterCard, Visa.
PRICES: [2016] per room B&B £135–£185, D,B&B £195–£235. Set dinner £32.50, à la carte £40–£45. 1-night bookings refused weekends Apr–Oct.

ROWSLEY Derbyshire

Map 3:A6

THE PEACOCK AT ROWSLEY

In well-kept gardens reaching to the River Derwent, where wild trout dart through the water, this stylish 17th-century manor house is run with 'high standards'. Owners Lord and Lady Edward Manners live at nearby Haddon Hall; the staff are 'friendly', 'efficient', 'helpful'. Choose among individually styled bedrooms, each with a modern marble bathroom and an antique piece or two. (Rooms facing the busy road have double-glazed windows.) 'Overlooking the garden, our lovely, quiet, superior room had a good-sized bathroom with plenty of storage space (though the shower could have had better water pressure).' Eat in: chef Dan Smith's 'generously portioned' modern dishes are 'first class'. 'We enjoyed a tender venison cobbler; lamb rump came with a brilliant dish of peas, lettuce and baby onions braised with cured lamb belly – the tastiest vegetable dish I've ever had.' 'Excellent', sophisticated pub classics (burgers and wild garlic gnocchi among them) may be taken in the bar with a local ale or custom cocktail. Don't forget Fido: dogs are welcomed with treats and a bowl, even a biscuit at turn-down. (PA, and others)

Bakewell Road
Rowsley
DE4 2EB

T: 01629 733518
F: 01629 732671
E: reception@thepeacockatrowsley.com
W: www.thepeacockatrowsley.co.uk

BEDROOMS: 15.
OPEN: all year except 2 weeks Jan.
FACILITIES: lounge, bar, 2 dining rooms, free Wi-Fi, in-room TV (Freeview), civil wedding licence, ½-acre garden on the river, unsuitable for disabled.
BACKGROUND MUSIC: none.
LOCATION: village centre.
CHILDREN: not under 10 at weekends.
DOGS: allowed in bedrooms only (food and water bowls provided).
CREDIT CARDS: MasterCard, Visa.
PRICES: [2016] per room B&B from £190, D,B&B from £265. À la carte £45. 1-night bookings sometimes refused.

RUSHLAKE GREEN Sussex

Map 2:E4

STONE HOUSE

Old-fashioned hospitality never goes out of style at Jane and Peter Dunn's late Tudor ancestral manor house standing in 'beautifully kept' gardens and great swathes of secluded grassland. Enter through stone gates and up the drive twisting past the lake. Inside the gabled building, the Dunns run their 'delightful' small hotel with much charm and personal attention. Public rooms have plenty to admire: antiques, portraits and paintings; family photographs; vintage china and old silver; liberal spreads of chintz. Lay your head in one of the 'comfortable', staunchly traditional bedrooms, each with its own character and biscuit barrel. In the evening, Jane Dunn's 'top-notch' dinners are 'simple and pleasing', with 'wonderfully fresh' produce from the walled kitchen garden, perhaps grilled artichoke hearts, sun-dried tomatoes, bocconcini, fresh basil pesto. 'Afterwards, Mr Dunn paid us a visit in the library (dressed in a three-piece suit, no less!) and chatted to us by the log fire.' The estate is ripe for exploration: sit in the summer house, or taste strawberries in the garden; ask for a picnic to eat in the grounds. More reports, please.

Rushlake Green
TN21 9QJ

T: 01435 830553
F: 01435 830726
E: stonehousehotel@aol.co.uk
W: www.stonehousesussex.co.uk

BEDROOMS: 7.
OPEN: all year except 23 Dec–1 Jan, 15 Feb–7 Mar.
FACILITIES: drawing room, library, dining room, billiard room, free Wi-Fi, in-room TV (Freeview), 850-acre estate (6½-acre garden, farm, woodland, croquet, shooting, pheasant/clay-pigeon shooting, 2 lakes, rowing, fishing), unsuitable for disabled.
BACKGROUND MUSIC: none.
LOCATION: 4 miles SE of Heathfield, by village green.
CHILDREN: not under 9.
DOGS: allowed in bedrooms, not in public rooms.
CREDIT CARDS: MasterCard, Visa.
PRICES: [2016] per room B&B £140–£299. À la carte £35. 1-night bookings refused weekends 16 May–1 Sept.

RYE Sussex

JEAKE'S HOUSE

♥César award since 1992

There's charm a-plenty at Jenny Hadfield's B&B on cobbled Mermaid Street, its interior a characterful mix of low beams, blazing fires, dark panelling, labyrinthine passages and steep stairs. In a former Cinque Ports town rich in literary associations, the 17th-century wool store was from 1924 the 'deeply cherished home' of American writer Conrad Aiken. With the adjoining men's club and the Elders House, it has been restored by the 'very nice' owner. Bedrooms, all with fluffy towels, dressing gowns and a hospitality tray, are named after distinguished visitors; the best have a king-size four-poster bed and sitting area. (Some guests have wished for more storage space.) There is an atmospheric bar (just jot down what you drink), a parlour equipped with board games, and a 'very special' piano ('we are always pleased to hear people playing it,' the owner says). At a 'splendid' breakfast in a grand galleried room ('discreet' background music is played), help yourself to the buffet on the sideboard; Richard Martin cooks local sausages, Rye rarebit, scrambled eggs sprinkled with chives from the garden. (PM, and others)

Mermaid Street
Rye
TN31 7ET

T: 01797 222828
E: stay@jeakeshouse.com
W: www.jeakeshouse.com

BEDROOMS: 11.
OPEN: all year.
FACILITIES: parlour, bar/library, breakfast room, free Wi-Fi, in-room TV (Freeview), unsuitable for disabled.
BACKGROUND MUSIC: chamber music in breakfast room.
LOCATION: central, car park (£3 per 24 hours, advance booking).
CHILDREN: not under 8.
DOGS: allowed, on leads 'and always supervised' (£5 a night), not in breakfast room.
CREDIT CARDS: Diners, MasterCard, Visa.
PRICES: [2016] per room B&B £95–£150. 1-night bookings sometimes refused.

SEE ALSO SHORTLIST

ST IVES Cornwall

Map 1:D1

BOSKERRIS HOTEL

St Ives in summer, for all its charms, is crowded. But stroll along the Coastal Path, or take the train one stop to Carbis Bay, and you can be sitting here on the sun terrace, drink in hand, gazing out to the lighthouse that inspired Virginia Woolf. Marianne and Jonathan Bassett have gone for boutique chic at their 1930s hotel, with 'big glass doors', 'clean, light open spaces', and shades of cream, sand and sea. Most bedrooms have an ocean view; all are well supplied with a cafetière, bottled water, magazines, bathrobes and slippers. Splurge on the spacious 'celebration' room, with a sunken bath in the room. At breakfast tuck in to 'a better-than-average buffet' with fresh fruit, freshly squeezed orange juice and home-made muesli; a 'delicious' full English uses locally sourced ingredients, with 'lovely Cornish-made brown sauce'. Lazy afternoons call for a Cornish cream tea anywhere you care to sit; in the evening, ask for 'good advice' about local restaurants, or enjoy a simple supper 'with a hint of the Med'. More reports, please.

25% DISCOUNT VOUCHERS

Boskerris Road
Carbis Bay
St Ives
TR26 2NQ

T: 01736 795295
E: reservations@boskerrishotel.co.uk
W: www.boskerrishotel.co.uk

BEDROOMS: 15. 1 on ground floor.
OPEN: mid-Mar–mid-Nov, restaurant closed Sun/Mon.
FACILITIES: lounge, bar, breakfast room, supper room, free Wi-Fi, in-room TV, decked terrace, 1½-acre garden.
BACKGROUND MUSIC: all day in public rooms.
LOCATION: 1½ miles from centre (20 mins' walk), car park.
CHILDREN: not under 10.
DOGS: not allowed.
CREDIT CARDS: MasterCard, Visa.
PRICES: [2016] per room B&B £150–£280. À la carte £30. 1-night bookings sometimes refused in high season.

SEE ALSO SHORTLIST

ST LEONARDS-ON-SEA Sussex

Map 2:E4

ZANZIBAR INTERNATIONAL HOTEL

🏅César award since 2016

Yearning for Morocco's charms? Keen on Manhattan's city-slick style? Check in to Max O'Rourke's 'splendidly quirky' hotel on the Sussex seafront, where bedrooms are inspired by far-off travels. There's an informal, 'relaxed' ambience throughout: 'First names are used from the start; we were given drinks in the small garden while our suitcases were carted upstairs.' Pick a bedroom as if spinning a globe; with views of the sea or over the tropical garden (even a 'Zen garden', in one case), rooms 'vary hugely'. 'Spacious Antarctica had white walls and a chandelier like icicles; a window-side chaise longue and sofa looked through big windows towards the sea. A small fridge held drinks and goodies.' In the popular restaurant, Pier Nine, seafood is the draw: the morning's catch is listed on the menu. 'Delicious, utterly unpretentious' dishes might include 'very fresh' sea bass, charred baby gem, clam and potato broth. Alfresco meals can be taken in the small garden by the bar. In the morning, breakfast (ordered the night before) is accompanied by a note suggesting an outing for the day.

9 Eversfield Place
St Leonards-on-Sea
TN37 6BY

T: 01424 460109
E: info@zanzibarhotel.co.uk
W: www.zanzibarhotel.co.uk

BEDROOMS: 8. 1 on ground floor.
OPEN: all year.
FACILITIES: bar, restaurant, free Wi-Fi, in-room TV (Freeview), garden, beach across road, unsuitable for disabled.
BACKGROUND MUSIC: 'easy listening' in bar, restaurant.
LOCATION: seafront, 650 yds W of Hastings pier, free parking.
CHILDREN: not under 5.
DOGS: allowed in bedrooms. (cleaning fee), not in public rooms.
CREDIT CARDS: Amex, MasterCard, Visa.
PRICES: [2016] per room B&B from £99. Set dinner £34.50, à la carte £35.

ST MARY'S Isles of Scilly

STAR CASTLE

♉César award since 2009

Visitors new and old continue to award gold stars to the Francis family's characterful hotel, in a 16th-century castle above Hugh Town, with 'stunning views' over the islands. 'The immensely high standards are maintained,' says a trusted Guide correspondent in 2016. 'The staff are a cohesive, contented, well-managed team.' Choose among bedrooms in the castle and 'fine, comfortable' chalet-style buildings in the grounds. 'Our cosy castle room (they remembered our favourite) had been redecorated and updated. There were fresh flowers, a super tea tray, an exceptionally comfy bed – everything one could wish for after a long day birdwatching.' 'Look forward to dinner' in the 'atmospheric' restaurant or airy conservatory. 'We expected superb fish dishes, and they were, but the meat offerings were equally wonderful.' Guests who 'couldn't face a five-course meal' this year appreciated the option to choose 'any permutation' off the menu. Wake to a 'spectacular' breakfast spread; a 'fabulous' kedgeree; 'memorable' smoked haddock. (Abigail Kirby-Harris, Andrew Butterworth, Rosemary and Nick Wright)

25% DISCOUNT VOUCHERS

The Garrison
St Mary's
TR21 0JA

T: 01720 422317
F: 01720 422343
E: info@star-castle.co.uk
W: www.star-castle.co.uk

BEDROOMS: 38. 27 in 2 garden wings.
OPEN: all year, B&B only Nov–mid-Feb except Christmas/New Year.
FACILITIES: lounge, bar, 2 restaurants, free Wi-Fi, in-room TV (Freeview), civil wedding licence, 3-acre grounds (covered swimming pool, 12 by 4 metres, tennis), beach nearby, unsuitable for disabled.
BACKGROUND MUSIC: none.
LOCATION: ¼ mile from town centre, boat (2¾ hours)/helicopter.
CHILDREN: welcomed, no under-5s in restaurants in evening (children's dinner at 5.30 pm).
DOGS: allowed in garden rooms, not in restaurants or lounge.
CREDIT CARDS: Amex, MasterCard, Visa.
PRICES: [2016] per person B&B (Nov–mid-Feb) from £75, D,B&B from £89. À la carte £34.50.

ST MAWES Cornwall

Map 1:E2

IDLE ROCKS

Perched 'truly on the water', Karen and David Richards's sophisticated hotel is 'just the place to unfurl after the stresses of the day-to-day', visitors say. 'Well-chosen' decor in the public spaces 'sets the style': vibrant coastal colours ('lots of blue') throughout, along with bold paintings, huge flower planters, squashy cushions, 'up-to-date' glossy magazines. A children's playroom brims with toys and puzzles. Go barefoot in the individually styled bedrooms – all the better to feel the pile of 'expensive rugs' on smooth wooden floors. Against an airy palette, find 'splendid' pillows and 'gorgeous' flourishes (glasswork, bleached coral, heavy throws in natural fibres). 'Our bathroom had a motion-sensor-operated night light – a fantastic addition.' An evening turn-down service leaves 'tidiness everywhere'. In the lively restaurant, chef Guy Owen's modern menu draws from the local larder; consider wild bream alla romana, barbecued vegetables. A separate oyster menu has them butter-poached, with a lemongrass velouté, or in a chilli-ginger preparation. Breakfast has 'excellent marmalade', artisan bread, eggs all ways. (Abigail Kirby-Harris)

Harbourside
St Mawes
TR2 5AN

T: 01326 270270
E: reservations@idlerocks.com
W: www.idlerocks.com

BEDROOMS: 19. 4 in adjacent annexe, 1 suitable for disabled.
OPEN: all year.
FACILITIES: lounge, restaurant, kids' room, boot room, free Wi-Fi, in-room TV (Sky), terrace.
BACKGROUND MUSIC: all day in public areas.
LOCATION: central, on the harbour.
CHILDREN: all ages welcomed.
DOGS: allowed in 2 bedrooms, not in public rooms.
CREDIT CARDS: all major cards.
PRICES: [2016] per room B&B £200–£380. Set menu £45, à la carte £47.50. 1-night bookings sometimes refused weekends.

SEE ALSO SHORTLIST

ST MAWES Cornwall

Map 1:E2

TRESANTON

♌ César award since 2009

Atop a steep hill, a higgledy-piggledy path leads to this cluster of houses forming a 'faultless' hotel whose panoramic views reach across Falmouth Bay towards St Anthony's lighthouse. Owner/designer Olga Polizzi has retained the hotel's yachting origins (it was once a clubhouse), drawing connections to the sea everywhere: blue-and-white fabrics and tiles, lazy deckchairs, original Cornish seascapes, a mosaic of Poseidon. The adventurous might charter Pinuccia and take the luxury of the hotel on a day sea trip. Individually decorated bedrooms ('relaxed, but not overdone') are spread across the property, some reached up stairs through meandering gardens. Rooms might have a crow's nest terrace, a balcony with deckchairs; all but two are sea-facing. A cinema, a playroom and garden Wendy house will keep youngsters busy. In the 'superb' all-white restaurant, chef Paul Wadham's Mediterranean menu features the day's catch, perhaps brill, broccoli, pancetta, new potatoes. Book ahead for the popular summer barbecues. There is a sister hotel: Hotel Endsleigh, Milton Abbot (see entry).

27 Lower Castle Road
St Mawes
TR2 5DR

T: 01326 270055
F: 01326 270053
E: manager@tresanton.com
W: www.tresanton.com

BEDROOMS: 30. In 5 houses.
OPEN: all year, except 2–3 weeks Jan.
FACILITIES: 2 lounges, bar, restaurant, cinema, playroom, conference facilities, free Wi-Fi, in-room TV (Freeview), civil wedding licence, terrace, ¼-acre garden, 48-foot yacht, unsuitable for disabled.
BACKGROUND MUSIC: none.
LOCATION: on seafront, valet parking (car park up hill).
CHILDREN: all ages welcomed, no under-6s in restaurant in evening.
DOGS: allowed in some bedrooms, and in dogs' bar, not in sitting rooms or restaurant.
CREDIT CARDS: Amex, MasterCard, Visa.
PRICES: [2016] per room B&B from £255. À la carte £45. 1-night bookings refused peak weekends.

SEE ALSO SHORTLIST

SALCOMBE Devon

Map 1:E4

SALCOMBE HARBOUR HOTEL

With chic interiors decorated to 'an impressive sea theme', designers pushed the boat out when it came to the redevelopment of this 'attractive' Victorian waterside hotel on a 'wonderful' Devon estuary. There are 'many lovely touches': maritime stripes and shades of blue; wide terraces for alfresco dining; in-room binoculars to take in the 'stunning' views. Throughout, staff are 'professional and willing to please'. Choose from four floors of bedrooms, many overlooking the water; 'decanters of gin and sherry in the room are a nice touch, with ice and lemon delivered each evening'. 'Our room, which had a balcony facing the beaches across the estuary, was difficult to fault.' There's 'a good ambience' in the Jetty restaurant, where chef Alex Aitken cooks seasonal dishes with an emphasis on 'high-quality' ingredients and locally caught fish – say, paupiette of sole, Salcombe crab fondue, wilted greens. 'Very good' breakfasts include avocado on sourdough toast; grilled kippers with caper beurre noisette. Tuck in, then head out to explore the coastline or sail to secluded coves – it'll be gin o'clock before you know it.

Cliff Road
Salcombe
TQ8 8JH

T: 01548 844444
E: salcombe@harbourhotels.co.uk
W: www.salcombe-harbour-hotel.
   co.uk

BEDROOMS: 50. 2 suitable for disabled.
OPEN: all year.
FACILITIES: bar/lounge, Jetty restaurant, free Wi-Fi, in-room TV, civil wedding licence, spa (indoor swimming pool, 15 by 5 metres, fitness suite, treatment rooms), private moorings.
BACKGROUND MUSIC: in public areas.
LOCATION: town centre.
CHILDREN: all ages welcomed.
DOGS: allowed in some bedrooms, not in public rooms.
CREDIT CARDS: all major cards.
PRICES: [2016] per room B&B £169–£545. À la carte £45. 1-night bookings sometimes refused.

SEE ALSO SHORTLIST

SEAHAM Co. Durham

SEAHAM HALL

'A wonderful place, combining luxury, style and high standards with a pleasantly friendly and relaxed approach.' This serene, 'civilised' Georgian country house close to the sea is 'popular with all ages', say trusted Guide correspondents who celebrated 'a very special wedding anniversary in this very special place' in 2016. (They are doing rather better than Lord Byron and Anne Isabella Milbanke, who were married in the upstairs drawing room in 1815 and separated a year later.) Stay in contemporary, individually styled bedrooms, each stocked with fluffy bathrobes, classy toiletries, a capsule coffee-maker. 'Our spacious suite had a huge bed with a wonderfully soft duvet – utter luxury.' The views are of 'extensive grounds, beautifully landscaped', and of the sea. Sit down to a light, pan-Asian meal in the Ozone restaurant, or dine more formally on surprising modern dishes (perhaps ox cheek, hay-baked beetroot, pickled brambles) in Byron's Restaurant. Feeling overindulged? Reached via a peaceful, all-wood corridor, the Serenity Spa has 'all the facilities imaginable', including 'a large pool, lovely just for relaxing in'. (Pauline and Stephen Glover)

25% DISCOUNT VOUCHERS

Lord Byron's Walk
Seaham
SR7 7AG

T: 0191 5161400
E: hotel@seaham-hall.com
W: www.seaham-hall.com

BEDROOMS: 20. 1 suitable for disabled.
OPEN: all year.
FACILITIES: lift, 2 lounges, bar, 2 restaurants, private dining room, conference facilities, free Wi-Fi, in-room TV (Sky, BT), civil wedding licence, spa (treatment rooms, outdoor hot tubs, sun terrace, fitness suite, 20-metre heated swimming pool), 37-acre grounds (terraces, putting green).
BACKGROUND MUSIC: all day in public areas.
LOCATION: 5 miles S of Sunderland.
CHILDREN: all ages welcomed.
DOGS: not allowed.
CREDIT CARDS: Amex, MasterCard, Visa.
PRICES: [2016] per room B&B from £195, D,B&B from £255. Market menu £30, à la carte £50. 1-night bookings sometimes refused weekends.

SEAHOUSES Northumberland

Map 4:A4

ST CUTHBERT'S HOUSE

'What a find!' enthuses a regular Guide reader, of this 'brilliant' B&B in a 'lovingly restored' Presbyterian church on the 'beautiful' Northumberland coast. 'Great hosts' Jill and Jeff Sutheran live in the manse next door. Part of the church's former sanctuary, the Cuthbert room still contains the original harmonium, wooden pillars and tall windows; it is the communal heart of the B&B, with the breakfast room at one end and sofas at the other (lots of local information, too). Fancy a drink? Help yourself to the well-stocked honesty bar, which includes botanically brewed soft drinks and the house beer. Bedrooms are 'spacious' and 'comfortable', provided with dressing gowns and slippers; the Bede room, on the ground floor, is suitable for guests with mobility issues. Breakfast makes a feature of the local smoked fish. Try kipper pâté, or 'the best-ever' kedgeree, made with oak-smoked haddock from the village smokehouse. In the evening, the hosts have plenty of restaurant recommendations to share. Listen out for music nights: themselves musicians, the Sutherans organise occasional folk concerts. (GM, and others)

192 Main Street
Seahouses
NE68 7UB

T: 01665 720456
E: stay@stcuthbertshouse.com
W: www.stcuthbertshouse.com

BEDROOMS: 6. 2 on ground floor, 1 suitable for disabled.
OPEN: all year, except Christmas/ New Year, 'holiday periods in winter'.
FACILITIES: lounge, breakfast room, free Wi-Fi, in-room TV (Freeview), small garden.
BACKGROUND MUSIC: none.
LOCATION: 1 mile from harbour.
CHILDREN: not under 12.
DOGS: not allowed.
CREDIT CARDS: MasterCard, Visa.
PRICES: [2016] per room B&B £110–£125. 1-night bookings sometimes refused.

SHAFTESBURY Dorset

Map 2:D1

LA FLEUR DE LYS

Schoolgirls are a rarer sight today at this former girls' boarding school, now restaurant-with-rooms, in historic Shaftesbury, but education is still important: tutored wine-tasting weekends can be arranged. Mary Griffin-Shepherd is the 'friendly, hands-on' front-of-house at the ivy-clad stone building; husband, David, and Marc Preston are the much-praised chefs. 'It continues to be excellent,' a returning guest says this year. The seasonal dishes, served in the 'lovely' dining room, might include 'well-executed' crab mousse, samphire; seared Sika venison, apples, shallots, prunes. 'Try as much of the menu as possible.' The bedrooms are named after different varieties of grape. Sauvignon is 'small, but clean and well equipped'; 'immaculate' Shiraz is liked for its 'large, very comfortable' bed. Superior rooms have a sofa and a laptop computer. Guests in all rooms enjoy home-made biscuits, a fridge with fresh milk and bottles of water. Tuck in to an 'excellent' breakfast (freshly squeezed orange juice, porridge, marmalade in pots, a napkin to keep toast warm) before setting off to explore the 'friendly little town steeped in history'. (John Barnes, CB, and others)

25% DISCOUNT VOUCHERS

Bleke Street
Shaftesbury
SP7 8AW

T: 01747 853717
E: info@lafleurdelys.co.uk
W: www.lafleurdelys.co.uk

BEDROOMS: 8. 1 on ground floor.
OPEN: all year.
FACILITIES: lounge, bar, dining room, conference room, free Wi-Fi, in-room TV (Freeview), small courtyard garden.
BACKGROUND MUSIC: none.
LOCATION: N edge of historic town centre.
CHILDREN: all ages welcomed.
DOGS: not allowed.
CREDIT CARDS: Amex, MasterCard, Visa.
PRICES: [2016] per room B&B from £100, D,B&B from £175. Set meals from £29. 1-night bookings sometimes refused.

SHEFFIELD Yorkshire

Map 4:E4

✿ BROCCO ON THE PARK   NEW

César award: city hotel of the year

'What a joy to discover this stylish city hotel,' Guide inspectors enthuse in 2016. In a 'buzzy' neighbourhood beside Endcliffe Park, Tiina Carr has 'spruced up' this 'handsome' red brick building with a 'vibrant' 'Scandi-chic' interior. 'Our spacious room had a white-painted fireplace, a splendid king-size bed with good linen, louvred shutters on the windows; an enormous double-ended bath and excellent storage in the large bathroom. A couple of welcoming cupcakes awaited. Despite the double glazing, there was some road noise from busy Hunter's bar, out front.' Lit candles flicker in the restaurant at dinnertime; guests may eat alfresco on the terrace in the summer. Daily blackboard specials supplement the 'interesting' menu (many vegetarian, gluten-free options). 'We enjoyed tasty crab cakes; pork belly with crispy crackling and especially good red cabbage.' A guest in a wheelchair was 'gracefully accommodated, without fuss'. Join locals in the café at breakfast (charged extra), where 'extensive' choices include 'beautifully grilled' bacon, sourdough toast.

92 Brocco Bank
Sheffield
S11 8RS

T: 0114 266 1233
E: hello@brocco.co.uk
W: www.brocco.co.uk

BEDROOMS: 8. 1 suitable for disabled.
OPEN: all year.
FACILITIES: reception area, bar, restaurant, free Wi-Fi, in-room smart TV, civil wedding licence, terrace (barbecue), bicycle hire.
BACKGROUND MUSIC: in restaurant, plus Sunday jazz afternoons.
LOCATION: 1½ miles W of city centre.
CHILDREN: all ages welcomed.
DOGS: not allowed.
CREDIT CARDS: Amex, MasterCard, Visa.
PRICES: [2016] room £90–£230. Cooked breakfast from £7, à la carte £40.

SEE ALSO SHORTLIST

SHREWSBURY Shropshire

Map 3:B4

THE SILVERTON

NEW

Just over the Welsh Bridge from the historic town centre, David Cheshire and Donna Miles's 'excellent-value' restaurant-with-rooms is liked for its 'great, friendly service' and 'modern, almost minimalist' rooms. 'It ticked all the boxes,' say trusted Guide readers this year. Individually decorated bedrooms (some compact) have a modern shower room; two may be connected to form a family suite. 'Everything about our spotless, beautifully appointed room shouted "quality". It had large, double-glazed sash windows; a super-comfy bed; modern furnishings; up-to-date tech. The lovely bathroom had a drench shower, and fluffy towels on the heated towel rail.' Rooms at the front of the building may have some traffic noise (earplugs are provided). Modern meals (perhaps pan-fried duck breast, savoy cabbage, dauphinoise potatoes, poached pear) are served all day in the restaurant. 'A jazz guitarist was playing in the bar at dinnertime. We chose their steak deal – two sirloins cooked to perfection, with a bottle of house wine, and a lovely Malteser cheesecake dessert.' Theatre Severn is around the corner; pre-theatre menus are available. (Ian Malone)

9–10 Frankwell
Shrewsbury
SY3 8JY

T: 01743 248000
E: bookings@thesilverton.co.uk
W: www.thesilverton.co.uk

BEDROOMS: 7. 1 suitable for disabled.
OPEN: all year.
FACILITIES: lift, bar, restaurant, free Wi-Fi, in-room TV, terrace.
BACKGROUND MUSIC: live music every Fri and Sat night.
LOCATION: 10-min. walk from centre.
CHILDREN: all ages welcomed.
DOGS: not allowed.
CREDIT CARDS: MasterCard, Visa.
PRICES: [2016] per room B&B £75–£135. Pre-theatre menu £14, à la carte £30.

SEE ALSO SHORTLIST

SIDMOUTH Devon

Map 1:C5

HOTEL RIVIERA

'What a difference the details make!' Regular Guide contributors agree, finding service at Peter Wharton's traditional hotel 'consistently excellent'. At this fine Regency terrace overlooking Lyme Bay, visitors receive a 'warm' welcome from 'very friendly, professional staff who remember your name, and take time for a little chat when appropriate'. Bedrooms are 'spotless' and 'well equipped', the bathrooms 'very modern'. ('My one quibble was the scarcity of available sockets.') The sound of waves lapping the beach reaches seafront rooms. Dinner is 'a delight': chef Martin Osedo's 'inviting' daily-changing menus might include 'perfectly portioned, beautifully presented' dishes such as seared king scallops, apple compote, celeriac. Several vegetarian options are available. While guests dine, the bed is turned down, the teapot cleaned, the curtains are drawn. In the morning, an 'extensive and absolutely delicious' breakfast awaits. Served at the table in the 'timeless' dining room, it includes juice and freshly brewed coffee, fruit compote and cereals, poached haddock, eggs any way, hot toast 'that comes at the precise time you want it'. (TL)

The Esplanade
Sidmouth
EX10 8AY

T: 01395 515201
F: 01395 577775
E: enquiries@hotelriviera.co.uk
W: www.hotelriviera.co.uk

BEDROOMS: 26.
OPEN: all year.
FACILITIES: lift, lounge, bar, restaurant, function facilities, free Wi-Fi, in-room TV (Freeview), terrace, opposite pebble/sand beach (safe bathing).
BACKGROUND MUSIC: in bar and restaurant at mealtimes, occasional live piano music in bar.
LOCATION: central, on the esplanade.
CHILDREN: all ages welcomed.
DOGS: small dogs allowed in some bedrooms, not in public rooms except foyer.
CREDIT CARDS: all major cards.
PRICES: [2016] per person B&B £109–£194, D,B&B £129–£215. Set dinner £39–£43, à la carte £44.

SEE ALSO SHORTLIST

SOAR MILL COVE Devon

Map 1:E4

SOAR MILL COVE HOTEL

Family owned, family run, exuberantly family friendly, Keith Makepeace's 'welcoming' hotel stands in rolling countryside above a valley running down to the shore. Continuity gives it 'a pleasant, settled feel': they still serve the 'divine' pavlova Mr Makepeace's mother once made for Audrey Hepburn. Take a clotted cream tea on the terrace, then explore the many diversions outdoors and in: lawn and table tennis, a heated saltwater swimming pool, a spa, and 'lovely walks to the beach, with its craggy rocks' (borrow a pair of binoculars for dolphin-spotting). At dinner, tuck in to seaside-fresh fish and seafood alongside much locally sourced produce: chef Ian MacDonald's market-style menus might include Cornish Yarg and Exmoor Blue cheese soufflé; Cornish hake, baby spinach, samphire, soft-poached egg. Pick one of the modern bedrooms to call your own: varying room layouts suit parents with children, or couples wanting privacy; all have French windows opening on to a private patio leading to the garden. In the morning, a cheering breakfast includes local sausages, Salcombe smokies, home-made conserves, freshly squeezed juices. (CE)

Soar Mill Cove
TQ7 3DS

T: 01548 561566
E: info@soarmillcove.co.uk
W: www.soarmillcove.co.uk

BEDROOMS: 22. All on ground floor.
OPEN: all year, except New Year, Jan.
FACILITIES: lounge, 2 bars, restaurant, coffee shop, free Wi-Fi in reception, in-room TV (Freeview), indoor swimming pool (15 by 10 metres), treatment room (hairdressing, reflexology, aromatherapy, etc), civil wedding licence, 10-acre grounds (tennis, children's play area), sandy beach.
BACKGROUND MUSIC: none.
LOCATION: 3 miles SW of Salcombe.
CHILDREN: all ages welcomed (children's tea, baby-listening service, games room, children's entertainment in summer).
DOGS: allowed in bedrooms, coffee shop.
CREDIT CARDS: Amex, MasterCard, Visa.
PRICES: [2016] per room B&B from £125, D,B&B from £195. À la carte £35. 1-night bookings refused holiday weekends.

SOMERTON Somerset

Map 1:C6

THE LYNCH COUNTRY HOUSE

In extensive gardens on the edge of this medieval market town, former jazz musician Roy Copeland's 'elegant, understated, very comfortable' B&B hits the right note. It is ably managed by Lynne Vincent. Choose among the country-style bedrooms in the Grade II listed Georgian house and converted coach house across the courtyard: all rooms come with bathrobes, bottled water, a tea tray. Each has its own character – some are in the eaves, with a skylight; one has a four-poster bed and huge windows overlooking the grounds; all have a generous sprinkling of flowery prints. The 'beautiful' house has plenty of interest: climb to the observation deck at the top for far-reaching views of town and countryside; stroll in the gardens – 'worth a visit in their own right' – looking out for the resident swans on the lake. In the morning, sit down to a 'superb' breakfast: bread from a local bakery, fresh berries in season, hot dishes cooked to order. Dinner's 'not a problem': The White Hart (see Shortlist entry) is a five-minute walk away. More reports, please.

4 Behind Berry
Somerton
TA11 7PD

T: 01458 272316
F: 01458 272590
E: enquiries@
   thelynchcountryhouse.co.uk
W: www.thelynchcountryhouse.co.uk

BEDROOMS: 9. 4, in coach house, on ground floor.
OPEN: all year, only coach house rooms at Christmas and New Year, no breakfast 25 Dec/1 Jan.
FACILITIES: breakfast room, small sitting area, free Wi-Fi, in-room TV (Freeview), ¾-acre grounds (lake), unsuitable for disabled.
BACKGROUND MUSIC: none.
LOCATION: edge of town.
CHILDREN: all ages welcomed.
DOGS: allowed (not unattended) in 1 coach house room, not in public rooms.
CREDIT CARDS: Amex, MasterCard, Visa.
PRICES: [2016] per room B&B single £70–£95, double £80–£125.

SEE ALSO SHORTLIST

SOUTHAMPTON Hampshire

Map 2:E2

THE PIG IN THE WALL

'Smart', 'stylish' and 'shabby chic', this well-liked B&B is 'an eye-opening treat' in the busy port city, Guide inspectors say. Part of Robin Hutson's growing litter of Pig hotels, it receives praise for its 'well-thought-out' design and its 'delightful, efficient' staff. The 19th-century building is 'charmingly' set into the ancient city walls near the docks; inside, the reception area (wood floors, vintage china, a stuffed owl) works overtime as breakfast room, lounge and popular deli bar. 'Large and small pots of herbs were peppered about; people enjoyed nibbles and drinks by an open fire.' 'Everything works well' in the bedrooms: 'Our room had a beamed ceiling, original decorative iron fireplace, a bathtub in the bedroom (I would have preferred a sofa). We slept well, on crisp linens, in our superking-size bed.' The deli counter serves 'good-looking' snacks and drinks from midday until 10 pm. Better yet, book in at sister hotel The Pig, Brockenhurst (see entry) for dinner – transport's provided. In the morning, boil your own eggs at the continental buffet breakfast; 'good' coffee is served by the cup.

8 Western Esplanade
Southampton
SO14 2AZ

T: 02380 636900
E: info@thepighotel.com
W: www.thepighotel.com

BEDROOMS: 12. 2 on ground floor.
OPEN: all year.
FACILITIES: open-plan lounge/bar/deli counter, free Wi-Fi, in-room TV (Freeview), unsuitable for disabled.
BACKGROUND MUSIC: in public areas.
LOCATION: on the outskirts of the city.
CHILDREN: all ages welcomed.
DOGS: not allowed.
CREDIT CARDS: MasterCard, Visa.
PRICES: [2016] room £130–£190. Breakfast £10.

SEE ALSO SHORTLIST

STAMFORD Lincolnshire

Map 2:B3

THE GEORGE

'Very much a town hotel' ('at teatime it was full of people taking tea; in the morning, it was heaving with coffee drinkers'), this popular spot attracts many return guests who praise the 'friendly welcome' and the 'pleasant, unfussy' service. 'Consistently good, the place is run like a well-oiled machine, with an army of well-trained staff.' 'Although I travelled alone, I wasn't neglected at all.' Bedrooms vary in size; each has a handmade bed and bathrobes. 'Our large room – almost like a private apartment – had a half-tester bed, a sofa and two comfy chairs; a gleaming, modern bathroom; a peaceful garden view. Both windows opened to allow a through breeze.' 'The morning delivery of tea or coffee to the room is an excellent and enjoyable tradition.' There's plenty of opportunity to eat well: 'excellent' dinners, including veggie options, in the 'traditional' Oak Restaurant ('where the beef on the silver trolley and the dessert display are particular attractions'); 'tasty sandwiches' in the York Bar; breakfast cooked to order in the Garden Room. 'Our informal Garden Room dinner – of lobster spaghetti and summer pudding – was faultless.' (Josie Mayers, Helen Ann Davies, Lynn Wildgoose, Peter Anderson)

71 St Martins
Stamford
PE9 2LB

T: 01780 750750
F: 01780 750701
E: reservations@
  georgehotelofstamford.com
W: www.georgehotelofstamford.com

BEDROOMS: 45.
OPEN: all year.
FACILITIES: 2 lounges, 2 bars, 2 restaurants, 4 private dining rooms, business centre, free Wi-Fi, in-room TV (Sky, Freeview), civil wedding licence, 2-acre grounds (courtyard, gardens), only public areas suitable for disabled.
BACKGROUND MUSIC: none.
LOCATION: ½ mile from centre.
CHILDREN: all ages welcomed.
DOGS: allowed, not unattended in bedrooms, only guide dogs in restaurants.
CREDIT CARDS: all major cards.
PRICES: [2016] per room B&B £145–£260. À la carte £50.

SEE ALSO SHORTLIST

STANTON WICK Somerset

THE CARPENTER'S ARMS

Tap into 'friendly efficiency' at this well-liked inn: Guide readers returning this year tell us 'it was better than ever'. Charmingly hewn from a row of miners' cottages, it greets travellers with 'appealing' flower baskets. Inside, enter into 'a maze of thoroughly attractive rooms full of nooks and crannies' and an air of enduring constancy: low beams, exposed stone, solid wood, strong tartans, dark leather armchairs. Up 'steep' stairs, the bedrooms are as modern as the pub is traditional: bright, contemporary decor, with 'good' fittings and lighting; 'a fiercely effective heated towel rail' and lots of storage in the bathroom. In the popular pub ('busy every night – it's obviously well known'), Chris Dando's 'imaginative yet unfussy' menu 'spoils for choice' with, perhaps, herby Parmesan-crusted cod, chorizo-olive hash, roasted red pepper. A 'memorable' breakfast – with hot toast, 'excellent' poached eggs, a fruit platter, good coffee – is served at table, 'which makes a pleasant change from the usual buffet scrum'. Well placed for travel to Bath or Bristol (it's 20 minutes from the airport) and further afield. (MH, Jeannette Bloor, K and PR)

Wick Lane
Stanton Wick
BS39 4BX

T: 01761 490202
F: 01761 490763
E: carpenters@buccaneer.co.uk
W: www.the-carpenters-arms.co.uk

BEDROOMS: 13.
OPEN: all year except evenings 25/26 Dec, 1 Jan.
FACILITIES: bar, snug, 2 restaurants, function room, free Wi-Fi, in-room TV (Freeview), patio, secure parking, only public areas suitable for disabled.
BACKGROUND MUSIC: none.
LOCATION: 8 miles S of Bristol, 8 miles W of Bath.
CHILDREN: all ages welcomed.
DOGS: allowed in bar and outside areas.
CREDIT CARDS: Amex, MasterCard, Visa.
PRICES: [2016] per room B&B single from £75, double from £110, D,B&B single from £97.50, double from £155. À la carte £36.50.

STRATFORD-UPON-AVON Warwickshire   Map 3:D6

CHERRY TREES

'It oozes quality.' 'They made us feel like royalty.' 'Unreservedly recommended.' A chorus of praise this year for this 'fabulous' B&B, in a 'superb' spot 'convenient for the town and surrounding countryside'. Across the footbridge from the RSC Theatre, 'marvellous' hosts Tony Godel and Royd Laidlow receive a standing ovation for their 'friendly' welcome and the 'delicious' home-baked cake they offer to arriving guests. Bedrooms are 'clean' and 'tastefully decorated'; all have bathrobes, a Roberts radio, tea- and coffee-making facilities, home-made biscuits, helpful local information. 'Quiet and elegant, our comfortable suite had a private conservatory and a view on to the carefully tended water garden.' Wake refreshed: breakfast, with juice and freshly ground coffee, is as you like it. 'Generous, with very good choice', the spread includes fruit, Drambuie cream porridge, a selection of omelettes, a full English with award-winning sausages; granola, bread and marmalade are all home made. Popular with theatregoers; Tony Godel, a former stage manager, speaks with enthusiasm about the latest productions. (Wayne Ewing, Melinda Varcoe, Sharon Stuthard)

Swan's Nest Lane
Stratford-upon-Avon
CV37 7LS

T: 01789 292989
E: cherrytreesstratforduponavon@
    gmail.com
W: www.cherrytrees-stratford.co.uk

BEDROOMS: 3. All on ground floor.
OPEN: 4 Mar–3 Dec.
FACILITIES: breakfast room, free Wi-Fi, in-room TV (Freeview), ½-acre garden.
BACKGROUND MUSIC: none.
LOCATION: central, near river.
CHILDREN: not under 12.
DOGS: not allowed.
CREDIT CARDS: MasterCard, Visa.
PRICES: per room B&B £115–£135. 1-night bookings sometimes refused.

SEE ALSO SHORTLIST

STUDLAND Dorset

THE PIG ON THE BEACH

♀César award since 2016

The fourth addition to Robin Hutson's drove, this little Pig, in a 'rambling', turreted Gothic manor house, is 'a relaxed version of a country hotel, noticeably enjoyed by guests of all ages'. 'The welcome could not have been bettered,' Guide inspectors say. 'We were greeted with a smile and charming efficiency.' Take your pick from bedrooms in the 'imaginatively converted' main house, dovecotes and shepherds' huts: each is individually styled with mismatched furniture, vintage touches, woollen blankets. 'Our room had an enormous, comfy bed, good lighting, a large wardrobe; reclaimed-wood floors, retro prints, a Roberts radio. The huge windows overlooked grazing sheep.' After a morning on the white sands of Studland Bay, relax on 'squashy' sofas in the 'delightfully quirky' public rooms. In the conservatory dining room, Andy Wright's 'simple, appetising' dishes, perhaps chargrilled chicken, purple mizuna, garden pickles, use produce from the three kitchen gardens. Expect 'a treasure trove' at breakfast. Sister Pigs make their homes in Brockenhurst, Southampton and Pensford (see entries).

Manor House
Manor Road
Studland
BH19 3AU

T: 01929 450288
E: info@thepighotel.com
W: www.thepighotel.com

BEDROOMS: 23. Some on ground floor, 2 Dovecot hideaways, Harry's Hut and Pig Hut in grounds.
OPEN: all year.
FACILITIES: bar, lounge, snug, restaurant, private dining room, free Wi-Fi, in-room TV (Freeview), 2 treatment cabins, garden, unsuitable for disabled.
BACKGROUND MUSIC: all day in public areas.
LOCATION: above Studland Beach.
CHILDREN: all ages welcomed.
DOGS: not allowed.
CREDIT CARDS: MasterCard, Visa.
PRICES: [2016] room £170–£310. Breakfast £10–£15, à la carte £35. 1-night bookings refused weekends, Christmas, New Year.

STURMINSTER NEWTON Dorset

Map 2:E1

PLUMBER MANOR

♥ César award since 1987

An ancestral home under the care of the
Prideaux-Brune family, this 'wonderfully quiet'
17th-century country house in 'lovely, well-
cared-for' gardens has been a hotel since 1972.
Its many devotees love its eccentricities and the
unfailing warmth and bonhomie of Richard
Prideaux-Brune as front-of-house. 'Richard
welcomed us and looked after us beautifully.'
There is 'a timeless feel' about the faded, old-
fashioned setting, all log fires, antique sofas,
and portraits in gilded frames: 'It is indeed a
true escape.' Less liked is a sense, shared by
some guests, that the house has escaped the
modern world. 'One of the charms of Plumber
is its lack of "smart" or "chic". However,
"genteel dilapidation" can be taken too far.'
'Comfortable', staunchly traditional bedrooms
are floral and homely, with shortbread biscuits.
The formal dining rooms remain 'exquisite'.
Here, Brian Prideaux-Brune's daily-changing
menu, which might include roast guineafowl,
black cherries, cinnamon, is 'fantastic' – like
the house over its many years, 'the chef hasn't
changed, either'. (Humphrey and Frances
Norrington, and others)

25% DISCOUNT VOUCHERS

Sturminster Newton
DT10 2AF

T: 01258 472507
F: 01258 473370
E: book@plumbermanor.com
W: www.plumbermanor.com

BEDROOMS: 16. 10 on ground floor in
courtyard.
OPEN: all year except Feb.
FACILITIES: snug, bar, dining room,
gallery, free Wi-Fi, in-room TV
(Freeview), 1-acre grounds (garden,
tennis, croquet, stream).
BACKGROUND MUSIC: none.
LOCATION: 2½ miles SW of
Sturminster Newton.
CHILDREN: all ages welcomed.
DOGS: allowed in 4 bedrooms, not in
public rooms.
CREDIT CARDS: all major cards.
PRICES: [2016] per room B&B
£160–£240. Set dinner from £30.

SWAFFHAM Norfolk

Map 2:B5

STRATTONS

♛César award since 2003

Find all manner of eccentricities and theatrical touches at Les and Vanessa Scott's good-natured, family-friendly hotel. A bohemian, eco-friendly place, the Grade II listed Palladian-style house is managed by the Scotts' daughter, Hannah, and her husband, Dominic Hughes, with 'friendly, helpful' staff. 'Quirky' and 'imaginative', bedrooms in the main house and converted outbuildings have a carved four-poster bed here, a mermaid mosaic there, a Moroccan-style tented ceiling elsewhere still. There are antiques and art, original period features; even a private decked balcony or courtyard garden. Have children in tow? Spacious suites are ideal for a family; games, books and toys are readily available in the lounge. In the restaurant, Jules Hetherton relies on a network of foragers and local producers for the seasonal ingredients in her 'excellent' modern British dishes. Characteristic dishes: beetroot tarte Tatin, herby garden salad; cocoa-spiced pollack, Jerusalem artichokes, mussels. Tuck in – then ask Les Scott, a keen runner, about his favourite routes down forest trails. More reports, please.

4 Ash Close
Swaffham
PE37 7NH

T: 01760 723845
E: enquiries@strattonshotel.com
W: www.strattonshotel.com

BEDROOMS: 14. 6 in annexes, 1 on ground floor.
OPEN: all year except 1 week at Christmas.
FACILITIES: drawing room, reading room, restaurant, free Wi-Fi, in-room TV (Freeview), terrace, café/deli, 1-acre garden, unsuitable for disabled.
BACKGROUND MUSIC: all day in public areas.
LOCATION: central, parking.
CHILDREN: all ages welcomed.
DOGS: allowed in some bedrooms (£10 per day), lounges, not in restaurant.
CREDIT CARDS: Amex, MasterCard, Visa.
PRICES: [2016] per room B&B from £109, D,B&B from £163. À la carte £30. 1-night bookings refused weekends, 3-night min. at bank holidays.

SWALLOWCLIFFE Wiltshire

Map 2:D1

🦢 THE ROYAL OAK

NEW

César award: newcomer of the year

The Cinderella story is writ large in this 'magnificent' pub-with-rooms, an 'elegant' thatched-roof inn in a wooded valley. A group of villagers saved the derelict 19th-century building, the tale goes – and 'what a conversion it's turned out to be!' say Guide inspectors in 2016. 'We were welcomed with charm and warmth. Inside, superbly lit public areas wouldn't be out of place in the smartest glossies: stunning, yet comfortable, custom-designed furniture, Persian-style rugs, well-chosen modern paintings in tune with the rural setting.' Serene bedrooms overlook the village or the garden; two adjoining rooms are suitable for a family. 'Everything was immaculate in our large, well-lit room: an emperor-size bed, good bedside lamps, filter coffee, six sorts of tea; in the bathroom, fluffy towels on heated rails.' Come hungry for chef Mark Treasure's 'sophisticated', 'satisfying' pub classics. 'We loved the brill with a clever garnish of buckwheat, dried fig and crème fraîche.' Mornings, wake to 'delicious yogurt with fresh berries, chunky slices of home-baked bread, generous servings of salmon and scrambled eggs'.

Swallowcliffe
SP3 5PA

T: 01747 870211
E: hello@royaloakswallowcliffe.com
w: www.royaloakswallowcliffe.com

BEDROOMS: 6. 1 suitable for disabled.
OPEN: all year.
FACILITIES: lift, bar, dining room, Oak Room, free Wi-Fi, in-room TV (Freeview), garden.
BACKGROUND MUSIC: none.
LOCATION: 2 miles SE of Tisbury.
CHILDREN: all ages welcomed.
DOGS: 'friendly, well-behaved' dogs allowed in 1 room, public rooms (treats, towels provided).
CREDIT CARDS: Amex, MasterCard, Visa.
PRICES: [2016] per room B&B from £100. À la carte £28.

SWINBROOK Oxfordshire

Map 3:D6

THE SWAN INN

The setting is 'heavenly', say Guide inspectors this year: the rustic inn stands by a bridge over the River Windrush, a cricket pitch up the road; in the spring, newborn lambs bleat in the fields. Debo Mitford, the late Dowager Duchess of Devonshire, spent her childhood in this village; the inn is decorated with black-and-white family photographs. Enter through the cosy restaurant (flowers, oak settles, mismatched furnishings), where locals gather for real ales and seasonal, gastropubby meals – perhaps 'a generous helping of asparagus soup; delicious hake fillet on spicy chickpea dhal'. In fine weather, the garden fills with jolly guests while chickens roam free. 'Delightful' bedrooms are in converted stables by the garden and in a refurbished cottage on the waterfront. 'We'd booked a room in the cottage because we wanted the views – and, my goodness, we had them, in a lovely room with three aspects.' Be cheered by breakfast: 'on the buffet, dried-fruit compote, a bowl of honey, a big jug of the most freshly squeezed juice; excellent bacon and sausage; a lovely fried egg'. Landlords Archie and Nicola Orr-Ewing also run The King's Head Inn, Bledington (see entry).

25% DISCOUNT VOUCHERS

Swinbrook
OX18 4DY

T: 01993 823339
E: info@theswanswinbrook.co.uk
W: www.theswanswinbrook.co.uk

BEDROOMS: 11. 7 on ground floor, 5 in riverside cottage.
OPEN: all year except Christmas/New Year.
FACILITIES: bar, restaurant, free Wi-Fi, in-room TV (Freeview), garden, orchard, unsuitable for disabled.
BACKGROUND MUSIC: in bar and restaurant.
LOCATION: 2 miles E of Burford.
CHILDREN: all ages welcomed.
DOGS: not allowed.
CREDIT CARDS: MasterCard, Visa.
PRICES: [2016] per room B&B £125–£195, D,B&B £185–£255. À la carte £35.

TALLAND BAY HOTEL

There are, 'quite literally', fairies at the bottom of the garden at Teresa and Kevin O'Sullivan's 'friendly' clifftop hotel, on a 'remote' country road 'with spectacular views of the sea'. 'A welcoming spot with happy, smiley staff, it has a stylish sense of quirk and humour, all tastefully done. There's lots of artwork throughout, and plenty of outside seating areas to admire the view,' say Guide inspectors in 2016. No two bedrooms are the same – some are 'up different staircases', others are in cottages; one, accessed through the dining room, 'was remarkably convenient when it came to meals'. A 'New England-style' sea-view room is 'lovely and light, with chairs to sit in, cup of tea in hand, by the windows'. Another, 'warm and comfortable', has a 'huge' claw-footed bath in the 'large' bathroom, 'but the bedroom blinds didn't keep out the lights left on in the car park all night'. Eat in: 'The food was wonderful, and served in generous portions – lots of fish, an amuse-bouche at the start and a palate-cleanser at the end.' (Suzanne Lyons, and others)

Porthallow
Talland-by-Looe
PL13 2JB

T: 01503 272667
F: 01503 272940
E: info@tallandbayhotel.co.uk
W: www.tallandbayhotel.co.uk

BEDROOMS: 23. 4 in cottages, 6 on ground floor.
OPEN: all year.
FACILITIES: lounge, bar, restaurant, brasserie, free Wi-Fi, in-room TV (Freeview), civil wedding licence, patio, 2-acre garden.
BACKGROUND MUSIC: in bar and restaurant.
LOCATION: 2½ miles SW of Looe.
CHILDREN: all ages welcomed.
DOGS: allowed, not in restaurant during mealtimes.
CREDIT CARDS: all major cards.
PRICES: [2016] per room B&B £120–£280, D,B&B £190–£360. À la carte £47. 1-night bookings refused weekends in peak season.

TAPLOW Berkshire

CLIVEDEN HOUSE

'Expensive but worth every penny,' say guests seduced by the 'beautiful' grounds, 'stunning' bedrooms, 'superb' meals and 'attentive, personable' staff at this history-rich Italianate mansion on the River Thames. 'Service was exceptional throughout our stay, down to the person who poured the milk in my husband's teacup at breakfast.' Enter the Great Hall, with its panelled ceiling, massive fireplace, suits of armour, paintings and antiques; then check in to one of the handsome bedrooms 'lacking in nothing'. 'Opulent Lady Astor overlooks the gardens, Lord Astor is more austere; there are many others, all different,' say Guide inspectors. More bedrooms have been redecorated this year as part of the hotel's extensive refurbishment; three new rooms have been added. In the original drawing room, overlooking the 19th-century parterre, delight in chef André Garrett's 'excellent' modern meals, perhaps grilled asparagus, crisp pheasant's egg; English rose veal, Porthilly oyster tartare. The informal Astor Grill, which opened in spring 2016, serves classic American and British dishes. Under the same private ownership as Chewton Glen, New Milton (see entry). (AT, and others)

Bourne End Road
Taplow
SL6 0JF

T: 01628 668561
F: 01628 661837
E: reservations@clivedenhouse.co.uk
W: www.clivedenhouse.co.uk

BEDROOMS: 48. Some on ground floor, plus 3-bed cottage in grounds.
OPEN: all year.
FACILITIES: Great Hall, library, 2 restaurants, private dining rooms, free Wi-Fi, in-room TV (Freeview), civil wedding licence, spa, indoor and (heated) outdoor swimming pools, terrace, tennis, 376-acre National Trust gardens.
BACKGROUND MUSIC: none.
LOCATION: 20 mins from Heathrow, 40 mins Central London.
CHILDREN: all ages welcomed.
DOGS: not allowed in restaurants, spa or parts of garden.
CREDIT CARDS: all major cards.
PRICES: [2016] per room B&B £495–£2,175, D,B&B £615–£2,295. Tasting menu £97.50, à la carte £72.50. 1-night bookings occasionally refused.

TEFFONT EVIAS Wiltshire

Map 2:D1

HOWARD'S HOUSE

♧César award since 2010

In an 'unspoilt' rural village close to the River Nadder, this old stone house seems made for lazy days and unhurried evenings. From croquet rounds in the 'charming' garden, abloom in season, to late-evening coffee and dominoes in the fire-warmed sitting room, 'the whole feeling is of comfort and homeliness'. A long-time favourite of Guide readers, it receives praise for the 'faultless service' and 'excellent food'. 'We had a wonderful stay,' say guests this year. Check in to pleasingly decorated bedrooms with countryside, courtyard or garden views; the best, a newly refurbished top-floor room, has an enormous bed and two seating areas. In the evening, find out why 'the food is a great attraction'. Putting the spotlight on locally sourced, seasonal ingredients, chef (and co-owner) Nick Wentworth's modern, 'essentially English' menus might include roasted loin of Sika deer, creamed savoy cabbage, braised carrots. Start the day right with an 'outstanding' breakfast of freshly squeezed juices, yogurts, compotes and your choice of cooked dishes – croquet players need sustenance, too. (John C Walton, A and PC)

25% DISCOUNT VOUCHERS

Teffont Evias
SP3 5RJ

T: 01722 716392
E: enq@howardshousehotel.co.uk
W: www.howardshousehotel.co.uk

BEDROOMS: 9.
OPEN: all year except 23–27 Dec.
FACILITIES: lounge, snug, restaurant, function facilities, free Wi-Fi, in-room TV, 2-acre grounds (garden terrace, croquet), river, fishing nearby, only restaurant suitable for disabled.
BACKGROUND MUSIC: in dining room at mealtimes.
LOCATION: 10 miles W of Salisbury.
CHILDREN: all ages welcomed.
DOGS: allowed (£15 surcharge) in bedrooms, not in public rooms.
CREDIT CARDS: Amex, MasterCard, Visa.
PRICES: [2016] per room B&B single £120, double from £190. Set dinner £27–£32.50, tasting menu £65, à la carte £45.

TEMPLE SOWERBY Cumbria

Map 4: inset C3

TEMPLE SOWERBY HOUSE

In a pretty conservation village, 'helpful', 'hospitable' hosts Julie and Paul Evans run their relaxed small hotel with 'enthusiasm and professionalism'. The Grade II listed mansion stands in extensive gardens with a croquet lawn and space for raspberries, blueberries and redcurrants to grow wild. Inside, the country house feeling continues in traditionally styled rooms filled with antiques and flower-print fabrics. 'Our superior room was excellent, with a glorious view over the village green and beyond. The bathroom had a splendid spa bath.' In the restaurant overlooking the walled garden, Daniel Przekopowski, the new chef, uses seasonal ingredients and home-grown herbs and soft fruit in his 'tempting' canapés and 'high-quality' monthly menus. 'The slow-braised blade of beef was expecially fine.' There are quiet lanes and scenic drives all around; the Evanses have plenty of walking advice to share, and will lend the unprepared a map. Prefer to explore other terroirs? Book in at the popular wine weekends, for a taste of further-away lands. (Alan and Edwina Williams)

25% DISCOUNT VOUCHERS

Temple Sowerby
CA10 1RZ

T: 017683 61578
F: 017683 61958
E: stay@templesowerby.com
W: www.templesowerby.com

BEDROOMS: 12. 2 on ground floor, 4 in coach house (20 yds).
OPEN: all year except Christmas.
FACILITIES: 2 lounges, bar, restaurant, conference/function facilities, free Wi-Fi, in-room TV (Freeview), civil wedding licence, 1½-acre garden (croquet), unsuitable for disabled.
BACKGROUND MUSIC: none.
LOCATION: village centre.
CHILDREN: not under 12.
DOGS: allowed in coach house rooms (not unattended), not in public rooms or gardens.
CREDIT CARDS: MasterCard, Visa.
PRICES: [2016] per room B&B single £105–£115, double £145–£165, D,B&B single £150–£160, double £220–£240. Set dinner £33–£43. 1-night bookings occasionally refused.

TETBURY Gloucestershire

Map 3:E5

CALCOT MANOR

♥ César award since 2001

White-glove service may be the norm at any luxury hotel, but even the youngest guests receive white-mitten treatment at this exceptionally family-friendly spot. The 14th-century farmhouse, part of the small Calcot Hotels group, has an Ofsted-registered nursery, high teas and play areas; the vast countryside all around is ripe for exploration, with bicycles for all ages available to borrow. Dedicated accommodation for families includes thoughtful in-room touches such as blackout blinds and a baby-listening device. A group spanning three generations recently found the hotel 'an inspired choice': 'The staff were friendly and helpful; the lounges well appointed; the gardens admirable. We all enjoyed using the spa.' 'Comfortable' bedrooms – each fresh and modern-rustic – have magazines, fresh fruit, biscuits and all the latest tech. (Child-free guests might prefer to book a room in the main house.) In the Conservatory restaurant, sit down to modern meals including inspired vegetarian options, perhaps peppered couscous, vegetable bhajis, aubergine and chilli chutney, wild garlic flat bread. Breakfast is 'top of the class'.

Tetbury
GL8 8YJ

T: 01666 890391
E: reception@calcot.co
W: www.calcot.co

BEDROOMS: 35. 10 in cottage, 13 around courtyard, on ground floor.
OPEN: all year.
FACILITIES: lounge, 2 bars, 2 restaurants, crèche, free Wi-Fi, in-room TV (Sky, Freeview), civil wedding licence, 220-acre grounds (tennis, heated outdoor 8-metre swimming pool, children's play area, spa with 16-metre swimming pool).
BACKGROUND MUSIC: in restaurants.
LOCATION: 3 miles W of Tetbury.
CHILDREN: all ages welcomed.
DOGS: allowed in courtyard bedrooms, not in public rooms.
CREDIT CARDS: Amex, MasterCard, Visa.
PRICES: [2016] per room B&B from £249, D,B&B from £329. À la carte £40. 1-night bookings refused weekends.

SEE ALSO SHORTLIST

TISBURY Wiltshire
Map 2:D1

THE BECKFORD ARMS

There's good reason why Dan Brod and Charlie Luxton's 'attractive' pub-with-rooms is 'very popular', say regular Guide readers. 'Sensitively refurbished to match modern expectations', the ivy-covered inn has a 'relaxing' ambience with log fires and 'comfy' sitting rooms. In summer, the 'charming' terrace and garden come into their own, with a pétanque piste and hammocks. 'Well-informed' staff are 'personable and unobtrusively attentive'. Take your pick of 'country-chic' bedrooms (some 'unthrillingly small') in the main building and two 'luxurious' lodges down the lane, each with a 'comfortable' bed, 'lovely, fresh' linen, 'interesting' natural toiletries, and 'thoughtful touches' including fresh milk and home-made biscuits. 'Full marks for fresh coffee and a cafetière, instead of instant!' Meals are 'imaginatively prepared' and 'beautifully presented': perhaps pan-fried sea trout, cockle and clam broth, samphire at dinner; 'outstanding' local yogurt and home-made breads at breakfast. 'Ask for a map of the lovely walks, with magnificent views, around the estate.' The Talbot Inn, Mells (see entry), is under the same ownership. (Robert Grimley, Sue and John Jenkinson)

Fonthill Gifford
Tisbury
SP3 6PX

T: 01747 870385
E: info@beckfordarms.com
W: www.beckfordarms.com

BEDROOMS: 10. 2 in lodges nearby.
OPEN: all year except 25 Dec.
FACILITIES: sitting room, bar, restaurant, private dining room, free Wi-Fi, in-room TV, function facilities, 1-acre garden.
BACKGROUND MUSIC: light background jazz in public areas.
LOCATION: in village, 1 mile N of Tisbury.
CHILDREN: all ages welcomed.
DOGS: allowed in 1 bedroom, public areas.
CREDIT CARDS: MasterCard, Visa.
PRICES: [2016] per room B&B from £95. À la carte £30–£35. 1-night bookings sometimes refused.

SEE ALSO SHORTLIST

TITCHWELL Norfolk

Map 2:A5

BRIARFIELDS
NEW

Walkers, birdwatchers and dog owners flock to this family-friendly hotel on the north Norfolk coast, its vista stretching across salt marshes and the sea. It receives a full entry thanks to a regular Guide reader who enjoyed 'four good breakfasts and four excellent dinners' over a 'thoroughly enjoyable' stay this year. Manager Peter McGeown leads a team of 'exceptionally well-trained, helpful' staff. Most of the neat bedrooms, each with a modern bathroom, are set around a quiet courtyard; three spacious suites are ideal for a family. Summertime calls for Pimm's in the suntrap courtyard or on the decked terrace, while children scramble in the playground; when the wind picks up, take refuge by the wood-burners inside – there are books, board games, real ales, local sea buckthorn gin. In the restaurant, super-local dishes use Norfolk seafood (perhaps Brancaster mussels), and meat from farms barely 15 miles away. There's much to explore in the area: the RSPB Titchwell Marsh nature reserve is down the road; the Royal West Norfolk Golf Club is a five-minute drive away; a private path leads to the beach. (Helen Anthony)

Main Road
Titchwell
PE31 8BB

T: 01485 210742
F: 01485 210933
E: info@briarfieldshotelnorfolk.
co.uk
W: www.briarfieldshotelnorfolk.
co.uk

BEDROOMS: 23. 20 around the courtyard, 1 suitable for disabled.
OPEN: all year.
FACILITIES: bar, dining room, snug, TV lounge (Sky), free Wi-Fi in public areas, in-room TV, meeting facilities, 5-acre garden (play area).
BACKGROUND MUSIC: all day in bar and restaurant.
LOCATION: in village, 6 miles W of Burnham Market.
CHILDREN: all ages welcomed (family rooms).
DOGS: allowed in some bedrooms, bar.
CREDIT CARDS: MasterCard, Visa.
PRICES: per room B&B from £80, D,B&B from £105. À la carte £30.

TITCHWELL Norfolk

Map 2:A5

TITCHWELL MANOR

The audacious interiors at this modern hotel on the north Norfolk coast nicely complement the ever-changing vista across marshes and the sea. (Afternoon tea, with retro 'Crunchie' teacakes, makes a nice accompaniment, too.) A 'friendly' place, the converted Victorian farmhouse has been owned by Ian and Margaret Snaith for nearly 30 years. 'Comfortable' bedrooms are in the main house and converted outbuildings. Pick one to suit – some are bright and cheery, others more restrained; some are snug, others are ideal for a family. At garden's end, the privacy-please Potting Shed bedroom has a log-burner and a veranda, a freestanding roll-top bath in the room. The Snaiths' son, Eric, a self-taught chef, has been in charge of the kitchen since 2003. Feed on tapas and informal meals in the 'pleasant' Eating Rooms, or sit down to modern dishes in the Conservatory overlooking the walled garden – there are 'plenty of options'. Eric Snaith's posh chippy (halloumi and spinach arancini with your beer-battered whiting, perhaps) is two miles up the coastal road. Birdwatchers, delight: the RSPB reserve is on the doorstep. More reports, please.

nr Brancaster
Titchwell
PE31 8BB

T: 01485 210221
E: info@titchwellmanor.com
W: www.titchwellmanor.com

BEDROOMS: 27. 12 in herb garden, 4 in converted farm building, 1 in Potting Shed, 2 suitable for disabled.
OPEN: all year.
FACILITIES: lounge, bar, restaurant, conservatory, free Wi-Fi, in-room TV (Freeview), civil wedding licence, ¼-acre walled garden.
BACKGROUND MUSIC: in public rooms.
LOCATION: 5 miles E of Hunstanton.
CHILDREN: all ages welcomed (sand pit, games, DVDs).
DOGS: allowed in some rooms, public rooms (£10 a night).
CREDIT CARDS: Amex, MasterCard, Visa.
PRICES: [2016] per room B&B £125–£235, D,B&B £185–£295. Set menus £55–£65, à la carte £30.

TITLEY Herefordshire

Map 3:C4

THE STAGG INN

🏆 César award since 2013

The Stagg made history in 2001 as the first pub in Britain to earn a Michelin star – a coup for Nicola and Steve Reynolds, who'd taken on the abandoned inn just three years before, and have run it with grace and flair ever since. 'They have the right balance: the food, service and ambience are superb,' writes a fellow Guide hotelier. 'Everyone is so friendly, helpful and gracious that visitors cannot fail to feel cosseted.' The 'lovely' old inn is 'full of nooks and crannies (as well as unexpected steps to trap the unwary)'; dried hops hang from the beams, while book-stuffed alcoves invite a good rummage. Locals fill the cosy pub (real ales, local gins, sophisticated snacks); in the dining rooms, Steve Reynolds's flavourful, pretension-free meals might include Herefordshire beef fillet, smoked mash. 'Leave room for pudding: the home-made ice creams and sorbets deserve a mention.' Spend the night in 'quiet' rooms at the back of the inn, or in the 'beautifully furnished', antique-packed Georgian vicarage down the country road (the hosts offer to drive the distance). (Richard Morgan-Price, Mary Hewson)

25% DISCOUNT VOUCHERS

Titley
HR5 3RL

T: 01544 230221
E: reservations@thestagg.co.uk
W: www.thestagg.co.uk

BEDROOMS: 6. 3 at Old Vicarage (300 yds).
OPEN: all year except 24–26 Dec, 1 Jan, 1 week in Jan/Feb, first 2 weeks Nov, restaurant closed Mon, Tues.
FACILITIES: bar, dining room, small outside seating area (pub), sitting room, 1½-acre garden (Old Vicarage), free Wi-Fi, in-room TV (Freeview), unsuitable for disabled.
BACKGROUND MUSIC: none.
LOCATION: on B4355 between Kington and Presteigne.
CHILDREN: all ages welcomed.
DOGS: allowed in pub, some pub bedrooms.
CREDIT CARDS: Amex, MasterCard, Visa.
PRICES: [2016] per room B&B £70–£140. À la carte £35. 1-night bookings occasionally refused at bank holiday weekends.

TUDDENHAM Suffolk

Map 2:B5

TUDDENHAM MILL

Beyond the rustic weatherboard exterior of this historic 18th-century mill, find 'stylish' bedrooms, 'good' modern meals – and a handy, in-room stock of home-made biscuits ready for the taking. The restaurant-with-rooms is owned by the small East Anglia-based Agellus Hotels group; Malcolm Wyse is manager. Each of the 'luxurious' rooms, sleekly monochrome, has its own character: three, in the mill, have exposed beams and an oversized stone bath; loft suites, accessed via external stairs, have a balcony; other rooms, overlooking millstream or water meadow, have a private patio. All have an 'ultra-modern' bathroom with 'high-quality extras' like dressing gowns and top-end toiletries. Evenings, book a spot for dinner in the candlelit restaurant. Chef Lee Bye uses seasonal ingredients to create inventive dishes based on local produce: Norfolk quail, hazelnuts, smoked garlic, pak choi; Denham lamb chop, asparagus, burnt aubergine, ricotta. A vegetarian guest was 'particularly well looked after'. Next day, after an 'excellent' breakfast, take to the open countryside: hybrid bicycles are available to borrow; walking and cycling paths, surrounded by wildlife and heathland, abound. (EJH)

High Street
Tuddenham
IP28 6SQ

T: 01638 713552
E: info@tuddenhammill.co.uk
W: www.tuddenhammill.co.uk

BEDROOMS: 15. 12 in 2 separate buildings, 8 on ground floor, 1 suitable for disabled.
OPEN: all year.
FACILITIES: bar, restaurant, 2 function rooms, free Wi-Fi, in-room TV (Freeview), 12-acre grounds (petanque, chipping and putting green, bicycles to borrow).
BACKGROUND MUSIC: 'modern' in bar and restaurant.
LOCATION: in village, 8 miles NE of Newmarket.
CHILDREN: all ages welcomed.
DOGS: welcomed in some bedrooms (£15 a night).
CREDIT CARDS: MasterCard, Visa.
PRICES: [2016] per room B&B £185–£345, D,B&B £235–£395. À la carte £38, early dining (Sun–Fri 6.30–7.30 pm) £19.50, tasting menu £55. 2-night min. stay at weekends.

TWO BRIDGES Devon
Map 1:D4

PRINCE HALL

Chris Daly's 18th-century mansion on Dartmoor makes for a 'friendly, relaxing' hotel, its 'delightful' staff and 'laid-back' attitude attracting many return guests. (It's said that Arthur Conan Doyle was inspired to write The Hound of the Baskervilles while staying at the house; today, better-behaved dogs are made very welcome, with all manner of treats.) In 2016, regular Guide correspondents on a second visit found 'comfy' armchairs and an open fire in the lounge – 'lovely and warm on a cold March day'. Bedrooms, named after local tors, are light, airy, beautifully furnished. 'Ours (Yestor) was large, with plenty of storage space, and stunning views across Dartmoor from the two armchairs.' In the dining room, 'gone are the white tablecloths and china; in are paint-distressed tables and pottery plates, to encourage a more relaxed feel'. Dogs and their owners may eat in the bar; in fine weather, take drinks and meals on the terrace. 'The food was heavenly – sea bass and sole cooked to perfection.' At breakfast, 'plenty of high-quality options' accompany the leaf tea ('hurrah!') and home-baked bread. (GC)

25% DISCOUNT VOUCHERS

Two Bridges
PL20 6SA

T: 01822 890403
E: info@princehall.co.uk
W: www.princehall.co.uk

BEDROOMS: 8. Plus Shepherd's Hut in grounds.
OPEN: all year.
FACILITIES: 2 lounges, dining room, free Wi-Fi in bar/lounge, civil wedding licence, terrace, 5-acre grounds, only ground floor suitable for disabled.
BACKGROUND MUSIC: 'easy listening' in restaurant and lounges.
LOCATION: 1 mile E of Two Bridges.
CHILDREN: not under 10.
DOGS: allowed (treats; facilities for food storage and dog washing; pet-friendly garden and grounds), not in restaurant.
CREDIT CARDS: MasterCard, Visa.
PRICES: [2016] per room B&B £115–£220, D,B&B £170–£255. Set dinner £39.50–£47.50. 1-night bookings sometimes refused.

ULLSWATER Cumbria

Map 4: inset C2

HOWTOWN HOTEL

♀César award since 1991

Take a step back in time to a gentler age. This 17th-century stone farmhouse has been home for 112 years to the Baldry family, who welcome guests with legendary kindness. 'Thoroughly cosseting, it unashamedly sticks to its old-fashioned values – and it's all the better for that,' say Guide inspectors. The situation is isolated: in a hamlet served by the steamers that cruise Ullswater. The escape is absolute: no Wi-Fi, no telephone signal, no email (write or phone to book). A blazing fire, oil paintings and sets of china ('everything displayed with care and pride') set the tone; a grandfather clock strikes a homely note. In the 'spotless', 'well-decorated' country-style bedrooms, find woolly blankets, fringed lampshades, Imperial Leather soap. The day begins with a tap of the brass knocker on the bedroom door and the delivery of a pot of loose-leaf tea. The 9 am gong is the summons to breakfast. Explore the 'very special' setting, taking in the 'fantastic' views over the fells, then return in time for new chef Colin Akrigg's 'very nicely cooked' four-course dinner at 7 pm. 'A great experience.'

25% DISCOUNT VOUCHERS

Ullswater
CA10 2ND

T: 01768 486514
W: www.howtown-hotel.com

BEDROOMS: 15. 4 in annexe, plus 4 self-catering cottages.
OPEN: Mar–1 Nov.
FACILITIES: 3 lounges, TV room, 2 bars, dining room, tea room, no Wi-Fi, 2-acre grounds, 200 yds from lake (private foreshore, fishing), walking, sailing, climbing, riding, golf nearby, unsuitable for disabled.
BACKGROUND MUSIC: occasionally in lounge.
LOCATION: 4 miles S of Pooley Bridge, bus from Penrith station 9 miles.
CHILDREN: all ages welcomed (no special facilities, £5 per night).
DOGS: allowed in some bedrooms (£4 per night charge), not in public rooms.
CREDIT CARDS: none.
PRICES: [2016] per person B&B £99. Set dinner £30. 1-night bookings sometimes refused.

ULVERSTON Cumbria

Map 4: inset C2

THE BAY HORSE

César award since 2009

'A place that draws us back.' A regular Guide reader, in 2016, paid a third visit to Robert Lyons and Lesley Wheeler's former staging post on the Leven estuary. 'The obvious delights are the position – right at the water's edge across from Morecambe Bay – and the subsequent views.' Inside, 'the owners make you feel very welcome.' The rooms aren't huge ('remember, it's a pub-with-rooms'), and a guest this year thought housekeeping could be better, but each room is 'adequate and comfortable', with board games, books and magazines. Six estuary bedrooms, at a slight premium, have French doors opening on to a terrace. 'Those views make up for the size of the room.' Downstairs, 'the pub is warm, cosy and welcoming', with log fires, comfy seating and fun ornaments. Afternoon tea is 'a home-made treat'. Book ahead for dinner (a single sitting) in the candlelit conservatory, where Robert Lyons's 'well-presented', 'full-flavoured' dishes – perhaps braised Lakeland lamb shank – are 'extremely good'. Next morning, enjoy an 'exceptional' cooked breakfast. 'Terrific value for money.' (Christine Hodgkin, and others)

Canal Foot
Ulverston
LA12 9EL

T: 01229 583972
F: 01229 580502
E: reservations@thebayhorsehotel.
co.uk
W: www.thebayhorsehotel.co.uk

BEDROOMS: 9.
OPEN: all year, restaurant closed Mon midday (light bar meals available).
FACILITIES: bar lounge, restaurant, free Wi-Fi, in-room TV (Freeview), picnic area, unsuitable for disabled.
BACKGROUND MUSIC: in bar and restaurant.
LOCATION: 1½ miles from town centre.
CHILDREN: not under 9.
DOGS: allowed, not in restaurant (except assistance dogs).
CREDIT CARDS: all major cards.
PRICES: [2016] per room B&B £95–£120, D,B&B (min. 2 nights on weekends) £155–£180. À la carte £40. 1-night bookings refused busy weekends Apr–Sept.

UPPER SLAUGHTER Gloucestershire

Map 3:D6

LORDS OF THE MANOR

🏆César award since 2015

In 'attractive' gardens, 'just as fetching in winter frost as in the spring', this honey-stoned former rectory welcomes guests into plush luxury (with, some visitors point out, a price tag to match). Take tea and 'scrumptious' cakes in 'grand old English style' in the 'comfortable' lounges; the panelled bar is 'just the place for cocktails and excellent canapés'. 'We were looked after beautifully,' say Guide readers this year. Michael Obray is the new manager; the staff are 'efficient, smiling', 'wonderfully kind'. 'I felt a little weak on arrival, and they brought me home-made biscuits in the room.' Bedrooms – some cosy, others more generous – are individually furnished, and look out over lawns, Cotswold hills or the village. Careful selection is advised: guests this year found theirs dim, with a difficult bathroom. The restaurant, where Richard Picard-Edwards's Michelin-starred dinners include a 'spectacular' tasting menu, has 'crisp linens and service to match'. 'The guineafowl consommé was one of those dishes that stay in one's memory long after the plate has been carried back to the kitchen.' (F and IW, Sophie Harrowes, and others)

Upper Slaughter
GL54 2JD

T: 01451 820243
F: 01451 820696
E: reservations@lordsofthemanor.com
W: www.lordsofthemanor.com

BEDROOMS: 26. 16 in converted granary and stables, 1 on ground floor.
OPEN: all year.
FACILITIES: drawing room, lounge bar, restaurant, library, games room, free Wi-Fi, in-room TV (Freeview), civil wedding licence, terrace, 8-acre grounds, unsuitable for disabled.
BACKGROUND MUSIC: none.
LOCATION: in village, 2 miles N of Bourton-on-the-Water.
CHILDREN: all ages welcomed, no under-15s in restaurant in evening (high tea served).
DOGS: allowed in some bedrooms, not in restaurant.
CREDIT CARDS: all major cards.
PRICES: [2016] per room B&B £195–£510, D,B&B £325–£640. Set menu £72.50, tasting menu £85.

UPPINGHAM Rutland

LAKE ISLE HOTEL & RESTAURANT

Find peace, tranquillity and a finely cooked English beef fillet at Janine and Richard Burton's 'well-run' hotel and restaurant on the High Street of this 'lovely' market town. (It is named after the meditative WB Yeats verse in which the Irish poet evokes a rustic serenity.) The restaurant is popular with locals, who come for chef Stuart Mead's 'imaginative' modern dishes, perhaps smoked and cured mackerel, Bleue d'Artois potatoes, wasabi salt, capers; roast chicken, wild mushrooms, scorched cabbage, barley risotto. Eat well, then retire to one of the modest modern bedrooms upstairs or in courtyard cottages, to spend the night. Each is equipped with a tea tray and home-baked biscuits; the best have a whirlpool bath. There's 'notably good choice' at breakfast: choose from compotes, fruits and natural yogurt; freshly baked croissants and home-made preserves; Scotch kippers; salmon and smoked haddock fishcakes. A fine base for exploring the area; for those yearning to follow in Yeats's soil-encrusted footsteps, ancient woodland, protected wildlife sites and the Rutland Water nature reserve are within a half-hour's drive. More reports, please.

16 High Street East
Uppingham
LE15 9PZ

T: 01572 822951
F: 01572 824400
E: info@lakeisle.co.uk
W: www.lakeisle.co.uk

BEDROOMS: 12. 2 in cottages.
OPEN: all year, restaurant closed Sun night, Mon lunch.
FACILITIES: lounge, bar, restaurant, free Wi-Fi, in-room TV (Freeview), unsuitable for disabled.
BACKGROUND MUSIC: in restaurant.
LOCATION: town centre.
CHILDREN: all ages welcomed.
DOGS: allowed in cottage rooms, not in public areas.
CREDIT CARDS: MasterCard, Visa.
PRICES: [2016] per room B&B £90–£110, D,B&B £156–£176. À la carte £35.

VENTNOR Isle of Wight

Map 2:E2

HILLSIDE

Gert Bach's modern hotel stands on a steep hill over the seaside resort. ('Guests with sufficiently strong legs won't find it too inconvenient.') 'Enduring first impressions were of clean Scandinavian decor and airy rooms flooded with light,' write guests this year. 'Everything carried conviction, from the white walls and dazzling abstract paintings, to the pale wooden floors, Hans Wegner wishbone chairs, and crisp Le Klint lampshades.' Most of the bedrooms, some snug, look out to sea. 'We were delighted by our room. Our bed was comfortable, though the bedside lighting could have been better; the adequately sized shower room had good-quality towels. There is so little traffic on the road outside that we were untroubled by its noise.' No coffee or tea is allowed in the bedrooms: take hot drinks in the lounges. An 'excellent' dinner ('though the menu changed little over our stay') is served from 7 pm; the Hillside Bistro, in town, has 'a similar, if slightly spicier, menu'. At breakfast, sample the house's home-made butter, yogurt and conserves, even its own blend of coffee. The 'narrow' car park 'calls for thoughtful parking'. (Tom and Sarah Mann, and others)

25% DISCOUNT VOUCHERS

151 Mitchell Avenue
Ventnor
PO38 1DR

T: 01983 852271
E: mail@hillsideventnor.co.uk
W: www.hillsideventnor.co.uk

BEDROOMS: 12. Plus self-catering apartment.
OPEN: all year, restaurant closed Sun dinner.
FACILITIES: restaurant, coffee room, quiet room, conservatory, free Wi-Fi, in-room TV, terrace, 5-acre garden (beehives), unsuitable for disabled.
BACKGROUND MUSIC: 'subdued', in restaurant in evening.
LOCATION: above town centre.
CHILDREN: over-12s welcomed.
DOGS: not allowed.
CREDIT CARDS: MasterCard, Visa.
PRICES: [2016] per person B&B £73–£93. À la carte £26. 2-night min. bookings preferred.

SEE ALSO SHORTLIST

VERYAN-IN-ROSELAND Cornwall

THE NARE

❦ César award since 2003

'Pretty well perfect', Toby Ashworth's seaside hotel on the Roseland peninsula, founded nearly 30 years ago by his grandmother, continues to please. 'The ethos is a little old-fashioned,' which is much of the hotel's appeal for regular visitors: sheets or duvets are provided according to guests' tastes; a valet is available to unpack bags on arrival; silver service is the rule in the dining room. Homely, 'comfortable' bedrooms, many with a balcony or private terrace for the best sea views, are 'a pleasure to be in'. No two are the same, but all have fresh flowers, armchairs, plenty of magazines. 'We had to change rooms in the middle of our stay (my mistake), but it was managed with the minimum of fuss and inconvenience.' Come dinnertime, chef Richard James serves a 'delicious' daily-changing five-course table d'hôte menu. 'They encourage gentlemen to wear jacket and tie at dinner, but with no overt disapproval if you don't.' Less formal meals are served in the nautical Quarterdeck restaurant. Travelling with family? The facilities are ideal: croquet, a safe beach, a 'superb' heated outdoor swimming pool. (David Lodge)

Carne Beach
Veryan-in-Roseland
TR2 5PF

T: 01872 501111
E: stay@narehotel.co.uk
W: www.narehotel.co.uk

BEDROOMS: 37. Some on ground floor, 1 in adjacent cottage, 5 suitable for disabled.
OPEN: all year.
FACILITIES: lift, lounge, drawing room, sun lounge, gallery, study, bar, library, light lunch/supper room, 2 restaurants, conservatory, free Wi-Fi, in-room TV (Freeview), indoor 10-metre swimming pool, gym, 2-acre grounds, heated 15-metre swimming pool, tennis, sandy beach.
BACKGROUND MUSIC: none.
LOCATION: S of Veryan, on coast.
CHILDREN: all ages welcomed, no under-7s in restaurant in evening.
DOGS: allowed in bedrooms, not in public areas (except assistance dogs).
CREDIT CARDS: Amex, MasterCard, Visa.
PRICES: [2016] per room B&B £290–£835. Set dinner £50, à la carte £50.

WAREHAM Dorset

Map 2:E1

THE PRIORY

♛César award since 1996

'Delightful' riverside gardens, 'stunning' views, 'excellent' meals and an 'exceptionally friendly' atmosphere keep guests returning to this well-loved country hotel in a former 16th-century priory. It is owned by the Turner family; 'staff are admirable – however do they manage to remember all the guests' names?' 'Well-equipped, comfortable' bedrooms are in the main house and a converted boathouse on the riverbank. 'Our mini-suite had a four-poster bed (without fussy drapes); armchairs and a sofa; ample wardrobes in a separate dressing area; a bowl of fresh fruit. The balcony overlooked the garden; to the side we could see across the river to the bridge.' After canapés in the bar, in the beamed drawing room or alfresco on the terrace, tuck in to chef Stephan Guinebault's much-praised modern dishes, served in the 'atmospheric' Abbot's Cellar restaurant. A typical dish: loin of rose veal, truffle cream potato, roasted root vegetables. 'Breakfast in the Garden Room was very good indeed: eggs just right; delicious porridge.' Lush gardens lead to the River Frome; in spring, 'bulbs flower anywhere they can get a foothold'. (E and RP, BB)

25% DISCOUNT VOUCHERS

Church Green
Wareham
BH20 4ND

T: 01929 551666
F: 01929 554519
E: admin@theprioryhotel.co.uk
W: www.theprioryhotel.co.uk

BEDROOMS: 18. Some on ground floor (in courtyard), 4 suites in boathouse.
OPEN: all year.
FACILITIES: sitting room, drawing room, snug bar, 2 dining rooms, free Wi-Fi, in-room TV (Freeview), 4½-acre gardens (croquet, river frontage, moorings, fishing), unsuitable for disabled.
BACKGROUND MUSIC: pianist in drawing room Sat evenings 'and special occasions'.
LOCATION: town centre.
CHILDREN: not under 12.
DOGS: not allowed.
CREDIT CARDS: Amex, MasterCard, Visa.
PRICES: [2016] per room B&B £220–£380, D,B&B £265–£425. Set dinner £48.50.

WELLS Somerset

STOBERRY HOUSE

Tim and Frances Meeres Young rescued this 18th-century coach house from ruin 20 years ago and transformed it into an 'altogether excellent' luxury B&B with a sweep of 'beautifully laid out' grounds. 'Several hours could easily be spent idling about the carefully planted gardens, anticipating what delight is around the next corner.' Find colourful prints, fresh flowers, packed bookshelves, board games in the sitting rooms; a well-equipped pantry has all the necessities for making light snacks. In the main house and studio (a stroll across the lawns), the 'comfortable, well-appointed' bedrooms are individually designed. 'What a lovely surprise to discover we could park alongside our well-equipped studio suite.' The truly romantic can arrange intimate picnics or afternoon teas in the gardens or on the grassy knoll overlooking Wells cathedral. Expect a 'superb' breakfast with a full ('and I do mean "full"') English and an 'unrivalled' continental spread: yogurts, Somerset cheeses, salami, freshly baked breads, Scotch pancakes, home-made jams; porridge has its own menu. 'Frances cooks much of it, using produce from her potager.' (Geoffrey Bignell, Peter Rogers)

Stoberry Park
Wells
BA5 3LD

T: 01749 672906
F: 01749 674175
E: stay@stoberry-park.co.uk
W: www.stoberryhouse.co.uk

BEDROOMS: 5. 1 in studio cottage.
OPEN: all year except 2 weeks over Christmas and New Year.
FACILITIES: 3 sitting rooms (1 with pantry), breakfast room, orangery, free Wi-Fi, in-room TV (Freeview), 6½-acre garden in 25 acres of parkland, unsuitable for disabled.
BACKGROUND MUSIC: none.
LOCATION: outskirts of Wells.
CHILDREN: all ages welcomed (in studio suite).
DOGS: not allowed.
CREDIT CARDS: Amex, MasterCard, Visa.
PRICES: [2016] per room B&B (continental) £65–£155. Cooked breakfast £5.50, à la carte £35.

WEST END Surrey

Map 2:D3

THE INN AT WEST END

NEW

Locals flock to this 'attractive', 'well-run' and well-liked pub/restaurant-with-rooms, adjacent to Bisley, for coffee and a chat in the morning – when they're not swapping excess allotment produce for wine and real ales, that is. 'We were impressed by the professionalism and genuine friendliness of the staff,' Guide readers said in 2016. After 15 years as publicans, in spring 2015, 'hands-on' owners Gerry and Ann Price added 12 bedrooms; each is 'bright and modern without being trendy'. 'While the pub stands on a busy road, the rooms are well set back on a courtyard garden. We were not bothered by traffic noise,' said Guide inspectors, who liked their 'spacious, well-appointed' room. Other guests were similarly pleased: 'We had a very comfortable bed; the bathroom, practically designed, had an excellent shower.' At dinner, find out why the locals gather. Served in the bar and restaurant, chef Mark Baines's 'excellent' modern cooking (perhaps crispy buttermilk pheasant, sweet potato, house slaw) is accompanied by an 'unusual' wine list. Awake to 'a large choice' of cooked dishes, including an 'excellent' kedgeree. (John Saul, Edward Mirzoeff, and others)

42 Guildford Road
West End
nr Woking
GU24 9PW

T: 01276 485842
E: gerryprice@btconnect.com
W: www.the-inn.co.uk

BEDROOMS: 12. 1 suitable for disabled.
OPEN: all year.
FACILITIES: pub/restaurant, wine shop, free Wi-Fi, in-room TV (Freeview), patio, courtyard garden.
BACKGROUND MUSIC: none.
LOCATION: 6 miles W of Woking.
CHILDREN: welcomed, if old enough to take their own room.
DOGS: allowed.
CREDIT CARDS: all major cards.
PRICES: [2016] per room B&B from £125, D,B&B from £185 ('but ask for offers'). À la carte £35.

WEST HOATHLY Sussex

Map 2:E4

THE CAT INN

♧ César award since 2014

Andrew Russell has elevated innkeeping to a real 'craft': his popular 16th-century free house is well stocked with fare from local microbreweries and English vineyards. 'Andrew is hands-on and welcoming; he knows all about hospitality, and it shows.' There is 'great attention to detail everywhere': a 'lovely' log fire in the grate, posies on wooden dining tables; in the 'well-equipped' bedrooms, find 'beautiful' antique furniture, reading material, a capsule coffee-maker with fresh milk, 'a well-stocked tea chest on the landing'. 'Room One, our favourite, is spacious yet cosy, with a spotless bathroom. It overlooks the village church, whose tower is occupied by garrulous jackdaws.' Chef Alex Jaquemin's 'buzzing' restaurant has a 'great atmosphere'. The 'varied', 'decently priced' menu has daily specials, perhaps roasted stone bass fillet, spätzle, brown shrimp, wild mushrooms. (Vegan options clearly marked.) Guide readers this year 'cannot overstate how good the breakfast is'. Don't let the name fool you: a 'much-loved' cocker spaniel greets newcomers to the bar, where dogs are welcomed. (Angie Davies, Barrie Wilkinson)

25% DISCOUNT VOUCHERS

North Lane
West Hoathly
RH19 4PP

T: 01342 810369
E: thecatinn@googlemail.com
W: www.catinn.co.uk

BEDROOMS: 4.
OPEN: all year except Christmas, restaurant closed Sun evening.
FACILITIES: bar, 3 dining areas, free Wi-Fi, in-room TV (Freeview), terrace (alfresco meals), unsuitable for disabled.
BACKGROUND MUSIC: none.
LOCATION: in village.
CHILDREN: not under 7.
DOGS: not allowed in dining room.
CREDIT CARDS: MasterCard, Visa.
PRICES: [2016] per room B&B from £120. À la carte £28.

WHASHTON Yorkshire

Map 4:C3

THE HACK & SPADE

'Well worth finding', Jane and Andy Ratcliffe's 'unpretentious' inn welcomes weary travellers with 'comfortable' rooms and 'good meals'. Down a single-track lane, the refurbished 19th-century ale house is in a tiny, 'utterly peaceful' village, with 'views of the valley and rolling hills' ('the most noise you'll hear is from a passing tractor or the school bus'). Expect a hearty welcome, if not from the local domino club, who gather in the pub once a week, then certainly from the 'enthusiastic', 'chatty' owners. 'Jane looked after us well.' In the candlelit restaurant, dine on 'generous' portions of Jane Ratcliffe's accomplished pub dishes, perhaps local black pudding, grilled goat's cheese, onion relish; pan-fried pork tenderloin, cider, caramelised apples. Retire afterwards to an 'uncluttered' room with 'a cool, contemporary feel'. Overlooking countryside or village green, bedrooms are well equipped with bathrobes, Fairtrade teas, ground coffee and a cafetière. In the morning, start the day with 'very good' coffee and a well-cooked breakfast, then ask the hosts for insider advice on nearby walks – this is a prime spot for exploring the Yorkshire Dales. (PB, RB)

Whashton
DL11 7JL

T: 01748 823721
E: reservations@hackandspade.com
W: www.hackandspade.com

BEDROOMS: 5.
OPEN: all year except Christmas/New Year, last 2 weeks Jan, restaurant closed Sun–Wed.
FACILITIES: lounge, restaurant, free Wi-Fi, in-room TV (Freeview), garden, only restaurant suitable for disabled.
BACKGROUND MUSIC: 'soft' in dining room in evening.
LOCATION: 4 miles NW of Richmond.
CHILDREN: not under 7.
DOGS: not allowed.
CREDIT CARDS: MasterCard, Visa.
PRICES: [2016] per room B&B £120–£130. À la carte £25.

WHITEWELL Lancashire

Map 4:D3

THE INN AT WHITEWELL

There are 'superb' rooms, 'attentive' staff and 'cream-tea scones just as they should be' at this 'comfortable', well-loved country hotel above the Forest of Bowland. 'I hope it never changes,' says a return visitor this year. The River Hodder rushes past the garden; within the 18th-century inn and romantically restored coach house, choose one of the 'impressive' bedrooms in which to lay your head. (Ask for a room with a restored Victorian cabinet bath in the 'enormous' bathroom – 'perhaps not for the faint-of-heart, but uniquely characterful'.) 'Our beautiful room had an excellent view over the river to the valley. A bonus: the comfortable sofa by the peat fire, so we could toast our toes.' 'Everything is pretty near perfect' in the dining room, where long-serving chef Jamie Cadman's modern dishes, perhaps venison carpaccio or whole roasted poussin, use plenty of local meat and game. 'I had the lamb shank, and they were happy to serve alternative vegetables to those listed on the menu.' Hungry for something more casual? In the bar, 'the famous fish pie never disappoints'. (Mike Craddock, Lynn Wildgoose)

Whitewell
BB7 3AT

T: 01200 448222
F: 01200 448298
E: reception@innatwhitewell.com
W: www.innatwhitewell.com

BEDROOMS: 23. 4 (2 on ground floor) in coach house, 150 yds.
OPEN: all year.
FACILITIES: 3 bars, restaurant, boardroom, private dining room, free Wi-Fi, civil wedding licence, 5-acre garden, 7 miles fishing (ghillie available), unsuitable for disabled.
BACKGROUND MUSIC: none.
LOCATION: 6 miles NW of Clitheroe.
CHILDREN: all ages welcomed.
DOGS: allowed, not in dining room.
CREDIT CARDS: MasterCard, Visa.
PRICES: per room B&B single £95–£210, double £132–£260. À la carte £40.

WILMINGTON Sussex

Map 2:E4

CROSSWAYS HOTEL

'The sheer number of returnees bears witness' to the 'warm welcome' at Clive James and David Stott's 'cheerful, meticulously informal' restaurant-with-rooms at the foot of the South Downs national park. 'The essentials remain unchanged,' writes a faithful guest of his annual visit. 'David and Clive are friendly, chatty, but never intrusive. Well-judged details are typical of the spirit of this very attractive place.' The hosts have 'spruced up' their Georgian house, with upgraded bath- and shower rooms; a second gazebo has been added in the garden. Bedrooms are 'comfortable, pleasant, sparkling clean'. Go for the best – a spacious room with a private balcony overlooking the duck pond. Come dinnertime, settle in happily. 'The restaurant is clearly the centrepiece; eating there is a treat.' In David Stott's 'excellent' dishes (perhaps guineafowl, flageolet beans, bacon), savour the taste of the place – there's game from nearby estates, fish from Hastings, vegetables from the garden. 'Breakfast is superb – it does make a difference that all the food is locally sourced.' Book early for Glyndebourne ('very good' packages). (Richard Parish, Charles Medawar)

Lewes Road
Wilmington
BN26 5SG

T: 01323 482455
F: 01323 487811
E: stay@crosswayshotel.co.uk
W: www.crosswayshotel.co.uk

BEDROOMS: 7. Plus self-catering cottage and apartment.
OPEN: all year except 20 Dec–late Jan, restaurant closed Sun/Mon.
FACILITIES: breakfast room, restaurant, free Wi-Fi, in-room TV (Freeview), 2-acre grounds (duck pond), unsuitable for disabled.
BACKGROUND MUSIC: occasionally, in dining areas.
LOCATION: 2 miles W of Polegate on A27.
CHILDREN: not under 12.
DOGS: not allowed.
CREDIT CARDS: Amex, MasterCard, Visa.
PRICES: [2016] per room B&B £145–£165, D,B&B £220–£240. Set dinner £43.

WINDERMERE Cumbria

Map 4: inset C2

CEDAR MANOR

NEW

'Gracious', 'sincere' owners Caroline and Jonathan Kaye run their well-liked small hotel with warmth and personality, agree guests in 2016. 'They're an energetic, hands-on couple who work well and closely with their small team of excellent staff.' The 19th-century country retreat 'cleverly combines period features with a pleasing modern design'. There's 'a high-end luxury feel' throughout, and a 'relaxed' atmosphere where 'everyone mingles over cocktails for hours'. 'Superbly appointed' bedrooms have 'plenty of thoughtful touches – chocolate eggs over Easter weekend; an elegantly typed note about the clocks changing'. In the candlelit restaurant, Roger Pergl-Wilson's modern dinners, with 'generous' servings of 'varied home-baked breads', are 'excellent' (leave room for the 'imaginative desserts and home-made petits fours'). Wake to a heartening breakfast, served at table: home-made jams and marmalade; 'delicious' prunes soaked in brandy and Earl Grey tea; a good choice of cooked dishes. Pack a lunch of 'generously filled sandwiches' for a walk through woodland to the lake. (Pauline and Stephen Glover, John Firrell, and others)

Ambleside Road
Windermere
LA23 1AX

T: 01539 443192
E: stay@cedarmanor.co.uk
W: www.cedarmanor.co.uk

BEDROOMS: 10. 1 suite in coach house.
OPEN: all year except 18–26 Dec, 3–19 Jan.
FACILITIES: 2 lounges, restaurant, free Wi-Fi, in-room TV (Freeview), patio, ¼-acre garden, unsuitable for disabled.
BACKGROUND MUSIC: 'quietly' in lounge and restaurant.
LOCATION: 5-min. walk from town centre.
CHILDREN: all ages welcomed.
DOGS: not allowed.
CREDIT CARDS: MasterCard, Visa.
PRICES: [2016] per room B&B £135–£425, D,B&B £214–£504. Set dinner £39.95. 2-night min. stay at weekends preferred.

WINDERMERE Cumbria

Map 4: inset C2

GILPIN HOTEL AND LAKE HOUSE

César award since 2000

'Our favourite small hotel – simply the best run we've ever stayed at.' The Cunliffe family's 'great' country house hotel continues to please Guide readers. 'Family run, it makes for a personal, amiable experience.' Visitors praise the 'friendly, attentive' staff and the 'thoughtfulness they exercise in making their guests happy'. 'They're clearly intent on providing what guests want, rather than what they want them to have.' Sit in the elegant lounge (books, magazines, plump sofas); wander in the 'lovely' grounds (Victorian flower gardens, ancient trees, llama paddock). Most of the 'well-equipped' bedrooms are in the Edwardian main house; others are at the Lake House, which has its own spa, lake and boathouse. In 2016, five cedar-clad spa lodges sprang up in the grounds, with private treatment areas and views, from outdoor hot tubs, of the Lake District moors. Await evening: chef Hrishikesh Desai's modern menus are 'superb'. 'The turbot with shrimps and artichokes was the nicest meal we'd had in a long time.' 'An absolute joy.' (Wolfgang Stroebe, Christopher Harris, Peter Govier)

Crook Road
Windermere
LA23 3NE

T: 015394 88818
E: hotel@gilpinlodge.co.uk
W: www.thegilpin.co.uk

BEDROOMS: 31. 6 in orchard wing, 5 in spa lodges in grounds, 6 in Lake House (½ mile from main house).
OPEN: all year.
FACILITIES: bar, 2 lounges, 3 dining rooms, free Wi-Fi, in-room TV (Freeview), civil wedding licence, 22-acre grounds (ponds, croquet), spa for Lake House residents (treatment rooms, salt snug, hot tubs, 20-metre heated pool), free access to nearby country club, unsuitable for disabled.
BACKGROUND MUSIC: in dining rooms.
LOCATION: on B5284, 2 miles SE of Windermere.
CHILDREN: not under 7.
DOGS: allowed in 2 bedrooms (£30 a night), not in public rooms.
CREDIT CARDS: all major cards.
PRICES: [2016] per room B&B from £255, D,B&B from £334. Set dinner £58. 1-night bookings refused weekends, bank holidays.

WINDERMERE Cumbria

Map 4: inset C2

HOLBECK GHYLL

Overlooking Lake Windermere, Stephen and Lisa Leahy's ivy-clad Victorian hunting lodge is 'an enjoyable oasis', say Guide readers this year. The atmosphere – 'friendly, relaxed, not stuffy in the slightest' – may be timeless, but changes have been afoot. Darren Cornish, who won high praise at Oak Bank, Grasmere (see entry), is now the chef; his modern British menus place an emphasis on local ingredients. 'We were given four amuse-bouche in the lounge, and a very good appetiser of curry-spiced carrot soup. The meal got better and better, through crab, duck, mackerel and beef, with an excellent sorbet in between. We liked the long, interesting wine list – there were plenty available by the glass.' In the 'very pleasant' bedrooms, locally distilled damson gin accompanies the 'stunning' views over the lake or fells. 'The stock of biscuits was replenished while we were at dinner – a nice touch.' At breakfast, ask for a table overlooking the lake – a fine partner to the fruit, muesli and 'crispy' pastries; dark-roast coffee and leaf tea; eggs Benedict with a 'well-seasoned' hollandaise sauce. (Alasdair Adam, A and BB)

Holbeck Lane
Windermere
LA23 1LU

T: 015394 32375
E: stay@holbeckghyll.com
W: www.holbeckghyll.com

BEDROOMS: 29. 1 suitable for disabled, 13, including 3 suites, outside the main house, plus 2-bedroom and 4-bedroom cottages.
OPEN: all year except 2 weeks Jan.
FACILITIES: 2 lounges, bar, restaurant, private dining rooms, conference facilities, free Wi-Fi, in-room TV, civil wedding licence, small spa, 17-acre grounds (tennis, putting, croquet, jogging track).
BACKGROUND MUSIC: piano in lounge and restaurant in evening.
LOCATION: 4 miles N of Windermere.
CHILDREN: all ages welcomed, not under 8 in restaurant.
DOGS: allowed in lodge rooms (£25 per stay, VIP package £50).
CREDIT CARDS: Amex, MasterCard, Visa (charge for credit card use).
PRICES: [2016] per room B&B from £170, D,B&B from £270. Set dinner £68, gourmet menu £88.

WOLD NEWTON Yorkshire

Map 4:D5

THE WOLD COTTAGE

Rather grander than its name suggests, Katrina and Derek Gray's Grade II listed Georgian manor house stands in large landscaped gardens within acres of farmland; the wildlife-rich woodland of the Yorkshire Wolds extends beyond. 'An atmosphere of calm' presides. Arrive to tea and home-made cake in the sitting room before heading up to spacious bedrooms traditionally decorated in country style. Some rooms have views of the grounds; all are stocked with thoughtful extras: garden blooms, a radio, chocolates, biscuits, waffle robes, cotton buds. 'We always sleep well here.' The hostess's evening meals, perhaps accompanied by local beers, may be served by arrangement. Breakfast, with 'a wide range' of locally sourced produce, is taken communally. Expect home-baked bread, Yorkshire black pudding, bacon and sausages from the local butcher, tomatoes freshly picked from the on-site greenhouse. Children might enjoy playing at a mini version of The Good Life: they can feed carrots to the family pony, and meet the sheep (and spring lambs) on the farm. This is ideal walking and cycling country; the coast is nearby. More reports, please.

25% DISCOUNT VOUCHERS

Wold Newton
YO25 3HL

T: 01262 470696
F: 01262 470696
E: katrina@woldcottage.com
W: www.woldcottage.com

BEDROOMS: 6. 2 in converted barn, 1 on ground floor, 2 self-catering cottages.
OPEN: all year.
FACILITIES: lounge, dining room, free Wi-Fi, in-room TV (Freeview), 3-acre gardens (croquet) in 240-acre grounds (farmland, woodland).
BACKGROUND MUSIC: at breakfast in dining room.
LOCATION: just outside village.
CHILDREN: all ages welcomed.
DOGS: not allowed.
CREDIT CARDS: MasterCard, Visa.
PRICES: [2016] per person B&B £50–£90. 1-night bookings refused weekends.

WOLTERTON Norfolk

THE SARACEN'S HEAD

In a 'beautifully rural' setting ('satnav was useful'), 'friendly' hosts Janie and Tim Elwes have created a 'very special' atmosphere at their 'lovely', unusual Georgian inn. ('There's no reason why, in 1806, the architect GS Repton should have designed the inn in the exotic style of a Tuscan farmhouse except, perhaps, that it seemed like a fun idea,' the owners say.) The Elweses 'run a tight ship in a relaxed manner', with 'faultless' service, say guests this year. Rub shoulders with locals over Norfolk ales in the bar, then consume 'generous portions' of chef Mark Sayers's 'honest' dishes, perhaps tomato and Norfolk Dapple cheese tart; grilled wild sea bass, samphire. Food miles are proudly stated on the menu (the roast loin of Wolterton lamb comes from 200 yards away). 'Quiet and comfortable', simply designed bedrooms, including a family room, have a modern bathroom; all look over green countryside. 'The coffee at breakfast was the best ever.' The coast is nearby; at Wroxham, hire a day boat to explore the Broads. (Judith and John Albutt)

Wall Road
Wolterton
NR11 7LZ

T: 01263 768909
F: 01263 768993
E: info@saracenshead-norfolk.
co.uk
W: www.saracenshead-norfolk.
co.uk

BEDROOMS: 6.
OPEN: all year except 24–27 Dec, 2 weeks late Feb/early Mar, restaurant closed Sun evening, Mon in Nov–Apr.
FACILITIES: lounge, bar, restaurant, free Wi-Fi, in-room TV (Freeview), courtyard, 1-acre garden, unsuitable for disabled.
BACKGROUND MUSIC: in bar and dining rooms.
LOCATION: 5 miles N of Aylsham.
CHILDREN: all ages welcomed.
DOGS: allowed in bedrooms, back bar, not in restaurant.
CREDIT CARDS: MasterCard, Visa.
PRICES: [2016] per room B&B £100, D,B&B £160. À la carte £32.

WOOTTON COURTENAY Somerset

Map 1:B5

DUNKERY BEACON
COUNTRY HOUSE

'It gets better and better,' say returning guests
in 2016, of Jane and John Bradley's 'lovely,
peaceful' small hotel on Exmoor. 'Instantly
relaxing', the Edwardian hunting lodge
has 'beautiful views' towards the summit of
Dunkery Beacon. Guests praise the 'friendly'
hosts, whose 'unobtrusive attention to detail
is evident at all times'. 'Clean, comfortable'
bedrooms, some in the eaves, are individually
and tastefully styled; all are well supplied with
fresh milk, locally ground coffee, chilled spring
water. Most evenings, 'pre-dinner drinks bring
guests together before they dine at their own
table – it's all very harmonious'. John Bradley is
a keen forager whose 'accomplished' menus use
'good, largely local ingredients' – try carpaccio
of Holnicote venison, Parmesan tuile, micro
herbs; wild mushroom risotto, wilted pousse.
'John's delicious cooking and Jane's knowledge
of wine combine excellently.' Afterwards,
spend a clear night stargazing – Exmoor is a
designated dark-sky area free of artificial light;
the hotel has a telescope ready for stellar action.
(Andrew and Hannah Butterworth, John
Livingstone-Learmonth, and others)

25% DISCOUNT VOUCHERS

Wootton Courtenay
TA24 8RH

T: 01643 841241
E: info@dunkerybeacon
accommodation.co.uk
W: www.dunkerybeacon
accommodation.co.uk

BEDROOMS: 8. 1 on ground floor.
OPEN: mid-Feb–2 Jan, restaurant
closed Sun/Mon/Tues.
FACILITIES: lounge, restaurant,
breakfast room, free Wi-Fi in public
areas, some bedrooms), in-room TV
(Freeview), limited mobile phone
reception, ¾-acre garden (alfresco
meals), unsuitable for disabled.
BACKGROUND MUSIC: in restaurant
in evening.
LOCATION: 4 miles SW of Dunster.
CHILDREN: not under 10.
DOGS: allowed in 2 bedrooms (£5 per
night), not in public rooms.
CREDIT CARDS: MasterCard, Visa.
PRICES: [2016] per room £80–£145,
D,B&B £127–£192. Set dinner
£23.50–£26.95. 1-night bookings
refused Fri/Sat.

WORCESTER Worcestershire

Map 3:C5

THE MANOR COACH HOUSE   NEW

'Upgrade! Upgrade!' In 2016, trusted Guide correspondents exuberantly called for a full entry for Sylvia and Terry Smith's welcoming B&B, in 'a lovely rural location' close to the town centre and Worcester cathedral. 'Extremely comfortable', the modestly furnished bedrooms (one a duplex family suite with a kitchenette) are in converted outbuildings set around a courtyard. 'Drive to the door of any one of the bedrooms, to be surrounded by delight – old cart wheels and farm paraphernalia in front, an immaculate spring garden behind, with daffodils, currants and magnolias in bloom. Our spacious, immaculate room had a wide bed, ample storage space, good lighting, an easy chair; a tidy bathroom with everything we needed.' Terry Smith is 'rightly proud of his breakfasts': berries, diced fruit, 'delicious' ginger yogurt, a hot breakfast 'cooked with utmost care'. 'I was on a fussy diet, but every peculiarity was catered for. Terry told us that the last guests to leave had to finish everything laid out on the sideboard – in another life, I would've had a good try.' 'An astonishing bargain.' (Michael Bourdeaux)

Hindlip Lane
Hindlip
Worcester
WR3 8SJ

T: 01905 456457
E: info@manorcoachhouse.co.uk
W: www.manorcoachhouse.co.uk

BEDROOMS: 5. All in converted outbuildings, 3 on ground floor, 1 suitable for disabled.
OPEN: all year except Christmas.
FACILITIES: breakfast room, free Wi-Fi, in-room TV (Freeview), 1-acre garden.
BACKGROUND MUSIC: none.
LOCATION: 2 miles from city centre.
CHILDREN: all ages welcomed, by arrangement.
DOGS: not allowed.
CREDIT CARDS: all major cards.
PRICES: [2016] per room B&B single £59, double £85.

YARM Yorkshire

Map 4:C4

JUDGES

Guests roundly praise the 'professionalism and charm' of the Downs family's 'brilliant' country house hotel. The Victorian pile stands in 'lovely manicured parkland' on the edge of the North Yorkshire moors. Within, the 'dedicated' staff are 'unstarchy', 'friendly', 'extremely attentive'. Downstairs, find swagged curtains, prints of famous paintings, 'comfortable' sofas and armchairs. Traditionally decorated bedrooms are individually styled. 'Our spacious room had beautiful blue chintz on the walls and bedding, plus a decanter of sherry along with the usual coffee and teas – wonderful.' Book a room with a spa bath for 'a fabulous foam soak of Hollywood starlet proportions'. Beds are turned down in the evening; set your shoes out for an old-fashioned shine. After 'unusual' canapés and pre-dinner drinks, sit down to a 'delicious' dinner, perhaps of hand-dived scallops, sweetcorn purée, Yorkshire chorizo, pickled leeks; fillet of dry-aged beef, pressed potato, Wye Valley asparagus. At breakfast, 'the view over the park – its trees in blossom, the squirrels on the lawns – is delightful'. 'It was just like a home away from home, only better.' (FW, Lesley Hutchinson, Alan Bates, Gillian Caldwell)

25% DISCOUNT VOUCHERS

Kirklevington Hall
Kirklevington
Yarm
TS15 9LW

T: 01642 789000
F: 01642 782878
E: reception@judgeshotel.co.uk
W: www.judgeshotel.co.uk

BEDROOMS: 21. Some on ground floor.
OPEN: all year.
FACILITIES: lounge, bar, restaurant, private dining room, free Wi-Fi, in-room TV (Freeview), function facilities, business centre, civil wedding licence, 36-acre grounds (paths, running routes), access to local spa and sports club, unsuitable for disabled.
BACKGROUND MUSIC: none.
LOCATION: 1½ miles S of centre.
CHILDREN: all ages welcomed.
DOGS: not allowed.
CREDIT CARDS: all major cards.
PRICES: [2016] per room B&B from £145, D,B&B from £220. À la carte £35.

YORK Yorkshire

Map 4:D4

MIDDLETHORPE HALL & SPA

'The 21st-century's answer to staying at
Downton Abbey', this 'elegant', 'well-run'
William and Mary mansion continues to win
accolades from guests who deem it 'superb'.
The 'lovely old house' standing in 'extensive',
'tranquil' gardens ('a real joy to behold') is
owned by the National Trust; Lionel Chatard,
the long-serving manager, heads a team of
'friendly', 'efficient', 'discreet' staff. 'The
charming staff addressed us by name, and
ensured we had everything we could possibly
want.' 'Spacious' public rooms, reached via
'fire-lit' halls, are 'beautifully furnished' with
antiques. In the 'well-staffed' dining room,
Ashley Binder, the new head chef, cooks a 'first-
class' modern menu (though a guest this year
wished for a more frequently changing selection
of dishes). Well fed, retire to traditionally
decorated bedrooms ('creaky' floorboards; 'soft
stripes and florals' from 'yesteryear') spread out
between the main house, the restored 18th-
century courtyard and cottages in the gardens;
umbrellas are provided. 'It's top of the tree – our
favourite hotel.' (Jane Bailey, Richard Morgan-
Price, Caroline Faircliff, Harry Medcalf)

Bishopthorpe Road
York
YO23 2GB

T: 01904 641241
F: 01904 620176
E: info@middlethorpe.com
W: www.middlethorpe.com

BEDROOMS: 29. 17 in courtyard, 2 in
garden, 1 suitable for disabled.
OPEN: all year.
FACILITIES: drawing room, sitting
rooms, library, bar, restaurant, free
Wi-Fi, in-room TV (Freeview),
civil wedding licence, 20-acre
grounds, spa (10 by 6 metre indoor
swimming pool).
BACKGROUND MUSIC: none.
LOCATION: 1½ miles S of centre.
CHILDREN: over-6s welcomed.
DOGS: allowed in garden suites, not
in public rooms.
CREDIT CARDS: Amex, MasterCard,
Visa.
PRICES: [2016] per room B&B from
£143, D,B&B from £218. Set dinner
£69, à la carte £43. 1-night bookings
refused weekends in summer.

SEE ALSO SHORTLIST

ZENNOR Cornwall

Map 1:D1

THE GURNARD'S HEAD

♔César award since 2009

'A great place to experience rugged west Cornwall with the wind straight off the Atlantic', this mellow, family-friendly inn beside the Coastal Path is well liked for its 'character' and 'generosity'. It is owned by the Inkin brothers, whose inspired ventures also include The Old Coastguard, Mousehole, and The Felin Fach Griffin, Felin Fach, Wales (see entries). 'Well run' and 'laid-back', it invites escape and relaxation. With fresh flowers, Welsh blankets and paperbacks, the cosy bedrooms are slightly retro around the edges – but they're all the better for it. 'The rooms have a Roberts radio but no TV, and indeed no mobile reception. Wonderful!' In the lively pub (Cornish ales, bare floorboards, local art, log fires), soak in the buzzy atmosphere with locals and tourists. Max Wilson took over as chef in 2016; taste the coast in his 'excellent-value' seasonal menus including, perhaps, foraged nettle and mint gazpacho; ray wing, crushed potatoes, chard, samphire. In the morning, a breakfast of 'honest fare' includes Cornish apple juice, home-made jam and soda bread, kippers or a full English with hog's pudding. (Chris Savory, and others)

25% DISCOUNT VOUCHERS

Treen
Zennor
TR26 3DE

T: 01736 796928
E: enquiries@gurnardshead.co.uk
W: www.gurnardshead.co.uk

BEDROOMS: 7.
OPEN: all year except 24/25 Dec.
FACILITIES: bar, restaurant, lounge area, free Wi-Fi, 3-acre garden (alfresco dining), unsuitable for disabled.
BACKGROUND MUSIC: Radio 4 at breakfast, selected music at other times, in bar and restaurant.
LOCATION: 7 miles SW of St Ives, on B3306.
CHILDREN: all ages welcomed.
DOGS: allowed, not in dining room.
CREDIT CARDS: MasterCard, Visa.
PRICES: [2016] per room B&B £115–£180, D,B&B £165–£230. Set menus £16–£19, à la carte £19.

25%
DISCOUNT VOUCHER

THE GOOD HOTEL GUIDE 2017
Use this voucher to claim a 25% discount off the normal price for bed and breakfast at hotels with a 25% DISCOUNT VOUCHERS sign at the end of the entry. **You must request a voucher discount at the time of booking and present this voucher on arrival. Further details and conditions overleaf.** Valid to 10th October 2017.

25%
DISCOUNT VOUCHER

THE GOOD HOTEL GUIDE 2017
Use this voucher to claim a 25% discount off the normal price for bed and breakfast at hotels with a 25% DISCOUNT VOUCHERS sign at the end of the entry. **You must request a voucher discount at the time of booking and present this voucher on arrival. Further details and conditions overleaf.** Valid to 10th October 2017.

25%
DISCOUNT VOUCHER

THE GOOD HOTEL GUIDE 2017
Use this voucher to claim a 25% discount off the normal price for bed and breakfast at hotels with a 25% DISCOUNT VOUCHERS sign at the end of the entry. **You must request a voucher discount at the time of booking and present this voucher on arrival. Further details and conditions overleaf.** Valid to 10th October 2017.

25%
DISCOUNT VOUCHER

THE GOOD HOTEL GUIDE 2017
Use this voucher to claim a 25% discount off the normal price for bed and breakfast at hotels with a 25% DISCOUNT VOUCHERS sign at the end of the entry. **You must request a voucher discount at the time of booking and present this voucher on arrival. Further details and conditions overleaf.** Valid to 10th October 2017.

25%
DISCOUNT VOUCHER

THE GOOD HOTEL GUIDE 2017
Use this voucher to claim a 25% discount off the normal price for bed and breakfast at hotels with a 25% DISCOUNT VOUCHERS sign at the end of the entry. **You must request a voucher discount at the time of booking and present this voucher on arrival. Further details and conditions overleaf.** Valid to 10th October 2017.

25%
DISCOUNT VOUCHER

THE GOOD HOTEL GUIDE 2017
Use this voucher to claim a 25% discount off the normal price for bed and breakfast at hotels with a 25% DISCOUNT VOUCHERS sign at the end of the entry. **You must request a voucher discount at the time of booking and present this voucher on arrival. Further details and conditions overleaf.** Valid to 10th October 2017.

CONDITIONS

1. Hotels with a **25% DISCOUNT VOUCHERS** sign have agreed to give readers a discount of 25% off their normal bed-and-breakfast rate.
2. One voucher is good for the first night's stay only, at the discounted rate for yourself alone or for you and a partner sharing a double room.
3. Hotels may decline to accept a voucher reservation if they expect to be fully booked at the full room price.

- - - ✂ - - - - - - - - - - - - - - - - - - -

CONDITIONS

1. Hotels with a **25% DISCOUNT VOUCHERS** sign have agreed to give readers a discount of 25% off their normal bed-and-breakfast rate.
2. One voucher is good for the first night's stay only, at the discounted rate for yourself alone or for you and a partner sharing a double room.
3. Hotels may decline to accept a voucher reservation if they expect to be fully booked at the full room price.

- - - ✂ - - - - - - - - - - - - - - - - - - -

CONDITIONS

1. Hotels with a **25% DISCOUNT VOUCHERS** sign have agreed to give readers a discount of 25% off their normal bed-and-breakfast rate.
2. One voucher is good for the first night's stay only, at the discounted rate for yourself alone or for you and a partner sharing a double room.
3. Hotels may decline to accept a voucher reservation if they expect to be fully booked at the full room price.

- - - ✂ - - - - - - - - - - - - - - - - - - -

CONDITIONS

1. Hotels with a **25% DISCOUNT VOUCHERS** sign have agreed to give readers a discount of 25% off their normal bed-and-breakfast rate.
2. One voucher is good for the first night's stay only, at the discounted rate for yourself alone or for you and a partner sharing a double room.
3. Hotels may decline to accept a voucher reservation if they expect to be fully booked at the full room price.

- - - ✂ - - - - - - - - - - - - - - - - - - -

CONDITIONS

1. Hotels with a **25% DISCOUNT VOUCHERS** sign have agreed to give readers a discount of 25% off their normal bed-and-breakfast rate.
2. One voucher is good for the first night's stay only, at the discounted rate for yourself alone or for you and a partner sharing a double room.
3. Hotels may decline to accept a voucher reservation if they expect to be fully booked at the full room price.

- - - ✂ - - - - - - - - - - - - - - - - - - -

CONDITIONS

1. Hotels with a **25% DISCOUNT VOUCHERS** sign have agreed to give readers a discount of 25% off their normal bed-and-breakfast rate.
2. One voucher is good for the first night's stay only, at the discounted rate for yourself alone or for you and a partner sharing a double room.
3. Hotels may decline to accept a voucher reservation if they expect to be fully booked at the full room price.

SCOTLAND

Dunnottar Castle, near Stonehaven, Aberdeenshire

LOCH MELFORT HOTEL

Calum and Rachel Ross's 'lovely', 'good-value' hotel on the Argyll coast overlooks a 'peaceful' bay, with islands beyond. 'There's something magical about the light, at all times and in all weathers, in this most stunning setting. Who could wish for more?' say Guide inspectors in 2016. Arrive by boat, if you will – four private moorings are available. Staff are 'friendly, interesting', 'knowledgeable about the local area'; bedrooms are in the main house and a cedar-framed annexe connected by a walkway. 'The decor was dated, but our annexe room was comfortable, clean and well kept, with nice, soft towels in the small bathroom.' Take pre-dinner drinks in the lounge (super-local Crinan gin and Loch Fyne beer are worth a try), then sit down to a 'tasty, beautifully presented' dinner while 'the light fades over the islands'. 'We chose local oysters in tempura batter, guineafowl on a delicious risotto. A light lemon dessert was perfect, along with heaps of local cheeses.' 'Well-cooked' breakfasts, including 'delicious' local smoked haddock, are 'served efficiently'. 'I had the "wee breakfast" – what I'd call a "full Scottish"!'

Arduaine
PA34 4XG

T: 01852 200233
F: 01852 200214
E: reception@lochmelfort.co.uk
W: www.lochmelfort.co.uk

BEDROOMS: 25. 20 in Cedar Wing annexe, 10 on ground floor, 1 suitable for disabled.
OPEN: all year except Mon–Wed Nov–Mar, 3 weeks Dec/Jan, open Christmas/New Year.
FACILITIES: sitting room, library, bar/bistro, restaurant, free Wi-Fi, in-room TV, wedding facilities, 17-acre grounds (including National Trust for Scotland's Arduaine Garden).
BACKGROUND MUSIC: modern Scottish in restaurant and bistro.
LOCATION: 19 miles S of Oban.
CHILDREN: all ages welcomed (under-2s free).
DOGS: allowed in 6 bedrooms (£9 per night), not in public rooms.
CREDIT CARDS: MasterCard, Visa.
PRICES: [2016] per person B&B £79–£143, D,B&B £114–£164, £30 single supplement. Set menu £42.

AUCHENCAIRN Dumfries and Galloway   Map 5:E2

BALCARY BAY HOTEL

'Graeme Lamb's beautiful hotel is one of our favourites,' writes a Guide reader this year, of this 'peaceful, well-maintained' place in an 'idyllic' setting by the water. 'The staff are so helpful – they brought in all our cases from the car. In fact, practically all guest requests seem to be granted: we've never had anything refused.' Elaine Ness, the 'expert', long-serving manager, is much appreciated. Bedrooms have views to Hestan Island, or over the garden where 'resident pheasant' Charlie perambulates of a morning; three ground-floor rooms have a private seafront patio. In the 'cosy' lounge, find a log fire, books, 'and fresh magazines!' The hands-on host takes orders for drinks and dinners; in the sea-facing dining room, chef Craig McWilliam's 'up-to-date' meals ('with a nod to old-fashioned tastes') draw a well-mixed crowd. A typical dish: seared guineafowl breast, lyonnaise potato, ratatouille. Breakfast has home-made rolls, local honey, seasonal preserves; scrambled eggs 'with a deep orange yolk'; 'very good' coffee. Twitchers, take note: four RSPB reserves are within driving distance. 'Superb value.' (Dr Mabel Tannahill, and others)

Shore Road
Auchencairn
DG7 1QZ

T: 01556 640217
F: 01556 640272
E: reservations@balcary-bay-hotel.
    co.uk
W: www.balcary-bay-hotel.co.uk

BEDROOMS: 20. 3 on ground floor.
OPEN: 4 Feb–2 Dec.
FACILITIES: 2 lounges, bar, conservatory, restaurant, free Wi-Fi (lounge only), in-room TV (Freeview), 3-acre grounds.
BACKGROUND MUSIC: none.
LOCATION: on shore, 2 miles SW of village.
CHILDREN: all ages welcomed.
DOGS: allowed in bedrooms, not in public rooms.
CREDIT CARDS: MasterCard, Visa.
PRICES: per person B&B £77–£93, D,B&B £86–£122 (min. 2 nights). 1-night bookings usually refused weekends.

SEE ALSO SHORTLIST

AULDEARN Highland

Map 5:C2

BOATH HOUSE

♔César award since 2013

Once thought of as the most beautiful Regency house in Scotland (it was designed by Aberdeen architect Archibald Simpson), this 'wonderful' luxury hotel is owned and run by the Matheson family. Original architectural features are a unique backdrop to the continually changing exhibition of Scottish artwork staged around the house. 'Well-equipped' bedrooms are individually styled with tartan accents and the odd antique. In the 'delightful' grounds, pick any one of the interconnected paths down to the natural lake, through the wild flower meadow and into the walled garden; secluded seating areas dot the lawns. After canapés and aperitifs, sit down to Charlie Lockley's 'beautifully cooked, no-choice' menus in the 'elegant' dining room. The Michelin-starred chef prepares succinctly described dishes – perhaps langoustine, amaranth, hazelnut; lamb, black olive, kale – using organic produce from the kitchen garden. 'I loved it.' Breakfast is 'as elegant and well presented as dinner'. Start the day off right with fruit smoothies; porridge with fruit compote and crème fraîche; home-baked bread slathered with 'delicious' marmalade. (BW)

Auldearn
IV12 5TE

T: 01667 454896
F: 01667 455469
E: info@boath-house.com
W: www.boath-house.com

BEDROOMS: 8. 1, in cottage (50 yds), suitable for disabled.
OPEN: all year.
FACILITIES: 2 lounges, whisky bar/library, orangery, restaurant, health/beauty spa, free Wi-Fi, in-room TV (Freeview), wedding facilities, 22-acre grounds (woods, gardens, meadow, streams, trout lake).
BACKGROUND MUSIC: none.
LOCATION: 2 miles E of Nairn.
CHILDREN: all ages welcomed, not under 8 in dining room at dinner.
DOGS: allowed in some bedrooms, not in public rooms.
CREDIT CARDS: Amex, MasterCard, Visa.
PRICES: [2016] per room B&B single £190–£260, double £285–£365, D,B&B £380–£450. Set dinner £45–£70.

BALLANTRAE Ayrshire

Map 5:E1

COSSES COUNTRY HOUSE

From the watercolour paintings and home-made fruitcake to the woodland and garden dotted with 'daffodils everywhere', countryside charisma fills this gracious guest house on the edge of Crailoch Burn. It is run 'in a charming manner' by Susan and Robin Crosthwaite, who have 'lovingly furnished' their one-time farmhouse with antiques, books and 'pretty extras'. Arrive to afternoon tea, then amble around the estate – black Labrador Monty may be your guide. In the evening, Robin Crosthwaite serves aperitifs by the log fire before a communal dinner; the hostess (author of A Country Cook's Garden in South West Scotland) uses plenty of home-grown and locally sourced food in her 'delicious' daily-changing menus. 'After the meal, we had a wonderful surprise when crossing the courtyard to our room: a magnificent, starry night sky.' 'Breakfast was served in the kitchen at a time to suit us; it was lovely to chat with Susan as she cooked. The table had been set with pretty crockery; there was everything you could wish for – garden fruit compote, home-made muesli, any cooked dish you could think of.' More reports, please.

Ballantrae
KA26 0LR

T: 01465 831363
F: 01465 831598
E: staying@cossescountryhouse.com
W: www.cossescountryhouse.com

BEDROOMS: 3. All on ground floor, 2 across courtyard.
OPEN: Easter–Nov.
FACILITIES: drawing room, dining room, games room (table tennis, darts), free Wi-Fi, in-room TV (Freeview), 12-acre grounds.
BACKGROUND MUSIC: none.
LOCATION: 2 miles E of Ballantrae.
CHILDREN: not under 12.
DOGS: allowed by arrangement in 1 suite, not in public rooms.
CREDIT CARDS: MasterCard, Visa.
PRICES: per person B&B £55–£70, D,B&B £90–£110.

KINLOCH HOUSE

Amid the log fires, hunting trophies, gilt-framed paintings and decorative china, find 'calm and tranquillity' at this 'wonderfully relaxing' traditional country house hotel (Relais & Châteaux) surrounded by green hills and paddocks. Claim a spot in the inviting public rooms to call your own: play board games by the fireplace (Scottish malt optional); pick a book off the shelves and settle into a tartan-covered armchair. The staff are discreet and efficient. 'If you want something, just ask at reception and it happens straight away.' Spacious bedrooms are staunchly, sumptuously traditional in style, with fresh flowers, chocolates and Scottish toiletries; there are antique dressing tables, brass lamps, swathes of richly coloured damask or floral chintz. Nibble on canapés before sitting down to chef Steve MacCallum's 'excellent' country house menus, served at tables laid with white linens, crystal and silver. Typical dishes: terrine of chicken livers, date chutney, toasted brioche; slow-cooked beef feather blade, creamed leeks, wild mushrooms. Perthshire surrounds: castles glower nearby; walks and cycling trails abound; fishing on the River Tay can be arranged. (WW)

Dunkeld Road
Blairgowrie
PH10 6SG

T: 01250 884237
F: 01250 884333
E: reception@kinlochhouse.com
W: www.kinlochhouse.com

BEDROOMS: 15. 4 on ground floor.
OPEN: all year except last 2 weeks Dec, open New Year.
FACILITIES: bar, lounge, drawing room, conservatory, dining room, private dining room, free Wi-Fi, in-room TV (Freeview), wedding facilities, 28-acre grounds.
BACKGROUND MUSIC: none.
LOCATION: 3 miles W of Blairgowrie, on A923.
CHILDREN: all ages welcomed, no under-6s in dining room at night.
DOGS: not allowed.
CREDIT CARDS: Amex, Mastercard, Visa.
PRICES: [2016] per room B&B from £210, D,B&B from £316. Set dinner £53. 1-night bookings refused at busy periods.

BROADFORD Highland

TIGH AN DOCHAIS

Neil Hope and Lesley Unwin's 'excellent and unpretentious' B&B shines out on the Isle of Skye. Designed by RIBA award-winning architects, the modern building has 'wonderful' views of Broadford Bay and the Cuillin mountains from every room – look out for seabirds and local wildlife (binoculars supplied). Guests enter the B&B via a galvanised footbridge to the lounge and dining areas on the upper floor. Bright and 'very clean', these shared spaces have a cathedral ceiling and solid oak flooring with underfloor heating; the book-lined lounge has plump red sofas and a log-burning stove. Admire the landscape from the 'good-sized, well-equipped', tartan-accented bedrooms on the floor below; each leads to larch decking through sliding doors. The 'friendly' hosts provide plenty of 'helpful information' on local walks, beachcombing and kayaking. In the morning, Neil Hope cooks a 'delicious' breakfast, taken communally. Choose from home-made bread and muffins, yogurt, locally smoked haddock, organic sausages and Achmore cheeses. An 'excellent', 'good-value' evening meal can be arranged in advance; restaurants are within walking distance.

13 Harrapool
Broadford
IV49 9AQ

T: 01471 820022
E: hopeskye@btinternet.com
W: www.skyebedbreakfast.co.uk

BEDROOMS: 3. All on ground floor.
OPEN: Mar–Nov.
FACILITIES: lounge, dining area, free Wi-Fi, ½-acre garden, unsuitable for disabled.
BACKGROUND MUSIC: traditional, occasionally, at breakfast.
LOCATION: 1 mile E of Broadford.
CHILDREN: all ages welcomed.
DOGS: not allowed.
CREDIT CARDS: MasterCard, Visa.
PRICES: [2016] per room B&B £105. Set dinner £25.

BRODICK Ayrshire

Map

KILMICHAEL COUNTRY HOUSE

César award since 2016

Be prepared for shrieks of greeting as you turn in to the wooded drive of this 'very special' small mansion, the oldest house on Arran – and that's just from the peacocks! Inside the house, owners Geoffrey Botterill and Antony Butterworth extend a 'personable' but less vociferous welcome, with offers of tea and home-made shortbread. 'The atmosphere is that of a well-cared-for home; the ornaments, pictures and books help enhance this welcoming feeling.' Choose among 'comfortably furnished' bedrooms, each with original features and an antique bed. 'Attractive and restful, ours had plenty of space. There were fresh garden flowers, a CD-player with a selection of music; the large, airy bathroom had masses of piping hot water.' Gather with fellow guests at 7 pm for drinks and canapés in the lounge, before tucking into Antony Butterworth's 'absolutely first-class' set – but flexible – menu (vegetarians, have no fear). In-season ingredients are locally sourced; salad comes from the potager; all is 'beautifully presented'. In the morning, wake to home-made jam, 'delicious compotes', eggs from Kilmichael ducks and hens.

Glen Cloy
Brodick
KA27 8BY

T: 01770 302219
E: enquiries@kilmichael.com
W: www.kilmichael.com

BEDROOMS: 4.
OPEN: Apr–Oct, restaurant close᠁
Sun–Tues.
FACILITIES: 2 drawing rooms, din᠁
room, free Wi-Fi (in drawing
rooms), in-room TV, 4-acre grou᠁
(burn), unsuitable for disabled.
BACKGROUND MUSIC: none.
LOCATION: 1 mile SW of village.
CHILDREN: not under 12.
DOGS: not allowed in public room᠁
on lead in grounds.
CREDIT CARDS: Diners, MasterCa᠁
Visa.
PRICES: [2016] per room B&B sing᠁
£98, double £163–£205. Set dinn᠁
£45. 1-night bookings sometime᠁
refused Sat.

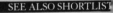

SEE ALSO SHORTLIST

CALLANDER Perth and Kinross

Map 5:D2

POPPIES HOTEL AND RESTAURANT

Set back from the A84, in a small town on the edge of Loch Lomond and the Trossachs national park, this Victorian mansion has been turned by John and Susan Martin into a warm and comfortable hotel. The Martins are hands-on hosts who show great attention to detail, Guide inspectors say. Spacious bedrooms are 'tastefully decorated' in an understated style; some have a sofa bed to accommodate a family. Choose a room at the front for views across the road to meadows and river, with a distant shadow of hills. Time for a tipple? The oak-crafted bar stores more than 120 local and regional malt whiskies – ask the hostess about her specially selected whisky trails. In the candlelit restaurant, David Low, the new chef, adds a gentle twist to traditional Scottish produce. Consider medallions of Balquhidder venison, turnip fondant, wilted spinach; herb-crusted rack of Dornoch lamb, roasted courgette, potato cake. Come morning, an 'excellent' breakfast is fuel for exploring Walter Scott's 'Rob Roy country'. 'Ideally located for exploring a beautiful, accessible part of the country.' More reports, please.

25% DISCOUNT VOUCHERS

Leny Road
Callander
FK17 8AL

T: 01877 330329
F: 01877 332679
E: info@poppieshotel.com
W: www.poppieshotel.com

BEDROOMS: 9. 1 on ground floor.
OPEN: 27 Jan–25 Dec.
FACILITIES: bar, restaurant, free Wi-Fi, in-room TV (Freeview), small front garden, unsuitable for disabled.
BACKGROUND MUSIC: in bar and restaurant.
LOCATION: ½ mile from town centre.
CHILDREN: all ages welcomed.
DOGS: allowed in 2 bedrooms, not in public rooms.
CREDIT CARDS: Amex, MasterCard, Visa.
PRICES: [2016] per room B&B single £55–£80, double £80–£115, D,B&B £20 added per person. Early evening menu (6 pm–7 pm) from £14.50, à la carte £30.

DUNVALANREE IN CARRADALE

A stay at Alan and Alyson Milstead's restaurant-with-rooms, on the Mull of Kintyre, is an object lesson in the importance of a warm welcome, and of those extra in-room touches praised by Guide readers – complimentary home-made shortbread, bathrobes, binoculars, a brimming information folder. 'They show real thought for guests.' While rooms on the upper floors have 'magnificent' sea views to Arran's mountains, bedrooms may require careful selection: a guest in 2016 thought her ground floor room needed sprucing up. Alan Milstead is an 'ebullient' host, who 'encourages conversation between guests' as they gather for drinks at 7 pm. In the dining room overlooking cliff-top garden and ocean, Alyson Milstead, 'a talented cook', plans her 'varied' menus around local fish, shellfish and farm produce. 'It's clever, interesting food, excellently cooked.' Try monkfish, pancetta, lemon cream sauce; Kintyre venison, red onion, orange. (A post-prandial walk from the Edwardian house down to tranquil Port Righ bay is an excellent digestif.) At breakfast, juice is freshly squeezed; eggs come from the Milsteads' hens; 'home-made potato scones are a treat'. (JN, and others)

25% DISCOUNT VOUCHERS

Port Righ
Carradale
PA28 6SE

T: 01583 431226
E: book@dunvalanree.com
W: www.dunvalanree.com

BEDROOMS: 5. 1 on ground floor suitable for disabled.
OPEN: all year except Christmas.
FACILITIES: lounge, dining room, free Wi-Fi, in-room TV (Freeview), wedding facilities, terrace.
BACKGROUND MUSIC: in dining room, Radio 2 in morning, jazz in evening.
LOCATION: on edge of village 15 miles N of Campbeltown.
CHILDREN: all ages welcomed.
DOGS: allowed in bedrooms and lounge.
CREDIT CARDS: MasterCard, Visa.
PRICES: per person B&B £50–£70, D,B&B £73.50–£88.50. Set dinner £29.

CHIRNSIDE HALL

There's a 'cheerful' ambience at Tessa and Christian Korsten's 19th-century mansion, in vast grounds with views stretching across the countryside to the Cheviot hills. 'Tessa welcomed us as old friends,' say guests this year, on their sixth annual visit. Traditionally furnished and homely, the 'well-maintained' house has deep sofas in the public rooms, and hunting trophies on the walls (the place is popular with shooting parties). 'With an open fire on a damp July afternoon, the two lounges felt warm and comfortable.' Tables are set with white linens and fresh flowers in the evening, when chef Tim Holmes's 'straightforward', daily-changing menu includes home-baked bread ('the star of the show') and game from the estate, typically loin of roe deer, Scottish girolles, celeriac purée, fondant potato. 'We thoroughly enjoyed our dinners.' Settle in, afterwards, to one of the 'large and airy' bedrooms with 'far-reaching views', each equipped with bathrobes, blackout blinds and tea- and coffee-making facilities. Mornings, breakfast has 'good choice': home-made muesli, fruit compotes and crème fraîche, 'real' Eyemouth kippers. 'Well located for exploring the Borders.' (AB, GC)

Chirnside
TD11 3LD

T: 01890 818219
F: 01890 818231
E: reception@chirnsidehallhotel.com
W: www.chirnsidehallhotel.com

BEDROOMS: 10.
OPEN: all year except Mar.
FACILITIES: 2 lounges, dining room, private dining room, free Wi-Fi, in-room TV (Freeview), billiard room, fitness room, library/conference rooms, wedding facilities, 5-acre grounds, unsuitable for disabled.
BACKGROUND MUSIC: none.
LOCATION: 1½ miles E of Chirnside, NE of Duns.
CHILDREN: all ages welcomed.
DOGS: allowed in bedrooms (not unattended), not in public rooms.
CREDIT CARDS: Amex, MasterCard, Visa.
PRICES: [2016] per room B&B £180, D,B&B £240. À la carte £40.

COLONSAY Argyll and Bute

Map 5:D1

THE COLONSAY

Carefree informality and an unpretentious ambience reign at this white-painted 18th-century inn, minutes up a single-track road from the ferry. It is owned by Jane and Alex Howard; Ivan Lisovyy manages a 'young, friendly' staff. Rub elbows with locals and tourists in the 'buzzy' bar (malt whiskies, locally brewed island beer, occasional Scottish music evenings); 'the lounge is cosy when a lovely log fire is burning'. At dinner, find fresh island produce – Colonsay shellfish, salad from the kitchen garden. 'We liked the unusual house-cured beetroot gravadlax; scallops and a generous portion of langoustines were delicious.' Trusted Guide readers this year noted 'variable' meals over a short stay. Simply furnished bedrooms have a homey feel; some can be snug. 'Our large, well-lit, sea-facing room had two comfortable armchairs, plenty of storage; a modern bathroom (but a feeble shower). Two windows looked across to Jura. The big, metal-framed bed, though comfortable, had noisy springs, reminding me of the old-fashioned beds at boarding school.' Breakfast in the 'bright' dining room is uplifting: 'good OJ and coffee; lovely scrambled eggs, hot-smoked salmon'.

25% DISCOUNT VOUCHERS

Isle of Colonsay
PA61 7YP

T: 01951 200316
F: 01951 200353
E: jane@colonsayestate.co.uk
W: www.colonsayholidays.co.uk

BEDROOMS: 9.
OPEN: mid-Mar–1 Nov, Christmas, New Year, check-in days Fri, Sat, Sun, Wed, Thurs.
FACILITIES: conservatory, lounge, log room, bar, restaurant, free Wi-Fi on ground floor, accommodation unsuitable for disabled.
BACKGROUND MUSIC: sometimes in restaurant, occasional live music in bar.
LOCATION: 400 yds W of harbour.
CHILDREN: all ages welcomed.
DOGS: allowed in 2 bedrooms, public rooms except restaurant.
CREDIT CARDS: MasterCard, Visa.
PRICES: per room B&B £75–£150, D,B&B £30 added per person. À la carte £25–£30.

CONTIN Highland

COUL HOUSE

A long drive on a single-track country road leads to this Georgian house built for a baronet, today an 'outstanding' traditional hotel owned by Stuart and Susannah Macpherson. Step into the large hall, its stag's head over the open fireplace, to be greeted by 'friendly and professional' staff. Beyond, find a cosy drawing room and a lounge bar ideal for 'stretching out in, by the log fire, after a bracing walk'. In the octagonal formal dining room (a showpiece, with an ornate plastered ceiling and huge windows), chef Garry Kenley serves 'a very good lobster' – and more besides. His 'enjoyable' menus have a modern touch, perhaps including wild mushroom pâté, aubergine caviar; Baharat-spiced lamb rump, caponata, rosemary potato cake. Bedrooms vary in size and shape, though all are traditionally decorated, with antiques, paintings, an old-fashioned bathroom; choose one with views towards the Strathconon mountains. Bring your dog, or borrow residents Alfie and Bella for 'a spectacular walk': you can't miss the Douglas fir planted in 1827 by plant hunter David Douglas himself – it still stands in the grounds. (HM, and others)

Contin
IV14 9ES

T: 01997 421487
F: 01997 421945
E: stay@coulhouse.com
W: www.coulhousehotel.com

BEDROOMS: 21. 4 on ground floor, 1 suitable for disabled.
OPEN: all year except 24–26 Dec.
FACILITIES: lounge bar, drawing room, front hall, restaurant, free Wi-Fi, in-room smart TV, conference/wedding facilities, 8-acre grounds (children's play area, 9-hole pitch and putt).
BACKGROUND MUSIC: 'mixed' in bar, classical in restaurant.
LOCATION: 17 miles NW of Inverness.
CHILDREN: all ages welcomed, discounts up to age 15.
DOGS: allowed (£5 per day).
CREDIT CARDS: all major cards.
PRICES: [2016] per room B&B single £95–£105, double £175–£325. À la carte £35.

DUNVEGAN Highland

Map 5:C1

THE THREE CHIMNEYS AND THE HOUSE OVER-BY

♀César award since 2001

'We had a fantastic stay, with an excellent welcome; dinner was as good as we'd hoped.' At 'the back of beyond' – 'which is, of course, part of its charm' – Shirley and Eddie Spear's low-built, whitewashed restaurant-with-rooms overlooks Loch Dunvegan. Much has changed since the Spears opened their doors in 1985, but a constant has been their passion for Scottish produce and tradition. Head chef Scott Davies sources everything possible locally to create dishes with a Nordic accent – halibut, duck, carrot, mussels, lamb, dulse, parsnip, ewe's cheese – each dish bespeaking confidence in exceptional raw materials. Eat well, then sleep over in 'superb, crisply furnished', loch-facing bedrooms, each with patio doors leading to a garden with seating. At breakfast, the buffet of the past has been dispensed with; wake, now, to a three-course affair with home-baked cinnamon buns, seasonal fruit compotes, and your choice of ham and haddie omelette, Mallaig peat-smoked salmon, Lochalsh haggis or eggs from local crofts. Magical Dunvegan Castle is across the water. (Susan Willmington)

Colbost
Dunvegan
IV55 8ZT

T: 01470 511258
F: 01470 511358
E: eatandstay@threechimneys.co.uk
W: www.threechimneys.co.uk

BEDROOMS: 6. All on ground floor (5 split-level) in separate building, 1 suitable for disabled.
OPEN: all year except 12 Dec–13 Jan.
FACILITIES: lounge/breakfast room (House Over-By), main lounge, restaurant, free Wi-Fi, in-room TV (Freeview), garden on loch.
BACKGROUND MUSIC: in House Over-By lounge, 'for different moods and times of day'.
LOCATION: 4 miles W of Dunvegan.
CHILDREN: no under-5s at lunch, no under-8s at dinner, tea at 5 pm.
DOGS: not allowed.
CREDIT CARDS: Amex, MasterCard, Visa.
PRICES: [2016] per room B&B £345. Tasting menu £90, à la carte £65.

DUROR Argyll and Bute

Map 5:D1

BEALACH HOUSE

♕ César award since 2009

Along a rough track 'with not a sign of habitation', Jim and Hilary McFadyen have posted encouraging notices ('You're on the right road!') to arriving guests. 'You wonder if there's anything at the end; what you find is a lovely white house in a very pretty garden,' say Guide inspectors in 2016. The 'large, rambling' former croft is 'completely isolated, but warm and cosy, with a good welcome'. 'We loved it.' Take tea and home-made flapjacks in the lounge ('comfortable' sofas, books, games, a large TV), then head to 'clean, tastefully furnished' bedrooms. 'Though compact, ours was comfortable, with a good shower in the bathroom. Nice touches: a quirky teapot, local guides, a container of emergency sewing supplies.' Hilary McFadyen's 'delicious' family-style dinners are 'competently' served in the 'attractive' dining room. 'The hosts were happy for us to have friends join us for dinner. Hilary sent us the menu in advance, we brought our own wine, and had a lovely meal with home-baked bread and fresh vegetables.' In the morning, a 'well-cooked and -presented' breakfast includes a daily special.

Salachan Glen
Duror
PA38 4BW

T: 01631 740298
E: enquiries@bealachhouse.co.uk
W: www.bealachhouse.co.uk

BEDROOMS: 3.
OPEN: Mar–Oct, dining room closed Mon evening.
FACILITIES: lounge, conservatory, dining room, free Wi-Fi, 8-acre grounds, unsuitable for disabled.
BACKGROUND MUSIC: none.
LOCATION: 2 miles S of Duror, off A828.
CHILDREN: not under 14.
DOGS: not allowed.
CREDIT CARDS: MasterCard, Visa.
PRICES: per room B&B £90–£110, D,B&B £150–£170. Set dinner £25–£30. Min.2-night bookings in July and Aug.

EDINBURGH

THE BONHAM

In a 'quiet' residential area within walking distance of Princes Street, this 'reasonably priced', 'very satisfactory' hotel is a 'civilised' retreat, even during the hubbub of the Festival. Now part of the privately owned Principal Hayley group, it's a bright, lively place, the Edwardian panelled walls hung with modern art. 'Lovely' bedrooms, some compact, are individually styled; the best, and largest, have a separate sitting room with bay windows overlooking Drumsheugh Gardens. 'My large room had a splendid view over the Edinburgh rooftops.' There is no guest lounge, but the cosy Consulting Room bar – its name a nod to the building's past as a medical clinic – is just what the doctor ordered for afternoon tea, a midday snack, a sundowner or a nightcap. Dine in: in the restaurant, chef Marco Nobrega's modern Scottish dishes might include pressed duck and sloe gin terrine, pickled vegetables; beetroot and goat's cheese gnocchi, candied walnuts, red chard. At breakfast, help yourself to home-made fruit compotes, smoked Scottish salmon, cheeses, cold meats; hot dishes, including vegetarian options, are served at table. (Charles Elliott, E and JG)

35 Drumsheugh Gardens
Edinburgh
EH3 7RN

T: 0131 274 7400
E: bonham.reservations@
     principal-hayley.com
W: www.townhousecompany.com

BEDROOMS: 49. 6 on ground floor, 1 suitable for disabled.
OPEN: all year, restaurant closed Mon/Tues lunch.
FACILITIES: lift, reception lounge, bar, restaurant, free Wi-Fi, in-room TV (Freeview), wedding facilities, parking.
BACKGROUND MUSIC: jazz and classical in public areas.
LOCATION: West End.
CHILDREN: all ages welcomed.
DOGS: allowed in bedrooms (£30 charge), not in public rooms.
CREDIT CARDS: Amex, MasterCard, Visa.
PRICES: [2016] per room B&B from £140. À la carte from £27.50. 1-night bookings sometimes refused.

SEE ALSO SHORTLIST

ERISKA Argyll and Bute

ISLE OF ERISKA HOTEL, SPA AND ISLAND

Ⓠ César award since 2007

Rumble across a bridge at the mouth of Loch Creran to reach this 'simply faultless' Victorian baronial mansion, a luxury spa hotel with a Michelin-starred restaurant, on a private pleasure island. 'A magical place,' say guests in 2016. 'In heavy rain and high winds, log fires in the public rooms meant there wasn't a hint of chilliness. The attentive staff were devoted to making sure we had a wonderful time.' (In finer weather, there's much outdoor diversion: croquet, golf, archery, kayaking; walks 'till you meet the sea'.) Bedrooms are 'well furnished'; for extra space and seclusion, choose one with a private garden. 'Our comfortable superior room had a modern country house theme; an adequate, though dated, bathroom with posh toiletries. Nice touches: comforting hot-water bottles at turn-down; early-morning tea or coffee; a free daily newspaper of our choice.' In the dining room, sample new chef Paul Leonard's 'exceptional, inventive take on Scottish ingredients', perhaps Scrabster halibut or Mallaig langoustines, all with 'good vegetable accompaniments'. (David Birnie)

Benderloch
Eriska
PA37 1SD

T: 01631 720371
F: 01631 720531
E: office@eriska-hotel.co.uk
W: www.eriska-hotel.co.uk

BEDROOMS: 25. 5 spa suites, 2 cottages, 2 Hilltop Reserves, some on ground floor, 2 suitable for disabled.
OPEN: all year except Jan.
FACILITIES: drawing room, reception room, main hall, library, free Wi-Fi, in-room TV, leisure centre, heated swimming pool, gym, wedding facilities, tennis, 350-acre private island, 6-hole par 22 golf course.
BACKGROUND MUSIC: none.
LOCATION: 12 miles N of Oban.
CHILDREN: all ages welcomed (special evening meal arrangements), no under-5s in leisure centre.
DOGS: allowed, not in public rooms or spa suites.
CREDIT CARDS: Amex, MasterCard, Visa.
PRICES: [2016] per room B&B £350–£480, D,B&B £450–£580. Set dinner £55. 2-night min. stay, 'with rare exceptions'.

GRASSHOPPERS

Hop along to this 'brilliant', budget-friendly spot – 'just like a very upmarket hostel' – popular with the young and young-at-heart. The entrance, on an 'anonymous, un-hotel-like office block' beside Central Station, may seem overwhelmingly urban, but step in and take the lift to the top: cool Scandinavian interiors, a friendly welcome and sweet treats await (think of gingerbread slices one day, home-made ice cream another). 'We loved the views and the little touches, especially the cakes on arrival.' Cheery, high-ceilinged bedrooms (some snug) are kitted out with bottled water, fresh milk, a tube of Smarties; stylish bathroom 'pods' have a power shower and Scottish toiletries. 'We found our room quiet, despite it looking out over the dramatic glass roof of the train station.' Four nights a week, stay in for a simple supper (pea, asparagus and parmesan risotto; braised Tuscan sausage and mash) – or see the hip in-house city guide for dinner recommendations close by. In the morning, an 'excellent' breakfast buffet is supplied by local producers and delis: yogurts, fruits, freshly baked breads; cheeses and cold meats; traditional Scottish porridge. (AD and J Lloyd, and others)

6th floor Caledonian Chambers
87 Union Street
Glasgow
G1 3TA

T: 0141 222 2666
F: 0141 248 3641
E: info@grasshoppersglasgow.com
W: www.grasshoppersglasgow.com

BEDROOMS: 29.
OPEN: all year except 4 days at Christmas, no evening meals Fri–Sun.
FACILITIES: breakfast/supper room, free Wi-Fi, in-room TV (Sky), unsuitable for disabled.
BACKGROUND MUSIC: none.
LOCATION: by Central Station.
CHILDREN: all ages welcomed.
DOGS: allowed.
CREDIT CARDS: Amex, MasterCard, Visa.
PRICES: [2016] per room B&B £85–£125, D,B&B £100–£140. À la carte £17.

SEE ALSO SHORTLIST

GLENFINNAN Highland

GLENFINNAN HOUSE HOTEL

There's a touch of magic and romance on the 'idyllic' shores of Loch Shiel, where stands the MacFarlane family's 'lovely, traditional' hotel. It is well managed by Manja and Duncan Gibson. Bedrooms are 'comfortably furnished', and have original fittings. Garden-view rooms have an 'enormous' spa bath, underfloor heating. 'As returning guests, we were welcomed with chocolates and a handwritten note – a nice touch.' 'The atmosphere is akin to staying in a friend's Highland home,' say the hosts, so no room keys, televisions, telephones. ('We asked for a key, though, and there was no hesitation providing one.') 'Roaring' log fires contribute to 'the warmth and comfort of the place'; fresh flowers and Jacobite-themed paintings add colour. In the bar and restaurant, classically trained chef Duncan Gibson brings a French twist to the 'excellent' Scottish menu ('some superb daily specials'). Try a 'hot pot' of traditional haggis; vegetarian haggis comes with clapshot (mashed potatoes and turnips with chive). Young guests are welcomed: there are children's menus and indoor and outdoor play areas. (A and EW, Lynn Wildgoose)

Glenfinnan
PH37 4LT

T: 01397 722235
F: 01397 722249
E: availability@glenfinnanhouse.com
W: www.glenfinnanhouse.com

BEDROOMS: 14.
OPEN: 24 Mar–5 Nov.
FACILITIES: drawing room, bar/lounge, playroom, restaurant, wedding facilities, free Wi-Fi, 1-acre grounds (play area), unsuitable for disabled.
BACKGROUND MUSIC: Scottish in bar and restaurant.
LOCATION: 15 miles NW of Fort William.
CHILDREN: all ages welcomed.
DOGS: allowed, not in restaurant or drawing room.
CREDIT CARDS: Amex, MasterCard, Visa.
PRICES: [2016] per room B&B single £70–£80, double £140–£240. À la carte £25–£35.

GLENFINNAN Highland

Map 5:C1

THE PRINCE'S HOUSE

Ina and Kieran Kelly have nurtured a loyal following: guests come to this small hotel at the head of Loch Shiel for the 'friendly' welcome, 'attentive' service and 'outstanding' cooking. As a 17th-century 'change house', it provided shelter and a change of horse for travellers heading to and from the coast. Today, it is a gateway into the western Highlands, and a fine-dining experience. 'The superb meal was the highlight of our stay,' say Guide contributors this year. The 'excellent', traditionally furnished bedrooms have a 'very comfortable' bed and 'lots of storage space'; the best has a Jacobean four-poster and views across the hills (a honeymoon favourite, say the hosts). The oldest part of the building houses the wood-panelled restaurant. Here, Kieran Kelly – 'a talented chef par excellence' – cooks 'some of the finest food we have ever eaten'. His innovative Scottish menu might include terrine of wild duck, chutney apple, hibiscus syrup; pan-seared West Coast scallops, fennel–crème fraîche velouté. Breakfast has freshly squeezed orange juice; 'excellent' porridge. Walks from the front door. (AJG, Ralph Wilson)

25% DISCOUNT VOUCHERS

Glenfinnan
PH37 4LT

T: 01397 722246
E: princeshouse@glenfinnan.co.uk
W: www.glenfinnan.co.uk

BEDROOMS: 9.
OPEN: mid-Mar–end Oct, 27 Dec–2 Jan, restaurant open Easter–end Sept, New Year.
FACILITIES: restaurant, bistro/bar, free Wi-Fi, in-room TV (Freeview), small front lawn, only bar suitable for disabled.
BACKGROUND MUSIC: in restaurant and bar.
LOCATION: 17 miles NW of Fort William.
CHILDREN: all ages welcomed.
DOGS: allowed in bar.
CREDIT CARDS: Amex, MasterCard, Visa.
PRICES: [2016] per room B&B £75–£90 single, £130–£180 double/twin, £175–£200 four-poster. Set menu (in restaurant) £45, à la carte (in bistro) £28.

GRANTOWN-ON-SPEY Highland

Map 5:C2

CULDEARN HOUSE

'Probably the best small hotel we've visited,' a guest says this year. Next to woodland, William and Sonia Marshall's Victorian country hotel is 'a well-run and caring operation'. 'The hands-on hosts gave us a very warm welcome.' Fans like the traditional atmosphere. There are plenty of books and ornaments; an open fire burns in the marble fireplace; original features have been retained. From first- and second-floor bedrooms, look out over greenery and local woodland. 'Our spacious bedroom was extremely comfortable and very well appointed'; bathrooms are 'immaculate'. Guests gather in the 'well-decorated' lounge for amuse-bouche and drinks before dinner. In the dining room, Sonia Marshall's 'superb' daily-changing four-course dinner might include game terrine, home-made onion marmalade, sweet poached pear; fillet of sea bream, orange and ginger glaze. Wake up to 'generous' servings of coffee at breakfast; an 'excellent' poached egg and kipper are cooked to order. The hotel is on the Speyside Malt Whisky Trail: whisky aficionados have an 'extensive and impressive' list of fine malts and rare single-barrel casks to choose from.

Woodlands Terrace
Grantown-on-Spey
PH26 3JU

T: 01479 872106
F: 01479 873641
E: enquiries@culdearn.com
W: www.culdearn.com

BEDROOMS: 6. 1 on ground floor.
OPEN: all year.
FACILITIES: drawing room, dining room, free Wi-Fi, in-room TV (Freeview), ¾-acre garden, unsuitable for disabled.
BACKGROUND MUSIC: none.
LOCATION: edge of town (within walking distance).
CHILDREN: not under 10.
DOGS: not allowed.
CREDIT CARDS: MasterCard, Visa.
PRICES: per person B&B £75–£85, D,B&B £100–£125. À la carte £45.

SEE ALSO SHORTLIST

GORDON'S

Food is the focus at Maria and Gordon Watson's restaurant-with-rooms in a 19th-century terrace house near Lunan Bay. Maria Watson provides 'a very warm welcome' and supervises the 'friendly' service front-of-house. Gordon Watson and son Garry 'brilliantly deliver' in the 'small but lovely' dining room (chandeliers, tartan curtains, white table linens). Their 'excellent', concise, modern British menu emphasises local, seasonal fare and classic cooking techniques ('right up there with the best of London!'). Try scallops, crispy chicken wings, Jerusalem artichoke; roast Gressingham duck breast, crisp confit leg, herb gnocchi – all accompanied by 'warm, light, moreish' home-baked bread. In warm weather, lighter bites and drinks may be taken in the small garden and patio. 'We were wonderfully looked after.' Well nourished, head for 'tastefully decorated', 'spotlessly clean' bedrooms, each individually styled. 'Ours had a very comfortable bed and everything we needed.' Want more space for lounging about? A contemporary suite in the courtyard might suit. In the morning, a 'wonderful' breakfast has 'the best scrambled eggs'. (Jim Grover, RG)

Main Street
Inverkeilor
DD11 5RN

T: 01241 830364
E: gordonsrest@aol.com
W: www.gordonsrestaurant.co.uk

BEDROOMS: 5. 1 on ground floor in courtyard annexe.
OPEN: all year except Jan, 1 week Sept.
FACILITIES: lounge, restaurant, free Wi-Fi in reception, in-room TV, small garden and patio, unsuitable for disabled.
BACKGROUND MUSIC: none.
LOCATION: in village.
CHILDREN: not under 12.
DOGS: not allowed.
CREDIT CARDS: MasterCard, Visa.
PRICES: per room B&B £110–£159. Set dinner £57.

IONA Argyll and Bute

Map 5:D1

ARGYLL HOTEL

On this 'very special' island off the Isle of Mull, 'charming' owners Wendy and Rob MacManaway create a homely, relaxing atmosphere at their 'informal' 19th-century former crofter's cottage, its lawns tumbling down to the rocky shoreline. 'It's a lovely place to stay, with a character and charm of its own.' Two cosy lounges (one with an open fire, the other with a piano) have wide water views – pick a book off the shelves and settle in. Some bedrooms may be 'compact', but all have immaculate linens on a wooden bedstead, and views over sea, garden or courtyard. Save space for chef Richard Shwe's 'creative', 'imaginative', 'delicious' super-local dishes: Mull venison, garden carrot terrine, venison sausage roll, blueberry mayonnaise at dinner; home-made tattie scones and hogget sausages supplied by island crofters at breakfast. Admirers praise the place with a near-religious fervour: 'We loved sitting in the garden with a glass of wine before dinner, watching the boats and the views across the Sound of Iona – simply heavenly.' Another fan: 'Being here makes a committed atheist feel holy!' (RS, RM)

25% DISCOUNT VOUCHERS

Isle of Iona
PA76 6SJ

T: 01681 700334
E: reception@argyllhoteliona.co.uk
W: www.argyllhoteliona.co.uk

BEDROOMS: 17. 7 in extension.
OPEN: Apr–late Oct.
FACILITIES: 3 lounges (1 with TV), conservatory, dining room, free Wi-Fi in dining room and west lounge, wedding facilities, beachfront garden, unsuitable for disabled.
BACKGROUND MUSIC: contemporary Scottish, 'gentle' jazz in dining room.
LOCATION: village centre.
CHILDREN: all ages welcomed.
DOGS: up to 2 allowed, not in dining room or sun lounge.
CREDIT CARDS: MasterCard, Visa.
PRICES: B&B per room £67–£185. À la carte £30. 1-night bookings sometimes refused.

KILBERRY Argyll and Bute

Map 5:D1

KILBERRY INN

César award since 2010

Life is 'very relaxing' at this well-regarded restaurant-with-rooms along a scenic single-track stretch in a remote, rustic spot. At the red-roofed former cottage, owners Clare Johnson and David Wilson have built a reputation for their warm welcome. 'David is brilliant at front-of-house, encouraging a lot of craic between the guests,' a regular visitor says. He presides over the 'wee' bar and cosy dining room (stone walls, an open fire, works by local artists); Clare Johnson has a Michelin Bib Gourmand for her 'very good' modern cooking. No foams and gels here – 'the focus is on flavour,' the chef says. 'We particularly enjoyed whole langoustine; crab cakes; apple and celeriac soup.' 'Simple yet comfortable' bedrooms are actually 'little cottages' set around a 'very attractive' Mediterranean-style courtyard garden. At breakfast, expect more 'high-quality ingredients': home-made granola, toast with home-made marmalade and jams, honey from Kilberry Castle. Order a packed lunch for a day of otter- and seal-spotting on nearby beaches. A handy stop for travellers en route to the islands of Islay and Jura. (GC)

Kilberry, by Tarbert
PA29 6YD

T: 01880 770223
E: relax@kilberryinn.com
W: www.kilberryinn.com

BEDROOMS: 5. All on ground floor.
OPEN: Tues–Sun 18 Mar–mid-Dec.
FACILITIES: restaurant, snug (wood-burning stove), variable Wi-Fi (Kilberry is a Wi-Fi 'not-spot'), in-room TV (Freeview), unsuitable for disabled.
BACKGROUND MUSIC: in restaurant at lunch and dinner.
LOCATION: 16 miles NW of Tarbert, on B8024.
CHILDREN: no under-12s.
DOGS: allowed by arrangement in 1 bedroom, not in public rooms.
CREDIT CARDS: MasterCard, Visa.
PRICES: [2016] per room D,B&B £215. À la carte £37. 1-night bookings sometimes refused.

KILCHRENAN Argyll and Bute

Map 5:D1

ARDANAISEIG

The scene is pure theatre: the Scottish baronial mansion, built in 1834, with turrets, chimneys and crow-stepped gables, stands against a backdrop of Loch Awe. Inside, owner Bennie Gray, an antiques dealer, has filled the place with 'eccentricity' and 'a pleasingly old-fashioned air of country house grandeur'. Enter into the 'unstuffy' atmosphere of a private house – albeit one abounding in oil paintings, statuary, 'quirky' objets d'art. The 'magnificent' drawing room has mirrors, 'beautiful' antique tables, a 'fine-looking' Bechstein grand piano. From each of the public rooms, take in 'superb, romantic views' over lawns, down to the loch and over to the peak of Ben Lui. The bedrooms, each different, all 'beautifully furnished', were the work of a set designer for Scottish Opera. For a night under the stars, book the converted boathouse in 'a glorious position' on the water. Come dinnertime, chef Colin Cairns's 'excellent' dinner is served in the 'elegant' dining room (white napery, candles, silver) – try the 'perfectly tender' beef. Mornings, after a 'tasty' breakfast, borrow bikes and wellingtons to explore the extensive grounds and 'pretty' loch-side bay.

Kilchrenan
PA35 1HE

T: 01866 833333
F: 01866 833222
E: hello@ardanaiseig.com
W: www.ardanaiseig.com

BEDROOMS: 19. Some on ground floor, 1 in Boatshed, 1 self-catering cottage.
OPEN: Easter to New Year.
FACILITIES: drawing room, library/bar, restaurant, free Wi-Fi, in-room TV (Freeview), wedding facilities, 120-acre grounds on loch, unsuitable for disabled.
BACKGROUND MUSIC: none.
LOCATION: 4 miles E of Kilchrenan.
CHILDREN: all ages welcomed.
DOGS: allowed 'for a small fee'.
CREDIT CARDS: all major cards.
PRICES: [2016] per room B&B £217–£330, D,B&B from £277. À la carte from £30, tasting menu £60.

KILLIECRANKIE Perth and Kinross

KILLIECRANKIE HOTEL

25% DISCOUNT VOUCHERS

🏆César award since 2011

'There is a wonderful balance of hospitality and efficiency at this long-established hotel,' say regular Guide correspondents, of Henrietta Fergusson's much-liked 19th-century dower house, at the entrance to the beautiful, wooded Pass of Killiecrankie. 'We visit every year – it has never failed us,' other admirers agree in 2016. 'The rooms are comfortable and well furnished, staff are friendly and helpful, the food is excellent.' Summertime calls for cream teas in the 'beautifully kept' garden: 'It's a delightful setting, with a wonderful variety of bird life.' Relax in refurbished, individually styled bedrooms made countryside-comfy with fresh flowers, Egyptian cotton sheets, fluffy towels and good toiletries. A nice touch: beds are turned down at night. In the dining room, sample chef Mark Easton's daily-changing menu, which makes inventive use of local produce and home-grown fruit and vegetables. Typical dishes: salad of locally cured gravadlax and crayfish; supreme of grouse, pommes Anna, savoy cabbage. 'Well placed for local attractions.' (Pauline and Stephen Glover, Alan and Edwina Williams)

Killiecrankie
PH16 5LG

T: 01796 473220
F: 01796 472451
E: enquiries@killiecrankiehotel.
co.uk
W: www.killiecrankiehotel.co.uk

BEDROOMS: 10. 2 on ground floor.
OPEN: 18 Mar–3 Jan.
FACILITIES: sitting room, bar with conservatory, dining room, breakfast conservatory, free Wi-Fi, in-room TV (Freeview), 4½-acre grounds (gardens, woodland), unsuitable for disabled.
BACKGROUND MUSIC: none.
LOCATION: hamlet 3 miles W of Pitlochry.
CHILDREN: all ages welcomed.
DOGS: allowed in some bedrooms, not in sitting or dining rooms.
CREDIT CARDS: Amex, MasterCard, Visa.
PRICES: [2016] per room B&B from £200, D,B&B £140–£320. Set dinner £42. 1-night bookings sometimes refused weekends.

KINCLAVEN Perth and Kinross

BALLATHIE HOUSE   **NEW**

Sporting prints abound, and display cabinets here showcase 'monster' fishing trophies – a sign of this country hotel's long association with salmon fishing. The 'lovely' 19th-century house, owned by the Milligan family, stands in a 'delightful' spot on the banks of the River Tay. 'Comfortable and quiet', it receives an upgrade to a full entry this year thanks to admiration from regular Guide readers. Come up the wooded drive to find gilt-framed paintings, tartan-upholstered sofas, open fires, an intimate, wood-panelled bar; there's 'plenty of space to sit'. Plenty of choice of accommodation, too: 'grander' main-house bedrooms have period features and a spacious bathroom; those in a riverside building (reached via a lit pathway through the garden) have a balcony or patio overlooking the water. 'We were there to fish and walk, so opted for the cheaper Sportsman's Lodge in the grounds. Our large, warm room was plainly furnished, but suitable for our purposes.' In the 'excellent' restaurant, chef Scott Scorer's 'skilfully prepared', 'fine' Scottish menus might include sautéed Pittenweem langoustines, pancetta, green pea velouté. 'We will return.' (Ralph Wilson, and others)

Kinclaven
PH41 4QN

T: 01250 883268
F: 01250 883396
E: email@ballathiehousehotel.com
W: www.ballathiehousehotel.com

BEDROOMS: 50 bedrooms. 16 in riverside building, 12 in Sportsman's Lodge, some on ground floor, 1 suitable for disabled.
OPEN: all year.
FACILITIES: drawing room, bar, restaurant, private dining rooms, free Wi-Fi, in-room TV (Freeview), wedding/function facilities, 900-acre estate (golf, fishing, shooting, sled-dog racing by arrangement).
BACKGROUND MUSIC: none.
LOCATION: 1½ miles SW of Kinclaven.
CHILDREN: all ages welcomed, no young children in restaurant in evening.
DOGS: allowed in some bedrooms (not unattended, £20 charge), not in public rooms.
CREDIT CARDS: MasterCard, Visa.
PRICES: [2016] per person B&B from £120, in Sportsman's Lodge, per person B&B from £70.

🏵 THE CROSS AT KINGUSSIE

César award: Scottish hotel of the year

In an 'interesting' spot in the Highlands, 'very friendly' hosts Celia and Derek Kitchingman run their 'lively' restaurant-with-rooms in a former tweed mill on the banks of the River Gynack. Guests consistently praise the Kitchingmans' hospitality. 'They served me an early breakfast when I arrived on the overnight sleeper train, and Derek insisted on driving me to the station on my last morning,' a Guide reader says in 2016. 'Comfortable' bedrooms in the 'lovely' building (wooden beams, stone walls) are decorated in rustic colours that recall the surrounding hills. 'Our large, airy room had plenty of storage, a modern bathroom; a small balcony overlooked the burn.' Settle in: there are books and DVDs to borrow; a south-facing riverside terrace is ideal for alfresco drinks; two lounges have games and log fires for rainy days. In the white-walled dining room, chef David Skiggs cooks a 'beautifully presented', 'very high-quality' menu, including, perhaps, lamb cannelloni, violet artichoke, rosemary jus. Wake up to a breakfast buffet of fruit, cereals, yogurt and freshly squeezed juice; 'good choices' of cooked dishes. (GC, Mike Benne)

Tweed Mill Brae
Ardbroilach Road
Kingussie
PH21 1LB

T: 01540 661166
E: relax@thecross.co.uk
W: www.thecross.co.uk

BEDROOMS: 8.
OPEN: closed Christmas and Jan, except Hogmanay.
FACILITIES: 2 lounges (wood-burning stove), restaurant, free Wi-Fi, in-room TV (Freeview), 4-acre grounds (terraced garden, woodland), only restaurant suitable for disabled.
BACKGROUND MUSIC: none.
LOCATION: 440 yds from village centre.
CHILDREN: all ages welcomed.
DOGS: not allowed.
CREDIT CARDS: Amex, MasterCard, Visa.
PRICES: [2016] per room B&B £100–£190, D,B&B £200–£280. Set dinner £55, tasting menu £60.

KIRKBEAN Dumfries and Galloway

Map 5:E2

CAVENS

'On a wild winter night, we received a warm welcome from owner/host/chef Angus Fordyce and his wife,' writes a regular Guide reader in 2016. 'Cavens is a winning example of the small "hands-on" country hotel genre, epitomised by Angus's willingness to drive out to rescue us from a flooded car incident.' Automobile adventuring aside, the Fordyce family's 18th-century manor house has a 'restful' atmosphere and 'friendly, smiling' staff. Admirers like the traditional decor and the sitting rooms filled with books, antiques, oil paintings, a grand piano. Bedrooms overlook the gardens and surrounding countryside; pick an 'Estate' room for extra space in which to luxuriate. At dinner, Angus Fordyce's market menu might include warm fennel salad; Galloway beef, red wine marmalade. Bon vivants might enjoy a digestif and home-made petits fours by the log fire. Ask to see the small private wine cellar – the host is pleased to conduct a tour. Breakfasts are 'particularly good, with plenty of choice'. The extensive grounds, including a new kitchen garden, offer ample space to roam. (Dick Pugh, and others)

25% DISCOUNT VOUCHERS

Kirkbean, by Dumfries
DG2 8AA

T: 01387 880234
F: 01387 880467
E: enquiries@cavens.com
W: www.cavens.com

BEDROOMS: 6. 1 on ground floor.
OPEN: Mar–Nov, exclusive use by groups at New Year.
FACILITIES: 2 sitting rooms, dining room, meeting facilities, free Wi-Fi, in-room TV (Freeview), 10-acre grounds, unsuitable for disabled.
BACKGROUND MUSIC: light classical all day in one sitting room, dining room.
LOCATION: in village.
CHILDREN: all ages welcomed (cots provided).
DOGS: allowed by arrangement, not in public rooms or unattended in bedrooms.
CREDIT CARDS: MasterCard, Visa.
PRICES: [2016] per room B&B £100–£200, D,B&B £150–£300. Set dinner £25, à la carte £35. 1-night bookings refused Easter, bank holidays.

GLENHOLME COUNTRY HOUSE

Just outside the fishing port of Kirkcudbright, this 'interesting and charming' guest house inspires acclaim: 'I can't decide if it is idiosyncratic, characterful, tasteful or cosmopolitan – probably all four,' writes an admirer. The Victorian mansion is as bookish and arty as one might expect from Jennifer and Laurence Bristow-Smith, the former an artist, the latter a writer and retired diplomat. Explore the 'well-thumbed' library, whose chimney breast is wallpapered with pages from an old dictionary; admire the artefacts from the hosts' extensive travels; when the weather demands it, get cosy by the log fire in the sitting room. Large gardens invite further investigation. Bedrooms are named after Victorian political figures; Curzon has 'every comfort', plus 'spectacular views'. The 'very good' dinners (strictly bring-your-own-bottle) are served communally in 'a dining room to die for'. 'Guests are invited to say what they do or cannot eat, and we build a menu based on that,' the hosts say. Breakfast is 'very good, with home-made conserves and lots of fruit'; hot dishes are cooked to order. (DW, and others)

Tongland Road
Kirkcudbright
DG6 4UU

T: 01557 339422
E: info@glenholmecountryhouse.
   com
W: www.glenholmecountryhouse.
   com

BEDROOMS: 4.
OPEN: all year except Christmas, New Year.
FACILITIES: library, lounge, dining room, hall, free Wi-Fi, 2-acre garden (formal gardens, vegetable plot, orchard), unsuitable for disabled.
BACKGROUND MUSIC: none.
LOCATION: 1 mile N of town.
CHILDREN: not under 12.
DOGS: not allowed.
CREDIT CARDS: MasterCard, Visa.
PRICES: [2016] per room B&B single £90–£100, double £100–£125. Set dinner £35. 1-night bookings sometimes refused in high season.

KYLESKU Highland

KYLESKU HOTEL

César award since 2014

'Absolutely charming' owners, 'wonderful' food and an atmosphere of 'informal warmth' draw fans to this well-loved hotel in 'one of the wildest and most beautiful locations'. The loch-side, white-painted 17th-century inn is 'run with enthusiasm' by Sonia Virechauveix and Tanja Lister. Frazzled minds find calm in this 'peaceful spot': sit by the 'roaring' fire in the lounge, which has 'plenty of reading material to occupy quieter moments'. Among the 'very stylish' bedrooms, loch-facing rooms, with their 'ever-changing seascapes', are the first to go – 'book well in advance'. A 'fantastic' extension finished in 2015 'blends well with the superb setting', and 'enables every diner to see the spectacular view across the loch'. The daily catch, brought from boats on the slipway in front of the hotel, informs Sonia Virechauveix's French-inflected menu. 'It's not glamorous, but very tasty – seafood heaven.' Vegetarians rejoice: plenty of interesting options, perhaps a spinach and ricotta strudel. 'The attention to detail in the restaurant is exceptional.' Tanja Lister is on hand at breakfast to help guests plan their day. (BW, CA, and others)

Kylesku
IV27 4HW

T: 01971 502231
E: info@kyleskuhotel.co.uk
W: www.kyleskuhotel.co.uk

BEDROOMS: 11. 4 in annexe, 1 suitable for disabled.
OPEN: mid-Feb–end Nov.
FACILITIES: lounge, bar, restaurant, free Wi-Fi in bar and lounge, in-room TV (Freeview), small garden (tables for outside eating).
BACKGROUND MUSIC: in afternoon and evenings, in bar and half the dining area.
LOCATION: 10 miles S of Scourie.
CHILDREN: all ages welcomed (cot £10, extra bed £25).
DOGS: allowed (£10 a night), but not unattended in bedrooms.
CREDIT CARDS: MasterCard, Visa.
PRICES: [2016] per room B&B £105–£160. À la carte £45.

LANGASS LODGE

In 'a paradise for wildlife, especially birds', Amanda and Niall Leveson Gower have been hosting guests for 20 years at their 'handsome' small hotel. The former shooting lodge stands alone above Langass sea loch, and has views of Ben Eaval. Within its white-painted walls, the atmosphere is relaxed, informal, 'friendly'. 'Stylishly decorated', the main house has a 'cosy' bar (stag's head, wood-burning stove, 'a traditional feel'), a 'bright, airy' dining room and a 'light, conservatory-like' sitting room. At every turn, admire 'fabulous' views over the 'pretty' garden and across the water. Take your pick of bedrooms in the main lodge or in a 'barn-like' extension set into the hillside, and reached via a covered walkway. 'Our spacious hillside bedroom had large, comfy beds and armchairs, fancy throws, rugs on wooden floors; French windows opened on to a little terrace.' At dinner, Hugh Sawyer, the new chef, focuses on fresh local fish; try the Langass seafood platter – with lobster, for a treat. 'Angela suggested walks and provided maps'; a favourite is a 'wonderful' circuit up Ben Langass, with 'great views over loch and mountains'.

Locheport
Isle of North Uist
HS6 5HA

T: 01876 580285
F: 01876 580385
E: langasslodge@btconnect.com
W: www.langasslodge.co.uk

BEDROOMS: 11. Some in modern extension, 1 suitable for disabled.
OPEN: spring–31 Oct.
FACILITIES: lounge, bar, restaurant, free Wi-Fi, in-room TV (Freeview), 11-acre garden in 200-acre grounds.
BACKGROUND MUSIC: in public rooms.
LOCATION: 7½ miles SW of Lochmaddy.
CHILDREN: all ages welcomed.
DOGS: not in restaurant.
CREDIT CARDS: Amex, MasterCard, Visa.
PRICES: [2016] per room B&B single £80–£115, double £95–£155. À la carte £40.

THE ALBANNACH

Come hungry. Overlooking Lochinver Bay, this modest restaurant-with-rooms is owned and run by self-taught chefs/patrons Lesley Crosfield and Colin Craig, who hold a Michelin star for their modern Scottish cooking. Nearly everything here is locally sourced, including the tableware. 'It is a showcase for all things local, free-range and wild,' the chefs say. Fans are more succinct: 'It is excellent.' Using produce from local crofters and the catch landed at the town's harbour, the daily-changing five-course menu might include garden beetroot soufflé; roast wild turbot, white and green asparagus, black potatoes. (The chefs are happy to discuss food dislikes and allergies before planning the set menu.) Aperitifs and post-dinner petits fours are taken in the conservatory ('a good place to lounge around with a book'). Sleep soundly in 'lovely' bedrooms with views of the gardens and mountains beyond. Every room in the 200-year-old Highland house is different: one has a private terrace; two, with a sofa bed, can accommodate a family. The Caberfeidh pub in the village, under the same ownership, has sharing plates and local seafood. (BW, and others)

Baddidarroch
Lochinver
IV27 4LP

T: 01571 844407
E: info@thealbannach.co.uk
W: www.thealbannach.co.uk

BEDROOMS: 5. 1 in byre.
OPEN: 10 Feb–20 Nov, 16 Dec–4 Jan. Closed Mon, Mon–Wed in winter.
FACILITIES: snug, conservatory, dining room, free Wi-Fi, in-room TV (Freeview), ½-acre garden.
BACKGROUND MUSIC: none.
LOCATION: ½ mile from village.
CHILDREN: not under 12.
DOGS: not allowed.
CREDIT CARDS: Diners, MasterCard, Visa.
PRICES: [2016] per room D,B&B single £225, double £305–£385. Set dinner £72. 1-night bookings generally refused Sat.

THE DOWER HOUSE

♀️César award since 2008

Cheerful wisteria and flower-filled gardens greet visitors to this Georgian stone cottage-orné, 'well located outside Inverness'. Guests praise the 'wonderful hospitality' from owners Mena and Robyn Aitchison: 'They are such lovely people, and they try hard to please.' 'A home away from home', the 'pleasant, peaceful' guest house has a lived-in feel: the lounge brims with 'interesting objects' – antiques, Persian rugs and Chinese vases, well-stocked bookshelves and potted plants. The 'cosy' bedrooms are individually decorated, and have a shower or Victorian roll-top bath. Each room faces the gardens, which are 'wonderful to walk in; there are benches everywhere'. A guest with moderately limited mobility was well accommodated this year. 'My small room was well suited to me and had an excellent walk-in shower. A handrail leading down three small steps to the bedroom would have been helpful.' In the evenings, sit down to 'exceptional' no-choice menus: Robyn Aitchison is a 'superb' cook. Breakfast is 'first rate': proper porridge; eggs from resident hens. (Charles Elliott, Helen Anthony)

Highfield
Muir of Ord
IV6 7XN

T: 01463 870090
F: 01463 870090
E: info@thedowerhouse.co.uk
W: www.thedowerhouse.co.uk

BEDROOMS: 4. All on ground floor.
OPEN: Apr–Oct.
FACILITIES: lounge, dining room, snug/TV room, free Wi-Fi, in-room TV (Freeview), wedding facilities, 5-acre grounds, unsuitable for disabled.
BACKGROUND MUSIC: none.
LOCATION: 14 miles NW of Inverness, 1 mile N of Muir of Ord.
CHILDREN: no under-5s at dinner (high tea at 5 pm).
DOGS: allowed in bedrooms (not on bed or furniture), not in public rooms.
CREDIT CARDS: MasterCard, Visa.
PRICES: [2016] per room B&B from £145, D,B&B from £221.

BARLEY BREE

'The efficient and friendly staff are a great asset' at this popular restaurant-with-rooms, say Guide inspectors in 2016. Occupying a 19th-century coaching inn on the 'very quiet' main street of a pretty conservation village, it is run by French owner/chef Fabrice Bouteloup and his Scottish wife, Alison, a wine expert. 'We were warmly welcomed and shown to our room. Everything was spotlessly clean and inviting. Our bed had a billowy duvet; there were plenty of towels in the small, functional bathroom.' Take pre-dinner drinks in the snug lounge; a convivial dinner ('pleasantly noisy at times') is served in an 'attractive' room 'decorated with outdoorsy tools reflecting the rural surroundings'. 'The menu is small – only four choices for each course – so you know it's being freshly cooked. It was all very tasty – a broccoli-and-asparagus amuse-bouche with a bite of haggis; rabbit with pear and foie gras; a delicious pannacotta with rosewater jelly and blackberry sorbet.' At breakfast, 'we were immediately brought a pot of tea'; 'there was lots of toast from home-baked bread, and home-made marmalade and raspberry jam.'

6 Willoughby Street
Muthill
PH5 2AB

T: 01764 681451
F: 01764 910055
E: info@barleybree.com
W: www.barleybree.com

BEDROOMS: 6.
OPEN: all year except Christmas, 2 weeks July, restaurant closed Mon, Tues.
FACILITIES: lounge bar, restaurant, free Wi-Fi, in-room TV (Freeview), small terrace and lawn, unsuitable for disabled.
BACKGROUND MUSIC: in lounge bar and restaurant.
LOCATION: village centre.
CHILDREN: all ages welcomed (family room, children's menu).
DOGS: not allowed.
CREDIT CARDS: MasterCard, Visa.
PRICES: per room B&B from £95. À la carte £40.

THE MANOR HOUSE

There are 'dramatic' views of the ferries on Oban bay from Leslie and Margaret Crane's 'excellent' hotel, to be sure, but there's much interest within the Georgian stone mansion as well, say guests this year. 'We enjoyed a relaxing break. The standards are high; the staff are very friendly and helpful; the food, from hearty Scottish breakfasts to well-balanced dinners, is first class.' Take coffee or tea in the 'spacious' lounges and well-stocked bar; on a fine day, lunch on the terrace overlooking the harbour. Bedrooms may be snug, but are 'well appointed' in country house style, and stocked with bottled water, fruit, cookies and coffee. Go for one of the best, with binoculars to take in the 'wonderful' views. In the elegant dining room (white linens, fresh flowers, candles), long-serving chef Shaun Squire 'makes good use of local produce' in his daily-changing menus. Typical dishes: quail's egg, crisp Brie, asparagus; veal cordon bleu, Orkney Cheddar, smoked ham, olive oil mash. Lighter meals, perhaps West Highland fish soup, are served in the bar. The harbour and ferry terminal are a stroll away.

Gallanach Road
Oban
PA34 4LS

T: 01631 562087
F: 01631 563053
E: info@manorhouseoban.com
W: www.manorhouseoban.com

BEDROOMS: 11. 1 on ground floor.
OPEN: all year except 25/26 Dec.
FACILITIES: 2 lounges, bar, restaurant, free Wi-Fi, in-room TV (Freeview), wedding facilities, 1½-acre grounds, access to nearby gym, unsuitable for disabled.
BACKGROUND MUSIC: traditional in bar and dining room.
LOCATION: ½ mile from centre.
CHILDREN: not under 12.
DOGS: allowed by arrangement, not in public rooms.
CREDIT CARDS: all major cards.
PRICES: [2016] per room B&B £120–£250, D,B&B £195–£325. Set dinner £37.50–£42.50.

SEE ALSO SHORTLIST

PEAT INN Fife

Map 5:D3

THE PEAT INN

NEW

'Luxurious', 'relaxing', 'warmly welcoming', Katherine and Geoffrey Smeddle's rustic restaurant-with-rooms receives rave reviews from trusted correspondents, whose reports earn it a full entry in the Guide. Past the 'blazing' log fire in the 'lovely' reception lounge, savour Geoffrey Smeddle's modern, Michelin-starred dishes. 'Every course was delicious and beautifully served, from the halibut to the pork cheek to the steak to the chocolate dessert. While busy, the restaurant has an unhurried feel.' Staff are 'impeccable'; 'catering for our gluten-intolerant friend wasn't a problem'. Afterwards, put your feet up in 'well-kept', 'very special' suites in the separate residence ('extremely comfortable' beds, 'attractive' bathrooms, garden views). 'We were glad not to have to drive home on a dark winter's night.' Breakfast is served in the suite. 'Two cheerful ladies came at the agreed time and set it out in our sitting room. It was the perfect amount for the morning after a big meal: soft-boiled eggs, granola, yogurt, smoked haddock; plenty of toast and croissants, with home-made preserves.' 'A comfortable base for touring the coastal villages nearby.' (Jackie and Hugh Tunstall-Pedoe, Colin Adams)

Peat Inn
KY15 5LH

T: 01334 840206
F: 01334 840530
E: stay@thepeatinn.co.uk
W: www.thepeatinn.co.uk

BEDROOMS: 8. All suites, on ground floor in annexe, 7 split-level.
OPEN: all year except 1 week Christmas, 1 week Jan, open New Year, restaurant closed Sun/Mon.
FACILITIES: lounge, restaurant, free Wi-Fi, in-room TV, ½-acre garden.
BACKGROUND MUSIC: in restaurant at mealtimes.
LOCATION: 6 miles SW of St Andrews.
CHILDREN: all ages welcomed.
DOGS: only guide dogs allowed.
CREDIT CARDS: Amex, MasterCard, Visa.
PRICES: [2016] per room B&B from £195, D,B&B from £325 (including tasting menu). Set dinner £50, tasting menu £70.

PITLOCHRY Perth and Kinross

Map 5:D2

CRAIGATIN HOUSE AND COURTYARD

Minutes away from some of Scotland's best distilleries, Andrea and Martin Anderson's 19th-century home has been 'superbly' converted into an award-winning B&B. The Andersons now celebrate ten years at the helm (they arrived as guests in 2007 and never looked back). Expect a hearty greeting: 'Martin welcomed us warmly, showed us to our room and gave us great advice about the local area,' says a reader this year. Choose from bedrooms in the main house or in the converted stables. Each is individually decorated; biscuits, handmade locally, are a delicious accent. 'Our delightful courtyard suite was well appointed and spotlessly clean; the light, bright sitting area had extremely comfortable chairs. Although the room is nearest to the road, we were not disturbed by traffic noise.' The dining room and lounge occupy the double-height, light-filled cedarwood extension that overlooks the 'beautifully kept' gardens. In the morning, sit down to 'excellent' service and a varied breakfast menu; a reader recommends the 'divine' Arnold Bennett omelette, with fresh smoked haddock and cheese. (Deborah Connell)

165 Atholl Road
Pitlochry
PH16 5QL

T: 01796 472478
E: enquiries@craigatinhouse.co.uk
W: www.craigatinhouse.co.uk

BEDROOMS: 14. 7 in courtyard, 2 on ground floor, 1 suitable for disabled.
OPEN: Mar–Dec, closed Christmas.
FACILITIES: lounge, 2 dining rooms, free Wi-Fi, in-room TV (Freeview), 2-acre garden.
BACKGROUND MUSIC: at breakfast.
LOCATION: central.
CHILDREN: not under 13.
DOGS: not allowed.
CREDIT CARDS: MasterCard, Visa.
PRICES: [2016] per room B&B £98–£125. 1-night bookings refused Sat.

SEE ALSO SHORTLIST

PITLOCHRY Perth and Kinross

Map 5:D2

DALSHIAN HOUSE

'Warm and welcoming', Martin and Heather Walls's 'absolutely beautiful' 18th-century house stands in 'tranquil' woodland and gardens – all the better to relax, unwind and keep a keen eye out for red squirrels, rabbits and all manner of wild birds. On cool days, sit by the wood-burning stove in the elegant lounge; there are books and magazines to borrow. B&B accommodation is in smartly decorated bedrooms that mix traditional furnishings with bold modern flourishes; each has a hospitality tray. Travelling with family? Ask for one of two spacious rooms in the eaves, set up with extra single beds for a group. Breakfast is 'a great start to the day'. Help yourself to vanilla-scented pears, cinnamon-dusted berry compote, Earl Grey-infused figs, home-baked marmalade muffins; spoon porridge with a nip of local Edradour whisky; order a Stornoway black pudding Benedict, or scrambled eggs with Dunkeld smoked salmon. Afterwards, stroll into the Victorian town to explore (during the annual Autumn Festival, there's much animation till late), or embark on a forest ramble – the Wallses are happy to advise. (Sharon Methven)

25% DISCOUNT VOUCHERS

Old Perth Road
Pitlochry
PH16 5TD

T: 01796 472173
E: dalshian@btconnect.com
W: www.dalshian.co.uk

BEDROOMS: 7.
OPEN: all year except Christmas.
FACILITIES: lounge, dining room, free Wi-Fi, in-room TV (Freeview), 1-acre garden, unsuitable for disabled.
BACKGROUND MUSIC: none.
LOCATION: 1 mile S of centre.
CHILDREN: all ages welcomed.
DOGS: allowed by arrangement, not in public rooms.
CREDIT CARDS: MasterCard, Visa.
PRICES: [2016] per person B&B £35–£45.

SEE ALSO SHORTLIST

PITLOCHRY Perth and Kinross

Map 5:D2

THE GREEN PARK

♥ César award since 2015

It's the attention to detail that wins praise from Guide readers at the McMenemie family's 'surprising, impressive' traditional hotel on the banks of Loch Faskally. In each of the public rooms, discover plenty to occupy lazy days: binoculars and a book of Scottish birds 'thoughtfully' left in the sun lounge; a daily afternoon tea buffet of hot drinks and home-made cakes in the main lounge; thousands of books to borrow, on shelves throughout the Victorian house. Everywhere, too, experience the 'informality', 'warmth' and 'incredibly personal service' that keep regular guests coming back. Most of the good-sized bedrooms overlook the lawns stretching down to the water; original paintings provide the finishing touch. In-room fridges are new this year. In the dining room, angle for a much-in-demand window table with a view of the loch. Chef Chris Tamblin's 'superb' French-inflected Scottish menu (perhaps including pan-fried venison, roast chestnuts) is 'cheerfully' served. Three breakfast buffet tables carry 'the greatest range of choices we have ever seen'; cooked dishes are served at the table. (Anthony Bradbury, and others)

Clunie Bridge Road
Pitlochry
PH16 5JY

T: 01796 473248
F: 01796 473520
E: bookings@thegreenpark.co.uk
W: www.thegreenpark.co.uk

BEDROOMS: 51. 13 on ground floor, 1 suitable for disabled.
OPEN: all year except Christmas.
FACILITIES: 2 lifts, 3 lounges, library, bar, restaurant, free Wi-Fi, in-room TV (Freeview), 3-acre garden.
BACKGROUND MUSIC: none.
LOCATION: ½ mile N of town centre.
CHILDREN: all ages welcomed.
DOGS: allowed, not in public rooms.
CREDIT CARDS: MasterCard, Visa.
PRICES: [2016] per person B&B £80–£91, D,B&B £91–£116. Set menus £25–£29.

SEE ALSO SHORTLIST

PITLOCHRY Perth and Kinross

Map 5:D2

KNOCKENDARROCH HOTEL & RESTAURANT

'A feeling of friendliness' is in the air at Struan and Louise Lothian's 'cheerful', 'welcoming' small hotel, in an 'attractive' town 'well placed for exploring Perthshire'. The staff are 'unobtrusive' and obliging: 'We mentioned that we'd be going for a walk before dinner, and the receptionist gave us a map and route suggestions,' Guide inspectors report. Most of the 'fresh, tasteful' bedrooms in the 'beautiful' Victorian villa have panoramic views of the burgh and surrounding hills. 'Our room overlooking the front of the house had a good-sized bed, comfortable armchairs, lots of storage space; the well-equipped bathroom had plenty of hot water.' Bedrooms on the top floor have a small balcony and binoculars to take in the view. Downstairs, there are two roaring fires, Scottish contemporary art and a comprehensive whisky cabinet in the lounges. Be 'spoilt for choice' by chef Graeme Stewart's 'original' daily-changing menu (including 'beautifully presented' Perthshire lamb, and vegetarian options). Breakfast has 'everything you could wish for', including 'masses of toast', home-made preserves. 'We felt very well looked after.'

25% DISCOUNT VOUCHERS

Higher Oakfield
Pitlochry
PH16 5HT

T: 01796 473473
E: bookings@knockendarroch.co.uk
W: www.knockendarroch.co.uk

BEDROOMS: 12. 1 on ground floor.
OPEN: Feb–20 Dec.
FACILITIES: 2 lounges, restaurant, free Wi-Fi, in-room TV (Freeview), 2-acre woodland garden, unsuitable for disabled.
BACKGROUND MUSIC: in restaurant in evening.
LOCATION: central.
CHILDREN: not under 10.
DOGS: not allowed.
CREDIT CARDS: Amex, MasterCard, Visa.
PRICES: [2016] per room B&B £145–£220, D,B&B £160–£275. Set dinner £42. 1-night bookings sometimes refused on Sat.

SEE ALSO SHORTLIST

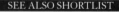

POOLEWE Highland

Map 5:B1

POOL HOUSE

Time for something completely different. On the shores of Loch Ewe, this 'quirky' guest house is run by two generations of the 'charming' Harrison family; it is filled with two generations of character and whimsy. The 300-year-old house brims with antiques and curios; admirers also like the gentlemen's billiard table, Victorian piano, open fires and well-stocked library. 'It has all the attributes of a small boutique hotel of outstanding quality,' a Guide reader writes. Each of the four suites has a lounge and views across the bay. 'We watched otters from the window of our sunny, spacious sitting room.' A single (and singular) bedroom was added this year: accessed via a private garden entrance, it has a hand-painted antique two-poster bed, and a marble bathtub set between carved pillars. In the nautical-themed dining room (a seven-foot gilded compass; hand-painted stars on the ceiling), four-course modern Scottish dinners are 'cooked to perfection'. Typical dishes: garlicky local squid, herbed vermouth; pan-fried Goosnargh duck, wild mushrooms, port-and-shallot sauce. Green-fingered guests, check out the shoreline kitchen garden and subtropical ornamentals. (JH)

by Inverewe Garden
Poolewe
IV22 2LD

T: 01445 781272
E: stay@pool-house.co.uk
W: www.pool-house.co.uk

BEDROOMS: 5.
OPEN: Easter–Nov.
FACILITIES: reception room, drawing room/library, dining room, private dining room, billiard/whisky room, free Wi-Fi in public areas, in-room TV (Freeview), ½-acre garden, unsuitable for disabled.
BACKGROUND MUSIC: none.
LOCATION: 6 miles NE of Gairloch.
CHILDREN: not under 14.
DOGS: allowed in some bedrooms and billiard/whisky room.
CREDIT CARDS: Amex, MasterCard, Visa.
PRICES: [2016] per room B&B £225–£375. Set menu £45. 1-night bookings refused weekends.

PORT APPIN Argyll and Bute

Map 5:D1

THE AIRDS HOTEL

Take a breathtaking drive through Glencoe to this former ferry inn (Relais & Châteaux) on Loch Linnhe, with the Morvern mountains beyond. Shaun and Jenny McKivragan were guests here in 2002, and so loved the place that they bought it. The white-painted building stands in a 'gorgeous' setting with wide views of the peaceful surroundings. Inside, smartly dressed staff, though 'very pleasant', add to the 'rather formal' atmosphere. Enter through the conservatory, its vista stretching over the loch; further in, find log fires, books, fresh flowers and a mix of antiques and contemporary pieces in the lounges. Recently redecorated bedrooms are kitted out with iced water in silver jugs, a decanter of Whisky Mac, swanky toiletries, top-end bedlinen; most overlook the water. At dinner, new chef Chris Stanley's 'beautifully' presented dishes – perhaps stone bass, truffle, Pink Fir Apple potatoes, wild leek – are served with ceremony. There's an 'impressive' menu at breakfast, including porridge 'and a wee dram'. In-room massages are offered, but the greatest tonic is the fresh air (bikes, wellies and packed lunches available). (J and MB, and others)

Port Appin
PA38 4DF

T: 01631 730236
E: airds@airds-hotel.com
W: www.airds-hotel.com

BEDROOMS: 11. 2 on ground floor, plus 2 self-catering cottages.
OPEN: all year, restaurant closed Mon/Tue Nov–Jan (open Christmas and New Year).
FACILITIES: 2 lounges, conservatory, whisky bar, restaurant, civil wedding licence, free Wi-Fi, in-room TV (Freeview), spa treatments, ½-acre garden (croquet, putting), mountain bike hire, unsuitable for disabled.
BACKGROUND MUSIC: none.
LOCATION: 20 miles N of Oban.
CHILDREN: all ages welcomed, no under-8s in dining room in evening (children's high tea).
DOGS: allowed in bedrooms (not unattended, £10 a day), not in public rooms.
CREDIT CARDS: MasterCard, Visa.
PRICES: [2016] per room DB&B £305–£520.

SEE ALSO SHORTLIST

KNOCKINAAM LODGE

Sheltered by a horseshoe of wooded hills, and edged by a private beach on the coast of the Rhinns of Galloway, Sian and David Ibbotson's 19th-century former hunting lodge is a popular choice for special occasions. Newlyweds this year attest to the staff's 'attention to detail, professionalism and friendliness'. Others praise the 'excellent' customer service. The 'secluded' setting is full of possibilities, romantic and strategic. Book the Churchill suite, where the former PM stayed while planning the D-Day landings in 1944: the original fireplace and 100-year-old enamelled bath in which he soaked are still there; the super-king-size sleigh bed, walk-in shower and a seating area are newer. Other bedrooms – some snug, all different – have much charm; many have views over the sea. In the candlelit restaurant, chef Tony Pierce's 'superb' tasting menu is modern Scotland on a plate. Relish his 'elegant' dishes, perhaps grilled fillet of native salmon, pickled fennel, pink grapefruit and coriander; roast canon of Galloway lamb, black pudding crust, garlic pomme purée. Breakfast, with freshly baked bread and home-made preserves, is praised. (Helen Helmers, and others)

25% DISCOUNT VOUCHERS

Portpatrick
DG9 9AD

T: 01776 810471
F: 01776 810435
E: reservations@knockinaamlodge.com
W: www.knockinaamlodge.com

BEDROOMS: 10.
OPEN: all year.
FACILITIES: 2 lounges, bar, restaurant, free Wi-Fi, in-room TV (Freeview), wedding facilities, 30-acre grounds, only restaurant suitable for disabled.
BACKGROUND MUSIC: 'easy listening'/classical in restaurant in evening.
LOCATION: 3 miles S of Portpatrick.
CHILDREN: welcomed, no under-12s in dining room after 7 pm (high tea at 6).
DOGS: allowed in some bedrooms, not in public rooms.
CREDIT CARDS: Amex, MasterCard, Visa.
PRICES: [2016] per person D,B&B single £175–£325, double £145–£220. 1-night bookings sometimes refused.

PORTREE Highland

Map 5:C1

VIEWFIELD HOUSE

César award since 1993

Soak in the house-party atmosphere at the Macdonald family's country pile, a 'fabulous' house standing peacefully in acres of mature wooded gardens, with views of Portree Bay. Continuing a welcoming tradition started by his grandmother, Hugh Macdonald receives guests with a friendly, informal, 'attentive' air, offering drinks and cream teas. There's much to admire in the Victorian interior: antiques, oil paintings, colonial memorabilia, hunting trophies; a grand piano sits by huge windows in the log fire-warmed drawing room. Traditionally styled bedrooms, most with an en suite bathroom in a converted dressing room, vary in size; for a languid soak, ask for a room with a bathtub. There's no TV in the bedrooms (a communal TV room's just the ticket if the tennis is on), but there's plenty of diversion all around: nurse a malt whisky while browsing the collection of books, play croquet on the lawn, walk up the hill for views of the Sound; the town is a ten-minute stroll away. Evenings, 'fantastic' dinners of rustic dishes are served, by arrangement, under the gaze of gilt-framed portraits. More reports, please.

Viewfield Road
Portree
Isle of Skye
IV51 9EU

T: 01478 612217
F: 01478 613517
E: info@viewfieldhouse.com
W: www.viewfieldhouse.com

BEDROOMS: 11. 1, on ground floor, suitable for disabled.
OPEN: early Apr–mid-Oct.
FACILITIES: drawing room, morning/TV room, dining room, free Wi-Fi, 20-acre grounds (croquet, swings).
BACKGROUND MUSIC: none.
LOCATION: S side of Portree.
CHILDREN: all ages welcomed.
DOGS: allowed in bedrooms, not in public rooms.
CREDIT CARDS: MasterCard, Visa.
PRICES: [2016] per person B&B £65–£90. Set dinner £25.

RANNOCH STATION Perth and Kinross

Map 5:D2

MOOR OF RANNOCH HOTEL

♻ César award since 2015

Life slows down at this 'beautifully remote' hotel, which stands amid the 'captivating wild scenery' of uninhabited moorland. Scott Meikle and Stephanie Graham are the 'professional but refreshingly laid-back' owners; expect a 'relaxed' warmth and genuine hospitality. 'We took the sleeper train from London. Scott met us on the platform and took our bags; a lovely breakfast was waiting at the hotel.' The absence of 'modern-day essentials' (like Wi-Fi and a mobile phone signal) encourages a 'convivial' atmosphere, devotees say. 'There are always such interesting people to chat with.' Nonetheless, 'despite the intimacy of the place, we felt we had space to relax'. Straightforward bedrooms are 'well equipped', 'quiet', 'just big enough'; each has 'stunning' views. 'While Scott is the consummate host, Steph is the talented chef.' Her 'good-value' 'slow-food' dinners have 'sensible flavour combinations – scallops with cauliflower, venison with juniper, etc'. In the morning, as the mist hangs over the moor, sit down to a 'hearty, freshly cooked' breakfast served with home-made tattie scones or warm toast. (KD, Joel Mumford, Mark Slaney, DS)

Rannoch Station
PH17 2QA

T: 01882 633238
E: info@moorofrannoch.co.uk
W: www.moorofrannoch.co.uk

BEDROOMS: 5.
OPEN: 11 Feb–end Oct.
FACILITIES: lounge, bar, dining room, no Wi-Fi, unsuitable for disabled.
BACKGROUND MUSIC: none.
LOCATION: on a single-track, dead-end road, 40 miles W of Pitlochry.
CHILDREN: all ages welcomed.
DOGS: welcomed.
CREDIT CARDS: all major cards.
PRICES: per room B&B from £140. Set meals £24–£30.

RATHO Midlothian

THE BRIDGE INN AT RATHO

Walk along the 'pretty' towpath of the historic Union Canal and look in on the 'huge, interesting' walled garden in the grounds of Ratho Hall – 'it's the source of much of the delightful food you'll eat' at Graham and Rachel Bucknall's 'characterful' restaurant-with-rooms on the water. The heart of this pretty village, the 'lively' pub has 'smart' public rooms warmed by open fires, a 'many-windowed' dining room overlooking the canal, a terrace for alfresco meals; 'an easy, informal air' throughout. Upstairs, the bedrooms are neatly rustic, with modern touches. 'Ours was small, but not cramped, with a large, comfortable bed (only one bedside table and lamp, though). The good-sized bathroom had fluffy towels, a deep freestanding bath, Scottish-made toiletries.' Food in the 'popular' restaurant doesn't get more local, with those home-grown vegetables, and pork from the rare breed pigs raised just across the canal. It's all 'delicious': rolled pork loin, toasted oats, roast apple sauce at dinner; home-made sausages and tattie scones at a 'generous' breakfast. Summer Sundays, take a lunch cruise up the canal – a real sailor's delight.

27 Baird Road
Ratho
EH28 8RA

T: 0131 333 1320
F: 0131 333 3480
E: info@bridgeinn.com
W: www.bridgeinn.com

BEDROOMS: 4.
OPEN: all year, no accommodation 24/25 Dec.
FACILITIES: 2 bars, restaurant, free Wi-Fi, in-room TV (Freeview), terrace (beer garden, boat shed), only bar and restaurant suitable for disabled.
BACKGROUND MUSIC: 'relaxed' all day, live music Sat nights.
LOCATION: in village, 7 miles W of Edinburgh.
CHILDREN: all ages welcomed.
DOGS: allowed in bar only.
CREDIT CARDS: Amex, MasterCard, Visa.
PRICES: [2016] per room B&B from £85. À la carte £30. 1-night bookings sometimes refused.

ST OLA Orkney Islands

Map 5:A3

THE FOVERAN

A passion for all things Orcadian is evident in this award-winning restaurant-with-rooms overlooking Scapa Flow. From the art and craft pieces on display in the lounge, to the stone-ground beremeal flour in the home-baked bere bunno loaf, local wins the day. (The traditional Orkney chair in the fire-warmed lounge is 'more comfortable than it looks'.) Unpretentious and relaxed, this is a family affair: chef/patron Paul Doull and his wife, Helen, bought the single-storey hotel in 2000; they run it with Paul's brother, Hamish, and sister-in-law, Shirley. 'Friendly, helpful' staff welcome guests into the spacious dining room overlooking countryside and sea. Here, fish and Kirkwall Bay shellfish, North Ronaldsay mutton, Orkney beef and locally made cheeses are mainstays of the short menu, along with the odd slug of peaty Highland Park whisky. The locals, who 'rate it highly for a night out', can't be wrong – try crispy Grimbister Farm cheese, plum and ginger dip; sea bass, prawns, pak choi. Retire, afterwards, to simple, pretty bedrooms, some looking over the bay. At breakfast, sausages and black pudding come from local suppliers, preserves are home made.

St Ola
Kirkwall
KW15 1SF

T: 01856 872389
F: 01856 876430
E: info@thefoveran.com
W: www.thefoveran.com

BEDROOMS: 8. All on ground floor.
OPEN: Apr–early Oct, by arrangement at other times, restaurant closed variable times in Apr, Oct.
FACILITIES: lounge, restaurant, free Wi-Fi, in-room TV, 12-acre grounds (private rock beach), unsuitable for disabled.
BACKGROUND MUSIC: local/Scottish traditional in restaurant.
LOCATION: 3 miles SW of Kirkwall.
CHILDREN: all ages welcomed.
DOGS: not allowed.
CREDIT CARDS: MasterCard, Visa.
PRICES: [2016] per person B&B single £77, double from £57, D,B&B single £102, double from £82. À la carte £35.

SCARISTA Western Isles

Map 5:B1

SCARISTA HOUSE

🏅 César award since 2012

In a 'remarkable' setting on the remote west coast of Harris, this 'peaceful' whitewashed manse soothes frazzled souls with the 'wonderfully laid-back, professional' hospitality within. It is owned by Neil King and Patricia and Tim Martin. Guide correspondents praise its 'characterful simplicity'. The house has rugs on wooden floors, comfortable sofas, art on the walls; log fires burn in cosy public rooms. Peruse 'the wealth of books' in the downstairs library (joined, perhaps, by the resident dog and cat); in the pet-free drawing room, find the quiet writing desk with an inspiring view of the ocean. Take in the sea views, too, from any of the bedrooms spread out between the main house and adjacent Glebe House, each thoughtfully decorated with furniture and fabrics that reflect the history of the place. Come dinnertime, the 'fantastic' no-choice menus can be adapted for most dietary needs with notice. Wild, organic and home-produced ingredients are used as much as possible; fish and game feature – Stornoway halibut, Harris Minch langoustines, Lewis quail's eggs, garden-fresh vegetables. 'Superb' breakfasts.

Scarista
Isle of Harris
HS3 3HX

T: 01859 550238
E: bookings@scaristahouse.com
W: www.scaristahouse.com

BEDROOMS: 6. 3 in annexe.
OPEN: Mar–14 Dec.
FACILITIES: 2 sitting rooms, 2 dining rooms, free Wi-Fi in most bedrooms and all public areas, wedding facilities, 1-acre garden, unsuitable for disabled.
BACKGROUND MUSIC: none.
LOCATION: 15 miles SW of Tarbert.
CHILDREN: all ages welcomed, early supper provided for young children.
DOGS: allowed by arrangement.
CREDIT CARDS: Amex, MasterCard, Visa.
PRICES: [2016] per room B&B £220–£245. Set meals £44–£52.

SLEAT Highland

Map 5:C1

TORAVAIG HOUSE

Take in 'fine views' over the Sound of Sleat from Ken Gunn and Anne Gracie's 'friendly' small hotel. Better yet, take to the high seas with the owners, who offer guests trips aboard their yacht to the islands of Rhum and Eigg. Back on land, settle in by the wood fire in the 'lovely' lounge (a glass of malt whisky in hand, if it suits) before heading into the smart restaurant for dinner. Here, new chef Fin Wood's modern menus use plenty of super-local produce – just-landed lobsters and langoustines, lamb and venison from island crofts, home-grown salads and herbs. Come bedtime, lay your head in one of the contemporary, 'nicely decorated' bedrooms overlooking the sound or the surrounding hills. Individually styled, each room is warm and restful, with a 'good' shower in a compact bathroom; the best bedroom (of a 'generous' size) has a bay window with a sea view. Good options at breakfast: Skye smoked salmon, Mallaig kippers, French toast and berries. Duisdale House nearby (see Shortlist) is under the same ownership. More reports, please.

Knock Bay
Sleat
Isle of Skye
IV44 8RE

T: 01471 820200
F: 01471 833404
E: info@skyehotel.co.uk
W: www.toravaig.com

BEDROOMS: 9.
OPEN: Mar–Nov.
FACILITIES: lounge, dining room, free Wi-Fi, in-room TV (Freeview), wedding facilities, 2-acre grounds, unsuitable for disabled.
BACKGROUND MUSIC: none.
LOCATION: 7 miles S of Broadford.
CHILDREN: not under 12.
DOGS: not allowed.
CREDIT CARDS: MasterCard, Visa.
PRICES: [2016] per person B&B £94–£149, D,B&B £143–£198. Set dinner £49, à la carte £40.

SEE ALSO SHORTLIST

STRATHTAY Perth and Kinross

RIVERWOOD   **NEW**

'Chill out' and join the red squirrels, pheasants and partridges who call this leafy conservation village home. Up a long driveway, 'ever-attentive' hosts Ann and Alf Berry welcome guests to their modern B&B, in 'beautiful, extensive gardens' that stretch, languidly, to the River Tay. 'All very relaxing.' Step inside and slip into something more comfortable: guests are asked to take off their shoes in the house 'for a homely environment'; slippers are provided. 'Spacious' bedrooms in the Arts and Crafts-style home are tastefully decorated in neat, neutral shades; each has a large bed, a flat-screen TV and top-end extras such as Scottish-made toiletries and a capsule coffee machine. Book a seat at the table for Ann Berry's three-course dinners, served by candlelight on selected nights each week. Breakfast, which may be taken alfresco in good weather, is 'wonderful': try the locally smoked salmon and potato rösti, or home-made griddle pancakes. The B&B has brown trout fishing rights over a 125-metre stretch of the river; tee-timers have complimentary access to the Strathtay Golf Club, minutes away. (Richard Danzey)

Strathtay
Pitlochry
PH9 0PG

T: 01887 840751
E: info@riverwoodstrathtay.com
W: www.riverwoodstrathtay.com

BEDROOMS: 7. 4 suites on ground floor.
OPEN: 6 Feb–19 Dec, New Year.
FACILITIES: lounge/dining room, library, free Wi-Fi, in-room TV (Freeview), 4½-acre grounds (lawns, woodland, fishing).
BACKGROUND MUSIC: 'easy listening' in dining room at mealtimes.
LOCATION: in the village, 9½ miles SW of Pitlochry.
CHILDREN: over-12s welcomed.
DOGS: not allowed.
CREDIT CARDS: Diners, MasterCard, Visa.
PRICES: [2016] per room B&B £110–£160, D,B&B (on selected nights) £170–£220.

STRATHYRE Perth and Kinross

Map 5:D2

CREAGAN HOUSE

Regular guests speak with fondness of Cherry and Gordon Gunn's 'delightful' B&B, in an extended 17th-century farmhouse. Cherry Gunn is a 'welcoming, vivacious' hostess who is 'meticulous in everything she does'; the couple run their enterprise with 'commitment and passion'. Take tea with 'delicious' home-baked shortbread biscuits in the lounge on arrival, then relax in 'spotlessly clean' bedrooms decorated in a traditional style 'in keeping with the rest of the hotel'. 'Cherry remembered the room we'd liked on a previous visit,' say returning guests this year. 'The largest of their bedrooms, Larch, has a comfortable double bed, a large wardrobe with proper wooden hangers, a selection of books; a lovely Highland view from the dormer window. The faux-medieval decor will divide opinion.' 'Generous portions' of the host's 'excellent' Scottish-inflected French menu are served in the 'imposing' dining room. Come morning, 'very good' breakfasts (with Gordon Gunn's 'creamy' scrambled eggs and 'lovely' bacon) can be a leisurely affair; afterwards, join red squirrels and 'prolific birdlife' along a 'pleasant' woodland path to an 'idyllic' seating spot. (RS, Alan and Edwina Williams)

25% DISCOUNT VOUCHERS

Strathyre
FK18 8ND

T: 01877 384638
E: eatandstay@creaganhouse.co.uk
W: www.creaganhouse.co.uk

BEDROOMS: 5. 1 on ground floor.
OPEN: 7 Apr–23 Oct, closed Mon–Thurs.
FACILITIES: lounge, restaurant, private dining room, free Wi-Fi, in-room TV (Freeview), 1-acre grounds.
BACKGROUND MUSIC: none.
LOCATION: just N of village.
CHILDREN: all ages welcomed.
DOGS: not allowed in public rooms.
CREDIT CARDS: Diners, MasterCard, Visa.
PRICES: per person B&B single £90–£100, double £67.50–£77.50.

STRONTIAN Highland

Map 5:C1

KILCAMB LODGE

'Hurray! This is how a good hotel should be,' crow Guide inspectors in 2016. 'You immediately feel, as you walk in the door, that they're keen to make you feel at home.' Sally and David Ruthven-Fox's stone house is in remote countryside on the shores of Loch Sunart. 'Everything is beautifully presented; there are fresh flowers everywhere.' 'Paul Arcari, the manager, greeted us and showed us around; the next day, he shook our hands before we left.' Choose among 'smart, well-furnished' bedrooms overlooking loch or garden – one opens on to a private balcony. 'Ours had a large bed covered in cushions; fluffy towels and lovely toiletries in the bathroom. After dinner, they brought us a Thermos of fresh milk, ready for the morning.' In the restaurant, chef Gary Phillips's 'fancy', 'impeccably served' menus might include 'excellent lamb cutlets and venison' ('shame there wasn't more variety from one day to the next'). Informal meals are taken in the brasserie. Come morning, tuck in to an 'extensive' breakfast, then step aboard the vintage Dunkirk 'little ship' for a wildlife trip on the loch.

Strontian
PH36 4HY

T: 01967 402257
F: 01967 402041
E: enquiries@kilcamblodge.co.uk
W: www.kilcamblodge.co.uk

BEDROOMS: 11.
OPEN: all year except Jan, restaurant closed Mon/Tues in Nov, Feb.
FACILITIES: drawing room, lounge, bar, restaurant, brasserie, free Wi-Fi, in-room TV (Sky), wedding facilities, 22-acre grounds, unsuitable for disabled.
BACKGROUND MUSIC: in restaurant and brasserie in evening.
LOCATION: edge of village.
CHILDREN: all ages welcomed (travel cots, high chairs).
DOGS: allowed in 4 bedrooms, not in public rooms (£10 per night).
CREDIT CARDS: MasterCard, Visa.
PRICES: per room B&B £150–£325, D,B&B £250–£425. À la carte £45.

THORNHILL Dumfries and Galloway

Map 5:E2

TRIGONY HOUSE

The 'beautiful, rolling hills and farmland' surrounding Jan and Adam Moore's hotel are just the thing to set tails wagging. Guide inspectors (and their cockapoo) in 2016 found a 'friendly, cheerful' spot where canine companions are welcomed with treats and allowed 'everywhere but the dining room'. 'With relaxed access for dogs, a pretty garden, and good walking country all around, the hotel is well suited for dog owners.' Bedrooms vary in size, though all have home-made shortbread and 'real' coffee. A guest in a wheelchair found the ground-floor conservatory room 'ideal'. 'Our room, plain but fresh, was small – though fine for a night. Everything was spotless and well cared for. We had a comfortable double bed, a small wardrobe, a good-sized bathroom (poor water pressure, alas).' Choose from Adam Moore's 'interesting' rustic menu in the dining room – perhaps 'unusual' curried mackerel; 'beautifully cooked' guineafowl; 'inviting' desserts. Dogs may devour a sausage with their owners in the bar. In the morning, enjoy a 'lovely' breakfast before walkies: 'perfectly cooked' hot dishes ('but why the cold plates?'); 'delicious' home-made granola, fruit, yogurt.

Closeburn
Thornhill
DG3 5EZ

T: 01848 331211
F: 01848 331303
E: info@trigonyhotel.co.uk
W: www.trigonyhotel.co.uk

BEDROOMS: 9. 1 on ground floor.
OPEN: all year except 25–27 and 31 Dec.
FACILITIES: lounge, bar, dining room, free Wi-Fi, in-room TV (Freeview), wedding facilities, 4-acre grounds, unsuitable for disabled.
BACKGROUND MUSIC: jazz in bar in evening.
LOCATION: 1 mile S of Thornhill.
CHILDREN: all ages welcomed.
DOGS: 'well-behaved' dogs welcomed.
CREDIT CARDS: all major cards.
PRICES: per room B&B from £120, D,B&B from £170. À la carte £35. 1-night bookings sometimes refused Sat.

THURSO Highland

Map 5:B2

FORSS HOUSE

An unusual Georgian house in wooded grounds, sitting above a meander in the River Forss, Ian and Sabine Richards's hotel was once home to Major CRE Radclyffe – author, game hunter, falconer. The eccentric crenellated entrance hall was built for him as a trophy room. Step inside to be 'warmly' greeted by Anne Mackenzie, manageress extraordinaire. 'What a lovely character!' writes a reader this year. Staff are 'naturally friendly and welcoming'. Bedrooms are well equipped (fresh fruit, and fresh milk for tea), if slightly old-fashioned. 'Ours was large and airy, with a two-seater sofa and plenty of storage.' At dinner, sample chef Andrew Manson's 'unusual combinations', with produce from the sea and neighbouring estates. 'We enjoyed Caithness Cheddar soup with nettle dumplings; a starter of roe deer, beetroot and chestnut tart. The chefs went the extra mile to present a very pretty veggie meal the evening I didn't fancy meat.' Breakfast in the conservatory includes 'a good range of hot and cold dishes using quality ingredients'. Whisky lovers, settle in – there's a choice of 300 bottles in the bar. (GC)

25% DISCOUNT VOUCHERS

Forss
Thurso
KW14 7XY

T: 01847 861201
F: 01847 861301
E: anne@forsshousehotel.co.uk
W: www.forsshousehotel.co.uk

BEDROOMS: 14. 3 in main house on ground floor, 4 in River House, 2 in Sportsmen's Lodge.
OPEN: all year except 23 Dec–4 Jan.
FACILITIES: dining room, breakfast room, lounge, bar, free Wi-Fi, in-room TV (Freeview), meeting room, wedding facilities, 19-acre grounds with river and waterfall.
BACKGROUND MUSIC: in public areas in morning and evening.
LOCATION: 5 miles W of Thurso.
CHILDREN: all ages welcomed (under-5s free).
DOGS: allowed in Sportsmen's Lodge only.
CREDIT CARDS: all major cards.
PRICES: [2016] per room B&B single £99–£135, double £135–£185, D,B&B single £137–£170, double £205–£260. À la carte £35.

TIRORAN HOUSE

The surroundings are vast: well-kept lawns
lead to thick woodland; there are waterfalls,
a tumbling burn, an old Victorian trout pond
and a private beach. Inside this pretty Victorian
hunting lodge, however, things shrink down
to a human scale, as hosts Laurence and Katie
Mackay create a 'house-party atmosphere',
encouraging guests to mingle over drinks and
nibbles in one of the 'charming' sitting rooms.
Come dinnertime, new chef Michael Scotford
serves an extensive menu focusing on Scottish
produce: try island seafood terrine, Scottish
pork belly; Loch Awe sea trout, seared kale,
beurre blanc. On Sundays, a simpler supper is
served, perhaps rib of Aberdeen Angus beef
with all the trimmings (vegetarian options
are available). Bedrooms, each with its own
style, are traditionally decorated with touches
of countryside florals; book one with views
over the garden and loch. In the morning,
wake to breakfast choices including a full
Scottish, Loch Fyne kippers and locally smoked
haddock, then head out to explore. Ask about
ranger-accompanied forest wildlife walks – the
white-tailed Mull eagles are a sight to see. More
reports, please.

25% DISCOUNT VOUCHERS

Tiroran
Isle of Mull
PA69 6ES

T: 01681 705232
F: 01681 705232
E: info@tiroran.com
W: www.tiroran.com

BEDROOMS: 11. 2 on ground floor,
4 in annexes, plus 2 self-catering
cottages.
OPEN: all year except Nov–Feb, open
New Year.
FACILITIES: 2 sitting rooms, dining
room, conservatory, free Wi-Fi,
in-room TV (Freeview), 17½-acre
gardens in 56-acre grounds, beach
with mooring, wedding facilities,
unsuitable for disabled.
BACKGROUND MUSIC: none.
LOCATION: N side of Loch Scridain.
CHILDREN: all ages welcomed.
DOGS: allowed (not unattended) in
4 bedrooms, not in public rooms.
CREDIT CARDS: MasterCard, Visa.
PRICES: [2016] per room B&B
£175–£230. Sunday set dinner £36,
à la carte £35–£45.

THE CEILIDH PLACE

'Lovely, warm and welcoming, it is one of our favourite places to stay.' Formed from a collection of whitewashed cottages in a fishing village, Jean Urquhart's unusual bookshop-with-rooms began in 1970 as a café in a boatshed, where musicians could sing for their supper. Fans like the informal, bohemian atmosphere that has been conserved. The 'gorgeous, rambling' lounge (redecorated in winter 2015/16) has original artwork, a log fire, an honesty bar, and a pantry where guests help themselves to tea and coffee. 'They take literature seriously': besides the bookshop and the 'wee' library in the parlour, each of the 'tasteful but rustic' bedrooms has a small collection of books selected by friends and past guests (but no television). Basic, bunk-bedded rooms in the Bunkhouse across the road accommodate larger parties. In the 'lively' café/bar, chef Scott Morrison uses mainly local produce in his 'eclectic Scottish fusion' menu, perhaps including 'fresh local fish'; haggis-in-a-pot with cream and whisky. A fine base for day-trips by the sea, and scenic drives – to arboretums, waterfalls and even bone caves – in the area. (RS, and others)

25% DISCOUNT VOUCHERS

12–14 West Argyle Street
Ullapool
IV26 2TY

T: 01854 612103
F: 01854 613773
E: stay@theceilidhplace.com
W: www.theceilidhplace.com

BEDROOMS: 13. 10 with facilities en suite, plus 11 in Bunkhouse across road.
OPEN: all year except two weeks Jan.
FACILITIES: bar, parlour, coffee shop, restaurant, bookshop, conference/function facilities, free Wi-Fi, civil wedding licence, 2-acre garden, only public areas suitable for disabled.
BACKGROUND MUSIC: 'eclectic' in public areas.
LOCATION: village centre (large car park).
CHILDREN: all ages welcomed (under-5s free).
DOGS: allowed.
CREDIT CARDS: MasterCard, Visa.
PRICES: per person B&B £64–£88 (rooms in Bunkhouse from £24). À la carte £26.

SEE ALSO SHORTLIST

WALLS Shetland

BURRASTOW HOUSE

Watch the Arctic terns tumble above Wester Sound in this 'beautiful, peaceful, unusual' spot, where Pierre Dupont runs a laid-back hotel in his 18th-century house. 'His kindness, hard work and willingness to please are essential ingredients to the hotel's success,' a regular Guide contributor says this year. 'Staying here is like staying in someone's home: past the weather-beaten facade, the comfortable public rooms have a well-worn feel. Everything is very informal – if you want something, ask Pierre!' Bedrooms in the main house overlook the water, where otters fish. 'Our large, light, modern room in the extension had beautiful views; a good bathroom.' Guests help themselves from the drinks cabinet, recording, in a notebook, what they've had. At dinner, 'everything that can be is home made'. 'The cooking is consistently good. There is no smoke, foams and fanciness here: we enjoyed an excellent fish soup, and delicious halibut with hollandaise sauce; desserts included a lovely home-made rhubarb pie.' Breakfast, with 'good' coffee, toasted home-baked bread and home-made marmalade, is 'a wonderful start to the day'. (David Birnie)

Walls
Shetland
ZE2 9PD

T: 01595 809307
E: info@burrastowhouse.co.uk
W: www.burrastowhouse.co.uk

BEDROOMS: 7. 3 in extension, 2 on ground floor.
OPEN: Apr–Oct.
FACILITIES: sitting room, library, dining room, free Wi-Fi in library, in-room TV (Freeview), 'weak mobile phone signal', wedding facilities, unsuitable for disabled.
BACKGROUND MUSIC: none.
LOCATION: 2 miles from Walls, 27 miles NW of Lerwick.
CHILDREN: all ages welcomed (under-13s half price).
DOGS: not allowed.
CREDIT CARDS: MasterCard, Visa.
PRICES: [2016] per person B&B £60, D,B&B £95.

WALES

Beach in north-west Wales accessed via a traditional hand-crafted gate

HARBOURMASTER HOTEL

♥ César award since 2005

'A bustling place, popular with locals and visitors', Glyn and Menna Heulyn's small hotel stands on the quayside of this pretty fishing village. It remains a favourite among Guide readers. 'It continues to be an enjoyable place to stay,' say returning guests this year. 'The staff are exceptional, and the place is still personally managed, which makes a huge difference. Customers are truly welcomed and looked after.' Pick one of the stylish, colourful bedrooms (Welsh blankets, posh toiletries, a Roberts radio); the best have panoramic views of the harbour and sea. 'Our large first-floor suite had lovely new chairs – we could've sat in them all day.' In fine weather, harbourfront animation 'adds to the atmosphere': 'watching the children catching crabs while their parents sit on the harbour wall in the sunshine is like holidays used to be'. Blend in with locals in the 'buzzy' bar, or book ahead to try chef Ludo Dieumegard's 'excellent' dishes, perhaps 'very, very tender' local lamb rump, in the breezy restaurant. Breakfast is worth waking for: pancakes, organic porridge, 'particularly fine smoked salmon and scrambled eggs'. (Lynn Wildgoose)

Pen Cei
Aberaeron
SA46 0BT

T: 01545 570755
F: 01545 570762
E: info@harbour-master.com
W: www.harbour-master.com

BEDROOMS: 13. 2 in cottage, 1 suitable for disabled.
OPEN: all year except 24 (evening)–26 Dec.
FACILITIES: lift, bar, restaurant, free Wi-Fi, in-room TV (Freeview), small terrace, pebble beach (safe bathing nearby).
BACKGROUND MUSIC: all day in bar.
LOCATION: central, on the harbour.
CHILDREN: under-5s in cottage only.
DOGS: not allowed.
CREDIT CARDS: all major cards.
PRICES: per room B&B from £120, D,B&B from £170. Set dinner £35, à la carte £35. 1-night bookings refused weekends in high season, min. 2-night stay for D,B&B rate.

TREFEDDIAN HOTEL

'A hotel with heart and soul', this long-time favourite overlooking Cardigan Bay has been 'well run' by the Cave family and 'unfailingly cheerful' staff for more than a century. Guide readers, many regulars, praise the sense of continuity and the long-held standards. 'My son (age 21) and I (age 54) were the youngest there for most of our stay. Did we care? Not one bit. The hotel is busier with young families during the school holidays, but it's refreshing, out of season, to go somewhere that maintains tradition.' Take your pick of the light, bright bedrooms, each 'immaculately clean and welcoming', many with views of the sea. 'The ones with a balcony are ideal in the summer.' (Ring to discuss room choices beforehand: guests in 2016 thought some single rooms weren't to the standard of the doubles.) Food is 'excellent': 'well-cooked' fish; 'generous' breakfasts. 'Although there is a dress code in the restaurant, the hotel takes a relaxed view.' Head out with a packed lunch, or stay put and enjoy the many diversions – a swimming pool, a putting green and plenty more. (Peter and Kay Rogers, Stephen and Jane Marshall, Dorothy Brining)

Tywyn Road
Aberdyfi
LL35 0SB

T: 01654 767213
F: 01654 767777
E: info@trefwales.com
W: www.trefwales.com

BEDROOMS: 59. 1 suitable for disabled.
OPEN: all year except 4 Dec–13 Jan.
FACILITIES: lift, lounge bar, study, family lounge, adult lounge, restaurant, games room (snooker, table tennis, air hockey), free Wi-Fi, in-room TV (Freeview), indoor swimming pool (6 by 12 metres), beauty salon, 15-acre grounds (lawns, sun terrace, tennis, putting green).
BACKGROUND MUSIC: none.
LOCATION: ½ mile N of village.
CHILDREN: all ages welcomed.
DOGS: allowed in 1 lounge, some bedrooms.
CREDIT CARDS: MasterCard, Visa.
PRICES: [2016] per person B&B from £65, D,B&B £74–£158. Set dinner £29.50. 2-night min. stay preferred (but check for 1-night availability).

THE ANGEL HOTEL

A 'fine' hotel with 'professional yet friendly' staff, this renovated 19th-century coaching inn is owned and run by the local Griffiths family. It is a 'classy' place decorated with 'an eye for good taste', say inspectors in 2016. (Good humour, too – look out for 'amusing' curtains printed with 'amply petticoated ladies being wooed by sexy lute-players'.) Mingle with locals in the 'handsome' public rooms: 'very much a town hotel', The Angel welcomes visitors who come for drinks and casual dinners at the Foxhunter Bar, or for the 'renowned' afternoon tea. Bedrooms are in the main building, and adjacent mews and restored cottages nearby. 'Our room was wonderfully comfortable and well lit, with an expansive bathroom. A sofa faced the big wall-mounted TV screen; the hospitality tray had Fairtrade teas. We appreciated the overnight shoeshine.' Service is 'exquisite' in the Oak Room restaurant, where chef Wesley Hammond serves a 'short but enticing' menu, including 'pecan pie good enough for Louisiana'. Wake to an extensive breakfast menu – 'enough to satisfy a Welsh XV prop forward' – with breakfast cocktails and good vegetarian options.

15 Cross Street
Abergavenny
NP7 5EN

T: 01873 857121
F: 01873 858059
E: info@angelabergavenny.com
W: www.angelabergavenny.com

BEDROOMS: 32. 2 in adjacent mews, plus two 2-bedroom cottages.
OPEN: all year except 24–27 Dec.
FACILITIES: lift, lounge, bar, tea room, restaurant, private function rooms, free Wi-Fi, in-room TV (Freeview), civil wedding licence, courtyard.
BACKGROUND MUSIC: in restaurant and tea room.
LOCATION: town centre.
CHILDREN: all ages welcomed (cots free of charge, Z-beds for under-12s £26).
DOGS: allowed in some bedrooms (£25 charge), not in restaurant or tea room.
CREDIT CARDS: Amex, MasterCard, Visa.
PRICES: [2016] per room B&B from £99, D,B&B from £149. Set dinner £25, à la carte £30. 1-night bookings sometimes refused.

ABERGAVENNY Monmouthshire

Map 3:D4

🏆 THE HARDWICK **NEW**

César award: restaurant-with-rooms of the year

'A contented buzz' fills this 'sophisticated yet unpretentious' restaurant-with-rooms in an 'attractive' sheep-grazed setting. Here, chef/patron Stephen Terry and his wife, Joanna, 'extremely hands-on' hosts, lead a team of 'friendly, efficient' staff. Guide inspectors in 2016 found leather sofas and vintage touches in the bar; in the 'packed' dining room, 'smartly dressed staff kept things running smoothly'. 'The long, interesting menu, and well-priced, well-chosen wine list, make decisions difficult. We enjoyed grilled Wye valley asparagus, buffalo mozzarella, broad beans; roast hake fillet, brown shrimps; perfect mashed potatoes.' 'Very good' bedrooms are in a modern, Scandi-inspired courtyard extension. 'Ours had a comfortable bed, crisp sheets, a Welsh tweed throw; ample storage; design books and magazines by the sofa. In the smart bathroom: good towels, a huge walk-in shower.' At breakfast, 'no need for tramping up to a buffet'. Sit down to 'excellent' freshly squeezed orange juice; 'very good' cafetière coffee; 'super, buttery scrambled eggs on sourdough toast'. 'Linen napkins were a bonus.'

Old Raglan Road
Abergavenny
NP7 9AA

T: 01873 854220
E: info@thehardwick.co.uk
W: www.thehardwick.co.uk

BEDROOMS: 8. 5 on ground floor, 1 suitable for disabled.
OPEN: all year.
FACILITIES: bar, restaurant, private dining facilities, free Wi-Fi, in-room TV, courtyard, small garden.
BACKGROUND MUSIC: 'unintrusive' in public areas.
LOCATION: 2¾ miles S of Abergavenny.
CHILDREN: all ages welcomed.
DOGS: not allowed.
CREDIT CARDS: MasterCard, Visa.
PRICES: [2016] per room B&B single (Mon–Thurs) £115, double £135–£150. Set dinner (Mon–Thurs) £20–£25, à la carte £35.

PORTH TOCYN HOTEL

♔ César award since 1984

'We had a great time,' say guests this year of the Fletcher-Brewer family's 'lovely, wacky' hotel overlooking Cardigan Bay. Neither cutting-edge contemporary nor superbly stylish, the hotel has a 'friendly', 'old-school' feel that endears it to its admirers. Nick Fletcher-Brewer is the 'jolly, jokey' manager. Country antiques, books, watercolours and prints give the 'unfussy' bedrooms individual character; most have 'amazing' sea views. Interconnecting rooms have been designed with families in mind. Gather with fellow guests for aperitifs in the snug bar, then settle down to Louise Fletcher-Brewer and Ian Frost's 'outstanding' dinners – perhaps sea-salt-and-beetroot-cured salmon, caper popcorn, quail egg, citrus crème fraîche; pan-fried pork tenderloin, apple mash, baked courgettes. 'We appreciated the option of "light-bite" suppers alongside three-course dinners.' Plenty of opportunity to work it all off: the 'lovely' swimming pool awaits; the Wales Coastal Path runs in front of the hotel; the beach is a five-minute walk away. 'Highly recommended.' (GC, Carol and Geoffrey Jackson, and others)

Bwlch Tocyn
Abersoch
LL53 7BU

T: 01758 713303
F: 01758 713538
E: bookings@porthtocynhotel.co.uk
W: www.porthtocynhotel.co.uk

BEDROOMS: 17. 3 on ground floor.
OPEN: week before Easter–early Nov.
FACILITIES: sitting rooms, children's rooms, small bar, dining room, free Wi-Fi, in-room TV (Freeview), 20-acre grounds (swimming pool, 10 by 6 metres, heated May–end Sept, tennis), call to discuss disabled access.
BACKGROUND MUSIC: none.
LOCATION: 2 miles outside village.
CHILDREN: all ages welcomed (high tea for under-5s; no babies or young children at dinner).
DOGS: not allowed in public rooms.
CREDIT CARDS: MasterCard, Visa.
PRICES: [2016] per room B&B single £80–£95, double £110–£190. Set dinner £47. 1-night bookings occasionally refused.

GWESTY CYMRU

Expect a 'warm welcome' at Huw and Beth
Roberts's 'excellent' hotel, on the lively Victorian
promenade of this historic market town. The
Robertses have given their Grade II listed
terrace house a striking, modern interior and
a strong sense of Welsh identity: signs are
bilingual; much of the furniture is handmade in
Wales; the restaurant highlights local produce.
Oil canvasses hang in the smart bedrooms, each
taking an element of the surrounding landscape
as inspiration (terracotta and bronze for Pen
Dinas, white for the foaming surf of the sea).
'The rooms overlooking the sea are very good,
with chairs in the bay window so you can enjoy
the passing scene.' Up three flights of stairs, a
beamed room under the eaves with a sofa bed
can accommodate a family. In the evenings, chef
William Ainsworth cooks modern dishes with
a Welsh touch. His menus might include crispy
squid, Halen Môn chilli and garlic sea salt; local
lamb rump in a mint, honey and Welsh mustard
crust. 'Freshly cooked', breakfast is 'excellent'.
The animation of the town centre is within an
easy stroll. (DK)

19 Marine Terrace
Aberystwyth
SY23 2AZ

T: 01970 612252
F: 01970 623348
E: info@gwestycymru.co.uk
W: www.gwestycymru.co.uk

BEDROOMS: 8. 2 on ground floor.
OPEN: all year except 22 Dec–2 Jan,
restaurant closed for lunch Tues.
FACILITIES: small bar area,
restaurant, seafront terrace, free
Wi-Fi, in-room TV (Freeview),
secure parking (book in advance),
unsuitable for disabled.
BACKGROUND MUSIC: 'easy listening'
in reception and restaurant.
LOCATION: central, on seafront.
CHILDREN: all ages welcomed at
lunch, no under-5s to stay or in
restaurant in evenings.
DOGS: not allowed.
CREDIT CARDS: MasterCard, Visa.
PRICES: per room B&B £70–£150.
À la carte £35.

BRYNIAU GOLAU

🏅 César award since 2014

'A real haven' on the edge of Snowdonia national park, this small guest house is run by 'charming hosts' Katrina Le Saux and Peter Cottee. Their 'beautiful' Victorian house overlooks Bala lake. Tastefully refurbished in period style, it has an easy, mellow atmosphere, ideal for 'those who love peace and quiet'. Relax in front of the log fire in the spacious sitting room; sip pre-dinner drinks on the terrace while soaking in the sunset over the Arenig mountain. The 'beautifully appointed, spotlessly clean' bedrooms are named after local mountains: two, Berwyn and Arenig, have a four-poster bed; in Aran, lie back in the large bath with views over the lake. Stay in for dinner: Peter Cottee cooks 'high-quality, unpretentious' meals by arrangement two nights a week, perhaps onion tart, home-made chutney; pan-fried sole, aubergine compote, sautéed asparagus, gratin potatoes. Breakfast, taken communally, is noteworthy: home-made bread and preserves; honey from the hosts' bees. 'Lovely walks in the area'; stroll halfway around the lake, then hop aboard the steam train to return. More reports, please.

25% DISCOUNT VOUCHERS

Llangower
Bala
LL23 7BT

T: 01678 521782
E: katrinalesaux@hotmail.co.uk
W: www.bryniau-golau.co.uk

BEDROOMS: 3.
OPEN: Mar–Dec (not Christmas).
FACILITIES: sitting room, dining room, free Wi-Fi, ½-acre garden (terrace), unsuitable for disabled.
BACKGROUND MUSIC: none.
LOCATION: 2 miles SE of Bala.
CHILDREN: babes in arms, and over-10s welcomed.
DOGS: not allowed.
CREDIT CARDS: MasterCard, Visa.
PRICES: [2016] per room B&B £110–£120, D,B&B £170–£180. Set dinner £30. 1-night bookings refused weekends.

LLWYNDU FARMHOUSE

At the end of a jiggledy single-track road up a steep hill, Paula and Peter Thompson's 'very family-friendly', 'super little hotel' stands out for its simplicity and folksy charm. With oak beams, stone walls, log fires and well-used furnishings, the 16th-century farmhouse and 18th-century granary appeal to guests who come for the 'splendid' welcome and 'laid-back' atmosphere. Characterful, 'spotlessly clean' bedrooms reflect the age of the buildings; some have small windows (guests this year thought their room gloomy). For a laugh, choose the room with a walk-in wardrobe in what might once have been a latrine. Gather for aperitifs in the homey lounge – 'a wood-burner makes it cosy' – then sit down to Peter Thompson's 'commendable' candlelit dinner. Local ingredients give the flavour of the place (try Welsh rarebit with Cenarth smoked cheese; pan-fried hake, king prawns, capers); an 'interesting' wine list rounds out the 'very good' meal. 'With a good bottle of Pouilly-Fumé and the enchanting views across Cardigan Bay, it was a magical evening.' A fine base to explore a 'lovely part of the country'. (P and CM, and others)

Llanaber
Barmouth
LL42 1RR

T: 01341 280144
F: 01341 281236
E: intouch@llwyndu-farmhouse.
   co.uk
W: www.llwyndu-farmhouse.co.uk

BEDROOMS: 6. 3 in granary, 1 on ground floor.
OPEN: all year except 25/26 Dec, restaurant closed Sun and Wed.
FACILITIES: lounge, restaurant, free Wi-Fi, in-room TV (Freeview), ¼-acre garden in 4-acre grounds, unsuitable for disabled.
BACKGROUND MUSIC: 'occasionally and on demand' in dining room.
LOCATION: 2 miles N of Barmouth.
CHILDREN: all ages welcomed (free for under-2s).
DOGS: not allowed.
CREDIT CARDS: MasterCard, Visa.
PRICES: per room B&B £110–£130, D,B&B £160–£195. Set dinner £25–£35. 1-night bookings sometimes refused weekends and in peak season.

THE BULL

A 'well-run' hotel, this Georgian rebuild of a centuries-old inn (formerly Ye Olde Bulls Head) mixes ancient and modern, from the convivial beamed bar to the stylish Loft restaurant under the eaves. Staff are 'pleasant', 'friendly', 'efficient', 'unhurried'. Choose from bedrooms in the main house, a converted hayloft and a refurbished town house. Some are traditional, others are more contemporary; all have a coffee machine, Welsh biscuits, fresh milk. 'Our spacious Townhouse suite was beautifully furnished, but more personal touches – perhaps magazines, local information or an odd painting – wouldn't have been misplaced.' Ring to discuss before booking: a ground-floor room in the main building was considered 'gloomy', though its bathroom was 'clean and well maintained'. Book for a 'fantastic', 'first-rate' dinner in the restaurant, where chef Hefin Roberts features Anglesey produce in his modern menus. Informal meals may be taken in the 'cheerful' brasserie – though guests finding the piped music too loud in the evening thought the room 'better suited for breakfast', when the atmosphere is calmer. (Neville Kenyon, Mary Coles)

Castle Street
Beaumaris
LL58 8AP

T: 01248 810329
F: 01248 811294
E: info@bullsheadinn.co.uk
W: www.bullsheadinn.co.uk

BEDROOMS: 25. 2 on ground floor, 1 in courtyard, 13 in The Townhouse adjacent, 1 suitable for disabled.
OPEN: all year, but limited opening in Christmas period. Loft restaurant closed lunch, Sun–Tues nights.
FACILITIES: lift (in The Townhouse), lounge, bar, brasserie, restaurant, free Wi-Fi, in-room TV (Freeview), courtyard, charging station for electric cars.
BACKGROUND MUSIC: 'upbeat, contemporary' in brasserie.
LOCATION: central.
CHILDREN: all ages welcomed, no under-7s in restaurant.
DOGS: allowed in some bedrooms, bar and lounge.
CREDIT CARDS: MasterCard, Visa.
PRICES: [2016] per room B&B double £90–£145, D,B&B from £170. Set dinner (restaurant) £49.50, à la carte (brasserie) £28.

BRECHFA Carmarthenshire

Map 3:D2

TY MAWR

♔ César award since 2011

Unpretentious, rustic, homey, this small country hotel sits peacefully on the edge of the Brechfa forest. Annabel and Stephen Thomas are the 'hospitable' owners (who also extend a warm welcome to visiting dogs). Charm is in the beams, fireplaces and thick stone walls of the 16th-century farmhouse; the walls are hung with works (many for sale) by local Carmarthenshire artists. Simply decorated, the 'comfortable', 'immaculate' bedrooms have 'all the amenities you might expect'. Drop off your bags, then head outside – forest walks await (watch out for woodpeckers); the country paths are made for leisurely rambles. Feeling lazy? In fine weather, take afternoon tea on the patio, or play croquet in the 'manicured' garden leading down to the river. Build up an appetite: come dinnertime, Stephen Thomas's 'super-local food' uses plenty of produce in season. His wholesome dishes might include slow-roasted shoulder of Welsh lamb, wild garlic, cavolo nero; saffron- and honey-poached pear, home-made honeycomb ice cream. In the morning, wake to a buffet of fresh fruit salad, cereals, local yogurts; hot dishes cooked to order. (GC, and others)

25% DISCOUNT VOUCHERS

Brechfa
SA32 7RA

T: 01267 202332
E: info@wales-country-hotel.co.uk
W: www.wales-country-hotel.co.uk

BEDROOMS: 6. 2 on ground floor, 1 with private access.
OPEN: all year.
FACILITIES: sitting room, bar, breakfast room, restaurant, free Wi-Fi, in-room TV (Freeview), 1-acre grounds, unsuitable for disabled.
BACKGROUND MUSIC: classical in restaurant during dinner.
LOCATION: village centre.
CHILDREN: not under 12.
DOGS: by arrangement (no charge), not allowed in breakfast room, restaurant.
CREDIT CARDS: Amex, MasterCard, Visa.
PRICES: [2016] per room B&B £115–£130, D,B&B £160–£175. Set dinner £25–£30. 1-night bookings occasionally refused on Sat in summer.

THE COACH HOUSE `NEW`

Wake to a cheering discovery at this modern B&B, a short walk from the centre: 'the longest breakfast menu I've ever seen'. 'Pleasant and helpful', Tony Morris-Davies and Marc Pearce-Hopkins are the owners who 'make it all so comfortable', say regular Guide readers, whose recommendation earns the B&B a full entry. The hosts have 'beautifully decorated' their refurbished 19th-century coaching inn with 'carefully arranged objets d'art – ceramics, shells, driftwood'. Bedrooms vary in size. 'Our mini-suite had a large bed, a sofa, a rocking chair; a spacious bathroom; a fridge with drinks and chocolate. The bedside lights were a trifle dim. We were impressed by muted floor lights designed to be left on all night for bathroom expeditions without disturbing one's partner. Double glazing kept out any road noise.' Evening snacks ('gorgeous variations on Welsh rarebit; a nice salad with an omelette') are 'a big plus'. In the morning, work your way through that breakfast menu. 'The pièce de résistance? Pikelets piled high with cream and fresh berries, almost too beautiful to eat.' (Jill and Mike Bennett)

12 Orchard Street
Brecon
LD3 8AN

T: 01874 640089
F: 01874 623464
E: thecoachhousebrecon@gmail.com
W: www.coachhousebrecon.wales

BEDROOMS: 6.
OPEN: all year.
FACILITIES: sitting area, breakfast room, free Wi-Fi, in-room TV, garden, drying room, secure bicycle storage, unsuitable for disabled.
BACKGROUND MUSIC: classical and Welsh harp music.
LOCATION: ½ mile from town centre.
CHILDREN: not under 16.
DOGS: not allowed.
CREDIT CARDS: none.
PRICES: [2016] per room B&B £80–£160. 1-night bookings refused weekends in high season.

CARDIGAN Ceredigion

Map 3:D2

CAEMORGAN MANSION `NEW`

'Inviting' rooms, 'outstanding' dinners and a 'friendly' atmosphere make this small guest house an ideal base for exploring the coast and countryside of Cardigan Bay. Its owners, Beverley and David Harrison-Wood, spent years renovating the old mansion. Today, guests are welcomed in smart, modern rooms – with home-made biscuits to sweeten the deal. Choose among individually styled bedrooms (two in the eaves), each with a large bed and thoughtful touches including bathrobes and slippers, a tea-and-coffee machine. Looking for a quiet night in? Books and DVDs are available to borrow. 'We overslept in the superb bed.' Book ahead for dinner in the dapper, red-painted restaurant, its central log-burner creating a cosy, 'tranquil' ambience. Here, David Harrison-Wood's modern European dishes might include sautéed scallops, bacon, sage; pork fillet, brandy-prune sauce, seasonal vegetables. Breakfast the next morning, including a full Welsh, is 'a delight'. Set out, afterwards, for the Wales Coastal Path, keeping your eyes peeled for dolphins in the bay; beaches are within easy reach. (Deborah Moberly Harris, Brian Smith, Peter Wood)

Caemorgan Road
Cardigan
SA43 1QU

T: 01239 613297
F: 01239 393070
E: guest@caemorgan.com
W: www.caemorgan.com

BEDROOMS: 5.
OPEN: all year except Christmas.
FACILITIES: bar, restaurant, free Wi-Fi, in-room TV (Freeview), function facilities, 2-acre gardens, unsuitable for disabled.
BACKGROUND MUSIC: none.
LOCATION: ½ mile N of town centre.
CHILDREN: not under 16.
DOGS: not allowed.
CREDIT CARDS: MasterCard, Visa.
PRICES: [2016] per room B&B from £120. À la carte £30. 1-night bookings often refused peak weekends.

GLIFFAES

🏅 César award since 2009

Pheasants scatter on the lawn around this Italianate mansion standing 'proudly' by the River Usk, where Guide inspectors in 2016 found 'a fine house filled with warm, amiable staff'. 'Clearly a popular place', the 'superb' sporting hotel has been in the same family for three generations; Susie and James Suter are now in charge. 'It never fails to please,' say guests this year, on their twelfth visit. 'Things don't change, which suits us.' The drawing rooms have 'a casual grandeur' ('interesting' paintings, fresh flowers, books and magazines); the conservatory, with palms and wicker chairs, has a colonial feel. Summer Sundays call for lazy lunches, alfresco on the terrace. Borrow a pair of wellies and follow the 'impressive' walk among 'magnificent' specimen trees, then return for Karl Cheetham's modern dinners, perhaps 'very nice' chicken and wild mushroom ravioli. Period bedrooms, decorated in country house style, each have their own character; splurge on one with a balcony overlooking 'the handsome lichen-printed stone terrace, the rushing river and the hills beyond'. (Michael and Pauline Bastick, and others)

25% DISCOUNT VOUCHERS

Gliffaes Road
Crickhowell
NP8 1RH

T: 01874 730371
F: 01874 730463
E: calls@gliffaes.com
W: www.gliffaeshotel.com

BEDROOMS: 23. 4 in cottage annexe, 1 on ground floor suitable for disabled.
OPEN: all year except Jan.
FACILITIES: 2 sitting rooms, conservatory, bar, dining room, free Wi-Fi, in-room TV, civil wedding licence, 33-acre garden (tennis, croquet, private stretch of the River Usk for fly fishing).
BACKGROUND MUSIC: jazz/classical in bar in evening.
LOCATION: 3 miles W of Crickhowell.
CHILDREN: all ages welcomed.
DOGS: not allowed indoors (kennels available).
CREDIT CARDS: all major cards.
PRICES: [2016] per room B&B £135–£290, D,B&B £215–£373. À la carte £42. 1-night bookings refused high-season weekends.

DOLFOR Powys

THE OLD VICARAGE

There is 'an atmosphere of heart-warming hospitality' at Helen and Tim Withers's small guest house, enveloped in the vast Montgomeryshire countryside. Arrive to afternoon tea and home-baked cake, taken by the cheering fire in cool weather, then settle in to one of the pretty bedrooms, each filled with rustic style and 'lacking nothing'. All are different: Teme has a deep roll-top bath, ideal for soaking in after a day's walking; the two-bedroom Severn suite, with king-size beds, accommodates a family. Sip a house cocktail and nibble at tasty snacks in the lounge before sitting down to Tim Withers's 'simple, no-nonsense' dinner (served six nights a week), perhaps including Welsh lamb, rice, spring vegetables; home-made ice cream. Breakfast is countryside-hearty, too, and sourced from local suppliers: traditionally cured kippers; omelettes with laver bread; eggs from the free-range hens in the garden. The hosts are 'dedicated to sustainability': hire a bicycle (complete with repair kit and accessories), plug in your electric vehicle for charging; receive a discount if you arrive by public transport. (Johan Van den Berg, and others)

Dolfor
SY16 4BN

T: 01686 629051
F: 01686 207629
E: tim@theoldvicaragedolfor.co.uk
W: www.theoldvicaragedolfor.co.uk

BEDROOMS: 4.
OPEN: all year except last 3 weeks Dec, dining room closed Sun.
FACILITIES: drawing room, dining room, free Wi-Fi, in-room TV (Freeview), 1½-acre garden, unsuitable for disabled.
BACKGROUND MUSIC: none.
LOCATION: 3 miles S of Newtown.
CHILDREN: all ages welcomed.
DOGS: not allowed.
CREDIT CARDS: Amex, MasterCard, Visa.
PRICES: [2016] per person B&B £37.50–£60, D,B&B £67.50–£90. Set dinner £25–£30. 1-night bookings sometimes refused.

Y GOEDEN EIRIN

♀ César award since 2008

A Bechstein grand piano presides over the beamed breakfast room in this granite former cowshed, today a modest, characterful B&B run by Eluned Rowlands. Come and explore: the house is filled with Welsh- and English-language books; the walls are hung with works by Welsh painters including Kyffin Williams and Gwilym Prichard. The whole is as much a paean to Welsh culture as it is a reflection of its Tregarth-born hostess – an academic, art collector and gourmand – and her late husband, the author and musician John Rowlands. (Even the name 'Y Goeden Eirin' – 'The Plum Tree' – is a homage to the collection of stories by Gwynedd writer John Gwilym Jones.) Two of the rustic bedrooms, with a shower room of local slate, are in a renovated outbuilding just across the lawn; a spacious room in the main house has a settee and a desk, a bathtub in the bathroom. All are stocked with cafetière coffee, herbal tea, sherry, fruit, Welsh cakes. Breakfast on home-baked bread and home-made preserves; local eggs, bacon and sausages are cooked on the Aga. Rugged Snowdonia awaits.

Dolydd
LL54 7EF

T: 01286 830942
E: eluned.rowlands@tiscali.co.uk
W: www.ygoedeneirin.co.uk

BEDROOMS: 3. 2 in annexe.
OPEN: all year except Christmas/New Year.
FACILITIES: breakfast room, lounge, free Wi-Fi, in-room TV (Freeview), 20-acre pastureland, electric car charging point, unsuitable for disabled.
BACKGROUND MUSIC: none.
LOCATION: 3 miles S of Caernarfon.
CHILDREN: not under 12.
DOGS: not allowed.
CREDIT CARDS: none, cash or cheque payment requested on arrival.
PRICES: per room B&B single £65, double £90–£100.

EGLWYSFACH Powys

Map 3:C3

YNYSHIR HALL

'Everything is exquisite' at this 'very welcoming' country house retreat (Relais & Châteaux), where goldfinches, song thrushes and blackbirds flit about the 'beautiful' grounds leading to a vast bird reserve. Queen Victoria once owned the 16th-century manor house and cherished its gardens, but for many guests, Joan Reen – who, with her husband, Rob, filled the home with warmth and personality until her death in 2016 – was the one they hailed. Today, John and Jennifer Talbot, with manager Anand Rathod, carry on her work. 'It's all spot on,' say guests this year. Each of the 'comfortable' bedrooms has its own character, with an 'opulent' four-poster here or an antique brass bedstead there. For extra space to lounge about, choose a garden suite with a patio and views of the gardens and mountains. Walking country surrounds: stomp about the rugged Cambrian ridges, or head for Borth beach, then return for Gareth Ward's 'superlative' Michelin-starred tasting menus, which might include wild duck, salt pear, shiso; scampi, black garlic, rhubarb. 'We simply murmured in delight as we ate.' (Richard Morgan-Price, FT)

Eglwysfach
SY20 8TA

T: 01654 781209
F: 01654 781366
E: info@ynyshirhall.co.uk
W: www.ynyshirhall.co.uk

BEDROOMS: 10. 2 garden suites, 1 in studio annexe, 3 on ground floor, 1 suitable for disabled.
OPEN: all year except first 3 weeks Jan.
FACILITIES: drawing room, bar lounge, restaurant, free Wi-Fi, in-room TV (Freeview), civil wedding licence, treatment rooms, 12-acre gardens in 1,000-acre bird reserve.
BACKGROUND MUSIC: in bar and restaurant.
LOCATION: 6 miles SW of Machynlleth.
CHILDREN: all ages welcomed, not under 9 in restaurant in evening.
DOGS: allowed in some bedrooms (£25 per night), not in public rooms.
CREDIT CARDS: Amex, MasterCard, Visa.
PRICES: [2016] per room B&B £335–£970, D,B&B £435–£1,070. Set dinner £55, tasting menus £89–£120. 1-night bookings refused Christmas/New Year.

🏵 AEL Y BRYN

César award: Welsh guest house of the year

The 'genuine warmth' that imbues Robert Smith and Arwel Hughes's much-loved rural B&B impressed Guide inspectors in 2016 as much as it does returning guests, who rave about the hosts' 'enthusiasm, support, flexibility and desire to please'. 'Everything – the comfort, the design, the cuisine, Robert and Arwel's relations with their guests – is idiosyncratically personal.' Arrive to 'great pots of tea and tiered platters of Arwel's home-baked treats (including a couple of Welsh cakes for good measure)'. In 'comfortably jumbly' gardens, the house is filled with paintings, sculptures, bibelots; 'the snug library is a hideout for book lovers'. 'Our spacious, well-furnished bedroom came supplied with travel guides and books, an exhaustive tea tray, a packed information binder; the window seat surveyed a painterly landscape.' A 'sociable' dinner of 'refined comfort food' ('and plenty of it!') may be served, by arrangement. 'We woke to a royal breakfast: fresh chrysanthemums on the table; an impressive buffet spread; perfectly prepared eggs. We felt very spoiled.' (GM Jones, HM Lusby, Michael Frayn, and others)

25% DISCOUNT VOUCHERS

Eglwyswrw
SA41 3UL

T: 01239 891411
E: stay@aelybrynpembrokeshire.
   co.uk
W: www.aelybrynpembrokeshire.
   co.uk

BEDROOMS: 4. All on ground floor.
OPEN: all year except Christmas/
New Year.
FACILITIES: library, music room, dining room, conservatory (telescope), free Wi-Fi, in-room TV (Freeview), courtyard, 2½-acre garden (wildlife pond, stream, bowls court).
BACKGROUND MUSIC: 'easy listening'/ classical in music room in evening.
LOCATION: ½ mile N of Eglwyswrw.
CHILDREN: not under 14.
DOGS: not allowed.
CREDIT CARDS: Amex, MasterCard, Visa.
PRICES: [2016] per room B&B £100–£130. Set dinner £24–£28.

FELIN FACH Powys

Map 3:D4

THE FELIN FACH GRIFFIN

♥César award since 2013

'I'd be very happy if this were my local,' says a Guide inspector in 2016, of the Inkin brothers' 'charming' pub-with-rooms. 'The relaxed atmosphere belies the fact that the owners [and long-serving manager, Julie Bell] run a professional operation with great care for details.' Come in to mismatched armchairs and a 'roaring' log fire, then check in to one of the smart, country-style bedrooms: each has fresh flowers, natural toiletries, local art, Welsh blankets. 'Our room was small, with just enough space for the double bed, but the bathroom was nicely furnished, with a powerful shower. Plenty of books and magazines; filter coffee, leaf tea, lovely shortbread biscuits. We were given fresh milk, too – a big plus.' In the 'appealing, shabby-chic' dining room, 'amazing', 'inventive' meals are well catered for by the lush kitchen garden. 'My veggie dish of shaved asparagus and charred cabbage was delicious.' Super-local breakfasts might include a 'marvellous' spiced-fruit compote. Sister inns The Gurnard's Head, Zennor, and The Old Coastguard, Mousehole (see entries), share the same spirit.

25% DISCOUNT VOUCHERS

Felin Fach
LD3 0UB

T: 01874 620111
E: enquiries@felinfachgriffin.co.uk
W: www.felinfachgriffin.co.uk

BEDROOMS: 7.
OPEN: all year except 24/25 Dec.
FACILITIES: bar area, dining room, breakfast room, private dining room, no Wi-Fi, limited mobile phone signal, 3-acre garden (stream, kitchen garden, alfresco dining), only bar/dining room suitable for disabled.
BACKGROUND MUSIC: Radio 4 at breakfast, 'easy listening' at other times, in bar and restaurant.
LOCATION: 4 miles NE of Brecon, in village on A470.
CHILDREN: all ages welcomed (games, books, children's menu).
DOGS: allowed in bedrooms, not in restaurant.
CREDIT CARDS: MasterCard, Visa.
PRICES: [2016] per room B&B £130–£170, D,B&B £185–£225. Set menu £28.50.

THE MANOR TOWN HOUSE

Close to the lively town square, the smart, powder-blue facade of Helen and Chris Sheldon's 'friendly' Georgian town house gives no clue to the vast sea view that unfurls behind it. Order a cream tea on the terrace, and look out over the harbour of Lower Town (transformed into Llareggub in the 1971 film Under Milk Wood). The house is immaculate yet homey, its two lounges hung with work by Welsh artists. One has a thoughtfully stocked honesty bar, the other a collection of books and DVDs. Bedrooms, some overlooking the sea, are individually styled; each has dressing gowns, posh toiletries, a comfortable bed with crisp linens. Families are readily accommodated. Breakfast is a treat, with locally made bread and pastries, waffles, fresh fruit, Greek yogurt and a daily cooked special. The owners are happy to advise on eating spots, day-trips and local places of interest. There's plenty to hold a visitor's attention in this old fishing town, including music festivals in May and July, a food festival in November. The Pembrokeshire Coastal Path runs through the wooded valley below the garden.

11 Main Street
Fishguard
SA65 9HG

T: 01348 873260
E: enquiries@manortownhouse.com
W: www.manortownhouse.com

BEDROOMS: 6.
OPEN: all year except 23–28 Dec.
FACILITIES: 2 lounges, breakfast room, free Wi-Fi, in-room TV (Freeview), small walled garden, unsuitable for disabled.
BACKGROUND MUSIC: classical at breakfast.
LOCATION: town centre.
CHILDREN: all ages welcomed.
DOGS: not allowed.
CREDIT CARDS: MasterCard, Visa.
PRICES: [2016] per room B&B £85–£120. 1-night bookings sometimes refused peak weekends.

GLYNARTHEN Ceredigion

Map 3:D2

PENBONTBREN

♔César award since 2012

A night in a threshing barn may not sound like the last word in luxury, but 'there's nothing to find fault with' at this B&B conversion of a 19th-century livestock farm, where hens wander and chuckle in the 'beautiful' grounds. Richard Morgan-Price and Huw Thomas are the 'friendly', hands-on hosts. Choose to sleep in stables, mill, barn or granary – in each case, find an 'immaculate' suite with a large bed (twins available), a capsule coffee-maker, fresh milk, high-end toiletries, a separate sitting room and private outside space. There's no private lounge in the 'bijou' garden room, made countryside chic in soothing creams and whites; instead, step out on to a terrace with a covered pergola, right in the middle of the garden. Order breakfast in bed, or head for the breakfast room, in another converted barn, where tables are laid with 'crisp white linen'. Here, sip glasses of freshly squeezed orange juice while tucking into organic yogurt and a wide choice of cooked dishes: kippers, local smoked salmon, a 'traditional Welsh' with laver bread, eggs every way. More reports, please.

25% DISCOUNT VOUCHERS

Glynarthen
SA44 6PE

T: 01239 810248
F: 01239 811129
E: contact@penbontbren.com
W: www.penbontbren.com

BEDROOMS: 6. 5 in annexe, 1 in garden, 3 on ground floor, 1 family suite, 1 suitable for disabled.
OPEN: all year except Christmas.
FACILITIES: breakfast room, free Wi-Fi, in-room TV (Freeview), 7-acre grounds.
BACKGROUND MUSIC: none.
LOCATION: 5 miles N of Newcastle Emlyn.
CHILDREN: all ages welcomed.
DOGS: allowed in some bedrooms, not in breakfast room.
CREDIT CARDS: MasterCard, Visa.
PRICES: per room B&B £99–£125. 1-night bookings sometimes refused weekends.

CASTLE COTTAGE

How times change: steps from the medieval castle, Glyn and Jacqueline Roberts's 'impressive' restaurant-with-rooms occupies two of Harlech's oldest buildings, described in 1798 as a cheerless spot offering no bed, just a dirt floor strewn with rushes. Today, Guide readers praise the 'excellent' contemporary rooms, each well equipped with a king-size bed, tea and coffee, fresh fruit, Welsh spring water, slippers. Three have a sofa bed, ideal for a child; some have 'wonderful' views of sea and mountains. The tables are laid with white linens at dinner; after canapés in the bar, sit down to Glyn Roberts's modern Welsh menus, including, perhaps, grilled Milford Haven cod, vanilla salt, saffron potatoes; herb-roasted loin of lamb, bubble and squeak, buttered carrots. At breakfast, muesli and jam are home made, juice is freshly squeezed, yogurt and honey are local, hot dishes are cooked to order. Well placed for touring the coast; beaches and fishing spots are within easy reach. Have boots made for walking? The town is within Snowdonia national park: gentle strolls and challenging hikes abound. (Mary Coles, IM)

25% DISCOUNT VOUCHERS

Y Llech
Harlech
LL46 2YL

T: 01766 780479
E: glyn@castlecottageharlech.co.uk
W: www.castlecottageharlech.co.uk

BEDROOMS: 7. 4 in annexe, 2 on ground floor.
OPEN: all year except Christmas and 3 weeks Nov, restaurant closed Sun–Wed in winter months.
FACILITIES: bar, lounge, restaurant, free Wi-Fi, in-room TV (Freeview), unsuitable for disabled.
BACKGROUND MUSIC: radio at breakfast, 'discreet' CDs at dinner in bar/restaurant.
LOCATION: town centre.
CHILDREN: all ages welcomed (child sharing parents' room £15).
DOGS: not allowed.
CREDIT CARDS: MasterCard, Visa.
PRICES: per room B&B £130–£175. Set menus £35–£40, tasting menu £45.

THE FALCONDALE

25% DISCOUNT VOUCHERS

'You won't be disappointed,' writes a reader in 2016, of Chris and Lisa Hutton's 'classy hotel', a Victorian Italianate mansion standing in extensive landscaped grounds. 'The staff are like friends'; the whole is 'very welcoming' – not least to Fido, who can dine off his own menu alongside you in the conservatory. Public rooms are tastefully, traditionally furnished, with 'interesting' pictures, magazines and a baby grand piano. Bedrooms vary in size and outlook ('each has its own character'), but all are comfortable, in country house style. The best has a Juliet balcony and views over the Teifi valley dotted with sheep; a room with two double beds is ideal for a family. In the 'elegant' dining room, chef Justin Heasman's menu showcases Welsh produce, with crab and lobster from Cardigan Bay, artisan cheeses, home-grown herbs. 'Delicious' dishes might include rack of spring lamb, rosemary jus, port jelly; Perl Las cheese and leek risotto. Sample the 'comprehensive' buffet at breakfast. A good countryside base for exploring West Wales; Cardigan Bay is 40 minutes' drive away. (Angela Williams, Frederic Jones, Glen Ellis)

Falcondale Drive
Lampeter
SA48 7RX

T: 01570 422910
E: info@thefalcondale.co.uk
W: www.thefalcondale.co.uk

BEDROOMS: 18.
OPEN: all year.
FACILITIES: lift, bar, 3 lounges, conservatory, restaurant, free Wi-Fi, in-room TV (Freeview), civil wedding licence, terrace, 14-acre grounds (lawns, woodland), unsuitable for disabled.
BACKGROUND MUSIC: classical in restaurant and lounges.
LOCATION: 1 mile N of Lampeter.
CHILDREN: all ages welcomed.
DOGS: allowed, not in main dining room.
CREDIT CARDS: MasterCard, Visa.
PRICES: [2016] per room B&B £100–£190, D,B&B £170–£260. Set dinner £42.

LLWYN HELYG

'The antithesis of "Welsh cosy"', this stone-built house in neat gardens is run as a 'superb, if glossy, luxury B&B' by Fiona and Caron Jones. 'A bit Milan-meets-Dallas, it has an undeniable "wow" factor', with a 'massive' entrance hall, 'stylishly furnished' sitting areas 'in large hallways and intimate rooms', and 'spacious' bedrooms up the 'impressive' Imperial staircase. 'Genuinely helpful', the Joneses are 'warm, welcoming, unassuming' hosts. 'Caron offered help with luggage when we arrived, and later ferried us to and from the restaurant for dinner.' Settle in to bedrooms well equipped with dressing gowns, slippers, a spa bath in the bathroom. 'Ours was elegant: crisp, top-quality bedlinen and plump pillows; lovely rugs; a luxurious bathroom in beige marble. We looked out on to magnificent countryside.' Music buffs, rejoice: the raftered Listening Room, complete with 'squashy' sofas and an extensive vinyl collection, has 'the best sound system we've heard outside the Albert Hall'. In the 'bright' breakfast room, a 'fresh, good-quality' spread is 'elegantly presented' on fine china. The 'absolutely wonderful' National Botanic Garden of Wales is a ten-minute drive away.

Llanarthne
SA32 8HJ

T: 01558 668778
E: enquiries@
llwynhelygcountryhouse.co.uk
W: www.llwynhelygcountryhouse.co.uk

BEDROOMS: 3.
OPEN: all year except 10 days over Christmas.
FACILITIES: 4 lounges, listening room, breakfast room, free Wi-Fi, in-room TV (Freeview), 3-acre garden, unsuitable for disabled.
BACKGROUND MUSIC: none.
LOCATION: 8 miles W of Llandeilo, 9 miles E of Carmarthen.
CHILDREN: not under 16.
DOGS: not allowed.
CREDIT CARDS: MasterCard, Visa.
PRICES: [2016] per room B&B £135–£155.

LLANDRILLO Denbighshire

Map 3:B4

TYDDYN LLAN

César award since 2006

Meadows, mountains and Michelin-starred meals attract visitors to Susan and Bryan Webb's 'lovely', rural restaurant-with-rooms. The mellow-stone Georgian gentry house has a homey elegance, with open fires, armchairs, a peaceful decor. The hostess's 'vibrant personality lifts the whole place'; 'service is relaxed and excellent'. Pretty, 'comfortable' bedrooms have a traditional country charm – find tea and coffee facilities, home-baked biscuits, robes and slippers. Each room has its own character: one has an antique four-poster bed, a sitting area, garden views; another has French doors opening on to a private patio. In the evening, sample 'substantial' canapés before tasting Bryan Webb's 'fabulous' daily-changing menus, including, perhaps, 'beautifully tender grouse'; 'a generous portion of stuffed rabbit leg'. 'The only downside is that by pudding time we were a wee bit full.' Young gastronomes are welcomed: ask for smaller portions off the regular menu, or a sensible children's selection. Come morning, a notable breakfast is fuel for the many walks around. (Mary Coles, PA, and others)

25% DISCOUNT VOUCHERS

Llandrillo
LL21 0ST

T: 01490 440264
F: 01490 440414
E: info@tyddynllan.co.uk
W: www.tyddynllan.co.uk

BEDROOMS: 13. 3 with separate entrance, 1, on ground floor, suitable for disabled.
OPEN: all year except 3 weeks Jan, restaurant closed Mon and Tues, Jan–Mar.
FACILITIES: 2 lounges, bar, 2 dining rooms, free Wi-Fi, in-room TV (Freeview), civil wedding licence, 3-acre garden.
BACKGROUND MUSIC: none.
LOCATION: 5 miles SW of Corwen.
CHILDREN: all ages welcomed.
DOGS: allowed in some bedrooms (£10 per night), not in public rooms.
CREDIT CARDS: Amex, MasterCard, Visa.
PRICES: per room B&B £190–£320, D,B&B £290–£420. Set dinner £60, tasting menus £75–£90.

BODYSGALLEN HALL AND SPA

♀César award since 1988

The name may mean 'house among thistles', but the 'meticulously kept' combination of manicured lawns, knotted gardens and meadow flowers tells otherwise. Flourishing, too, is the praise guests reserve for this 'beautiful', 'ancient' mansion under the stewardship of the National Trust. 'It hasn't changed one bit in the 20 years we've been going there, and that's how I hope it stays,' says a trusted Guide correspondent this year. 'The sofas are comfortable; the place is warm, quiet and peaceful; the staff are super-friendly, super-professional, immaculately turned out.' Beyond the public rooms ('lovely' original fireplaces, fresh flowers, leather-bound books), bedrooms in the main hall and in cottages in the grounds are furnished with antiques and original paintings. 'Our cottage suite was immaculate – a bit tired around the edges, but it's like going to stay with a favourite relative.' Come dinnertime, suit up for John Williams's 'superb' modern menu. 'Some may find it a little formal, but we dressed up, dined in for five nights (they kindly altered the menu), and drank gallons of fair-priced wine. Loved it!' (Richard Morgan-Price, and others)

The Royal Welsh Way
Llandudno
LL30 1RS

T: 01492 584466
F: 01492 582519
E: info@bodysgallen.com
W: www.bodysgallen.com

BEDROOMS: 31. 16 in cottages, 1 suitable for disabled.
OPEN: all year, restaurant closed Mon lunch.
FACILITIES: hall, drawing room, library, bar, dining room, free Wi-Fi, in-room TV (Sky, Freeview), civil wedding licence, 220-acre park (gardens, tennis, croquet), spa (16-metre swimming pool).
BACKGROUND MUSIC: none.
LOCATION: 2 miles S of Llandudno and Conwy.
CHILDREN: no under-6s in hotel, under-8s in spa (set swimming times).
DOGS: not allowed.
CREDIT CARDS: Amex, MasterCard, Visa.
PRICES: [2016] per room B&B £180–£385. À la carte £55. 1-night bookings sometimes refused.

SEE ALSO SHORTLIST

OSBORNE HOUSE

Behind the stone portico and bay windows of this 'atmospheric' 19th-century seafront house, find a wealth of period detail and ornament – paintings, lamps, antique furniture, clocks, figurines. It is the little sister of the Empire Hotel round the corner; both are run by Elyse Waddy (née Maddocks, a scion of the Maddocks family, who have been here since 1946) and her husband, Michael. The 'beautifully furnished' suites have antiques, oriental rugs on bare floorboards, a comfy sitting room with a fireplace, and a marble bathroom. First-floor rooms overlook 'the elegant sweep of the Victorian buildings and wide promenade'; those on the second floor take in 'the bay and the cliffs in all their glory'. Head to the Empire to use the spa and saltwater swimming pool. The all-day bistro, with its fluted pillars and chandeliers, is 'far more elegant than many hotel restaurants; you feel it's a special occasion, eating here'. Typical dishes: crab, prawn and crayfish fishcakes; roasted lamb shank. Mornings, ask for a continental breakfast to be served in the suite, or stroll to the Empire for a full Welsh. (BW)

17 North Parade
Llandudno
LL30 2LP

T: 01492 860330
F: 01492 860791
E: sales@osbornehouse.com
W: www.osbornehouse.co.uk

BEDROOMS: 6.
OPEN: all year, except 10 days Christmas, open New Year.
FACILITIES: sitting room, bar, café/bistro, free Wi-Fi, unsuitable for disabled.
BACKGROUND MUSIC: in public rooms.
LOCATION: on promenade.
CHILDREN: not under 14.
DOGS: not allowed.
CREDIT CARDS: all major cards.
PRICES: [2016] per room B&B £125–£175, D,B&B £155–£205. À la carte £26. 1-night bookings sometimes refused.

SEE ALSO SHORTLIST

THE LAKE

'It's like going home,' writes a regular Guide reader this year, who considers Jean-Pierre Mifsud's country house hotel 'a regular haunt'. The 19th-century hunting and fishing lodge stands in extensive lawns stretching down to a lake on the River Irfon. Inside, find inviting sofas and armchairs amid antiques, paintings and original features. The 'comfortable' grand lounge, with fresh flowers, up-to-date magazines and views across the lawns, is just right for bara brith at afternoon tea. Fans praise the 'superb' staff: 'The young team are great fun and all very pleasant.' Choose among traditionally styled bedrooms (up a 'creaky old staircase') in the main house, and more contemporary accommodation in the purpose-built lodge. In the evening, settle into the 'first-class' dining room for new chef Stephen Crichton's modern Welsh menus, perhaps mushroom risotto, Parmesan, hazelnut cream; fillet of mackerel, beetroot, oyster. A 'good' breakfast is served in the modern orangery: smoked fish, a selection of cereals, a full Welsh with laver bread. Northcote Manor, Burrington, England (see entry), is under the same ownership. (Richard Morgan-Price, Michael and Pauline Bastick)

25% DISCOUNT VOUCHERS

Llangammarch Wells
LD4 4BS

T: 01591 620202
F: 01591 620457
E: info@lakecountryhouse.co.uk
W: www.lakecountryhouse.co.uk

BEDROOMS: 30. 12 suites in adjacent lodge, 7 on ground floor, 1 suitable for disabled.
OPEN: all year.
FACILITIES: 3 lounges, orangery, restaurant, free Wi-Fi, in-room TV, spa (15-metre swimming pool, restricted hours for under-16s), civil wedding licence, 50-acre grounds (tennis).
BACKGROUND MUSIC: none.
LOCATION: 8 miles SW of Builth Wells.
CHILDREN: all ages welcomed, no under-8s in spa.
DOGS: allowed (£10 charge).
CREDIT CARDS: Amex, MasterCard, Visa.
PRICES: [2016] per room B&B £195–£260. Set dinner £45.

LLYSWEN Powys

Map 3:D4

LLANGOED HALL

There's 'birdsong in the air' and 'a great atmosphere of peace' at this 'glorious' country house hotel, in large gardens descending to the River Wye, say Guide inspectors. The Jacobean mansion (Relais & Châteaux) once belonged to Sir Bernard Ashley; his 'fabulous' collection of art and antiques is displayed throughout, alongside fresh flowers, open fires and many Laura Ashley prints. Staff are 'impeccable': 'everyone addressed us by name'. Overlooking the valley, traditional bedrooms are supplied with sherry, fresh fruit and water. 'Spacious and lovely, our deluxe room had a chandelier, a sofa, two big squashy chairs; a claw-footed bath in the bathroom. The canopied bed had been made with blankets and sheets, as we'd requested.' Chef Nick Brodie's dinners, well supplied by the organic kitchen garden, are an event (though a guest this year hungered for larger portions). 'The menus are elaborate and expensive, but the food, such as an exquisite veggie concoction to complement the turbot, was superb. I couldn't cope with the fancy asparagus starter so asked for a small portion plainly done. "No problem" – and it was delicious.'

Llyswen
LD3 0YP

T: 01874 754525
F: 01874 754545
E: enquiries@llangoedhall.com
W: www.llangoedhall.co.uk

BEDROOMS: 23.
OPEN: all year.
FACILITIES: great hall, morning room, library, bar/lounge, restaurant, billiard room, function rooms, free Wi-Fi, in-room TV (Freeview), civil wedding licence, 23-acre gardens and parkland, unsuitable for disabled.
BACKGROUND MUSIC: none.
LOCATION: 12 miles NE of Brecon.
CHILDREN: all ages welcomed, only 'well-behaved children' in dining room (babysitting can be arranged).
DOGS: allowed in bedrooms with £120 professional allergy clean, heated kennels available.
CREDIT CARDS: Amex, MasterCard, Visa.
PRICES: [2016] per room B&B £145–£600, D,B&B £250–£750. Four-course table d'hôte menu £75, tasting menus £95–£125.

PEN-Y-GWRYD HOTEL

♀César award since 1995

Why visit the Pullees' 'eccentric' and 'old-fashioned' hotel at the foot of Snowdonia? Well, because it's there. It was run by the same family back in 1953 when it hosted Sir Edmund Hillary and Tenzing Norgay as they trained to climb Everest, and not a lot has changed since then. Built in 1810, the farmhouse-turned-coaching inn retains the spirit of a mountaineers' hostel, 'safe from the relentless grind of modernity'. Wi-Fi has found its way into the common areas, TV into some bedrooms, but even now not all rooms have an en suite bathroom. The compensations are many, not least the beauty of the surroundings and the hotel's own swimming lake, sauna and chapel. Lounge about in three snugs, with a reliquary of Everest memorabilia, a dartboard and table tennis. The cooked breakfast is 'hearty'. Lunch in the bar might be soup, quiche, smoked duck salad. At night, when the gong sounds, head to the dining room, shake out your starched napkin and tuck in to a sustaining set dinner 'fit for explorers'. Long may they keep the log fires burning.

Nant Gwynant
LL55 4NT

T: 01286 870211
E: escape@pyg.co.uk
W: www.pyg.co.uk

BEDROOMS: 18. 1 on ground floor, 5 in annexe.
OPEN: Mar–mid-Nov, occasional weekends Dec, New Year.
FACILITIES: lounge, bar, games room, dining room, free Wi-Fi in games room, in-room TV (Freeview) in some rooms, chapel, 1-acre grounds (natural swimming lake, sauna), unsuitable for disabled.
BACKGROUND MUSIC: none.
LOCATION: between Beddgelert and Capel Curig.
CHILDREN: all ages welcomed.
DOGS: allowed in some bedrooms (£10 charge).
CREDIT CARDS: MasterCard, Visa.
PRICES: [2016] per person B&B £45–£75, D,B&B £70–£100. Set dinner £25. 1-night bookings often refused weekends.

NARBERTH Pembrokeshire

THE GROVE

♛César award since 2016

'Unfussy', 'warm', 'genuine', Neil Kedward and Zoë Agar's stylish country hotel stands in 'flourishing' gardens near the coast. Step into the 18th-century mansion: there are oil paintings and watercolours, sofas and easy chairs, lots of books, 'a table with a chessboard all set up and ready to go'. In the main house and three garden cottages, choose one of the 'luxurious' bedrooms; each has its own character, with art, antiques and views of the grounds or vast countryside. Six cottage suites opened in spring 2016, some with a private garden. Gather in the lounges or on the sun terrace for pre-dinner canapés. In the restaurant ('smart white tablecloths, shiny table settings'), 'unusual flavours and tastes' – perhaps Welsh lamb, boulangère potato, sheep curd, confit fennel – are 'much enjoyed'. Come morning, start the day with 'excellent' pastries and 'a good selection for the muesli brigade'; scrambled eggs receive 'top marks'. Have little ones in tow? They'll find plenty to do, with boules, croquet and garden tree swings; the sandy beach at Saundersfoot is within a 20-minute drive. (MC, DB, and others)

25% DISCOUNT VOUCHERS

Molleston
Narberth
SA67 8BX

T: 01834 860915
E: info@thegrove-narberth.co.uk
W: www.thegrove-narberth.co.uk

BEDROOMS: 26. 12 in cottages in the grounds, some on ground floor.
OPEN: all year.
FACILITIES: 3 lounges, bar, 3 restaurant rooms, free Wi-Fi, in-room TV (Sky), civil wedding licence, 26-acre grounds.
BACKGROUND MUSIC: in public areas.
LOCATION: 1 mile S of Narberth.
CHILDREN: all ages welcomed, no under-10s in restaurant after 7 pm.
DOGS: allowed in 3 bedrooms, not in main building.
CREDIT CARDS: Amex, MasterCard, Visa.
PRICES: [2016] per room B&B from £210, D,B&B from £318. Tasting menu £89, à la carte £59.

SEE ALSO SHORTLIST

CNAPAN

'Exceptionally welcoming', 'traditional but not stuffy', this restaurant-with-rooms wins applause from Guide readers who enjoy the relaxed, friendly atmosphere and the 'well-informed' staff ('several of whom are family'). The pink-painted town house is minutes from the coast, in a 'fantastic area to explore'; Judith and Michael Cooper are the 'hard-working' owners. 'It's not a hip hotel, but very nice for that,' says a Guide reader this year. 'The Coopers are so friendly you almost feel you know them – they're always available for a chat.' 'The food is the main event': Judith Cooper's 'great' dinners, 'obviously very popular with locals', have been drawing visitors for more than 30 years. Clink glasses of prosecco in the secluded garden, then tuck in to 'delicious, unpretentious combinations of ingredients', perhaps roasted duck, soured cherry-port sauce, cannellini mash. Stay the night in a 'comfortable, fresh and bright' bedroom. 'Ours, with a sparkling new bathroom, was decorated with pictures by local artists; there were locally made blankets on the bed.' Breakfast brings home-made muesli and preserves, hot dishes cooked to order. (Jan Lund)

East Street
Newport
SA42 0SY

T: 01239 820575
F: 01239 820878
E: enquiry@cnapan.co.uk
W: www.cnapan.co.uk

BEDROOMS: 5. Plus self-catering cottage.
OPEN: Mar–mid-Dec, restaurant closed Mon and Tues.
FACILITIES: lounge, bar, restaurant, free Wi-Fi, in-room TV, small garden, only restaurant suitable for disabled.
BACKGROUND MUSIC: jazz/'easy listening' in evenings in dining room.
LOCATION: town centre.
CHILDREN: all ages welcomed.
DOGS: not allowed.
CREDIT CARDS: MasterCard, Visa.
PRICES: [2016] per room B&B £95, D,B&B £147. Set dinner £26–£33. 1-night bookings sometimes refused during peak season and some Saturdays.

NEWPORT Pembrokeshire

LLYS MEDDYG

There's 'an affable air' to Edward and Louise Sykes's 'smart' restaurant-with-rooms, in an 'appealing' Georgian coaching inn in this 'attractive' village. 'It is the best of its kind – small, family run, equally professional and personable. There's a strong ethos here – you sense that hospitality comes naturally to the Sykeses and their modest team. And the cooking is exceptional,' say Guide inspectors in 2016. There are three dining areas, each 'with its own spirit': the 'lively, popular' cellar bar; the 'charming' summertime-only kitchen garden; the modern-rustic dining room, 'all raw wood and Welsh art'. 'Everything was pretty without being precious. And what punchy flavours! Razor clams freshly foraged came as an amuse-bouche with black pudding; smoked duck breast in a spiced consommé was deep and subtle.' Head upstairs, afterwards, to 'chic', 'cosy' bedrooms 'comfortable as home' (some may have noise from the bar). In the morning, glasses of 'frothy, freshly squeezed orange juice' are brought to linen-clad tables; dig into 'fine' breakfast crêpes, 'blueberry jam made by Ed's brother', 'delicious' home-smoked salmon. (Agathe and Louis Homberg, and others)

25% DISCOUNT VOUCHERS

East Street
Newport
SA42 0SY

T: 01239 820008
E: info@llysmeddyg.com
W: www.llysmeddyg.com

BEDROOMS: 8. 1 on ground floor, 3 in mews annexe, plus a cottage.
OPEN: all year.
FACILITIES: bar, restaurant, kitchen garden dining area (open in summer holidays), sitting room, free Wi-Fi, in-room TV (Freeview), civil wedding licence, garden, unsuitable for disabled.
BACKGROUND MUSIC: in bar and dining room during meals.
LOCATION: central.
CHILDREN: all ages welcomed.
DOGS: allowed in 3 annexe bedrooms, bar.
CREDIT CARDS: MasterCard, Visa.
PRICES: [2016] per room B&B £100–£120, D,B&B £200–£220. À la carte £33.

PENALLY ABBEY   **NEW**

There's much that appeals at this 'superb' hotel, in a skilfully spruced-up late 18th-century Gothic house looking out to sea, say guests in 2016: 'friendly, helpful' staff; 'excellent' food; 'lovely' spots to lounge in; a good-natured atmosphere throughout. New owners Lucas and Melanie Boissevain have refurbished with panache, restoring period features and heritage detail. The inviting sitting room (flowers, books, magazines, log fire) calls for tea and a biscuit; a pretty terrace has 'great views' of the sea. From snug accommodation in the eaves to a spacious, refined room overlooking the water, bedrooms update a classically elegant look with easy charm. Sundown calls for a sit-down: sip a Welsh whisky or a local craft beer in the cosy bar, then sup on a modern menu in tune with the seasons, perhaps including a springtime rack of lamb, crushed Pembrokeshire potatoes, spinach and carrot purée. Breakfast on fruit, pastries and Welsh specialities such as laver bread, then set out to explore the large, attractive grounds: among the wild flowers, find an ancient well and the ruins of a medieval abbey.

Penally
SA70 7PY

T: 01834 843033
F: 01834 844714
E: info@penally-abbey.com
W: www.penally-abbey.com

BEDROOMS: 11. 4 in coach house (100 yds), 2 on ground floor.
OPEN: all year except first 2 weeks Jan.
FACILITIES: sitting room, snug bar, conservatory, restaurant, The Courtyard private function room, free Wi-Fi, in-room TV, civil wedding licence, in-room massages and beauty treatments, terrace, 6-acre grounds.
BACKGROUND MUSIC: in public areas.
LOCATION: 1½ miles SW of Tenby.
CHILDREN: all ages welcomed.
DOGS: allowed in bar, conservatory, sitting room, coach house bedrooms (not unattended), not in restaurant.
CREDIT CARDS: MasterCard, Visa.
PRICES: [2016] per room B&B from £125.

HOTEL PORTMEIRION

🏆 César award since 1990

Noël Coward wrote Blithe Spirit while staying at this Italianate village on the coast of Snowdonia national park – and a blithe spirit infuses the whole extraordinary caprice. Built over 50 years, from 1925, by Sir Bertram Clough Williams-Ellis, Portmeirion grew up behind this Victorian mansion, now a 'charming' hotel that 'combines old-world touches with stylish modernity'. Stay in the main hotel, the Victorian-Gothic Castell Deudraeth, or one of the village buildings, their 'brightly coloured exteriors' inspired by the Italian Riviera. The hotel rooms are traditionally styled, with antique and new furniture; more contemporary Castell rooms have views of estuary, countryside and gardens. Dine informally in Castell Deudraeth's brasserie, or in the curvilinear Art Deco hotel dining room, where the 'amazing' modern cooking is 'a major highlight'. Guide readers praise the comfort, the 'wonderful views', the 'extremely friendly' service and the 'very good breakfast', while the situation itself – with Portmeirion's shell grotto, bell tower, dog cemetery, pan-tiled temple and more besides – is without compare.

25% DISCOUNT VOUCHERS

Minffordd
Penrhyndeudraeth
Portmeirion
LL48 6ER

T: 01766 770000
F: 01766 770300
E: reception@portmeirion-village.com
W: www.portmeirion-village.com

BEDROOMS: 57. 14 in hotel, some on ground floor, 1 suitable for disabled; 11 in Castell Deudraeth, 32 in village.
OPEN: all year.
FACILITIES: hall, lift, 3 lounges, bar, restaurant, brasserie in Castell, beauty salon, free Wi-Fi, in-room TV, civil wedding licence, 170-acre grounds, heated swimming pool (May–Sept).
BACKGROUND MUSIC: none.
LOCATION: 2 miles SE of Porthmadog.
CHILDREN: all ages welcomed.
DOGS: not allowed.
CREDIT CARDS: Amex, MasterCard, Visa.
PRICES: [2016] per room B&B from £154, D,B&B from £219. Set menu (restaurant) £36–£45, à la carte £50. .

PWLLHELI Gwynedd

THE OLD RECTORY

At the end of a leafy drive, 'charming hosts' Gary and Lindsay Ashcroft run their 'superb' B&B with great attention to detail. The Georgian rectory stands in its own beautifully tended grounds; within, antiques, ornaments, paintings and tufted leather armchairs add to the peaceful, traditional atmosphere. Bedrooms have garden views and thoughtful extras, such as chocolates, sherry, good china on the tea tray; one has a freestanding tub in the bathroom. Breakfast is taken communally: expect home-made bread, jam and marmalade; juices and cereals from the buffet; cooked dishes with local meats and fish. Need a veggie breakfast? The hosts are happy to cater for special diets. Spend a lazy afternoon over tea and magazines in the sitting room overlooking the gardens (a log fire burns on cool days), or ask for a packed lunch and head out to explore: Snowdonia beckons; sandy beaches and cliff walks are within a five-minute drive; the Llyn Coastal Path is nearby. In the summer, rent the Ashcrofts' well-equipped, brightly painted hut at family-friendly Llanbedrog beach. (Michael Watkins, and others)

25% DISCOUNT VOUCHERS

Boduan
Pwllheli
LL53 6DT

T: 01758 721519
E: theashcrofts@theoldrectory.net
W: www.theoldrectory.net

BEDROOMS: 4. Plus a self-catering cottage and lodge.
OPEN: all year except Christmas.
FACILITIES: drawing room, dining room, free Wi-Fi, in-room TV (Freeview), 3-acre grounds, unsuitable for disabled.
BACKGROUND MUSIC: none.
LOCATION: 4 miles NW of Pwllheli.
CHILDREN: all ages welcomed.
DOGS: only assistance dogs allowed in house (kennel and run available).
CREDIT CARDS: MasterCard, Visa.
PRICES: [2016] per room B&B £75–£115. 1-night bookings refused some weekends, high season and bank holidays.

PWLLHELI Gwynedd

Map 3:B2

PLAS BODEGROES

César award since 1992

Roses, roses all the way: on the remote Lleyn peninsula, Chris and Gunna Chown's 'lovely' restaurant-with-rooms occupies a Georgian manor house whose name translates as 'Rosehip Hall' – a fitting moniker for this 'romantic' place embowered in woodland, with wisteria draped over the veranda. After 30 years on the frontline, the Chowns in 2016 brought in Camille and Chris Lovell as manager and chef. 'We'll stay in the background and assist when we can,' the owners say. Guide readers have long praised the 'relaxing ambience' and 'friendly staff' – an impression helped along, perhaps, by the home-made bara brith served at afternoon tea. All the bedrooms overlook the gardens; two of the suites accommodate a family. In the pretty blue dining room, Chris Lovell continues to highlight local produce in season, with fruit, vegetables and herbs from the kitchen garden. Characteristic of his 'imaginative, tasty' modern dishes: loin of Welsh lamb, sweetbreads, burnt honey, lavender curd. Spend the morning exploring the 'delightful' grounds: there are places to sit; a path leads through a yew tree gate to the stream. (MC)

Nefyn Road
Efailnewydd
Pwllheli
LL53 5TH

T: 01758 612363
F: 01758 701247
E: info@bodegroes.co.uk
W: www.bodegroes.co.uk

BEDROOMS: 10. 2 in courtyard cottage.
OPEN: all year except 3 Jan–6 Feb.
FACILITIES: lounge, bar, breakfast room, restaurant, free Wi-Fi, in-room TV (Freeview), 5-acre grounds, unsuitable for disabled.
BACKGROUND MUSIC: none.
LOCATION: 1 mile W of Pwllheli.
CHILDREN: all ages welcomed.
DOGS: allowed in some bedrooms, not in public rooms.
CREDIT CARDS: MasterCard, Visa.
PRICES: [2016] per room B&B £150–£190, D,B&B £249–£289. Set dinner £49. 1-night bookings sometimes refused bank holidays.

FAIRYHILL

Guide readers this year continue to be 'impressed' by the balance of 'informality and great efficiency' at Paul Davies and Andrew Hetherington's 'lovely, quiet' small hotel down peaceful country lanes. 'We felt well looked after and "at home" here.' 'Excellently located', the 18th-century Georgian mansion stands in 'lovely grounds full of wildlife'; wander round to find the ornamental lake, the old orchard, wide-spreading trees for reading under. Inside, the house is 'beautifully furnished and maintained, without being fussy'. Settle into 'comfortable, cosy' bedrooms: each is individually designed; all are thoughtfully stocked with organic teas, home-made Welsh cakes and 'loads of gadgets'. The tables are set with white linens and fresh flowers in the restaurant, where chef David Whitecross's modern British dishes are praised. 'We ate in, over six nights. Though the menu didn't change, there were daily specials and adequate choice. We loved the sea bass with samphire that one of the cooks collects from the salt marshes. The wine list is vast, but we were well advised by one of the waiters.' 'Good breakfasts, too.' (Humphrey Norrington, DG)

Reynoldston, Gower
SA3 1BS

T: 01792 390139
F: 01792 391358
E: postbox@fairyhill.net
W: www.fairyhill.net

BEDROOMS: 8.
OPEN: all year except 24–26 Dec and first 3 weeks Jan, open New Year, restaurant closed Mon and Tues, Nov–end Mar.
FACILITIES: lounge, bar, 3 dining rooms, meeting room, free Wi-Fi, in-room TV (Freeview), civil wedding licence, spa treatment room, 24-acre grounds, unsuitable for disabled.
BACKGROUND MUSIC: 'easy listening' in public areas at mealtimes.
LOCATION: 11 miles W of Swansea.
CHILDREN: not under 8.
DOGS: allowed in bedrooms (not unattended), not in public rooms.
CREDIT CARDS: MasterCard, Visa.
PRICES: [2016] per room B&B from £200, D,B&B (min. 2 nights) from £275. À la carte £49.50. 1-night bookings refused Sat.

SKENFRITH Monmouthshire

Map 3:D4

THE BELL AT SKENFRITH   **NEW**

In a 'postcard-worthy scene' of a 17th-century coaching inn by the stone bridge over the River Monnow, Guide inspectors in 2016 found a 'friendly', 'personable' spot, where owners Richard Ireton and Sarah Hudson are 'clearly invested in ensuring guests have a good time'. 'A jolly innkeeper, Richard greeted us at dinner, poured our drinks at the bar, and went round to chat at all the tables.' The bedrooms have been 'intelligently redecorated to suit contemporary tastes'. 'Ours, in the eaves, had exposed beams, metal-framed beds, cream carpeting over creaky floors. In the bathroom, a freestanding bathtub overlooked green countryside.' Come dinnertime, enjoy Joseph Colman's 'generous' portions of 'refined pub grub'. 'We loved rabbit three ways – confit leg, stuffed loin and pie – a hearty dish that sent us to bed happy.' ('The piped pop music, though, was at odds with the atmosphere.') Wake to a 'very good' breakfast 'overlooking the garden sloping into the hedges and hills'. A buffet holds home-made muesli and local yogurt; 'thick country toast and home-made berry jam' are served at table. (GC, and others)

Skenfrith
NP7 8UH

T: 01600 750235
F: 01600 750525
E: enquiries@skenfrith.co.uk
W: thebellatskenfrith.co.uk

BEDROOMS: 11.
OPEN: all year.
FACILITIES: sitting room, bar, restaurant, function facilities, free Wi-Fi, in-room TV (BT), terrace, garden, unsuitable for disabled.
BACKGROUND MUSIC: all day in bar and restaurant.
LOCATION: 9 miles W of Ross-on-Wye.
CHILDREN: all ages welcomed.
DOGS: 'well-behaved dogs' allowed in bedrooms, bar.
CREDIT CARDS: MasterCard, Visa.
PRICES: per room B&B from £150, D,B&B from £190. À la carte £28.

DOLFFANOG FAWR

At the foot of Cadair Idris, Lorraine Hinkins and Alex Yorke's 'exceptional' guest house is a 'superb' spot for walkers, anglers, cyclists and other guests in search of 'excellent' accommodation and 'simple, yet seriously good meals'. (Late-night star-lit soaks in the outdoor hot tub help, too.) The 18th-century farmhouse has comfy seats around a stone fireplace, and shelves of books and guides to pore over. On sunny days, sit in the lawned garden, its views stretching over tranquil countryside (look out for the odd escapee lamb from the neighbouring fields). Choose among the homely, well-thought-out rooms, each kitted out with Welsh blankets and local artwork; three have a window seat from which to take in the surrounding landscape of lake or hills. Most nights, the hostess cooks a communal dinner using local specialities such as Welsh Black beef, Snowdonia salt-marsh lamb and wild Dysynni sea trout, the whole accompanied by 'an unexpectedly good list of wines and craft beers'. Mornings, expect a 'generous' breakfast with award-winning sausages and home-baked bread; mountains, beaches and a historic steam train await. (GN)

Tal-y-llyn
Tywyn
LL36 9AJ

T: 01654 761247
E: info@dolffanogfawr.co.uk
W: www.dolffanogfawr.co.uk

BEDROOMS: 4.
OPEN: Mar–Oct, dining room closed Sun/Mon/Tues eve.
FACILITIES: lounge, dining room, free Wi-Fi (in most rooms, though temperamental), in-room TV (Freeview), 1-acre garden (hot tub), unsuitable for disabled.
BACKGROUND MUSIC: none.
LOCATION: by lake 10 miles E of Tywyn.
CHILDREN: not under 10.
DOGS: allowed in bedrooms (£5 per night) and lounge (if other guests don't mind).
CREDIT CARDS: MasterCard, Visa.
PRICES: [2016] per room B&B £100–£120, D,B&B £156–£176. À la carte £28. 1-night bookings sometimes refused.

THE WHITEBROOK

The bounty of the 'lovely' Wye valley – including foraged pennywort, hedge bedstraw and nasturtium tubers, 'all firsts for us!' – inspires the 'fresh, attractive' food at this modern, Michelin-starred restaurant-with-rooms run by chef/patron Chris Harrod and his wife, Kirsty. 'The experience is absolutely spot on, not least because of the kind and helpful staff.' Sample 'delicious' canapés before taking a seat in the 'atmospheric' restaurant ('well-spaced tables, proper tablecloths') for 'super', 'unpretentious' meals that are 'full of new flavours' – perhaps 'amazing' parsnip croquette, salsify, charlock; 'unusual' halibut, rainbow chard, foraged fennel. Fed well, retire to a 'restful' bedroom, upstairs in the 'refreshed' 17th-century drovers' inn. 'Our good-sized, well-decorated room had a big, comfy bed and two chairs; there were excellent toiletries and plenty of towels in the bathroom.' A 'small but comfortable' room overlooking the rear garden was less liked. At breakfast, tuck in to 'very freshly squeezed' orange juice, 'good' cafetière coffee, 'interesting' cooked options, including scrambled eggs 'elegantly served in a "bird's nest" of smoked salmon'. (T and GA, Pat and Jeremy Temple)

Whitebrook
NP25 4TX

T: 01600 860254
E: info@thewhitebrook.co.uk
W: www.thewhitebrook.co.uk

BEDROOMS: 8.
OPEN: all year except 26 Dec, first 2 weeks Jan, restaurant closed Mon, Tues midday.
FACILITIES: lounge/bar, restaurant, business facilities, free Wi-Fi in room, in-room TV (Freeview), terrace, 3-acre garden, River Wye 2 miles (fishing), only restaurant suitable for disabled.
BACKGROUND MUSIC: 'chill-out music' in restaurant.
LOCATION: 6 miles S of Monmouth.
CHILDREN: not under 12.
DOGS: only guide dogs allowed.
CREDIT CARDS: Amex, MasterCard, Visa.
PRICES: [2016] per room D,B&B £223–£334. Tasting menu £67, à la carte £54.

CHANNEL ISLANDS

St Peter Port, Guernsey

HERM

THE WHITE HOUSE

César award since 1987

'Walking is the thing' on this 'very green', car-free island: alight from the ferry and let a tractor bring your luggage to this 'truly lovely' hotel ('it's all part of the enjoyment'). 'Everything is in good condition,' say guests this year. 'The restaurant is large and airy; the gardens and swimming pool at their best; the view from the front lawn over the sea to Guernsey is wonderful. On a rainy day in June, cheerful coal fires burned in the lounge.' Guests are encouraged to 'escape the 21st century': there's no TV or telephone in the bedrooms ('good Wi-Fi', though); instead, most rooms have an ocean view and a balcony. 'We loved our bedroom, with its large windows and great views.' It's 'a good idea' to eat in: chef Karl Ginnever's daily-changing menus, 'much anticipated after a day in the open air', include a catch of the day, perhaps fillet of whiting, saffron potatoes, tandoori greens. At breakfast, tables are set with little dishes of home-made marmalade and Guernsey butter: 'We enjoyed the traditional English and the smoked haddock.' (Max Lickfold)

Herm
GY1 3HR

T: 01481 750075
F: 01481 710066
E: hotel@herm.com
W: www.herm.com

BEDROOMS: 40. 18 in cottages, some on ground floor.
OPEN: late Mar–early Oct.
FACILITIES: 3 lounges, 2 bars, 2 restaurants, conference room, free Wi-Fi, 1-acre garden (tennis, croquet, 7-metre solar-heated swimming pool), beach 200 yds, Herm unsuitable for disabled.
BACKGROUND MUSIC: none.
LOCATION: by harbour, air/sea to Guernsey, then ferry from Guernsey (20 mins).
CHILDREN: all ages welcomed.
DOGS: allowed in 2 bedrooms (£20 per dog per night), reception lounge, garden bar.
CREDIT CARDS: MasterCard, Visa.
PRICES: [2016] per person B&B from £72, D,B&B from £107. Set dinner £33.50. 1-night bookings refused Sat.

ST BRELADE Jersey

Map 1: inset E6

THE ATLANTIC HOTEL

'Just about perfect for a restful break – this is what a good hotel should be,' writes a reader this year of the Burke family's 'wonderfully maintained' luxury hotel on a headland above St Ouen's Bay. Opened in 1970 by Henry Burke, it is today under the stewardship of his son, Patrick. 'The hotel's greatest asset is its staff. They are right there when needed, but discreet when you don't need a fuss.' Bedrooms overlook the ocean or the neighbouring golf course; families might like the ground-floor garden studios, with a private terrace leading to the swimming pool and six acres of grounds. 'Our bedroom was smallish but beautifully appointed and very comfy.' Guests find the library and lounge areas 'so cosy'; the restaurant is 'quite wonderful'. Here, Michelin-starred chef Mark Jordan deploys the best island produce in such 'innovative (but not frightening!)' dishes as Jersey beef tartare, foie gras mousse, oyster ceviche; salad of St Ouen's Bay lobster, mango, lobster tempura, Ebene caviar. Work off the calories at the health club or on the tennis courts. The wildlife site of Les Mielles is nearby. (Peter and Anne Davies)

Le Mont de la Pulente
St Brelade
JE3 8HE

T: 01534 744101
E: patrick@theatlantichotel.com
W: www.theatlantichotel.com

BEDROOMS: 50. Some on ground floor.
OPEN: 5 Feb–2 Jan.
FACILITIES: lift, lounge, library, cocktail bar, restaurant, private dining room, fitness centre (swimming pool, sauna, mini-gym), free Wi-Fi, in-room TV (Sky), civil wedding licence, 6-acre garden (tennis, indoor and outdoor heated swimming pools, 10 by 5 metres), unsuitable for disabled.
BACKGROUND MUSIC: in restaurant, lounge and cocktail bar in evenings.
LOCATION: 5 miles W of St Helier.
CHILDREN: all ages welcomed.
DOGS: not allowed.
CREDIT CARDS: all major cards.
PRICES: [2016] per room B&B £150–£310, D,B&B £250–£410. Set dinner £55, tasting menu £85, à la carte £65.

SEE ALSO SHORTLIST

ST PETER Jersey

Map 1: inset E6

GREENHILLS

NEW

'Charming and elegant', the Seymour family's newly refurbished hotel in a 'lovely rural spot' earns a place in the Guide thanks to trusted readers who enjoyed a 'faultless' stay in 2016. Carmelita Fernandes and Joe Godinho, the managers, are 'much in evidence'; their staff are 'personable and attentive'. Country-style bedrooms, many overlooking the gardens, are supplied with bathrobes and home-made biscuits; ask for a poolside room, with French doors opening on to the pool terrace. 'Our very comfy bed had been made up with sheets and blankets as we'd requested. There was adequate storage space, excellent bedside lighting, a well-lit bathroom with a good-sized walk-in shower and heated towel rails.' On cool days, a log fire burns in the 'pleasant' bar; in the 'attractive' restaurant, chef Lukasz Pietrasz's 'first-class' modern menus showcase seasonal Jersey produce, including Jersey Royal potatoes – buttered, minted, chipped or fried. A network of walker-friendly country lanes surrounds the hotel; set out on a ramble, or simply find a spot in the flower-filled gardens or by the heated pool till teatime beckons. (Annette and Harry Medcalf)

Mont de L'École
St Peter
JE3 7EL

T: 01534 481042
E: reservations@greenhillshotel.
   com
W: www.seymourhotels.com/
   greenhills-hotel

BEDROOMS: 31 bedrooms. 10, on ground floor, suitable for disabled.
OPEN: all year except last Sun before Christmas–mid-Feb.
FACILITIES: 2 lounges, bar, restaurant, garden, terrace (alfresco meals), free Wi-Fi, in-room TV (Sky, Freeview), outdoor heated swimming pool, complimentary access to leisure club at sister hotel, The Merton.
BACKGROUND MUSIC: in public areas.
LOCATION: 8 miles NW of St Helier.
CHILDREN: all ages welcomed.
DOGS: allowed in some bedrooms.
CREDIT CARDS: Diners, MasterCard, Visa.
PRICES: [2016] per room B&B £94–£266. À la carte £40.

ST PETER PORT Guernsey

Map 1: inset E5

LA FRÉGATE

For Victor Hugo in exile, Guernsey was his 'rock of hospitality and freedom'. Guests today feel much the same way about La Frégate. Occupying a comprehensively refurbished 18th-century manor house with a modern extension, the hotel has 'fantastic views' over the town, harbour and Cornet Castle. Simon Dufty, who manages for private owners, has a steady hand on the tiller. From sleek, 'well-equipped' bedrooms, admire the vista across the sea to Sark and Herm; on a clear day, France shrugs on the horizon. 'Our balcony looked towards the neighbouring islands: magical.' Daylight pours into the well-regarded dining room, where chef Neil Maginnis uses plenty of local ingredients, in particular fish and shellfish, in his 'straightforward' menus. 'The food deserves all the accolades it has had.' Opt for Guernsey scallops, cauliflower, pancetta; seared brill fillet, leeks, mussels, beurre noisette. Vegetarians have plenty of imaginative options: smoked cheddar beignets; asparagus, sage and onion rösti. A path winds through terraced gardens to the waterfront; amble down – and puff back up (or take a taxi). Don't miss Hugo's Hauteville House, 'a poem in several rooms'. (JR)

25% DISCOUNT VOUCHERS

Beauregard Lane
Les Cotils
St Peter Port
GY1 1UT

T: 01481 724624
F: 01481 720443
E: enquiries@lafregatehotel.com
W: www.lafregatehotel.com

BEDROOMS: 22.
OPEN: all year.
FACILITIES: lounge/bar, restaurant, private dining/function rooms, free Wi-Fi, in-room TV (Freeview), patio (alfresco dining), ½-acre terraced garden, unsuitable for disabled.
BACKGROUND MUSIC: in bar.
LOCATION: clifftop, 5 mins' walk from centre.
CHILDREN: all ages welcomed.
DOGS: not allowed.
CREDIT CARDS: Amex, MasterCard, Visa.
PRICES: [2016] per room B&B £99.50–£420. Set dinner £28.50–£35, à la carte £47.50.

SEE ALSO SHORTLIST

ST SAVIOUR Jersey

LONGUEVILLE MANOR

Run with 'a personal touch', this 'luxurious', family-friendly hotel (Relais & Châteaux), in an extended 14th-century Norman manor house, has been owned by three generations of the Lewis family. 'The staff are professional and attentive, with plenty of smiles,' says a guest in 2016. Feel the laid-back atmosphere seep in: 'Guests seem to talk to one another more here than they do at other, similar establishments.' Choose among smart bedrooms, some fresh and modern, others more traditionally ornate; some superior rooms have a private patio leading to the garden. All have thoughtful touches: fresh fruit, magazines and board games; posh toiletries and scented candles. 'Our room was lovely, with a large, comfortable sitting area.' Chef Andrew Baird takes his pick of the produce from the hotel's Victorian kitchen garden, as well as from local suppliers; book a table for his 'imaginative' table d'hôte menus, served in the fine Oak Room. Snacks and lighter meals may be taken in the lounges or, in good weather, by the pool. 'Breakfast, from an extensive choice, was very tasty, especially the black pudding.' (Yvette Peart, JR)

Longueville Road
St Saviour
JE2 7WF

T: 01534 725501
F: 01534 731613
E: info@longuevillemanor.com
W: www.longuevillemanor.com

BEDROOMS: 30. 8 on ground floor, 2 in cottage.
OPEN: all year except 2 weeks in Jan.
FACILITIES: lift, 2 lounges, cocktail bar, 2 dining rooms, free Wi-Fi, in-room TV (Sky), function/conference/wedding facilities, spa, 18-acre grounds (croquet, tennis, outdoor heated swimming pool, woodland), sea 1 mile, unsuitable for disabled.
BACKGROUND MUSIC: in bar and restaurant.
LOCATION: 1½ miles E of St Helier.
CHILDREN: all ages welcomed (children's menus, treasure hunts, cookery courses).
DOGS: allowed, not in public rooms.
CREDIT CARDS: all major cards.
PRICES: [2016] per room B&B from £195, D,B&B from £285. Set dinner £45, 'discovery' menu £80, à la carte £60.

SARK

LA SABLONNERIE

'On our umpteenth-plus-one visit, we found it as wonderful as ever,' a devotee writes this year. When Elizabeth Perrée's parents opened their guest house in a 16th-century farmhouse in 1948, it had just three bedrooms. Today, there are 22, some in nearby cottages, all individually styled, with a neat, rustic feel. The low, whitewashed main building is swagged with roses. The 'helpful' staff are 'marvellous'. The whole is a picture of laid-back charm on this rugged, car-free 'paradise' island – 'like stepping back into the past'. There is no TV (though Wi-Fi can be arranged); guests relax in front of the log fire in the beamed lounge or, in good weather, 'on the many seats scattered' in the flower-filled gardens. 'I read lots of books, or write bits of books – which I could never do on a more hectic holiday.' Days are devoted, the hostess confirms, to daydreaming, wandering, exploring. In the restaurant, chef Colin Day's dinners are 'superb'. Guests enjoy classics with a twist, each made with the freshest local produce – meat from the family's farm, crab and lobster landed daily. Vegetarians are happily catered for. (John Barnes)

Little Sark
Sark, via Guernsey
GY10 1SD

T: 01481 832061
F: 01481 832408
E: reservations@sablonneriesark.com
W: www.sablonneriesark.com

BEDROOMS: 22. Some in nearby cottages.
OPEN: mid-Apr–Oct.
FACILITIES: 3 lounges, 2 bars, restaurant, Wi-Fi by arrangement, wedding facilities, 1-acre garden (tea garden/bar, croquet), Sark unsuitable for disabled.
BACKGROUND MUSIC: classical/piano in bar.
LOCATION: S part of island, boat from Guernsey (guests will be met at the harbour on arrival).
CHILDREN: all ages welcomed.
DOGS: allowed at hotel's discretion, but not in public rooms.
CREDIT CARDS: MasterCard, Visa.
PRICES: [2016] per person B&B £40–£115.50, D,B&B £79.50–£147. À la carte £49.50.

IRELAND

St Colman's Cathedral in Cobh, Co. Cork

BAGENALSTOWN Co. Carlow

Map 6:C6

LORUM OLD RECTORY

César award since 2014

There's no place like home – especially if home is Bobbie Smith's 'gracious' guest house, in a peaceful spot in the Barrow river valley. Admirers this year praise the 'attentive' service, 'friendly' atmosphere, 'great' food and 'exemplary comfort'. 'It was flawless.' 'Tastefully decorated', the stone-built 19th-century rectory is filled with fresh flowers, books, paintings, knick-knacks and eclectic personal touches; a grandfather clock ticks quietly in the hallway. Sit by the turf fire in the drawing room: large windows let in the Mount Leinster landscape. Generous bedrooms are individually decorated with antique furniture; some have a four-poster bed, some a fireplace; all have views of countryside and gardens. In the evening, residents meet in the lounge for aperitifs before sitting down to a communal dinner at a mahogany table set with silverware and candles. A member of Euro-Toques, the hostess is dedicated to preserving culinary traditions; her five-course dinners might include pork with Calvados; elderflower sorbet. At breakfast, try the home-baked bread with a full Irish. (Martyn Todd, Fergus Lawson)

Kilgreaney
Bagenalstown

T: 00 353 59 977 5282
E: bobbie@lorum.com
W: www.lorum.com

BEDROOMS: 4.
OPEN: Feb–Nov.
FACILITIES: drawing room, study, dining room, snug, free Wi-Fi, 1-acre garden (croquet) in 18-acre grounds, unsuitable for disabled.
BACKGROUND MUSIC: none.
LOCATION: 4 miles S of Bagenalstown on R705 to Borris.
CHILDREN: by arrangement.
DOGS: by arrangement, not in public rooms.
CREDIT CARDS: MasterCard, Visa.
PRICES: per room B&B €160, D,B&B €260.

BALLINGARRY Co. Limerick

THE MUSTARD SEED AT ECHO LODGE

'I've stayed in glitzier places. I've stayed in grander places. But I've never stayed at a more charming spot,' says a regular Guide reader of this 'lovely' restaurant-with-rooms in a pretty, rural village. A return visit this year found 'the same air of tranquil calm, and the same friendly, attentive service'. Still, there have been changes: John Edward Joyce, the long-serving restaurant manager, is the new owner; former owner Daniel Mullane will make 'occasional appearances', staff say. The 'enjoyable country house-party atmosphere' remains. Choose one of the 'very comfy', individually decorated bedrooms, ; some have views over garden and countryside. At dinner, chef Angel Pirev creates 'well-presented' dishes from local and home-grown produce, perhaps pan-fried trout, blue mussels, horseradish-pickled scallops, compressed cucumber and dill. 'As the bedroom didn't have tea- or coffee-making facilities, we were served tea in the sitting room by a cheerful housekeeper before breakfast.' The morning meal 'is a real treat': home-baked soda bread, stewed garden fruit, eggs from resident hens. (Dr Helena Shaw, Janet and Paul Mills)

Ballingarry

T: 00 353 69 68508
F: 00 353 69 68511
E: mustard@indigo.ie
W: www.mustardseed.ie

BEDROOMS: 16. 1, on ground floor, suitable for disabled.
OPEN: all year except 24–26 Dec.
FACILITIES: 3 public rooms, library, entrance hall, sun room, free Wi-Fi (in public areas, some bedrooms), in-room TV (Freeview), wedding facilities, 12-acre grounds.
BACKGROUND MUSIC: piano on occasion in restaurant.
LOCATION: in village, 18 miles SW of Limerick.
CHILDREN: all ages welcomed.
DOGS: allowed in 1 bedroom, not in public rooms.
CREDIT CARDS: Amex, MasterCard, Visa.
PRICES: [2016] per person B&B from €90, D,B&B from €129. Set menus €46–€60.

BALLYCASTLE Co. Mayo

STELLA MARIS

'I had an excellent stay.' In a 'dramatically beautiful' setting on the Wild Atlantic Way, Frances Kelly-McSweeney's hotel wins praise for its 'comfortable' rooms, its 'local and freshly prepared' meals and its 'cosy' atmosphere. The team of young, local staff is appreciated. 'Frances is permanently in place.' The long, seaward conservatory is an ideal place to sit over drinks or coffee, while gazing out over Bunatrahir Bay. 'There are books scattered around; binoculars available; it is totally tranquil,' writes a guest this year. Bedrooms have antique furniture and original features; most have sea views. In a series of small dining rooms, the tables are set with white linens at dinner. A trained chef, the Ballycastle-born hostess cooks a small, daily-changing menu of modern Irish dishes, perhaps 'moderate' portions of grilled prawns; local cod with a Parmesan crust. At breakfast, find a 'good pick-and-mix' buffet with fresh sliced fruits, porridge, smoked salmon; 'excellent' bacon; 'very good' bread. Enniscrone and Carne golf clubs are 40 minutes' drive away; a number of coastal walks are easily accessible. (Richard Parish)

Ballycastle

T: 00 353 96 43322
F: 00 353 96 43965
E: info@stellamarisireland.com
W: www.stellamarisireland.com

BEDROOMS: 11. 1, on ground floor, suitable for disabled.
OPEN: 28 Apr–9 Oct.
FACILITIES: lounge, bar, restaurant, conservatory, free Wi-Fi ('most dependable in public areas'), in-room TV (Freeview), wedding facilities, 2-acre grounds.
BACKGROUND MUSIC: none.
LOCATION: 1½ miles W of Ballycastle.
CHILDREN: not under 5.
DOGS: not allowed.
CREDIT CARDS: MasterCard, Visa.
PRICES: [2016] per person B&B from €75, D,B&B from €125. À la carte €35.

BALLYLICKEY Co. Cork

Map 6:D4

SEAVIEW HOUSE

Family antiques and fresh flowers create a homely feel of old-world elegance at Kathleen O'Sullivan's traditional hotel overlooking Bantry Bay. The 'vast collection' of ornaments and objets d'art in the spacious public rooms may strike some as old-fashioned, but a 'warm welcome' never goes out of style – admirers praise the restful surroundings and 'admirably efficient' staff. While away an afternoon with a book from the cosy library; take tea in the garden on a fine day; when cool evenings draw in, gather with fellow guests (and a glass of vintage port) by the roaring fire in the lounge. Individually decorated with antiques and fine art, bedrooms vary in size; a suite with a sofa bed can accommodate a family. Choose one with 'distant' views over the sea. Come dinnertime, settle into the restaurant overlooking the garden. Here, the daily-changing menus of 'decent' home cooking might include local specialities like Bantry Bay crab or West Cork lamb. An excellent base to explore the Beara peninsula; the Wild Atlantic Way is easily accessible. More reports, please.

25% DISCOUNT VOUCHERS

Ballylickey

T: 00 353 27 50073
F: 00 353 27 51555
E: info@seaviewhousehotel.com
W: www.seaviewhousehotel.com

BEDROOMS: 25. 2, on ground floor, suitable for disabled.
OPEN: 15 Mar–15 Nov.
FACILITIES: bar, library, 2 lounges, restaurant/conservatory, free Wi-Fi in public rooms, some bedrooms, in-room TV (Ericom), wedding facilities, 4-acre grounds, riding, golf nearby.
BACKGROUND MUSIC: none.
LOCATION: 3 miles N of Bantry and 7 miles SE of Glengarriff on N71.
CHILDREN: all ages welcomed, special menus and babysitting available.
DOGS: not allowed in public rooms.
CREDIT CARDS: MasterCard, Visa.
PRICES: [2016] per person B&B €70–€95, D,B&B €100–€110. Set dinner €35–€45.

BALLYMOTE Co. Sligo

Map 6:B5

TEMPLE HOUSE

A half-mile drive meanders through sheep-grazed parkland towards this Georgian mansion, on a vast estate including ancient woods and a ruined Knights Templar castle overlooking a lake. Within, discover all the trappings of a 'lived-in' ancestral home – portraits, antiques, family memorabilia. There have been Percevals here since 1665; present incumbents Roderick and Helena Perceval welcome guests with 'a warm handshake'. A 'sweeping' staircase leads to bedrooms of a positively stately size; all have a dressing table, large wardrobe, easy chairs, 'lots of prints of country scenes'. Beds are turned down while guests gather for drinks in the mirrored drawing room. Hobnob with fellow visitors at a large mahogany table while eating off 'a traditional dinner service with old silver'; no-choice, 'quality country -house dinners' (dislikes are discussed at booking) might include home-grown vegetables and 'generous portions' of lamb as local as it gets. Breakfast brings 'delicious' stewed fruits, 'excellent' black and white pudding, home-made marmalade. Set off for a stomp around the estate; on wet days, waterproofs and wellingtons are available to borrow.

Ballinacarrow
Ballymote
F56 NN50

T: 00 353 87 997 6045
E: stay@templehouse.ie
W: www.templehouse.ie

BEDROOMS: 6.
OPEN: Apr–mid-Nov.
FACILITIES: drawing room, dining room, table tennis room, free Wi-Fi, wedding facilities, 1½-acre garden, 1,000-acre estate, water sports on site, unsuitable for disabled.
BACKGROUND MUSIC: none.
LOCATION: 12 miles S of Sligo.
CHILDREN: all ages welcomed.
DOGS: not allowed.
CREDIT CARDS: all major credit cards.
PRICES: per room B&B €150–€210. Set dinner €49.

BALLYVAUGHAN Co. Clare

Map 6:C4

GREGANS CASTLE HOTEL   **NEW**

There isn't a castle at this chic country hotel, but the welcome guests receive is nearly royal. Peat fires warm the bar and 'gracious' drawing room; there are antiques, garden flowers, books to borrow, 'gorgeous, squashy' sofas. The house cat adds a sense of 'soothing' domesticity. On the edge of the Burren, with 'splendid' views to Galway Bay, it is 'magical'. Simon Haden was brought up here; today, he runs the 18th-century manor house with his wife, Frederieke McMurray. Pick one of the individually styled bedrooms overlooking garden, bay or mountains (some have a private garden area). Each has been brought up to date with 'voguish' colours and modern artwork. Most evenings, sample chef David Hurley's 'creative' Irish and European dishes, perhaps potato ravioli, bianchetto truffle, Parmesan; dry-aged Wicklow venison, braised shoulder, celeriac, roasted onion. Come breakfast, find a spread of home-baked organic breads and pastries, cheeses and cold meats, home-made jams and marmalades; orders for pancakes, eggs and fish dishes are taken at the table. Hop on one of the hotel bicycles afterwards – rural lanes unfurl all around.

Gragan East
Ballyvaughan
H91 CF60

T: 00 353 65 707 7005
E: stay@gregans.ie
W: www.gregans.ie

BEDROOMS: 21. 7 on ground floor, 1 suitable for disabled.
OPEN: mid-Feb–early Nov, restaurant closed Wed, Sun (except bank holiday weekends).
FACILITIES: drawing room, bar, dining room, free Wi-Fi, 15-acre grounds (ornamental pool, croquet), wedding facilities, safe sandy beach 4½ miles, golf, riding, hill walking nearby.
BACKGROUND MUSIC: all day in bar, during meals in dining room.
LOCATION: 3½ miles SW of Ballyvaughan.
CHILDREN: all ages welcomed, no under-7s in dining room at night.
DOGS: allowed in bedrooms with garden access, not in public rooms.
CREDIT CARDS: all major cards.
PRICES: [2016] per room B&B from €265, D,B&B from €395. Set menu €72.

BANGOR Co. Down

Map 6:B6

CAIRN BAY LODGE

Awake to the sun rising over the Irish Sea at
Chris and Jenny Mullen's carefree B&B, in an
'impressive' Edwardian villa in this seaside
resort town. 'Delightful, attentive' hosts,
the Mullens are well liked for their warmth
and ease with guests of all ages ('our young
daughters were made very welcome'). The
oak-panelled public areas are full of character:
kilim rugs, interesting prints, vintage shop signs,
steamer trunks-turned-coffee tables, plenty of
books and magazines. Take in the 'beautiful
views' from deep armchairs set before huge
windows. In the jaunty ground-floor Starfish
café, mingle with locals who drop in for light
lunches and weekend brunches of sweet corn
fritters, avocado, lime-chilli crème fraîche.
'Beautifully appointed, very comfortable'
bedrooms (a '50s-style lamp here, a collection of
antique mirrors there) have sea or garden views.
'My well-equipped en suite had everything that
might've been forgotten.' In the morning, choose
from a 'varied, imaginative' breakfast menu:
local honey, home-baked bread; Copeland Island
crab, scrambled egg, chilli jam. On the Mourne
Coastal Route; a good base for exploring the
Ards peninsula. More reports, please.

25% DISCOUNT VOUCHERS

278 Seacliff Road
Ballyholme
Bangor
BT20 5HS

T: 028 9146 7636
F: 028 9145 7728
E: info@cairnbaylodge.com
W: www.cairnbaylodge.com

BEDROOMS: 8.
OPEN: all year, café closed Sun, Mon.
FACILITIES: lounge, breakfast room,
café, free Wi-Fi, in-room TV
(Freeview), beauty salon, ¼-acre
garden, unsuitable for disabled.
BACKGROUND MUSIC: 9 am–4 pm
in café.
LOCATION: ¼ mile E of town centre.
CHILDREN: all ages welcomed.
DOGS: not allowed.
CREDIT CARDS: Amex, MasterCard,
Visa.
PRICES: [2016] per person B&B
£40–£50. 1-night bookings refused
weekends June–Sept.

CASTLEHILL Co. Mayo

Map 6:B4

ENNISCOE HOUSE

Find 'an otherworldly air of genteel shabbiness' and 'a somewhat Enid Blyton approach to things' at this 'countryside hideaway', gazing down 'a sweep of fields' to the lakeshore. Said to be the last great house of North Mayo, the faded-pink Georgian mansion is owned by 'accommodating' hostess Susan Kellett and her 'chatty, affable' son, DJ. 'They're genuinely kind people,' say Guide inspectors in 2016, who were plied with 'an excellent tea, with home-made blackcurrant jam, by an earthy fire'. 'Curio upon curio catches the eye in the enormous sitting rooms'; bedrooms are up a grand elliptical staircase. 'Our high-ceilinged Major's Room had wonderfully comfortable beds; lots of seating space; splendid views through huge windows. It was chilly our first night, despite the many heaters; in the glorious bathroom were mislabelled shower taps.' At dinner, Susan Kellett's 'well-cooked kitchen-garden fare' is 'delightfully retro': 'tomato and foraged wild garlic soup; flavoursome stuffed peppers; tasty baked salmon'. 'Breakfast was wonderful: a generous buffet, the best mushrooms I've ever eaten, porridge to die for; even home-baked vegan soda bread, and a jug of almond milk.'

25% DISCOUNT VOUCHERS

Castlehill
F26 EA34

T: 00 353 96 31112
F: 00 353 96 31773
E: mail@enniscoe.com
W: www.enniscoe.com

BEDROOMS: 6. Plus self-catering units behind house.
OPEN: Apr–end Oct, New Year.
FACILITIES: 2 sitting rooms, dining room, free Wi-Fi (in public rooms, some bedrooms), wedding facilities, 160-acre estate (3-acre garden, tea room, farm, heritage centre, conference centre, forge, fishing, woodland walks), unsuitable for disabled.
BACKGROUND MUSIC: none.
LOCATION: 2 miles S of Crossmolina.
CHILDREN: all ages welcomed.
DOGS: allowed in bedrooms, not in public rooms.
CREDIT CARDS: MasterCard, Visa.
PRICES: [2016] per person B&B €80–€120, D,B&B €130–€170. Set menus €45–€50.

CASTLELYONS Co. Cork

Map 6:D5

BALLYVOLANE HOUSE

♛ César award since 2009

There's 'an atmosphere of warm hospitality' and 'a genuine sense of welcome' at Justin and Jenny Green's historic, family-friendly country house in the North Cork countryside, say Guide inspectors in 2016. 'Magnificently furnished with antiques and fine art, the house nevertheless remains a family home (with children's music on the grand piano, for instance).' Treats abound in the characterful bedrooms: magazines, home-made cordial and chocolates, fancy coffee. 'Our spacious room had a large bed, ornate bedside tables, a marble fireplace with an eclectic selection of (mostly Irish) books; the bathroom, with a deep bath approached by mounting steps, was pure class.' The house-party atmosphere, perhaps steeped in glasses of the 'wonderfully fragrant' house gin, Bertha's Revenge, encourages guests to dine communally. 'We summoned up the courage to eat with strangers, and shared a fascinating, totally unpredicted evening of humour and common enthusiasms. The food, meanwhile – crab brûlée; beautifully rare sirloin steaks; lemon meringue pie – was immaculately, informally served.' In the morning, breakfast is 'splendid'.

Castlelyons
P61 FP70

T: 00 353 25 36349
F: 00 353 25 36781
E: info@ballyvolanehouse.ie
W: www.ballyvolanehouse.ie

BEDROOMS: 6. Plus 'glamping' tents May–Sept.
OPEN: all year except Christmas, New Year (self-catering only).
FACILITIES: hall, drawing room, honesty bar, dining room, free Wi-Fi, wedding facilities, 80-acre grounds (15-acre garden, croquet, 3 trout lakes, woodland, fields), unsuitable for disabled.
BACKGROUND MUSIC: none.
LOCATION: 22 miles NE of Cork.
CHILDREN: all ages welcomed (tree house, farm animals, games, high tea).
DOGS: allowed, but kept on lead during shooting season July–Jan.
CREDIT CARDS: MasterCard, Visa.
PRICES: per room B&B from €198, D,B&B from €258. Set dinner €60.

CLIFDEN Co. Galway

Map 6:C4

THE QUAY HOUSE

César award since 2003

'There's no reception as such – just a warm welcome, straight into first names, and an easy smile.' Guide inspectors in 2016 were 'charmed' by the 'generosity of spirit' at this 'well-run' B&B on the harbour's edge. Julia and Paddy Foyle are the 'delightful' hosts; their son, Toby, is 'a thoughtful cook'. The B&B is spread across four houses, including the 19th-century harbour master's house. 'There's a lot to look at': mismatched furnishings, framed pictures, giant mirrors, African hunting trophies, brass Indian lanterns. 'Our spacious triple room, with a large bathroom (and nice smellies), had a splendid outlook over the ever-changing harbour. A squashy sofa, electric fireplace and Juliet balcony made it a lovely place to rest.' Breakfast in the 'bright' conservatory is 'a fantastic start to the day': 'freshly squeezed orange juice, strong coffee, Irish cheeses, a fruit salad with fragrant mint leaves; perfect poached eggs. Toby beautifully rose to the challenge of vegan cooking, with dainty soldiers of sun-dried tomato bread, delicious mushrooms on garlicky wilted spinach.' Ask for 'excellent advice' about the area: 'Julia revolutionised our itinerary.'

Beach Road
Clifden

T: 00 353 95 21369
F: 00 353 95 21608
E: thequay@iol.ie
W: www.thequayhouse.com

BEDROOMS: 16. 3 on ground floor, 1 suitable for disabled, 7 studios (6 with kitchenette) in annexe.
OPEN: end Mar–end Oct.
FACILITIES: 2 sitting rooms, breakfast conservatory, free Wi-Fi, in-room TV (Freeview), small garden, fishing, sailing, golf, riding nearby.
BACKGROUND MUSIC: none.
LOCATION: harbour, 8 mins' walk from centre.
CHILDREN: all ages welcomed.
DOGS: not allowed.
CREDIT CARDS: MasterCard, Visa.
PRICES: [2016] per person B&B single €90–€120, double €70–€80.

CLIFDEN Co. Galway

Map 6:C4

SEA MIST HOUSE

'Warm and hospitable, with a ready laugh',
Sheila Griffin welcomes guests to her
'characterful', 'attractive' B&B in an 'engaging'
town. 'It's like staying with friends,' say Guide
inspectors in 2016, who were greeted by 'gossipy'
chickens, among 'masses of tulips and budding
flowers', in the 'much-loved' garden. The
cherry-red front door opens on to a 'lived-in'
space, with 'a sense of lightness and warmth
throughout': find 'art on the walls, framed old
photographs, collections of crockery, fascinating
books, a lovely reading nook, some quite
dangerous sofas – you sink into them and don't
want to leave'. Traditionally styled bedrooms
are upstairs. 'Ours was large and well lit, with
a compact shower in the clean, well-equipped
bathroom; a window seat overlooked the street
(virtually no noise at night). A large fitted
wardrobe had shelves and fixed hangers; the
supply of lovely biscuits was replenished daily.'
Wake to a 'marvellous' breakfast: an 'enormous'
buffet; 'delicious' cooked dishes (ordered the
night before). 'I'd requested a vegan option, and
got gorgeous potato pancakes with wild garlic
and fat field mushrooms; home-made preserves
accompanied fresh-off-the-griddle fruit scones.'

Seaview
Clifden
H71 NV63

T: 00 353 95 21441
E: sheila@seamisthouse.com
W: www.seamisthouse.com

BEDROOMS: 4.
OPEN: mid-Mar–end Oct.
FACILITIES: 2 sitting rooms,
conservatory dining room, mini-
library, free Wi-Fi, ¾-acre garden,
unsuitable for disabled.
BACKGROUND MUSIC: none.
LOCATION: just down from the main
square, on the edge of town.
CHILDREN: not under 4.
DOGS: not allowed.
CREDIT CARDS: Amex, MasterCard,
Visa.
PRICES: [2016] per person B&B
€40–€60.

CLONES Co. Monaghan

HILTON PARK

'Grand and glorious' Hilton Park is less a hotel than a stately ancestral home where one stays as a cherished guest. 'The Castle', as the antique- and painting-filled 18th-century Italianate mansion is known locally, is today run by ninth-generation Fred and Joanna Madden. Outside, there's fishing, boating, wild swimming, rambling, rounders. Inside, spacious bedrooms, some with floor-to-ceiling windows overlooking parkland, are furnished with family heirlooms. Books are everywhere – 'the accumulation of centuries of reading'. To fully soak in the atmosphere, ask for the bathroom with a freestanding bath overlooking the lake. Come dinnertime, gather with fellow guests around a mahogany table, with one of the family playing host. Fred Madden's four-course menu, supplied with meat and fish from the estate, and the large organic kitchen garden, might include garlic and thyme soufflé; rack of spring lamb, herb crust, quince and mint jelly. (Before a dessert of blackcurrant leaf panna cotta and poached rhubarb, spare a glance at the ornate plaster ceiling, inspired by an ancestor who sailed with Lord Nelson.) 'Simply the best.' More reports, please.

Clones

T: 00 353 47 56007
E: mail@hiltonpark.ie
W: www.hiltonpark.ie

BEDROOMS: 6.
OPEN: Mar–end Nov; groups only at Christmas/New Year.
FACILITIES: 3 drawing rooms, study, breakfast room, dining room, games room, free Wi-Fi (in public areas), wedding facilities, 600-acre grounds (3 lakes for fishing and wild swimming, golf course, croquet), unsuitable for disabled.
BACKGROUND MUSIC: none.
LOCATION: 4 miles S of Clones.
CHILDREN: all ages welcomed.
DOGS: not allowed.
CREDIT CARDS: all major cards.
PRICES: per person B&B from €90, D,B&B from €150. Set dinner €55.

DONEGAL TOWN Co. Donegal

Map 6:B5

ARD NA BREATHA

NEW

Theresa and Albert Morrow run their
'welcoming' traditional guest house on their
working farm, in green countryside between
Lough Eske and Donegal Town. 'Albert really
does farm – one morning he rose at 6 am to
lamb sheep before preparing breakfast – and
Theresa does a good job as front-of-house.' An
unpretentious, good-value spot, it earns a full
entry thanks to a long-time Guide reader, who
recommends it as 'an acceptable mid-way point
between the downmarket town hotels and the
luxury piles on the lough'. The rustic, beamed
restaurant has a snug bar (leather armchairs, a
turf fire); settle into the 'cosy' lounge, with books
and an honesty bar. Simple bedrooms, including
family rooms, are in a converted barn reached
via a covered walkway. 'Some might decry the
pine furniture and fittings as old fashioned,
but we thought our room, with a large bed and
small bathroom, was comfortable and cosy.' At
dinner, tuck in to Albert Morrow's 'satisfactory'
three-course menus, with lamb and vegetables
from the farm. Mornings, a 'fine' breakfast
awaits: 'fresh porridge, fresh berries, not a pre-
pack in sight'. (Esler Crawford)

Drumrooske Middle
Donegal Town

T: 00 353 74 972 2288
F: 00 353 74 974 0720
E: info@ardnabreatha.com
W: www.ardnabreatha.com

BEDROOMS: 6. All in converted barn.
OPEN: mid-Feb–end Oct.
FACILITIES: bar, lounge, restaurant,
free Wi-Fi, in-room TV (Freeview),
1-acre grounds, unsuitable for
disabled.
BACKGROUND MUSIC: in bar and
restaurant during breakfast and
dinner.
LOCATION: 1¼ miles NE of town
centre.
CHILDREN: all ages welcomed.
DOGS: allowed in bedrooms (not
unattended), not in public rooms.
CREDIT CARDS: MasterCard, Visa.
PRICES: per person B&B €35–€59. Set
dinner €39, à la carte €40.

SEE ALSO SHORTLIST

DUNLAVIN Co. Wicklow

Map 6:C6

RATHSALLAGH HOUSE

Come and be spoiled at the O'Flynns' large country house on the Wicklow/Kildare border, where the staff 'make you feel so welcome'. The house, converted from Queen Anne stables in 1798, stands in sweeping parkland with plenty of diversion (tennis in the walled garden, croquet on the front lawn, giant outdoor Jenga, bicycles to borrow, an 18-hole golf course). Inside, relax in a 'low-key' atmosphere, where turf and log fires burn in the traditionally furnished drawing rooms. The bedrooms are 'fabulous', with interesting prints and a seating area; look out for playful accents – dog-print wallpaper, a cheetah-emblazoned bedside lamp. Some spacious bedrooms in the main house have country views. At dinner, Abhishek Tiwari cooks modern Irish fare with international twists, using local produce and garden-fresh vegetables and herbs. Typical dishes: wild Wicklow pheasant and apricot terrine, plum purée chicory; grilled sea bass, bacon orzo-riso, pak choi, samphire. Some think breakfast's 'the best in the country' – load your plate with home-made soda bread, local hams and cheeses, and home-smoked fish, and judge for yourself. Popular for weddings. More reports, please.

25% DISCOUNT VOUCHERS

Dunlavin

T: 00 353 45 403112
F: 00 353 45 403343
E: info@rathsallagh.com
W: www.rathsallagh.com

BEDROOMS: 35. 21 in courtyards, 6 in gate lodges.
OPEN: all year except Christmas, Mon and Tues.
FACILITIES: 2 drawing rooms, bar, dining room, snooker room, free Wi-Fi, in-room TV (Freeview), wedding facilities, beauty therapy rooms, 500-acre grounds (golf course, tennis), 4-acre walled garden.
BACKGROUND MUSIC: none.
LOCATION: 2 miles SW of village.
CHILDREN: not under 6.
DOGS: allowed (in heated kennels), and with evidence of vaccinations.
CREDIT CARDS: all major cards.
PRICES: per room B&B €160–€200. À la carte €45.

GLASLOUGH Co. Monaghan

Map 6:B6

CASTLE LESLIE **NEW**

'I was charmed by its old-world, run-down
eccentricity when I visited some 20 years ago;
in that time, it has positively flourished,' says
a regular Guide correspondent in 2016 of the
Leslie family's history-rich hotel. Positively
sumptuous, too, are the slatherings of castle life:
open fires, gilt-framed portraits, leather-bound
books, a grand piano by huge picture windows,
confoundingly, a bathroom in a larger-than-life
doll's house. 'The staff are polite and attentive;
the entire place smacks of being well run.' The
whole stands in an acres-wide estate of rolling
countryside, ancient woods and lakes. There
are family heirlooms in the rooms; everywhere,
nooks and crannies for Scrabbling, chatting,
partaking of afternoon tea. Individually
designed bedrooms are characterful in the castle;
'smartly designed' and 'well lit' in the stone-built
lodge ('a splendidly labyrinthine Victorian pile');
spacious and ideal for families in the refurbished
mews on the estate. Take your pick of dinner
spots (craic and country dishes in the traditional
pub; modern menus in the restaurant); in the
morning, a 'typical Irish breakfast' has leaf tea,
and 'butter in a proper dish'. (Esler Crawford)

Glaslough

T: 00 353 47 88100
E: info@castleleslie.com
W: www.castleleslie.com

BEDROOMS: 121 bedrooms. 29 in
Lodge (some suitable for disabled),
11 in old stable mews, 12 in cottages
with self-catering facilities.
OPEN: all year except 23–27 Dec.
FACILITIES: drawing rooms, bar,
breakfast room, restaurant,
conservatory, billiard room, library,
cinema, free Wi-Fi, wedding/
conference facilities, spa, 14-acre
gardens in 1,000-acre grounds
(equestrian centre, tennis, walking
trails, wildlife, lakes, boating,
fishing).
BACKGROUND MUSIC: all day in public
areas of Lodge.
LOCATION: 7 miles NE of Monaghan.
CHILDREN: all ages welcomed.
DOGS: allowed on estate, not in
rooms (overnight in stables in
equestrian centre).
CREDIT CARDS: Amex, MasterCard,
Visa.
PRICES: [2016] per person B&B from
€62, D,B&B from €97. 1-night
bookings sometimes refused.

GOREY Co. Wexford

Map 6:D6

MARLFIELD HOUSE

'Ambitious' and 'very stylish', the Bowe family's Regency-style mansion (Relais & Châteaux) stands in extensive, 'well-kept' gardens, its 'inviting' interiors packed with fresh flowers, period paintings and antiques 'to fascinate the eye'. Guide inspectors in 2016 enjoyed a 'guest-centred' experience, with 'friendly, attentive' staff. There's plenty of space in which to lounge: low-slung armchairs sit by a fire; 'a grand piano in the imposing entrance hall adds a sense of style'. Check in to country house-style bedrooms, each with a marble bathroom. 'Our pleasing room, up two flights of stairs, had beautiful orchids, easy chairs, a super-king-size bed with a firm mattress and soft pillows. In the well-lit bathroom: a small bath, a reluctant shower.' Ruadhan Furlong's classic dishes, perhaps 'tender' scallops or 'expertly cooked' steak, are served in the Conservatory restaurant (white linens, Wedgwood china). 'We could've happily eaten our way through the tempting menu over successive nights.' Opt for informal meals in the Duck restaurant overlooking the kitchen garden. Come morning, wake to a 'sumptuous' breakfast with 'fine' leaf tea, then head out on an 'atmospheric' wooded walk in the grounds.

25% DISCOUNT VOUCHERS

Courtown Road R742
Gorey

T: 00 353 53 942 1124
E: info@marlfieldhouse.ie
W: www.marlfieldhouse.com

BEDROOMS: 19. 8 on ground floor.
OPEN: Feb–New Year, Conservatory restaurant closed Mon/Tues, Wed night/Sun night from Feb–mid-May, Oct–Dec, Duck restaurant closed Mon/Tues Jan–Apr, Oct–Dec.
FACILITIES: reception hall, drawing room, library/bar, 2 restaurants, free Wi-Fi, in-room TV (Freeview), wedding facilities, 36-acre grounds (gardens, tennis, croquet, wildfowl reserve, lake), unsuitable for disabled.
BACKGROUND MUSIC: all day in library/bar.
LOCATION: 1 mile E of Gorey.
CHILDREN: no under-8s at dinner (high tea, babysitting).
DOGS: allowed ('always on a lead') by arrangement, not in public rooms.
CREDIT CARDS: all major cards.
PRICES: [2016] per room B&B from €230, D,B&B from €350. Set dinner €42–€64.

KENMARE Co. Kerry

BROOK LANE HOTEL   **NEW**

There's 'a genuine sense of hospitality' at Una
and Dermot Brennan's small hotel, a short walk
from the centre of the pretty heritage town.
'Warm and friendly', it receives a full entry in
the Guide thanks to regular readers who praise
its 'comfortable accommodation' and 'value for
money'. Enter into a 'stylish' spot, all modern
art, mirrors, designer lighting; leather sofas
in alcoves encourage intimate conversation.
Evenings, mingle with locals in the popular
bar before sitting down to dinner in the busy,
informal restaurant. (Sister eatery, No. 35, is
a 15-minute walk away, in town.) Bedrooms
vary in size; a two-bedroom studio suits a
family. 'Our ground-floor room had attractive
armchairs, a super-king-size bed, a table and
an Anglepoise lamp; good bedside reading
lights. The spotless bathroom had wonderful
underfloor heating; double glazing kept traffic
noise to a minimum.' Enjoy a languid wake-
up – with freshly brewed coffee or tea delivered
to the room – then head to an 'immaculately
laid-out' breakfast, where the 'delightful,
articulate' hostess chats with guests. Ask for a
local walking guide – there's much to discover
in town and country. (Robert Gower)

Sneem Road
Kenmare

T: 00 353 64 664 2077
E: info@brooklanehotel.com
W: www.brooklanehotel.com

BEDROOMS: 22. 9 on ground floor,
1 suitable for disabled.
OPEN: all year except 24–26 Dec.
FACILITIES: lift, bar/restaurant,
library, free Wi-Fi, in-room TV,
wedding facilities.
BACKGROUND MUSIC: all day in public
areas.
LOCATION: 5-min. walk from town
centre.
CHILDREN: all ages welcomed.
DOGS: not allowed.
CREDIT CARDS: Diners, MasterCard,
Visa.
PRICES: per room B&B from €99,
D,B&B from €134. Set menus from
€35, à la carte €28.

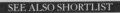

SEE ALSO SHORTLIST

LETTERFRACK Co. Galway

Map 6:C4

ROSLEAGUE MANOR

♔César award since 2010

'Mark Foyle, the owner, has seemingly endless enthusiasm for the Rosleague project. The energy he brings to it helps make it a very special place,' say regular Guide correspondents this year, of this pink-washed Regency manor house on the shores of Ballinakill Bay. With open fires, historical paintings and 'uniformly pleasant' staff, the hotel has a 'relaxed', old-world atmosphere. 'It somehow adapts to the mood of its guests: you can usually find convivial company if you want it, but you can sit quietly by a log and turf fire if you prefer.' Spacious bedrooms and suites are decorated in traditional country-house style, many with antiques; all have views of lough, gardens or forest. In the dining room, chef Emmanuel Neu cooks with home-grown produce and locally sourced ingredients – Cleggan Bay crab, line-caught mackerel, Leenane mountain lamb. Seafood, particularly, is praised. 'We had perfect plump scallops with cherry tomatoes and asparagus, hake with butter and capers, halibut with celeriac purée.' Breakfast on 'devilled kidneys and fresh fish alongside more conventional cooked dishes'. (Andrew Wardrop)

Letterfrack

T: 00 353 95 41101
F: 00 353 95 41168
E: info@rosleague.com
W: www.rosleague.com

BEDROOMS: 21. 2 on ground floor.
OPEN: mid-Mar–mid-Nov.
FACILITIES: 2 drawing rooms, conservatory/bar, dining room, free Wi-Fi, in-room TV (Freeview), wedding facilities, 25-acre grounds (tennis), unsuitable for disabled.
BACKGROUND MUSIC: none.
LOCATION: 7 miles NE of Clifden.
CHILDREN: all ages welcomed.
DOGS: 'well-behaved dogs' allowed.
CREDIT CARDS: MasterCard, Visa.
PRICES: [2016] per person B&B €75–€115, D,B&B €95–€145. Set dinner €36–€50. 1-night bookings sometimes refused.

LIMERICK Co. Limerick

NO. 1 PERY SQUARE

A fire burns in the marble fireplace, while candles flicker beside 'attractive' collections of books in Patricia Roberts's Georgian town house hotel overlooking the People's Park. Guide inspectors in 2016 received 'a cheerful greeting'. Gilt mirrors and 'a variety of art' hang on the walls; in the Park Room bar, sample light bites and a gin-and-tonic menu. Sash, the upstairs restaurant, is 'a very pleasant environment in which we enjoyed watching the world below pass by'. Fred Duarte cooks traditional dishes with a twist, perhaps 'tasty' sage, apple and hazelnut soup; sautéed chicken, lavender- and honey-roasted carrots. At bedtime, lay your head in one of the four 'elegant, spacious' period rooms (two overlook the square), with 'opulent' furnishings and fine original features – it's these, not the more ordinary Club Rooms ('rather small, needing better lighting; slippers and bathrobes provided') that 'lift the place'. At breakfast: home-made granola, freshly squeezed orange juice 'from tart oranges', 'unexceptional' scrambled eggs. Not quite ready for the bustling city? Book an organic treatment or Irish seaweed bath in the vaulted basement spa.

Georgian Quarter
1 Pery Square
Limerick

T: 00 353 61 402402
F: 00 353 61 313060
E: info@oneperysquare.com
W: www.oneperysquare.com

BEDROOMS: 20. 2 suitable for disabled.
OPEN: all year.
FACILITIES: lift, lounge, drawing room, restaurant, private dining room, free Wi-Fi, in-room TV (Freeview), wedding facilities, terrace, basement spa, deli/wine shop.
BACKGROUND MUSIC: in restaurant and lounge.
LOCATION: central.
CHILDREN: all ages welcomed.
DOGS: not allowed.
CREDIT CARDS: Amex, MasterCard, Visa.
PRICES: per room B&B from €195, D,B&B from €295. Set dinner €25–€29, à la carte €45.

LISDOONVARNA Co. Clare

Map 6:C4

SHEEDY'S

Guests arrive to tea, home-made biscuits and 'a warm welcome' at this 'excellent' family-run 18th-century country house near the Burren, where John and Martina Sheedy combine fine cooking (him) and a charming efficiency (her) to create their characterful retreat. Check in to one of the 'spacious', elegant bedrooms, each stocked with cookies, up-to-date magazines, bathrobes and slippers; for extra space, choose a junior suite with a large seating area. 'A feeling of well-being descends as you sit in the conservatory with a pre-dinner drink.' In the jaunty, tartan-floored restaurant, John Sheedy's 'formidable', French-inspired dishes – perhaps warm tart of St Tola goat's cheese, caramelised onions, figs – use herbs and vegetables from the hotel's garden, along with 'quality' ingredients from local farmers, fishermen, crofters and foragers. Informal meals, Irish whiskies and craft beers may be taken by the fire in the 'cosy', rustic bar. In the morning, wake to leaf teas and filter coffee; home-made jams, marmalades and breads; organic porridge served with Baileys. Tuck in, then ask the hosts for a map and head out into the dramatic scenery that surrounds. (AW)

Lisdoonvarna

T: 00 353 65 707 4026
F: 00 353 65 707 4555
E: info@sheedys.com
w: www.sheedys.com

BEDROOMS: 11. Some on ground floor, 1 suitable for disabled.
OPEN: Mar–Sept, closed 1 day a week in Apr.
FACILITIES: sitting room/library, sun lounge, bar, restaurant, free Wi-Fi, in-room TV (Freeview), ½-acre garden (rose garden).
BACKGROUND MUSIC: 'easy listening' at breakfast, light jazz at dinner.
LOCATION: 20 miles SW of Galway.
CHILDREN: not under 12.
DOGS: not allowed.
CREDIT CARDS: MasterCard, Visa.
PRICES: [2016] per room B&B €120–€180, D,B&B €220–€280. À la carte €47.

LONGFORD Co. Longford

VIEWMOUNT HOUSE

There's a quiet charm to Beryl and James
Kearney's 'extremely comfortable and well-
appointed' hotel, in a Georgian mansion on
the outskirts of town. Find original features,
period furniture, paintings and objets d'art
throughout. The vaulted sitting room was
once the kitchen (spot the old service bells);
the library has an open fire, old books, new
magazines. Past residents, the Barons Longford
family among them, are remembered in the
names of the elegant bedrooms. All have garden
views; there are feathered duvets, fresh flowers,
bottled water, handmade Irish toiletries; a fine
suite has an open fireplace with a mantel clock
and ornaments. The smart VM restaurant, in
converted stables, is 'rightly packed with locals
– it's clearly the place to go for a celebration'.
Here, chef Gary O'Hanlon serves seasonally
changing menus of 'superb' classic dishes with
a modern twist, perhaps braised lamb shank,
root vegetables espagnole, gremolata; pan-fried
Tory Island hake, beetroot and mushroom
ragout, roast pepper gel. At breakfast, sit down
to freshly squeezed orange juice, pancakes with
maple syrup, hot-smoked salmon, 'the freshest
eggs'. (M and RMD)

25% DISCOUNT VOUCHERS

Dublin Road
Longford

T: 00 353 43 334 1919
E: viewmt@iol.ie
W: www.viewmounthouse.com

BEDROOMS: 12. 7 in modern
extension, some on ground floor.
OPEN: all year except 29 Oct–8 Nov,
restaurant closed Mon, Tues, 25–27
Dec.
FACILITIES: reception room, library,
sitting room, breakfast room,
restaurant, free Wi-Fi, in-room TV,
wedding facilities, 4-acre grounds.
BACKGROUND MUSIC: none.
LOCATION: 1 mile E of town centre.
CHILDREN: all ages welcomed.
DOGS: not allowed.
CREDIT CARDS: Amex, MasterCard,
Visa.
PRICES: [2016] per person €70–€85,
D,B&B from €130. Set dinner €60
(early bird €35).

MAGHERALIN Co. Armagh

Map 6:B6

NEWFORGE HOUSE

César award since 2015

'Excellent in every way', John and Louise Mathers's 'gracious', traditionally decorated guest house has 'star quality', says a trusted Guide reader in 2016. The creeper-covered Georgian home has been in the Mathers family for six generations; today, after much sensitive restoration, its rooms are filled with tapestries, paintings, photographs and antiques. Arrive to home-made biscuits and freshly brewed tea or coffee in the drawing room; upstairs, step into an attractive bedroom overlooking the mature gardens. 'My room was elegantly furnished with a Victorian dressing table and a recently upholstered bucket-style chair and chaise longue; the bathroom was spotless.' Up-to-date technology and high-end toiletries are standard. Reserve a space for the host's 'delicious' three-course dinner, served Tuesday to Sunday at 8 pm. (Light meals of home-made soup and sandwiches are available the rest of the week.) Breakfast is 'superb': chilled, freshly squeezed orange juice, 'wonderfully yellow and sloppy' scrambled eggs, 'first-rate' spicy black pudding, toast from a home-baked loaf. (Robert Gower)

25% DISCOUNT VOUCHERS

58 Newforge Road
Magheralin
BT67 0QL

T: 028 9261 1555
E: enquiries@newforgehouse.com
W: www.newforgehouse.com

BEDROOMS: 6.
OPEN: Feb–Dec.
FACILITIES: drawing room, dining room, free Wi-Fi, in-room TV (Freeview), wedding facilities, 2-acre gardens (vegetable garden, wild flower meadow, orchard, woodland) in 50 acres of pastureland, unsuitable for disabled.
BACKGROUND MUSIC: in dining room.
LOCATION: edge of village, 20 miles SW of Belfast.
CHILDREN: under-1s and over-10s welcomed.
DOGS: not allowed.
CREDIT CARDS: Diners, MasterCard, Visa.
PRICES: [2016] per room B&B from £125, D,B&B from £205. À la carte £40.

MOUNTRATH Co. Laois

Map 6:C5

ROUNDWOOD HOUSE

Arrive to tea and home-made biscuits at Paddy and Hannah Flynn's family-friendly Georgian country house in parkland below the Slieve Bloom mountains. 'Lovely people', the hosts encourage an informal, house-party atmosphere in their handsomely lived-in family home, all heaving bookshelves, paintings, log fires and antique furnishings. Choose one of the eclectically furnished bedrooms: large rooms in the main house overlook the lawns and courtyards (look out for the tufted ducks); those in the Yellow House peer over the walled garden. All are cosy, with an electric blanket on the bed. Book ahead for a spot at Paddy Flynn's communal dinner, so the shopping – for super-fresh, super-local ingredients – can be done in time; dietary needs can be discussed but, in dinner-party style, 'we decide what you'll be having', the Flynns say. (Prefer to eat privately? Ask for the single table by the blazing fire in the study.) In the morning, breakfast on fruit compotes and slices of home-baked bread; griddle scones and a full Irish are hearty options. More reports, please.

Mountrath
R32 TK79

T: 00 353 57 873 2120
E: info@roundwoodhouse.com
W: www.roundwoodhouse.com

BEDROOMS: 10. 4 in garden building.
OPEN: all year except Christmas.
FACILITIES: drawing room, study/library, dining room, playroom, table tennis room, free Wi-Fi, wedding facilities, 18-acre grounds (garden, woodland), golf, walking, river fishing nearby, unsuitable for disabled.
BACKGROUND MUSIC: none.
LOCATION: 3 miles N of village.
CHILDREN: all ages welcomed.
DOGS: not allowed.
CREDIT CARDS: all major cards.
PRICES: [2016] per room B&B €95–€150. Supper (soup, cheese, dessert) €25, three-course set dinner €40 (Sun–Thurs), five-course set dinner €55 (all week).

MULTYFARNHAM Co. Westmeath

Map 6:C5

MORNINGTON HOUSE

'Gracious and enjoyable' hosts Anne and
Warwick O'Hara have long welcomed guests
to their 18th-century country house with tea
and home-baked cakes or biscuits. (The host's
home-made blueberry pancakes at breakfast are
a great draw, too.) The house has remained in
the family for more than 150 years; it retains a
gently old-fashioned charm, with its open fires,
antique furnishings, oriental rugs, paintings and
family photographs. Ask to play the grand piano
in the drawing room wallpapered in gold. At
night, candles are lit in the atmospheric dining
room, where Anne O'Hara's home-cooked
meals are communally served around the large
oak table. The hostess, a keen gardener, liberally
uses produce from the large walled garden and
greenhouse in her Irish dishes, perhaps carrot
and orange soup; herbed chicken, broccoli,
mashed potatoes. Spend the night in one of the
'comfortable', traditionally styled bedrooms –
most are 'spacious', with views over the gardens
and grounds. In the morning, enjoy a hearty
breakfast before striking out to explore. There
are resident donkeys and chickens to visit;
a path through the meadow leads to Lough
Derravaragh.

25% DISCOUNT VOUCHERS

Multyfarnham
N91 NX92

T: 00 353 44 937 2191
F: 00 353 44 937 2338
E: stay@mornington.ie
W: www.mornington.ie

BEDROOMS: 4.
OPEN: Apr–end Oct.
FACILITIES: drawing room, dining
room, free Wi-Fi in reception,
wedding facilities, 50-acre grounds
(¾-acre garden, croquet, bicycle
hire), unsuitable for disabled.
BACKGROUND MUSIC: none.
LOCATION: 9 miles NW of
Mullingar.
CHILDREN: all ages welcomed.
DOGS: not allowed in house.
CREDIT CARDS: all major cards.
PRICES: [2016] per person B&B
(double occupancy) €75, D,B&B
€120. Set dinner €45.

OUGHTERARD Co. Galway

Map 6:C4

CURRAREVAGH HOUSE

♔César award since 1992

Surely Ireland's oldest hotel in continuous family ownership, Henry and Lucy Hodgson's Victorian country house on the shores of Lough Corrib was taking paying guests as a sporting lodge in 1890. Not that it hasn't been updated since – 'several licks of paint have sharpened up the decor', writes one devotee on an annual visit this year. The manor house remains old-fashioned in the best sense, with antiques, button-back armchairs, fringed lamps, 'friendly and long-lasting staff' and 'contented guests – some nearly as long-lasting'. Bedrooms are spacious, with views of lough or mountains (who needs TV?). Henry Hodgson is an 'attentive', wryly amusing host; Lucy Hodgson cooks daily-changing, no-choice dinner menus. Guests, summoned by the gong, might find seared Corrib trout, rump of Connemara lamb, with inventive twists (here nori, there wood sorrel or redcurrant jus). Afternoon tea and an Edwardian-style breakfast with a 'frequently replenished buffet' contribute to a house-party atmosphere. Sausages are local, orange juice is freshly squeezed, soda bread is home baked. (Richard Parish)

Oughterard

T: 00 353 91 552312
F: 00 353 91 552731
E: mail@currarevagh.com
W: www.currarevagh.com

BEDROOMS: 12.
OPEN: 1 Apr–31 Oct.
FACILITIES: sitting room/hall, drawing room, library/bar with TV, dining room, free Wi-Fi, 180-acre grounds (lake, fishing, ghillies available, boating, swimming, tennis, croquet), golf, riding nearby, unsuitable for disabled.
BACKGROUND MUSIC: none.
LOCATION: 4 miles NW of Oughterard.
CHILDREN: all ages welcomed.
DOGS: allowed in 1 bedroom, not in public rooms.
CREDIT CARDS: all major cards.
PRICES: per person B&B €75–€90, D,B&B €110–€135. Set dinner €50.

RATHMULLAN Co. Donegal

Map 6:B5

RATHMULLAN HOUSE

Built as a summer retreat in 1820, this country house on the wooded shores of Lough Swilly has come up in the world since its 1940s hostel days of shared dormitories, sing-songs and potted-meat sandwiches. Today, Mark and Mary Wheeler run the fine hotel, the second generation of Wheelers to do so since 1962. There is plenty of space to sit in the series of lough-facing lounges (original ceiling mouldings, comfortable seating); pick a book from the library to read by the blazing turf fires. Individually decorated bedrooms are liberally furnished with antiques – the best, overlooking the lough or the gardens, have a balcony or patio. Travelling with little ones? Two-bedroom interconnecting suites, with a shared family bathroom, have enough space for six. Informal pizza dinners, washed down with Irish craft beers, are taken in the cellar Tap Room. 'Local produce is much in evidence' in the restaurant; try pan-seared Mulroy Bay scallops, garden artichoke, black pudding croquettes; roasted Greencastle-landed black sole, cured cucumber, confit potato. Afterwards, walk it all off with a woodland stroll that brings you to the sandy beach.

Rathmullan

T: 00 353 74 915 8188
F: 00 353 74 915 8200
E: info@rathmullanhouse.com
W: www.rathmullanhouse.com

BEDROOMS: 34. Some on ground floor, 1 suitable for disabled.
OPEN: Feb–Dec, 27 Dec–3 Jan.
FACILITIES: 4 sitting rooms, library, TV room, cellar bar/pizza parlour, restaurant, free Wi-Fi, in-room TV (Freeview), wedding facilities, 15-metre indoor swimming pool, 7-acre grounds (tennis, croquet).
BACKGROUND MUSIC: none.
LOCATION: ½ mile N of village.
CHILDREN: all ages welcomed.
DOGS: allowed in 1 bedroom, not in public rooms.
CREDIT CARDS: Amex, MasterCard, Visa.
PRICES: [2016] per person B&B €95–€175. À la carte €50. 1-night bookings sometimes refused.

RIVERSTOWN Co. Sligo

Map 6:B5

COOPERSHILL

♥César award since 1987

In a vast swathe of woodland and deer pastures, the 'easy grandeur and graciousness' of the O'Hara family's Georgian mansion is unmistakable. 'Helpful, welcoming' hosts Simon and Christina O'Hara are the seventh generation of the family to occupy the stately home. 'We like guests to feel they're visiting old friends who happen to have a country house,' they say, and guests reciprocate: 'conversations flow easily' between visitors. Log fires burn in the drawing room and dining room; original paintings and antiques abound. The traditionally furnished bedrooms bask in period elegance – two Georgian four-poster beds in the original master bedroom; a Victorian roll-top tub in the Yellow Room bathroom. Eat well in the dining room, where 'O'Hara ancestors look down from their portraits'. Christina O'Hara (regular guests will remember her as Chef McCauley) cooks home-grown feasts, perhaps including Coopershill venison medallions, juniper sauce. Breakfast has much choice: home-made bread and jams; a full Irish in any combination. Stroll about the estate, afterwards, crossing meadowland and river. (CG)

25% DISCOUNT VOUCHERS

Riverstown

T: 00 353 71 916 5108
E: reservations@coopershill.com
W: www.coopershill.com

BEDROOMS: 7.
OPEN: Apr–Oct, off-season house parties by arrangement.
FACILITIES: front hall, drawing room, dining room, snooker room, free Wi-Fi, wedding facilities, 500-acre estate (garden, tennis, croquet, woods, farmland, river with trout fishing), unsuitable for disabled.
BACKGROUND MUSIC: none.
LOCATION: 11 miles SE of Sligo.
CHILDREN: all ages welcomed.
DOGS: 'well-behaved' dogs allowed, not in public rooms.
CREDIT CARDS: MasterCard, Visa.
PRICES: per room B&B from €109, D,B&B from €163. Set dinner €54.

SHANAGARRY Co. Cork

Map 6:D5

BALLYMALOE HOUSE

César award since 1984

'Still the same little earthly paradise.' With 'outstanding' meals, 'comforting' log fires and 'effortless, round-the-clock attentiveness' from 'helpful' staff, this 'timeless' hotel provides an experience of 'top-quality hospitality'. 'It sets the bar high,' say Guide inspectors in 2016. Myrtle Allen's enterprise began as a modest restaurant in 1964; today it includes a cookery school, farm shop, music venue and much else. The founder, now in her 90s, is still a presence; daughter-in-law Hazel is manager. Pretty bedrooms vary in size and aspect. 'Our spacious room overlooking the garden had a king-size bed with luxurious sheets and a good, supportive mattress; a modern bathroom.' In the 'welcoming' restaurant, savour Gillian Hegarty's 'imaginative, yet unpretentious' cooking. 'Beautifully cooked loin of venison came with pouring jugs of horseradish and redcurrant sauces; savoury lentils accompanied a flavoursome duck.' Breakfast – 'probably the best I have enjoyed' – is a cheering event, with 'molten scrambled eggs, tender bacon, subtly spiced black and white pudding'. (Helge Rubinstein, Richard Parish, and others)

Shanagarry

T: 00 353 21 465 2531
F: 00 353 21 465 2021
E: res@ballymaloe.ie
W: www.ballymaloe.ie

BEDROOMS: 29. 9 in adjacent building, 4 on ground floor, 5 self-catering cottages suitable for disabled.
OPEN: all year, except Christmas Day.
FACILITIES: drawing room, 2 small sitting rooms, conservatory, 7 dining rooms, free Wi-Fi, wedding and conference facilities, 6-acre gardens, 300-acre farm, tennis, swimming pool (10 by 4 metres), cookery school nearby.
BACKGROUND MUSIC: none.
LOCATION: 20 miles E of Cork.
CHILDREN: all ages welcomed.
DOGS: allowed in 3 rooms with porch, not in public rooms.
CREDIT CARDS: Amex, MasterCard, Visa.
PRICES: [2016] per person B&B €100–€150. Set dinner €70–€75.

THURLES Co. Tipperary

Map 6:C5

INCH HOUSE

Trees grew out of the ground-floor windows of this 'imposing' Georgian mansion when John and Nora Egan rescued it from dereliction more than 30 years ago. Today, at the heart of a working cereals farm, the house, all polished wooden floors and 'a comfortable clutter everywhere', welcomes guests who come for the warm hospitality and the 'hearty' dinners. Mairin Byrne (daughter and manager) greets guests with 'charming efficiency' and an offer of tea and home-made cake. Up the 'magnificent' divided staircase, step into traditionally decorated bedrooms, each different from the other: find an antique half-tester bed in one, 'surprising' window seats in another. Follow local diners into the mullion-windowed restaurant, where chef John Barry's four-course menu emphasises 'country cooking'. Much produce comes from the farm or surrounds, in such dishes as honey-roasted confit of Irish duck leg, braised red cabbage, home-grown potatoes. Breakfast is 'excellent': 'lots of fruits, delicious freshly stewed rhubarb, porridge with a pot of honey, home-made bread and jam'. Walk it all off with a traipse through the grounds – the Egans' son, Joseph, has fashioned a trail. (EC)

Bouladuff
Nenagh Road
Thurles

T: 00 353 504 51348
E: info@inchhouse.ie
W: www.inchhouse.ie

BEDROOMS: 5.
OPEN: all year except Christmas, New Year and Easter, dining room closed Sun and Mon night.
FACILITIES: drawing room, restaurant, free Wi-Fi, in-room TV (Freeview), wedding facilities, 4-acre garden in 250-acre farm, unsuitable for disabled.
BACKGROUND MUSIC: Irish in evening in dining room.
LOCATION: 4 miles NW of Thurles on R498 to Nenagh.
CHILDREN: all ages welcomed.
DOGS: not allowed.
CREDIT CARDS: MasterCard, Visa.
PRICES: [2016] per room €120, D,B&B €170. À la carte €45.

SHORTLIST

The Shortlist complements our main section by including potential but untested new entries and appropriate places in areas where we have limited choice. It also has some hotels that have had a full entry in the Guide, but have not attracted feedback from our readers.

The Post House, Chewton Mendip

LONDON

Map 2:D4

THE ALMA, 499 Old York Road, Wandsworth, SW18 1TF. Tel 020 8870 2537, www.almawandsworth.com. Bedecked in classic Victorian brick and tile, this popular local pub (Young & Co's Brewery) is an unpretentious spot in south London. Andrew Taylor is the manager. Spacious accommodation is in a quiet coaching-house courtyard. Here, find stylish rooms with bespoke furnishings and state-of-the-art, environmentally friendly gadgetry (sensor-controlled air conditioning, a green key-card system). Looking for more room to spread out? Book the garden suite, with a private terrace and outdoor seating. Come dinnertime, settle in to the light, modern dining room at the back of the buzzy bar – local brews and gastropub classics are menu standards. Sleep in: breakfast is served till 11 am on weekends. Bar, restaurant (Sunday roasts). Free Wi-Fi, in-room TV (Freeview). Background music. Civil wedding licence. Function room. Complimentary use of Virgin spa and gym nearby. Children welcomed (cots, extra bed £15 per night). 23 bedrooms (2 on ground floor suitable for disabled). Per room B&B from £119. Dinner from £35. (Opposite Wandsworth Town railway station; 15 mins to Waterloo)

THE AMPERSAND, 10 Harrington Road, South Kensington, SW7 3ER. Tel 020 7589 5895, www.ampersandhotel.com. Museum hopper? Serious shopper? Material and educational riches of all kinds are easily reached from this eclectic, 'laid-back' South Kensington hotel. Its refreshing modern design was inspired by neighbouring museums and other Victorian landmarks; the rooms and suites are designated according to themes of astronomy, music, botany, ornithology and geometry. High-ceilinged bedrooms (some small; 16 allow smoking) have velvet fabrics, bright colours, an oversized bedhead; free soft drinks in the minibar. Sample cocktails and a modern Mediterranean menu in the basement restaurant, Apero, under the cellar arches; take light meals and afternoon tea in the drawing rooms. Bar, drawing rooms, restaurant, private dining room. Lifts. Business centre. Games room (table tennis). Gym. Free Wi-Fi, in-room TV. Contemporary background music. Guides and information on activities in Hyde Park (horse riding, inline skating) available. Public parking nearby (reservation required). Children (cots) and dogs welcomed. 111 bedrooms and suites (some suitable for disabled). Room from £170. À la carte breakfast £14. Dinner £32. (Underground: South Kensington)

THE ARCH LONDON, 50 Great Cumberland Place, Marble Arch, W1H 7FD. Tel 020 7724 4700, www.thearchlondon.com. The 'unfailingly helpful' staff and 'well-thought-through details' stand out at the Bejerano family's colourful modern hotel near Marble Arch. It has an 'intimate feel, despite its size' (it occupies seven Georgian town houses and two mews homes). The stylish, 'comprehensively equipped' bedrooms blend original features, fun textures, bold prints and the latest technology, while new British artwork hangs on the walls. In the 'excellent' Hunter 486 restaurant, chef Gary Durrant has developed a 'comprehensive' modern British menu inspired by the diversity of London's street food. 'We received superb service and splendid food every evening.' Enjoy an aperitif in the opulent martini 'library', or some afternoon fizz in the champagne lounge. Bar, brasserie, library (afternoon tea, cocktails), champagne salon. Gym. Free Wi-Fi, in-room TV (Sky). Background music. Valet parking. Children and dogs welcomed. 82 bedrooms (2 suitable for disabled). Room from £275. Breakfast £19–£24. Two-course dinner £19, three-course dinner £21. (Underground: Marble Arch)

BATTY LANGLEY'S, 12 Folgate Street, Spitalfields, E1 6BX. Tel 020 7377 4390, www.battylangleys.com. A Georgian extravaganza on a quiet cobbled street, Peter McKay and Douglas Blain's plush Spitalfields hotel (see also The Rookery and Hazlitt's, main entries) teems with sumptuous decoration and amusing eccentricities. It occupies two lovingly restored buildings dating from 1724, both now filled with rich fabrics, wood panelling, old portraits and polished antique furniture. (Even the bathrooms are decadent, with a copper shower screen here or a swan-shaped fixture there.) Sink into one of the inviting sofas in the well-stocked library; the Tapestry Room has an honesty bar and access to a small courtyard. Later, dream on a carved oak bed or a four-poster in one of the grandiose bedrooms. In the morning, sustenance is sweet: tea trays with yogurt, fruit and granola, fresh pastries and bagels are delivered to the room for breakfast. Library, tapestry

room. Meeting rooms. Lift. Free Wi-Fi, in-room TV. No background music. 29 bedrooms (1 suitable for disabled). Room from £330. Breakfast £11.95.

BERMONDSEY SQUARE HOTEL, Bermondsey Square, Tower Bridge Road, Bermondsey, SE1 3UN. Tel 020 7378 2450, www. bermondseysquarehotel.co.uk. In the shadow of the Shard, this modern, privately owned Bermondsey hotel is a few minutes' walk from a branch of the White Cube gallery, the Monmouth coffee roastery and an independent cinema (across the square). 'Reasonably sized' bedrooms have a wet room and a 'comfortable' bed 'with plenty of pillows and cushions'. Play a game of air hockey while the kitchen whips up 'very good, uncomplicated' British dishes in the all-day GB Grill & Bar; dine alfresco in fine weather. The continental breakfast has 'reasonable' coffee, a 'good' fruit salad. No alcohol is served, but guests may bring their own tipple for in-room drinking. Restaurant. Business functions. Lift. Free Wi-Fi, in-room TV. Background music. In-house tailor service. Children and dogs welcomed (boutique dog beds). 80 bedrooms (5 suites; family rooms; 4 suitable for disabled). Per room B&B from £99. Continental breakfast £9.95. (Underground: Bermondsey, Tower Hill)

THE BULL & THE HIDE, 4 Devonshire Row, Bishopsgate, EC2M 4RH. Tel 020 7655 4805, www.thebullandthehide. com. Check in with a pint at the copper-fronted bar in the lively ground-floor pub of this refurbished modern inn in the Square Mile. Standing on

Tudor foundations, it has served the neighbourhood as a tavern since the 1680s. It is now part of Richard Balfour-Lynn's Cunning Plan Pub Company. Seven crisply styled bedrooms on the upper floor have interesting textures and finishes; underfloor heating in the bathroom. Complimentary coffee and tea are in the well-stocked pantry. Tuck in to classic pub grub, served all day, in the bar; in the elegant Hide restaurant, try chef Kalifa Diakhaby's refined modern dishes – perhaps accompanied by a glass of wine from the owner's Hush Heath winery in Kent. Breakfast in the pub includes light bites and a wide selection of butties. The road is pedestrianised, but there may be some early-morning street noise as the City starts its day. Bar, restaurant (closed Sat lunch, Sun). Private dining. Free Wi-Fi and local telephone calls, in-room TV (Sky). Background music. 7 bedrooms. Room from £125. Breakfast £7.95. Dinner £38. Closed Christmas. (Underground: Liverpool Street)

CHARLOTTE STREET HOTEL, 15–17 Charlotte Street, Bloomsbury, W1T 1RJ. Tel 020 7806 2000, www. firmdalehotels.com. Spirited colours, sunny prints and fabrics, and a trove of Bloomsbury artists' original works set the scene at this exuberant Fitzrovia hotel (part of Tim and Kit Kemp's Firmdale Hotels group). Nick Hamdy is the manager. Choose among cheerful bedrooms varying in size – several can be connected to accommodate a family or group. Children aren't forgotten: they'll have a welcome gift, a mini-bathrobe, milk and cookies at bedtime; books, board games and DVDs are available to borrow. An all-day menu

is served in the 'bright' restaurant by 'attentive, pleasant and helpful' staff; a room-service selection is available. Sunday evenings, see what's showing in the small private cinema. Well located for Soho, the British Museum and West End theatres. Drawing room, library, Oscar bar, restaurant. Private dining/meeting rooms; 75-seat screening room; gym. Free Wi-Fi, in-room TV. No background music. Civil wedding licence. Children (cot, high chair, special cutlery, babysitting) and small dogs (by arrangement) welcomed. 52 bedrooms (family rooms; some rooms suitable for disabled). Room from £294. Breakfast £14–£26. Dinner £25–£34. (Underground: Goodge Street, Tottenham Court Road)

CITIZENM, 20 Lavington Street, Southwark, SE1 0NZ. Tel 020 3519 1680, www.citizenm.com. Style and budget friendly, this 'impressive' contemporary hotel, a branch of an international chain catering to 'mobile citizens', is 'excellent value for money'. It's conveniently located between Tate Modern and Borough Market, with easy links to the City. Self-service is standard – check yourself in and head straight to your room – though 'friendly and helpful' staff members are never far away. In the 'spotlessly clean' modular bedrooms, a large bed stands against a floor-to-ceiling window; a touch-screen tablet controls lighting, room temperature, window blinds and the television (which has free movies on demand). Work or play in the vast lobby and open-plan bar and canteen surrounded by modern art, Vitra furniture, Apple iMacs; public areas are accessible 24 hours a day. Sample 'divine' freshly squeezed clementine juice at breakfast, and 'probably the best breakfast coffee I can remember'. Open-plan lobby/bar/deli/work stations/seating areas. Meeting rooms. Lift. Free Wi-Fi, in-room TV. Children welcomed. 192 bedrooms (12 suitable for disabled). Room from £112. Breakfast from £13.95. Registered 'Citizens' receive the best available rate and a complimentary drink on arrival. (Underground: London Bridge, Southwark)

THE CONNAUGHT, Carlos Place, Mayfair, W1K 2AL. Tel 020 7499 7070, www.the-connaught.co.uk. Personalised treatment is de rigueur at this 'wonderful' late-Victorian luxury hotel (part of the Maybourne Hotel group), on a quiet corner of Mayfair. 'The service surpasses most hotels we've stayed in': butlers buttle, porters transport and waiters await your order. Lavish period features, antique pieces and bespoke modern furniture mingle throughout. Pick from classically styled or sleeker modern bedrooms, each with Italian bedlinen, cashmere blankets, state-of-the-art technology; all have a marble bathroom. Child-friendly flourishes, including home-made treats on arrival and personalised bathrobes, will please younger guests. Break up the afternoon with a lavish tea in the conservatory; come evening, indulge in the elegant wood-panelled restaurant, where Hélène Darroze has two Michelin stars for her fine French cooking (excellent vegetarian options). The award-winning spa is glamorous and soothing in equal measure. 2 bars, 2 restaurants. Art Deco-style ballroom. Swimming pool; fitness centre; spa (treatments, complimentary meditation classes). Moon Garden. Free Wi-Fi, in-room TV. Background music. Room service; butler service. Children welcomed (babysitting by arrangement). 119 bedrooms (30 in new wing; some suitable for disabled). Room from £480. Breakfast £26. (Underground: Bond Street)

COUNTY HALL PREMIER INN, Belvedere Road, Southbank, SE1 7PB. Tel 0871 527 8648, www.premierinn.com. The historic Portland stone-built former county hall is now a good-value riverside hotel overlooking the Thames, within steps of some of London's biggest landmarks. Double-glazing minimises street noise in the simply furnished bedrooms, each equipped with a desk, hospitality tray and basic bathroom. Breakfast is often busy. The Sea Life London Aquarium and the London Dungeon are in the same building; the Hayward Gallery and Royal Festival Hall are but five minutes' walk away. Self-service check-in. Lobby, bar, Thyme restaurant. Lift. Free Wi-Fi, in-room TV (Freeview). Background music. Conferences. Children welcomed. 314 bedrooms (some suitable for disabled). Room from £155. Meal deal (dinner and breakfast) £24.99 per person. (Underground: Waterloo)

COVENT GARDEN HOTEL, 10 Monmouth Street, Covent Garden, WC2H 9HB. Tel 020 7806 1000, www.firmdalehotels.com. As characterful and theatrical as the surrounding neighbourhood, this smart hotel (Firmdale Hotels group) is just round the corner from London's longest-running shows and a host of West End debuts. Guests praise its 'superb comfort and fantastic service'. Fresh flowers top the French stone fireplace in the wood-panelled drawing room; individually decorated bedrooms are hung with bold wallpaper and vintage prints. Each room has a granite-and-oak bathroom, some with a deep bathtub; many have views across the city's rooftops. Connecting rooms are available for families and groups. Saturday movie nights are hosted in the basement screening room. Modern menus in Brasserie Max can also be ordered as room service; the varied breakfast menu (extra charge) includes vegan options. Drawing room, library (honesty bar), restaurant. Meeting room. Screening room. Gym. Free Wi-Fi, in-room TV. No background music. Children (amenities, treats and activities) and small dogs (by arrangement) welcomed. 58 bedrooms. Room from £324. Breakfast £15–£30. Dinner £42. (Underground: Covent Garden, Leicester Square)

DORSET SQUARE HOTEL, 39–40 Dorset Square, Marylebone, NW1 6QN. Tel 020 7723 7874, www.firmdalehotels. com. Overlooking the original site of Thomas Lord's cricket ground, this Regency town house hotel is a peaceful getaway. The interior features the dynamic blend of colours, patterns and textiles that mark the hotel as one of the Firmdale Hotels group. Many of the individually styled bedrooms (some small) have leafy views of the garden square; all have a flat-screen TV and iPod docking station. Eat from the Mediterranean-inspired English brasserie menu, served in the popular all-day Potting Shed; take afternoon tea, and drinks from the honesty bar, in the high-ceilinged ground-floor drawing

room. Bringing children? Expect a warm welcome, with menus, toiletries and entertainment for young guests. Drawing room, brasserie. Lift. Free Wi-Fi, in-room TV. No background music. Room service. DVD library. Civil wedding licence. Dogs welcomed, by arrangement. 38 bedrooms (1 suitable for disabled; 2 ideal for a family). Room from £198. Continental breakfast buffet £10.50. (Underground: Marylebone)

DUKES LONDON, 35 St James's Place, St James's, SW1A 1NY. Tel 020 7491 4840, www.dukeshotel.com. Fancy a rakish drink? There's arguably no better spot than the place where Ian Fleming is said to have taken inspiration for James Bond's 'shaken, not stirred' tipple. The spy novelist once haunted the legendary Dukes bar at this discreet, quintessentially British town house hotel. Today, guests continue to gather for martinis and cocktails-of-the-month. At dinner, step in to the well-regarded Thirty Six restaurant for chef Nigel Mendham's modern English dishes. Afterwards, retire to one of the peaceful bedrooms – each has a marble bathroom; some have a seating area. Next day, ask for a picnic hamper to take to nearby Green Park. Fear not the British summer: the hamper comes with blankets, shrugs and a hot-water bottle. Drawing room, Dukes bar, champagne lounge, conservatory. Health club (steam room, gym, beauty treatments). Courtyard; cognac and cigar garden. Free Wi-Fi, in-room TV. Background music. 24-hour room service. Civil wedding licence; function facilities. Children welcomed (treats and amenities). 90 bedrooms, 15 suites (1 suitable for disabled). Per room B&B

from £346. Dinner £49. (Underground: Green Park)

ECCLESTON SQUARE HOTEL, 37 Eccleston Square, Belgravia, SW1V 1PB. Tel 020 3503 0691, www.ecclestonsquarehotel. com. Find gadgets and gizmos galore at Olivia Byrne's 'very stylish' modern hotel on an elegant garden square. 'It surpassed all our expectations,' say guests this year. 'Domesticated heaven', it has high ceilings, large windows, Murano glass chandeliers – and 'mostly intuitive' cutting-edge technology throughout. ('Super-friendly' staff are always on hand to help the less tech-savvy.) 'Comfortable', high-tech bedrooms (some compact, some with a private patio or balcony) have an iPad, electronically controlled curtains, an adjustable bed with massage settings. International guests also have use of a free mobile phone, with unlimited Internet access and free calls to selected countries. At dinner, a rather more analogue affair, pick and mix French-inspired tapas dishes in the restaurant. Drawing room, media lounge (oversized 3D TV), bar, restaurant (afternoon tea, brunch). Picnic baskets are available to enjoy in the garden square. Free Wi-Fi, in-room TV (Sky). Background music. Parking discounts. Children over 13 welcomed. 39 bedrooms. Per room B&B £210, D,B&B £229.50. Dinner from £19.50. (Underground: Victoria)
25% DISCOUNT VOUCHERS

THE FIELDING, 4 Broad Court, off Bow Street, Covent Garden, WC2B 5QZ. Tel 020 7836 8305, www.thefieldinghotel. co.uk. A 'simple, well-located place to stay', this 'remarkably quiet' small hotel is a hop, skip and grand jeté from the Royal Opera House. It is managed by Grace Langley, with 'helpful' staff, for private owners. Reached by narrow corridors, modest bedrooms have an en suite bath or shower room. 'Our first-floor double room was small but had all the necessities: a large bed, a clean bathroom; excellent lighting. A tea and coffee tray held biscuits and bottles of sparkling and still water; slippers and an eye mask were also provided. We slept undisturbed with the windows wide open.' Breakfast isn't served, but there are many eating places nearby. 'Relatively good value for its position.' Free Wi-Fi, in-room TV (Freeview). No background music. Free access to nearby spa and fitness centre. Children welcomed (travel cots). 25 bedrooms. Single room from £108, double room from £168. (Underground: Covent Garden)

41, 41 Buckingham Palace Road, Victoria, SW1W 0PS. Tel 020 7300 0041, www.41hotel.com. Expect to be royally greeted at this discreet luxury hotel (Red Carnation group) overlooking the grounds of Buckingham Palace. On the fifth floor of a historic building (also home to sister hotel The Rubens at the Palace), the hotel has the atmosphere of a private club, with public rooms of mahogany panelling and polished brass. Receive a glass of champagne by way of welcome; on departure, accept apples, rusks and bottles of water as a thoughtful send-off. Choose among the stylish black-and-white bedrooms, each with an opulent marble bathroom – all have magazines and books; scented candles and season-appropriate bathrobes; flowers, fresh fruit and a plate of home-made treats.

Complimentary afternoon tea and canapés are taken in the lounge; each evening till late, accept the invitation to 'plunder the pantry' for light meals and snacks. An extensive breakfast is served until 1 pm on Sundays. Room, butler and chauffeur service. Free Wi-Fi, in-room TV (Sky). Background music. Business functions. Children and dogs welcomed. 30 bedrooms and suites. Per room B&B from £388. (Underground: Victoria)

GREAT NORTHERN HOTEL, Pancras Road, King's Cross, N1C 4TB. Tel 020 3388 0800, www.gnhlondon.com. Looking to make good connections? Opening directly on to the Western concourse of King's Cross station, this elegant luxury hotel, a Victorian railway stopover, is within yards of the St Pancras International Eurostar terminus. The sweeping terracotta building, designed by Lewis Cubitt in 1851, adds glamour to the regeneration of a once-seedy neighbourhood. Modern and sleek, the high-ceilinged bedrooms (some compact) take design inspiration from old-time railway carriage sleepers. There are bespoke furnishings, tall windows, good soundproofing; some rooms have 'clubby' walnut wood-panelled walls and a vintage-style bathroom. A nice touch: a help-yourself pantry on each floor, where guests may make tea or coffee, or sample a home-made treat. A wide selection of magazines and books is available to borrow. Mark Sargeant serves 'excellent' food in the lively, all-day Plum + Spilt Milk restaurant; find light bites and cocktails in a glamorous Art Deco bar. 3 bars, restaurant, Kiosk food stall. Lift. Free Wi-Fi, in-room TV (Sky).

Background music. 91 bedrooms (some suitable for disabled). Per room B&B from £224. Dinner £26–£45. (Underground: King's Cross St Pancras, Euston)

HAM YARD HOTEL, One Ham Yard, Soho, W1D 7DT. Tel 020 3642 2000, www.firmdalehotels.com. The bubble-gum pinks and lime greens of Tim and Kit Kemp's large, modern hotel (part of the Firmdale Hotels group) call to mind its buzzy surroundings, near Piccadilly Circus. Floor-to-ceiling windows in the large bedrooms overlook the city or turn inward to a tree-filled courtyard; each has a handsome bathroom in granite and oak. Pull a book from the well-stocked library; bowl in the 1950s-style basement bowling alley; take a drink up to the rooftop terrace, where a lush garden filters out the city. The rooftop garden also supplies herbs and vegetables to the contemporary British restaurant. Breakfast (charged separately) has much choice, with an interesting selection of smoothies and freshly squeezed juices. Drawing room, library; theatre, bowling alley. Soholistic spa, gym. Lift. Rooftop terrace and garden. Free Wi-Fi, in-room TV. No background music. Valet parking (charge). Children welcomed (amenities, treats, entertainment). 91 rooms (6 suitable for disabled). Room from £380. Breakfast from £10. (Underground: Piccadilly Circus)

HAYMARKET HOTEL, 1 Suffolk Place, West End, SW1Y 4HX. Tel 020 7470 4000, www.haymarkethotel.com. In bustling Theatreland, this 'beautifully furnished' hotel (part of the Firmdale Hotels group) bursts with co-owner

Kit Kemp's distinctive decorative verve, its rooms punctuated with vivid fabrics, quirky furniture and a striking mix of contemporary and traditional art. Sarah Pinchbeck manages a team of 'the most helpful staff'. Swim in the 'stunning' heated indoor pool, then relax at the pewter poolside bar; afterwards, tuck in to chef Robin Reed's bistro dishes in the informal Brumus restaurant. Breakfast has an interesting menu: start the day right, with huevos rancheros or waffles with Canadian maple syrup. Conservatory, library, bar, Brumus restaurant. Indoor swimming pool, gym. Lift. Free Wi-Fi, in-room TV. No background music. Civil wedding licence. Children (amenities, treats and entertainment) and dogs (by arrangement) welcomed. 50 bedrooms (2 suites; 5-bedroom town house). Room from £384. Breakfast £25.50. Dinner £30. (Underground: Green Park, Piccadilly)

THE HOXTON HOLBORN, 199–206 High Holborn, WC1V 7BD. Tel 020 7661 3000, www.thehoxton.com/london/holborn. In a former office block, with good transport links across the city, this youthful, modern hotel is anything but workaday. Vintage touches and cleverly designed bedrooms add style to a zesty atmosphere. Bedrooms (Shoebox, Snug, Cosy and Roomy) have leather and wood accents; a Roberts radio and old Penguin Classics add to the retro feel. Each room has tea- and coffee-making facilities; a mini-fridge with fresh milk and bottled water; a guide to local attractions. Guests also have an hour's worth of free local and international phone calls. Take your pick of eating spots: Brooklyn-style Hubbard & Bell

has truffle chips, banana splits and food all day; Chicken Shop, in the basement, serves spit-roasted meats; Holborn Grind supplies coffee, cakes, pastries and sandwiches. Breakfast on the go is always an option: a breakfast bag (orange juice, banana, yogurt, granola pot) appears on the door handle in the morning. No pool or gym – but there's a nail bar. Complimentary newspapers in the lobby. Sister hotel The Hoxton Shoreditch (see next entry) accommodates guests looking east. Meeting/function rooms. Nail salon. Free Wi-Fi. Background music (live DJ nights). Children welcomed. 174 bedrooms (some suitable for disabled). Per room B&B from £109. (Underground: Holborn)

THE HOXTON SHOREDITCH, 81 Great Eastern Street, Shoreditch, EC2A 3HU. Tel 020 7550 1000, www.hoxtonhotels. com. There's a vibrant, high-energy atmosphere at this 'intensely stylish' hotel – ideal for its trendy neighbourhood. Communal spaces have exposed-brick walls, stone fireplaces, leather armchairs; an arcade-game theme mixes with industrial accents. Upstairs, 'well-equipped', good-value bedrooms have a 'decent' large bed, 'good lighting', 'proper' hangers; a 'splendid' bathroom. A perk: the room rate includes an hour's worth of free phone calls. Mealtimes, choose from the American-influenced menu at the 'excellent' all-day Hoxton Grill; the 'buzzy' bar, popular with locals, is open till late. In the morning, stretch your arm out the door: a breakfast bag containing a banana, a granola pot and a bottle of orange juice awaits outside. A sister hotel (see previous entry) brings guests closer to the hubbub of Oxford Circus. Weekly music and art events. Lounge, courtyard (with retractable roof). Lift. Meeting rooms. Shop. Free Wi-Fi. Background music. Children welcomed. 210 rooms (11 suitable for disabled). Per room B&B from £99. (Underground: Old Street)

H10 LONDON WATERLOO, 284–302 Waterloo Road, Waterloo, SE1 8RQ. Tel 020 7928 4062, www. hotelh10londonwaterloo.com. ¡Bienvenido! 'Friendly' staff give arriving guests a continental welcome and a complimentary glass of cava at this good-value Spanish chain hotel on busy Waterloo Road. The sleek, contemporary public rooms have striking photographic murals and a selection of newspapers and magazines; bright bedrooms (some compact) on the upper floors have 'good' double glazing (making traffic noise 'bearable'). Go all the way to the top: here, the best rooms have a panoramic vista of the urban landscape. Feel sky-high over cocktails in the eighth-floor Waterloo Sky bar; indulge in 'outstanding' modern Spanish dishes in the restaurant, where the service is 'prompt and friendly'. Mornings, find a 'considerable' breakfast buffet; 'excellent' cooked dishes. The South Bank is 15 minutes' walk away. Lounge, bar, Three O Two restaurant. Leisure centre (gym, sauna, hydromassage shower; treatments). Meeting rooms. Free Wi-Fi, in-room TV. 177 bedrooms. Per room B&B from £147. Dinner £30. (Underground: Waterloo)

INDIGO, 16 London Street, Paddington, W2 1HL. Tel 020 7706 4444, www.ihg. com/hotelindigo. Contemporary style and quirky elegance mix at this modern hotel in a collection of converted town houses. Part of the InterContinental Hotels group, it stands opposite a small garden square within easy reach of Paddington station and express trains to Heathrow. Up the glass staircase and down colourful corridors, bedrooms (some small) are decorated with plush fabrics and photographic murals of neighbouring Hyde Park and Little Venice. Each room has an espresso machine, complimentary soft drinks; a spa-inspired shower. Light sleepers, ask for a room at the back (earplugs provided). Lounge/lobby, bar, brasserie. Terrace. Fitness studio. Free Wi-Fi, in-room TV. Background music. Children welcomed. 64 bedrooms (some with private balcony or terrace; 2 suitable for disabled). Per room B&B from £205. (Underground: Paddington)

THE KENSINGTON, 109–113 Queen's Gate, Kensington, SW7 5LR. Tel 020 7589 6300, www.doylecollection. com/hotels/the-kensington-hotel. In a terrace of classic white-stucco Victorian town houses, this 'sophisticated' museum-district hotel (part of the Doyle Collection) has been refurbished with a cool, glamorous interior. Open fires burn in many of the 'uncluttered' reception rooms; modern art sits comfortably within heritage decor. Choose a bedroom to suit – they vary in size, but all have a capsule coffee machine and a marble bathroom with top-end toiletries. Feeling peckish? Afternoon tea (including gluten-free options) is served in the 'expansive' drawing room; detox milkshakes, juices and custom smoothies are available. For a more substantial meal, try chef Steve Gibbs's seasonal modern dishes in the restaurant or the clubby bar. 3 drawing rooms, K bar, Town House restaurant, Juicery. Meeting rooms. Fitness suite; spa treatment room. Free Wi-Fi, in-room TV. No background music. Children welcomed (arrival gift, board games, DVDs, tepees; family rooms). 150 bedrooms and suites (some suitable for disabled). Room from £255. Continental breakfast £15. (Underground: South Kensington)

KNIGHTSBRIDGE HOTEL, 10 Beaufort Gardens, Knightsbridge, SW3 1PT. Tel 020 7584 6300, www.firmdalehotels.com. A retreat from bustling Knightsbridge, this handsome town house hotel (part of the Firmdale Hotels group) is on a quiet, tree-lined street minutes from Hyde Park. Contemporary British art and specially commissioned ceramics and fabrics add character to the two cosy sitting rooms. The bright, colourful bedrooms are individually designed in co-owner Kit Kemp's bold style; each has a granite-and-oak bathroom; most have views of Beaufort Gardens or the city skyline. In lieu of a restaurant, room-service menus are available all day in the sitting rooms or bedroom. Take afternoon tea in the drawing room or library; a Princes and Princesses tea for children has jellies and milkshakes. Museum-hop in nearby South Kensington, then come back to relax with a cocktail, an in-room massage or a choice of beauty treatments. Drawing room, library, bar. Free Wi-Fi, in-room TV. No background music. Room service. Civil wedding licence. Children (amenities, books, board games, DVDs, treats) and small dogs (by arrangement)

welcomed. 44 bedrooms. Room from £288. À la carte breakfast £3.50–£14.50. (Underground: Knightsbridge)

THE MAIN HOUSE, 6 Colville Road, Notting Hill, W11 2BP. Tel 020 7221 9691, www.themainhouse.co.uk. See London through a local's eyes, at Caroline Main's personally run guest house in bohemian Notting Hill. It was conceived for 'the independent traveller', the hostess says: rather than breakfast in, explore the neighbourhood, with discounts at the nearby deli and artisan bakery; bring workout togs to take advantage of special day rates at the local BodyWorksWest health club (pool, gym). The elegant Victorian house has period features, antique furnishings and an airy, uncluttered feel. Spacious suites occupy an entire floor; they are well equipped with purified water, guides and maps, umbrellas, adaptor plugs, a fridge. A complimentary newspaper and morning coffee or tea are brought to the room or served on the balcony. Roof terrace. Free Wi-Fi, in-room TV. No background music. DVD library. Reasonable rates for chauffeur service to airports. Well-behaved children welcomed. 3 bedrooms. Room per person £55 (min. 3-night stay). (Underground: Notting Hill Gate)

THE MONTAGUE ON THE GARDENS, 15 Montague Street, Bloomsbury, WC1B 5BJ. Tel 020 7637 1001, www.montaguehotel.com. Opposite the British Museum, this 'attractive, well-run' hotel, with its own trove of treasures and intriguing history, is a fine match for its exalted neighbour. Dirk Crokaert manages 'enthusiastic' staff for the Red Carnation group. In the lavish public rooms, draped curtains frame the windows; the ceilings are hung with crystal chandeliers; bold floral prints adorn the furnishings. The 'very comfortable', well-equipped bedrooms follow suit, with gilded mirrors and hand-crafted furniture. Children are spoiled with games, DVDs, a mini-bathrobe and slippers. Seasonal fare characterises chef Martin Halls's menu in the informal Blue Door Bistro; in good weather, enjoy an alfresco meal on the Garden Grill terrace. Lounge, bar, 2 conservatories. Terrace. Designated outdoor smoking area. Free Wi-Fi, in-room TV. Classic/contemporary background music in public areas; pianist in Terrace bar in evening except Sun. Civil wedding licence. Children and dogs (special treats) welcomed. 100 rooms and suites (1 suitable for disabled). Per room B&B single from £258, double from £328. Dinner £37. (Underground: Russell Square)

THE NADLER KENSINGTON, 25 Courtfield Gardens, Kensington, SW5 0PG. Tel 020 7244 2255, www.thenadler.com. Nights at the museum are within reach in this white stucco hotel aimed at the style-conscious budget traveller. Part of the Nadler Hotels group (see also The Nadler Liverpool, Shortlist entry), the modern hotel provides no-frills 'affordable luxury' in a leafy residential setting. The simply furnished, studio-style bedrooms have a mini-kitchen (microwave, fridge, sink, cutlery), independently controlled heating and air conditioning. Travelling with family? Ask for a larger room with a sofa bed. There's no restaurant or bar, but local eating spots are all around – and guests receive discounts at many

of them. In the morning, a continental breakfast (£8.50) may be delivered to the room, by arrangement. Hire city bikes nearby; ask to borrow a helmet. Reception lobby. Music library, games. Access to local Fitness First gym. Free Wi-Fi, in-room TV. Background music. Children welcomed. 65 bedrooms (some with bunk bed; 1 suitable for disabled). Room from £138. (Underground: Earl's Court, Gloucester Road)

QBIC HOTEL, 42 Adler Street, Whitechapel, E1 1EE. Tel 020 3021 3300, london.qbichotels.com. Bright colours and Scandinavian design teem at this modern Dutch chain hotel not far from Brick Lane. Encouraged by crisply efficient staff, the lively atmosphere reflects the animation of surrounding streets known for curry houses, proper bagels and young creatives. In the stylish, no-frills bedrooms, plug into British and European sockets; connect using the Skype-ready television. The shower room is cleverly tucked behind the well-designed headboard of the large, organic-wool bed. There's no restaurant or bar; a row of vending machines has vacuum-packed stews, organic crisps, locally brewed beers; breakfast (included in the room rate) is a 'grab bag' of juice, fruit and a cereal bar. Socialise or work in the enormous lounge: blond wood flooring, rugs, mismatched furniture, all-day complimentary tea/coffee. Lounge (open to non-residents), bar. Lift. Free Wi-Fi, in-room TV. Children welcomed (connecting rooms, baby cots). 171 rooms (some suitable for disabled). Room £98–£146. Breakfast buffet £7.95. (Underground: Aldgate East, Whitechapel)

THE ROYAL PARK HOTEL, 3 Westbourne Terrace, Paddington, W2 3UL. Tel 020 7479 6600, www.theroyalpark. com. 'We really like this hotel.' A 'comfortable, homely' atmosphere permeates this elegant town house hotel, where antique furniture and original oil paintings add a 'gracious' feel to the public spaces. 'Extremely nice' staff take care of guests' needs. Bedrooms (each with a 'spacious' limestone shower room or bathroom) are well equipped with bathrobes and slippers; many rooms look down the tree-lined avenue or over a private mews. Dine from an eclectic European menu in Kiyan restaurant; next morning, enjoy a lie-in with an 'excellent' breakfast in bed. Bar, restaurant. Lift. Business/function facilities. Garden; terrace. Free Wi-Fi, in-room TV. Room service. Limousine service. Children welcomed. 48 bedrooms. Per room B&B (including welcome drink) from £173. Dinner £22. (Underground: Paddington, Lancaster Gate)

ST JAMES'S HOTEL AND CLUB, 7–8 Park Place, St James's, SW1A 1LS. Tel 020 7316 1600, www.stjameshotelandclub. com. In a peaceful cul-de-sac close to Green Park, this luxurious Victorian hotel (Althoff Hotels) combines sumptuously decorated rooms with a Michelin-starred restaurant – a mix that's just right for the chic Mayfair streets close by. Find handmade wallpaper, Murano glass chandeliers and black lacquer accents in the stylish bedrooms; two of the best have a private terrace with views over the city's rooftops. Chef William Drabble's modern French cooking wins acclaim in the boldly decorated restaurant,

Seven Park Place; light lunches and pre- and post-theatre suppers are taken in William's Bar & Bistro. For a more whimsical touch, book a place at the chef's afternoon tea, which, devised in collaboration with Hamleys toy store, is based on popular parlour games – domino biscuits and snakes-and-ladders petits fours. Lounge, bar, bistro, restaurant (closed Sun, Mon). 4 private dining rooms; function rooms. Free Wi-Fi, in-room TV. No background music. Children welcomed (dedicated kids' concierge; cot £36; extra bed £60). 60 bedrooms (10 suites; 2 suitable for disabled). Per room B&B from £335, D,B&B from £449. Dinner £63. (Underground: Green Park)

ST PAUL'S HOTEL, 153 Hammersmith Road, Hammersmith, W14 0QL. Tel 020 8846 9119, www.stpaulhotel. co.uk. A former boys' school built in 1884, this smartly converted hotel today showcases the impressive arches, terracotta brickwork and Romanesque style that typify architect Alfred Waterhouse's designs. (Discerning guests will recognise similarities with his more famous creation, the Natural History Museum.) Some of the modern bedrooms retain an original fireplace; all have a bathroom decked in marble. Toast the end of school days over a champagne afternoon tea; at dinnertime, take a seat in Melody restaurant over a varied menu of European dishes. Bar, restaurant (open to non-residents); garden. Lift. Free Wi-Fi, in-room TV. Background music. Room service. Business/function/wedding facilities. Limited parking (reservation necessary). Children welcomed (extra bed). 35 bedrooms (1 suitable for disabled).

Double room from £186. Breakfast £12.50. Dinner £50. (Underground: Hammersmith, Kensington Olympia, Barons Court)

SLOANE SQUARE HOTEL, 7–12 Sloane Square, Chelsea, SW1W 8EG. Tel 020 7896 9988, www.sloanesquarehotel. co.uk. 'We're so glad we stayed,' say Guide readers this year. 'Ideally located for west London, the hotel is part of the lively Sloane Square scene. The staff are wonderfully efficient; comfortable rooms and friendliness are the order of the day.' Choose among 'smart', 'cleverly designed' bedrooms, each 'well equipped' with a capsule coffee machine and a minibar 'filled with things you might actually want'. Rooms at the front overlook the bustling square; those at the rear have views on to a beautiful Art Deco church. A 'promptly delivered' room-service meal may be ordered from the 'bustling' Côte brasserie next door. 'Good cooked dishes' at breakfast. Cadogan Hall and the Royal Court Theatre are nearby. Brasserie, bar. Meeting rooms. Lift. Free Wi-Fi, local and national phone calls, in-room TV. Background music. Room service. Parking (charge). Children welcomed. 102 bedrooms. Room £189–£375. Full English breakfast £9.95. (Underground: Sloane Square)

SOFITEL LONDON ST JAMES, 6 Waterloo Place, St James's, SW1Y 4AN. Tel 020 7747 2210, www.sofitel.com. The mainly French staff add to the continental air at this handsome neoclassical hotel, part of the international Sofitel hotel group. In a 'wonderful' location just off Pall Mall, it is managed by Nicolas Pesty. Variously sized bedrooms are 'exceptionally comfortable'; they have a desk, a minibar, tea- and coffee-making facilities; luxury toiletries in the bathroom. Descend twin spiral staircases into Le Balcon brasserie for 'excellent' Franco-British dishes; live harp music accompanies afternoon tea and old-world cocktails in the popular Rose Lounge. Mornings, tuck in to a 'delicious' breakfast buffet, then set out to explore: many of the city's cultural landmarks are within walking distance. Lounge, bar, restaurant. Spa (treatments); gym. Business facilities. Free Wi-Fi, in-room TV. Background music. Room service. Valet parking. Children welcomed (babysitting on request). 183 rooms (1 suitable for disabled; some interconnecting). Room from £224. Breakfast £25. (Underground: Charing Cross, Piccadilly Circus)

THE SOHO HOTEL, 4 Richmond Mews, off Dean Street, Soho, W1D 3DH. Tel 020 7559 3000, www.firmdalehotels. com. If cats are connoisseurs of comfort, none are more so than Fernando Botero's ten-foot-high sculpture of a bronze feline, which has found its home in the lobby of this glamorous Firmdale hotel. The flamboyantly furnished public rooms are adorned with fresh flowers and modern art; individually styled bedrooms follow suit, with plush upholstery, a riot of colour and texture, floor-to-ceiling windows, a luxurious bathroom. Families are welcomed: children will find an array of books, board games, DVDs; a mini-bathrobe; milk and cookies at bedtime. Spend a lazy afternoon in the small cinema; regular Sunday film events include lunch, tea or dinner. Drawing room (honesty bar), library, bar, Refuel restaurant, 4 private dining rooms. Lift. Gym. Beauty treatment rooms. 2 screening rooms. Free Wi-Fi, in-room TV. Background music. DVD library. Civil wedding licence. Children (high chair, special cutlery, cot, extra bed; babysitting) and small dogs (by arrangement) welcomed. 96 bedrooms and suites (4 suitable for disabled). Also 4 apartments. Room from £330. Breakfast from £13. Set dinner £20.50. (Underground: Leicester Square)

SOUTH PLACE HOTEL, 3 South Place, Bishopsgate, EC2M 2AF. Tel 020 3503 0000, www.southplacehotel.com. 'Just what we were looking for.' Guide readers celebrating a special occasion this year praised the 'friendly' service and style of this modern luxury hotel in the City. With interiors designed by Terence Conran, its pedigree shows: 'The lobby and bar have a distinctly cool, European feel. Our beautiful, quiet room had original artwork, bespoke furniture, state-of-the-art lighting; the bathroom was a dream. And how lovely to find that the soft drinks in the minibar, our welcoming tea and coffee, and the morning paper were all included in the room rate.' Choose between a number of eating, drinking and merry-making options: 3 South Place bar and grill; a rooftop terrace with a retractable roof; the Michelin-starred Angler restaurant, much liked for its seafood menu (closed Sat lunch and Sun; Christmas period). 'We enjoyed our breakfast of fresh pastries, compote and toast.' 4 bars, 2 restaurants, Le Chiffre residents' lounge and games room (books, magazines, games, turntable, cocktails); 'secret' garden.

Lift. Gym; steam, sauna, treatment room. 5 private dining and meeting rooms. Free Wi-Fi, in-room TV. Background music (live DJ Fri and Sat nights in bars). Civil wedding licence. Children (cot; interconnecting rooms) and small/medium-size dogs welcomed. 80 bedrooms, studios and suites (4 suitable for disabled). Per room B&B £185–£465. Dinner £50. (Underground: Liverpool Street, Moorgate)

THE STAFFORD, 16–18 St James's Place, St James's, SW1A 1NJ. Tel 020 7493 0111, www.thestaffordhotel.co.uk. The red-brick facade of these three Victorian town houses hides a long and intriguing history: the buildings have been home, at various times, to a nanny of Queen Victoria's children, several troops of Allied officers, and a heroine of the French Resistance. Today, it is a sophisticated hotel, with individually designed bedrooms in the main houses, and suites spanning the converted mews and carriage houses. Swathed with memorabilia from its wartime guise as a bomb shelter, the 350-year-old wine cellar hosts regular tastings of its massive wine collection. Stateside paraphernalia and celebrity photographs festoon the characterful American Bar. Breakfast has plenty of choice, including waffles with maple syrup. At lunch and dinner, chef Carlos Martinez cooks modern dishes in the elegant Lyttleton restaurant. The National Gallery and Green Park are a short walk away. Lounge, bar, restaurant. Courtyard. Lift. Free Wi-Fi, in-room TV. No background music. Civil wedding licence, function facilities. Parking (charge). Children welcomed. 104 bedrooms (11 in Carriage House;

26 in Mews; 1 suitable for disabled). Chauffeur-driven hotel car (3 pm–8 pm, by arrangement). Per room B&B from £411. (Underground: Green Park)

TEN MANCHESTER STREET,
10 Manchester Street, Marylebone, W1U 4DG. Tel 020 7317 5900, www. tenmanchesterstreethotel.com. Tucked behind a neighbourhoody garden square, this red-brick Edwardian hotel (City & Country Hotels) has the discreet atmosphere of a gentleman's club, and attentive, welcoming staff. Choose among 'comfortable', individually designed bedrooms; four courtyard rooms open on to a private terrace with seating, music and heaters. Modern Italian cuisine is served all day in Dieci restaurant. Cigar aficionados, take note: there's a walk-in humidor, a sampling room, an all-weather smoking terrace, and a contentedly masculine cigar room with portraits and rich leather chairs. Regent's Park is ten minutes' walk away. Lounge/bar. Free Wi-Fi, in-room TV (Sky). No background music. Children welcomed. 24-hour room service; chauffeur service. 44 bedrooms (9 suites). Per room B&B £165–£375. Dinner £45. (Underground: Baker Street, Bond Street, Marylebone)

TOWN HALL HOTEL & APARTMENTS,
Patriot Square, Bethnal Green, E2 9NF. Tel 020 7871 0460, www.townhallhotel. com. Art Deco meets the decorative cutting edge at this fashionable, award-winning hotel in quickly-brightening-up Bethnal Green. Built in the heyday of Edwardian architecture, the Grade II listed former town hall is liked for its stylish interiors – look out for the ornate moulded ceilings,

stately staircases and marble pillars, all carefully restored. Throughout, too, find a team of 'friendly, helpful' staff. Choose among bedrooms individually styled with vintage furniture and homey touches, such as a sheepskin rug. All are provided with top-end toiletries and 'barista-quality' coffee. (Ask for a goldfish companion for the night.) 'Our large, airy apartment had an excellent kitchen; a modern bathroom with lots of storage space; large, opening windows.' Join trend-setting locals and tuck in to a casual meal at the light-filled Corner Room, or book a seat for chef Lee Westcott's well-regarded five- or seven-course modern dinner menus in the Typing Room restaurant. A room-service menu is available 24 hours a day. Free shuttle bus to Liverpool Street and Bank on weekday mornings. Parking can be difficult. Cocktail bar, 2 restaurants. 'Gorgeous' indoor swimming pool, gym (open 6 am to midnight). Lift. Free Wi-Fi. Background music. Civil wedding licence. Function facilities. Children welcomed. 98 bedrooms and studios (4 suitable for disabled). Room from £172. Breakfast from £15. (Underground: Bethnal Green)

ENGLAND

ALDEBURGH Suffolk
Map 2:C6
DUNAN HOUSE, 41 Park Road, IP15 5EN. Tel 01728 452486, www. dunanhouse.co.uk. Take an arty retreat hidden in Suffolk woodland. Simon Farr and Ann Lee, an artist and a potter, welcome B&B guests to their colourful Victorian house filled with their own eye-catching artwork. Spacious

bedrooms have garden or river views; bird chorus serves as a gentle alarm clock. A family room on the top floor has a smaller connecting room with a single bed. Communal breakfasts include stewed fruit from the garden, home-made jams and marmalade, and eggs freshly laid by the hens that roam in the garden – all of it charmingly served on the hostess's hand-turned crockery. A ten-minute walk gets you into town; a footpath beyond the front gate leads to the marshes and the river. Ask about the house's pioneering heritage – it has a fascinating history. ½-acre garden. Free Wi-Fi, in-room TV. No background music. Parking. Children welcomed. Resident cats. 4 bedrooms (1 family room). Per room B&B £70–£100. 2-night min. stay preferred. Closed Christmas.

ALFRISTON Sussex
Map 2:E4

DEANS PLACE, Seaford Road, BN26 5TW. Tel 01323 870248, www. deansplacehotel.co.uk. On the outskirts of a 'delightful' village of ancient inns and medieval buildings, this 'handsome', 'extensively modernised' old farmhouse stands in 'well-maintained' ornamental gardens, with 'many secluded spots in which to read or enjoy some privacy'. Guide inspectors in 2016 praised its 'high-quality' dinners and 'splendid' outdoor areas (croquet lawn, putting area, swimming pool). Bedrooms are 'clean and comfortable' ('though they'd benefit from some updating'); most have views across the gardens to the hills beyond. Sample small plates and classic pub favourites all day in the bar and on the terrace. In the 'attractive' restaurant, a 'small but well-balanced menu' of

modern British dishes is 'attentively' served. At breakfast, 'I ordered a full English and was rewarded with a plate that would be the envy of most transport cafés, containing an enormous portion of all one would expect.' An 'excellent' option for weddings and conferences. Bar, restaurant. Function rooms. Free Wi-Fi, in-room TV (Freeview). Civil wedding licence. Terrace. 4-acre garden. Outdoor swimming pool (12 by 6 metres, May–Sept). Background music ('played on a loop, niggled after a while'). Children and dogs (in some bedrooms, £5 a night) welcomed. 36 bedrooms (1 suitable for disabled). Per room B&B from £100, D,B&B from £170. Dinner £38.
25% DISCOUNT VOUCHERS

WINGROVE HOUSE, High Street, BN26 5TD. Tel 01323 870276, www. wingrovehousealfriston.com. Run with a small, friendly team, Nick Denyer's welcoming restaurant-with-rooms occupies an elegant 19th-century house embraced by a colonial-style veranda. The stylish bedrooms are 'perfection'. Dressed in attractive grey, brown and navy hues, some have a high, metal-framed bed, some a white-panelled bath. Take in the views of the village green and surrounding countryside through prettily shuttered windows, or ask for one of two rooms with a heated balcony. In the candlelit restaurant, chef Matthew Comben's 'top-quality' modern European dinners use seasonal produce from local farms and the South Downs. Breakfast has fruit salad, croissants, home-made jams. Festive terraces (one with heat lamps) have tables and seating. Lounge/ bar (extensive gin menu), restaurant (closed Mon–Fri lunch; special diets catered for). Free Wi-Fi, in-room TV (Freeview). Background music. 20 mins' drive from Glyndebourne. Children welcomed. 7 bedrooms (2 with access to balcony). Per room B&B £120–£200. Dinner £35.

ALKHAM Kent
Map 2:D5

THE MARQUIS AT ALKHAM, Alkham Valley Road, CT15 7DF. Tel 01304 873410, www.themarquisatalkham. co.uk. Close to the cliffs of Dover, this white-painted countryside restaurant-with-rooms is an excellent stopping point on the way to the Channel Tunnel, and a destination in itself. Manager David Harris (for Bespoke Hotels) is now at the helm. Smartly decorated, it has exposed brickwork, wooden floors, contemporary fabrics and furnishings. Book a table for chef Andrew King's seasonal à la carte dishes, or to sample his Kent-inspired four- and seven-course tasting menus. (Vegetarian menus are available.) Afterwards, stay the night in a modern bedroom – each room has a 'large, comfortable' bed and underfloor heating; some have views over the Alkham valley. Rooms at the back are quietest. Extensive breakfasts; afternoon tea; Sunday lunch. Lounge/bar, restaurant (closed Mon lunch); small garden. Free Wi-Fi, in-room TV (Freeview). Civil wedding licence. Background music. Children (no under-8s in restaurant) welcomed. On a busy road 4 miles W of Dover. 10 bedrooms (1 suitable for disabled; 3 rooms in 2 cottages, 3 mins' drive away). Per room B&B from £99, D,B&B from £179.
25% DISCOUNT VOUCHERS

APPLEDORE Devon
Map 1:B4

THE SEAGATE, The Quay, EX39 1QS. Tel 01237 472589, www.theseagate. co.uk. 'Dogs and muddy boots' are welcomed at this inviting quayside inn, which stands right on the South West Coastal Path as it snakes around the Torridge estuary. The white-painted 17th-century inn is managed by Phil and Jan Hills. Extensively refurbished, the simple, airy bedrooms (some beamed) have tea- and coffee-making facilities, and a modern bathroom. Children big and small might like the bunk bed in the family room. New chef Sean Sives cooks daily specials based on the day's catch; summer weekends, queue up for a shrimp or two off the barbecue. Two terraces have tables and seating, and impressive views across the water. At breakfast: local yogurts, fresh fruit, a good selection of cooked dishes. Open-plan restaurant/bar (local ales); 2 terraces, walled garden. Free Wi-Fi, in-room TV. 'Easy listening' background music. Parking. Children and dogs welcomed. 2 miles from Bideford. 10 bedrooms. Per room B&B single £70, double from £99. 2-night min. stay at weekends preferred. Dinner £24.
25% DISCOUNT VOUCHERS

ARMSCOTE Warwickshire
Map 3:D6

THE FUZZY DUCK, Ilmington Road, CV37 8DD. Tel 01608 682635, www. fuzzyduckarmscote.com. Blow away the city cobwebs at this 'comfortable home-away-from-home' in the Cotswolds. Sister-and-brother team Tania and Adrian Slater have stylishly refurbished the 18th-century coaching inn, retaining the distinctive flagstone floors, exposed

beams and original fireplaces. Named for different species of duck, each bedroom has luxury linens, woollen throws and complimentary goodies (the owners are behind beauty products company Baylis & Harding). Let the children entertain themselves with the dressing-up box; come nighttime, they'll love the loft bed above the bathroom (available in the largest room). Chef Richard Craven gives pub favourites a contemporary twist; a double-aspect fireplace separates a cosy private dining area from the main floor. Bar, restaurant (closed Sun eve and Mon). 1-acre garden. Free Wi-Fi, in-room smart TV. Background music. Children (special menu) and dogs (doggy welcome pack; home-made dog biscuits and snacks in the bar) welcomed. Hunter boots and guide books available to borrow. 4 bedrooms. Per room B&B from £130. Dinner £31.
25% DISCOUNT VOUCHERS

ARNSIDE Cumbria
Map 4: inset C2
NUMBER 43, The Promenade, LA5 0AA. Tel 01524 762761, www. no43.org.uk. Settle in to the window seat in the elegant lounge of Lesley Hornsby's modern seafront B&B to take in the panoramic views of the Kent estuary and the fells beyond. There are books, magazines and an honesty bar for company. Upstairs, find cool, contemporary bedrooms stocked with plenty of pillows and cushions; a hospitality tray with posh teas, freshly ground coffee and home-made biscuits; upscale toiletries in the bathroom. Two suites have binoculars for wildlife spotting. A generous breakfast includes home-made compotes, granola, locally

caught and smoked haddock; milk and eggs from a local farm. Light suppers of meat, cheese and smoked fish platters are available; in the summer, ask for a barbecue pack. Lounge, dining room. Garden, patio (alfresco drinks). Free Wi-Fi, in-room TV (Freeview). Background music. Children over 5 welcomed. 6 bedrooms. Per room B&B £125–£185.

ASTHALL Oxfordshire
Map 2:C2
THE MAYTIME INN, nr Burford, OX18 4HW. Tel 01993 822068, www. themaytime.com. A smithy once took care of horses at this 17th-century coaching inn near the River Windrush. Today, the pretty, mellow-stone building is more likely to host local villagers, gin drinkers, countryside walkers and ramble-weary dogs. Dominic Wood, the owner, has refurbished the airy space in a contemporary country style. With soaring rafters, leather sofas and tweed upholstery, the ground floor is divided into cosy dining areas where chef Roger Williams serves home-made rustic food and pub classics. Local brews, wines by the glass and a large range of gins are served in the bar or garden. Overlooking the courtyard, country-chic bedrooms have a neat modern bathroom; some have a free-standing bath. Bar, restaurant. Large terrace and garden (alfresco meals and drinks); outdoor bar; boules pitch. Free Wi-Fi, weak mobile signal, in-room TV (Freeview). Background music. Children and dogs welcomed. Resident dog, Alfie. 2 miles E of Burford. 6 bedrooms (all on ground floor). Per room B&B £95–£160, D,B&B (in low season) £135–£200.

AYSGARTH Yorkshire
Map 4:C3

STOW HOUSE, Leyburn, DL8 3SR. Tel 01969 663635, www.stowhouse.co.uk. Grab the lead, pack the pups and head for James Herriot country. A welcoming spot for 'well-behaved' dogs, Phil and Sarah Bucknall's refurbished old rectory has great walks from the door. The black-and-white tiled entrance hall leads into the warm, light-hearted B&B. Bedrooms are furnished with restraint yet have playful touches (a bronco bucks across a panel; a kangaroo winks from a wall mount). Painted in soothing colours, with wooden floors and views over the dales, the rooms are named after the art that hangs on the walls; the bathrooms, guests say, are enormous. Downstairs, seating areas are a riot of vibrant velvets or patterns, and there is a wood-burning stove; browse the many books over one of the hostess's made-to-order cocktails. In the morning, tuck in to meaty treats from the local butcher at breakfast. Dinner is available for groups of six or more; the friendly hosts can advise on walks, and nearby pubs and restaurants. Sitting room (honesty bar), snug, dining room. Free Wi-Fi, in-room TV (Freeview). No background music. Children and well-behaved dogs (in 5 rooms) welcomed. Resident animals. 7 miles W of Leyburn. 7 bedrooms (1 on ground floor). Per room B&B £110–£175. Closed 23–28 Dec.

25% DISCOUNT VOUCHERS

BAINBRIDGE Yorkshire
Map 4:C3

LOW MILL GUEST HOUSE, Low Mill, Leyburn, DL8 3EF. Tel 01969 650 553, www.lowmillguesthouse.co.uk. Jan and Neil McNair's unusual B&B is in their impressively restored late-18th-century corn mill on the River Bain, with glorious Wensleydale countryside stretching out beyond it. The water wheel still works today – admire the cogs and grindstones over tea and cake in the sitting room. Spacious bedrooms have exposed stone walls, soaring rafters, wooden floors and characterful features from the past. Each room has a wide bed, home-made biscuits and modern-day comforts (DVD player, iPod dock, radio alarm clock). For extra character, book the sympathetically converted Workshop Room, which retains the mill's original winding gear and pulley wheel (a wood-burning stove and gleaming copper bath are among its more up-to-date features). Jan McNair's two- or three-course rustic dinners are served from 6 pm to 7.30 pm in the candlelit dining room; wines are available by the glass. (Dietary requirements are catered for.) Next morning, find an excellent breakfast selection: home-made yogurt, berry compote, cereals, fresh and dried fruit; the cooked menu includes pancakes, home-baked Yorkshire ham, eggs from the neighbours' free-range hens. In warm months, the long riverside garden is an ideal place to sit. Lounge (board games, large DVD library), dining room (log fire). Garden. Free Wi-Fi. No background music. Parking. Children over 11 and dogs (not in dining room) welcomed. 3 bedrooms. Per room B&B £105–£180. Dinner £20–£25.

YOREBRIDGE HOUSE, Leyburn, DL8 3EE. Tel 01969 652060, www.yorebridgehouse.co.uk. Style influences from around the world bring international flair to this corner of a

pretty Yorkshire village. With lawns
sloping down to the water, the Victorian
stone-built school and headmaster's
house have stunning views of the River
Ure. Inside, well-travelled owners
Charlotte and David Reilly have filled
the rooms with inspiration from their
favourite places. Each bedroom is
different: Rahmoune repurposes an
antique Moroccan window as a striking
bedhead; Pienza's ornate wallpaper,
carved furniture and chandelier lend
an air of Italianate grandeur. Six rooms
across the courtyard have a private
terrace with a hot tub. Take afternoon
tea in the Master's Room, the bar or
the garden. In the candlelit restaurant,
chef Dan Shotton's fine menus are
strong on local produce. Lounge, bar,
garden room, restaurant (open to non-
residents). Free Wi-Fi (in public areas),
in-room TV (Sky). Civil wedding
licence. Background music. Children
and dogs (in 2 rooms, by arrangement)
welcomed. 2-acre grounds. 12 bedrooms
(4 in schoolhouse; plus The Barn Suite
in village, 5 mins' walk; ground-floor
rooms suitable for disabled). Per room
B&B £200–£295, D,B&B £310–£395.
Dinner £55.

BAINTON Yorkshire
Map 4:D5

WOLDS VILLAGE, Manor Farm,
YO25 9EF. Tel 01377 217698, www.
woldsvillage.co.uk. Here be dragons
– and painted sheep, wildflower pigs,
the remains of the Wicked Witch
of the East, and more besides, all
scattered in the courtyards and along
woodland trails deep in the Yorkshire
Wolds. Sally and Chris Brealey, with
Sally's mother, Maureen Holmes, run
their unusual enterprise on a Georgian

farmstead with a restaurant, tea shop, gift
shop and art gallery. Accommodation
is in a sympathetically designed new
barn made from reclaimed materials;
each of its soundproofed bedrooms
is decorated with a different historic
theme – Tudor, Victorian, Edwardian,
Art Deco. Country-style home cooking
is available throughout the day. Lounge,
bar, restaurant (closed Sun eve), tea
room. Craft and gift shop, art gallery,
art trail. Visitor information centre.
6-acre grounds. Free Wi-Fi, in-room TV
(Freeview). Background music. Children
welcomed (special menu; cots). 6 miles
W of Driffield. 7 bedrooms (3 on ground
floor, some suitable for disabled). Per
room B&B £100, D,B&B £140. Dinner £25.
Closed for 2 weeks from 28 Dec.
25% DISCOUNT VOUCHERS

BARNSLEY Gloucestershire
Map 3:E6

THE VILLAGE PUB, GL7 5EF. Tel 01285
740421, www.thevillagepub.co.uk.
The hub of the village, this stone-built
restaurant-with-rooms (Calcot Hotels)
is also a style hub, with country-chic
rooms and smartened-up drinking
and dining areas. Tuck in to chef John
Jewell's hearty pub classics – he uses
plenty of fruit and vegetables from the
kichen garden at sister hotel Barnsley
House, up the street (see main entry).
Bedrooms have a separate entrance
from the pub. Here, find old beams
and deep roll-top baths, perhaps a
four-poster bed. Light sleepers should
ask for a room away from the road.
In the morning, English farmhouse
breakfasts have home-made jams and
home-baked bread. Green-thumbed
guests, take note: there's complimentary
access to the famous Barnsley House

gardens designed by late horticulturalist Rosemary Verey. Bar, restaurant. Free Wi-Fi, in-room TV (Freeview). Background music. Children (cot, high chair; £25 supplement) and dogs welcomed. 4½ miles E of Cirencester. 6 bedrooms. Per room B&B from £99. Dinner £31.

BARNSTAPLE Devon
Map 1:B4

BROOMHILL ART HOTEL, Muddiford Road, EX31 4EX. Tel 01271 850262, www.broomhillart.co.uk. Intriguing sculptures stand along the steeply winding drive, and in the garden and heavily wooded grounds surrounding this 'quirky' small hotel. There's much to see within, too. Dutch owners Rinus and Aniet van de Sande have filled their imposing late-Victorian house with art of all kinds: 'interesting' paintings hang throughout; downstairs, a large gallery displays contemporary works. ('We spent a good hour looking at the excellent collection.') Each bedroom has a comfortable bed, plenty of storage space; many overlook the grounds and colourful outdoor sculptures. Mediterranean 'slow food' and tapas are served in the award-winning Terra Madre restaurant. Bar, restaurant (closed Sun–Tues; two-course early dinner for hotel guests 6 pm–7.30 pm Mon/Tues), library. Gallery (open to the public). Free Wi-Fi, in-room TV. Civil wedding licence. 10-acre grounds with sculpture park. No background music. Parking. Children (£15 charge) and dogs (by arrangement; £5 charge) welcomed. 4 miles N of Barnstaple. 6 bedrooms. Per room B&B single from £65, double £75–£135, D,B&B from £135. Closed 18 Dec–10 Jan.

BATH Somerset
Map 2:D1

BRINDLEYS, 14 Pulteney Gardens, BA2 4HG. Tel 01225 310444, www.brindleysbath.co.uk. There's a light, airy feel at this bijou B&B, all fresh flowers, calming hues and white-painted furniture. The Victorian villa, 'ideally' situated near the Kennet and Avon canal, is run by David Roberts and Laura Warington for Sarah and Michael Jones (who own Grays, see Shortlist entry). The handsomely styled bedrooms have a generous hospitality tray, and top-end toiletries in the modern bathroom; the best has a super-king-size bed, and city views from large windows. Take breakfast in a 'very smart and bright' room overlooking the 'well-kept' garden. The hearty blackboard menu includes local eggs, bacon and sausages; ask for vegetarian options. Lounge, breakfast room. Small garden. Free Wi-Fi, in-room TV (Freeview). No background music. Complimentary on-street parking permits. Children over 12 welcomed. 6 bedrooms (some are small). Per room B&B £135–£200. 2-night min. stay at weekends preferred. Closed Christmas.

DORIAN HOUSE, 1 Upper Oldfield Park, BA2 3JX. Tel 01225 426336, www.dorianhouse.co.uk. Music and a touch of romance await at this modern B&B owned by cellist Timothy Hugh and his wife, Kathryn; Robert and Lize Briers are the managers. Up the hill from the city centre (with 'fabulous' views over the Royal Crescent), the Victorian stone house is filled with an eclectic mix of Asian antiques, contemporary art and other intriguing artefacts. The bedrooms are named after composers; each has a power shower in the marble bathroom; some have a four-poster bed. Wake to freshly baked croissants and a choice of cooked options. Lounge (open fire), conservatory breakfast room/music library. Small, hilly garden. Free Wi-Fi, in-room TV (Freeview). Classical background music. Parking. Children welcomed. Ten mins' walk from the centre. 13 bedrooms (1 on ground floor). Per room B&B £109–£175.

GRAYS, 9 Upper Oldfield Park, BA2 3JX. Tel 01225 403020, www.graysbath. co.uk. Cool, calm and cocooning, this contemporary B&B occupies a large Victorian villa on the southern slopes of the city, a 15-minute walk from the centre. It is managed by James Grundy for the owners, Sarah and Michael Jones (see also Brindleys, Shortlist entry). Soft colours, architectural prints and French-style furniture give the bright rooms a continental ambience. One room has a modern four-poster bed, another triple bay windows; yet others, in the loft, are cosier. Most have views of the garden or the city skyline; all are supplied with bathrobes and posh toiletries. Breakfast brings cereals, yogurts, fruit, compotes; meaty and vegetarian options cooked to order. On-site parking is a plus. Lounge, breakfast room. Small garden. Free Wi-Fi, in-room TV (Freeview). No background music. Parking. Children over 12 welcomed. 12 bedrooms (4 on ground floor). Per room B&B £110–£205. 2-night min. stay at weekends preferred. Closed Christmas.

HARINGTON'S HOTEL, 8–10 Queen Street, BA1 1HE. Tel 01225 461728, www.haringtonshotel.co.uk. Peter and Melissa O'Sullivan's small hotel exudes wit and personality, from its boldly patterned wallpapers to its quirky decorative touches (a stag-head wall hook here, a rotary telephone there). Well-equipped bedrooms are on three upper floors; there's no lift, but the friendly staff offer help with luggage. Take your pick of eating and drinking places: hot drinks and light meals (including afternoon tea) are taken in the coffee lounge; the bar has Bath ales and cocktails. In Harry's Kitchen, chef Steph Box whips up a range of breakfast delights, from stacks of sweet pancakes to smoked kippers, a hearty burger or a traditional full English. Time for something a little different? Rent the private hot tub in the secluded courtyard – champagne optional. Lounge, breakfast room, café/bar. Small conference room. Hot tub (£7.50 per person per hour). Small courtyard. Free Wi-Fi, in-room TV. Room service. 'Easy listening' background music. Secure reserved parking nearby (£11 for 24 hrs). Children (in some rooms) by arrangement. 13 bedrooms, plus self-catering town house and apartments. Per room B&B £79–£203. 2-night min. stay some weekends.

PARADISE HOUSE, 86–88 Holloway, BA2 4PX. Tel 01225 317723, www. paradise-house.co.uk. David and Annie Lanz's B&B stands in award-winning gardens on a peaceful street. 'It's fair value, at a good address,' say Guide readers in 2016 who praised the 'world-class' breakfasts and 'charming, willing, if sometimes green' staff. Well equipped, and decorated in period or contemporary style, each bedroom has a modern bathroom; many also have good city views. 'Our deluxe room had a most comfortable super-king-size bed, and a fine view across Bath. It lacked storage, however.' Take in views of garden and city over pre-dinner drinks in the drawing room – the floor-to-ceiling windows capture everything. Drawing room, breakfast room. ½-acre garden. Free Wi-Fi, in-room TV (Freeview). No background music. Parking. Children (cot) welcomed. 15 mins' downhill walk to town. 12 bedrooms (4 on ground floor; family suite; 3 in annexe). Per room B&B £130–£220. 2-night min. stay at weekends. Closed Christmas Day.

THREE ABBEY GREEN, 3 Abbey Green, BA1 1NW. Tel 01225 428558, www. threeabbeygreen.com. Janeites, how quick will come the reasons for approving of Nici and Alan Jones's 'very comfortable' B&B? Swiftly enough, if you book one of the three charming bedrooms, all reached by a winding staircase, in the Jane Austen wing of this Grade II listed Georgian town house. The other rooms, in the main building, have original wood panelling, a mix of antique and contemporary furniture, a honeyed palette. 'Ours had a good bed and a lovely big bath.' At breakfast there are local jams, marmalades and compotes; vegetarian options. Close to the Abbey, the Roman Baths and the Pump Rooms – ask the friendly hosts for local information. Dining room. Free Wi-Fi (computer and printer available), in-room TV (Freeview). Background radio. Children welcomed. 10 bedrooms (3 in adjoining building; 2 on ground floor suitable for disabled; plus 1-bedroom apartment). Per room B&B £120–£240. 2-night min. stay at weekends. Closed Christmas.

VILLA MAGDALA, Henrietta Road, BA2 6LX. Tel 01225 466329, www. villamagdala.co.uk. 'Delightful' staff, 'fresh, modern' rooms and 'proper' kippers keep guests coming back to this 'terrific' B&B, in a Victorian villa whose 'quiet, leafy' setting is 'within walking distance of everything'. It is newly run, 'with charm and pride', by Ian and Christa Taylor, who also own Abbey Hotel (see main entry), across the river. There's a 'welcoming and generous' air about the place, say Guide readers this year. 'They absolutely know what they're doing. The airy, comfortable house has been decorated in crisp colours, with antiques here and there, and fresh flowers in the hall.' Past the hallway lined with books, stylish, 'spotless' bedrooms (Good, Better, Best, Fabulous) vary in size and aspect. Thoughtful touches: biscuits replenished each evening; 'a flask of fresh milk in an ice bucket to take up when you return after dinner'. In the morning, an extensive breakfast menu includes a glass of Buck's Fizz. Sun's out? Find the best spot on the terrace overlooking Henrietta Park. Breakfast room. Free Wi-Fi, in-room TV. 'Very quiet' background radio. Garden (deck chairs), terrace. Parking ('a big plus'). Children (in some rooms; cot; extra bed £45 per night) and dogs welcomed. Resident dog, Muttley. 20 bedrooms (some family rooms; 2-room suite on lower ground floor). Per room B&B £119–£279. Closed Christmas.

BAUGHURST Hampshire
Map 2:D2
THE WELLINGTON ARMS, Baughurst Road, RG26 5LP. Tel 0118 982 0110, www.thewellingtonarms.com.

A 'comfortable, low-key' place, this 18th-century former hunting lodge in the North Wessex Downs pleases guests with its laid-back atmosphere. (The hand-knit mohair tea cosies are pleasing, too.) It is owned by Jason King (the chef) and Simon Page. Stylishly converted bedrooms, some with soaring green-oak beams, are superbly kitted out with top-quality bedlinen, bathrobes, high-end toiletries, a capsule coffee machine and home-made biscuits; the handsome Cart House room, in a freestanding barn, looks out over neighbouring fields. Mealtimes, join the locals and visitors making tracks for the relaxed pub and dining room (wooden floors, exposed brickwork, retro-painted wood-panelled walls). Here, Jason King's 'extraordinary, unfussy' dishes use the bounty of vegetables, herbs and salads grown in the garden and polytunnel at the back. In the morning, the pub's free-range chickens supply eggs for the 'leisurely' breakfasts. Bar, restaurant (closed Sun eve). Garden. Available for private functions. Free Wi-Fi, in-room TV (Freeview). Background music. Children and dogs (£10 per night) welcomed. 4 bedrooms (3 in converted outbuildings). Per room B&B £100–£200. Dinner £35.

BEESANDS Devon
Map 1:E4

THE CRICKET INN, Kingsbridge, TQ7 2EN. Tel 01548 580215, www.thecricketinn.com. Facing the beach and a wide expanse of sea, this 19th-century inn on Start Bay is 'rightly popular' for its 'excellent' upmarket pub grub and stylish accommodation. The whole is a family concern: owners Rachel and Nigel Heath renovated and extended the building to include its airy, New England-style bedrooms; son Scott is the chef. At lunch and dinner, tuck in to fresh seafood including crab, lobster and scallops straight from the bay – it's all served by the 'friendly' staff. Spend the night in one of the seaside-inspired bedrooms, refurbished in 2016. Some are large enough to accommodate a family; most have sea views. Full Devonshire breakfasts. On the South West Coastal Path; the village has a large freshwater lake with a bird hide. Going walking? Ask about luggage transfers to your next destination. Bar, restaurant (alfresco dining). Private dining facilities. Free Wi-Fi, in-room TV. No background music. Parking. Children (special menu) and dogs welcomed. 7 bedrooms (4 in a new extension; 3 family rooms). Per room B&B £100–£130, D,B&B £140–£170.

BELPER Derbyshire
Map 2:A2

DANNAH FARM, Bowmans Lane, Shottle, DE56 2DR. Tel 01773 550273, www.dannah.co.uk. 'Charming' hosts Joan and Martin Slack do 'all they can to make guests welcome' at their rustic B&B on a 150-acre working farm in the Derbyshire Dales ('watch out for tractors!'). The stone-built house has plenty of character, with extensive gardens in which to get comfortably lost, and a spa cabin with a Finnish sauna and double steam shower. Visitors return for the 'lovely, spacious, beautifully clean' bedrooms overlooking garden and countryside; equally appreciated are bathrooms 'with all the luxury trimmings'. Want some alone time? Book the Secret Garden hut, on a secluded lawn with a screen of trees – its outdoor spa bath is perfect for midnight stargazing. 'Delicious, plentiful' farmhouse breakfasts include award-winning black pudding, locally made sausages, eggs from free-range hens. Supper platters with a selection of meats, cheeses, fish, salads, home-made bread and puddings can be arranged. 2 sitting rooms, dining room. Large walled garden. Meeting room. Licensed. Free Wi-Fi, in-room TV (Freeview). No background music. Parking. 2 miles from town. Children welcomed (£20 per night). 8 bedrooms (4 in adjoining converted barn; 3 on ground floor). Per room B&B £175–£295. Supper platter £18.95. 2-night min. stay on Fri, Sat. Closed Christmas.

BERWICK Sussex
Map 2:E4

GREEN OAK BARN, The English Wine Centre, BN26 5QS. Tel 01323 870164, www.englishwinecentre.co.uk. Wine lovers, set your sights on the 'smart' rooms in Christine and Colin Munday's reconstructed traditional Sussex barn, within easy reach of an impressive collection of English vintages. (The Mundays also own the adjacent wine centre and shop, which stocks more than 140 English labels.) Gather with fellow guests in the open-plan communal area on the ground floor (sofas, a bar, a baby grand piano). Stylish, modern bedrooms on the upper level have a large bed, designer fabrics, specially commissioned artwork. In the thatched Flint Barn restaurant, sample a wide choice of wines by the glass to accompany the seasonal English menus. Colin Munday organises regular wine tastings. Bar/lounge, terrace, restaurant (open lunch Wed–Sun; dinner Fri/Sat

or by prior arrangement). Wine shop. 3-acre garden with water features. Lift. Free Wi-Fi, in-room TV (Freeview). Civil wedding licence, functions. No background music. Children welcomed. 5 miles from Glyndebourne. 5 bedrooms (1 suitable for disabled). Per room B&B £120–£175. Dinner from £25.50. Closed Christmas, New Year.
25% DISCOUNT VOUCHERS

BEXHILL-ON-SEA Sussex
Map 2:E4

COAST, 58 Sea Road, TN40 1JP. Tel 01424 225260, www.coastbexhill.co.uk. 'Done up with care', Piero and Lucia Mazzoni's 'well-run' B&B is in a tidy Edwardian villa on a street sloping down to the seafront. Bright, modern bedrooms have a seating area, tea- and coffee-making facilities, bottled water, biscuits, wooden hangers ('praise be!'); 'nice smellies' in the 'clean' bathroom. The 'warm, friendly' hosts provide a good choice of hot dishes at breakfast, including pancakes with crème fraîche, fresh fruit and maple syrup, and vegetarian dishes – all served in a sunny room. 'A delight.' Convenient for shops, restaurants and the station. Lounge, breakfast room. Free Wi-Fi, in-room TV (Freeview). Soft background music. Children over 5 welcomed. Secure bicycle storage. 5 bedrooms. Per room B&B single from £70, double from £89.

BIBURY Gloucestershire
Map 3:E6

THE SWAN, nr Cirencester, GL7 5NW. Tel 01285 740695, www.cotswold-inns-hotels.co.uk. Pass meadows dotted with grazing cows and sheep on the way to this 17th-century former coaching inn, in a village that William Morris proclaimed to be the most beautiful in England. The inn (Cotswold Inns and Hotels) stands on the banks of the River Coln; most of the stylishly refurbished bedrooms overlook the water. Each room is different – some have a four-poster bed, others a spa bath – but all are well equipped with a capsule coffee machine and fancy toiletries. Splurge on one of the cottage suites, a short walk from the inn, each with a separate sitting room and private garden. Dine on modern European dishes in the brasserie; in summer, doors open on to a courtyard for alfresco dining. Lounge, bar (wood-burning stove), brasserie. ½-acre garden. Lift. Free Wi-Fi, in-room TV (Freeview). Civil wedding licence, functions. No background music. Children and well-behaved dogs (in some bedrooms; charge) welcomed. Trout fishing can be arranged. 22 bedrooms (4 in garden cottages, 1 with hot tub). Per room B&B £170–£290. Dinner from £29.50.

BISHOP'S CASTLE Shropshire
Map 3:C4

THE CASTLE HOTEL, Market Square, SY9 5BN. Tel 01588 638403, www. thecastlehotelbishopscastle.co.uk. 'We thoroughly enjoyed our stay – and our dog loved it, too.' Teeming with pastoral character, Henry and Rebecca Hunter's 'well-presented', refurbished 300-year-old hotel, built on an ancient castle bailey, is a refuge for walkers and cyclists seeking good-value Shropshire accommodation – and a fine selection of real ales to go with it. It is co-owned with Henry Hunter's parents, who own Pen-y-Dyffryn, Oswestry (see main entry). Climb the fine Georgian staircase to reach 'excellent', individually

designed bedrooms in a variety of sizes and styles. At lunch and dinner, enjoy chef Steve Bruce's bistro food in the casual bar areas or, more formally, in the 'handsome' oak-panelled restaurant (a fresh fish menu is added on Thursday and Friday). On sunny days, step outside: the large enclosed garden has a terrace with a pergola for alfresco dining. 3 bars (open fires; traditional pub games), dining room. Garden with fish pond, patio, terrace. Free Wi-Fi, in-room TV (Freeview). In-room spa treatments. Bicycle storage, mud room. No background music. Parking. Children (extra bed £25 per night) and dogs welcomed. 12 bedrooms (2 family rooms). Per room B&B £75–£190, D,B&B £102–£245. Closed Christmas Day.
25% DISCOUNT VOUCHERS

BISHOP'S TACHBROOK
Warwickshire
Map 2:B2

MALLORY COURT, Harbury Lane, CV33 9QB. Tel 01926 330214, www.mallory. co.uk. For a stab at the quintessential English country life, check in to this 'luxurious', 'relaxing' ivy-clad manor house (Relais & Châteaux), 'beautifully situated' for Warwick Castle and Stratford-upon-Avon. The 'extensive' landscaped gardens, complete with pond, formal Old English rose garden and bountiful kitchen garden, create a feeling of sanctuary. Long-serving manager Sarah Barker heads a team of 'quietly efficient, pleasantly professional' staff. Individually decorated bedrooms are in the main house and modern Knights' Suite annexe. Ring to discuss the best room choices before booking: some guests this year liked a 'spacious,

well-equipped' main-house room with 'a good view' over the garden; others found their annexe room 'smart but impersonal'. 'The turn-down service is meticulous. They left two bottles of water and a little bag of sweets, with an invitation to take them away the next day.' There's a choice of eating places: chef Paul Foster serves a 'fine' daily-changing menu in the 'excellent' oak-panelled restaurant (vegetarian tasting menu available); the 'light, stylish' brasserie has straightforward dishes (perhaps 'perfectly cooked' sweetbreads; 'spot-on' sea trout with cockles and shrimps) at 'reasonable' prices. Next morning, wake to a 'civilised, high-quality' breakfast. 2 lounges, brasserie (Thurs jazz nights), restaurant, terrace. Lift. Outdoor swimming pool, tennis court, croquet. Free Wi-Fi, in-room TV. Background music. Civil wedding licence, function facilities. Children welcomed. 31 bedrooms (11 in Knight's Suite, 2 suitable for disabled). Per room B&B from £169. Set dinner £49.50.
25% DISCOUNT VOUCHERS

BLACKBURN Lancashire
Map 4:D3
MILLSTONE AT MELLOR, Church Lane, Mellor, BB2 7JR. Tel 01254 813333, www.millstonehotel.co.uk. Guests receive 'a friendly welcome' at this stone-built former coaching house (Thwaites Inns of Character) in the Ribble valley. It is run by chef/patron Anson Bolton and his wife, Sarah. Book a table in the 'lively' restaurant – 'clearly the pub's main attraction is its food,' say Guide readers in 2016. The chef's 'excellent', 'confident' meals are cooked in 'a local Lancashire style'; a beer sommelier is on hand to pair

dishes with real ales. Stay the night in country-style bedrooms stocked with fresh milk, tea- and coffee-making facilities, and home-made biscuits. 'Ours was of a reasonable size, with good storage space. It faced the road, but wasn't too noisy. In the bathroom: fleecy bathrobes, a good shower.' Breakfast is a hearty affair, with fresh fruit, yogurts and freshly baked croissants, but one visitor thought it lacked the oomph of the evening meal. Residents' lounge (log fire), bar, restaurant (open to non-residents), terrace (alfresco dining). Free Wi-Fi, in-room TV. Background radio at breakfast ('but, as our table was next to the radio, we were able to turn it down'). Parking. Children welcomed. 23 bedrooms (6 in courtyard; 2 suitable for disabled). Per room B&B single £56–£100, double £62–£120. Dinner £30.

BLACKPOOL Lancashire
Map 4:D2
NUMBER ONE ST LUKE'S, 1 St Luke's Road, South Shore, FY4 2EL. Tel 01253 343901, www.numberoneblackpool.com. Minutes from Blackpool Pleasure Beach and the famous promenade, Mark and Claire Smith's 'beautiful' Art Deco B&B is 'very much recommended' for its good value and convenient location. The 'outstanding' modern bedrooms have a king-size bed; up-to-date gadgetry includes a large plasma TV, games console and remote-controlled lighting. Catch up on the latest soaps on the wall-mounted TV above the whirlpool bath; bathrooms also have a power shower and music system. Go big with the 'full Blackpool' at breakfast or opt for a lighter option (special diets are catered for). A large conservatory overlooks the garden. (See also Number

One South Beach, next entry.) Dining room, conservatory. Garden (hot tub). Putting green. Free Wi-Fi, in-room TV (Freeview). No background music. Parking. Free POD Point for charging electric vehicles. 2 miles from town centre. Children over 4 welcomed. 3 bedrooms. Per room B&B from £110.

NUMBER ONE SOUTH BEACH,
4 Harrowside West, FY4 1NW. Tel 01253 343900, www. numberonesouthbeach.com. Reach the attractions of Blackpool with a stroll down the promenade from this 'very comfortable,' modern hotel. Owners Janet and Graham Oxley and Claire and Mark Smith (see Number One St Luke's, previous entry) have done up the bedrooms with pizzazz; each has up-to-date gadgetry, including a TV in the bathroom. Go for one of the best, with a balcony and sea views. The 'excellent' hosts are 'very informative about what's going on in town'. Plenty of choice at breakfast. Lounge (oversized plasma TV), bar, restaurant. Lift. Pool table; indoor golf simulator. Meeting/conference facilities. Free Wi-Fi, in-room TV (Sky). Quiet classical background music. Parking. Children over 5 welcomed. 14 bedrooms (some suitable for disabled). Per room B&B £139–£175. Dinner £26–£30. 2-night min. stay at weekends in high season. Closed 26–31 Dec.

RAFFLES HOTEL & TEA ROOM, 73–77 Hornby Road, FY1 4QJ. Tel 01253 294713, www.raffleshotelblackpool. co.uk. A good-value option for the seaside resort, Graham Poole and Ian Balmforth's traditional hotel is close to the Winter Gardens, the promenade

and the beach. The flower-bedecked entrance welcomes visitors to the bay-fronted house; inside, find a spot to relax in the comfortable sitting room and homely bedrooms. Suites with a lounge and kitchenette can accommodate a family. Most afternoons, enjoy home-made cakes and snacks in the traditional English tea room. In the evening, feast on Ian Balmforth's three-course set dinners (requested in advance). Lounge, bar, breakfast room, tea room (closed Mon, and midweek out of season). Free Wi-Fi, in-room TV (Freeview). Background music. Parking. Children (cot; special rates for over-5s) and dogs (in some rooms, by arrangement) welcomed. 17 bedrooms and suites (some on ground floor). Per person B&B from £40. Set dinner £12.95. Closed Christmas.

BORROWDALE Cumbria
Map 4: inset C2
LEATHES HEAD HOTEL, Keswick, CA12 5UY. Tel 01768 777247, www. leatheshead.co.uk. There are 'superb' views and uninterrupted vistas across to Catbells, Skiddaw and Derwent Water from this secluded hotel at the head of the Borrowdale valley. A welcoming place, the country house was built for a ship-owner's daughter; today, it blends Edwardian elegance with modern touches. Jamie Adamson and Jane Cleary are the managers. Individually decorated bedrooms overlook countryside, valley or garden; two of the best, in the original master bedrooms, have armchairs by double-aspect bay windows. Get comfortable in the conservatory, beside the fire in the lounge, or in the intimate, smartly refurbished bar. In the restaurant,

sample Daniel Hopkins's fine-dining menus, which use plenty of locally grown and home-reared Cumbrian produce. Plan ahead for days out – packed lunches may be ordered the night before. Lounge, bar, dining room, drying room; conservatory, terrace. 3-acre grounds. Free Wi-Fi, in-room TV (Freeview). No background music. 4½ miles S of Keswick. 12 bedrooms (3 on ground floor; 1 suitable for disabled). Per room D,B&B from £145. 2-night min. stay at weekends. Closed Dec–Feb.

BOURNEMOUTH Dorset
Map 2:E2
THE GREEN HOUSE, 4 Grove Road, BH1 3AX. Tel 01202 498900, www. thegreenhousehotel.com. It's easy being green at this handsomely restored Grade II listed Victorian villa close to the seafront. Rescued from dereliction by co-owner Christopher Airey, the hotel is run with a commitment to environmental consciousness: the chic, modern interior is decorated with natural and organic materials, and eco paints and wallpaper; its furnishings are made from storm-felled trees; solar panels power an ecological energy system; bees make honey in the rooftop beehives. In the stylish bedrooms, find organic bedlinen; a jar of freshly baked biscuits. Choose from chef Andy Hilton's unfussy modern menu in the Arbor restaurant; in clement weather, the terrace is the place to be. Bar, restaurant. Terrace. Lift. Free Wi-Fi, in-room TV (Freeview). Civil wedding licence. Background music. Parking. Children (special menu; cot) welcomed. 32 bedrooms (1 suitable for disabled; 5 master doubles have an open-plan

bathroom). Per room B&B from £119, D,B&B from £165.

URBAN BEACH, 23 Argyll Road, BH5 1EB. Tel 01202 301509, www. urbanbeach.co.uk. A laid-back vibe characterises Mark Cribb's friendly small hotel near Boscombe beach. Sip a seasonal cocktail in the buzzy bar; in the popular bistro, pick from an à la carte menu of modern dishes. Sister restaurant Urban Reef, on the promenade, is a fun alternative – and hotel guests get priority booking. Bedrooms vary in size, from snug singles to a spacious triple-aspect room suitable for a family; all have tea- and coffee-making facilities, and DVDs to borrow. Ask the engaging staff about the best of Bournemouth – they pride themselves on showing off their seaside resort. Bar/bistro; covered seating deck with heaters. Free Wi-Fi, in-room TV. DVD and iTunes library. Background music. Complimentary use of local leisure club with gym, indoor pool, sauna and steam room. Limited on-site parking; free street parking. Children (special menu; cot, baby bath, extra bed, monitor, high chair; toys, activities) welcomed. 12 bedrooms. Wellies, umbrellas, universal phone charger available on request. 1 mile E of town centre. Per room B&B single £72, double £100–£180. Dinner £32. 2-night min. stay at weekends.
25% DISCOUNT VOUCHERS

BOWNESS-ON-WINDERMERE
Cumbria
Map 4: inset C2
LINDETH HOWE, Lindeth Drive, Longtail Hill, LA23 3JF. Tel 01539 445759, www.lindeth-howe.co.uk.

A fine base from which to potter about the south lakes, this Victorian country house was once the home of the celebrated author who wrote about the exploits of Peter Rabbit and Squirrel Nutkin. The hotel stands in large grounds with mature gardens, ponds and woodlands – space enough for present-day guests to find adventure of their own. 'Well-appointed' bedrooms have views across the garden or lake and fells; larger rooms can accommodate a family. In fine weather, take afternoon tea on the sun terrace or strike out on any of the many walks from the front door; on wet days, claim a spot in the sitting room with a book or board game. Come dinnertime, sit down to newly appointed chef Chris Davies's innovative British dishes in the candlelit dining room (good vegetarian choices). Sitting room, library, lounge bar, restaurant. Free Wi-Fi, in-room TV. Civil wedding licence. Pianist on Sat evenings. Sun terrace. 5-acre grounds. Indoor swimming pool, sauna, fitness room, treatment room. Electric bicycles for hire. Children welcomed (no under-7s in restaurant at night; children's high tea, babysitting available); 3 dog-friendly rooms. 34 bedrooms (2 on ground floor suitable for disabled). Per room B&B from £170, D,B&B from £240. Tasting menu £62.95, à la carte £35–£55. Closed 2–16 Jan.

BRANSCOMBE Devon
Map 1:C5

THE MASON'S ARMS, EX12 3DJ. Tel 01297 680300, www.masonsarms.co.uk. In a 'delightful' village close to the shingle beach, this popular pub-with-rooms occupies a creeper-covered 14th-century cider house and a row of cottages. It is managed by Alison Ede for St Austell Brewery Hotels & Inns. Locals and tourists come for the real ales in the 'cosy' bar (slate floors, stone walls, log fireplace); the 'fresh, excellent' cooking (including 'outstanding' fish dishes) keeps them in their seats. Bedrooms in the main building and garden cottages are 'comfortably furnished' with a 'good' bed, and a mix of antique and contemporary furniture; many have original features. Wake up with the inn's custom blend of Fairtrade coffee at breakfast; there's also a choice of continental and cooked options. The village is 'well placed' for visiting the coast; a ten-minute walk down a field path leads to the beach and the sea. Bar, restaurant. Garden with outdoor seating. Free Wi-Fi (in main bar only), in-room TV. No background music. Children and dogs (in some cottages, £10 per night) welcomed. 27 bedrooms (14 in cottages, some suitable for disabled). Per room B&B from £95. Dinner £30.

BRIGHTON Sussex
Map 2:E4

A ROOM WITH A VIEW, 41 Marine Parade, BN2 1PE. Tel 01273 682885, www.aroomwithaviewbrighton.com. Enjoy 'lovely' views down to the Palace Pier from Stephen Bull's 'immaculately presented', 'well-located' Georgian guest house in Kemp Town. Guests praise its 'cheerful, friendly' staff and 'thoughtful' touches. The 'light, airy, clean' bedrooms are well equipped (ear plugs in the bedside drawer, biscuits and a capsule coffee machine, dressing gowns, slippers); each has a 'comfy' bed and large windows. An attic room with a terrace is 'small but delightful'. Find good choice on the 'excellent' breakfast menu, including blueberry pancakes and 'highly recommended' double eggs Benedict, plus a wide buffet (all diets catered for). Steps from the beach; a few minutes' walk to the Lanes, restaurants and shops. 'Tight but useful' on-site parking. Lounge (gentle background music), breakfast room. Free Wi-Fi, in-room TV. Parking. 9 bedrooms. Per room B&B £125–£275.

DRAKES, 43–44 Marine Parade, BN2 1PE. Tel 01273 696934, www.drakesofbrighton.com. Sleek style, sea views and a good selection of sundowners come together at this modern seafront hotel near the pier. It is owned by Gayle and Andy Shearer; Richard Hayes manages a team of 'courteous, helpful' staff. Spread across the two Regency town houses, bedrooms are well equipped with magazines, freshly ground coffee, still and sparkling water; waffle robes and slippers in the bathroom. Go for glamour in the best room, where a free-standing bathtub has been set in front of the floor-to-ceiling windows looking out to sea. Start the night – or finish it off – with cocktails in Drakes Bar; in the 'smart' basement restaurant, newly promoted chef Andy Vitez serves modern British and European dishes, including interesting vegetarian options. Lounge/bar, restaurant. Meeting room. Free Wi-Fi, in-room TV (Sky). Civil wedding/partnership licence. Light background music. Limited on-site parking. Children welcomed. 20 bedrooms (2 on ground floor). Room £120–£360. Breakfast £6–£12.50. 4-course dinner £56. 2-night min. stay at weekends.
25% DISCOUNT VOUCHERS

FIVE, 5 New Steine, BN2 1PB. Tel 01273 686547, www.fivehotel.com. Close to the beach and pier, Caroline and Simon Heath's well-located modern B&B occupies a handsome Regency town house on a garden square. Many of the bright, well-equipped bedrooms (some snug) look towards the sea. Pick the hour and a breakfast picnic hamper appears at the door, containing muffins, cereals, yogurts, fruit, juice; decadent extras like champagne and breakfast cakes may be supplied. A room-only option lets guests sample breakfast or brunch in one of the many cafés nearby. Free Wi-Fi, in-room TV (Freeview). No background music. DVD library. Children over 5 welcomed. Bicycle storage. 10 bedrooms (some with sea views). Per person B&B £35–£60. 2-night min. stay at weekends.

PASKINS, 18–19 Charlotte Street, BN2 1AG. Tel 01273 601203, www.paskins.co.uk. Enjoy the seashore, then lay your head in this sustainability-savvy B&B occupying two stuccoed Grade II listed 19th-century houses in Kemp Town. Owners Susan and Roger Marlowe have had green credentials since before these were trendy. 'Comfortable', colourful bedrooms are immaculate; toiletries are certified cruelty-free. The hosts find inspiration in cuisine from across the world, and have long sourced produce locally; their 'delicious' organic breakfast menu, served in the Art Deco dining room, has 'unusual' choices, with excellent vegetarian and vegan options (including home-made meat-free sausages and fritters). Lounge, breakfast room. Free Wi-Fi. No background music. Children and dogs (by arrangement) welcomed. 19 bedrooms. Per person B&B £50–£75. Discounts to Vegetarian Society, Vegan Society and Amnesty International members.

BROCKENHURST Hampshire
Map 2:E2
DAISYBANK COTTAGE, Sway Road, The New Forest, SO42 7SG. Tel 01590 622086, www.bedandbreakfast-newforest.co.uk. Expect a sweet welcome at Ciaran and Cheryl Maher's chic hideaway in the New Forest: home-made cupcakes are offered on arrival. B&B accommodation is in the main Arts and Crafts house and a prettily converted cottage in the garden. Cosseting bedrooms have a wide bed, plantation shutters and all the mod cons (iPod dock, Roberts radio, silent mini fridge, capsule coffee machine); a well-designed bathroom or wet room. Some cottage suites have their own patio with access to the garden. Before retiring for the night, place your breakfast order in the flowerpot outside your room; awake to an Aga-fresh full Irish or New Forest breakfast, pancakes or home-baked soda bread (special diets are catered for). Brockenhurst locals, the hosts have a wealth of knowledge about the area, including helpful advice on pubs and restaurants. 2 sitting rooms, breakfast room. Free Wi-Fi, in-room TV (Freeview). No background music. Garden. Secure parking. Children over 10 welcomed. 10 mins' walk from village and station. 7 bedrooms (all on ground floor, some in Gardener's Cottage, some 'disabled friendly'). Per room B&B £100–£140. Closed for 1 week over Christmas period.
25% DISCOUNT VOUCHERS

BUCKDEN Cambridgeshire
Map 2:B4
THE GEORGE, High Street, PE19 5XA. Tel 01480 812300, www.thegeorgebuckden.com. The 'busy, buzzing' restaurant is 'a highlight' at this 'beautifully decorated' 19th-century coaching inn on the main street of a 'quaint' village, say Guide inspectors in 2016. The hotel and brasserie are owned by Anne and Richard Furbank; their staff are 'courteous', 'friendly', 'obliging'. Locals flock to the 'pleasing', 'family-friendly' dining room, where chef Benaissa El Akil's 'excellent' modern British dishes have a Mediterranean touch. 'The waiters were very attentive with a complex order.' The bedrooms may be 'a little old fashioned', with 'dim' lighting, but they have a 'comfortable' bed and a 'clean, modern' bathroom. 'I had a good night's sleep.' A 'nice' touch: a fruit bowl in the corridor. 'Excellent' coffee at breakfast; 'perfectly poached' eggs and smoked salmon are among the 'delicious' options. Bar, lounge, restaurant. Private dining rooms. Lift. Free Wi-Fi, in-room TV (Freeview). Background music. Civil wedding licence. Courtyard. Children welcomed. 12 bedrooms (3 suitable for disabled). Per room B&B £95–£150, D,B&B £150–£180. Dinner £35. Closed evenings of 25/26 Dec, 1 Jan.

BUCKFASTLEIGH Devon
Map 1:D4
KILBURY MANOR, Colston Road, TQ11 0LN. Tel 01364 644079, www.kilburymanor.co.uk. Countryside contentment settles over Julia and Martin Blundell's 'tastefully furnished' B&B, in a 17th-century longhouse whose impressive four-acre grounds

lead, through a meadow, to the River Dart. Each of the comfortable, spacious bedrooms has a fireplace, pleasing snaps of colour, bathrobes; Fairtrade tea, coffee and hot chocolate on the hospitality tray. Two rooms, in the converted barn across the courtyard, have their own entrance. Extensive breakfasts include the hostess's home-made marmalade, conserves and compotes; special dietary needs can be catered for. Evenings, the Blundells have local eateries to recommend. Wander in the peaceful garden: there are flower borders, fruit trees and a pond. Dining room (wood-burning stove). Garden, courtyard (outdoor seating). Free Wi-Fi, in-room TV (Freeview). No background music. Children over 8 welcomed. Resident dogs, Dillon and Buster. 1 mile from town; the South Devon Railway runs behind the house. Buckfast Abbey, otter sanctuary, butterfly farm nearby. Bicycle and canoe storage. 4 bedrooms (2 in converted stone barn across the courtyard; plus one 1-bedroom cottage). Per room B&B single from £65, double £80–£95. Credit cards not accepted.

BUDLEIGH SALTERTON Devon
Map 1:D5
ROSEHILL ROOMS AND COOKERY, 30 West Hill, EX9 6BU. Tel 01395 444031, www.rosehillroomsandcookery.co.uk. Coastal paths and cookery classes draw guests to Willi and Sharon Rehbock's immaculate B&B. The Victorian house is set in peaceful gardens with a sweeping view down to the sea. Inside, large bedrooms have a sofa, magazines, and home-made cakes or biscuits. On fine days, breathe in the fresh air: a large veranda wraps

around the house. Breakfast is taken communally. In the autumn and winter months, Willi Rehbock, a professional chef, hosts cooking classes on bread-making, seafood, Mediterranean cuisine and more. Dining room. Free Wi-Fi, in-room TV (Freeview). No background music. 4 bedrooms. Per room B&B from £120. 2-night min. stay.

BURFORD Oxfordshire
Map 2:C2
BAY TREE HOTEL, Sheep Street, OX18 4LW. Tel 01993 822791, www.cotswold-inns-hotels.co.uk/the-bay-tree-hotel. Step under the arch of wisteria draped across the entrance and into this 'lovely old building', as visitors have done for more than 400 years. It is now part of Michael and Pamela Horton's small Cotswold Inns and Hotels group; Mark Jelinek manages. Settle into a comfy armchair over a cup of tea in the smart, oak-panelled library (quirky lamps, well-stocked shelves, a roaring fire); head up the galleried staircase to a bedroom individually designed with jaunty checks, tweeds or hunting-themed fabrics. Rooms vary in size and style – ask for one with a four-poster bed or a feature fireplace. Bedrooms are well equipped with a capsule coffee machine, bathrobes and high-end toiletries. Some, with direct outdoor access, are dog-friendly, too. Dine in: the pleasing, light-filled restaurant is 'a very good eatery' serving modern British dishes; in fine weather, meals may be taken on the terrace. Library, bar, Bay Tree restaurant, patio (alfresco dining). Free Wi-Fi, in-room TV (Freeview). No background music. Civil wedding licence, function facilities. Walled garden (croquet). Children and

well-behaved dogs (charge) welcomed. 21 bedrooms (2 adjoining garden rooms on ground floor). Per room B&B from £145, D,B&B from £200.

BURWASH Sussex
Map 2:E4
PELHAM HALL, High Street, TN19 7ES. Tel 01435 882335, pelhamhall. co.uk. Matthew Fox has banished the humdrum at his cheering B&B in a meticulously restored medieval hall house. A collection of fine fabrics, eye-catching pottery, murals and antiques complements the 14th-century hammer beams and wattle-and-daub walls. Former servants' quarters now serve as a reception area; the inglenook kitchen now houses a bright, colourful library and honesty bar. No two bedrooms are alike. Phoenix has a balmy feel (tropical prints, hand-painted silks), and French doors opening on to a private patio. Split-level Labrador has groovily repurposed antiques, a private entrance, and magnificent Weald views from the sitting area. In the oldest wing, Bantham has interesting fittings, and a hand-finished mural by a local artist. Breakfast is served in the oak-floored dining room or in the garden on fine days: lumberjack pancakes, Spanish-style baked eggs, a full English; vegetarian alternatives available. Close to Bateman's and Great Dixter; pubs and restaurants within easy reach. Reception room, library/bar, dining room, patio (alfresco breakfasts). Free Wi-Fi, in-room TV. No background music. Garden. Children over 12 welcomed. 3 bedrooms. Per room B&B from £115. 2-night min. stay preferred. Closed Christmas, New Year. Credit cards not accepted.

BUXTON Derbyshire
Map 3:A6
HARTINGTON HALL, Hall Bank, Hartington, SK17 0AT. Tel 01298 84223, www.yha.org.uk/hostel/hartington. From annual beer and music festivals to year-round walking and cycling tours, discover plentiful amusement at this 'lovely' upmarket youth hostel in the Peak District. Standing in 'immaculate' grounds, the former Jacobean manor house offers 'amazing value', in a setting with period features galore (mullioned windows, oak panelling, stone fireplaces). The main building makes a charming backdrop for basic accommodation; the converted coach house and barn have more rooms, including self-catering suites. Board games, books and bicycles can be borrowed for children – or send young ones off to the jungle gym and goat pen in the grounds. Hearty, home-cooked breakfasts are taken in the restaurant (open to the public); a 'rural' menu is served at dinnertime. Packed lunches provided. 2 lounges, bar, restaurant. Games room, self-catering kitchen, drying room. Meeting rooms. Free Wi-Fi (YHA members, in public rooms only). Background music. Civil wedding licence. Extensive grounds: beer garden, pet area. Parking. Children welcomed (adventure playground, giant Connect 4). 20 mins' drive from Buxton. 35 bedrooms (10 in barn annexe, 5 in coach house; 1 suitable for disabled). Private room from £19. Breakfast £5.25, dinner from £11.95.

CAMBRIDGE Cambridgeshire
Map 2:B4
THE VARSITY HOTEL & SPA, 24 Thompson's Lane, off Bridge Street, CB5 8AQ. Tel 01223 306030, www. thevarsityhotel.co.uk. In the midst

of this seat of learning stands a 'very convenient' hotel on the River Cam. A collegiate air infuses the place: rooms, in graduating categories, are named after the different colleges; portraits of famed alumni gaze down at visitors; complimentary Saturday walking tours take in 'town and gown' landmarks. Guide readers this year praised the 'helpful' staff and warm welcome. 'Visitors are usually greeted by a retired college porter with a bowler hat – an elegant touch.' Take in 'wonderful' views from the modern, air-conditioned bedrooms, some with extra seating and a large four-poster bed. The restaurant specialises in meat and fish cooked on the grill. In warm months, find a spot on the rooftop terrace for a drink from the extensive cocktail menu. Breakfast ('really good') has lots to choose from. 'The valet parking works well.' Dining room, roof terrace (barbecue in season; open to non-residents). Lift. Glassworks health club and spa (spa bath overlooking the River Cam), gym. Free Wi-Fi, in-room TV. Background music (restaurant). Civil wedding licence, conference facilities. Valet parking service (parking charge), local car parks. Children welcomed. 48 bedrooms (3 suitable for disabled). Per room B&B (continental) from £255.

CANTERBURY Kent
Map 2:D5
CANTERBURY CATHEDRAL LODGE, The Precincts, CT1 2EH. Tel 01227 865350, www.canterburycathedrallodge.org. Guide inspectors this year liked the warm welcome and 'cheerful, helpful' staff at this 'very special' purpose-built B&B and conference centre in the 'beautiful, tranquil' grounds of the UNESCO-designated World Heritage site. Residents have private access to the cathedral precincts and 'awe-inspiring' grounds after hours. Simple, 'comfortably equipped' courtyard bedrooms have views across the lawns and gardens, or the cathedral ('I couldn't resist sitting on the window seat and just staring at the magnificence'). 'Small' bathrooms make clever use of space. 'We appreciated the good lighting and efficient blackout curtains; bonus points for the convenience of the iron and ironing board.' Some 'no-frills' rooms are on the second floor of the adjacent Burgate annexe (no lift, no views). The Refectory serves as a 'bright, airy' breakfast space; eat alfresco on the terrace when weather cooperates. 'Our eggs Norwegian and a vegetarian breakfast were well cooked and speedily presented.' Library (newspapers, 'packed' bookshelves, 'comfortable' sofas), breakfast room. Campanile garden. Meeting/function facilities. Lift. Free Wi-Fi, in-room TV (Freeview). No background music. Limited parking (pre-booking required). 35 bedrooms (1 suitable for disabled). Per room B&B £92–£169.

CHATTON Northumberland
Map 4:A3
CHATTON PARK HOUSE, New Road, nr Alnwick, NE66 5RA. Tel 01668 215507, www.chattonpark.com. Paul and Michelle Mattinson's stately Georgian house is a 'most welcoming' B&B in peaceful countryside. Homely and comfortable, spacious bedrooms (named after nearby villages) have bathrobes, slippers and space to sit. Stretch out in the 'very large' dual-aspect lounge; take a stroll in the manicured grounds. 'Superlative' breakfasts (ordered in advance) are just the thing to fuel a

ramble in Northumberland national park. The Mattinsons are on hand with local information and restaurant recommendations. Sitting room, cosy bar, breakfast room. 4-acre grounds; grass tennis courts (May–Sept). Free Wi-Fi, weak mobile telephone signal, in-room TV (Freeview). No background music. Parking. ½ mile from Chatton; Alnwick, Bamburgh and Holy Island are close by. 4 bedrooms (plus 2-bedroom self-catering stone lodge with private garden). Per room B&B from £139. Closed late Nov–Feb.

CHELTENHAM Gloucestershire
Map 3:D5

BEAUMONT HOUSE, 56 Shurdington Road, GL53 0JE. Tel 01242 223311, www.bhhotel.co.uk. A noble, white-painted Victorian merchant's house is now home to Fan and Alan Bishop's 'excellent' B&B. Well-appointed bedrooms on the first, second and lower ground floors (some refurbished in 2016) vary in size and style. Top-floor rooms have sloping ceilings; two themed rooms (Out of Africa and Out of Asia) have a spa bath in the bathroom; a family suite sleeps four. All rooms have a 'comfortable' bed, tea- and coffee-making facilities, bottled water and biscuits. Make a complimentary hot drink in the spacious lounge, or go for something stronger at the honesty bar. In good weather, take a coffee into the well-tended garden. Breakfast includes smoked fish, local sausages, American-style pancakes; have it brought to the room if you're after a more languid start to the day. The shops and restaurants of Montpellier Arcade are 25 mins' walk away. Lounge, dining room (background music), conservatory. Free Wi-Fi, in-room TV (Freeview, Sky). Parking. Children (cot; £30 per night charge) welcomed. 1 mile from centre. 16 bedrooms (2 family suites). Per room B&B £75–£284. 2-night min. stay on Sat night, and for Festivals and Cheltenham Gold Cup.

BUTLERS, Western Road, GL50 3RN. Tel 01242 570771, www.butlers-hotel. co.uk. True to form for a butler-themed B&B, Guy Hunter and Robert Davies offer 'consistently exceptional service' at this former gentleman's residence, 'an easy walk' from the town centre. The house has been embellished with classic hats and photographs, archival sporting periodicals and candlestick telephone;. Take tea and coffee in the 'comfortable, well-used' lounge stocked with newspapers, books and games. 'Nice touches' include a shoe-buffing cloth on the landing, and proper stationery in the lounge. 'Well-appointed' bedrooms (Jeeves, Hudson, Brabinger, etc) have a radio, a hospitality tray and ironing/pressing facilities. Breakfast ('too good') is taken in a high-ceilinged room overlooking the pretty walled garden. The hosts 'go to a lot of trouble to help' guests seeking advice on local sightseeing or restaurants. 10 mins' walk to the bus and railway stations. Drawing room, dining room (quiet radio in the morning); ¼-acre garden. Free Wi-Fi, in-room TV (Freeview). Parking. Children over 5 welcomed. 9 bedrooms. Per room B&B single £60–£75, double £85–£120. 2-night min. stay during weekends and festivals.

THE CHELTENHAM TOWNHOUSE, 12–14 Pittville Lawn, GL52 2BD. Tel 01242 221922, www.cheltenhamtownhouse. com. Off to the races? Doff your beau chapeau at this airy B&B – it's well located for the racecourse. The Regency house was designed by architect John Forbes, who was also responsible for the Pittville Pump Room nearby; owners Adam and Jayne Lillywhite have created a relaxing atmosphere within, with fresh flowers, newspapers and an honesty bar in the lounge. It is managed by Nathanial Leitch. Individually styled, the light, modern bedrooms range from compact 'economy' rooms to spacious studio apartments with a kitchen and a sofa bed. Good breakfasts. Two bicycles and helmets are available to borrow. Lounge, breakfast room. Sun deck. Lift. Free Wi-Fi, in-room TV (Freeview). No background music. DVD library. Parking (limited on-site; permits supplied for street). Children (family rooms; cot, extra bed, high chair, milk warming) welcomed. 26 bedrooms (5 studio apartments, 4 in annexe, one 2-bed suite). Per room B&B £58–£150.

No. 131, 131 The Promenade, GL50 1NW. Tel 01242 822939, www.no131. com. Friendly staff create a 'nice atmosphere' at this chic hotel on the promenade. The conscientiously restored Grade II* listed villa is owned by Sam and Georgina Pearman; Liz Greenstock is now the manager. Arrive in time for afternoon tea – there are home-made sausage rolls and Victoria sponge for the taking. Upstairs, bedrooms are individually, tastefully designed with sophisticated colours and original British artworks; 'very comfortable', they have a 'great' bed, a capsule coffee machine, interesting minibar snacks, a hot-water bottle. Rub shoulders with locals over tasty cocktails and sharing plates in the glamorous Crazy Eights bar; in the smart restaurant, new chef Alan Gleeson specialises in seafood and wood-fired prime cuts, using quality local ingredients. The Pearmans also own the Wheatsheaf, Northleach (see main entry). Drawing room, lounge, games room, bar, restaurant. Terrace (alfresco dining). Private dining rooms. Free Wi-Fi, in-room Apple TV. Background music. 'Very convenient' parking. Children welcomed. 11 bedrooms. Per room B&B from £150. Dinner £38.

No. 38 The Park, 38 Evesham Road, GL52 2AH. Tel 01242 822929, www. no38thepark.com. From the exceedingly well-equipped bedrooms to the smart-yet-rustic breakfast spread, this modish, modern B&B has much to like. Sam and Georgina Pearman (see previous entry) are the astute owners; Liz Greenstock manages. The Georgian town house stands opposite leafy Pitville Park. Inside, bedrooms are done up with original artwork, a mix of vintage and modern furniture, an antique radiator, a large bed. Some, entered via a shared doorway, are ideal for a family. Each is different, though all have a hot-water bottle, a capsule coffee machine, natural toiletries and diverting technology (iPod docking station, flat-screen TV with pre-loaded movie library). No evening meals are served, but sister restaurant The Tavern is a ten-minute walk away. At breakfast, the farmhouse buffet table is laid with cereals, pastries, fruit, cold cuts and juices. Sitting room, open-plan dining area, private dining room (a chef can be arranged). Free Wi-Fi, in-room Apple TV (Sky). Background music. In-room treatments. Small courtyard garden. Limited parking. Children (cots; extra bed £25 per night; childcare by arrangement) and dogs welcomed. 15 mins' walk from centre; on the A435 towards Evesham (front windows double glazed). 13 bedrooms. Per room B&B (continental) from £120.

CHESTER Cheshire
Map 3:A4
THE CHESTER GROSVENOR, Eastgate, CH1 1LT. Tel 01244 324024, www. chestergrosvenor.com. Chandeliers and fine oak panelling mark the impressive entrance hall of this Grade II listed luxury hotel fit for a duke. (Indeed, it is managed by Bespoke Hotels for the Duke of Westminster.) 'Well-appointed' bedrooms are elegantly styled in neutral tones; they have an 'outstandingly comfortable' bed; 'excellent' large towels in the marble bathroom. Call for tea or coffee: 'It's swiftly served, with lovely china cups and teapots, biscuits and fresh milk.' Feeling peckish? Light meals may be taken in Arkle bar and lounge; the 'attractive' brasserie has 'great' food at lunch and dinner. The Michelin-starred Simon Radley at The Chester Grosvenor is 'an experience not to be missed'. Close to the cathedral and the Eastgate Clock, the whole 'couldn't be more centrally placed'. Drawing room, gallery lounge, private dining room. Lift. Free Wi-Fi, in-room TV. Background music. Civil wedding licence; function facilities. Spa (crystal steam room, herb sauna, themed shower, ice fountain; 5 treatment rooms). Valet parking service; multi-storey car park at rear of hotel. Children (special menu; interconnecting family rooms; no under-12s in restaurant) welcomed. 80 bedrooms and suites (1 suitable for disabled). Per room B&B (continental)

from £185, D,B&B from £210 in brasserie, from £290 in restaurant. Set menus (in restaurant) £75 or £99.

ODDFELLOWS, 20 Lower Bridge Street, CH1 1RS. Tel 01244 345454, www. oddfellowschester.com. Rumour has it this listed neoclassical mansion is a former meeting place for the altruistic Independent Order of Odd Fellows. Today, it's Oddfellows by name and delightful by nature. Public spaces are jollied up with topsy-turvy lamps, boxing bunnies, typewriters, and oak panelling hand-painted with blue tits and foxes. No two bedrooms – in the main house and a modern annexe – are alike. One has a circular bed, another twin roll-top baths; one is inspired by illustrator Randolph Caldecott, another by cinematographer Peter Newbrook. Take drinks in the Secret Garden (artificial grass, fire pits, heated private booths) or the flamboyant lounge bar; come dinnertime, sample the modern, Mediterranean-inspired menu cooked by chefs Steven Tuke and Simon Radley (of the Chester Grosvenor, see previous entry). A bagged breakfast (croissant, natural yogurt, fresh orange juice, fruit) is delivered to the bedroom in the morning. Lobby, bar, restaurant, conservatory. Private dining room, terrace. Free Wi-Fi, in-room TV. Background music. Garden. Children (cot, extra bed £30 per night) welcomed. 18 bedrooms (14 in annexe; 1 suitable for disabled). Per room B&B from £125. Closed Christmas Day.

CHEWTON MENDIP Somerset
Map 2:D1
THE POST HOUSE, BA3 4NS. Tel 01761 241704, www.theposthousebandb.co.uk. A rustic French feel infuses this charming

English cottage. Near the cathedral city of Wells, 'excellent hostess' Karen Price has turned a 400-year-old former post office and bakery into a stylish B&B. Throughout, wild flowers are bright against cool heritage hues; rustic lime-plaster walls, original flagstone floors and low wooden beams complement well-designed touches (vintage prints, beautiful glassware). In the bedrooms, a supply of home-baked biscuits is topped up every day. Breakfast has fresh fruit salad, home-baked bread, locally sourced bacon and sausages. Fancy self-catering? The 'luxurious' Old Bakery is a good option: it has a stone fireplace and its own secluded, vine-covered courtyard. Bath, Cheddar Gorge, Longleat and Wookey Hole are all within easy reach. Sitting room, dining room. Mediterranean-style courtyard. Small garden. Free Wi-Fi, in-room TV (Freeview). No background music. Parking. Children over 8 welcomed. Resident dog, Monty. 2 bedrooms (plus 1 self-catering cottage). Per room B&B £90–£160. 2-night min. stay at weekends.

CHICHESTER Sussex
Map 2:E3

ROOKS HILL, Lavant Road, Mid Lavant, PO18 0BQ. Tel 01243 528400, www.rookshill.co.uk. In a village at the foot of the South Downs, Erling Sorensen has restored a former farmhouse to create his stylish B&B. Bedrooms, including a new room with a four-poster bed, have feather pillows, crisp linens, a hospitality tray with hot chocolate; a power shower in the bathroom. Double glazing keeps out road noise. In winter, make for the log burner in the cosy drawing room; in warm months, the wisteria-clad patio

is a pleasant place to sit. At breakfast, help yourself to juices, cereals, yogurts, local honey, a fresh fruit salad; wash down a traditional cooked dish with freshly ground coffee or a choice of teas. No evening meals are served, but restaurants and pubs are nearby. Good links to Goodwood, and to Chichester's theatre scene. Drawing room, breakfast room. Courtyard. Free Wi-Fi, in-room TV (Freeview). Classical background music. Parking. 4 miles N of city centre. 4 bedrooms (1 suitable for disabled). Per room B&B £95–£165. Closed Christmas, New Year's Day.

CHIDDINGFOLD Surrey
Map 2:D3

THE CROWN INN, The Green, Petworth Road, GU8 4TX. Tel 01428 682255, www.thecrownchiddingfold.com. There's a 'welcoming' atmosphere at Daniel and Hannah Hall's 'really nice' thatch-roofed 16th-century country inn, all medieval walls, 'massive' beams, inglenook fireplaces and 'delicious' pub grub. 'We like the fact that it hasn't been mucked around with, and is still sticking to its traditional character.' Take a seat in the popular bar and 'lovely' oak-panelled dining room for a local ale and a dish off the 'inviting' menu. Once a month, sharpen your trivia skills at the convivial pub quiz. Afterwards, retire to one of the characterful bedrooms, each 'well equipped and modern' against original sloping floors and handsome antique furnishings. Two rooms, across the courtyard, have French windows opening on to a private garden. Good choice at breakfast. Bar (open fire), snug, restaurant. Free Wi-Fi, in-room TV (Freeview). Background music.

Parking. Children (special menu) welcomed. 8 miles SW of Peterborough. 8 bedrooms (2 on ground floor). Per room B&B £95–£185.

CHILGROVE Sussex
Map 2:E3

THE WHITE HORSE, 1 High Street, PO18 9HX. Tel 01243 519444, www. thewhitehorse.co.uk. In the foothills of the South Downs, this 'simply lovely' spot has a smart, modern-rustic style, and 'simple but satisfying' meals. Under a constellation of mirrors in the dining room, find a place on a leather banquette and tuck in to chef Rob Armstrong's 'good-quality' dishes, firmly rooted in the surrounding countryside – he sources trout from nearby rivers and pigeon from local estates. 'Comfortable' bedrooms are kitted out with quirky design touches: old steamer trunks, wool blankets, sheepskin rugs and the occasional copper bathtub. All rooms open on to a courtyard with views of the land all around; two have a private patio with an outdoor hot tub. Bar, restaurant, private dining room. Free Wi-Fi, in-room TV. Soft background music. Function facilities. 2 patios, garden. Croquet. Parking. Helipad. Children (cot, no bedding supplied; charge for extra bed) and dogs (£15 per stay) welcomed. 15 bedrooms (all on ground floor; 2 in main building, 13 in rear annexe; 2 suitable for a family). 10 mins' drive from Chichester. Per room B&B from £99. Dinner £30.

CHURCH STRETTON Shropshire
Map 3:C4

VICTORIA HOUSE, 48 High Street, SY6 6BX. Tel 01694 723823, www. victoriahouse-shropshire.co.uk. 'We've found somewhere that meets all our needs: it's well priced, comfortable and convenient, with superb breakfasts.' A 'capable and wonderfully energetic' hostess, Diane Chadwick warmly welcomes B&B visitors with afternoon tea at her 'splendid' Victorian town house. In the individually styled bedrooms, find original artwork and an antique or two; complimentary sherry, teas, hot chocolate and biscuits help guests settle in to their stay. Most days, light lunches may be taken in the dining room, with home-cooked Scottish and Australian favourites based on recipes from family and friends; home-baked cakes and scones are available all day. Freshly cooked, locally sourced breakfasts. Cyclists and walkers welcomed. Lounge, dining room (midday meal served Wed–Sun), garden. Free Wi-Fi, in-room TV (Freeview). No background music. Pay-and-Display parking (deducted from hotel bill, or permits supplied). Children and well-behaved pets (£10 per night) welcomed. 6 bedrooms. Per room B&B £55–£90.
25% DISCOUNT VOUCHERS

CLEY-NEXT-THE-SEA Norfolk
Map 2:A5

CLEY WINDMILL, The Quay, NR25 7RP. Tel 01263 740209, www.cleywindmill. co.uk. Heed the call of adventure at Julian and Carolyn Godlee's characterful B&B and restaurant in a 19th-century grinding mill on the north Norfolk coast. Fortune favours the brave: expansive views of the salt marshes and the sea can be enjoyed throughout, but the most inspiring vistas are found from the top-floor Wheel Room, accessed via a ladder. Here, the climb is rewarded with a different panorama from each of the room's four windows. Scared of heights? Tuck yourself in to the library in the circular sitting room at the base of the mill. A country aesthetic adorns the bedrooms (upstairs and in converted outbuildings). In the evening, chefs Emma Pegden and Jimmi Cubitt serve a daily-changing menu at the candlelit communal dinner. The mill stands next to a bird sanctuary; regular birdwatching events are organised. Sitting room, restaurant (open to non-residents). ¼-acre garden. Free Wi-Fi, in-room TV (Freeview). Background music. Civil wedding licence. Children (in some rooms; early supper by arrangement) welcomed. 9 bedrooms (3 in converted boathouse and granary). B&B £159–£199. Set menu £32.50. 2-night min. stay on Fri and Sat nights.

COLWALL Worcestershire
Map 3:D5

COLWALL PARK HOTEL, Walwyn Road WR13 6QG. Tel 01684 540000, www. colwall.com. 'A charm all of its own.' Lovely landscaped gardens lead straight into the wilds of the Malvern Hills from this tranquil black-and-white Edwardian country house hotel. Laura Fish manages 'helpful, friendly and efficient staff'. Fresh flowers bring a taste of the outdoors into the chic, simply styled bedrooms (some small but still 'well furnished, with plenty of storage'). Spacious family suites have a separate bedroom for young guests. White-painted beams criss-cross the ceilings in public spaces. The attractive modern bar (log fire) serves fresh Italian coffee, light meals and a good selection of local ales and ciders. Eat well:

'excellent' modern British dishes at dinner; 'plenty of variety' at breakfast. 2 lounges (1 with TV), library, bar, restaurant. Free Wi-Fi, in-room TV (Freeview). No background music. Civil wedding licence. Conference facilities. 2-acre garden. Children (cot, extra bed £35 per night) and dogs (Mutts Membership). 22 bedrooms. Per room B&B £95–£160, D,B&B £145–£210.

CONSTANTINE Cornwall
Map 1:E2

TRENGILLY WARTHA, Nancenoy, TR11 5RP. Tel 01326 340332, www.trengilly. co.uk. In a secluded wooded valley near the Helford river, Will and Lisa Lea's family-friendly pub-with-rooms is reached 'down the narrowest of Cornish lanes'. It is a picture of rustic charm, with a lively bar popular with locals, and a lush garden sloping towards a sheltered pond (find a leafy nook in which to sit). Local fishermen and farmers provide the ingredients for Nick Tyler's classic menus, served in the bar, bistro or conservatory. Bedrooms are simply furnished in country style, with views over the large garden or the village. Lazy day? Borrow a DVD or two and hole up in your room – tea, coffee and biscuits are supplied. Award-winning breakfasts include a filling full Cornish. Bar (quiz nights), restaurant, private dining room, conservatory, terrace (alfresco dining). Games room. Free Wi-Fi, in-room TV. Live music in bar Sun night. 6-acre garden (sheltered pond). Children and dogs welcomed. Resident goat, Titch. 11 bedrooms (2 in garden annexe). Per person B&B single from £60, double from £84. Closed Christmas.

CONSTANTINE BAY Cornwall
Map 1:D2

TREGLOS HOTEL, Beach Road, nr Padstow PL28 8JH. Tel 01841 520727, www.tregloshotel.com. Popular with young and old, the Barlow family's traditional hotel has 'very helpful' staff and plenty to do. There are play areas, a games room, a spa and swimming pool; landscaped gardens buttress an 18-hole golf course; the sandy white beaches of Constantine Bay are close by. Take in fine coastal views from many of the 'comfortable' bedrooms – some have a balcony. At lunch and dinner, feast on 'imaginative' daily-changing menus in chef Gavin Hill's award-winning restaurant. 2 lounges, bar, conservatory, restaurant (smart/casual attire after 7 pm). Children's den, games room. Indoor swimming pool. Glo spa, spa treatments. Lift. Free Wi-Fi (variable signal), in-room TV (Freeview). Background music (optional). 1-acre grounds, sunken garden. Children (special menus) and dogs (in some rooms) welcomed. Parking. 3 miles W of Padstow. 42 bedrooms (1 on ground floor; 2 suitable for disabled; plus self-catering apartments in grounds). Per room B&B from £150. Set dinner £36. 2-night min. stay during some periods. Closed Nov–Feb.

25% DISCOUNT VOUCHERS

CORNWORTHY Devon
Map 1:D4

KERSWELL FARMHOUSE, nr Tornes, TQ9 7HH. Tel 01803 732013, www.kerswellfarmhouse.co.uk. Between Totnes and Dartmouth, Nichola and Graham Hawkins's B&B occupies a lavishly renovated 400-year-old longhouse. This is a homely, rustic spot, where rooms have been kitted out with fresh flowers, English oak fittings and a mix of antique and farmhouse furnishings. A collection of fine art (paintings, pottery, glassware) is exhibited in the milking-parlour-turned-gallery. Settle in to one of the comfortable bedrooms – all have teas and ground coffee, cotton bathrobes, novels and magazines. For extra lounging space, ask for the suite in the converted barn, with a separate sitting room and private garden. Morning brings warm fruit compotes, golden-yolked Eggs Royale, traditional Devon breakfasts; resident hens supply the eggs. Wake early to wander down the footpaths, past the newly restored pond, to reach woodland and riverside trails – it's the perfect time to catch sight of wildlife. 2 dining rooms, sitting room (honesty bar, including wines from local vineyard). Gallery. Free Wi-Fi, in-room TV. No background music. 14-acre grounds. Parking. Kayaking (1 kayak available to loan). Children over 12 welcomed. Resident dog, Bear. 4 miles from Totnes. 5 bedrooms (1 in adjacent barn; 1 on ground floor). Per person B&B £55–£70. 2-night min. stay preferred. Credit cards not accepted. Closed Nov–Apr.

CORSHAM Wiltshire
Map 2:D1

THE METHUEN ARMS, 2 High Street, SN13 0HB. Tel 01249 717060, www.themethuenarms.com. Ancient beams, heritage shades and craft brews draw admirers to Martin and Debbie Still's handsomely restored Georgian coaching inn, in an attractive market town. Past the solid stone facade, intimate dining areas have elm floorboards, exposed stone walls, log fires. The unfussy, Italian-inflected, all-day menu, cooked by Piero Boi, makes good use of local-area produce. Spend the night: the well-equipped bedrooms are crisply, tastefully decorated; each has comfy seating and a Roberts radio; perhaps a roll-top bath in the bathroom. A family suite sleeps four. More bedrooms (some suitable for disabled) were in the works as the Guide went to press. At breakfast, help yourself to freshly baked pastries, yogurt, compote, fruit salad, Wiltshire honey; good cooked options. Capability Brown-designed Corsham Court is up the High Street. 2 bars (West Country ales, Somerset cider brandy), lounge, restaurant, private dining room. Free Wi-Fi, in-room TV (Freeview). No background music. Large garden, courtyard (alfresco dining). Boules piste. Parking. Children (special menu) welcomed. 14 bedrooms (1 in annexe; family room). 8 miles NE of Bath. Per room B&B £120–£200, D,B&B from £125. Closed Christmas Day.

COVENTRY Warwickshire
Map 2:B2

BARNACLE HALL, Shilton Lane, Shilton, CV7 9LH. Tel 02476 612629, www.barnaclehall.co.uk. Rustic and welcoming, Rose Grindal's B&B, just five miles outside the city centre, charms with its nooks and crannies, low doorways and old oak beams. Bedrooms in the Grade II listed 16th-century farmhouse, though a touch old-fashioned, are large and comfortable; fresh flowers are all the dressing they need. Tasty breakfasts have lots of choice (special diets can be catered for, by arrangement). Sitting room (wood-burning stove), dining room. Free Wi-Fi, in-room TV. No background music. Garden, patio. Children (by arrangement) welcomed. Easy access from the motorway. 3 bedrooms. Per person B&B single £45–£55, double £75–£85. Credit cards not accepted. Closed Christmas.

COOMBE ABBEY, Brinklow Road, Binley, CV3 2AB. Tel 02476 450450, www.coombeabbey.com. After a turbulent past (including Gunpowder Plot machinations), peace has come to reign at this 'stunning' 12th-century Cistercian abbey. It is run by Ron Terry, with 'charming' staff, for Coventry City Council. Recent visitors were captivated by its 'character, eccentricity and individuality'. Deer may be spotted as you approach through 'well-maintained' parkland; cross a bridge into 'superb' formal gardens. Inside, sit back on one of the antique armchairs to take in the high-vaulted reception, with its carved stone pulpit and wrought-iron chandeliers. Long, atmospheric, dark red corridors, displaying 'magnificent' antiquities and china, lead to the sumptuous 'bedchambers'. Rooms may have a canopy bed, original moulding, Victorian bath, richly tiled waterfall shower; their leaded windows yield views over the courtyard, lawns or tree-lined drive. 'Classic, decently cooked' dishes are served in the conservatory dining room, candlelit at night. Bar, Garden Room restaurant, terrace. Private dining rooms. 500 acres of parkland, walking trails; wildlife. Free Wi-Fi, in-room TV. Room service. Functions; wedding/conference facilities. Paid parking (£5 per day). Children welcomed. 119 bedrooms. Per room B&B from £89, D,B&B from £159.

COVERACK Cornwall
Map 1:E2

THE BAY HOTEL, North Corner, nr
Helston, TR12 6TF. Tel 01326 280464,
www.thebayhotel.co.uk. A 'very
welcoming' hotel, on a bite-shaped cove
in the Lizard Peninsula. There's no
mobile reception – not even a landline
in the bedrooms. Instead, from lounge,
library, dining room and many of the
bedrooms, take in superb, uninterrupted
views of the shoreline. Victoria and
Nicholas Sanders are the new owners;
Zoe Holmes, the previous owners'
daughter, has stayed on as manager.
Lawned gardens on two levels lead to
the beach; a coastal path starts at the
foot of the drive. Fresh fish and lobsters
landed in the bay inspire new chef Chris
Conboye's cooking, in the candlelit
restaurant. Full Cornish breakfasts.
Lounge, bar/restaurant, conservatory.
Free Wi-Fi in public areas, in-room
TV (Freeview). Background music
(quiet classical music or blues). Large
sun terrace, garden. Parking. Children
over 12, and small to medium-size dogs
welcomed (dog-friendly beach). 14
bedrooms (1 on ground floor suitable
for disabled). Per room B&B £100–£250,
D,B&B £140–£290. Closed Nov–Feb.

CRAYKE Yorkshire
Map 4:D4

THE DURHAM OX, Westway, YO61 4TE.
Tel 01347 821506, www.thedurhamox.
com. A 300-year history of hosting
weary travellers backs this characterful
country pub. Over the past 15 years,
Michael and Sasha Ibbotson have
continued that tradition, with 'good-
quality, excellent-value dining and
accommodation' in the 'friendly' inn
and adjacent farm cottages. 'Even on

two cold January nights, it was busy.'
Eat in the flagstone-floored dining areas
or the all-weather garden room. Newly
promoted chef Robert Lacey cooks the
British pub classics and daily specials
on the blackboard menus. 'The food
is excellent, with an interesting and
varied choice.' Modern, country-style
bedrooms (some small) have a large bed,
pretty fabrics, exposed beams; a spacious
studio has sofas, a kitchen, an honesty
bar and a private balcony with views
across the Vale of York. Walks from
the door; walking guides available. 3
bars, restaurant, private dining room.
Free Wi-Fi, in-room TV. Background
music. Function facilities. 1-acre
grounds. Parking. Children (special
menu, high chairs) and dogs (in public
areas, some bedrooms) welcomed. 3
miles E of Easingwold. Convenient for
Park-and-Ride into York. 6 bedrooms
(1 suite, accessed via external stairs; 5 in
converted farm cottages; 2 on ground
floor), plus 3-bedroom self-catering
cottage in village. Per room B&B
£120–£150. Dinner £30.

CROSTHWAITE Cumbria
Map 4: inset C2

THE PUNCH BOWL INN, Lyth Valley,
nr Kendal, LA8 8HR. Tel 01539
568237, www.the-punchbowl.co.uk.
'Just what you want in a country inn
– good beer, excellent food and nice
bedrooms.' Richard Rose's 'fantastic'
300-year-old inn stands alongside
a stone church in the peaceful Lyth
valley. Individually designed bedrooms,
named after former vicars, have a
pleasing, rustic feel, perhaps with thick
wooden beams or pretty floral prints;
each has a heated-floor bathroom
with a free-standing roll-top bath and

separate shower. In the 'lovely, calm' restaurant, with its 'roaring' fire, sample chef Scott Fairweather's 'imaginative, well-executed' classic country dishes. Morning tea or coffee is brought to the room on request; a cream tea is offered every afternoon. 2 bars, 2 terraces, restaurant. Free Wi-Fi (in bar), in-room TV (Freeview). Background music. Civil wedding licence; conference facilities. Parking. 5 miles E of Bowness-on-Windermere. Children welcomed. 9 bedrooms. Per room B&B £105–£305. Dinner £35.

DARLINGTON Co. Durham
Map 4:C4

Headlam Hall, nr Gainford, DL2 3HA. Tel 01325 730238, www.headlamhall.co.uk. The family Robinson's handsome 17th-century country manor sits in beautiful walled gardens; further beyond, the working farm gently sprawls. It's 'a very pleasant place to stay', with its thick stone walls, huge fireplaces and traditional furnishings; its spa and nine-hole golf course. Refurbished bedrooms in the main building vary in size and character, with period decor, elegant fabrics and antique pieces; more contemporary spa rooms have superb views over the gardens, golf course and surrounding countryside. Chef Derek Thomson uses home-grown soft fruits, herbs and vegetables in his modern British dishes, served in the panelled dining room, the airy orangery and the spa brasserie. Bar, brasserie, lounge, drawing room, library. Private dining. Lift. Free Wi-Fi, in-room TV (Freeview). 'Easy listening'/jazz background music. Civil wedding licence/function facilities. Terraces, 4-acre garden, lake, ornamental canal. Spa (15 by 6 metre indoor pool, outdoor hydrotherapy pool, sauna, gym, treatment rooms). Tennis, 9-hole golf course, croquet. Parking. Children and dogs (in mews rooms only) welcomed. 8 miles W of Darlington. 38 bedrooms (9 in coach house, 6 in mews, 7 in spa; 2 suitable for disabled). Per room B&B single £100–£200, double £130–£230. Dinner £35. Closed 24–27 Dec.
25% DISCOUNT VOUCHERS

Houndgate Townhouse, 11 Houndgate, DL1 5RF. Tel 01325 486011, www.houndgatetownhouse. co.uk. A felt moose's head greets guests at Natalie Cooper's wittily finished guest house and restaurant on the western edge of town. The 18th-century town house (once a school and later municipal offices) mixes eye-catching wallpaper and bespoke furniture to stylish effect; specially commissioned artefacts and sculptures include an impressive long-tasselled chandelier (a nod to Stephenson's Locomotion No. 1 and Darlington's former railway fame). The whole is 'very nicely done'. Smart bedrooms are individually decorated; the best have a huge four-poster bed and a freestanding bath. Order bistro classics in the restaurant (until 8 pm); eat alfresco in the terraced courtyard in season; breakfast until noon on home-made granola, yogurt, berries, eggs all ways, a full English. Afternoon tea has home-baked breads and cakes. Lounge, bar (occasional jazz nights), Eleven restaurant (Saturday brunch, traditional Sunday lunch; closed Sun eve), courtyard. Lift. Free Wi-Fi, in-room TV (Freeview). Background music. Room service. Paid parking. Children (special menu, high chair, cot, extra beds) welcomed. Complimentary access to indoor swimming pool across the road. 8 bedrooms (1 suitable for disabled). Per room B&B £90–£145. 25% DISCOUNT VOUCHERS

DARTMOUTH Devon
Map 1:D4

BROWNS HOTEL, 27–29 Victoria Road, TQ6 9RT. Tel 01803 832572, www. brownshoteldartmouth.co.uk. A short walk from the waterfront, Clare and James Brown's modern town house hotel is liked for its informal atmosphere. Neat bedrooms vary in size, though all have a large bed, space to sit, artwork by local artists, designer lighting. Food and wine events (open to the public) are occasionally organised in the sleek, open-plan wine bar and shop; when the bar is closed, guests are offered complimentary pre- and post-dinner drinks. Sample Mediterranean-influenced meals in the bistro; tapas and light bites are available in the bar. Lounge, bar (complimentary tapas on Fri eve), restaurant (closed Sun–Thurs). Free Wi-Fi, in-room TV. Soft background jazz. Parking permits supplied. Children welcomed. 8 bedrooms. Per room B&B £150–£199. Dinner £32. 2-night min. stay in peak season. Closed Christmas, Jan.

STRETE BARTON HOUSE, Totnes Road, Strete, TQ6 0RU. Tel 01803 770364, www.stretebarton.co.uk. Stuart Litster and Kevin Hooper's B&B, in a 16th-century manor house, stands in the centre of a coastal South Hams village, its flamboyant interiors a pleasant surprise. Eastern-style calm infuses many of the bedrooms, with Buddhas, silks, tassels and bold prints, though the best have views that are wholly local – stretching towards the sea. Each room is well stocked with fresh flowers, magazines, coffee and tea, still and sparkling water and biscuits. In winter, lounge on squashy sofas and comfortable armchairs by the fire in the drawing room; when fine weather comes, loaf on the terrace overlooking the water. Seasonal fruit and local farm yogurts are served at breakfast. 5 miles SW of Dartmouth. Sitting room, breakfast room; 1/3-acre garden. Free Wi-Fi, in-room TV. No background music. In-room massages/spa treatments, by arrangement. Children over 8 and dogs (in cottage suite) welcomed. 6 bedrooms (1 in cottage annexe). Per room B&B £105–£195. 2-night min. stay preferred on Fri, Sat in peak season.

DONNINGTON Sussex
Map 2:E3

THE BLACKSMITHS, Selsey Road, nr Chichester, PO20 7PR. Tel 01243 785578, the-blacksmiths.co.uk. Clean lines and scrubbed wooden surfaces leave a voguish finish in Mariella and William Fleming's newly renovated village pub-with-rooms close to the Chichester canal towpath. The bright, airy bar has a Scandinavian vibe: pale wooden floors, pew benches, Nordic throw pillows. Upstairs, find a small seating area, a hospitality tray and framed bookshelves on the landing, where a bright orange fridge gives the otherwise muted interior a spot of colour. Named after regional birds (Skylark, Barnowl, Lapwing), the grey-and-white-painted bedrooms have handsome wallpaper, unusual prints, a large bed, plump armchairs; two have an original fireplace and a roll-top bathtub. The kitchen makes use of a thriving herb garden, the chicken flock and the Flemings' farm; seasonal British ingredients inspire a simple yet sophisticated menu. Bar, restaurant, garden patio, fire pits. Free Wi-Fi. Children and dogs welcomed. 3 bedrooms. Per room B&B £120–£150. Dinner £24. Closed Christmas, New Year's Eve.

DOVER Kent
Map 2:D5
WALLETT'S COURT, Westcliffe, St Margaret's-at-Cliffe, CT15 6EW. Tel 01304 852424, www. wallettscourthotelspa.com. 'Just the one night made us reluctant to ever leave.' The Oakley family's 'quaint and quirky' hotel is in a pretty hamlet near St Margaret's Bay. There's plenty of choice of accommodation: spacious traditional rooms in the white-painted Jacobean manor house; snug stable-block rooms overlooking the gardens and wild flower meadows; high-ceilinged Kentish barn suites; a crop of outbuildings, a wagon and tepees punctuating the extensive landscaped gardens, all with an outdoor fire pit. 'Delicious' five-course Kentish menus, devised by new chef Tom Dawson, are served in the oak-beamed restaurant. Breakfast in the conservatory includes eggs from resident hens, locally sourced bacon and sausages. 'I was uber-impressed with the cleanliness and service.' Restaurant (open to non-residents; closed Sun eve), lounge/bar. Library, conservatory, sun terraces. Free Wi-Fi (main house), in-room TV (Freeview). Classical background music. Civil wedding licence, functions. 12-metre indoor swimming pool (swim trainer). Spa (hydrotherapy massage,

sauna, steam room, fitness studio, indoor hot tub, treatment cabins, relaxation room). Tennis courts, badminton, croquet lawn, boules court, golf pitching range, jogging trail. Tree house. Children (baby-listening devices; high teas; £20 per child for an extra bed) and dogs welcomed. 10 mins' drive from the port and cruise terminal. 17 bedrooms (13 in converted farm buildings; plus 2 tepees in grounds). Per room B&B from £135, D,B&B from £215. Dinner £45. Closed Christmas.
25% DISCOUNT VOUCHERS

DULVERTON Somerset
Map 1:B5
THREE ACRES COUNTRY HOUSE, Ellersdown Lane, Brushford, TA22 9AR. Tel 01398 323730, www. threeacresexmoor.co.uk. Peace, comfort and a beautifully secluded position on the southern edge of Exmoor national park make Julie and Edward Christian's 1930s B&B 'a special place'. Also praised: 'The log fire and the chat.' Airy bedrooms have thoughtful extras like fresh milk and a silent-tick alarm clock; a ground-floor room has a small south-facing terrace and its own front door. Sample West Country breakfasts with home-made cheese-and-leek sausages, and fruit compotes made with berries from the garden. Ask for a light supper if you're staying in; for larger groups, a dinner party can be arranged. Bar (Exmoor gin), sitting room, breakfast room. Free Wi-Fi, in-room TV (Freeview). No background music. 2-acre grounds, sun terrace. Children (cot, high chair, toys, play equipment in garden) welcomed. 2 miles S of Dulverton. 6 bedrooms (1 on ground floor; 1 family suite, with extra beds in

small annexe). Per person B&B £45–£75. 2-night min. stay preferred.
25% DISCOUNT VOUCHERS

DUNWICH Suffolk
Map 2:B6
THE SHIP AT DUNWICH, St James Street, IP17 3DT. Tel 01728 648219, www. shipatdunwich.co.uk. Close to the beach and the RSPB reserve at Minsmere, this 'unspoiled, unpretentious' old inn is in an 'atmospheric' village, a once-important port until it was lost to the sea in medieval times. It is managed by Matthew Goodwin for the small Agellus Hotels group. A labyrinth of public rooms, still with their original wooden and stone floors, leads to the covered courtyard and large beer garden where stands an 800-year-old fig tree. The whole makes a charming setting for a pint of real ale and a dish from chef Sam Hanison's wide selection of pub favourites. Bedrooms (Good, Best, Marsh View Best) are spread across the main house and converted outbuildings; some have their own entrance and overlook the gardens or village. Ring to discuss room choices before booking: guests this year thought their Best room 'fine', despite noise from the kitchen extractor fan. Dogs are 'warmly welcomed' with a bowl of water and treats; they're allowed into the bar, conservatory and breakfast room (but not the dining room), as well as several bedrooms. Restaurant, bar, courtyard (alfresco dining). Free Wi-Fi, in-room TV (Freeview; smart TV in family rooms). No background music. Garden. Children and dogs welcomed. 16 bedrooms (4 on ground floor in converted stables; family rooms; 1 suitable for disabled). Per room B&B £115–£140. Dinner from £22.50.

EAST WITTON Yorkshire
Map 4:C4
THE BLUE LION, DL8 4SN. Tel 01969 624273, www.thebluelion.co.uk. Nurse a pint of real ale while warming your toes by the fire in Paul and Helen Klein's pleasing old stone coaching inn. A 'homely place with good atmosphere and good food', the traditional inn has flagstone floors, sturdy oak settles, old prints on the walls. Blackboard menus, displayed in the rustic restaurant (candlelit at night), include robust dishes using meat from local farms. Country-style bedrooms in the original building are cosy; larger, 'very quiet' rooms, with more modern furnishings, are housed across the courtyard in the converted stables. Most rooms have views of the surrounding dales. 'Very good value.' 2 bars, restaurant. Private dining room. Free Wi-Fi, in-room TV (Freeview). No background music. 1-acre garden, beer garden. Parking. Children (over-2s £15 per night) and dogs (in some rooms) welcomed. Resident dog, Sadie. 15 bedrooms (9 in courtyard annexe). Per room B&B £94–£129, D,B&B £135–£169.

EASTBOURNE Sussex
Map 2:E4
OCKLYNGE MANOR, Mill Road, BN21 2PG. Tel 01323 734121, www. ocklyngemanor.co.uk. Once the home of Peter Pan illustrator Mabel Lucie Attwell, this pink Georgian mansion is now a traditional B&B run by Wendy Dugdill. The stunning gardens are a highlight: amid the riot of flowers, the 18th-century gazebo and the ancient oak and ash form hidden alcoves in which to while away the hours. Traditionally styled bedrooms have views across the gardens; a modern bathroom. At

breakfast: home-baked bread, home-made marmalade, organic ingredients. A short walk from the town centre, 1¼ miles from the seafront. Free Wi-Fi, in-room TV (Freeview). No background music. Garden. Parking. 3 bedrooms. Per person B&B from £50. 2-night min. stay at weekends.

EASTON GREY Wiltshire
Map 3:E5

WHATLEY MANOR, SN16 0RB. Tel 01666 822 888, www.whatleymanor.com. Great lime trees line the 'impressive' approach to this luxury hotel and spa (Relais & Châteaux). It stands in lush, extensive gardens with woodland, wild flower meadows, sculptures, secluded arbours and a river. The Grade II listed 18th-century manor house has been restored by the Landolt family; large parts of the grounds have their roots in the original 1920s layout. Choose among 'spacious' bedrooms decorated with original artwork and a mix of antique and modern furniture; many overlook the gardens. In the Dining Room restaurant, chef Martin Burge has two Michelin stars for his modern menus (vegetarian tasting menu available); 'delicious' informal meals may be taken in the Swiss-style brasserie. 'Well-executed' breakfasts have a 'very good' buffet. 3 lounges, 2 bars, brasserie, restaurant (Wed–Sun, 7 pm–10 pm). Cinema. Gym, spa (hydrotherapy pool, mud chamber, salt scrub shower, Iyashi Dome). Free Wi-Fi, in-room TV. 'Ambient' background music. Civil wedding licence, conference facilities. 12-acre garden (picnics). Children over 12 and dogs (in some rooms, treats and toys provided; £30 per night) welcomed. 23 bedrooms and suites. Bicycles available to borrow. Per room B&B from £325. Set dinners £116 or £186. Brasserie dinner £35.

EDENBRIDGE Kent
Map 2:D4

HEVER CASTLE B&B, Hever TN8 7NG. Tel 01732 861800, www.hevercastle. co.uk. Sweep through a private gated entrance and into sumptuous B&B accommodation in these two Edwardian additions to 13th-century Hever Castle. Within the Astor and Anne Boleyn wings, leaded windows, moulded ceilings, grand chimney pieces, and corridors lined with paintings heighten the sense of grandeur. Characterful bedrooms blend original features and antiques with modern-day comfort; spacious bathrooms in limestone or marble have a roll-top bath or walk-in shower. In the inviting sitting room stocked with books and magazines, settle in to one of the deep sofas before the wood-burning stove. B&B guests have complimentary access to the castle and grounds during opening hours; after the public has left for the day, roam the peaceful gardens and ancient yew maze (some sections closed). Breakfast on locally smoked kippers or smoked salmon and scrambled eggs in a magnificent, light-filled room, with window seats to gaze across the orchard to the castle. The Moat restaurant serves lunch on days when the castle is open to the public. Lounge, billiards room. Free Wi-Fi. No background music. Parking. Gardens, lake walks. Tennis court. Adventure playground, water maze, rowing boats on the lake (depending on the season). Children (extra beds) welcomed. 2 mins' walk to village pub; 1½ miles from Hever station. 28

bedrooms (some on ground floor, some suitable for a family), plus self-catering Medley Court cottage. Per room B&B single £105–£120, double £165–£275.

EDINGTON Wiltshire
Map 2:D1

THE THREE DAGGERS, 47 Westbury Road, nr Westbury, BA13 4PG. Tel 01380 830 940, www.threedaggers.co.uk. There's much to like about this popular village pub-with-rooms on the outskirts of a village near the Uffington White Horse: 'lovely' staff, 'hearty' dinners, 'splendid, well-equipped' bedrooms. For craft-beer lovers, there's one thing, in particular, to love: an on-site microbrewery turning out artisanal, hops-based beverages at their freshest. 'We were impressed.' Find a spot in the 'well-populated' bar or dining room, where chef Kevin Chandler serves 'unpretentious, tasty' meals, perhaps a 'robust' dish of lamb rump, pearl barley risotto, cauliflower fritters. 'Well-thought-through' accommodation is reached via a separate entrance just yards from the pub. Here, 'comfortable' bedrooms, including a spacious room with a claw-foot bath in the bathroom, have a cool, modern-rustic feel. Resident guests share the use of a private sitting room with a squashy sofa, wood-burning stove and honesty bar; a kitchen has complimentary help-yourself extras (cereals, bread, eggs, milk, orange juice). Take a continental breakfast here in the morning, or order a cooked dish in the pub's conservatory. The garden leads straight to the village park. Bar (draught beers), dining area. Private dining room. Free Wi-Fi, in-room TV (Freeview). Background music. Garden (benches). Microbrewery, farm shop. Children

(special menu, colouring sets; cots, baby monitors; adjacent public play area) welcomed. 3 bedrooms. Per room B&B from £85. Dinner £25.
25% DISCOUNT VOUCHERS

EGTON BRIDGE Yorkshire
Map 4:C5

BROOM HOUSE, Broom House Lane, YO21 1XD. Tel 01947 895279, www.broom-house.co.uk. In the North York Moors national park, Georgina and Michael Curnow's 'high-quality' B&B makes a good base for walkers, mountain bikers, fisherfolk and seekers of the quiet life. Immaculate, 'very comfortable' bedrooms (some snug) are in the restored Victorian farmhouse and a modern extension; a self-contained cottage suite has a large lounge and private patio. All have views over the Esk valley – watch out for the North Yorkshire Moors Railway steam train, which runs along the perimeter of the garden. 'Excellent, freshly cooked' breakfasts include smoked haddock, Whitby kippers, home-made jams, fruit smoothies. Good pub food is a short stroll away, along the banks of the River Esk. Whitby Abbey and Castle Howard are nearby. Lounge, breakfast room. Free Wi-Fi, in-room TV (Freeview). Background music. Garden. ½ mile W of village. 7 bedrooms. Per room B&B £92–£152. Closed Dec–Feb. 2-night min. stay preferred.

ELTERWATER Cumbria
Map 4: inset C2

THE ELTERMERE INN, LA22 9HY. Tel 015394 37207, www.eltermere.co.uk. 'We enjoyed staying here.' Overlooking Elter Water, Mark and Ruth Jones's country hotel is liked for its 'helpful' staff, 'stunning' views and 'excellent' food. It is a family affair: daughter Aimee is the 'charming' manager; son Edward is chef. Take tea and cake by the 'beautiful' stone fireplace when you arrive – there's a 'traditional country atmosphere', with stuffed birds and 'interesting' pictures, in the 'comfortable' lounge and two bars. Elegant bedrooms (some small) have plenty of storage; most have views of Eltermere or the Langdale peaks. In the restaurant, chef Edward Jones's 'delicious' modern European cooking – perhaps including 'amazing' lamb chops – is 'nicely served and presented'. Overindulged? Opt for a 'very refreshing fruit jelly' to top it off. Head out on country walks from the front door; row into the lake from the private jetty. 2 lounges, bar, restaurant; terrace. Free Wi-Fi (in public areas). Contemporary background music ('not too much of a bother'). 3-acre garden. Complimentary passes for the spa at the Langdale Hotel (pool, hot tub, steam room), 10 mins' walk away. 2 miles from Grasmere. 12 bedrooms. Per room B&B £145–£295. Set dinner £28.50; à la carte £30–£40. Closed Christmas and New Year (restaurant open New Year's Eve). 2-night min. stay at weekends.

ELTON Cambridgeshire
Map 2:B4

THE CROWN INN, 8 Duck Street, nr Peterborough, PE8 6RQ. Tel 01832 280 232, www.thecrowninn.org. Meet your sweetheart underneath the spreading horse chestnut tree that fronts this 'thoroughly recommended' thatch-roofed country inn. Inside the 16th-century building, Gavyn Willimer has joined chef/patron Marcus Lamb in the kitchen, serving 'good', wholesome pub classics and Sunday roasts in the bar and restaurant. Named after local villages and landmarks, the 'well-equipped, modern' bedrooms (some above the pub) have tea- and coffee-making facilities, fresh milk, bottled water; two, across the courtyard, have French windows that open on to a private garden. Ask for a breakfast hamper to be delivered to the room; dinner hampers, too, may be arranged for guests staying in one of the garden rooms. Don't forget a packed lunch before heading off on a jaunt across the countryside. Bar (local ales, open fire), snug, restaurant. Free Wi-Fi, in-room TV (Freeview). Background music. Parking. Children (special menu) and dogs (in public areas) welcomed. 8 miles SW of Peterborough. 8 bedrooms (2 on ground floor). Per room B&B £110–£145, D,B&B £125–£195.

EVERSHOT Dorset
Map 1:C6

THE ACORN INN, 28 Fore Street, DT2 0JW. Tel 01935 83228, www.acorn-inn.co.uk. Thomas Hardy's Tupcombe eavesdrops in the inglenooks of this 16th-century inn, renamed the Sow and Acorn in The First Countess of Wessex. Under the real-life management of Jack and Alex MacKenzie, the refurbished inn (Red Carnation Hotels) retains the 'good atmosphere', beams, stone floors and log fires that the writer captures. (Surreptitious servants are few and far between.) Individually decorated bedrooms have been handsomely, lavishly styled with a traditional feel. Each given a Hardy-themed name, they have a comprehensive hospitality tray and a modern bathroom. Two interconnecting rooms can accommodate a family. The deep leather seats and selection of good ales in the Hardy bar attract 'faithful regulars'; chef Guy Horley serves hearty dishes in the restaurant. 'Good' Dorset breakfasts. An enormous copper beech tree shades the small patio and beer garden. Guests may use the spa facilities of sister hotel Summer Lodge, opposite (£15 charge). 2 bars (over 100 single malts; 39 wines by the glass), restaurant, lounge. Free Wi-Fi, in-room TV (Sky). Background music. Small beer garden, skittle alley. Children (cots, extra beds, baby changer, high chairs, children's menu) and dogs (£10 charge; treats) welcomed. 10 bedrooms. Per room B&B from £115, D,B&B from £175. 2-night min. stay at weekends during peak season.

FALMOUTH Cornwall
Map 1:E2

THE ROSEMARY, 22 Gyllyngvase Terrace, TR11 4DL. Tel 01326 314669, www. therosemary.co.uk. Lynda and Malcolm Cook's 'delightful' Edwardian town house, close to the beach, has 'fantastic' views across the garden towards Falmouth Bay. B&B accommodation (including two-bedroom suites suitable for a family) is in modern, well-appointed bedrooms – ask for one with a view of the sea. Cornish cream teas are served in the lounge; picnics, with slabs of home-baked cake, are available for a coastal ramble. 'Good-quality' breakfasts (all diets catered for). Lounge, bar, dining room. South-facing garden, sun deck. Free Wi-Fi, in-room TV. No background music. Children (travel cot £10; extra bed £25; high chair) and dogs (by arrangement) welcomed. 10 mins' walk to town. 8 bedrooms (two 2-bedroom suites). Per room B&B single

£50–£70, double £79–£157. 2-night min. stay preferred. 'Generally' closed early Nov–Jan, 'but call for availability over the winter'.

FOLKESTONE Kent
Map 2:E5

ROCKSALT, 4–5 Fish Market, CT19 6AA. Tel 01303 212070, www.rocksaltfolkestone.co.uk. Mark Sargeant's 'modish, imaginative' restaurant-with-rooms (co-owned with Josh de Haan) brings a new aesthetic to the traditional English seaside. The dining room's dark-timber-and-glass exterior, cantilevering over Folkestone's fishing harbour, holds a light-catching interior: lime-washed oak flooring, curved banquettes, floor-to-ceiling windows with views out to sea. A wide-ranging menu includes home-cured and -smoked fish dishes cooked by Simon Oakley; the lively bar has cocktails and light bites. While food is the focus, the rooms haven't been overlooked. 'Seaside chic' bedrooms in a building across the cobbled street are decorated with exposed brick, driftwood stools, hues of sand and sky. Each has an antique bed, a wet room, expansive views of the Channel (binoculars provided). A continental breakfast hamper is delivered to the room. Bar, restaurant (last orders by 5 pm in winter), terrace. Free Wi-Fi, in-room TV. No background music. Children welcomed. On-street parking. 4 bedrooms (1 family room). Per room B&B from £85. Dinner £25–£35.

FONTMELL MAGNA Dorset
Map 2:E1

THE FONTMELL, SP7 0PA. Tel 01747 811441, thefontmell.com. A burbling stream separates smart dining rooms from the buzz of the popular bar at this quirkily renovated roadside inn. Upstairs, appealing, country-cottage bedrooms have tea- and coffee-making facilities and a DVD-player; the best room, Mallyshag, has a super-king-size bed, a large sofa and a roll-top bath on a wooden dais. Downstairs, there's a welcoming atmosphere in the lively bar. Try a local beer or one of the weekly-changing guest ales, then step into the stylish dining room (its walls lined with books and wine bottles) for imaginative dishes and comfort food cooked by chef/patron Tom Shaw. On weekend evenings in summer, two wood-fired pizza ovens in the garden draw hungry locals. Bar, restaurant (closed Mon, Tues), large garden. Free Wi-Fi, in-room TV (Freeview). Background music. DVD library. Children (special menu; cot, extra bed £20 per night) and dogs (in 1 room) welcomed. 4 miles from Shaftesbury. 6 bedrooms. Per room B&B £60–£100.

FOWEY Cornwall
Map 1:D3
THE OLD QUAY HOUSE, 28 Fore Street, PL23 1AQ. Tel 01726 833302, www.theoldquayhouse.com. Wake to the sound of seagulls and views upon a sunlit bay at this chic, privately owned hotel, in a 'spectacularly' converted Victorian seamen's mission on the waterfront. There's much that's pleasing here, from the 'tastefully rejuvenated' public areas to the 'exceptionally friendly and helpful' staff and 'very good' food. 'Clean, fresh, contemporary' bedrooms, many with views over the estuary, are impressively well stocked: find biscuits and bottled water, books

and DVDs, local guides, earplugs, umbrellas and raincoats. 'I liked the fridge on the landing with little jugs of fresh milk – a thoughtful touch.' In the informal restaurant, chef Ryan Kellow cooks classic French dishes with a Cornish twist – try Fowey River oysters, local scallops, West Country cheeses. 'The sun streams into the restaurant at breakfast time.' Martin Nicholas is the manager. Help is offered with parking, 'a substantial walk away'. Open-plan lounge, bar, restaurant with seating area (closed for lunch Tues Easter–Sept). Free Wi-Fi, in-room TV. No background music. Civil wedding licence. Waterside terrace (alfresco dining). Children over 12 welcomed. Parking permits supplied. 11 bedrooms. Per room B&B £190–£335, D,B&B £265–£410. Set dinner £30–£37.50.
25% DISCOUNT VOUCHERS

GATWICK Sussex
Map 2:D4
LANGSHOTT MANOR, Ladbroke Road, Langshott, Horley, RH6 9LN. Tel 01293 786680, www.langshottmanor. com. 'An enjoyable experience, from check-in to check-out.' In 'peaceful' grounds close to Gatwick airport, this 'beautiful' Elizabethan timber-framed manor house (Alexander Hotels) is liked for its 'friendly' staff and 'very nice, well-presented' meals. Katie Savage is the manager. Pick one of the smartly decorated bedrooms to suit – some have an antique bathtub, others a four-poster bed, yet others a private patio garden; all have tea- and coffee-making facilities, bathrobes and slippers. In the elegant Mulberry restaurant overlooking the gardens, chef Phil Dixon's modern European dishes

are inspired by the seasons. Lighter meals and fireside afternoon teas may be taken in the lounges. Start the day with local pork-and-apple sausages, porridge with a dash of whisky. 3 lounges (piano background music), bar, restaurant, private dining room. Free Wi-Fi, in-room TV (Freeview). Civil wedding licence, conference facilities. 3-acre garden, terrace (alfresco dining), medieval moat. Croquet. Children and dogs (in 2 rooms, by arrangement; charge) welcomed. 22 bedrooms (15 in mews, a short walk across the hotel grounds). Per room B&B from £139, per person D,B&B from £99. Dinner £49.50, tasting menu £70. 2-night min. stay preferred.

GILSLAND Cumbria
Map 4:B3
THE HILL ON THE WALL, Brampton, CA8 7DA. Tel 01697 747214, www. hillonthewall.co.uk. Amblers, ramblers, ambition bikers and serious hikers receive an 'excellent' welcome at Elaine Packer's 'magnificent' B&B. The 'superb' Georgian farmhouse is in an outstanding hilltop location overlooking Hadrian's Wall near Birdoswald; French doors open on to a 'beautiful' walled garden. 'Elaine has thought of every comfort, from chocolates and all manner of teas on the hospitality trays, to sumptuous decoration and fabrics in all the rooms,' say Guide readers in 2016. Arriving guests are treated to tea and home-made cake beside a fire in the drawing room; later, retire to an 'elegant' bedroom well stocked with glossy magazines, cafetière coffee, a biscuit barrel. 'We slept in perfect peace.' 'Gigantic portions' of locally sourced, home-cooked Northumbrian

breakfasts, ordered the night before, are 'delicious' – 'the best I've had in a B&B'. Packed lunches available (£6). Lounge (library, wood-burning stove), breakfast room. Free Wi-Fi, in-room TV (Freeview). No background music. 1-acre garden, terrace. Parking; secure bicycle storage. Children over 10 welcomed. 1 mile W of Gilsland on the B6318. 3 bedrooms (1 on ground floor). Per room B&B £80–£90. Credit cards not accepted. Closed Dec–Feb.

WILLOWFORD FARM, nr Brampton, CA8 7AA. Tel 01697 747962, www. willowford.co.uk. Pull off the National Trail and into Liam McNulty and Lauren Harrison's B&B on a 100-acre organic farm: the longest-running stretch of uninterrupted Hadrian's Wall wends straight through the farmyard. The remains of a bridge and two turrets can still be seen from the old byre, which houses five cosily stylish, energy-efficient bedrooms. Each has exposed wooden beams, slate floors and antique furniture; a waterfall shower. Head to the Samson Inn in the village for dinner (under the same management; lifts offered); lamb from the farm appears on the menus. Packed lunches available (£6). Plenty of places for guests to walk, picnic and sit. Lounge/breakfast room. Free Wi-Fi, in-room TV. No background music. Children (family suite) welcomed; well-behaved dogs by arrangement (£5 charge; chickens and sheep on farm). Resident dog. ½ mile W of Gilsland, between Gilsland village and Birdoswald Roman fort. 5 bedrooms (all on ground floor). Per room B&B £88–£95. Closed Dec–Feb.

GRAFFHAM Sussex
Map 2:E3
WILLOW BARNS, nr Petworth,
GU28 0NT. Tel 01798 867493, www.
willowbarns.co.uk. The rough-hewn,
flint-and-brick exterior of Amanda
and William Godman's 'stylish' B&B
belies its age: it was built in 2010 using
traditional methods in flint and brick.
Countryside-fresh bedrooms each
have their own door opening on to a
serene courtyard; inside the rooms, find
fresh flowers, sweet treats, a 'gorgeous'
bathroom. The Godmans also own
the White Horse pub (adjacent),
which serves oven-baked pizzas and
home-made ice cream made with
produce from their farm. Cyclists
and riders welcomed; many footpaths
and bridleways nearby. Clay-pigeon
shooting can be organised. Sitting room
with log fire in the pub (restaurant
closed Sun eve, and Mon in Jan, Feb).
Free Wi-Fi, in-room TV (Freeview).
No background music. Large courtyard
garden, pub garden. Parking. Turnout
for visiting horses, by arrangement
(midweek only). 5 miles from Petworth.
Children over 12 welcomed. 6 bedrooms
(all on ground floor). Per room B&B
from £110 (2-night min. stay at peak
weekends). Dinner £25.
25% DISCOUNT VOUCHERS

GRANGE-IN-BORROWDALE
Cumbria
Map 4: inset C2
BORROWDALE GATES, CA12 5UQ.
Tel 017687 77204, www.borrowdale-
gates.com. In wooded grounds, the
Harrison family's Lakeland hotel near
Derwentwater is liked for its 'good
position', 'helpful staff' and 'tasty food'.
Several of the bedrooms have patio

doors leading to the garden; others have
a balcony; most have views over the
Borrowdale valley. In the elegant dining
room overlooking the fells, the cooking
is 'superb': try fell-bred Herdwick lamb
or Borrowdale trout at dinner; buttered
kippers or a full Cumberland at a plentiful
breakfast. Walking and climbing routes
straight from the door; a local bus runs
nearby. A complimentary round of golf
at Keswick Golf Club is offered to hotel
guests. Open-plan bar, dining room and
lounge (log fire), reading room. Lift. Free
Wi-Fi, in-room TV. No background
music. Wedding facilities (exclusive use
only). 2-acre grounds, terrace (alfresco
drinks). Children (£25 per night) and dogs
(in 4 rooms; £7 per night) welcomed. 25
bedrooms (10 on ground floor; 1 suitable
for disabled). Per person D,B&B £95–£137.
Closed Jan.
25% DISCOUNT VOUCHERS

GRANGE-OVER-SANDS Cumbria
Map 4: inset C2
CLARE HOUSE, Park Road, LA11 7HQ.
Tel 01539 533026, www.clarehousehotel.
co.uk. The Read family's loyal
following praises the 'personable'
staff, welcoming atmosphere and
'outstanding' food at this extended
Victorian house in 'delightful', well-
maintained gardens. Sit by the log fires
in the comfortable sitting rooms. Most
of the bedrooms have 'wonderful' views
over Morecambe Bay. Take morning
coffee and afternoon tea in the lounges
or garden. In the evening, chefs Andrew
Read and Mark Johnston cook four-
course menus of classic English and
French dishes (served between 6.30
pm and 7.30 pm). 2 lounges, dining
room (Sunday lunch; open to non-
residents). Free Wi-Fi, in-room TV. No

background music; brass band concerts take place on the bandstand throughout the summer. ¾-acre grounds (croquet, loungers, tables and benches). Mile-long promenade at the bottom of the garden (bowling green, tennis courts, putting green; easy access to ornamental gardens). Parking. Children (no special facilities) welcomed. 18 bedrooms (1 on ground floor suitable for disabled). Per person D,B&B £94.50–£100. Closed mid-Dec–mid-Mar.
25% DISCOUNT VOUCHERS

GRASSINGTON Yorkshire
Map 4:D3
GRASSINGTON HOUSE, 5 The Square, nr Skipton, BD23 5AQ. Tel 01756 752406, www.grassingtonhouse.co.uk. On a cobbled market square, Sue and John Rudden have added contemporary flair to their restaurant-with-rooms in a limestone Georgian house. Bedrooms are individually decorated: many have glamorous touches; some have a balcony or window seat. All are equipped with Fairtrade tea and coffee, home-made biscuits, waffle bathrobes, organic toiletries. 'Very enjoyable' classic English food is served in the smart restaurant and the fireside bar; alfresco meals may be taken on the terrace. The hosts' rare-breed pigs provide the restaurant with bacon, sausages and plenty of crackling. 'We were pleased with it in every way.' Lounge, bar, No. 5 restaurant; terrace. Free Wi-Fi, in-room TV. Background music. Civil wedding licence; functions. Children welcomed (travel cot, extra bed; £35 per night). Cookery master classes. Horse riding, cycle hire, fly fishing and shooting can be arranged. Parking. 9 bedrooms. Per room B&B £120–£140, D,B&B £195–£230. Dinner £35–£45. Closed Boxing Day–New Year.

GREAT LANGDALE Cumbria
Map 4: inset C2
THE OLD DUNGEON GHYLL, LA22 9JY. Tel 01539 437272, www.odg.co.uk. Weary fell walkers and climbers have found refuge in the comforting atmosphere and crackling fires at this unpretentious, dog-friendly inn for more than 300 years. Its 'glorious' situation, at the head of the Great Langdale valley, is hard to beat. It is managed by Jane and Neil Walmsley for the National Trust. 'Basic', country-style bedrooms (some snug) 'may not be the height of elegance, but they're very reasonably priced', and several have two or more beds to accommodate a family. Each room has a traditional feel (floral curtains, a brass bedstead); most have outstanding views of the surrounding fells. Savour tasty home-baked treats with morning coffee and afternoon tea in the residents' lounge; call in at the lively Hikers' Bar, once cow stalls, for real ales and a wide selection of malt whiskies. The occasional open-mic night is enjoyable compensation for the lack of TV and patchy mobile reception. Walking routes and packed lunches available. Residents' bar and lounge, dining room, Hikers' Bar ('straightforward' pub food; open to public); live music on first Wed of every month. Free Wi-Fi (in some rooms and public areas). No background music. Drying room. Beer garden. Parking. Children (special rates for over-5s) and dogs (£5 per night) welcomed. 1-acre garden. 12 bedrooms. Per person B&B from £58. Dinner £25. 2-night min. stay at weekends. Closed 24–26 Dec.

GURNARD Isle of Wight
Map 2:E2

THE LITTLE GLOSTER, 31 Marsh Road, PO31 8JQ. Tel 01983 298776, www. thelittlegloster.com. Seaside simplicity and a Scandinavian flair are found by the water's edge, just west of Cowes. Chef/patron Ben Cooke and his wife, Holly, run their charming restaurant-with-rooms here, all Nordic-inflected dishes, elegantly pared-down bedrooms and superb sea views in seemingly every direction. In the well-regarded restaurant, Ben Cooke and Jay Santiago use plenty of Isle of Wight produce, such as Bembridge crab and crayfish, and locally farmed meat; for a culinary punch, try the house-cured gravadlax with a choice of aquavit. Coastal-themed bedrooms in stripes and scrubbed wood are in a separate wing, with their own entrance. Travelling with family? Book the garden suite, which has a sitting room and a private terrace with access to the seaside garden. Lots of choice at breakfast: 'super' juices, home-made marmalade, healthy options, eggs all ways. Bar, restaurant (closed Sun eve, Mon; plus Tues/Wed, Oct–Apr). Free Wi-Fi, in-room TV (Freeview). Background music. Functions. Garden. Petanque court. Children (extra bed £30 per night) welcomed. 5 mins' drive from Cowes. 3 bedrooms (in adjoining building). Per room B&B £110–£240. Dinner £45–£55. Closed Christmas, Jan–mid-Feb.

HALIFAX Yorkshire
Map 4:D3

SHIBDEN MILL INN, Shibden Mill Fold, Shibden, HX3 7UL. Tel 01422 365840, www.shibdenmillinn.com. In the fold of the Shibden valley, Simon and Caitlin Heaton's 'very attractive' 17th-century country inn stands opposite the mill stream that once powered local industry. Glen Pearson is the manager. Newly refurbished and redesigned, bedrooms have a bright, homely feel, with good facilities: teas and coffees, towelling robes, a DVD-player (and access to a DVD library). In the atmospheric restaurant, chef Darren Parkinson uses Yorkshire fare in his seasonal and early-bird menus; specialities include steaks grilled in the charcoal oven and served with beef-dripping chips. Shibden Mill's in-house brew is a worthy accompaniment. 'Bustling' oak-beamed bar, restaurant. Private dining room. Small conference facilities. Free Wi-Fi, in-room TV (Freeview). Background music. DVD library. Patio (alfresco dining). Parking. Children welcomed (special menu). 2 miles NE of Halifax. 11 bedrooms. Per room B&B from £100, D,B&B from £182. Closed Christmas, New Year.

HARROGATE Yorkshire
Map 4:D4

STUDLEY HOTEL, 28 Swan Road, HG1 2SE. Tel 01423 560425, www. studleyhotel.co.uk. Orchids and dark-wood furnishings create a contemporary air at Bokmun Chan's town house hotel, close to Valley Gardens. Neat, modern bedrooms vary in size and amenities: smaller rooms have a compact shower room; superior rooms have a smart TV with on-demand movies. A spacious room with a sofa bed can accommodate a family. Sample chef Kenneth Poon's 'excellent' pan-Asian dishes in the popular Orchid restaurant; cocktails, sandwiches and sharing platters can be taken in the O Bar. Guests have access to a nearby leisure centre (gym, pool, steam rooms, sauna and treatments). Lounge, bar, restaurant. Lift. Free Wi-Fi, in-room TV. Patio (alfresco dining). Limited on-site parking; permits supplied. Children welcomed (high chairs, cots). 28 bedrooms. Per room B&B £90–£160.

HASTINGS Sussex
Map 2:E5

THE LAINDONS, 23 High Street, TN34 3EY. Tel 01424 437710, www.thelaindons.com. One for the coffee cognoscenti and everyone in between, this handsome Georgian coaching house hosts a modern B&B and well-respected coffee shop. Sara and Jon Young have brought a Scandinavian air to the Grade II listed building. Spacious, high-ceilinged bedrooms in blue, white and grey tones have a bespoke bed made locally using recycled wood; nautical touches (oars, Breton stripes, a seagull) link to the nearby sea. Sweet treats and freshly ground coffee are replenished daily. Leaf through magazines over a glass of fizz in the loft-level honesty bar overlooking Old Town chimney tops. In honesty baskets around the house, find local sparkling wine, beer, soft drinks and snacks. Breakfast on home-made granola, muesli and bread; 'puffy' pancakes and other cooked options. Down in the Coffee Bar and Roastery, B&B guests receive a discount on the extensive menu of brews and beans roasted on the premises by Jon Young. 5 mins' walk to the beach. Lounge, conservatory/breakfast room (gentle soul, jazz background music); coffee bar. Free Wi-Fi, in-room smart TV. Overnight parking permits supplied. Children over 10 welcomed.

5 bedrooms. Per room B&B £120–£140. Closed Christmas period–mid-Jan.

HEACHAM Norfolk
Map 2:A4

HEACHAM HOUSE, 18 Staithe Road, PE31 7ED. Tel 01485 579529, www.heachamhouse.com. Arrive to tea and home-made cake at Rebecca and Robert Bradley's beautifully presented B&B. Fresh flowers brighten the bedrooms in the red-brick Victorian house; two rooms have views of the village duck pond. Breakfast on home-baked bread, home-made preserves, award-winning sausages, and muffins served with crème fraîche and fruit compote. There's much to explore: the town is in an area famed for its miles of sandy beaches, salt marshes, sunset views and wonderful diversity of wildlife; the hosts offer good advice on places of interest. Walkers and cyclists are provided with drying (much appreciated on wet days) and secure storage. Sitting room, breakfast room. Free Wi-Fi, in-room TV (Freeview). No background music. Small front garden with seating. Parking. Bicycle storage. 3 miles from Hunstanton. Children over 14 welcomed. 3 bedrooms. Per room B&B £85–£95. Credit cards not accepted. Closed Christmas, New Year.

HELMSLEY Yorkshire
Map 4:C4

NO54, 54 Bondgate, YO62 5EZ. Tel 01439 771533, www.no54.co.uk. Lizzie Rohan's welcoming B&B, on the edge of the North York Moors national park, is 'a very good base' for exploring the 'wonderful' surrounding countryside. Pretty bedrooms ('quiet and well equipped') are set around a sunny courtyard filled with flowers in the summertime; each room has thick towels and a well-stocked hospitality tray. Come in, to be plied with tea and home-baked cake; in the morning, the much-praised communal breakfasts have home-baked muffins, smoked kippers, creamy porridge, roast Yorkshire ham with brown sugar and cloves. Dining/sitting room (open fire). Free Wi-Fi, in-room TV (Freeview). No background music. Small cottage garden and courtyard. Children over 12 welcomed. Resident dog. Picnics available. 3 rooms (on ground floor, in courtyard). Per person B&B £50.

HERTFORD Hertfordshire
Map 2:C4
NUMBER ONE PORT HILL, 1 Port Hill, SG14 1PJ. Tel 01992 587350, www. numberoneporthill.co.uk. 'Quirky and very individual', Annie Rowley's artfully styled B&B is in a Grade II listed Georgian town house mentioned in the Pevsner architectural guide to Hertfordshire. 'Fighting through the foliage of that packed little front garden, with the perfume of the roses still intense, was fun.' 'Immaculately kept' rooms brim with chandeliers, huge mirrors, vintage glassware and sculptures – 'an unbelievable collection'. Up the mahogany staircase, the light-filled drawing room is just the place to settle into, with a book or a nip of home-made sloe gin. Bedrooms (two petite, with a bathroom to match) are on the top floor. Each is supplied with bathrobes, slippers and an 'eclectic' selection of reading material, plus a host of treats – Belgian hot chocolate, sweet and savoury snacks. 'The double glazing was very good at keeping out the traffic noise', but there may be

creaks and bumps from other rooms. 'Superb' organic breakfasts are taken at a communal table, in the pretty courtyard garden, by the pond or under the wisteria; home-cooked dinners may be ordered in advance. Drawing room. Free Wi-Fi, in-room TV (Sky, Freeview). Radio 2 at breakfast. Front and back gardens. Limited street parking. Children over 12 welcomed ('exemptions made, if discussed, for younger children'). Resident Labrador, Presley. 5 mins' walk from the town centre. 3 bedrooms. Per room B&B £110–£130. Dinner £40. Closed Christmas.

HEXHAM Northumberland
Map 4:B3
THE HERMITAGE, Swinburne, NE48 4DG. Tel 01434 681248, www. thehermitagebedandbreakfast.co.uk. At the end of a long drive, guests are welcomed with a hot drink and home-baked cake at Katie and Simon Stewart's B&B, in a 'beautiful' stone-built house. 'Very traditional, just lovely', the house is decorated with antiques and old family pictures; find fresh flowers in the peaceful, 'very comfortable' bedrooms. The hosts are helpful with restaurant bookings, and can advise on circular walks on Hadrian's Wall nearby. Tennis fans, channel your inner Federer: besides manicured lawns, a vegetable patch and flower garden, the large grounds also include a tennis court. 'Excellent' communal breakfasts. Drawing room, breakfast room. Free Wi-Fi, in-room TV. No background music. 2-acre grounds, terrace, tennis court. Babes in arms, and children over 6 welcomed. Resident dogs. 7 miles N of Corbridge

(ask for directions). 3 bedrooms. Per person B&B single from £56, double from £95. Credit cards not accepted. Closed Nov–Feb.

HOOK Hampshire
Map 2:D3

TYLNEY HALL, Ridge Lane, Rotherwick, RG27 9AZ. Tel 01256 764881, www. tylneyhall.co.uk. 'We're always happy to return.' An extensive programme of restoration and preservation keeps this Grade II listed Victorian mansion in superlative condition. Surrounded by 'lovely, peaceful' countryside, the luxury hotel (Pride of Britain Hotels) has 'delightful, extensive grounds' and 'welcoming' staff who are 'always willing to help'. Climb a sweeping staircase to reach 'well-furnished and -serviced' bedrooms, each with a 'comfortable' bed. Golf carts ('always swift') ferry guests from the main house to cottage rooms in the grounds. Children are kept well entertained, with goody bags, games, exploration trails, a treasure hunt and special feed for the hotel's flock of ducks. Chef Stephen Hine's formal menu, including 'a delicious soufflé', is served in the wood-panelled Oak Room restaurant; take lighter meals in the lounge or on the terrace overlooking the gardens. Breakfast is 'excellent'. 2 lounges, bar, restaurant. Private dining rooms. Free Wi-Fi, in-room TV (Freeview). No background music. Room service. Civil wedding licence, conference/function facilities. Spa (sauna, treatment rooms, indoor and outdoor pools, gym). 66-acre grounds (gardens, parkland; walking and jogging trails; tennis, croquet, cricket; mountain bicycles to borrow). Children and dogs (in some rooms) welcomed.

112 bedrooms (some in cottages in the grounds; some suitable for disabled). Per room B&B from £250, D,B&B from £267.

HOPE Derbyshire
Map 3:A6

LOSEHILL HOUSE, Losehill Lane, Edale Road, S33 6AF. Tel 01433 621219, www. losehillhouse.co.uk. At the end of a leafy lane, this 'beautiful' hillside spa hotel has winning views across the Hope valley. The secluded white-painted Arts and Crafts house is run by Paul and Kathryn Roden, with 'attentive' staff. Choose among well-equipped, individually decorated bedrooms, each with comfy seating, plush bathrobes and locally produced biscuits; a complimentary newspaper is provided. Head off on walks across the valley, then come back to soak in the terrace hot tub as the sun goes down. Afterwards, take pre-dinner drinks and canapés in the lounge or bar. In the restaurant, chef Darren Goodwin serves 'excellent' modern dishes using Peak District produce whenever possible. 'Superb' breakfasts. Drawing room, bar, restaurant. Lift. Free Wi-Fi, in-room TV. Background music. Civil wedding licence; function/conferences; exclusive use. 1-acre garden; terrace. Spa (indoor swimming pool, outdoor hot tub, treatment rooms; open to non-residents). Parking. Children and dogs (in 2 rooms) welcomed. 23 bedrooms (4 with external entrance). Per room B&B from £160. Dinner £39.50. 2-night min. stay at weekends.

HUDDERSFIELD Yorkshire
Map 4:E3

THE THREE ACRES INN & RESTAURANT, Roydhouse, HD8 8LR. Tel 01484 602606, www.3acres.com. In wide

Pennine countryside, this roadside drovers' inn with 'tremendous views to all sides' wins praise for its fine Yorkshire meals – and the rooms in which to sleep them off. It is owned by Brian Orme, Neil Truelove and Neil's son, Tom. Hearty appetites are well catered for in the restaurant, where chef Tom Davies's contemporary British cuisine comes in 'trencher portions'; sample one of the seasonal cocktails – perhaps a spring rhubarb bellini – as accompaniment. In the main building and garden cottages, bedrooms vary in size, from a good-sized single room to a spacious family suite. Breakfast has home-made muesli, a choice of yogurts, dried fruit and nuts; local bacon and sausage; porridge with cream and golden syrup. Popular Sunday lunches. Bar, restaurant. Free Wi-Fi, in-room TV (Freeview). Background music. Civil wedding licence, small function/private dining facilities. Terraced garden, decked dining terrace. Well-behaved children (cots) welcomed. 6 miles from town centre (busy morning traffic); close to Yorkshire Sculpture Park and National Mining Museum. 17 bedrooms (1 suitable for disabled; 8 in adjacent cottages). Per room B&B £80–£200. Dinner £45. Closed evenings 25/26 Dec, midday 31 Dec, evening 1 Jan.

HUNSTANTON Norfolk
Map 2:A5

No. 33, 33 Northgate, PE36 6AP. Tel 01485 524352, 33hunstanton.co.uk. A sweeping remodel, by Jeanne Whittome, of her Victorian villa B&B has brought welcome flights of fancy to this patch of north Norfolk. Arrive to an afternoon cream tea in the cosy sitting room or on the lawn; later, settle in to one of the sophisticated bedrooms decorated in coastal whites and greys. Each has a large bed, seating and a dressing table; tea, Fairtrade cafetière coffee and biscuits; a drench shower, robes and a bathtub in the bathroom. Longing for the sea? Ask for the room with a balcony whose vista stretches towards the water. Take breakfast in bed with bagels or croissants, or eat in the bright, south-facing dining room; there are freshly baked breads and pastries, home-made granola and jams, all sourced from the hostess's deli in Thornham, the neighbouring village. B&B guests receive discounts at the deli. Sitting room, dining room. Free Wi-Fi, in-room TV (Freeview). No background music. Garden. Children (cot, high chair; extra bed £30) and dogs (not in dining room) welcomed. Parking. 5 bedrooms (1, 'disabled friendly', on ground floor with courtyard; plus 2 suites above the deli in Thornham (10 mins' drive). Per room B&B from £85.

ILMINGTON Warwickshire
Map 3:D6

THE HOWARD ARMS, Lower Green, CV36 4LT. Tel 01608 682226, www.howardarms.com. It's been suggested that this 400-year-old Cotswold stone inn was one of Shakespeare's haunts. Just a myth? Perhaps, but the bard would surely appreciate the polished flagstones, hearth fire and easy-going atmosphere that attract visitors today. Rob Jeal is the manager. Bedrooms in the main building are elegant and characterful: one has a hand-painted bedhead and pretty throw pillows; another a carved four-poster bed with thick tartan bedcoverings. Rooms in the garden wing are more modern. All have tea- and coffee-making facilities and shortbread biscuits. Choose from a blackboard menu of comfort food, sharing platters and the fish of the day in the popular pub and restaurant; finish with a 'wicked' pudding. Breakfast is 'particularly good'. A variety of walks from the village. Snug, bar, dining room. Free Wi-Fi, in-room TV (Freeview). 'Easy listening' background music. Patio/garden (alfresco dining). Parking. Children welcomed. 8 bedrooms (5 through separate door under covered walkway). Per room B&B from £90. Dinner £30.

ILSINGTON Devon
Map 1:D4

ILSINGTON COUNTRY HOUSE, nr Newton Abbot, TQ13 9RR. Tel 01364 661452, www.ilsington.co.uk. 'Off the beaten track – and worth finding', this 'delightful' Dartmoor hotel has been run by the Hassell family for four generations. The comfortable seating areas have wood-burning fires; a modern spa, with a hydrotherapy pool, is ideal for truly relaxing. Take in 'lovely' moorland views from any of the traditionally furnished bedrooms. Follow the locals to the Blue Tiger Inn for bistro food and snacks, or sample Mike O'Donnell's 'simple but delicious' British food in the dining room – the chef adds a European twist while focusing on local produce. 2 lounges, bar, restaurant, pub, conservatory. Spa (11 by 5 metre indoor pool). Lift. Free Wi-Fi, in-room TV (Freeview). Background music. Civil wedding licence, conference facilities. 10-acre grounds (croquet). Children (special menu; PlayStation; garden games)

and dogs (in ground-floor rooms; £8 per night) welcomed. 4 miles NE of Ashburton. 25 bedrooms (8 on ground floor; family suites). Per room B&B from £130, D,B&B from £194.

IRONBRIDGE Shropshire
Map 2:A1

THE LIBRARY HOUSE, 11 Severn Bank, TF8 7AN. Tel 01952 432299, www. libraryhouse.com. Near the River Severn, this peaceful, 'beautifully decorated' Grade II listed Georgian building, once the village library, is today a sweet B&B run by Sarah and Tim Davis. Bedrooms, named after writers, are well equipped with cotton waffle dressing gowns, and fresh milk for tea or coffee; the smallest room benefits from a private patch of garden terrace. The sitting room, with its original library shelves, recalls the building's past. Settle in here and browse from the sizeable collection of books – a wood-burning stove keeps things cosy. Well placed for visiting the World Heritage Site of Ironbridge Gorge and its museums. Sitting room, breakfast room. Free Wi-Fi, in-room TV (Freeview). No background music. Mature garden, courtyard. Parking passes supplied for local car parks. Restaurants and pubs nearby. Children welcomed by arrangement. Resident dog. 3 miles from Telford. 4 bedrooms (1 with private terrace). Per person B&B £75–£120.

KESWICK Cumbria
Map 4: inset C2

DALEGARTH HOUSE, Portinscale, CA12 5RQ. Tel 01768 772817, www. dalegarth-house.co.uk. Find a route to suit: great walks of all levels are to be found from the front door of Craig and Clare Dalton's friendly guest house. On an elevated spot, the Edwardian house has superb views of Derwentwater or the mountains from nearly every room. Choose among comfortable bedrooms decorated in restful hues; each has a flat-screen TV and a hospitality tray. Clare Dalton cooks daily changing, four-course dinners (with choices for each course), served at 7 pm. Special dietary requirements can be catered for, by prior request. Fill up on Cumbrian breakfasts; home-baked cakes at teatime will see you through till dinner. The hosts readily help to plan days out, with much local information . Lounge, bar, dining room. Free Wi-Fi, in-room TV (Freeview). Occasional background radio at breakfast, classical/'easy listening' at dinner. Garden. Parking. Bicycle storage. Children over 12 welcomed. 1½ miles W of Keswick. 10 bedrooms (2 on ground floor in annexe). Per person B&B £44–£55, D,B&B £67–£78. Closed mid-Dec–Feb. 2-night min. stay preferred.

Lyzzick Hall, Underskiddaw, CA12 4PY. Tel 01768 772277, www. lyzzickhall.co.uk. In an 'ideal position' on the lower slopes of Skiddaw, this family-friendly, early Victorian country hotel has 'well-equipped' bedrooms, and 'excellent food, pleasantly served, in the fine dining room'. It is run by the Fernandez and Lake families. Get right into the 'stunning' scenery of the Catbells and Borrowdale valley, with good walking and cycling routes. On return, claim a spot by the log fire in the lounge. Most bedrooms have 'glorious' views towards the Lakeland fells. In the elegant dining room

(candles, flowers, white linen), chef Ian Mackay cooks 'excellent' traditional and modern British dishes, including an inventive seven-course tasting menu. (No nuggets for children, either: rather than serving a set menu for young guests, the chef will cook 'whatever they fancy', the hosts say, depending on the fresh produce at hand.) Desserts are 'especially fine'. 'Plenty of choice at breakfast.' 'Thoroughly recommended.' 2 lounges, orangery, bar, restaurant (open to non-residents). 'Very good' indoor swimming pool; sauna, whirlpool bath. Free Wi-Fi, in-room TV. Background music. 4-acre landscaped grounds. Children welcomed (toys, books, play area). 2 miles N of Keswick. 30 bedrooms (1 on ground floor). Per person B&B from £79, D,B&B from £104. Closed Christmas, Jan.

KINGHAM Oxfordshire
Map 3:D6
Mill House Hotel, OX7 6UH. Tel 01608 658188, www.millhousehotel. co.uk. There's 'a warm atmosphere' at Paul and Maria Drinkwater's 'good-value' hotel, in a 'lovely old building' standing in extensive, 'well-kept' grounds that run down to the River Evenlode. A one-time flour mill (see the original fireplace and bread ovens in the lounge), the 18th-century building 'has changed for the better' since the Drinkwaters took over and began a programme of refurbishment – ask for one of the refreshed bedrooms. Service is 'prompt and courteous' in the restaurant, where the à la carte menu is 'well up to scratch'. In the bar, a good selection of lunches and suppers accompanies the real ales on tap. Light

snacks, cream teas and sandwiches are taken by an open fire in the lounge throughout the day, or on the terrace overlooking the trout stream. 'Excellent' breakfasts. 6 miles E of Stow-on-the-Wold. Complimentary pick-up and drop-off service at Kingham Station, a short drive away; local buses. Bar, restaurant; terrace. Free Wi-Fi, in-room TV. Live music 4 pm–7 pm on the first Sunday of every month. 10-acre gardens. Civil wedding licence. Children and dogs welcomed (charge). 21 bedrooms. Per room B&B from £120, D,B&B from £165.

KINGSBRIDGE Devon
Map 1:D4
THURLESTONE HOTEL, Thurlestone, TQ7 3NN. Tel 01548 560382, www.thurlestone.co.uk. The Grose family have delivered 'first-class' hospitality for over 120 years at their 'very good', family-friendly hotel, a five-minute walk from the sea. Many of the well-equipped bedrooms have 'wonderful' views over the large subtropical gardens and the coast. There's much diversion: croquet lawns, sun terraces, sports facilities, a spa; young guests also have a children's club during the school holidays. 'All the food is excellent': dress up for dinner in the restaurant; enjoy crab sandwiches and seafood platters at the terrace bar; drink real ales in the 16th-century pub; take an 'excellent' cream tea in the garden in fine weather. Lounges, bar, Margaret Amelia restaurant (open to non-residents), pub. Lift. Free Wi-Fi, in-room TV (Sky). No background music. Civil wedding licence, functions. Terrace, outdoor eating area. Spa (indoor swimming pool, laconium, fitness studio, treatments),

outdoor heated swimming pool (May–Sept). Tennis, squash, badminton, croquet, 9-hole golf course. Children and dogs (in some rooms; £8 per night) welcomed. 4 miles SW of Kingsbridge. 65 bedrooms (2 suitable for disabled; some with balcony, sea views). Per room B&B £200–£470 (2-night min. stay). Dinner £39.50.

KINGSWEAR Devon
Map 1:D4
KAYWANA HALL, Higher Contour Road, nr Dartmouth, TQ6 0AY. Tel 01803 752200, kaywanahall.co.uk. One of four 'butterfly' houses in Devon, Tony Pithers and Gordon Craig's ultra-modern home is all curving stairways, unexpected angles and walls of glass, the whole hidden at the end of a private drive amid 12 acres of woodland. Separate from the main house, the bedrooms, reached via steep steps, don't lack style, either. Neat and contemporary, they have floor-to-ceiling windows, abstract art, a private outdoor seating area. Thoughtful amenities include teas and an espresso machine, fudge and home-made biscuits, fresh milk and bottled water. Beds are turned down in the evening. Come morning, head for the main building for breakfast, served at a time to suit. There are fresh juices, locally baked bread, fresh berries or a fruit compote, and plenty of cooked options – with ingredients all sourced from within a five-mile radius. Breakfast room. Free Wi-Fi, in-room TV. No background music. 12-metre outdoor heated swimming pool. Parking. 1½ miles from Dartmouth (reached by passenger ferry). 4 bedrooms (in separate building). Per room B&B £155–£185. Closed Nov–mid-Mar.

KNARESBOROUGH Yorkshire
Map 4:D4

NEWTON HOUSE, 5–7 York Place, HG5 0AD. Tel 01423 863539, www. newtonhouseyorkshire.com. Denise Carter's welcoming B&B is in the centre of a charming market town, a few minutes' walk from Knaresborough Castle. From its secret passages to its (alleged) castle stones, the 300-year-old town house is home to some intrigue. The traditional bedrooms, however, are straightforwardly comfortable, and thoughtfully stocked with books, magazines, still and sparkling water, and a hospitality tray. In the evening, bars, pubs and restaurants are all a stroll away – the hostess has recommendations aplenty – but ask for a simple supper, and you might receive a bowl of soup, an omelette, a sandwich. Breakfast is an event. A Slow Food adherent, Denise Carter bakes her own sourdough bread and makes jams and compotes on the Aga; small-scale producers supply the eggs, milk, smoked fish, bacon and sausages on the menu. Sitting room (honesty bar, books, magazines, newspapers, games), dining room, conservatory. Small courtyard garden, 'wildlife' area with bird feeders. Free Wi-Fi, in-room TV (Freeview). Classic FM (breakfast). Parking. Children (cot, high chair, books, games and toys, family room) and dogs (in 2 stable block rooms with outside access; home-made treats) welcomed. 4 miles from Harrogate. 12 bedrooms (2 on ground floor, suitable for disabled; 2 in converted stables). Per room B&B single £60–£100, double £85–£125. **25% DISCOUNT VOUCHERS**

KNUTSFORD Cheshire
Map 4:E3

BELLE EPOQUE, 60 King Street, WA16 6DT. Tel 01565 633060, www. thebelleepoque.com. Raise the curtain on marble pillars, gilded figurines, Art Nouveau fireplaces and Venetian-glass mosaic floors at Matthew Mooney's 'theatrical' brasserie-with-rooms. (With its high tower – a memorial to author Elizabeth Gaskell – and Mediterranean-style rooftop garden, the scene makes a stunning background for the weddings that take place here.) Richard Walker is the manager. Overlooking the walled courtyard, the spacious, modern bedrooms are well equipped with bathrobes and an espresso machine. Refined à la carte and eight-course tasting menus are served in the restaurant; sit down to pub grub in the Victorian-style Rose and Crown, next door (also owned by the Mooneys). Small artisan producers and local farms supply the ingredients. Convenient for Tatton Park. Lounge/bar, restaurant (background jazz; closed Sun), 3 private dining rooms. Free Wi-Fi, in-room TV (Freeview). Civil wedding licence. Roof garden (alfresco dining), terrace. Parking. 7 bedrooms. Per room B&B (continental on weekdays) single £95, double £110–£115. Dinner £30.

LANCASTER Lancashire
Map 4:D2

THE ASHTON, Well House, Wyresdale Road, LA1 3JJ. Tel 01524 684600, www. theashtonlancaster.com. Bold textures, jewel hues, the occasional chicken running loose in the grounds – this elegant sandstone Georgian house is a fun showcase of James Gray's skills

as a former TV and set designer. The
B&B is highly ranked among fellow
hoteliers, who write: 'It was all superb.
James runs the establishment to such
high standards.' Guests are greeted
with drinks and a home-baked treat.
Each room has its own charm – an
enormous roll-top bath here, a double
shower there – and all are well thought
out, with bathrobes, posh toiletries, a
DVD-player and iPod docking station.
Ordered in advance, supper platters of
locally sourced meat, fish and cheese,
with chutneys and home-baked bread,
can be taken in the dining room or
bedroom. The generous breakfast
spread includes tasty muffins and a fresh
fruit salad; eggs come, of course, straight
from the hens in the garden. The host
is a fount of local information. Lounge,
dining room. Free Wi-Fi, in-room
TV (Freeview). Background music.
1-acre garden. Parking. Children over
6 welcomed. 1 mile E of city centre and
universities. 5 bedrooms (1 on ground
floor; some overlook the garden and
park). Per room B&B £110–£180. Closed
Christmas, New Year.

GREENBANK FARMHOUSE, Abbeystead,
LA2 9BA. Tel 01524 792063, www.
greenbankfarmhouse.co.uk. 'A haven'
for birdwatchers, peace-seekers and
lovers of the rustic life, Sally Tait's
'homely' B&B, a Victorian stone-built
house on a former cheese-making
farm, is set in rural tranquillity.
There are 'magnificent' views from
the conservatory lounge, not least of
passing swifts, swallows, curlews,
pheasants and partridges. Country-style
bedrooms have a spacious bathroom
and panoramic views of the river and
surrounding fells. In the conservatory

or cosy winter dining room, breakfast
has good choice – eggs from the
garden hens, cooked dishes using
local produce, 'delicious' home-baked
bread. Dining room, conservatory/
lounge. 6-acre grounds (some working
farmland), ½-acre lawned garden.
Free Wi-Fi, in-room TV (Freeview).
No background music. Parking.
8 miles from the city. 3 bedrooms. Per
person B&B single £50, double £70.
Credit cards not accepted.

LAVENHAM Suffolk
Map 2:C5
THE SWAN, High Street, CO10
9QA. Tel 01787 247477, www.
theswanatlavenham.co.uk. Three
timber-framed 15th-century buildings
form this surprisingly swanky hotel (TA
Hotel Collection) in a medieval village.
The open lounges blend ancient and
modern, with wood-burning stoves,
cosy pockets of sofas, and oak beams
suggesting partitions. Twisty-turny
corridors lead to country-house-style
bedrooms equipped with bathrobes,
bottled water and tea- and coffee-
making facilities. A characterful suite
has a separate lounge, original inglenook
fireplace and mullioned windows.
Choose from a number of dining
options: light bites in the Airmen's bar;
re-thought British favourites in the
'bright, modern' brasserie overlooking
the garden; refined contemporary dishes
in the Gallery restaurant (no children
under ten), helmed by chef Justin Kett.
Need a pick-me-up? Check in to the
Weavers' House Spa – post-massage
sorbets hit the right spot. Lounge, bar,
brasserie, restaurant. Spa (treatment
rooms, hot stone sauna, steam room,
outdoor hydrotherapy pool, garden

terrace). Free Wi-Fi, in-room TV (Freeview). Occasional background music. Civil wedding licence, private dining/function facilities. Courtyard, small garden. Children (early suppers) and dogs (in some rooms) welcomed. 45 bedrooms (some suitable for disabled). Per room B&B £155–£360.

LECHLADE Gloucestershire
Map 3:E6

THE FIVE ALLS, Filkins, GL7 3JQ. Tel 01367 860875, www.thefiveallsfilkins. co.uk. Quirky touches bring a splash of the unexpected to this mellow 18th-century refurbished dining-pub-with-rooms in the Cotswolds. It is owned by Lana and Sebastian Snow, who also own The Plough, Kelmscott, nearby (see main entry). Downstairs, original flagstone floors, stone walls and a huge fireplace with a wooden mantel are brightened by colourful textiles, Bill Brandt prints, vintage wallpaper, leather chesterfield sofas and enormous displays of flowers. Upstairs, four cosy, pale-hued bedrooms have a comfortable bed, a smart bathroom, local artwork on the walls. Other rooms, cottage-style, are in the garden. Book ahead for a slap-up feed: Sebastian Snow's long menus, featuring pub classics and dishes with an Italian influence, are popular locally. In fine weather, large parasols spring up around the picnic tables in the pretty garden – the ideal spot to go alfresco. Snug, bar, restaurant (2 dining rooms, closed Sun eve). Free Wi-Fi, in-room TV (Freeview). Background music. Garden. Children welcomed (special menus). 9 bedrooms (some family rooms, 5 in annexe). Per room B&B £95–£130. Dinner £28.

LEICESTER Leicestershire
Map 2:B3

HOTEL MAIYANGO, 13–21 St Nicholas Place, LE1 4LD. Tel 01162 518898, www.maiyango.com. Bespoke wood furnishings, commissioned artwork and bold colours have turned this 150-year-old former shoe factory into a chic hotel near the historic centre. Aatin Anadkat is the owner. Spacious bedrooms are equipped with a large bed and a modern bathroom; extras include organic tea and coffee, fresh milk, a snack tray and a DVD library. Take pre-dinner drinks with a side of fantastic city views in the Glass Bar overlooking Jubilee Square, then sample new chef Salvatore Tassari's modern fusion dishes in the informal, lantern-lit restaurant. The Maiyango Kitchen Deli around the corner serves 'convenience restaurant food', available to take away. Bar, cocktail lounge, restaurant (closed lunchtime Sun–Tues). Lift. Free Wi-Fi, in-room TV (Freeview). Background music. 24-hour room service menu. Function facilities. Cooking and cocktail classes. Roof terrace. Paid public parking nearby. 15 mins' walk to train station. 14 bedrooms (1 suitable for disabled). Per person B&B from £79, D,B&B from £111. Closed Christmas, New Year.
25% DISCOUNT VOUCHERS

LEWES Sussex
Map 2:E4

SKYHOUSE, Cuilfail, BN7 2BE. Tel 07468 691 860, www.skyhousesussex.com. A zero-carbon wonder in the countryside, Amy Burgess's modern B&B combines state-of-the-art eco-luxury, clean design and sustainable practice. The German-made eco-house is on a hillside overlooking the Transition Town of

Lewes (which makes clear its dedication to sustainable living); floor-to-ceiling windows bring in light and calm. To the rear, the back gate opens on to the South Downs, so the green hills seem to unfurl right up to the door. Spacious bedrooms with wide views of the downs have original art, bespoke fabrics and much smart tech: underfloor heating, sensor lighting, remote-controlled blinds. A healthy breakfast suits the healthy environment: find smoothie bowls of yogurt, fruit purée, seeds and berries alongside more classic options. Guests arriving on foot, or by bicycle or electric vehicle receive a 10% discount. 15 mins' walk to train station; 10 mins' walk to shops, bars and restaurants. Glyndebourne is easily reached, 3½ miles away. Living room. Lift. Free Wi-Fi, in-room smart TV. Garden. Children over 12 and dogs welcomed. 3 bedrooms (all on ground floor, 1 suitable for disabled). Per person B&B £160–£250.

LICHFIELD Staffordshire
Map 2:A2

SWINFEN HALL, Swinfen, WS14 9RE. Tel 01543 481494, www. swinfenhallhotel.co.uk. A minstrels' gallery graces the entrance foyer of the Wiser family's Grade II listed 18th-century manor house – a first glimpse of the 'elegant historic charm' of this 'excellent' small hotel. It stands in 'lovely, well-maintained' grounds including an extensive deer park. Inside, 'friendly' staff are 'committed to giving their guests a great experience'. Stuart Kennedy is the manager. Choose among 'well-appointed' bedrooms decorated in traditional or modern style – all are provided with freshly baked shortbread,

locally sourced mineral water, a house blend of ground coffee. Take afternoon tea, light meals and cocktails in the clubby lounge or wood-panelled Edwardian bar (its terrace overlooks the formal gardens and deer park). In the Four Seasons restaurant, sit at a table set with white linen for chef Ryan Shilton's 'first-class' à la carte and tasting menus using estate-reared venison and lamb, and produce from the Victorian walled garden and orchard. (Vegetarian menus are available.) Regular concerts, wine and jazz suppers, and gourmet nights. 2 miles S of Lichfield. Lounge, bar, cocktail lounge, restaurant; terrace. Private dining room, ballroom. Free Wi-Fi, in-room TV (Sky). Background music. Civil wedding licence. 100-acre grounds (formal gardens, woodlands, parkland, wild hay meadows, 45-acre deer park). Children welcomed (cots, high chairs). 17 bedrooms. Per room B&B single from £140, double from £170; D,B&B single from £185, double from £260.

LINCOLN Lincolnshire
Map 4:E5

THE CASTLE, Westgate, LN1 3AS. Tel 01522 538801, www.castlehotel.net. Guests are 'well looked after' by 'extremely pleasant, welcoming' staff at this smartly refurbished hotel, a former school built on the site of Lincoln's Roman Forum. Set in the historic Bailgate area, it's an excellent base from which to explore the city. 'Comfortable' modern bedrooms (some small) have views of the castle walls or the medieval cathedral; those in the 250-year-old Coach House are on the ground floor. Chef Mark Cheseldine serves 'good, beautifully presented' modern European dishes in the 'charming' panelled restaurant. Fancy something lighter? Head to the stylish, popular bar for bistro-style snacks. Good breakfasts. 2 small lounges, bar, Reform restaurant (evenings only). Free Wi-Fi, in-room TV. Background music. Massage and beauty treatments. Wedding/function facilities. Parking. Children welcomed. 18 bedrooms (some in attic, some in courtyard; 1 suitable for disabled); plus 1 apartment, and Castle Cottage (available for self-catering). Per room B&B single £90–£100, double £100–£150; D,B&B single £120–£135, double £130–£220. Dinner £32.95.

LITTLE ECCLESTON Lancashire
Map 4:D2

THE CARTFORD INN, Cartford Lane, PR3 0YP. Tel 01995 670166, www.thecartfordinn.co.uk. Discover cosy alcoves, a convivial bar, smart, rustic bedrooms and 'genuinely hospitable' staff at Julie and Patrick Beaumé's refurbished 17th-century coaching inn on the banks of the River Wyre. The individually decorated bedrooms are chic indeed, with eye-catching wallpapers, quirky features and top-end toiletries. Some have a Juliet balcony with riverside views; others, in the attic, have a skylight. A penthouse suite has a private rooftop terrace and a panorama of the Bowland Fells. Dine informally in the bar and by the fireside – cask ales, craft beers, signature cocktails and custom-made soft drinks are worthy accompaniments – or take a seat in the River Lounge, where chef Chris Bury cooks classic British dishes with a French touch. During the summer months, eat alfresco on the terrace while the river rushes by. Want to

take it all home with you? Stop in at the deli, TOTI (Taste of the Inn), for international and Lancashire treats including breads, cakes and pastries straight from the inn's kitchen. Bar, restaurant, delicatessen. Free Wi-Fi, in-room TV (Freeview). Background music. Terrace. Parking. The train station, at Poulton-le-Fylde, is a short drive away; Blackpool is 7 miles SW. 15 bedrooms (some in riverside annexe, 1 family room, 1 suitable for disabled). Per room B&B £80–£230. Closed Christmas Day.

LIVERPOOL Merseyside
Map 4:E2

HARD DAYS NIGHT, Central Buildings, North John Street, L2 6RR. Tel 01512 361964, www.harddaysnighthotel.com. A must for fans of the Fab Four, this Beatles-themed hotel has 'a strong dash of personality'. Inside the grand Grade II listed building, original paintings, statues, photographs and artful references to the Liverpool band come together in the bedrooms and public spaces. 'Friendly' staff are on hand to help if you need somebody. Each of the individually designed bedrooms has a large bed, 'good fittings' and a monsoon shower in the bathroom; some have a private balcony. Quietest rooms face away from the street. Shake it up with dinner in Blakes restaurant (decorated with Sir Peter Blake's iconic artwork), where traditional British dishes have a contemporary twist. Lounge (live music on Fri and Sat nights), Bar Four cocktail bar, brasserie, restaurant (open to non-residents; closed Sun, Mon lunch). Art gallery. Lift. Free Wi-Fi, in-room TV (Sky). Background music. Civil wedding licence; function facilities.

Close to the Cavern Club; tours can be arranged. Parking discounts. Children welcomed (special menu). 110 bedrooms (1 suitable for disabled). Per room B&B from £140, D,B&B from £154. Closed Christmas.

HOPE STREET HOTEL, 40 Hope Street, L1 9DA. Tel 0151 709 3000, www. hopestreethotel.co.uk. Opposite the Philharmonic Hall, in the vibrant cultural quarter, this handsome modern hotel is 'a real find'. 'It's a fine example of change for the better, in a city that's being revived so well,' say Guide readers in 2016. Mary Colston is the manager. With exposed brick walls, vintage metal supports and old beams, the former Victorian coach factory retains a characterful atmosphere in its 'light, airy' public areas. Most of the 'tastefully decorated' bedrooms have 'fantastic' views of the river, the cathedral or the city skyline. Dine on chef David Critchley's 'delicious' modern dishes in the London Carriage Works restaurant; cocktails, sandwiches and sharing plates may be taken in the residents' lounge. 'The breakfast menu provides many choices, some of gargantuan size.' 'At the end of our stay, the 25-minute walk – nearly all downhill – to Lime Street station was a good way to finish an excellent break.' Lounge, bar, restaurant. Private dining. Lift. Gym, treatment rooms. Free Wi-Fi, in-room TV (Sky). Background music. 24-hour room service. Civil wedding licence, functions. Limited parking nearby (£10 charge). Children (special menu) and dogs (£15 per night) welcomed. 89 bedrooms (some interconnecting; 2 suitable for disabled). Per room B&B from £114.

THE NADLER LIVERPOOL, 29 Seel Street, L1 4AU. Tel 0151 705 2626, www. thenadler.com. The Ropewalks area is a lively backdrop for this stylish hotel in a converted printworks. A sister to The Nadler Kensington, London (see Shortlist), it offers good-value, 'practical and efficient' accommodation in the city centre. Each of the smart, modern bedrooms has a well-equipped mini-kitchen with tea, coffee, a microwave, a fridge, crockery and cutlery. Coming with a larger group? Ask for the Secret Garden suite – spread over two levels, it has bathrobes, slippers and a private garden area. Enjoy continental breakfasts (ordered in advance) and a complimentary coffee in the lounge. There is no bar or restaurant, but guests are offered discounts at local restaurants, bars and clubs. Lounge, meeting room. Lift. Free Wi-Fi, 30 mins of free local and national landline calls per day, in-room TV. Background music. Vending machines. Parking discounts. Children welcomed. 106 bedrooms (some suitable for disabled). Room from £49. Breakfast £7.

LUDLOW Shropshire
Map 3:C4

SHROPSHIRE HILLS, Aston Munslow, SY7 9ER. Tel 01584 841565, www. shropshirehillsbedandbreakfast.co.uk. Enjoy a sweet welcome at Chris and Linda Baker's country B&B where visitors are greeted with tea and cake. (The treats keep coming, well after guests arrive: 'Linda made sure that I was never short of her delicious gluten-free cakes and biscuits,' a guest reports this year.) 'Spacious', 'spotlessly clean' bedrooms are well equipped with fresh milk, teas, ground coffee, locally hand-woven wool throws; two have views of the Shropshire hills. 'Ours had been furnished to a very high standard and had wonderful views across the valley. Everything that we needed was there.' Breakfast includes home-grown tomatoes; home-made jams and compotes made from garden fruit; eggs from the Bakers' chickens. Tuck in, then visit the three alpacas that graze in the paddock. Rambles from the doorstep include the Corvedale Three Castles Walk; the surrounding conservation village is well positioned for walking the Shropshire Way along the slopes of Wenlock Edge. Walkers and cyclists are welcomed – there are changing and drying facilities and a boot room. Lounge/dining room. Free Wi-Fi, in-room TV (Freeview). No background music. 2-acre garden, terrace (outdoor seating). 8 miles NE of Ludlow. 3 bedrooms (all with separate entrance from main house). Per room B&B £98–£125. 2-night min. stay preferred. Closed Dec–Easter.

LUPTON Cumbria
Map 4: inset C2

THE PLOUGH, Cow Brow, LA6 1PJ. Tel 01539 567700, www.theploughatlupton. co.uk. Old-world country charm combines with state-of-the-art facilities at Paul Spencer's smartly refurbished 18th-century coaching inn, in a hamlet close to Kirkby Lonsdale. Susannah Harris is the manager. A relaxed atmosphere prevails in the historic pub – settle in to a squashy sofa under the old oak beams with a fresh pint of cider, or warm yourself before the wood-burning stove. At lunch and dinner, chef Matt Adamson cooks refined pub food and plenty of steaks, with a good vegetarian selection for balance. Upstairs, inviting country-style bedrooms come in a host of shapes and sizes: Hutton, a family suite, has superb views over Farleton Knott; Torsin has dual-aspect windows and an oversized bathroom with a monsoon shower, roll-top slipper bath, double washbasins and feature lighting. Ideally placed for exploring the Lake District and the Yorkshire Dales. Lounge, bar, restaurant. Free Wi-Fi (signal variable), in-room TV (Freeview). Background music. Civil wedding licence. Terrace, garden. Parking. Children and dogs (in 1 room) welcomed. 5 mins' drive from M6 junction 36. 6 bedrooms (family room). Per room B&B £155–£195. Dinner £30. No overnight guests 24/25 Dec.
25% DISCOUNT VOUCHERS

LYME REGIS Dorset
Map 1:C6

DORSET HOUSE, Pound Road, DT7 3HX. Tel 01297 442055, www. dorsethouselyme.com. A short walk from the historic Cobb, Lyn and Jason Martin's B&B welcomes guests with stylish calm. Modern, breath-of-fresh-air bedrooms, most with sea views, have wooden floors and subtle colours; a couple have a sofa bed to accommodate a child or two. In the smart, log-burner-warmed sitting room or outside on the veranda, mingle over a glass of local sparkling wine or Dorset gin from the honesty bar; grab one of the Welsh blankets if the weather turns cool. Breakfast takes centre stage. Eaten communally at a large scrubbed table, the morning meal includes freshly ground coffee, home-made granola, Aga-cooked options. Organic produce is used whenever possible; all diets can be catered for, with advance notice. 'Muddy boots are welcome,' the hosts say; there are maps and wellies for walkers to borrow. Snug (honesty bar, newspapers, magazines), breakfast room. Free Wi-Fi, in-room TV (Freeview). Background music. Veranda. Children welcomed (£15 for 1 child, £25 for 2). 5 bedrooms. Closed Christmas. Per room B&B £105–£160.

LYNMOUTH Devon
Map 1:B4

SHELLEY'S, 8 Watersmeet Road, E35 6EP. Tel 01598 753219, www. shelleyshotel.co.uk. Kippers are always on the menu at Jane Becker and Richard Briden's well-liked, traditional B&B in an 18th-century house with fine views over Lynmouth Bay. (The house is named after Percy Bysshe Shelley, who brought his child bride, Harriet, here in 1812 for their honeymoon.) Bedrooms may seem old-fashioned, with a retro metal bedstead and a floral or patchwork bedcovering, but the sea views are timeless – ask for a room with a private balcony. Generous breakfasts are taken in the light-filled conservatory with an expansive vista across the bay. Short walk to the harbour. Lounge, bar, conservatory breakfast room. Courtyard garden. Free Wi-Fi, in-room TV. No background music. Children over 12 welcomed. 11 bedrooms (1 on ground floor). Per room B&B £85–£125. 2-night min. booking preferred. Closed Dec–Mar.

LYTHAM Lancashire
Map 4:D2

THE ROOMS, 35 Church Road, FY8 5LL. Tel 01253 736000, www. theroomslytham.com. Within walking distance of shops, restaurants and the sea, Jackie and Andy Baker's Fylde coast B&B pleases with its modern rooms and generous breakfasts. 'Beautifully fitted', bedrooms are equipped with up-to-date technology (digital radio, iPod docking station, flat-screen TV); stylish wet rooms (one with a bathtub) have a rain shower and underfloor heating. A tasty breakfast, served in the walled garden when weather permits, has freshly blended smoothies, locally baked bread, Buck's Fizz; a praiseworthy array of cooked dishes includes local sausages, smoked haddock fish-cakes, pancakes, waffles and eggs Benedict, Arlington or Florentine. The 'helpful' hosts have plenty of local knowledge to share – including where to find the best pizza-and-jazz combos in town. Breakfast room (background TV). Free Wi-Fi, in-room TV (Freeview). Decked garden. Children welcomed. 5 bedrooms ('lots of stairs'), plus 2-bed serviced apartment. Per room B&B single £90–£110, double £110–£140.

MALVERN WELLS Worcestershire
Map 3:D5

THE COTTAGE IN THE WOOD, Holywell Road, WR14 4LG. Tel 01684 588860, www.cottageinthewood.co.uk. 'You'd be hard pressed to find a hotel with a more impressive view.' At the end of a steep uphill drive, Julia and Nick Davies's 'guest-centred' hotel is 'perched high' on the east side of the Malverns. Guide inspectors in 2016 found traditionally furnished bedrooms, 'appetising' meals, 'efficient, welcoming' staff – and a vista that 'stretches for miles' across the plains towards the distant Cotswolds. Choose between bedrooms in the main 16th-century dower house, a garden cottage and the more modern Coach House – each differs in character and aspect. 'Our first-floor room in the coach house, though dated, maximised the view, with French doors opening on to a small balcony. Tea- and coffee-making facilities included fresh milk; mineral water was provided. Binoculars, too – a good touch.' The restaurant 'enjoys the stunning view' through large Georgian windows ('though the muzak did little for dining equanimity'). Mornings, 'generous' portions of 'buttery' scrambled eggs perk up a 'standard' breakfast. On a clear day, walk straight from the hotel grounds into the woods and up on to the Malvern Hills – from the top, gaze across Herefordshire and peer into Wales. Bar, lounge, restaurant; terrace (alfresco meals and drinks). Private dining, meeting facilities. Free Wi-Fi, in-room TV (Freeview). Children and dogs (£10 per night, in some bedrooms) welcomed. 7-acre grounds, with direct access to the Malvern hills. 30 bedrooms (4 in Beech Cottage, 19 in Coach House; 10 on ground floor; 1 suitable for disabled). Per room B&B £80–£198, D,B&B £150–£295 (plus 2% surcharge for credit-card payments on check-out).

MANCHESTER
Map 4:E3
DIDSBURY HOUSE, Didsbury Park, Didsbury Village, M20 5LJ. Tel 0161 448 2200, www.didsburyhouse.co.uk. With fresh flowers, books and low sofas by the fire, this stylish modern hotel is steeped in a relaxed, home-away-from-home atmosphere. The Victorian villa (part of the Eclectic Hotels group; see Eleven Didsbury Park, next entry) stands in a leafy urban village not far from the city centre; the airport is within easy reach. Individually styled bedrooms mix modern touches (prints, feature wallpaper) and original features (high windows, delicate cornices); many have a freestanding roll-top bath. Lie in on the weekends, when breakfast is served until noon. At aperitif o'clock, take alfresco drinks on the walled terrace (heated in cool weather). The city centre is easily reached by 'quick train'; otherwise, 'a cab ride from the centre late at night'. 'Good walks' in the botanic gardens, nearby. 2 lounges, bar, breakfast room. Meeting room. Gym. Walled terrace with water feature. Free Wi-Fi, in-room TV (Sky). 'Chill-out' background music. Exclusive use for weddings/functions. Children welcomed. 27 bedrooms. Room £150–£270. Breakfast £14–£16.

ELEVEN DIDSBURY PARK, 11 Didsbury Park, Didsbury Village, M20 5LH. Tel 0161 448 7711, www.elevendidsburypark.com. Sink into a sofa in the large, airy sitting rooms here, or find a lounger or hammock in the walled garden. This stylishly refurbished Victorian town house hotel has plenty of space in which to loll. Part of the Eclectic Hotels group (see Didsbury House, previous entry), the modern hotel is in a peaceful suburb close to the city centre. Elegant bedrooms range in size from snug Classic rooms (with a walk-in monsoon shower) to the lofty Veranda suite (whose French doors lead to a private balcony). A deli menu takes the place of a restaurant; it has sandwiches and steaks, served anywhere you wish to sit. Convenient for the airport (ten minutes' drive). 2 lounge/bars. Gym, treatment room. Free Wi-Fi, in-room TV (Sky). Background music.

Wedding/conference facilities. Veranda, large walled garden. Parking. Children and 'well-behaved' dogs welcomed. 20 bedrooms (1 on ground floor, suitable for disabled). Per room B&B from £138.

MARAZION Cornwall
Map 1:E1

GODOLPHIN ARMS, West End, TR17 0EN. Tel 01736 888510, www. godolphinarms.co.uk. St Michael's Mount beckons across the sandy causeway from James and Mary St Levan's 'unpretentious', 'superbly located' beachside inn. Robin Collyns, the manager, heads a team of 'obliging, efficient' staff. 'Modern', light-filled bedrooms, decorated in a style inspired by the coast, are hung with local artwork, and well supplied with bathrobes and high-quality toiletries; many have sea views; some have a balcony. Two suites of adjoining bedrooms accommodate a family. (Ring to discuss room choices: guests have commented on 'steep' stairs leading to some bedrooms.) There's no private residents' lounge, but find a spot in any of the informal drinking and dining areas: a log-burner-warmed space with easy chairs and comfy sofas; a relaxed beach bar and terrace; an airy glass-and-zinc extension which opens out for alfresco dining in good weather. Food is served all day: full Cornish breakfasts, cake-based elevenses, sharing platters, cream teas, Newlyn crab sandwiches, and a 'good' menu of daily specials including the seafood catch of the day. 2 bars, split-level dining area; 2 terraces. Free Wi-Fi, in-room TV (Sky). 'Easy listening' background music. Wedding/function facilities. Buckets, spades and fishing nets available to borrow.

Parking. Children (cot; extra bed £25 per night) and dogs (in some rooms) welcomed. 4 miles E of Penzance. 10 bedrooms (2 suites). Per room B&B £160–£250. Dinner £27.

MARCHAM Oxfordshire
Map 2:C2

B&B RAFTERS, Abingdon Road, OX13 6NU. Tel 01865 391298, www.bnb-rafters.co.uk. Receive a warm welcome at Sigrid Grawert's B&B on the edge of a pretty Oxfordshire village. Dainty accents, leafy plants, feature wallpaper and high-end technology round out the stylish bedrooms; the bathrooms have a power shower. Choose a room to suit: one has a freestanding bath and a private balcony; a single room has a water bed. In fine weather, enjoy the garden from a new outdoor seating area. Organic breakfasts, taken communally, include freshly squeezed orange juice, eggs Benedict, home-baked bread, home-made jams and marmalade; whisky porridge is a speciality. Vegetarian and special diets are catered for. Lounge, breakfast room. Free Wi-Fi, in-room TV (Freeview). No background music. Garden. Parking. Children over 12 welcomed. 3 miles W of Abingdon. 4 bedrooms. Per room B&B single from £57, double from £99. Closed Christmas, New Year. 2-night min. stay on bank holiday weekends.

MARGATE Kent
Map 2:D5

THE READING ROOMS, 31 Hawley Square, CT9 1PH. Tel 01843 225166, www.thereadingroomsmargate.co.uk. Louise Oldfield and Liam Nabb have artfully restored this 200-year-old town house on a Georgian square around the corner from the Turner Contemporary. Come in to stripped wooden floors, enormous sash windows, original shutters, rough stone fireplaces and vintage plasterwork – plus a fine selection of reading material, of course: local history books, Penguin paperbacks, glossy magazines. B&B accommodation is in expansive bedrooms, each occupying an entire floor. Each has its own character, but all have a large French-style bed, sprigs of blossoms, a 'cavernous' bathroom with a freestanding roll-top bath. Much-praised 'piping-hot' breakfasts – accompanied, perhaps, by a glass of carrot and ginger juice – are 'beautifully served' in the bedroom, at a table by the huge window. Free Wi-Fi, in-room TV. No background music. Parking vouchers available. 3 bedrooms. Per room B&B £150–£180. 2-night min. stay at weekends and on bank holidays.

MATLOCK Derbyshire
Map 3:A6

THE MANOR FARMHOUSE, Manor Farm, Dethick, DE4 5GG. Tel 01629 534302, www.manorfarmdethick.co.uk. To venture into Gilly and Simon Groom's 'excellent', 'wonderfully quiet' B&B is to step in to rustic peace and tranquillity. The 'very comfortable' Grade II* listed 16th-century stone house is on a sheep farm between two dales, in a spot where lambs gambol, and pheasants cross the maze of winding lanes. Two of the large, country-style bedrooms are in the beamed hayloft; another, on the ground floor of the main house, has direct access to the garden. Breakfast is taken around the large refectory table in the original Elizabethan kitchen – expect fresh local ingredients and

home-grown produce, prepared for all diets. Chatsworth House, Hardwick Hall and Haddon Hall are within easy reach. Sitting rooms (TV, games), breakfast room. Free Wi-Fi, in-room TV. No background music. 1-acre grounds. Parking, bicycle/motorcycle storage. Drying facilities. Children over 5 welcomed. 2 miles E of Matlock; collection from railway/bus station can be arranged. 4 bedrooms (1 on ground floor, suitable for disabled). Per room B&B £80–£95. 2-night min. stay on Sat, Apr–Oct.

MATLOCK BATH Derbyshire
Map 3:B6

HODGKINSON'S HOTEL, 150 South Parade, DE4 3NR. Tel 01629 582170, www.hodgkinsons-hotel.co.uk. 'A haven' in the centre, Chris and Zoe Hipwell's 'very special' Grade II listed town house hotel has 'superb views' of the valley, and 'challenging walks' from the door. Its quirky Victorian interior (tiled entrance hall, ornate glasswork, the original wood-and-glass bar) has great atmosphere – ask to explore the hotel's cellars, once used by Job Hodgkinson, the Victorian-era homeowner, to store his locally brewed beer. Traditionally furnished bedrooms may have river views or a four-poster bed; the walnut-trimmed bathrooms have a roll-top bathtub or an Edwardian-style walk-in shower. Dine on chef Leigh Matthews's 'excellent' modern British menus in the restaurant; at breakfast, choose from varied options, including omelettes, kedgeree and a full vegetarian. A large terraced garden surveys village rooftops, the view stretching to the granite cliffs and River Derwent beyond. Sitting room, bar, restaurant (open to non-residents; closed Sun eve). Free Wi-Fi, in-room TV. Background music/radio. Garden. Limited on-site parking; additional parking nearby. Children (extra cot/bed £10) and dogs (by arrangement, £10 per night) welcomed. 8 bedrooms. Per room B&B £50–£145, D,B&B £76–£171. Closed Christmas.

MEVAGISSEY Cornwall
Map 1:D2

PEBBLE HOUSE, Polkirt Hill, PL26 6UX. Tel 01726 844466, www.pebblehousecornwall.co.uk. The panoramic sea views from Andrea and Simon Copper's modern B&B stretch over Mevagissey Bay to historic Chapel Point and beyond, but turn your attention inside for a moment: this sleekly designed, child-free retreat invites calm contemplation. (A glass of champagne, offered on arrival, calls for consideration, too.) Each of the contemporary bedrooms has a 'seriously comfortable' bed and retro furniture; all but one have vast glass doors leading to a Juliet balcony or terrace overlooking the water. In the morning, the commanding views rival the host's impressive breakfasts: generous carafes of freshly squeezed orange juice, home-made granola, yogurt-and-compote sundaes, eggs lots of ways. When the weather cooperates, step outside: the terrace is just the place for Cornish cream teas, light snacks and drinks. Ask for a picnic before heading out on the South West Coastal Path. Breakfast room. Free Wi-Fi, in-room TV (Sky). Background music at breakfast. Terraced grounds. Parking. 10 mins' steep uphill stroll from the village. Bicycle storage, drying room.

No children under 16. 6 bedrooms (1 on ground floor). Per room B&B £120–£215.

TREVALSA COURT, School Hill, PL26 6TH. Tel 01726 842468, www.trevalsa-hotel.co.uk. On the cliff of a 'stunningly beautiful' cove, Susan and John Gladwin's 'superb' Arts and Crafts hotel is a lovely coastal retreat with 'friendly, well-trained' staff. 'Spectacular' views from the subtropical gardens 'seem to stretch to the sea'; to put your toes in the water, descend steep steps to the secluded sandy beach. Cheery, simply furnished bedrooms have a hospitality tray and DVD-player; the best have seating space and views of the sea. When the weather turns cool, sit by the fire in the lounge stocked with books and games. At lunch and dinner, try chef Adam Cawood's 'exceptionally good' cooking using produce sourced straight from the sea or nearby farms. The Coastal Path runs past the end of the garden. Lounge, bar, restaurant (light jazz background music). Free Wi-Fi, in-room TV (Freeview). 2-acre garden (summer house). Children (cot; extra bed £15 per night) and dogs (under supervision) welcomed. 10 mins' downhill walk to village. 15 bedrooms (3 on ground floor; family suite accessed from outside). Per room B&B £120–£260, D,B&B £170–£315. Closed end Nov–mid-Feb.
25% DISCOUNT VOUCHERS

MIDHURST Sussex
Map 2:E3

THE CHURCH HOUSE, Church Hill, GU29 9NX. Tel 01730 812990, www.churchhousemidhurst.com. Fina Jurado has instilled 'the attitude of a private house' in her large B&B, formed of four cottages with 13th-century origins, in the centre of the attractive market town. There's a relaxed elegance in the wide-planked wooden flooring, antique furniture and large, open-plan ground floor, where a fire blazes in the hearth. Guests are greeted with tea and home-made cake, and invited to 'chill'. A modern glass-and-oak staircase leads to stylishly rustic bedrooms, each stocked with fresh flowers and natural bath products. The suites are masterpieces: one has soaring beamed ceilings, another a mezzanine and velvet chaise longue, yet another a study overlooking the garden. Lazy mornings are made for the hostess's cooked-to-order breakfasts, served at a time to suit. Gather with fellow guests at a huge oak table; jams and marmalades are home made. Private dinner parties can be arranged. Sitting room/dining room, conservatory with TV. Free Wi-Fi, in-room TV (Sky). No background music. Garden. Children welcomed. 5 bedrooms (1 on ground floor). Per room B&B single from £70, double £140–£160. Closed Christmas.

MILLOM Cumbria
Map 4: inset C2
Broadgate House, Broadgate, Thwaites, LA18 5JZ. Tel 01229 716295, www.broadgate-house.co.uk. The gardens bloom in a riot of colour around Diana Lewthwaite's peaceful guest house, with the Lakeland fells as a dramatic backdrop. Home to the Lewthwaite family for almost 200 years, the fine, white-painted Georgian house has grand public rooms filled with antique furniture, sumptuous fabrics and an original fireplace. Spacious

bedrooms, decorated in a busy country-house style, are full of colour and pattern; each has a separate bathroom with a throne loo and freestanding bath. Designed as a series of 'garden rooms', the two-acre grounds include terraces, a croquet lawn, a walled garden and an 'oasis' with a palm tree. A cosseting base for exploring the Lake District. Sitting room (wood-burning stove), dining room, breakfast room. Free Wi-Fi in reception. No background music. 4 miles from town; beaches nearby. 5 bedrooms. Per room B&B single £55, double £95. Dinner (by arrangement) £25. No credit cards accepted. Closed 1–23 Dec.
25% DISCOUNT VOUCHERS

MISTLEY Essex
Map 2:C5
The Mistley Thorn, High Street, CO11 1HE. Tel 01206 392821, www.mistleythorn.co.uk. A good base for exploring Constable country, this congenial restaurant-with-rooms is run by chef/proprietor Sherri Singleton and her husband, David McKay. (The former 18th-century coaching inn has an interesting history – it was built on the foundations of the home of Witchfinder General Matthew Hopkins.) A soft palette and little extras (dressing gowns, luxury toiletries, home-made biscuits) adorn the comfortable bedrooms; four have views down the Stour estuary. Light sleepers may want to ask for a room away from traffic noise. Mersea oysters are a highlight in the smart restaurant, whose 'unpretentious' menu focuses on locally landed seafood and meats from nearby Sutton Hoo. (Vegetarians have interesting options to choose from.) Popular Sunday lunches.

Sherri Singleton also holds cookery workshops at the Mistley Kitchen next door (special room rates for those attending). Bar, restaurant (background jazz). Free Wi-Fi, in-room TV. Outdoor seating. Children (special menu, cot) and small/medium dogs (in 3 rooms; £5 per night charge) welcomed. 11 bedrooms (3 in annexe). Per room B&B £100–£125, D,B&B £135–£195.

MORETON-IN-MARSH
Gloucestershire
Map 3:D6

THE OLD SCHOOL, Little Compton, GL56 0SL. Tel 01608 674588, www. theoldschoolbedandbreakfast.com. Gather up your pencils and books: there'll be no sums in Wendy Veale's Victorian schoolhouse B&B – just a warm welcome over tea and home-made cake. Relax in the old assembly hall, now a spacious open-plan sitting/dining room; upstairs, browse the library in the vaulted drawing room while light filters in through the oversized church-style window. Pretty bedrooms, decorated in country style, have fresh flowers, complimentary refreshments, bathrobes, a super-king-size bed; bathrooms are stocked with thick, fluffy towels. A food writer and stylist, Wendy Veale cooks tasty communal breakfasts using eggs from the hens in the garden; freshly ground coffee and local honey round out the feast. Ask about light suppers, four-course dinners or picnic hampers; the amenable hostess can cater for special requests. 2 sitting rooms, dining room (BYO bottle at dinner), laundry room. Free Wi-Fi (computer available). No background music. 1-acre garden (pergolas, patios, fish pond, orchard;

bantam hens; pet rabbits, cat). Parking. 3 miles E of Moreton-in-Marsh. 4 bedrooms (1 on ground floor). Per room B&B from £120. 2-night min. stay at weekends. Dinner £32.

MULLION Cornwall
Map 1:E2

POLURRIAN BAY HOTEL, Polurrian Road, TR12 7EN. Tel 01326 240421, www. polurrianhotel.com. From swimming pools to spa treatments, from a cinema to a Sunday morning breakfast club, there are 'excellent' diversions for all ages at this modern clifftop hotel (Luxury Family Hotels) above a sandy bay on the Lizard peninsula. Yvonne Colgan is the manager. 'Well-appointed, comfortable' bedrooms have stunning views of the coastline; many have space for an extra bed or cot; some are interconnecting. 'Freshly cooked and plentiful' meals are available all day in the 'impressive' Vista lounge or more formal restaurant; on balmy afternoons, find a table on the terrace for an alfresco lunch. The days are full: choose between tennis courts, an adventure playground, a games room, garden exploration; the beach is a short stroll away. Vista lounge, snug, dining room (background music), cinema. The Den (nursery for children 6 months–8 years old), the Blue Room (older children; video games, pool, table football). Spa (9-metre pool). Lift. Free Wi-Fi, in-room TV. Civil wedding licence, functions. 12-acre grounds, terrace. Children (special menu; baby equipment) and dogs (in some rooms; £15 per night) welcomed. 41 bedrooms (some on ground floor, 1 suitable for disabled). Per room B&B £120–£570. Dinner £35–£40. 2-night min. stay in peak season.

NEWBY BRIDGE Cumbria
Map 4: inset C2

THE SWAN HOTEL & SPA, The
Colonnade, LA12 8NB. Tel 015395
31681, www.swanhotel.com. The River
Leven rushes past this family-friendly
hotel, spa and popular local pub, on
its way out to Morecambe Bay. Take
advantage of the riverside location and
arrive by boat – there are sheltered
moorings for guests. Amble about the
grounds: the owners, the Bardsley
family, have made the sweeping gardens
a welcoming scene, just right for playing
hide-and-seek at any age. Inside the
17th-century former coaching inn,
much has been refreshed following
extensive refurbishment in 2016. Smart
bedrooms are decorated in modern
country style, with liberal sprinklings
of floral prints. Ask for a room at the
front for the river view; those at the
back gaze out upon the lawn. There's
something for everyone: family suites
of interconnecting rooms have toys,
books and video games; adults-only
top-floor suites have a super-king-size
bed, and a double-ended bath in the
bathroom. In the atmospheric pub or
the River Room restaurant, choose
among pub classics and modern dishes
on chef Claire Asbury's menu. The
ample breakfast has good vegetarian
options. Fell Foot park, on the shores
of Lake Windermere, is nearby. Sitting
room, library, Swan Inn 'pub', River
Room restaurant, breakfast room. Free
Wi-Fi, in-room TV (Sky). Background
music. Civil wedding licence, function
facilities. 10-acre grounds, terrace. Spa
(treatments), indoor pool, hot tub, sauna,
steam room; gym. Parking; mooring.
Children welcomed (adventure
playground, nature trail, milk and
cookies before bed). 54 bedrooms (some
interconnecting, some suitable for
disabled), plus 5 self-catering cottages.
Per room B&B from £129. 2-night
min. stay on bank holiday weekends.
Dinner £32.

NEWMARKET Suffolk
Map 2:B4

BEDFORD LODGE, Bury Road,
CB8 7BX. Tel 01638 663175, www.
bedfordlodgehotel.co.uk. 'Altogether
delightful.' Returning guests this
year especially recommend the
'superb service', 'lovely gardens' and
'excellent breakfast' at this 'beautiful'
country house close to the racecourses.
Originally a Georgian hunting lodge
built for the sixth Duke of Bedford,
it has been a family-run hotel since
the 1940s. The 'excellent' bedrooms
(some small) have sumptuous accents
and textiles against a neutral palette,
and views of the stables or gardens;
several are interconnecting; all are
well supplied with mineral water,
juices, chocolates and posh toiletries.
Chef James Fairchild serves an eclectic
modern menu in Squires restaurant,
including 'the best cheese soufflé
anywhere'; in balmy weather, the terrace
is just the thing for dining alfresco. Be
sure to wander the impressive grounds
buttressing paddocks and training
stables – the rose gardens in season have
plenty to sniff at. Sitting room, library,
restaurant (open to non-residents), bar.
Private dining. Free Wi-Fi, in-room
TV (Sky). Background music. Civil
wedding licence, function facilities.
3-acre grounds, terrace. Spa (treatments,
tanning). Gym (sauna, steam room, hot
tub). Parking. Children welcomed. 77
bedrooms (some interconnecting, some

suitable for disabled, 6 suites). Per room B&B £180–£235. 2-night min. stay on bank holiday weekends. Dinner £32.

NEWQUAY Cornwall
Map 1:D2
THE HEADLAND HOTEL, Headland Road, TR7 1EW. Tel 01637 872211, www.headlandhotel.co.uk. Surf's up at this large, family-friendly hotel, standing just up from the beach, with spectacular views over Fistral Bay. The red-brick Victorian hotel, run by the Armstrong family, is as impressive and imposing as the 12-foot swells (spring and autumn) that merit the in-house surf academy. Find coastal views and coastal hues in most of the bedrooms; the best have a private balcony. Children have plenty of diversion: the surf school on the beach, buckets and spades to borrow, games and DVDs for the asking. Newquay lobster stars in the restaurant; informal meals are served on the beach-facing terrace. Lounges, bar, 2 restaurants (background music; alfresco dining), veranda. Free Wi-Fi, in-room TV. Civil wedding licence, conference/ event facilities. 10-acre grounds. 3 tennis courts, 2 heated swimming pools (indoor and outdoor), table tennis, croquet, putting, boules. Surf school. Spa (Cornish salt steam room, sauna, aromatherapy showers, hot tub). Gym. Children (bunk beds) and dogs (£20 per night charge) welcomed. 96 bedrooms (12 suites; 1 room suitable for disabled), plus 39 self-catering cottages in the grounds. Per room B&B £110–£395.

LEWINNICK LODGE, Pentire Headland, TR7 1QD. Tel 01637 878117, www. lewinnicklodge.co.uk. On the edge of a rocky headland, Pete and Jacqui Fair's voguish restaurant-with-rooms stands apart. Dan Trotter is the manager. Designed in soothing (or 'Spartan', says one guest) colours, sleek, well-equipped bedrooms have a 'comfortable', large bed and home-made biscuits; a power shower, slipper bath and, in some, views of the sea from the tub. Chef Rich Humphries produces 'uncomplicated but sufficiently tasty' Cornish feasts in the 'busy', 'informal' open-plan restaurant and bar, where the daily catch dictates his daily-changing specials; floor-to-ceiling windows open on to a large decked terrace jutting over the sea. Good walks from the door; Fistral Beach is nearby. Bar, restaurant (open to non-residents). Lift. Free Wi-Fi, in-room TV. Occasional background music/radio. In-room treatments. Parking. Children (extra bed on request; 20% charge for 3- to 11-year-olds) welcomed; dogs (in some rooms, £15 per night) by arrangement. 2½ miles from town centre. 11 bedrooms (some suitable for disabled; 1 family suite). Per room B&B £145–£240. Dinner £29.

NORTHALLERTON Yorkshire
Map 4:C4
CLEVELAND TONTINE, Staddlebridge, DL6 3JB. Tel 01609 882671, www. theclevelandtontine.co.uk. A once-upon-a-time travellers' inn, this Victorian house is today a 'comfortable, modern' hotel with 'decadent' bedrooms and 'delicious' food. 'Quirky and individual', it is now part of the Provenance Inns group (along with sister hotel The Carpenters Arms, Felixkirk, see main entry). Bedrooms are individually styled, some with 'dramatic' wallpaper; all have 'good-quality' drinks, home-made shortbread, magazines. 'Ours, warm

and comfortable, had a barley-twist bed, a desk, two '60s-style swivel chairs, a wardrobe with ample hanging space; a spacious bathroom. Secondary glazing did a good job soundproofing the room from the A19.' 'Bistro favourites are handled with flair' in the candlelit dining room divided by a 'wonderful' stone fireplace; at breakfast, served on mix-and-match vintage crockery in the 'splendid, light-filled' drawing room, find leaf tea, local sausages, 'toast thickly sliced from a proper loaf'. Lounge, bar, bistro. Function rooms, private dining. Free Wi-Fi, in-room TV (Freeview). Background music. Room service. Garden. Parking. 8 miles NE of Northallerton. Children welcomed (cot £10; extra bed £20–£80). 7 bedrooms. Per room B&B from £150, D,B&B from £230. Dinner £45.

NORWICH Norfolk
Map 2:B5
NORFOLK MEAD, Church Loke, Coltishall, NR12 7DN. Tel 01603 737531, www.norfolkmead.co.uk. 'Truly "boutique" and extremely comfy', James Holliday and Anna Duttson's 'stylish', wisteria-hung Georgian house is in a 'near-perfect' position in grounds that sweep down to the River Bure. There's 'a great atmosphere', say Guide readers in 2016. 'We had the warmest welcome from the energetic, cheerful, local staff, who are proud to be part of this venture.' Bedrooms vary in size and style, though all are supplied with a hospitality tray, dressing gowns, slippers and natural toiletries. A sophisticated suite has French doors leading to a balcony overlooking garden and river; the cottage and summer houses in the grounds perfectly accommodate families

and larger groups. Leisurely pursuits abound: hire the hotel's boat for a picnic and a lazy potter along the Norfolk Broads; count swans on the private lake. At dinner, tuck in to Anna Duttson's 'excellent' modern British dishes; in the morning, breakfast – 'so good' – includes home-made cereals, fruit compotes, a choice of cooked options. Take afternoon tea and aperitifs in the pretty walled garden when the weather's fine. Lounge, bar, snug, restaurant. Private dining. 2 beauty treatment rooms (10 am–7 pm). Free Wi-Fi, in-room TV (Freeview). Background music. Civil wedding licence. Conference/wedding facilities. Walled garden, fishing lake (swans, geese); off-river mooring. Children (cot, extra bed; £35 per night) and dogs (in some outside rooms; £20 per night charge) welcomed. 7 miles NE of Norwich. 15 bedrooms (2 in cottage, 3 in summer houses). Per room B&B from £135. Dinner £35–£37.

OUNDLE Northamptonshire
Map 2:B3
LOWER FARM, Main Street, Barnwell, PE8 5PU. Tel 01832 273220, www. lower-farm.co.uk. Fresh air and wholesome living are the name of the game at this 'excellent' B&B on the Marriott family's small arable farm. A former milking parlour and old stables, arranged around a central courtyard, have been converted into pretty bedrooms, simply furnished. There's limited Wi-Fi and no mobile signal, making contact with the outside world blissfully difficult. Instead, get back to the land: walk the Nene Way footpath which runs through the farm; there are plenty of other tracks and cycleways to explore. 'Friendly, accommodating'

Caroline Marriott is host; husband Robert and his brother, John, manage the farm. Copious farmhouse breakfasts include a steak-and-eggs special. Breakfast room (background radio/CDs). Courtyard garden with seating. Free Wi-Fi (limited), in-room TV (Freeview). Parking. Children, and dogs (in 2 rooms) welcomed. 3 miles from Oundle. 10 bedrooms (on ground floor; family rooms; 1 suitable for disabled). Per person B&B £50.
25% **DISCOUNT VOUCHERS**

OXFORD Oxfordshire
Map 2:C2

THE BELL AT HAMPTON POYLE, 11 Oxford Road, Hampton Poyle, OX5 2QD. Tel 01865 376242, www.thebelloxford.co.uk. Contemporary design and a timeless, pubby feel combine in this spruced-up honey-stone roadside inn in a small village near Oxford. It is owned by George Dailey; Suzy Minichova is the manager. The building dates, in parts, from the mid-1700s; its large log fire, beams, flagstone floors and cosy snugs add much atmosphere. Sit down to pizzas, grilled fish and pub classics in the restaurant (an open kitchen means you can watch the chefs at work), then retire to one of the bright, modern bedrooms supplied with tea- and coffee-making facilities and high-end toiletries. 2 bars (background music), library (private parties), restaurant; terrace. Free Wi-Fi, in-room TV (Freeview). Wedding, function facilities. Parking. Children (by arrangement) and dogs (not in bedrooms) welcomed. 4 miles N of Oxford. 9 bedrooms (1 on ground floor). Per room B&B (continental) single from £95, double from £120. Dinner £35

(£15 3-course set menu Mon–Thurs, 6 pm–7.30 pm).

BURLINGTON HOUSE, 374 Banbury Road, OX2 7PP. Tel 01865 513513, www.burlington-hotel-oxford.co.uk. Wake up with an appetite. In a leafy suburb north of Summertown, this 'cheerfully decorated' B&B, in a large, refurbished Victorian merchant's house, is gaining a reputation for its delicious breakfasts. There's freshly ground coffee, home-made granola and yogurt, and 'excellent' home-baked bread. Try the marmalade omelette – a speciality. The bedrooms, divided between the main house and the Japanese courtyard, are decorated in a contemporary style. Some may be snug, but all have a comprehensive refreshment tray with home-made biscuits. Nes Saini is the 'extremely efficient' manager. Sitting room, breakfast room. Free Wi-Fi, in-room TV. No background music. Small Japanese garden. Limited parking. Children over 12 welcomed. 15 minutes outside the city; frequent buses into the centre. 12 bedrooms (4 on ground floor; 2 in courtyard). Per room B&B from £70. Closed 20 Dec–5 Jan.

VANBRUGH HOUSE HOTEL, 20–24 St Michael's Street, OX1 2EB. Tel 01865 244622, www.vanbrughhousehotel.co.uk. Pristine yet unfussy, this sophisticated B&B near the Oxford Union is handsomely outfitted in natural fabrics, exposed stone and soothing, grey-painted wood panelling. David Robinson is the manager. Spread over two buildings dating from the 17th and 18th centuries, the inviting bedrooms are individually styled along three themes – Georgian,

Eclectic, and Arts and Crafts. Each has a fireplace, hand-crafted furniture, a media hub, and a minibar with fresh milk and complimentary drinks and snacks. Splurge on the best rooms – the Vicarage Suite and the Nicholas Hawksmoor Room – which have a private garden and terrace area. The 'secret' garden is one of Oxford's best kept. Breakfast can be taken there, or in the basement restaurant. Set lunches are served until 2 pm (2 courses £9.95; 3 courses £12.95). Breakfast room, small terrace. Free Wi-Fi, in-room TV (Freeview). No background music. Park-and-Ride recommended. Children welcomed. 7 mins' walk from rail station. 22 bedrooms (1 suitable for disabled). Per room B&B from £114. 2-night min. stay at weekends.

PENZANCE Cornwall
Map 1:E1

ARTIST RESIDENCE, 20 Chapel Street, TR18 4AW. Tel 01736 365664, www. artistresidence.co.uk. In the heart of historic Penzance, there's 'great fun' to be had at Justin and Charlotte Salisbury's Grade II listed 17th-century Georgian house, say trusted Guide readers this year. 'Lively' and bright, the modern hotel, standing on a narrow street leading down to the sea, has character in its vintage touches, eccentric finishes and great walls of 'intriguing' artwork. Hannah Smith is the manager. Organic toiletries and a Roberts radio come as standard in the vibrantly decorated rooms. 'Our medium Arty room – fairly snug, but fine for an overnight stay – was a vivid peacock blue, with leaves of gold. There was a comfortable super-king-size bed with good linen and

pillows; a shower room with plenty of space for toiletries.' There's a choice of eating places in town, but pop in to the 'informal', 'quirky' Cornish Barn restaurant (closed Sun/Mon in winter): 'undoubtedly popular', it has 'tasty' sharing plates, and meats straight from the smokehouse. Coffees, cocktails and Cornish ales and lagers are found in the new bar/lounge. The Salisburys also own an Artist Residence in London and one in Brighton (see main entries). Bar/lounge, Cornish Barn restaurant. Conference room. Free Wi-Fi, in-room TV (Freeview). Background music. Small courtyard garden with bar, table tennis and table football. Children (cots, but no bedding supplied; charge for over-3s) and dogs (in 2 ground-floor rooms; £10 charge) welcomed. 10 mins' walk from railway station; 5 mins' walk from seafront. 13 bedrooms, plus 4 self-contained apartments next door. Per room/apartment B&B £79–£280. Dinner £20–£25.

VENTON VEAN, Trewithen Road, TR18 4LS. Tel 01736 351294, www. ventonvean.co.uk. Chic and cheerful, Philippa McKnight and David Hoyes's stylish B&B is a ten-minute stroll from the seafront. Eye-catching colours, vintage furniture and arty features give it a modern feel, the whole set against the original features (stained-glass panels, original cornices, fireplaces) of the Victorian stone-built house. Potter in the lovely gardens; borrow a book in the sitting room; admire the many well-considered details – flamboyant pineapple sconces, towers of books and a collection of assorted crockery among them. In each of the spacious, inviting bedrooms, find a king-size bed, digital radio, tea and coffee tray, eco-friendly toiletries, bathrobes; a row of interesting wall hooks takes the place of a wardrobe. 'Exemplary' breakfasts have plenty of options, from the local (Newlyn smoked fish) to the more exotic (home-made corn tortillas with refried beans). Vegetarians and vegans are spoiled for choice. Sitting room, dining room (background music). Free Wi-Fi, in-room smart TV. Garden. Children over 5 welcomed. 5 bedrooms (1 with adjoining single room, suitable for a family). Per room B&B £81–£128. Closed Christmas Day, Boxing Day, 4–31 Jan.

PRESTON Lancashire
Map 4:D2
BARTON GRANGE HOTEL, 746–768 Garstang Road, Barton, PR3 5AA. Tel 01772 862551, www.bartongrangehotel. co.uk. Once the country home of a cotton mill owner, this sympathetically extended manor house hotel has been run by the Topping family for 65 years. Daniel Rich is the manager. Modern bedrooms are spread across the main house and a cottage in the grounds; each is stocked with bottled water, a coffee machine and minibar. Handy for families, some deluxe rooms sleep six. Chef Steve Hodson gives traditional dishes a modern twist in the Walled Garden bistro. In the morning, help yourself from a buffet breakfast, or order a 'grab-and-go' breakfast bag to take away. Lounge, snug, bistro/ wine bar; private dining. Lift. Free Wi-Fi, in-room TV (Sky). 'Easy listening' background music. Leisure centre ('nice' indoor swimming pool, sauna, gym). Pool/bar billiards. Civil wedding licence; conferences. Parking.

Children welcomed. Barton Grange Garden Centre, in the same ownership, is nearby. A few mins' drive from the M6; 6 miles from the city centre. 51 bedrooms (8 in the Garden House in the grounds; 1 suitable for disabled; family rooms). Per person B&B from £101, D,B&B from £126.

RAMSGATE Kent
Map 2:D6
THE FALSTAFF, 16–18 Addington Street, CT11 9JJ. Tel 01843 482600, www.thefalstafframsgate.com. Two Regency town houses combine to form this 'rather nice' modern hotel, a 19th-century public house, near the harbour. Its smartly refurbished rooms have been decorated with heritage shades and a judicious collection of vintage furnishings, oriental rugs and fine prints. Each room is different: one has a large bathroom with a bathtub; another a sitting area, and a writing desk in an antechamber. Dog treats and a bed await travelling hounds in Room 8; two interconnecting rooms create a spacious family suite. Head to the café or bar for breakfast or casual meals ('good, personable' service); the chic restaurant offers more substantial fare, with British favourites updated with European flair. Don't leave hungry: local produce and home-made snacks, including potted mackerel, pork pies, scotch eggs, jams and marmalades, can be purchased in the deli next door. Bar, restaurant, café, shop. Private dining room. Free Wi-Fi, in-room TV (Freeview). Background music. Small garden (summer barbecues). Children and dogs (in ground-floor room; bed, treats) welcomed. 8 bedrooms (1 on ground floor), plus 2 self-catering

apartments. Per room B&B £90–£140. Dinner £30–£45.

RICHMOND Yorkshire
Map 4:C3
EASBY HALL, Easby, DL10 7EU. Tel 01748 826066, www.easbyhall.com. Ease into one of the luxurious B&B suites at Karen and John Clarke's Georgian country house above the ruins of Easby Abbey. In a separate wing from the main house, the spacious suites are filled with plush fabrics, cushions, throws and vintage furniture; each has a log-burner or an open fire – even a champagne fridge, should the occasion call for it. Tear yourself away to explore the large grounds: three distinct gardens are flanked by a short woodland walk, an orchard and a breezy paddock. Come in, afterwards, to afternoon tea in the large drawing room. In the morning, a leisurely breakfast is served at a time to suit. Wake to a spread of home-made preserves, compote from the kitchen garden, poached pears from the orchard; local bacon; eggs from resident hens. Richmond is an easy stroll away, along the banks of the Swale. Drawing room, dining room. Gardens. Free Wi-Fi, in-room TV (Freeview). No background music. Children, well-behaved dogs, and horses (paddocks, loose boxes, stables) welcomed. 3 bedrooms (1, on ground floor, has easy access for disabled guests), plus 2-bedroom self-catering cottage. Per room B&B £180. Dinner £40–£60. Credit cards not accepted.

RIPLEY Surrey
Map 2:D3
BROADWAY BARN, High Street, nr Woking, GU23 6AQ. Tel 01483 223200, www.broadwaybarn.com. Mindi McLean's B&B, in a refurbished 200-year-old building, is ideally placed for the attractions of a historic Surrey village, where Londoners once cycled in droves to take in the clean country air. (Guests today could instead take in dinner at Michelin-starred Drake's restaurant, next door.) Imaginatively decorated bedrooms are supplied with fresh flowers, dressing gowns, slippers, chocolates and home-made shortbread; bathrooms, with underfloor heating, are stocked with complimentary toiletries. Wake to breakfast in the conservatory overlooking the walled garden: there's fresh fruit, home-baked bread, home-made granola and preserves; cooked daily specials; a selection of '300-calorie' options. Heathrow's Terminal 5 is a 20-minute drive away. Conservatory sitting room/breakfast room (quiet background music). Free Wi-Fi, in-room TV (Freeview). Garden. 2 miles from RHS Wisley. Children over 12 welcomed. 4 bedrooms (plus self-catering cottages and a villa). Per room B&B £110.

RYE Sussex
Map 2:E5
THE GEORGE IN RYE, 98 High Street, TN31 7JT. Tel 01797 222114, www.thegeorgeinrye.com. One of Rye's oldest coaching inns remains 'warm and welcoming' nearly 450 years after it first opened. A 'pleasant' place, it is owned by Alex and Katie Clarke, who have refurbished it with style. (A style so successful that the Clarkes opened The Shop Next Door for guests to buy the bedspreads, mohair throws and bespoke headboards used in the bedrooms.) The ramble of interconnecting buildings surrounds a central courtyard; amid the exposed stonework and characterful low ceilings, nooks and crannies reveal surprises – look out for the 18th-century wig store disguised

as a dumbwaiter. 'Well-appointed, comfortable' bedrooms have designer fabrics and wallpaper, and singular furniture. There might be a slipper chair here, a collection of Penguin Classics there; many rooms have a copper or zinc bath in the bathroom. Earplugs are provided to counter the early-morning seagulls. Eat in: real ales, English wines and bar snacks in the pub; modern, Mediterranean-influenced menus ('rich in seafood') in the George Grill restaurant. 'Good' breakfasts. Guest lounge, bar (log fire), restaurant. Free Wi-Fi, in-room TV (Freeview). 'Easy-listening' background music. Civil wedding licence, function facilities (the original Regency ballroom has chandeliers and a minstrels' gallery). Decked courtyard garden (alfresco meals). Children (cot, extra bed; £10–£20 per night) welcomed. 34 bedrooms (some in annexe across a courtyard). Per room B&B from £125. Dinner £60.

THE HOPE ANCHOR, Watchbell Street, TN31 7HA. Tel 01797 222216, www. thehopeanchor.co.uk. A former watering hole for sailors, shipbuilders and smugglers, this small, traditional hotel at the end of a cobbled street looks out across the quayside, the Romney Marshes, Camber Castle and beyond to the sea. It is run by Christopher George, with 'pleasant' staff. The simply furnished bedrooms may seem dated, but they are 'warm' and 'comfortable', and equipped with a tea tray, a clock radio and slippers. At dinner, sample chef Kevin Santer's traditional English dishes, cooked 'with a hint of French'; a catch of the day often comes straight from Rye Bay. Lounge, bar (snack menu), dining room. Private dining

room. Free Wi-Fi, in-room TV (Freeview). Background music. Room service. Wedding facilities. Parking permits supplied. Children (special menu; cot, monitor, high chair; over-5s £30 per night) and dogs (in some rooms) welcomed. 16 bedrooms (1 in roof annexe; 2 apartments, 1 on ground floor with patio; 1 cottage 10 yards away). Per room B&B £98–£185.

THE SHIP INN, The Strand, TN31 7DB. Tel 01797 222233, www.theshipinnrye. co.uk. In a 'good position' in the town, Karen Northcote's 'charming', cheerful inn occupies a former warehouse for storing contraband seized from 16th-century smugglers. Theo Bekker is the manager. In the quirky, modern bedrooms, a comfortable bed and mismatched furniture stand on characterful uneven wooden floors; all rooms have a shower, some have a bath; no two are alike. Downstairs in the popular bar and restaurant ('the noise didn't reach our room'), chef John Tomlinson's cooking 'goes well beyond pub grub', with 'delicious' seasonal specials, fish fresh from Hastings, produce from local suppliers and bread from an artisan baker. 'Breakfast is taken seriously.' Residents' lounge (board games, books, DVDs), bar, restaurant. Private dining room. Free Wi-Fi, in-room TV (Freeview). Background music. Small terrace with picnic benches. Pay-and-display parking nearby. Children (cots; extra bed £10 per night) and dogs (£10 per night) welcomed. Close to Rye Harbour Nature Reserve and Camber Sands. 10 bedrooms. Per room B&B £110–£125. Dinner £26. 2-night min. stay on Sat. Closed Christmas Day.

ST EWE Cornwall
Map 1:D2
LOWER BARNS, Bosue, nr St Austell, PL26 6EU. Tel 01726 844881, www.lowerbarns.co.uk. Deep in the Cornish countryside, Janie and Mike Cooksley bring together one-of-a-kind furnishings and a bold maelstrom of textures to create a zingy, upbeat feel in their rural home. Eye-catching bedrooms are designed to surprise and delight, with a freestanding slipper bath or a cleverly custom-made breakfast bar; there are addictively cheery colour combinations everywhere you look. Each room – including three suites, each with its own private garden – is as different as can be: pick Nook for its private outdoor sauna; book duplex Hayloft for its heaps of space; slip into cosy Hideaway, and emerge only for breakfast. No matter the choice, find a Roberts radio, comfy seating, towelling dressing gowns, DVDs, teas and coffees. There's plenty of space in which to luxuriate: daytime, picnic in the large, south-facing garden; nights, gaze at the starlit sky from the outdoor hot tub. In the conservatory overlooking the garden, gather with fellow guests to breakfast on fresh fruit compotes, warm muffins, local smoked fish, farm sausages, eggs 'any way you like'. An informal three-course set dinner may be served, in the garland-lit garden 'shack', by arrangement (special diets catered for; background music). Breakfast room/conservatory, dining room. Free Wi-Fi, in-room TV. Civil wedding licence. Small function facilities. Gym. Therapy room (treatments). Outdoor hot tub. Close to Gorran Haven beach; 1 mile from the Lost Gardens of Heligan. Parking. Children and dogs (in 2 suites, with own bedding) welcomed. Resident owl, Woody. 8 bedrooms (4 in the grounds, 1 suitable for disabled). Per room B&B £115–£225. Dinner £35. 2-night min. stay at weekends.
25% DISCOUNT VOUCHERS

ST IVES Cornwall
Map 1:D1
BLUE HAYES, Trelyon Avenue, TR26 2AD. Tel 01736 797129, www.bluehayes.co.uk. Standing high above Porthminster beach, Malcolm Herring's homely small hotel enjoys sweeping views over the bay, from the harbour and island to Godrevy lighthouse. Inside, there are seascapes, tropical palms, sofas to stretch out on. Each of the simply furnished bedrooms in the white-painted 1920s house benefits from the views – choose a room with a balcony, a roof terrace or a patio. Light suppers (salads, dressed crab, a lobster platter) may be taken in the dining room or on the terrace. On a fine day, find a spot by the balustrade to take in the vista over breakfast, then descend through the landscaped gardens to join the Coastal Path beachward. 2 lounges, bar, dining room. Free Wi-Fi, in-room TV (Freeview). No background music. Civil wedding licence. Small functions. Room service. Terrace, garden. Parking. Children over 10 welcomed. 6 bedrooms. Per room B&B £130–£270. Supper from £17. Closed Nov–Feb.

HEADLAND HOUSE, Headland Road, Carbis Bay, TR26 2NS. Tel 01736 796647, www.headlandhousehotel.co.uk. Mark and Fenella Thomas's stylish B&B brings together cake, the coast and Cornish chic. Escape the bustle of St Ives proper and arrive to home-baked treats at this three-storey Edwardian house overlooking Carbis Bay. Smart, restful bedrooms have a breezy seaside feel in coastal blues and calming shades of white; some have views over the water. Each has its own character: one has a secluded garden with a table and chairs, another has broad skylights for stargazing from the bathtub. There's a hammock in the garden, books to borrow; in the evening, a complimentary glass of sherry or port awaits. Organic Cornish breakfasts are served in a conservatory with panoramic views over the bay. Early start? Ask for a continental breakfast bag. St Ives is a scenic five-minute train journey away, or a 30-minute walk along the Coastal Path. Beach 600 yards; 1½ miles from St Ives. Snug lounge (bar, board games, magazines), conservatory breakfast room. Free Wi-Fi, in-room TV (Freeview). No background music. Large front garden, terrace. Parking. No children under 16. 9 bedrooms (3 off the courtyard garden at the rear). Per room B&B £95–£160. 2-night min. stay preferred. Closed Nov–first half Mar.

TREVOSE HARBOUR HOUSE, 22 The Warren, TR26 2EA. Tel 01736 793267, www.trevosehouse.co.uk. Between the beach and the town, Angela and Olivier Noverraz run their 'beautifully appointed' B&B with flair. The whitewashed terrace house is an appealing, design-conscious space: find flourishes of mid-century modern in the snug lounge; sip a cocktail while sitting on one of the deep-cushioned Eames-style chairs as an open fire burns. Shades of surf and sand sweep across the bedrooms, where flashes of vintage mingle with the latest gadgetry;

each room has a large, comfortable bed and organic toiletries. Breakfast on the terrace overlooking the Warren on a balmy morning, or in the bright breakfast room when there's a squall. Whatever the weather, tuck in to a feast of organic treats, with granola, home-made preserves, farl loaves, 'smoothie shots' and all manner of veggie-friendly cooked choices. Snug (newspapers, magazines, books, honesty bar), breakfast room. In-room treatments. Picnic hampers. Free Wi-Fi, in-room TV (Freeview). Background music. Terrace. Limited parking close by. Children over 12 welcomed. 6 bedrooms (1 in annexe behind the house). Per room B&B from £155. Closed mid-Dec–early Mar.

ST MAWES Cornwall
Map 1:E2
THE ST MAWES HOTEL, 2 Marine Parade, TR2 5DW. Tel 01326 270 170, www.stmaweshotel.com. One for seafarers, not-a-carers, families and friends, David and Karen Richards's newly refurbished harbourside pub-with-rooms takes in the big blue bay, over to St Anthony's Head. Ben Bass is manager and chef. There's an informal feel to the place, as locals drop in throughout the day; join them over cocktails, sharing plates and hearty meals (lobster and chips, home-made pizza) in the lively bar and Upper Deck restaurant. Spend the night in one of the coolly casual bedrooms decorated in fresh, modern hues; ask for one facing the sea, and listen as the waves sweep to the shore. Sophisticated big-sister hotel Idle Rocks (see main entry) is up the street. Bar, restaurant. Function room. Cinema. Free Wi-Fi, in-room TV (Freeview). Background music. Children (travel cot; charge) and small,

well-behaved dogs (in 2 rooms; bed, towel, bowl, treats, maps of local walks; £30 per stay) welcomed. 7 bedrooms (family rooms). Per room B&B from £175, D,B&B from £235. 2-night min. stay on Sat night.

ST MELLION Cornwall
Map 1:D3

PENTILLIE CASTLE, Paynters Cross, Saltash, PL12 6QD. Tel 01579 350 044, www.pentillie.co.uk. Feel like lord or lady of the manor at the Coryton family's 'magnificent' castellated mansion in extensive woodland gardens on the banks of the River Tamar. Built in 1698, the 'lovingly restored' building, today a grand country B&B, has belonged to the family for nearly 300 years. Spacious bedrooms have glorious countryside or valley views. The sumptuous suite has a dramatic four-poster bed. 'Splendid' breakfasts include home-made jams, granola, breads and compotes; sausages from local farms; honey from bees in the grounds. Formal three-course dinners are occasionally organised (non-residents welcomed); on other nights, ask about a light 'DIY' supper to warm up in the Aga. Free access to the historic gardens; picnics by arrangement. Drawing room (honesty bar), morning room, dining room. Free Wi-Fi, in-room TV. No background music. Civil wedding licence. 55-acre grounds, terrace. Heated outdoor swimming pool (Apr–Sept). Children welcomed (cot £10 for first night; extra beds for over-2s £25 for first night, £15 for subsequent nights). Dogs allowed (in heated boot room only; on a lead in the gardens). 20 mins' drive from Plymouth. 9 bedrooms (1 suitable for disabled). Per room B&B £145–£230. Dinner (selected

nights) £29.50. Open Christmas and New Year for exclusive hire only.

SALCOMBE Devon
Map 1:E4

SOUTH SANDS, Bolt Head, TQ8 8LL. Tel 01548 845 900, www.southsands.com. Nautical but nice, this 'beautifully designed' hotel injects New England flair into a secluded cove on South Sands beach. Soak up the 'relaxed and informal' atmosphere in the lounge, surrounded by beachy ornaments and original art; in fine weather, sip a cocktail on the terrace overlooking the estuary. Named after sailing boats, bedrooms are decorated in coastal pastels; ask for one with views of the sea (rear ones can hear traffic). Travelling with family? Beach suites with an open-plan living and dining area are ideal. The popular beachside restaurant emphasises fresh local seafood, with stunning estuary views a welcome garnish. Stephen Ball is the manager. Lounge, bar, restaurant (background music); terrace. Free Wi-Fi, in-room TV (Freeview). Civil wedding licence. Parking. Electric bicycles to borrow. Children and dogs (in some bedrooms; £12.50 per night) welcomed. Beaches and coastal paths. 27 bedrooms (5 beach suites; some on ground floor; 2 suitable for disabled). Per room B&B £170–£385. Dinner £35. 2-night min. stay at weekends.

SALISBURY Wiltshire
Map 2:D2

LEENA'S GUEST HOUSE, 50 Castle Road, SP1 3RL. Tel 07814 897907, www.leenasguesthouse.co.uk. Find comfortable, good-value accommodation at the Street family's modest B&B a short stroll, along riverside footpaths, from the centre. Traditionally decorated bedrooms in the Edwardian house have original features, including handsome stained-glass windows. Gary Street cooks 'excellent' breakfasts with plenty of choice; organic raspberries and redcurrants from the garden are available in season. The communal fruit bowl is regularly replenished – help yourself to one of your five-a-day. The accommodating, multilingual hosts like to practise their French, German and Suomi when possible. Lounge, breakfast room. Free Wi-Fi, in-room TV (Freeview). No background music. Garden. Parking. Children welcomed. 15 mins' walk to centre. 6 bedrooms (1 on ground floor; 2 family suites). Per room B&B £75–£110. Credit cards not accepted. Closed Christmas, New Year.

SPIRE HOUSE, 84 Exeter Street, SP1 2SE. Tel 01722 339213, www.salisbury-bedandbreakfast.com. The cheery chartreuse front door, a bold contrast to the austere flint brick, is an auspicious greeting to 'friendly, welcoming' Lois and John Faulkner's small, 'very nice' B&B. Brightly decorated inside, the Grade II listed 18th-century town house is opposite the cathedral close wall – 'very handy' not only for the cathedral, but also for the 'great places to eat' nearby. 'Lovely' bedrooms are 'pleasant to be in'; two overlook the quiet walled garden. The Faulkners have ready advice on restaurants, pubs and places to visit in the city. A continental breakfast, delivered to the room, includes juice, fresh fruit and locally baked pastries or granola slices; give in to a slice of cake in the afternoon. Garden. Free Wi-Fi, in-room

TV (Freeview). No background music. Parking opposite. Children over 11 welcomed. 4 bedrooms. Per room B&B £100. Closed Christmas.

SCARBOROUGH Yorkshire
Map 4:C5
PHOENIX COURT, 8–9 Rutland Terrace, Queens Parade, YO12 7JB. Tel 01723 501150, www.hotel-phoenix.co.uk. Given 'a warm welcome', guests this year were pleasantly surprised by Alison and Bryan Edwards's unassuming guest house overlooking North Bay and the beach. 'On arrival we wondered what we'd let ourselves in for, as it seemed a seaside boarding house. However, it's in a good central position and has its own car park. We slept well and had a great breakfast cooked to order in the morning. And the bill! At that price, you just can't complain.' Bedrooms (many with sea views) may be 'plain', but they have 'clean linen and lovely towels'. 'We had more room than we've had in far more expensive hotels.' Breakfast has home-baked bread, and home-made jams and marmalade; Yorkshire smoked kippers, tofu-and-mushroom sausages, bacon from local farms. A continental breakfast may be taken in the bedroom. Amblers and ramblers, ask the friendly hosts for route information and car-free itineraries; there are also drying facilities on site, and packed lunches, with home-baked rolls and cakes (£6 per person). Lounge, bar area, breakfast room (background radio). Free Wi-Fi, in-room TV (Freeview). Parking. Children welcomed (£10 per night; high chair). 10 mins' walk from the town centre. 13 bedrooms (9 with sea views; 1 on ground floor; 2 family rooms). Per room B&B

single £36–£40, double £50–£66. Closed Dec–Jan except New Year.
25% DISCOUNT VOUCHERS

SEDGEFORD Norfolk
Map 2:A5
MAGAZINE WOOD, Peddars Way, PE36 5LW. Tel 01485 570422, www. magazinewood.co.uk. Part country retreat, part boutique hotel, Pip and Jonathan Barber's self-contained B&B suites are wholly luxurious. There are just three very chic, very private suites, each with its own entrance and a terrace for watching spectacular sunsets across the countryside. An in-room tablet computer acts as online concierge: order breakfast, download a newspaper, plan a day of exploration. Extra comforts include mood lighting, a sumptuous bed, a deep bath in the bathroom; books, DVDs and a pair of binoculars are thoughtful touches. A well-equipped dining area in the room is stocked with posh muesli and cereals, organic yogurts, fruits, juice and croissants; a cooked breakfast (charged extra), ordered the night before, may be delivered to the door. 5 miles from Hunstanton; beaches, pubs and restaurants are close by. Free Wi-Fi, in-room TV (on-demand movies). No background music. 3-acre grounds (parkland, woodland). Parking. Infants (cots) and dogs (1 per room; £10 per night) welcomed. Resident dog, Gin. 3 suites (all on ground floor, 2 in converted barn). Per room B&B (continental) £105–£129. Cooked breakfast £5–£7.

SETTLE Yorkshire
Map 4:D3
SETTLE LODGE, Duke St, BD24 9AS. Tel 01729 823258, www.settlelodge. co.uk. Delve into the fells from this substantial Victorian B&B – it's an ideal gateway into the Three Peaks and the Dales. Amanda and Eduardo Martinez are the hospitable owners, who greet guests with tea and home-made cake. 'Spacious' bedrooms have a tea tray, DVD-player and large bed (much needed after one of the more strenuous walks from the door); one of the better rooms has a huge bay window with views towards High Hill. In the morning, breakfasts are 'delicious, with generous portions'. Ask about eating places and walking routes – the hosts have a wealth of information and will gladly provide maps. Sitting room, dining room. Free Wi-Fi, in-room TV. Garden, terrace. Parking. 5 mins' walk from the town centre and train station. 7 bedrooms. Per room B&B £70–£95.

SHANKLIN Isle of Wight
Map 2:E2
RYLSTONE MANOR, Rylstone Gardens, Popham Road, PO37 6RG. Tel 01983 862806, www.rylstone-manor.co.uk. 'In a lovely setting', Mike and Carole Hailston's small hotel stands in a public clifftop park with steps leading down to the shoreline of Sandown Bay. Traditionally decorated bedrooms in the 19th-century gentleman's residence vary in size and aspect; some have glimpses of the sea through trees. In the ornate, chandelier-lit dining room, Mike Hailston cooks a short, seasonal menu of modern and classic dishes. 'The fish – so fresh – was perfect every night.' On summer evenings, take a moment in the secluded private garden – it's 'a pleasant place to sip wine'. Drawing room (books, games), bar lounge, dining room. Free Wi-Fi, in-room TV (Freeview). Optional background music.

Terrace, ¼-acre garden in 4-acre public gardens. Direct access to sand/shingle beach. No children under 16.
9 bedrooms. Per room B&B from £135, D,B&B from £193. 2-night min. stay in peak season. Closed 9 Nov–7 Feb.
25% **DISCOUNT VOUCHERS**

SHEFFIELD Yorkshire
Map 4:E4

LEOPOLD HOTEL, 2 Leopold Street, Leopold Square, S1 2GZ. Tel 01142 524000, www.leopoldhotelsheffield. com. A modern hotel now occupies this sympathetically converted, Grade II listed former boys' grammar school close to the cathedral. Echoes of the building's history ring in the arched doorways, old school photos and ranks of coat pegs. Modern bedrooms have top-of-the-class technology (iPod docking station, digital radio, flat-screen TV); the best also have bathrobes and a capsule coffee machine. Enjoy meals and drinks on the terrace overlooking bustling Leopold Square, then stay out late on a non-school night – breakfast is served till late on the weekends. Well located for the city's shops and theatres. Part of Small Luxury Hotels of the World. Lounge bar, dining room. Private dining rooms. Free Wi-Fi, in-room TV. Background music. 24-hour room service. Civil wedding licence; conference/function facilities. Fitness suite. Terrace. Parking discounts in public car park nearby. Children welcomed. 90 bedrooms (5 suitable for disabled). Room from £90. Breakfast £7.95–£12.95.

SHERBORNE Dorset
Map 2:E1

THE EASTBURY HOTEL, Long Street, DT9 3BY. Tel 01935 813131, www. theeastburyhotel.co.uk. Off the main street, Paul and Nicky King's 'very pleasant' hotel hides behind a 'lovely' large walled garden filled with little pathways, nooks and crannies to become lost, and then found, in. Choose among bedrooms decorated in modern or traditional style – some overlook the courtyard; one has a private garden; all are 'very comfortable'. In the Conservatory restaurant, chef Matt Street uses garden-fresh salads and herbs in his 'very good cooking'. Splurge on a seven-course tasting menu with an accompanying wine flight – or step out and eat alfresco on the terrace in good weather. Sherborne Abbey is close by. Drawing room, lounge, bar, library, conservatory restaurant (background music). Private dining. Free Wi-Fi, in-room TV (Freeview). Wedding, function facilities. Terrace, garden. Golf breaks. Children (special meals by request; cots £8.50; extra beds £20) and dogs (£10 per night) welcomed. 23 bedrooms (3 with external access; 1 suitable for disabled). Per room B&B single from £85, double from £155. Tasting menu £55.
25% **DISCOUNT VOUCHERS**

THE KINGS ARMS, North Street, Charlton Horethorne, DT9 4NL. Tel 01963 220281, www.thekingsarms. co.uk. Chef/patron Sarah Lethbridge and her husband, Anthony, run their much-refurbished country pub and hotel in a pretty village close to the Somerset-Dorset border. There are sofas, newspapers, local artwork, a wood-burning stove; a terrace to take in wide views of the countryside. Come in for a pint and a chat; stay for the modern dishes, many cooked in a Josper charcoal oven. Spend the night in one of the colourful, individually styled bedrooms – they're well equipped with towelling bathrobes, tea- and coffee-making facilities, a DVD-player. Snug, bar, restaurant. Lift. Free Wi-Fi, in-room TV (Freeview). No background music. Functions. Terrace, garden, croquet lawn. Shooting parties. Free use of sports centre in Sherborne (4 miles); discounts at Sherborne Golf Club. Clay-pigeon shooting can be arranged. Parking. Children welcomed (special menu; cots, extra beds). 10 bedrooms (1 suitable for disabled; 1 interconnecting family room; 3 accessible by lift). Per room B&B £135–£250. Dinner £26–£30.

SHREWSBURY Shropshire
Map 3:B4

CHATFORD HOUSE, Chatford, Bayston Hill, SY3 0AY. Tel 01743 718301, www.chatfordhouse.co.uk. 'Warm and friendly' hostess Christine Farmer plies guests with treats at her 'first-class' B&B in a Grade II listed 18th-century farmhouse. 'We were spoiled with her delicious home-made cake.' Sleep in traditional, country-cottage-style bedrooms supplied with fresh flowers, magazines and a hospitality tray; each has 'wonderful' views across the garden and the Wrekin. Aga-cooked breakfasts use eggs from the resident hens; there are also home-made jams and compotes and local honey. The countryside's calling: explore the pretty garden and orchard; make friends with the hens, ducks, geese, sheep and cattle that live on the Farmers' smallholding. Sitting room, breakfast room (open fire). Free Wi-Fi, in-room TV. No background music. Garden; orchard. Parking. Children welcomed (high chair, cot).

Resident dogs. Close to the Shropshire Way. 5 miles S of Shrewsbury; within walking distance of Lyth Hill. 3 bedrooms. Per room B&B single from £60, double from £75. Credit cards not accepted.

GROVE FARM HOUSE, Condover, SY5 7BH. Tel 01743 718544, www.grovefarmhouse.com. Garden-fresh flowers and home-made shortbread await in the inviting, country-style bedrooms at Liz Farrow's peaceful B&B. The third-generation proprietor maintains a tranquil, welcoming atmosphere at her three-storey Georgian house, greeting arriving guests with tea and cake. At breakfast, feast on the hostess's home-made bread, granola and blueberry muffins; cooked options use eggs from home-reared chickens, and meats from nearby farms. Ask for dinner recommendations and tips on walks through beautiful parkland and wooded areas close by. Lounge, dining room. Free Wi-Fi, in-room TV (Freeview). No background music. ½-acre garden. Parking. Children welcomed. 6 miles S of Shrewsbury. 4 bedrooms, plus 2 self-catering suites with log burner, private courtyard, optional food hamper. Per room B&B £95. 2-night min. stay May–Sept. Closed Christmas, New Year.

THE INN AT GRINSHILL, High Street, Grinshill, SY4 3BL. Tel 01939 220410, www.theinnatgrinshill.co.uk. The Shropshire Way goes through sandstone quarries, leading to the front door of this 'delightful' 18th-century coaching inn. 'Excellent hosts' Victoria and Kevin Brazier have created a welcoming hub for locals and visitors. The popular wood-panelled bar has books and games, comfy sofas, an open fire – just the place for a pint of real ale and a dish off the bistro menu. In the modern restaurant and pleasant garden room, new chef Joshua Huxtable gives seasonal, local fare an Australian slant. Stay the night in one of the 'charming' bedrooms, then ask for a map in the morning – rural walks abound. 2 bars, garden room, restaurant (closed Sun eve, Mon and Tues; optional background music/radio). Free Wi-Fi, in-room TV (Freeview). Functions. Rose garden with fountain. Parking. Children welcomed (extra bed £35). 8 miles N of Shrewsbury. 6 bedrooms. Per room B&B single £89.50, double £119.50. D,B&B £79.50 per person (based on 2 people sharing). Closed Christmas Day. **25% DISCOUNT VOUCHERS**

LION AND PHEASANT, 50 Wyle Cop, SY1 1XJ. Tel 01743 770345, www. lionandpheasant.co.uk. Modernised with 'a simple but sure touch', this 16th-century coaching inn ('handy for the town centre') is on one of the oldest streets in town. It is owned by Dorothy Chidlow; Jim Littler manages, with 'pleasant, helpful' staff. Wend through the warren of smartly styled, beamed corridors to the 'well-furnished, well-equipped' bedrooms (some overlooking the river; some snug). Double glazing and earplugs help dampen early-morning traffic noise, but light sleepers might want to ask for one of the quieter rooms at the back of the hotel. Shropshire produce features on à la carte and bar menus served in several dining areas – the bar (oak floors, wide benches), the inglenook room (flagstone floors, open fire), the split-level restaurant (bare

tables, cosy nooks). Dion Wyn Jones is the new chef. 2 bars, restaurant, function room. Free Wi-Fi, in-room TV (Freeview). Background music. Room service. Garden terrace (alfresco dining). Children welcomed (high chairs; extra bed £15 per night). Narrow entrance to car park. 22 bedrooms. Per room B&B £99–£225, D,B&B from £95.50 per person (based on 2 people sharing). Closed Christmas Day, Boxing Day.

SIDLESHAM Sussex
Map 2:E3

THE CRAB & LOBSTER, Mill Lane, PO20 7NB. Tel 01243 641233, www.crab-lobster.co.uk. Rustic chic and a pared-back sensibility create a peaceful enclave in this modern-day inn overlooking the Pagham Harbour nature reserve. Renovated by owners Sam and Janet Bakose, the whitewashed 16th-century pub has squashy sofas, intimate corners, flagstone floors and original hearths. Sophie Harwood is the manager. Choose one of the comfortable, smartly designed bedrooms to suit: a cosy one in the eaves peers into the sky; some larger superior rooms have binoculars to take in views across the countryside to the sea. Tramp through the fields and gently sloping hills to build up an appetite for chef Clyde Hollett's fresh local fish, crab and lobster; celebrate the day with fizz from the local vineyard. Breakfast has honey from Sidlesham bees. Bar, restaurant (background music). Free Wi-Fi, in-room TV (Freeview). Terrace, small garden. Children welcomed (£30 per night). 4 miles S of Chichester. 6 bedrooms (2 in adjoining cottage). Per room B&B £165–£280. Dinner £37.50. 2-night min. stay at weekends.

SIDMOUTH Devon
Map 1:C5
VICTORIA HOTEL, The Esplanade,
EX10 8RY. Tel 01395 512651, www.
victoriahotel.co.uk. 'Old-fashioned in
the best sense of the word', this large,
traditional hotel overlooking the bay
is popular with visitors who return for
the 'immaculate' bedrooms, 'delightful'
gardens, Saturday-night dinner dances
and host of amenable staff. Plump sofas
by the bay windows in the sun lounge
overlook the esplanade; benches tucked
among the flowers in the garden invite
an alfresco sit-down; there are indoor
and outdoor swimming pools, a tennis
court, a golf course. Some of the bedrooms
have a balcony; all have a chocolate on
the pillow after the turn-down team
passes through. Dress up for dinner in
the Jubilee restaurant, where a live band
plays every night; in the informal White
Room restaurant, chef Stuart White puts
his classical French training to work on a
modern menu. Sun lounge, lounge bar, 2
restaurants. Free Wi-Fi, in-room TV (Sky,
Freeview). Background music. Room
service. Spa, sauna, treatments. Outdoor
and indoor swimming pools. Tennis court,
snooker, putting. Gift shop. Parking.
Children welcomed. 61 bedrooms (3
poolside suites). Single room £140–£160,
double room £195–£370. Breakfast £18.
Dinner £42. 2-night min. stay.

SISSINGHURST Kent
Map 2:D5
THE MILK HOUSE, The Street,
TN17 2JG. Tel 01580 720200, www.
themilkhouse.co.uk. 'Attractive inside
and out', Dane and Sarah Allchorne's
'excellent' pub-with-rooms has 'plenty
of atmosphere'. A cheerful, informal
spot, it's equally pleasing for its modish

interiors as it is for its good-humoured,
village-hub feel. (The wood-fired pizza
oven on the terrace is a nice touch,
too.) Tuck in to Dane Allchorne's
uncomplicated, seasonal pub fare in
the bar or on the sunny terrace or
lawn; more adventurous dishes (lime-
seared red snapper, pickled cucumber,
peashoot salad) are served in the smartly
rustic dining room. Up the stairs, airy
bedrooms (Byre, Buttery, Churn and
Dairy) are painted in dairy creams and
milky whites; a family room sleeps four.
Mornings, a copious breakfast ('very
good, but a little slow') is just right for
the half-mile walk to Sissinghurst Castle
garden. Bar, restaurant ('easy listening'
background music, closed Sun eve).
Private dining. Free Wi-Fi, in-room
TV (Freeview). Sun terrace and large
garden (alfresco meals, pond, children's
play area). Parking. Children welcomed
(special menu). 4 bedrooms (1 family
room). Per room B&B £80–£140. 2-night
min. stay at weekends.

SISSINGHURST CASTLE FARMHOUSE,
nr Cranbrook, TN17 2AB.
Tel 01580 720992, www.
sissinghurstcastlefarmhouse.com. Vita
Sackville-West created the gardens of the
Sissinghurst estate as a refuge dedicated
to beauty. Now restored by the National
Trust, Sue and Frazer Thompson's
Victorian farmhouse B&B is a refuge
dedicated to tranquillity. Taking in views
of sunrise or sunset, restful, country-style
bedrooms are decorated with pictures
and a mix of contemporary and period
furniture. Arrive to tea and home-
baked cake in the sitting room or the
sunny garden, then strike out to explore
ancient woodland, historic gardens or the
castle's Elizabethan tower. Farmhouse

breakfasts include Kentish apples and pears, locally smoked bacon and salmon, hearty sausages. Picnic lunches. Sitting room (books, magazines), dining room. Lift. Free Wi-Fi, in-room TV. No background music. Small functions. ¾-acre garden. Children welcomed. Resident dog. 7 bedrooms (1 suitable for disabled). Per room B&B £150–£200. 2-night min. stay at weekends, Easter–Sept. Closed Dec–Feb.

SNETTISHAM Norfolk
Map 2:A4

THE ROSE & CROWN, Old Church Road, nr King's Lynn, PE31 7LX. Tel 01485 541382, www.roseandcrownsnettisham. co.uk. Roses ramble up the whitewashed 14th-century walls of Jeannette and Anthony Goodrich's quintessential English inn, creating a pretty beacon when they're in bloom. Inside, low beams, leaning walls, twisting passages and cosy pockets combine with friendly staff to create a relaxed, family-friendly atmosphere that's popular with locals. Pleasant, cheering bedrooms are stocked with magazines, books, luxury toiletries, fresh milk and tasty home-made biscuits, as well as a bible of local information. In the different dining areas, pick between classic pub favourites and more daring fare; whichever you choose, chef Jamie Clarke uses game from local estates, and freshly caught mussels, oysters, lobster and crab. On fine days, the sunny walled garden is the place to be. Beaches nearby. 3 bar areas, 3 dining areas, lounge ('laid-back and low-key' background music). Free Wi-Fi, in-room TV (Freeview). Walled garden (alfresco meals and drinks, children's play area). Children (high

chair, colouring sets; cot £10 per night) and 'well-behaved' dogs welcomed. 16 bedrooms (2 on ground floor; 2 suitable for disabled). Per room B&B single £100–£120, double £120–£140. 2-night min. stay at peak times.

SOMERTON Somerset
Map 1:C6

THE WHITE HART, Market Place, TA11 7LX. Tel 01458 272273, www. whitehartsomerton.com. A total revamp of this 16th-century pub-with-rooms, in a village on the edge of the Somerset Levels, has exposed stone walls, left wooden floors bare and unveiled patchwork tiling, resulting in a contemporary, rustic-chic look throughout. It is managed by Kirsty Schmidt for the Draco Pub Company. Topping the pub, bedrooms at the front overlook the 13th-century church and the market square; at the back, views are of the pretty rear garden. Each room is stocked with fresh coffee and tea, and organic toiletries; some have just enough space to fit in a child's bed or cot. At lunch and dinner, 'fresh, simple' dishes support West Country suppliers – 'a model of what local and organic food should be'. Dine in the conservatory dining room, or go alfresco in the courtyard. Light meals and snacks are available throughout the day in the buzzy bar. Select from a good range of locally brewed beer and cider, then sit back with a newspaper beside an open fire. The Swan, Wedmore (see Shortlist entry), is under the same ownership. Bar, restaurant (closed Sun eve; 3 dining areas). Large courtyard garden. Free Wi-Fi, in-room smart TV. 'Easy listening' background music. Children (special menu) and dogs (in one room) welcomed. 8 bedrooms. Per room B&B from £85, D,B&B from £165.

SOUTH BRENT Devon
Map 1:D4

GLAZEBROOK HOUSE, Glazebrook, TQ10 9JE. Tel 01364 73322, www.glazebrookhouse.com. Curiouser and curiouser, Pieter and Fran Hamman's 'cheerful' 19th-century manor house on the southern edge of Dartmoor national park teems with collections and vintage pieces – 'all rather fun'. The reception desk is in the shape of a Spitfire wing; drums, china plates, hats, silver tea trays and old street signs adorn the walls; chandeliers, an emu skeleton and a stuffed flamingo decorate the hall. 'Zany' bedrooms are named after characters from Alice in Wonderland: a fluffy bed in White Rabbit is made of sheepskin; Caterpillar has a butterfly reading desk and views over the garden. All rooms come with complimentary minibar items, including chocolates and mini-bottles of wine; bathrooms are luxurious. 'Our large room overlooked the garden, nice and bright on a sunny day. There were two chandeliers, three suitcases mounted on the wall, an enormous bed with plenty of cushions – but only one armchair.' Choose from the list of locally brewed beers and speciality cocktails in the 'cosy' bar. In the 'pleasant, bright and airy' dining room, chef Anton Piotrowski (who earned a Michelin star in 2015 at his Plympton gastropub) cooks 'unusual', 'enjoyable' modern British dishes and eight-course tasting menus. Drawing room, bar, library, restaurant ('unobtrusive' background music). Wine and whisky tasting room. Free Wi-Fi, in-room TV (Freeview). Civil wedding licence, function facilities. 3½-acre mature garden, Chef's Kitchen Patio, terrace. 'Ample' parking. 1 mile SW of town centre. Children over 16 welcomed. 8 bedrooms (1 on ground floor; 1 suitable for disabled). Per room B&B from £199. Dinner £40. Closed 2 weeks Jan.
25% DISCOUNT VOUCHERS

SOUTH MOLTON Devon
Map 1:C4

ASHLEY HOUSE, 3 Paradise Lawn, EX36 3DJ. Tel 01769 573444, www.ashleyhousebedandbreakfast.com. Devotees of the blue plaque, take note: Nicky Robbins's Victorian villa bears one honouring Lord Samuel Widgery, the Lord Chief Justice of England from 1971 to 1980, who was born in the house. Now on the official South Molton Heritage Trail, the handsomely restored former gentleman's residence has three rooms for B&B guests, each high-ceilinged and smartly styled. Bedrooms contain antiques, contemporary pieces, original photography and artwork, a fireplace; tall windows afford wide countryside views. Devonshire breakfasts have home-made preserves, eggs from resident hens, fruit and vegetables from the garden, locally sourced bacon and sausages. Breakfast/sitting room (wood-burning stove). Free Wi-Fi, in-room TV (Freeview). Classical background music. Large garden. Parking. Children over 14 welcomed. Resident dog, Cassie. 3 bedrooms. Per person B&B £75–£105.

SOUTHAMPTON Hampshire
Map 2:E2

WOODLANDS LODGE HOTEL, Bartley Road, SO40 7GN. Tel 02380 292257, www.woodlands-lodge.co.uk. 'A perfect

little hotel, ideal for those with dogs.'
Travelling pets are as well looked after
as their human companions at Imogene
and Robert Anglaret's dog-friendly
hotel in the New Forest. Most of the
spacious, country-style bedrooms have
views over the gardens and woodland.
Some have a working fireplace, one
has a four-poster bed, another has a
double shower in the bathroom. Dogs
receive a treat, a blanket and a towel;
there's an outdoor tap for cleaning
mucky paws. An all-day snack menu is
served in the conservatory, the lounge
or the bedroom. Between 6.30 pm and
8.30 pm, sit down to dinner in Hunters
restaurant – the seasonal menus use fruit
and vegetables from the walled kitchen
garden. Lounge, bar, conservatory,
restaurant. Free Wi-Fi (in public areas),
in-room TV (Freeview). 'Easy listening'
background music in the evening;
Radio 2 during the day (optional). Civil
wedding licence, business facilities.
3-acre garden. Children (cot, extra bed)
and dogs (in some rooms) welcomed. 1
mile from Ashurst village (train station);
15 mins' drive from Southampton.
17 bedrooms (2 with garden access; 1
suitable for disabled). Per room B&B
from £89, D,B&B from £149.

STAMFORD Lincolnshire
Map 2:B3
THE BULL AND SWAN AT BURGHLEY,
High Street, St Martins, PE9 2LJ. Tel
01780 766412, www.thebullandswan.
co.uk. A riotous coterie of 17th-century
gentlemen – The Honourable Order
of Little Bedlam – is said to have met
and imbibed heavily at this old coaching
inn. Today, a more honourable order
of regulars and visitors props up the
refurbished bar. It is managed by Jen

Totty for the small Hillbrooke Hotels
group (see The Master Builder's,
Beaulieu, main entry). The inviting pub
has an open fire, exposed stone, panelled
walls, cheeky wallpaper; find a spot in
one of the three buzzy dining areas to
sample chef Phil Kent's modern pub
grub. Named after the pseudonyms
of the Order's great members, the
characterful bedrooms are well supplied
with crisp linen and smart fabrics; fancy
tea and 'proper' coffee; biscuits, bottled
water, a mini-bottle of organic vodka.
Breakfast has home-made muesli,
pastries, cured meats and cheeses, cloudy
apple juice; a long list of cooked options,
including veggie sausages. Sunday
roasts; early dinners. Burghley House
can be reached via a cross-country walk.
Bar with 3 dining areas. Private dining/
meeting room. Free Wi-Fi, in-room
TV (Freeview). Background music.
Courtyard garden with seating (alfresco
meals). Parking (narrow entrance).
Children (aged 3–13 £20 per night;
special menu) and dogs (in 3 rooms; dog
bed, bowls, special treats, room-service
menu; £20) welcomed. 9 bedrooms
(some can accommodate a family). Per
room B&B £85–£180, D,B&B £135–£220.

STOKE BY NAYLAND Suffolk
Map 2:C5
THE CROWN, Park Street, CO6 4SE.
Tel 01206 262001, www.crowninn.net.
'A delightful find.' In Constable country,
Richard Sunderland's pub and hotel is
liked for its 'characterful' restaurant
and 'smart, modern' bedrooms. 'Well-
cooked and -presented' brasserie-style
food is served all day alongside real
ales and a 'near-outstanding' wine
list; interesting vegetarian options
are available. In a separate clapboard

building, well-equipped bedrooms in country or contemporary style have a 'very smart bathroom' – ask for a room with a view of the countryside and Constable's boundless sky. Excellent walking nearby. Bar, restaurant, terrace. Wine shop. Free Wi-Fi, in-room TV (Freeview). No background music. Children welcomed (not allowed in restaurant after 8 pm; special menu; extra beds; £10 charge may apply). 11 bedrooms (some on ground floor; 3 with private terrace; 1 suitable for disabled). Per room B&B from £125, D,B&B from £145. Closed Christmas Day, Boxing Day.

STOWMARKET Suffolk
Map 2:C5

BAYS FARM, Earl Stonham, IP14 5HU. Tel 01449 711286, www. baysfarmsuffolk.co.uk. Stephanie and Richard Challinor's restored 17th-century farmhouse B&B stands in extensive, award-winning grounds, the whole swathed by lovely countryside. Outside, wander through the orchard, wild flower garden and fruit and vegetable gardens; within, find bedrooms individually designed in pretty pastels or masculine stripes. Each is well equipped with bottled water, an espresso machine, a choice of DVDs. Can't tear yourself away from the gardens? Book the shepherd's hut in the grounds: overlooking the newly landscaped moat, it has a king-size bed, up-to-date gadgetry, an oversized shower and a wood-burner. Wake to a fine communal breakfast, served in the former dairy (the oldest part of the house) at a time to suit. Bread, marmalade and jams are home made; cooked breakfasts come with dry-cured

Suffolk bacon. Snacks and a farmhouse supper are available. Reception hall, drawing room (open fire), dining room (background music). Free Wi-Fi, in-room TV (Freeview). 4-acre garden (included in the National Gardens Scheme). No children under 12. Resident dog. 4 miles E of Stowmarket. 5 bedrooms (1 in adjacent building, 1 in shepherd's hut). Per room B&B £80–£130. Dinner £25. 2-night min. stay on summer weekends.

STRATFORD-UPON-AVON
Warwickshire
Map 3:D6

WHITE SAILS, 85 Evesham Road, CV37 9BE. Tel 01789 550469, www.white-sails.co.uk. Tim and Denise Perkin's B&B, on the outskirts of Stratford, has lots of little extras to make guests feel at home: complimentary sherry, espresso coffee and home-made treats in the lounge are regularly replenished. Bedrooms are well supplied with bathrobes, a DAB radio/iPod docking station, home-baked cake, a silent fridge with chilled water and fresh milk. 'Our room was clean and comfortable, but we would have liked some comfy chairs.' In warm months, stay a moment – for a midsummer daydream – in the garden and cushion-strewn summer house. Good choice at breakfast includes home-made granola, and smoked haddock with poached eggs. Small lounge, dining room. Free Wi-Fi, in-room TV (Freeview). No background music. Garden. Parking. Bicycle storage. 1 mile W of centre (on a bus route); within walking distance of Anne Hathaway's cottage and gardens. Stratford racecourse nearby. Children over 12 welcomed. 5 bedrooms

(1 on ground floor). Per room B&B £110–£130 (2-night min. stay preferred at weekends). Closed Christmas Day, New Year.

TENBURY WELLS Worcestershire
Map 3:C5

THE TALBOT INN, Newnham Bridge, WR15 8JF. Tel 01584 781941, www.talbotinnnewnhambridge.co.uk. 'A super all-round stay.' Fields of growing hops surround this red-brick former coaching inn in the Teme valley; inside the 19th-century building, order a local real ale or cider in the hop-hung bar. At lunch and dinner, chef Jacob Vaughan cooks an 'excellent, varied' menu, perhaps 'an enjoyable sirloin steak with all the trimmings'. Long country walks leave you famished? Pop in for an 'early bird' supper before retiring to one of the 'modern, bright and immaculately kept' bedrooms. 'Ours, of a good size, had a super-king-size bed, soft linen and pillows, a flask of fresh milk for hot drinks. In the natural-stone bathroom: a walk-in shower and lovely, fluffy towels.' Barnaby Williams is the 'hard-working, ever-present' host; his staff are 'friendly' and 'efficient'. 3 dining areas (optional background music), snug, bar. Free Wi-Fi, in-room TV (Freeview). Small function facilities. Garden. Parking. Children (extra beds; £10 per night) and dogs (allowed in 3 rooms; £10 per night) welcomed. Off the A456, 4 miles from Tenbury Wells. 7 bedrooms. Per room B&B £70–£110. Dinner £30, three-course 'early bird' supper £15 (Mon–Fri). 2-night min. stay at weekends May–Sept. Closed 2–12 Jan.
25% DISCOUNT VOUCHERS

TETBURY Gloucestershire
Map 3:E5

THE ROYAL OAK, 1 Cirencester Road, GL8 8EY. Tel 01666 500021, www.theroyaloaktetbury.co.uk. Family-friendly, dog-friendly, all around fun and lively, Chris York and Kate Lewis's pub-with-rooms attracts locals and passers-by with its real ales, updated pub menu, and bright-and-breezy vibe. The jukebox gets the thumbs-up, too. The buzzy bar and raftered restaurant occupy the 18th-century stone inn – here, chef Richard Simms's cooking, including a noteworthy vegan menu, is inspired by the seasons and the 'superb' Cotswold producers. In the summer months, the informal atmosphere spills outside, when food is served from a vintage Airstream trailer on the terrace. Rustic bedrooms are in a separate building across the courtyard. Pick a top-floor room for the views across the valley; for more space, lounge in the Oak Lodge mezzanine suite, which has leather armchairs and a wood-burner. Bar, restaurant (closed Sun eve), private dining/meeting room. Free Wi-Fi, in-room TV (Freeview). Background music, monthly live music sessions. Large garden (boules pitch). Parking. Bike shed. Children (special menu; games; not after 8 pm in restaurant; beds £30 per night) and dogs (in ground-floor rooms; £10 per night) welcomed. 6 bedrooms (1 suitable for disabled). Per room B&B £85–£170. Dinner £25. 2-night min. bookings preferred. Closed 1–2 weeks Jan.
25% DISCOUNT VOUCHERS

THORNTON HOUGH Merseyside
Map 4:E2

MERE BROOK HOUSE, Thornton Common Road, Wirral, CH63 0LU. Tel 07713 189949, www.merebrookhouse.co.uk. On the edge of a village in the centre of the Wirral peninsula, Lorna Tyson and her husband, Donald (a farmer), have transformed an Edwardian country house into a relaxed B&B ('no notices/rules anywhere!') and small events venue. Built by a Liverpool brewer in the late 19th century, the house stands in mature grounds with a sunken dell, a large pond, and paddocks where calves graze. Beyond, woodland stretches down to the Mere Brook. Choose between individually decorated bedrooms spread between the original building and a converted coach house across the patio: most have views over the gardens or fields; one has its own patio; another a large private balcony. Each building has its own lounge; guests also have the use of a kitchen to store food and prepare meals. Feeling peckish? Help yourself to complimentary home-made cakes, cheese, fruit juice, tea and coffee whenever the desire strikes. Breakfast is served in the conservatory overlooking the pond, using super-local ingredients: honey from the garden beehives; milk from the Tysons' dairy cows; home-produced apple juice using fruit from the orchard. 3 lounges, conservatory, dining room. Guest kitchens. Free Wi-Fi, in-room TV (Freeview). Wedding/function facilities. 1-acre garden (benches, gazebo) in 4-acre grounds (pond, paddocks). Children welcomed (extra beds). Within 20 mins' drive of Liverpool and Chester. 8 bedrooms (4 in coach house; 3 on ground floor, 1 suitable for disabled). Per room B&B £75–£130.

THORPE MARKET Norfolk
Map 2:A5
THE GUNTON ARMS, Cromer Road, NR11 8TZ. Tel 01263 832010, www. theguntonarms.co.uk. Stumble upon Stubbs engravings or discover Damien Hirst paintings at art dealer Ivor Braka's sophisticated yet 'relaxed' pub-with-rooms. Tracey Manning is the manager. The 'interesting' flint-stoned, red-gabled inn sits on the edge of a historic deer park. Within, find wood-panelled walls, open fires, and 'lovely' country-house bedrooms decorated with handmade wallpaper, Turkish rugs and antique furniture. There's no television in the bedrooms (go to the two lounges for that); instead, take in bucolic views over the park, with the Roberts radio as musical accompaniment. A downstairs pantry has juice, tea and coffee. At lunch and dinner, chef Stuart Tattersall's meals are hearty and rustic. The speciality: 'chunks of meat' (steaks, ribs of beef, Barnsley chops, venison from the estate) cooked on a grill set over a huge open fire in the Elk dining room – 'as if in a medieval banqueting hall'. 2 restaurants (closed Sun), lounge, bar. Free Wi-Fi. Background music. Children (cot; extra bed £15 per night) and dogs (£10 per night) welcomed. 5 miles from Cromer. 8 bedrooms. Per room B&B £95–£185 (2-night min. stay at weekends). Dinner from £35. Closed Christmas Day.

THURNHAM Kent
Map 2:D5
THURNHAM KEEP, Castle Hill, nr Maidstone, ME14 3LE. Tel 01622 734149, www.thurnhamkeep.co.uk. Swan about in country house splendour at Amanda Lane's 'very impressive' B&B, in an Edwardian house built from the ruins of Thurnham Castle. The hostess offers a sweet welcome, with home-baked treats for afternoon tea; up the oak staircase, home-made

shortbread and seasonal fruits picked from the gardens are left in the 'beautiful', traditionally furnished bedrooms. Each room has an antique bed; two have a huge, original Edwardian bath in the bathroom; all have wide views over the extensive grounds and surrounding countryside – look out for pheasants. Communal breakfasts have home-made jams, honey from the garden's bees and eggs from resident hens. Arrange supper in advance or venture out to one of the many pubs nearby. Oak-panelled sitting room (wood-burning stove), dining room, conservatory. Billiard room (in the old chapel). Free Wi-Fi, in-room TV (Freeview). No background music. 7-acre terraced garden, pond, kitchen garden, dovecote, summer house. Terrace (alfresco breakfasts). Heated outdoor swimming pool (June–early Sept). Tennis, croquet. Parking. 3 miles from Maidstone. Children over 12 welcomed. 3 bedrooms. Per room B&B £130–£160. Closed mid-Dec–Feb.

TISBURY Wiltshire
Map 2:D1
THE COMPASSES INN, Lower Chicksgrove, nr Salisbury, SP3 6NB. Tel 01722 714318, www.thecompassesinn. com. Settle comfortably into rustic life at Susie and Alan Stoneham's traditional English pub, a cosy retreat with great country walks – the whole, contentedly, 'in the middle of nowhere'. There are nooks and crannies aplenty in the thatch-roofed 14th-century inn: come in to stone walls, low ceilings and huge beams; wooden settles and a log fire; real ales, malt whiskies, a blackboard menu of seasonal, locally inspired meals. Simply furnished,

country-style bedrooms are accessed separately; each has a hospitality tray and a modern bathroom. Well located for jaunts to Longleat, Stonehenge and Wilton House. Bar, restaurant (closed Mon lunch New Year–Easter). Free Wi-Fi, in-room TV (Freeview). No background music. Small functions. Front and rear gardens. Children (baby monitor, babysitting; over-3s £25 charge) and dogs welcomed. 2 miles E of Tisbury. 4 bedrooms, plus adjacent 2-bed cottage. Per room B&B from £95 (2-night min. stay on summer and bank holiday weekends). Dinner from £26. Closed Christmas Day, Boxing Day.

TOLLARD ROYAL Wiltshire
Map 2:E1
KING JOHN INN, SP5 5PS. Tel 01725 516207, www.kingjohninn.co.uk. Cheery pots of herbs or flowers welcome guests to this refurbished Victorian pub, in a pretty village on the edge of Cranborne Chase. It is now part of Cirrus Inns; Adam Wilson is the manager. The focus on updated British cuisine remains: in the 'enticing' dining area, or in the terraced garden on fine days, choose from menus rich in game and other local meat and produce. 'Pleasing', 'restful' bedrooms have a charming country feel, with pale colours, well-picked antiques, home-made shortbread and a selection of books; each is brought bang up to date with a flat-screen TV, all-natural bath products, fancy teas and an espresso machine. Most are in the main house, up a 'steep, narrow' stairway; some, in the former coach house, are steps away on a gravelled path (umbrellas provided). Get the day started with fresh orange juice and 'proper' toast

at breakfast. Popular with shooting parties – the Ashcombe and Rushmore estates are moments away. Lounge, bar, restaurant. Free Wi-Fi, in-room TV. Garden (outdoor functions; music licence). Parking. Children and dogs (by prior arrangement) welcomed. 6 miles W of Shaftesbury. 8 bedrooms (some on ground floor, 3 in coach house). Per room B&B from £90. Dinner from £20.

TORQUAY Devon
Map 1:D5
THE 25, 25 Avenue Road, TQ2 5LB. Tel 01803 297517, www.the25.uk. A flamboyant streak runs through Andy and Julian Banner-Price's refurbished Edwardian villa behind Torre Abbey. B&B accommodation is in bedrooms strikingly decorated with statement lighting fixtures and bold colours, each different as can be. Two rooms have a lounge; one has a separate dressing area; one has a groovy, fake zebra head – and black-and-white armchairs to match. Whichever is picked, all rooms have little extras such as home-made biscuits, bathrobes and slippers, a silent fridge with fresh milk and bottled water, an iPad. Arrive to tea and home-made cake in the drawing room; in the morning, knock back fruit smoothie shots at breakfast before tucking in to fruit salad, home-made yogurt and granola, scrambled eggs cooked with double cream and butter. The B&B is a short walk through gardens to the seafront; the main harbour, with shops, restaurants, bars and a theatre, is close by. Drawing room, dining room. Free Wi-Fi, in-room TV (Freeview). 'Easy listening' background music. Computer for guests' use. Sunny patio. Parking. No children under 18. Resident dog,

Patsy. 6 bedrooms. Per room B&B £99–£159. Closed Dec, Jan.
25% DISCOUNT VOUCHERS

TRESCO Isles of Scilly
Map 1: inset C1
NEW INN, TR24 0QQ. Tel 01720 422849, www.tresco.co.uk. Beachy hues, a 'relaxed' environment and the sound of the ocean create an away-from-it-all atmosphere at this cosy inn, the only pub on Robert Dorrien-Smith's private, car-free island. Robin Lawson manages 'pleasant, efficient' staff. A hub of the community, the 'traditional, deliberately unchanged' country pub has mismatched seating, a 'well-stocked' bar, a wood-burning stove; in good weather, eat under a canopy in the 'very pretty' garden. 'The peaceful residents' sitting area is calm, contemporary and comfortable, with books and velvet sofas. Bedrooms, recently renovated, are all lovely,' trusted Guide readers say this year. Some rooms in the main building may be snug; those in the modern annexe, which cost more, are more spacious. In the Michelin-approved pub, Alan Hewitt serves bar favourites with a twist (crab claws, partridge sausage rolls), using local produce and the catch of the day. Music, beer and cider festivals are held annually. The 'amazing' Abbey Garden is a ten-minute walk away. 2 bars (background music), residents' lounge, restaurant. Free Wi-Fi, in-room TV (Freeview). Patio (alfresco eating), pavilion, garden. Heated outdoor swimming pool ('very appealing, as one has to be stalwart to brave the sea'). Children welcomed. 16 bedrooms (some with terrace, some with sea views). Per person B&B from £60. Dinner from £44.

TROUTBECK Cumbria
Map 4: inset C2

BROADOAKS, Bridge Lane, LA23 1LA.
Tel 01539 445566, www.
broadoakscountryhouse.co.uk. Tracey
Robinson and Joanna Harbottle's 'very
welcoming' Lake District retreat is in
a 19th-century stone-and-slate country
house set in extensive landscaped
grounds, the views stretching towards
Windermere. 'Gorgeous' bedrooms
(some compact) are individually styled
with bold wallpaper and antique
furniture; some have a roll-top bath
or sunken spa bath in the bathroom.
A new suite in the grounds provides
generous accommodation for a
family or a large group: there are two
bedrooms, two bathrooms, a lounge
and a private patio. Take afternoon
tea in the new orangery; sample
pre-prandial canapés in the music
room – and don't forget to look up
at the decorative vaulted ceiling. In
Oaks brasserie, chef Sharon Elders
combines 'excellent' modern French
dishes with Cumbrian favourites,
using much local produce; good
vegetarian options. Music room
(vintage Bechstein piano, log fire), bar,
restaurant, orangery. Free Wi-Fi, in-
room TV (Freeview). Soft background
music. Civil wedding licence. 8-acre
grounds, stream. Complimentary
access to nearby spa (swimming
pool); 5 mins' drive. Children over
5, and dogs (in some rooms; £25 per
night) welcomed. Resident cockapoo,
Molly. 2 miles N of Bowness-on-
Windermere. 20 bedrooms (some
on ground floor; 5 in coach house; 3
detached garden suites, 5 mins' walk
from house). Per room B&B from
£155, D,B&B from £185.

TUNBRIDGE WELLS Kent
Map 2:D4

HOTEL DU VIN TUNBRIDGE WELLS,
Crescent Road, TN1 2LY. Tel 08447
489266, www.hotelduvin.com. Take not
the waters but, rather, the wines in this
'excellent' outpost of the du Vin group,
occupying an 18th-century sandstone
mansion in a Georgian spa town. Period
details mix with smart styling in the
modern bedrooms; some overlook
Calverley Park; all have a well-stocked
minibar. 'The lounges have the genteel
air of an 18th-century manor': find a
spot to nurse a pre-dinner drink in the
clubby bar; play board games among
the antiques in the lounge. A 'cigar
bothy' might please dedicated smokers.
Head to the informal dining room for
reliable bistro dishes; alfresco meals may
be taken on the 'fine' garden terrace
with views across the park. Bar, bistro,
lounge. Private dining room. Free
Wi-Fi, in-room TV. No background
music. Function facilities. 1-acre garden
(boules), terrace (alfresco dining).
Vineyard. Limited parking. Children
and dogs welcomed. Close to the station.
34 bedrooms (4 in annexe). Per room
B&B from £130, D,B&B from £170.

UPTON MAGNA Shropshire
Map 3:B5

THE HAUGHMOND, Pelham Road,
nr Shrewsbury, SY4 4TZ. Tel 01743
709918, www.thehaughmond.co.uk.
Mel and Martin Board's contemporary
coaching inn has brought new life to a
once-derelict pub. Along with a popular
bar/brasserie, there's now a coffee
shop, a village store, straightforward
B&B rooms and, for a special occasion,
Basils restaurant, which seats just 16
in a modern-rustic barn conversion. A

self-taught cook, Martin Board works with chef David Martin on both the brasserie's informal meals and the restaurant's five-course tasting menus (with an optional wine flight). Dine on fine country cooking (a vegetarian menu is available), then sleep well in one of the comfortable bedrooms above the bar. Each is simply decorated but thoughtfully supplied with bottled water, a hot drinks tray, toiletries, a smart TV with on-demand movies; one, in the eaves, has a Juliet balcony with views across the fields. Bar/brasserie, conservatory, breakfast room. Basils restaurant (booking essential; open Thurs, Fri, Sat eves; Sat lunch; £40). Function facilities in purpose-built barn. Free Wi-Fi, in-room smart TV. No background music. ½-acre garden, terrace. Parking. Children (travel cots, baby monitors) and dogs (£10 per night, own bedding required; must be on lead at all times in public areas) welcomed. 4 miles E of Shrewsbury. 5 bedrooms. Closed Christmas Day, New Year's Day. Per room B&B £90–£120.
25% DISCOUNT VOUCHERS

VENTNOR Isle of Wight
Map 2:E2

THE ROYAL HOTEL, Belgrave Road, PO38 1JJ. Tel 01983 852186, www. royalhoteliow.co.uk. 'Excellent as always', this grande dame of traditional seaside hotels continues to please visitors who come for its 'olde-worlde charm', says a regular Guide reader this year. Philip Wilson manages 'superb', 'very friendly' staff for William Bailey, the owner. 'Comfortable and well kept', the 185-year-old hotel stands in subtropical gardens close to the seafront and town centre. The best of the country-house-style bedrooms – each dressed in rich velvets, silks and toile de jouy – overlook the grounds and Ventnor Bay. Sit down to chef Steven Harris's 'absolutely excellent' seasonal, modern menus in the restaurant; lunch and afternoon tea may be taken in the bar, conservatory or geranium-scented terrace. In summer, head to the clifftop Riviera Terrace – the panoramic views are the ideal partner to a custom-packed picnic hamper. Lounge, bar, restaurant, conservatory. Lift to some rooms. Free Wi-Fi (public areas), in-room TV. Background music, pianist during peak-season weekends. Civil wedding licence, function rooms. In-room massages, beauty treatments. 2-acre grounds, outdoor heated swimming pool (May–Sept), Riviera Terrace (summer only). Sandy beach nearby (hilly walk). Parking. Children (baby listening; children's high tea; 3–8s £35 per day; 9–15s £50 per day) and dogs (£25 per day) welcomed. 52 bedrooms (1 suitable for disabled). Per room B&B £190–£290, D,B&B £260–£360. Dinner £40. 2-night min. stay at peak weekends. Closed 2 weeks Jan.
25% DISCOUNT VOUCHERS

WADDESDON Buckinghamshire
Map 2:C3

THE FIVE ARROWS, High Street, HP18 0JE. Tel 01296 651727, www. thefivearrows.co.uk. Near the gates of Waddesdon Manor, this half-timbered, ornately patterned Grade II listed building was built in 1887 to house the architects and craftsmen working on the manor itself. Today a hotel with 'comfortable', smartly styled bedrooms, it is run by the Rothschild family trust for the National Trust. Rooms in the main house and converted coach house vary in size and decor (those in the main house are more traditional); some may display contemporary artworks, others may have Edwardian antique furnishings from the family collection. Light sleepers, ring to discuss room choices before booking: guests in a room overlooking the main road reported a barely-there 'hum' of traffic ('it didn't disturb us'); others found the road noise insistent. 'Good' seasonal menus are served in the busy restaurant or courtyard garden ('but the menu didn't change during our three-night stay'). A well-chosen selection of Rothschild wines is fine accompaniment. 'We loved the wine list.' A popular venue for weddings and exclusive-use events. Hotel guests receive a complimentary ticket for the grounds of Waddesdon Manor. Bar, restaurant. Free Wi-Fi, in-room TV (Freeview). No background music. Civil wedding licence. 1-acre garden. Children welcomed. 16 bedrooms (5 in Old Coach House, 3 in courtyard on ground floor). Per room B&B from £116, D,B&B from £165. **25% DISCOUNT VOUCHERS**

WARTLING Sussex
Map 2:E4

WARTLING PLACE, Herstmonceux, nr Hailsham, BN27 1RY. Tel 01323 832590, www.wartlingplace.co.uk. Rowena and Barry Gittoes create 'a wonderful atmosphere' at their 'very comfortable' B&B, in a Grade II listed Georgian rectory convenient for Glyndebourne. Surrounded by large, 'well-kept' gardens, the house is tastefully furnished with interesting prints and pictures; in the drawing room overlooking the grounds, find a spot on the comfy

sofas. Well-appointed bedrooms have bathrobes, 'real' coffee and Fairtrade tea, a digital radio, an iPod dock; borrow DVDs for relaxed nights in. An 'excellent' breakfast, served in the spacious dining room or in the bedroom, includes fresh fruit, cereals, honey from local bees; cooked dishes use locally sourced ingredients such as home-grown salads, and smoked salmon from a fishery half an hour away. An evening meal or a late supper is available, by arrangement; in summer, ask about a picnic hamper before striking out to explore. The B&B is on the edge of the Pevensey Levels nature reserve; quiet beaches are minutes away. 'We were delighted.' Drawing room, dining room (honesty bar, CD player). Free Wi-Fi (main house), in-room TV (Freeview). No background music. 3-acre garden. Parking. Children and dogs (in cottage only) welcomed. 5 miles E of Hailsham. 4 bedrooms (plus 2-bedroom self-catering cottage; suitable for disabled). Per room B&B £130–£165.

WARWICK Warwickshire
Map 3:C6

PARK COTTAGE, 113 West Street, CV34 6AH. Tel 01926 410319, www. parkcottagewarwick.co.uk. Flowers bloom along the front of Janet and Stuart Baldry's 'good-value' B&B in a 15th-century black-and-white timber-framed building at the entrance to Warwick Castle. Inside, oak beams and sloping floors speak of its long history; the breakfast room, with its original sandstone floor, was once the castle dairy. Most of the traditionally styled bedrooms are up a steep, narrow staircase. Each room has its own character: one has a 300-year-old four-

poster bed, another a king-size spa bath; a ground-floor room opens on to the pretty patio garden. Little gestures are pampering, such as the minty chocolates guests recently found when returning from a night out. In the breakfast room, an antique Welsh dresser is laden with cereals, yogurts, fruit, juices; a generous full English is 'perfectly cooked'. Cafetière coffee or a pot of Yorkshire tea is brought to the table. Reception/sitting area, breakfast room. Free Wi-Fi, in-room TV (Freeview). No background music. Small garden (patio, tables and seating). Parking. Children welcomed. On the A429 into town; the racecourse is nearby. 8 bedrooms (2 on ground floor; 2 family rooms). Per room B&B single £55–£80, double £80–£99. Closed Christmas, New Year.
25% DISCOUNT VOUCHERS

WATCHET Somerset
Map 1:B5

SWAIN HOUSE, 48 Swain Street, TA23 0AG. Tel 01984 631038, www.swain-house.com. Ancient mariners and young romantics, follow Coleridge's footsteps to this charming harbour town – then step into Annie and Jason Robinson's chic B&B. Remodelled from an 18th-century town house and shop, it is swathed in muted shades of grey, white and stone; its slate floors, silver velvet sofa and hefty wood dining table bestow warm sophistication. Upstairs, well-thought-out bedrooms are simply done with style: find a large bed, a mural based on an Old Master painting, graphite-coloured carpets, sash windows. Bathrooms have robes, a roll-top slipper bath and a large walk-in shower. Jason Robinson serves praiseworthy breakfasts (including American-style pancakes with

fruit, yogurt and maple syrup, and other vegetarian options). A light charcuterie board supper is available on request, as is a lunchtime picnic hamper with a rug. Lounge, dining room. Free Wi-Fi, in-room TV (Freeview). No background music. 7 miles from Dunster Castle; West Somerset Steam Railway. 4 bedrooms. Per room B&B £135. Closed Christmas.

WATERGATE BAY Cornwall
Map 1:D2

WATERGATE BAY, On the beach, TR8 4AA. Tel 01637 860543, www.watergatebay.co.uk. By a two-mile stretch of sandy beach, Will Ashworth's large, energetic hotel brings together heaps of activities for water-sports enthusiasts, families and the less adventurous. Mark Williams is the manager. The on-site Extreme Academy specialises in surfing, kitesurfing, wave skiing, stand-up paddleboarding and handplaning; the leisure complex, Swim Club, has a 25-metre ocean-view infinity pool, a hot tub, a fitness studio and treatment rooms (open to day members). There are swim clinics, yoga breaks, weekend beach fitness classes; age-appropriate children's play areas – inside, outside, with paint under fingernails and sand between the toes. Choose, too, between a number of eateries: Zacry's for modern American cuisine; the Living Space for sharing platters and seasonal salads; the Beach Hut for a classic surf 'n' turf. Sleep it off in one of the contemporary, coastal bedrooms outfitted in bright colours and stripy fabrics (many face the sea), then wake up the next day for more. Lounge/bar, 3 restaurants. Free Wi-Fi, in-room TV (Freeview). Background music.

Civil wedding licence. Terrace, sun deck. Indoor/outdoor swimming pool. Surf school. Treatment rooms. Children and dogs (in some rooms; £15 per night; dog-friendly beach) welcomed. 5 miles from Newquay. 69 bedrooms (family suites; 2 suitable for disabled). Per room B&B from £145, D,B&B from £195. Dinner £36.50.

WEDMORE Somerset
Map 1:B6
THE SWAN, Cheddar Road, BS28 4EQ. Tel 01934 710337, www.theswanwedmore.com. Guide readers praise the 'lovely, informal atmosphere' at this popular pub-with-rooms (Draco Pub Company), a 'friendly community hub' in this pretty village. 'Ideal for a one-night stay', 'smart' modern bedrooms (Small, Medium, Big) come well equipped with freshly ground coffee and a cafetière, a stash of old-fashioned sweets, 'super' toiletries. Catch up on the world with a daily newspaper over a local ale by the bar fire; in warm weather, the terrace calls for Pimm's and home-made lemonade. Chef Tom Blake cooks 'very good', unfussy dishes using locally reared meat, and Somerset produce in season. 'Breakfast is a real treat with lots of options', including home-cured bacon and freshly baked bread. The White Hart, Somerton (see Shortlist entry), is under the same ownership. Bar (wood-burning stove), restaurant (closed Sun eve). Free Wi-Fi, in-room TV. DVD library. 'Eclectic' background music. Function facilities. Terrace, garden (wood-fired oven and barbecue). Parking. Children and dogs (in bar and garden only) welcomed. 6 bedrooms. Per room B&B £85–£125. Dinner from £28.

WESTBROOK Herefordshire
Map 3:D4
WESTBROOK COURT B&B, nr Hay-on-Wye, HR3 5SY. Tel 01497 831752, www.westbrookcourtbandb.co.uk. Beyond Kari and Chris Morgan's 'rambling' 17th-century farmhouse stands a sleek, black, timber-clad former stable transformed into five stylish B&B suites. All around, there are extraordinary views over the Wye valley. Spacious and light-filled, each suite has zingy splashes of colour, and local touches showcasing the hostess's roots in interior design. Pick one to suit: four suites have a mezzanine bedroom overlooking Merbach Hill; one, with a sofa bed, can accommodate a family. All have a lounge area, and a private terraced deck angled to catch the sun. On the weekend, gather in the Morgans' cheery farmhouse kitchen for a communal breakfast, with home-baked bread, home-made jam, local meats, and eggs from the garden hens; during the week, a sumptuous breakfast hamper (pastries, smoked salmon, freshly boiled eggs, fruit, yogurt pots) is brought to the bedroom. Communal breakfast room/kitchen. Free Wi-Fi ('slow – welcome to rural life!'), in-room TV (Freeview). No background music. 5-acre grounds, terrace. Cycle and kayak storage. Children welcomed (cot – linen not provided; extra bed £15 per night). 3 miles E of Hay-on-Wye. 5 bedrooms (1 family room; 1 suitable for disabled). Per room B&B £85–£150. Credit cards not accepted.

WHEATHILL Shropshire
Map 3:C5
THE OLD RECTORY, nr Ludlow, WV16 6QT. Tel 01746 787209, www.theoldrectorywheathill.com. Izzy Barnard's handsome Georgian B&B in beautiful Shropshire countryside is a

cheerful rural retreat, made special with lots of little touches: home-made treats on arrival, wild flowers throughout the house, knitted cosies on the boiled eggs at breakfast. Curl up on a sofa in front of a warming fire; potter in the acres of garden. Immaculate bedrooms are airy and full of comforts. Light supper trays or a candlelit four-course dinner may be requested in advance. Breakfast on preserves of home-grown summer fruit, orange-yolked duck eggs from the resident flock, home-cured bacon. The B&B is horse and hound approved: loose boxes and hay, plus acres of riding country and good walks, keep animals happy – ask for guides and route cards detailing nearby bridleways. Drawing room, dining room, sauna (in cellar). Free Wi-Fi, in-room TV (Freeview). No background music. In-room treatments by arrangement. 7-acre gardens. Boot room. Loose boxes, tack room. Children (by arrangement), dogs (£10 per night in boot room) and horses (£20 per night) welcomed. Resident dogs and cat. 7 miles E of Ludlow. 3 bedrooms. Per room single B&B from £75, double £90–£130. Dinner £35. 2-night min. stay preferred. Closed Christmas, Jan.

WHITSTABLE Kent
Map 2:D5
THE CRESCENT TURNER HOTEL, Wraik Hill, CT5 3BY. Tel 01227 263506, crescentturner.co.uk. With wide views of the Kent coast, this privately owned red-brick bolthole is named after the British master who immortalised the region. Prints of JMW Turner's works hang in the airy, rustic lounge, above squashy sofas and a wood-burning stove; the spacious terrace looks across the garden to the sea. Glitzy touches (a mirrored bedside table, an animal-print throw, a bright yellow bedhead) add a touch of zing to the bedrooms; many rooms have coastal or countryside views. In the restaurant, chefs David Thorman and Shane Martin serve the best of local produce – including super-local oysters – in their modern British dishes. In seaside season, reserve the hotel's beach hut on Whitstable beach (charged extra) – it comes complete with kitchen, lounge and three canoes. Bar/lounge, restaurant (open to non-residents), function room. Free Wi-Fi, in-room TV (Freeview). Soft instrumental background music. Civil wedding licence. 2¼-acre garden, terrace, gazebo. Children welcomed (family rooms). Parking. 'A short drive' or a 30-minute stroll to the town. 16 bedrooms. Per room £99–£220. Dinner £35.

WILMSLOW Cheshire
Map 4:E3
KINGSLEY LODGE, 10 Hough Lane, SK9 2LQ. Tel 01625 441794, www.kingsleylodge.com. Fresh flowers, scented candles and original works of art fill the bedrooms at Jeremy Levy and Cliff Thomson's luxurious B&B, in a remodelled 1950s Arts and Crafts house within easy walking distance of the town centre and station. Handcrafted antiques sit comfortably with more modern pieces in the spacious lounge; in the elegant bedrooms, find many thoughtful touches: bathrobes, slippers, top-end toiletries. Outside is as serene as in: the tranquil grounds include ponds, a pine wood, a formal parterre and a seating deck with a water cascade. Lounge (honesty bar), breakfast room, meeting room. Free Wi-Fi, in-room TV. DVD library. No background music.

2-acre garden, patio. Parking. Children over 13 welcomed. Close to Manchester airport. 6 bedrooms. Per room B&B £115–£340.

WINCHCOMBE Gloucestershire
Map 3:D5

THE LION INN, 37 North Street, GL54 5PS. Tel 01242 603300, www.thelionwinchcombe.co.uk. In 'a lovely old town' below the Cotswold hills, this 'fine modern inn' houses a popular bar and restaurant, and modern-rustic bedrooms 'decorated with wit and imagination'. It is newly part of the small Epicurean collection of inns in the south of Britain; Tom Noori and Sue Chalmers are the managers. Locals and visitors throng the 'laid-back', buzzy bar (stone walls, flagstone floors, a log fire) for craft ales and slices of 'delicious' home-baked cake; among the auction finds, there are newspapers, board games, and armchairs to sink into. Imaginative gastropub dishes are cooked by chef Alex Dumitrache. Characterful bedrooms, some beamed, some chandeliered, are decorated in fresh, light shades, with large vases of flowers. There's no TV or radio – Scrabble and cards are provided instead. Rooms above the bar or in the courtyard may have pub noise until closing time. Bar, snug, restaurant. Free Wi-Fi. Background music. Courtyard garden. Children (high chairs) and dogs (£15 charge) welcomed. 7 bedrooms (2 accessed by external staircase). Per room B&B from £80. Dinner £30. 2-night min. stay preferred.

WINCHESTER Hampshire
Map 2:D2

HANNAH'S, 16a Parchment Street, SO23 8AZ. Tel 01962 840623, www.hannahsbedandbreakfast.co.uk. Time your arrival to tea: mid-afternoons at this B&B off the High Street, Hannah McIntyre lays out a spread of freshly baked treats for guests. Candle-scented, flower-filled, its shelves lined with books to borrow, the B&B wins fans for its pleasing, country-style bedrooms, each with a super-king-size bed, space to sit and a bathtub big enough for two. Greet the day in style in the spacious, beamed breakfast room: the hostess serves home-made jams and granola, specially blended teas and coffees, generous platters of bacon, sausages, eggs and roast tomatoes. Open from Thursday to Sunday; book for a long weekend, and leave only when the cake runs out. Breakfast room, library (honesty bar); terrace with seating. Free Wi-Fi, in-room TV (Freeview). Background music. Resident cat, Leyla. Children over 12 welcomed. 3 bedrooms. Per room B&B £185–£205. Closed Mon–Wed; week before Christmas–end Jan.

THE OLD VINE, 8 Great Minster Street, SO23 9HA. Tel 01962 854616, www.oldvinewinchester.com. Ashton Gray's 'lovely', 'quiet' Grade II listed 18th-century inn stands opposite the cathedral green, with all the blessings a guest might need: 'enthusiastic, friendly and knowledgeable' staff, 'good, imaginative' food' and a 'wonderfully comfortable' bed – 'and all at a fair price', say Guide readers in 2016. Designer fabrics and wallpapers, and a mix of antique and modern furniture infuse elegance into the well-equipped bedrooms; each is supplied with water, soft drinks and an espresso machine. A top-floor suite has views of the cathedral. 'Our beautiful room, Zoffany, had everything one could wish for.' Hampshire produce takes centre stage on the menu in the oak-beamed restaurant, where an open fire burns in cool weather. Settle into the bar with a pint of real ale, or take a cocktail out to the small, flower-filled patio or the bright conservatory. 'We walked across the green to the cathedral to listen to evensong – magic.' 'We hope to return.' Bar ('easy listening' background music), restaurant. Free Wi-Fi, in-room TV (Freeview). Children welcomed (cot; over-3s £40 per night; no under-6s in restaurant and bar). Permits supplied for on-street parking. 6 bedrooms (1 family room; self-contained 2-bed apartment with garage, in annexe). Per room B&B single £120–£180, double £150–£200. Dinner £25–£30. Closed Christmas Day.

THE WYKEHAM ARMS, 75 Kingsgate Street, SO23 9PE. Tel 01962 853834, www.wykehamarmswinchester.co.uk. 'A top-rate example of a pub-with-rooms', this 18th-century coaching inn (Fuller's Hotels and Inns) is a warm, characterful spot, all log fires and local ales; old school desks tucked in nooks and crannies; pictures, ale mugs and kitschy breweriana. Jon Howard is the manager; the staff are 'helpful and friendly'. Well-equipped, individually decorated bedrooms, some with a four-poster bed, are reached via a narrow staircase; others are in a 16th-century building opposite. 'Mine was above the bar; there was perfectly bearable background noise – only talking, no music – till just after 11 pm.' Chef Gavin Sinden serves modern British dishes and pub classics in the wood-panelled dining room. 'Breakfast was excellent, with outstanding local black pudding.' Bar (local ales), 2 restaurants, 2 function rooms; small patio with seating. Free Wi-Fi (in public areas), in-room TV. No background music. Children over 12, and dogs (in 2 bedrooms; not in restaurant; £7.50 per night) welcomed. Parking. 14 bedrooms (7 in annexe). Per room B&B from £149, D,B&B from £189.
25% DISCOUNT VOUCHERS

WOODBRIDGE Suffolk
Map 2:C5
THE CROWN, The Thoroughfare, IP12 1AD. Tel 01394 384242, www.thecrownatwoodbridge.co.uk. A 'very well-thought-out' revamp by designer David Bentheim has given this 'extremely comfortable and welcoming' 16th-century coaching inn its chic, breezy air – Suffolk by way of Nantucket and Copenhagen. In the centre of a thriving market town near the Deben estuary, it is run by Garth Wray for the TA Hotel Collection. Mix with locals and newcomers in the glass-roofed bar, where a wooden sailing skiff catches the eye; there are cocktails, Suffolk brews and new chef Daniel Perjesi's 'excellent' brasserie-style dishes. Stay the night, afterwards, in one of the 'cool' bedrooms styled in neutral tones and shades of grey; modern lighting is 'excellent throughout'. The thoughtful staff are praised: 'I asked for direction on my onward journey, and the manager made me a three-page itinerary.' 4 dining areas, bar. Private dining. Free Wi-Fi, in-room TV (Sky). Background music; monthly jazz evenings. Courtyard garden. Parking. Children welcomed. 10 bedrooms.

Per room B&B £120–£200, D,B&B
£180–£245.
25% DISCOUNT VOUCHERS

WOODSTOCK Oxfordshire
Map 2:C2

THE FEATHERS, 16–20 Market
Street, OX20 1SX. Tel 01993 812291,
www.feathers.co.uk. In the centre
of a 'handsome' market town, this
characterful town house hotel, formed
from a row of diverse buildings, is
made lively with modern colours, bold
wallpapers and a collection of more
than 400 gins from around the world.
It is managed by Dominic Bishop for
Premier Cru Hotels. 'The unusual
structure of the building means that
clusters of rooms are reached by a
series of winding staircases with
lovely wooden banisters. It makes the
experience intimate, private.' Pick
among individually styled bedrooms
(there are five categories); many have
antique furniture, uneven floors and
quirky additions. There are no tea- or
coffee-making facilities in the room,
but order a tea tray, or take afternoon
tea and morning coffee in the lounge or
on the terrace. In the restaurant, tables
are 'smartly laid' for chef Ian Matfin's
'sophisticated' dinners'. Study,
Courtyard gin bar, restaurant (closed
Sun, Mon night). Free Wi-Fi, in-
room TV (Freeview). Background
music. Functions. Picnic hampers.
Free long-term parking within
walking distance. Children and dogs
(in some rooms) welcomed. Close to
Blenheim Palace. 21 bedrooms (5 in
adjacent town house; 1 suitable for
disabled; 1 suite has a private steam
room). Per room B&B from £159,
D,B&B from £239.

WOOLACOMBE Devon
Map 1:B4

WATERSMEET, EX34 7EB. Tel 01271
870333, www.watersmeethotel.co.uk.
There are 'fantastic' views across the
bay to Lundy Island from Amanda
James's 'relaxed' traditional hotel above
Woolacombe Bay. Once an Edwardian
gentleman's retreat, the 'comfortable'
hotel today welcomes guests who come
for the 'well-cooked' food and the
'excellent' walks to be had along the
Coastal Path. All but three bedrooms
look out to sea; some have a wooden
balcony or a garden terrace. Each room
is supplied with bottled water, upmarket
toiletries, bathrobes and a season-
appropriate duvet, though some guests
think 'the lighting could be better'. Take
afternoon tea in the 'spacious' lounge,
or on the terrace in good weather; come
evening, dine on classic British dishes
in the restaurant overlooking the bay.
Simpler meals may be taken in the airy
bistro. Lounge, bar, restaurant, bistro;
terrace (alfresco meals and drinks).
Function room. Lift. Free Wi-Fi, 'weak'
mobile phone reception, in-room TV
(Freeview). Background music. Room
service. Civil wedding licence. ½-acre
garden. Heated indoor and outdoor
swimming pools. Treatment room.
Sandy beach below. Children welcomed
(early dinners). 29 bedrooms (3 on
ground floor, 1 suitable for disabled).
Per room B&B £160–£300, D,B&B
£230–£370.

WROXTON Oxfordshire
Map 2:C2

WROXTON HOUSE HOTEL, Silver Street,
nr Banbury, OX15 6QB. Tel 01295
730777, www.wroxtonhousehotel.com.
'The little things count' at this 'friendly',

'good-value' hotel on the edge of a charming, honey-hued village three miles west of Banbury: 'The perfectly spreadable room-temperature butter made our day.' Ably run within the Best Western group by John and Gill Smith, the 'exquisite' thatched-roof manor house, dating back to 1649, has many original features (inglenook fireplace, oak beams). 'Comfortable, spotless' bedrooms are in the main house and a more modern wing; there are three room categories, but all have bottled water, a refreshment tray, a desk and an easy chair. 'Delicious, imaginative' daily-changing modern menus are served by head chef Marc Ward in the restaurant; find home-made jams, marmalade and chutney at breakfast. 'We were impressed.' 2 lounges, bar, 1649 restaurant. Private function rooms. Free Wi-Fi, in-room TV (Sky, Freeview). Civil wedding licence. Background music. Terrace. Parking. Children welcomed. 32 bedrooms (7 on ground floor; 3 in adjoining cottage). Per room B&B from £118, D,B&B from £174. 2-night min. stay at weekends.

YORK Yorkshire
Map 4:D4

BAR CONVENT, 17 Blossom Street, YO24 1AQ. Tel 01904 643238, www.bar-convent.org.uk. 'Unlike any other hotel in which I have stayed.' Founded as a school for girls in 1686, this unusual Grade I listed Georgian building houses England's oldest active convent and quirky, good-value accommodation. It is managed by Lesley Baines. Enter through the 'magnificent' glass-roofed hall, then seek out the 18th-century domed chapel and the library full of antique Catholic texts. Newly

redecorated, the spotless bedrooms have a 'wickedly' comfortable bed and access to a shared, fully equipped kitchen. Pick one to suit – there are many single rooms and two family rooms; some share a bathroom; street-facing rooms have air conditioning. Some rooms were redesigned in a restful palette, with a mosaic-tiled shower room, by Olga Polizzi (who owns Hotel Endsleigh, Milton Abbot, and Tresanton, St Mawes – see main entries). Breakfast, morning coffee, light lunches and afternoon tea are taken in the 'slightly utilitarian' café; for dinner in the evenings, many of the city's restaurants and cafés are within walking distance. Do check out the living heritage centre, which includes a multimedia history of the convent. Sitting rooms (on each floor, with TV), games room (small snooker table, board games), kitchen. Licensed café. Meeting rooms. Museum, shop. Chapel. Lift to 1st and 2nd floors. Free Wi-Fi, in-room TV (Freeview). No background music. Catholic wedding, function facilities. ½-acre garden. 20 bedrooms (some suitable for disabled). Per room B&B single £42–£67, double £96–£120. Closed Sun, Easter, 18 Dec–18 Jan.

THE BLOOMSBURY, 127 Clifton, YO30 6BL. Tel 01904 634031, www.thebloomsburyguesthouse.com. Tea and home-baked cake await at this 'friendly', 'beautifully decorated' B&B, in a Victorian house within walking distance of historic York Minster and the city centre. It is run by Matthew Townsley and Paul Johnson, who have newly taken over from Matthew's parents, Tricia and Steve Townsley, as they ease into retirement. Up the staircase (built in 1870), light spills into the 'lovely' bedrooms through large sash windows. Each room is different, but all have tea- and coffee-making facilities, a TV, a radio alarm clock, and a shower- or bathroom. In the morning, the dining room is 'a pleasure to have breakfast in' – sample sausages and thick-cut bacon from the local butcher, whose shop is minutes away. Sitting room, dining room (optional background music). Free Wi-Fi, in-room TV (Freeview). Terrace, flowery 'secret' courtyard garden. Parking. 1 mile to city centre. Children welcomed (no special facilities). Resident Yorkshire terrier, Harvey, 'who loves to meet and greet guests'. 7 bedrooms (1 on ground floor). Per room B&B £80–£90. 2-night min. stay at weekends in summer. Closed Christmas, New Year. Credit cards not accepted.

25% DISCOUNT VOUCHERS

SCOTLAND

ABERDEEN
Map 5:C3

ATHOLL HOTEL, 54 King's Gate, AB15 4YN. Tel 01224 323505, www.atholl-aberdeen.co.uk. Well located for city business and day trips to Royal Deeside, this privately owned hotel in a Victorian Gothic Revival building has a relaxing atmosphere and hospitable staff. Gordon Sinclair is the manager. Traditionally decorated bedrooms have plaid bedcovers and cushions; some rooms are large enough to accommodate a family. Sample chef Scott Craig's classic Scottish fare in the restaurant, the bar or the homely lounge. Breakfast brings tattie scones, Finnan haddies, Scottish buttery. The city centre is a short bus journey eastwards from the residential neighbourhood; the airport

is a 15-minute drive away. Lounge, bar, restaurant; patio. Lift to first floor. Free Wi-Fi, in-room TV (Sky Sports). Background music. Weddings, functions. Parking. 1½ miles W of the city centre. Castles, golf courses, whisky trails and beaches within reach. Children welcomed (special menu; £10 per night). 34 bedrooms (2 suitable for disabled). Per room B&B £70–£140. Dinner £25–£30.

ALLANTON Scottish Borders
Map 5:E3

ALLANTON INN, nr Duns, TD11 3JZ. Tel 01890 818260, www.allantoninn.co.uk. Guide readers like the 'warm welcome' and 'good ambience' at Katrina and William Reynolds's 'very good-value' restaurant-with-rooms, at the centre of a rural Scottish Borders village. 'The owners are totally involved, the accommodation is comfortable, and the food and service are first class.' Decorated with contemporary local artwork, well-equipped bedrooms in the stone-built 18th-century coaching inn have coffee- and tea-making facilities, Scottish biscuits, a useful information folder; Scottish-produced toiletries and 'a good power shower' in the bathroom. Join locals in the informal, rustic restaurant or bar, where chef Craig Rushton cooks a mix of modern and classic dishes. In the morning, breakfast is 'very good': Eyemouth kippers, home-made granola, home-baked bread; Katrina Reynolds's jams and marmalade. Day permits for trout and salmon fishing on the Whiteadder are available. Bar (30 different gins), restaurant (background music). Free Wi-Fi, in-room TV (Freeview). Beer garden. Children welcomed (high chairs, cots, toys and games). 6 bedrooms (1 family suite). Per room B&B single from £65, double from £75. Dinner £28. Closed Christmas, Boxing Day.

ALYTH Perth and Kinross
Map 5:D2

TIGH NA LEIGH, 22–24 Airlie Street, PH11 8AJ. Tel 01828 632372, www. tighnaleigh.com. Chris and Bettina Black's 'friendly' guest house, in a 'surprisingly large and pretty garden', is just what the doctor ordered, say regular Guide readers in 2016. The stone-built Victorian villa (once a doctor's home) stands on a street leading into the small town. Inside, there are 'sizeable' lounges with maps, books and guides to borrow, and neat, homely bedrooms varying in size and style. 'We had the largest bedroom, with an enormous four-poster bed, two easy chairs, a padded bench, adequate storage space; a spa bath in the good-sized bathroom. The bay window faced the street, but double glazing kept noise out.' A 'good' dinner may be 'well cooked' by Chris Black, by arrangement; vegetarians and other guests on a special diet are catered for 'with the same gusto' as meat eaters. Wake to a choice of cooked dishes at breakfast, with home-made jams and marmalades, perhaps a garden rhubarb and plum compote. 'Pleasant' hosts who are 'anxious to help in any way', the Blacks offer advice for distillery visits, castle visits and tours, nature and heritage trails, and many outdoor activities. They'll ensure you're well prepared, too – ask about a packed lunch or a gourmet picnic hamper to take with you. Lounge (log fire), TV room, reading room, conservatory dining room ('muted' background music). Free Wi-Fi,

in-room TV (Freeview, Sky Sports). Drying facilities. Computer for guests' use. Garden (pond). Children over 12 and dogs (£7.50; bedding not provided) welcomed. Resident cats. 5 bedrooms (1 on ground floor). Per person B&B £44.50–£65. Closed Oct–Jan.

APPLECROSS Highland
Map 5:C1

APPLECROSS INN, Shore Street, IV54 8LR. Tel 01520 744262, www.applecross. uk.com/inn. Magnificent views of the isles of Skye and Raasay, and the freshest of seafood, reward stout-hearted visitors to Judith Fish's white-painted hostelry. It stands at the end of an 11-mile stretch of single-track road, on the shores of the Applecross peninsula. A lively spot, the bar has a wood-burning stove and a large selection of malt whiskies. In the small dining room, chef Robert MacRae's daily-changing blackboard menus include plenty of garden produce, and fish and shellfish from Applecross Bay. In spring and summer, a retro food truck on the shore caters to locals and visitors hungry for ice creams, cakes, coffees and classic inn dishes. Basic bedrooms are clean and comfortable, with sea views; there may be some noise from the pub. Cyclists, walkers, kayakers and campers are made very welcome. Bar (draft ales; background music), dining room. Free Wi-Fi. Shoreside beer garden. Bicycle storage. Plenty of wildlife and local walks. Children (special menu, games; not allowed in bar after 8.30 pm; over-5s £10 per night) and dogs (in 2 rooms; £10 per stay) welcomed. 7 bedrooms (1 on ground floor for assisted access). Per person B&B from £65 (based on 2 people staying). Dinner £20–£30. Closed for accommodation for 2 weeks over Christmas and New Year.

ARINAGOUR Argyll and Bute
Map 5:C1
COLL HOTEL, Isle of Coll, PA78 6SZ. Tel 01879 230334, www.collhotel. com. In large gardens overlooking the bay, Kevin and Julie Oliphant's small hotel is in the only village on the small Hebridean Isle of Coll. Their daughter, Laura, is the manager. The cosy bars are the lively hub of the community; in the restaurant, Julie Oliphant and chef Graham Griffiths cook uncomplicated dishes specialising in freshly caught seafood. Smartly refurbished, understated bedrooms have home-made biscuits, rainy-day board games and sea kelp products; four also have spectacular views across the bay to the Treshnish Isles, Mull, Staffa, Iona and Jura. Come nightfall, be starry-eyed: Coll is a Dark Sky island with no artificial light pollution; bedrooms are supplied with a glow-in-the-dark skyscope; moon and star maps are available to borrow. Complimentary pick-up from and drop-off to the ferry pier. Lounge, 2 bars (darts, pool table, open fires), restaurant, small residents' lounge, residents' dining room. Free Wi-Fi, in-room TV (Freeview). No background music. Complimentary morning coffee and afternoon tea. Garden (decking, plenty of seating; pétanque). Helipad. Bicycles and helmets available to borrow. Children welcomed (special menu; buckets, spades). 1 mile from the ferry pier; 3-hour ferry journey from Oban. 6 bedrooms. Per room B&B single £70, double £120–£150. Dinner £25–£30. Closed Christmas; house parties only at New Year.
25% DISCOUNT VOUCHERS

ARISAIG Highland
Map 5:C1
THE OLD LIBRARY LODGE AND RESTAURANT, PH39 4NH. Tel 01687 450651, www.oldlibrary.co.uk. Spotting Nessie is so passé: the next challenge is the monster of Loch nan Ceall. With 'wonderful' views from the bedrooms at Mags and Allan Ritchie's laid-back restaurant-with-rooms, you just might catch a glimpse before breakfast. 'Comfortable' bedrooms in the converted 200-year-old stables are simply decorated, with bright throw pillows adding a dash of colour. 'Ours was clean and perfectly adequate, with an attractive modern shower room.' Rooms at the front look all the way to the Small Isles; four at the back have a neat balcony with a table and chairs, overlooking the small terraced garden. The bistro-style restaurant is 'excellent', with a French twist to the modern Scottish menu ('but most of the food was served with chips'). 'I'd go back tomorrow for another of those wonderful chocolate fondants served with home-made Drambuie ice cream.' 'Appetising' breakfasts include Scottish choices, with black pudding and haggis. 'Fascinating' lochside walks. Residents' lounge, restaurant. Free Wi-Fi. Traditional background music. Terraced garden. Children and dogs welcomed. 10 mins' drive from the ferry to and from the Isle of Skye. 6 bedrooms. Per person B&B from £60. Closed Jan.

AUCHENCAIRN Dumfries and Galloway
Map 5:E2
HAZLEFIELD HOUSE, DG7 1RF. Tel 01556 640597, www.hazlefieldhouse. co.uk. 'We had a fantastic stay.' Guests in 2016 'really enjoyed' Moyra and Rod

Davidson's 'relaxing' Georgian B&B, in tranquil farmland with uninterrupted views across the Solway Firth. Set amid extensive lawns and wooded grounds, the 'beautifully presented' B&B has 'a real sense of warmth and welcome' – 'the hosts make it special'. 'Everything is comfortably furnished, with a wood-burner in the living room and books everywhere, which we loved.' Large, 'well-appointed' bedrooms have thoughtful touches, such as a hot-water bottle and a choice of bedding. 'Excellent' home-cooked dinners, based on local and home-grown produce, are available on request (BYOB, no corkage charge). An 'ample and beautifully arranged' breakfast includes home-made marmalade, and honey from hives in the garden. Sitting room/study, dining room. Free Wi-Fi, in-room TV (Freeview). No background music. 4-acre grounds. Drying and storage facilities. Parking. 2 miles from village. 3 bedrooms (1 on ground floor). Per room B&B £80–£90. Closed Christmas, New Year.

BALLYGRANT Argyll and Bute
Map 5:D1

KILMENY COUNTRY HOUSE, Isle of Islay, PA45 7QW. Tel 01496 840668, www.kilmeny.co.uk. 'Fabulous hosts' Margaret and Blair Rozga welcome arriving guests with tea and home-baked cakes at their handsomely furnished 19th-century house in a 300-acre expanse of farmland. Each of the antique-filled, country house-style bedrooms has its own character: two ground-floor rooms have French doors leading to a small, sheltered garden; a suite with its own entrance has a kitchen, and an extra-large bathroom with twin basins, a slipper bath and a walk-in shower. From each room, take in 'spectacular views' over the Islay countryside – complimentary dram of whisky in hand. Come morning, Margaret Rozga's cooking 'is not to be missed' – her tasty breakfasts include home-made bread, oatcakes and preserves. 'Nothing short of excellent.' Drawing room, dining room, sun lounge. Free Wi-Fi, in-room TV (Freeview). No background music. ½-acre garden. ½ mile S of Ballygrant; 10 mins' drive to Port Askaig, for the ferry to the Isle of Jura. Children over 6 welcomed. 5 bedrooms (2 on ground floor). Per room B&B £138–£168. Credit cards not accepted. Closed Nov–Feb.

BARCALDINE Argyll and Bute
Map 5:D1

ARDTORNA, The Mill Farm, PA37 1SE. Tel 01631 720125, www.ardtorna. co.uk. Cresting a small hill, with uninterrupted views to the sea, Sean and Karen O'Byrne's secluded, eco-friendly spot brings Scandinavian style to Loch Creran. The super-modern, open-plan space is filled with splashes of colour against light wood furniture; floor-to-ceiling windows in every bedroom open to stunning sunsets. B&B accommodation is in neat, contemporary bedrooms, each with a king-size bed and underfloor heating. All are supplied with fluffy bathrobes, oversized towels and little extras – hand-made chocolates, complimentary treats in the mini-fridge. Arrive to sweet pastries at teatime; whenever the desire strikes, reach for the help-yourself coffee, malt whisky and home-made whisky cream liqueur in the hallway. Breakfast, in the glass-fronted dining room looking towards the water, has plenty of interesting choices: home-made soda bread, oatcakes, pesto scrambled eggs, a Scottish platter with Stornoway black pudding and tattie scones – all washed down with a freshly blended fruit smoothie or a custom-made Bloody Mary. The hosts have plenty of advice on local itineraries; alternatively, stay on site for a traditional longbow lesson taught by Sean O'Byrne, a former world champion. Dining room. Free Wi-Fi, in-room TV (Freeview). No background music. 1-acre farmland (archery range). Day passes available for the spa, gym and golf course at the Isle of Eriska Hotel (charged extra; see main entry). Children over 12 allowed. 10½ miles N of Oban. 4 bedrooms. Per person B&B £60–£85. 3-night min. stay preferred in twin rooms. Closed Dec–Feb.

BORVE Isle of Harris
Map 5:B1
PAIRC AN T-SRATH, HS3 3HT. Tel 01859 550386, www.paircant-srath. co.uk. Commanding views from Lena and Richard MacLennan's modest guest house on the Isle of Harris stretch over the sound of Taransay; on a clear day, see as far as St Kilda. The house stands on a working croft overlooking the beach at Borve. Inside, find Harris tweed in the simply furnished bedrooms and, in the sitting room, shelves of books to borrow. After a day of hill walking, golfing, cycling, beachcombing or kiting, ease tired muscles in the sauna, then sit down to a home-cooked three-course dinner – perhaps with Harris lobster or scallops from Uist – served by candlelight. Sitting room, dining room (open to non-residents;

no dinners served Sat, May–Sept). Free Wi-Fi. No background music. Sauna. 10 mins' drive from Tarbert ferry terminal. Children and dogs (in 1 room, by prior arrangement) welcomed. Resident dogs. 4 bedrooms. Per person B&B £54. Dinner £37. Closed Christmas, New Year.

BRAE Shetland
Map 5: inset A2
BUSTA HOUSE, ZE2 9QN. Tel 01806 522506, www.bustahouse.com. Make up your own Gothic romance in this characterful small hotel on the sheltered shore of Busta Voe. Most of the house was built in the 1700s, with parts dating back to 1588; it has a quirky layout, creaky floors, lots of stairs, an open peat fire and a friendly ghost. Joe and Veronica Rocks run the show with warmly welcoming staff. Traditionally furnished bedrooms, named after islands around the coast of mainland Shetland, overlook the gardens or the harbour. Choose from an extensive selection of malt whiskies in the bar before tucking in to a generous dinner; informal meals are taken in the lounges. 2 lounges, bar/dining area, Pitcairn restaurant (background music). Free Wi-Fi, in-room TV. Computer for guests' use. Weddings. Garden. Children welcomed. 22 bedrooms. Per room B&B £115–£170. Dinner from £35. Closed for 2 weeks over Christmas and New Year.

BRAEMAR Aberdeenshire
Map 5:C2
CALLATER LODGE, 9 Glenshee Road, AB35 5YQ. Tel 01339 741275, www. callaterlodge.co.uk. Julian and Katy Fennema's granite-built Victorian

shooting lodge is just over a caber's toss from the centre of a town famed for its Highland Games. Comfortable, simply furnished bedrooms are well supplied with guidebooks, local sweets and a daily home-baked treat; find Scottish toiletries, dressing gowns and pre-warmed towels in the bathroom. The B&B is well located for hill walkers and explorers of Royal Deeside; the welcoming hosts provide good route information and substantial packed lunches of sandwiches, home-baked goodies, fruit and a flask of tea. Come evening, return to a comfy seat by the wood-burner in the sitting room, with one of more than 55 malt whiskies. Breakfast is 'extremely good': salmon from Loch Fyne, eggs from resident hens, freshly cooked tattie scones, home-made preserves. Golf courses nearby; Scotland's largest ski resort, Glenshee, is ten minutes' drive away. Sitting room, dining room. Licensed. Free Wi-Fi, in-room TV (Freeview). No background music. 1-acre grounds (mature Scots pine trees, red squirrels, free-range hens). Drying room. Resident dogs. Braemar Gathering (Sept). Children over 8 welcomed. 9 miles S of Braemar. 6 bedrooms (1 family room). Per person B&B from £40.

BRIDGEND Argyll and Bute
Map 5:D1
BRIDGEND HOTEL, PA44 7PJ. Tel 01496 810212, www.bridgend-hotel.com. Roll out the barrel: whisky-sampling opportunities are but moments from this small hotel in a tranquil village close to most of the island's distilleries. It is managed by Lorna McKechnie for the Islay Estates Company. Surrounded by greenery, the hotel has a homely

atmosphere inside, with Islay tablet fudge and locally made toiletries in the tastefully decorated bedrooms. Tuck in to traditional Scottish cuisine in the garden-view restaurant; find pub grub and Islay ales in Katie's Bar; sit down to tea and home-baking in the tartan-carpeted lounge. The hotel has complimentary access to bank fishing, and preferential rates for boats on Islay Estate's trout-fishing lochs. Walkers and cyclists are welcomed (drying room). Lounge, bar, restaurant. Free Wi-Fi, in-room TV (Freeview). Traditional background music. Weddings. Garden, terrace. Children (cot, high chair; extra bed £20 per night) and well-behaved dogs welcomed. Parking. 11 bedrooms (1 family room with bunk bed). Per room B&B from £95, D,B&B from £115. Closed Feb.

BRODICK Ayrshire
Map 5:E1
AUCHRANNIE HOUSE HOTEL, Auchrannie Road, Isle of Arran, KA27 8BZ. Tel 01770 302234, www. auchrannie.co.uk. 'A very special holiday experience.' Part of the Johnston family's large, child-friendly resort, this 19th-century country house, one of two hotels on the extensive estate, has modern bedrooms and 'plush lounges to relax in'. Richard Small is the manager. Choose among the many diversions at the Isle of Arran resort, including three restaurants and two leisure clubs; flip a coin to decide who gets a spa day while the children explore the play barn, splash in the pool or visit the library. When it's time to refuel, head to the informal Brambles for grills, sharing platters and West Coast seafood, check out the laid-back Cruize bar/brasserie

for its child-friendly atmosphere, or sample Scottish-themed tapas at eighteen69, the conservatory restaurant (open for dinner Thurs–Mon). Bar, 3 restaurants. Spa (20-metre indoor pool, steam room, spa bath; gym). Free Wi-Fi, in-room TV (Freeview). Background music. Civil wedding licence, function facilities. 60-acre grounds. Tennis, badminton, bowls; fitness studio; snooker room. Parking. 5 miles from town. Complimentary bus service to and from the ferry terminal 1 mile away. Children (special menu; play barn, outdoor play/picnic area, children's swimming pool, library) and dogs (in some rooms) welcomed. 28 bedrooms (some suitable for disabled), plus Spa Resort rooms and 30 self-catering lodges. Per room B&B from £69, D,B&B from £99.

BRUICHLADDICH Argyll and Bute
Map 5:D1

LOCH GORM HOUSE, Isle of Islay, PA49 7UN. Tel 01496 850139, www.lochgormhouse.com. With stunning vistas across Loch Indaal to the island of Jura, Fiona Doyle's 'gorgeous' stone-built house on the northern shore of Islay is 'a pleasure to stay at'. The 'great' hostess is an accomplished florist and the house is filled with 'magnificent' flower arrangements. Two of the 'sumptuously furnished' bedrooms have spectacular sea views; another overlooks the peaceful garden. Take a drink outside in the summer months; in winter, have a glass by the fire in the large drawing room. Generous breakfasts are 'delicious'. The village distillery is half a mile away; sandy beaches, historic sites and good walks are all close by. Wellies, coats and beach towels are provided;

there are drying facilities, too. Drawing room, dining room. Free Wi-Fi, in-room TV (Freeview). No background music. 1-acre garden. Children welcomed (cot). 3 bedrooms. Per room B&B from £135. Closed Jan–Feb.
25% **DISCOUNT VOUCHERS**

CRINAN Argyll and Bute
Map 5:D1

CRINAN HOTEL, PA31 8SR. Tel 01546 830261, crinanhotel.com. Artist Frances Macdonald and her husband, Nick Ryan, have run their laid-back hotel with 'friendly informality' for nearly half a century. The large, white-painted building is in a 'spectacular position' overlooking the sea and a canal lock. 'Filled with wonderful art', it holds contemporary art exhibitions in its top-floor gallery. Simply furnished bedrooms, each hung with the works of a different Scottish artist, have 'marvellous' views of the rugged coast – ask for one with a private balcony. (Consider discussing room choices before booking – guests this year thought their room needed refreshing.) Watch the daily catch being landed, then served, in the popular, lively Seafood Bar ('it was lovely to know our meal had been caught within hours of eating'). In the loch-facing Westward restaurant, settle in to a menu strong on local seafood. Summer weekends, book a seat in the rooftop restaurant, Lock 16, for a platter of jumbo prawns, devoured while the sun sets over the loch. Feeling inspired? Ask about a painting trip on the hotel's 40-foot motor boat, skippered by the owners' son, the artist Ross Ryan. 2 lounges, bar/bistro, 2 restaurants, coffee shop. Art gallery. Lift. Free Wi-Fi, in-room TV. No background music.

Wedding, function facilities. ¼-acre garden (sheltered spots, spectacular views), patio. Treatment room (health and beauty). Children (£35 per night) and well-behaved dogs (by arrangement; own bedding required; £10 per night; not allowed in Westward restaurant) welcomed. Boat trips can be organised. 6 miles from Lochgilphead. 21 bedrooms (1 suitable for a family). Per room B&B £170–£280, D,B&B £210–£360. Closed Christmas, 4 Jan–end Feb.
25% DISCOUNT VOUCHERS

CUMNOCK Ayrshire
Map 5:E2
DUMFRIES HOUSE LODGE, Dumfries House Estate, KA18 2NJ. Tel 01290 429920, www.dumfrieshouselodge.com. 'We were encouraged to treat the place as our country home.' On the edge of the 2,000-acre Dumfries House estate, this historic 18th-century factor's house was remodelled into a 'luxurious' guest house in 2012. It is managed by Kathleen McLeod for the Prince's Trust. 'Beautifully furnished in grand country house style', it has cosy drawing rooms with open log fires. Traditional bedrooms (some compact) are filled with antiques and hung with period prints and pictures. Each has its own character: two snug single rooms are in the attic; one of the best rooms, with a country cottage feel, has patio doors that open on to the courtyard garden. Guests with limited mobility should discuss room choices before booking: a visitor this year discovered three sets of stairs between the front door and his ground-floor room. Breakfast is served till 10 am. Private tours of Dumfries House – 'a must' – can be booked (£25). Lounge, snug, study, breakfast room. Private function room. Free Wi-Fi, in-room TV (Freeview). No background music. Courtyard gardens in 2,000-acre estate. Children welcomed (though no family rooms). 22 bedrooms (some on ground floor, 13 in courtyard gardens, 1 suitable for disabled), plus 2 self-catering cottages. Per room B&B £85–£150. Closed Dec.

DALKEITH Midlothian
Map 5:D2
THE SUN INN, Lothianbridge, EH22 4TR. Tel 0131 663 2456, www.thesuninnedinburgh.co.uk. The humble, white-painted frontage of this former coaching house on the road to Edinburgh belies the handsomely refurbished interior of the Minto family's 'down-to-earth' gastropub-with-rooms. The original fireplace and old beams have been retained, but modern touches – stylish wallpaper, tweed scatter pillows, cheeky bibelots – bring the rooms bang up to date. Dine on well-regarded pub grub, cooked by chef Barry Drummond with a contemporary twist, in the dining room; the covered courtyard hosts barbecues and spritzers in summer. Work off the meal with a walk through the large grounds, then return to one of the thoughtfully designed bedrooms, each made different with bold prints and hand-crafted furniture. All the rooms are supplied with home-made biscuits, a Roberts radio, a selection of DVDs; the lavish suite has a copper bath big enough for two at the foot of the modern four-poster bed. Light sleepers, take note: the quietest rooms face away from the street. Bar, restaurant (background music; open log fire in winter). Free Wi-Fi, in-room TV (Sky).

Garden. Parking. Children welcomed (special menu). 7 miles S of Edinburgh; National Mining Museum and Dalkeith Country Park are close by. 5 bedrooms (1 suite). Per room B&B £95–£150. Dinner £30.

DERVAIG Argyll and Bute
Map 5:D1

KILLORAN HOUSE, Isle of Mull, PA75 6QR. Tel 01688 400362, www. killoranhouse.co.uk. Amid heather-clad volcanic rocks, Janette and Ian McKilligan's purpose-built guest house on the Isle of Mull stands as a beacon for hill walkers and dog walkers alike. Its hillside position affords excellent countryside rambles, as well as panoramic views over the village and Loch Cuin. Spacious, country-style bedrooms, all on the first floor, have tea- and coffee-making facilities and home-baked treats; find plenty of books, maps and local information in the study. Sit in a comfy armchair in the lounge for pre-dinner drinks, or admire the wonderful views from the decked balcony. Ian McKilligan's daily-changing three-course menu, inspired by local produce, is served in the dining room at 7.30 pm. Lounge, study, dining room. Free Wi-Fi, in-room TV (Freeview). 2 acres of garden/woodland. Parking. Children over 13 and well-behaved dogs welcomed. 1 mile SW of Dervaig on the Calgary road. 5 bedrooms. Per room B&B single £95, double £125–£135. Dinner £33. Closed Nov–Feb.

DORNOCH Highland
Map 5:B2

2 QUAIL, Castle Street, IV25 3SN. Tel 01862 811811, www.2quail.com. Kerensa and Michael Carr's 'very pleasant, comfortable and quiet' guest house occupies a carefully preserved late-Victorian sandstone building close to the cathedral and the Royal Dornoch Golf Club. The elegant Edwardian furnishings, largely family antiques, create a welcoming atmosphere; in cool evenings, sit by the wood-burning stove with one of the many books in the lounge. Well-proportioned bedrooms have tea- and coffee-making facilities and a radio alarm clock; a power shower in the bathroom. Michael Carr, a trained chef, cooks a 'delicious' breakfast; fellow golf enthusiasts, rest assured – breakfast is served from 7 am ('for those with an early tee time'). Dinner menus are tailored to guest preferences. Beautiful stretches of sandy beaches are a short distance away. Lounge/library, dining room. Licensed. Free Wi-Fi, in-room TV (Freeview). No background music. 'Babes in arms' and children over 10 welcomed. 3 bedrooms. Per room B&B £80–£120, D,B&B £101–£141. Closed Christmas.

DULNAIN BRIDGE Highland
Map 5:C2

MUCKRACH COUNTRY HOUSE HOTEL, nr Grantown-on-Spey, PH26 3LY. Tel 01479 851227, www.muckrach. com. Zesty colours and a cheery atmosphere fill the Cowap family's restored Victorian shooting lodge in the Cairngorms national park. Come in to wood-panelled public areas decorated with local artwork, bright modern furnishings and Scottish flourishes; on fine days, find a seat under a large parasol on the slated terrace overlooking pond and pastureland. Named for the region's whisky centres, glamorous heather-toned bedrooms are styled with a crystal chandelier and textured wallpaper; each is supplied with bathrobes, a hospitality tray and the latest gadgetry (smart TV, iPod dock, ceiling speakers). A coffee shop by day, the conservatory doubles as restaurant by night; come dinnertime, book a candlelit table for chef Rayner Muller's 'home-style cooking with a twist'. Whisky is taken seriously here: in the low-lit bar, work your way through more than 70 choices – perhaps with a haggis bonbon or two. Drawing room, library, bar, conservatory restaurant/coffee shop (open to non-residents). Meeting room. Private dining room. Free Wi-Fi, in-room TV (Freeview). Background music. Weddings. 1-acre garden, terraced patio. Drying room. Fishing, shooting, cycling, walking, birdwatching. Children (cots; extra bed £50 charge) and well-behaved dogs (£35 charge) welcomed. 5 miles from Grantown-on-Spey. 13 bedrooms (2 interconnecting rooms suitable for a family; 2 dog-friendly rooms in adjacent building). Per room B&B £99–£309. Dinner £27. Closed Christmas, New Year.

EDINBANE Highland
Map 5:C1

GRESHORNISH HOUSE, Isle of Skye, IV51 9PN. Tel 01470 582266, www.greshornishhouse.com. 'The combination of a very comfortable lounge and a decent range of malts gives this a house-party feel.' Neil and Rosemary Colquhoun's 'highly enjoyable' lochside B&B is in a remote, 'idyllic' location on the Isle of Skye, surrounded by secluded grounds. Mingle with fellow guests around the squashy sofas and log fire in the drawing room; play chess, snooker or two-piano duets in the billiard room. Named after Scottish islands, bedrooms in the Georgian (with Victorian additions) house have 'gorgeous' views of the loch or the garden. In the evening, chef Andrew Macpherson serves an 'excellent' dinner of Scottish classics, by arrangement. The Colquhouns have lived here for nearly 15 years and have much local information to share. 'A highlight was discovering some really unusual destinations, thanks to Neil's in-depth knowledge of Skye.' Drawing room, bar, conservatory, dining room (non-residents welcomed, closed Mon), billiard room. 10-acre grounds. Free Wi-Fi (limited), in-room TV. No background music. Tennis court, croquet lawn. Parking. Children welcomed; dogs by arrangement (£10 per night). Resident Labrador, Soay. Grazing sheep. 8 miles E of Dunvegan. 6 bedrooms (plus 2 attic rooms for family group). Per room B&B £140–£190. Dinner £29.50–£35. 2-night min. stay preferred. Closed Nov–Easter.

EDINBURGH
Map 5:D2

THE BALMORAL, 1 Princes Street, EH2 2EQ. Tel 0131 556 2414, www.roccofortehotels.com/the-balmoral-hotel. Get on board with this city-centre landmark: one of the great railway hotels, this grand Victorian building is today a luxury enterprise (Rocco Forte Hotels) with impressive public spaces, sleek, modern bedrooms and a Michelin-starred restaurant. Franck Arnold is the manager. A kilted doorman ushers guests inside; upstairs, find understated bedrooms with a bathroom of Italian marble. Most rooms have views of Edinburgh Castle. There's plenty of space in which to luxuriate – take afternoon tea under the glass dome and Venetian chandelier of the Palm Court; find your place on one of the tweed sofas in the whisky bar, where there are more than 400 malts, blends and vintages to sip. Sample chef Jeff Bland's much-praised, French-inflected modern Scottish cooking in Number One restaurant; lively Hadrian's brasserie is ideal for informal eating. Crane your neck to peer at the hotel's clock – an iconic feature of the city skyline – before you go: it has been set three minutes fast since 1902, to ensure no one misses their train. Drawing room, 3 bars, restaurant, brasserie. Free Wi-Fi, in-room TV. No background music. Civil wedding licence, conferences. 15-metre indoor swimming pool. Spa (treatment rooms, sauna, gym, exercise studio). Room service; 24-hour concierge. Valet parking. Children welcomed (special menus, amenities). 188 bedrooms (3 suitable for disabled; 20 suites). Per room B&B £252–£790. Dinner £68–£75.

BROOKS HOTEL EDINBURGH, 70–72 Grove Street, EH3 8AP. Tel 0131 228 2323, www.brooksedinburgh.com. The sights of the city are within easy reach from this recently restyled 1840s West End hotel. It is owned by Andrew and Carla Brooks (see also Brooks Guesthouse, Bristol, main entry). A cosy sitting room, with honesty bar, invites lounging: there are newspapers, magazines, board games; an open fire when the weather is brisk. Bedrooms vary in size (there are four categories, plus family rooms that sleep four), but all are pleasingly, understatedly styled, and come equipped with a tea tray,

an iPod docking station and a DVD-player. There is no restaurant, but a short room-service menu of comfort food includes fish pie, prawn curry, vegetable lasagne. Sleep in till late – Scottish breakfasts, with haggis and tattie scones, are served until 11 am at the weekend. Lounge (honesty bar; jazz/contemporary background music), breakfast room. Private dining room. Free Wi-Fi, in-room TV (Freeview). Small conferences. Courtyard garden. Paid parking nearby (£12 per day). Close to the Edinburgh International Conference Centre. Children welcomed (cots, high chairs; extra bed £20). 46 bedrooms (some in annexe; 1 suitable for disabled). Per room B&B £69–£189. Closed 23–27 Dec.

CITYROOMZ EDINBURGH, 25–33 Shandwick Place, EH2 4RG. Tel 0131 229 6871, cityroomz.com. No fancies or frills here – this good-value option is popular for its central location, cheerful, modern decor and straightforward rooms. Fifteen minutes' walk from Haymarket station, and close to all the city's major attractions, it has comfortable bedrooms equipped with tea- and coffee-making facilities, blackout curtains or blinds, an iron and ironing board, and a laptop safe. There are plenty of restaurants nearby; alternatively, eat a takeaway meal in the dining room (crockery and cutlery provided). In the morning, start the day with a continental breakfast buffet (charged extra) in the bright dining area, or take it to go as a breakfast bag with coffee and pastries. Discounts for parking at Castle Terrace car park, close by. Dining room. Lift. Free Wi-Fi, in-room TV (Freeview). Background music. Children welcomed. 72 rooms (9 family rooms with bunk bed). Room £75–£120. Breakfast £7.95.

94DR, 94 Dalkeith Road, EH16 5AF. Tel 0131 662 9265, www.94dr.com. Escape the crowds at Paul Lightfoot and John MacEwan's stylish Southside guest house, a short walk or bus ride from the centre. Sleek bedrooms in the restored Victorian town house have a mix of contemporary and traditional furniture, and modern Scottish artwork; one, which connects to a 'wee dram' (a smaller room with a bunk bed), is ideal for a family. Front-facing rooms have panoramic views of the Salisbury Crags and Arthur's Seat, while those at the back look over the walled gardens towards the Pentland hills. On-screen action and adventure are a DVD away (ask to browse the film library). Come morning, Paul Lightfoot, a trained chef, serves organic breakfasts, including a daily special; breakfast boxes can be brought to the room. The gregarious hosts are eager to help with restaurant, theatre and concert bookings, car hire and guided tours. Lounge (honesty bar), drawing room, breakfast room. Walled garden. Free Wi-Fi, in-room TV (Freeview, Netflix). No background music. Children over 3 welcomed (books, DVDs, games, Xbox). Resident labradoodle, Molli. Pop-up dining event twice a month. 10 mins by bus from the city centre; bicycles are available to borrow. 6 bedrooms (1 interconnecting family room). Per room B&B £80–£200. 2-night min. stay preferred. Closed Christmas Day.

PRESTONFIELD, Priestfield Road, EH16 5UT. Tel 0131 225 7800, www. prestonfield.com. 'An orgy for the senses', James Thomson's opulently decorated baroque mansion, next to Royal Holyrood Park, is a more-is-more celebration of gilded furniture, lavish flower arrangements, swags, velvets and brocades, leather-panelled rooms and black-kilted staff. It is managed by Alan McGuiggan. It has art- and antique-filled bedrooms, each seemingly more indulgent than the other. All have a remarkable bed and views over parkland; a welcome bottle of champagne adds sparkle – if more is needed. Chef John McMahon serves Scottish cuisine in the glamorous Rhubarb restaurant; afternoon tea is taken by a log fire, on the terrace or in a 'Gothic' tea house. More intimate, but no less atmospheric, The Witchery by the Castle (see Shortlist entry), in Edinburgh Old Town, is under the same ownership. 2 drawing rooms, sitting room, salon, library, whisky bar, Rhubarb restaurant. 4 private dining rooms. Lift. Free Wi-Fi, in-room TV. Background music. Civil wedding licence, function facilities. 20-acre grounds (gardens; croquet, putting; secure dog run; paddocks and woodland walk). Terraces, tea house. Parking (reserved parking for disabled). Children (high chair; babysitting by arrangement) and dogs welcomed. 23 bedrooms (5 suites; 1 suitable for disabled). Per room B&B from £335.

THE RAEBURN, 112 Raeburn Place, Stockbridge, EH4 1HG. Tel 0131 332 7000, www.theraeburn.com. Heritage melds with modern at this revamped Georgian house, in the hip and happening Stockbridge neighbourhood. Handsome, practically dashing, bedrooms have an oversized tweed bedhead, and a deep-pile rug on wooden floors; each has a Victorian-style bathroom with a marble shower and vintage-style tiling. Downstairs, the public areas attract the city's smart set: the clubby library has leather seating and floor-to-ceiling shelves of books; the stylish bar (cocktail central) has a terrace for outdoor drinking and dining; the sophisticated brasserie serves Scottish favourites like cullen skink and game pie. The Royal Botanical Gardens are a stroll away. Bar, restaurant, library (available for functions); terrace. Private dining area, conference room. Background music. Free Wi-Fi, in-room TV (Freeview). Garden. Children welcomed (extra beds, cots). 15 mins' walk to the city centre. 10 bedrooms (1 suitable for disabled). Per room B&B £135–£150. Dinner £25. Closed Christmas Day.

THE RUTLAND HOTEL, 1–3 Rutland Street, EH1 2AE. Tel 0131 229 3402, www.therutlandhotel.com. Medical pioneer Sir Joseph Lister once lived in this 19th-century building steps from the top of Princes Street, but there's nothing clinical about the voguish hotel that occupies it today. Steven Simpson manages for owner Nic Wood. With rich fabrics, bold patterns and ornate mirrors, colourful bedrooms have a touch of the baroque – though they're supplied with amenities just right for today: bathrobes, a fully stocked minibar, filter coffee, unusual teas; home-baked shortbread to nibble on arrival. Order hotdogs and small plates in the laid-back Huxley Bar (a fine spot for people-watching); in the smart Kyloe restaurant, chef John Rutter specialises in prime steaks from top Scottish

producers. Most surprising, perhaps, is the Edinburgh Gin Distillery in the basement. Take tours and classes during the day; come evening (Tues–Sun, 5 pm until late), the space morphs into the popular Heads and Tales bar and gin emporium, with a tempting menu of custom cocktails and small bites. 2 bars, restaurant (open to non-residents); private dining room. Lift. Free Wi-Fi, in-room TV (Freeview). Background music. Discounted parking at Castle Terrace car park, nearby. Children welcomed (special menu; iPad in restaurant; £35 charge for bed for over-4s). 11 bedrooms, plus 5 serviced apartments in adjacent buildings. Per room B&B from £135. Dinner £40. Closed Christmas Eve, Christmas Day.
25% DISCOUNT VOUCHERS

SOUTHSIDE GUEST HOUSE, 8 Newington Road, EH9 1QS. Tel 0131 668 4422, www.southsideguesthouse.co.uk. Between the Meadows and Holyrood Park, Franco and Lynne Galgani's welcoming B&B is within easy walking distance of the university and the Old Town; there is a frequent bus service to most destinations in the city. Many original features of the Victorian terraced house have been restored. Well-thought-out bedrooms have comfortable seating and pampering extras; the best have a four-poster bed and an espresso machine. Look forward to bedtime: the friendly hosts offer guests a whisky nightcap. In the morning, 'proper' breakfasts include a daily special, vegetarian options and Buck's Fizz. Breakfast room (light classical background music – 'mostly Bach'). Free Wi-Fi, in-room TV. Limited parking nearby, by prior arrangement. Children over 10 welcomed. 8 bedrooms. Per room B&B single £80–£90, double £100–£160. 2-night min. stay preferred. Closed Christmas.

25% **DISCOUNT VOUCHERS**

TIGERLILY, 125 George Street, EH2 4JN. Tel 0131 225 5005, www. tigerlilyedinburgh.co.uk. There's a swish sense of fun at this playful hotel in New Town, its restrained Georgian exterior giving way to spirited prints, jewel tones and mirror-ball surfaces. Popular with locals, its two bars are opulent and animated (chandeliers, an ever-evolving cocktail list) – just right for a street popular for shopping and nights out. Dine in – the busy restaurant serves a modern menu including steaks and sharing platters – then head to one of the jazzy bedrooms supplied with a pre-loaded iPod and an extensive DVD library. Each is different: a sultry room in black and white has a working fireplace; a glamorous suite has a sleek, modern four-poster bed. 2 bars (resident DJs), restaurant (background music). Lift. Free Wi-Fi, in-room TV. Children welcomed (cot; babysitting by arrangement). 33 bedrooms (some smoking). Per room B&B from £195. Dinner £37.

23 MAYFIELD, 23 Mayfield Gardens, EH9 2BX. Tel 0131 667 5806, www.23mayfield.co.uk. 'We couldn't fault it.' Ross Birnie's 'fantastic' three-storey Victorian house is a short walk from the centre. Original stained-glass windows, polished dark wood and heavy drapes add gravitas to the proceedings, but the sumptuous velvet chaise longues, oversized Connect

Four and Xbox don't let things get too serious. Debate the next move over a game of chess in the drawing room, or settle in to one of the leather sofas with a book from the shelves (wearing gloves, please – the oldest tomes date to the 1740s). Elegant bedrooms are equipped with handcrafted mahogany furniture, quality linen and bathrobes, luxury toiletries. 'My only grouse: showers only – no baths.' Breakfast is hearty; choose from clootie dumplings, tattie scones, haggis, 'a particularly enjoyable smoked herring'. A small back garden has a decked sitting area and a gazebo. Breakfast room (background music), club room. Free Wi-Fi, in-room TV (Freeview). Garden. Children over 3 welcomed. 1 mile S of the city centre; frequent bus service from bus stop just outside; restaurants within walking distance. 7 bedrooms. Per room B&B £80–£170. 2-night min. stay preferred. Closed Christmas.

21212, 3 Royal Terrace, EH7 5AB. Tel 0131 523 1030, www.21212restaurant. co.uk. The Michelin star is the obvious draw, but the bedrooms at Paul Kitching and Katie O'Brien's restaurant-with-rooms are no slouch, either. Light and airy, the large, sleek bedrooms occupy the upper floors of this listed town house, a five-minute walk from the centre. Handsomely styled in forest hues, they have an ample seating area and plenty of storage; their high windows afford impressive views over the city or rear gardens. Take time for pre- and post-dinner drinks in the first-floor drawing room, where oversized windows give good views across Royal Terrace and its gardens to the Firth of Forth and beyond. Afterwards, head into the award-winning restaurant to sample Paul Kitching's intriguing modern menus. Drawing room, restaurant (closed Sun, Mon); private dining rooms. Free Wi-Fi, in-room TV (Freeview). No background music. Children over 5 welcomed. 4 bedrooms. Per room B&B £95–£295. Dinner £55. Closed Christmas Day, Boxing Day, New Year. 2-night min. stay preferred.

THE WITCHERY BY THE CASTLE, Castlehill, The Royal Mile, EH1 2NF. Tel 0131 225 5613, www.thewitchery. com. Fall under the thrall of this dramatic restaurant-with-suites by the gates of Edinburgh Castle, where bewitching candlelit rooms, secret doors, and plenty of nooks and crannies fill the conjoined 16th- and 17th-century buildings. It is owned by James Thomson (see Prestonfield, Edinburgh, Shortlist entry); Jacquie Sutherland is the manager. Astonishing and atmospheric – think tapestries, painted ceilings, antique candlesticks, even a suit of armour – the two dining rooms serve theatrical splendour with their modern Scottish menus. The sumptuous, Gothic-style bedrooms carry on in the same vein. Most are swathed in antique velvet drapes and gold-laced brocade; a tapestry-lined entrance leads into the Turret Suite, whose lucky residents will find a collection of stags' antlers, an oak-panelled bathroom and exceptional views over the city's rooftops. A bottle of champagne is presented on arrival; in the morning, a breakfast hamper is delivered to the room. 2 dining rooms (the Witchery and the Secret Garden). Free Wi-Fi. Background music. Terrace. No children under 18. 9 suites. Per room B&B £325–£395. Dinner £55.

FORT WILLIAM Highland
Map 5:C1
THE LIME TREE, Achintore Road, PH33 6RQ. Tel 01397 701806, www. limetreefortwilliam.co.uk. Guests 'keep coming back' to this well-liked small hotel, restaurant and modern art gallery in a former manse near the town centre. The owner, David Wilson, is a visual artist; his work is displayed, along with that of other artists, throughout the hotel. 'Well designed and decorated', bedrooms overlook garden or loch. Pick one of the best: a smart, understated room with a four-poster king-size bed and views over the water to the hills beyond. Come dinnertime, aptly named chef Andrew Cook adds 'wonderful new ideas' to modern European menus with Scottish overtones. 3 lounges (a map room has books and guides), restaurant (jazz/Scottish background music). Gallery. Free Wi-Fi, in-room TV (Freeview). No background music. Garden with seating area. Drying room; bicycle storage. 5 mins' walk to town centre. Children and supervised dogs (daily charge) welcomed. Resident dog. 9 bedrooms (1 family room; some in modern extension). Per room B&B £90–£120. Dinner £50. Closed last 3 weeks Nov, Christmas, last 3 weeks Jan.

GLASGOW
Map 5:D2
BLYTHSWOOD SQUARE HOTEL, 11 Blythswood Square, G2 4AD. Tel 0141 248 8888, www.blythswoodsquare.com. The former headquarters of the Royal Scottish Automobile Club – 'a lovely building in a beautiful square' – is now home to a slick hotel with a hidden spa below and a clubby atmosphere up above. Murray Thomson is the manager.

'We were impressed with the charm and quiet efficiency of the staff,' say Guide readers in 2016. Red-velvet nooks and modern furnishings offset the sweeping staircase, dramatic public spaces, and original marble floors and pillars. In the 'very comfortable' bedrooms, an opulent bathroom gives 'a real touch of luxury'. Find well-executed meals in the popular restaurant, and well-mixed cocktails in the even more popular bar; champagne afternoon teas are served in the salon. 'Great' breakfasts include a Bloody Mary station. Part of the Principal Hayley group; The Bonham, Edinburgh (see main entry), is under the same ownership. 3 bars, salon, restaurant. Private screening room. Lift. Free Wi-Fi, in-room TV (Sky). Background music. Spa (2 relaxation pools, treatment rooms, rasul mud chamber). Civil wedding licence. Valet parking (from £27.50 for 24 hours). Children (special menu, cot, sofa beds, extra bed; 6–12s £30 per night) and dogs (in some bedrooms; £30) welcomed. 10 mins' walk to Buchanan Street. 100 bedrooms (some suitable for disabled). Per room B&B from £152.

15GLASGOW, 15 Woodside Place, G3 7QL. Tel 0141 332 1263, www.15glasgow.com. Lorraine Gibson's 'well-located' town house B&B is equidistant between the city centre and the fashionable West End. Greenery surrounds: the listed Georgian house nudges the edge of Kelvingrove Park; guests are given access to the leafy private garden across the road; the Botanic Gardens are a good stroll away. Inside, all is elegantly pared down, from the restored original fireplaces and intricate cornicing to the wooden shutters, stained glass and oak panelling. Spacious, high-ceilinged bedrooms have tall windows, mood lighting and a super-king-size bed; Tunnock's teacakes are a sweet gesture. Order breakfast the evening before – it's brought to the room at an agreed time, or can be had, communally, in the lounge. Free Wi-Fi, in-room TV (Freeview). No background music. Small garden. Parking. Children over 5 welcomed (extra bed £20). 5 bedrooms. Per room B&B £130–£165.

GRANTOWN-ON-SPEY Highland Map 5:C2

THE DULAIG, Seafield Avenue, PH26 3JF. Tel 01479 872065, www.thedulaig. com. Returning guests this year praise the 'unfussy feel and understated elegance' of Carol and Gordon Bulloch's 'gorgeous' B&B in an Edwardian country house ten minutes' walk from town. 'Simply wonderful', the hosts welcome guests with the help of the 'cake fairy', who leaves daily freshly baked treats in the spacious, tasteful bedrooms. The house is furnished with a mix of Arts and Crafts antiques and contemporary furniture; the comfortable drawing room has an open log fire. Extensive Scottish breakfasts include haggis, home-made potato scones, and eggs from the Bullochs' brood of free-range Black Rock hens; porridge is served with heather honey, cream and whisky. Packed lunches available. Drawing room, dining room (optional background music). Free Wi-Fi, computer available, in-room TV (Freesat). 1½-acre garden (pond, summer house), veranda. Parking (garage for motorbikes and bicycles). Children over 12 welcomed.

3 bedrooms. Per room B&B £135–£180 (based on two people sharing). Closed Christmas, New Year.

GULLANE East Lothian
Map 5:D3

GREYWALLS, Muirfield, EH31 2EG. Tel 01620 842144, www.greywalls.co.uk. Teatime and tee time are amply provided for at the Weaver family's elegant, 'well-located' hotel (Relais & Châteaux). It is a golfer's paradise, on the edge of Muirfield golf course, with nine other courses nearby. Inside the crescent-shaped stone house designed by Sir Edwin Lutyens, Edwardian dark wood and pale fabrics create a homely atmosphere – a fine backdrop for afternoon tea, with loose-leaf blends, sweetmeats and champagne. (In good weather, move the feast to the tranquil walled gardens, attributed to Gertrude Jekyll.) Each of the traditionally styled bedrooms is individually decorated with antiques and artwork; choose one looking to the Firth of Forth, or over the gardens and farmland to the Lammermuir hills. In Chez Roux restaurant, chef Lee Lawrie's classic French dishes emphasise local ingredients; lighter meals may be taken in the bar/lounge. Duncan Fraser is the manager. Bar/lounge, drawing room, library, conservatory, Chez Roux restaurant (open to non-residents). Free Wi-Fi, in-room TV (Freeview). No background music. Treatments. 6-acre garden. 15 mins' walk to sea. Weddings/ functions. Children (extra bed and breakfast £85) and dogs (in lodges only) welcomed. 23 bedrooms (4 on ground floor; 6 in lodges nearby). Per room B&B single from £85, double from £235. Dinner £40–£45.
25% DISCOUNT VOUCHERS

INNERLEITHEN Scottish Borders
Map 5:E2

CADDON VIEW, 14 Pirn Road, EH44 6HH. Tel 01896 830208, www. caddonview.co.uk. Stephen and Lisa Davies's 'friendly' guest house and restaurant in the Tweed valley is ideally located for walking, fishing, cycling and golf. Tea and home-baked cakes await arriving guests. Neat bedrooms in the handsome Victorian house vary in size and style; all have plenty of wardrobe space, complimentary toiletries in the shower- or bathroom, tea- and coffee-making facilities, bottled water. Five nights a week, Stephen Davies serves a Scottish menu in the candlelit dining room; game such as venison, duck and partridge are used in season. (Room snacks are available when the restaurant is closed for dinner on Sunday and Monday.) A leisurely breakfast is served until 10 am. Drawing room (books, guides, games), dining room (background music; no dinner Sun, Mon). Free Wi-Fi, in-room TV (Freeview). ½-acre mature garden. Storage for bicycles and fishing gear. Picnics available. Parking. Well-behaved children and dogs (in 1 bedroom, by arrangement; £5 per night charge) welcomed. Resident dogs. 8 bedrooms. Per room B&B £70–£110, D,B&B £130–£170. Closed Christmas.
25% DISCOUNT VOUCHERS

INVERNESS Highland
Map 5:C2

MOYNESS HOUSE, 6 Bruce Gardens, IV3 5EN. Tel 01463 233836, www. moyness.co.uk. Handy for the town centre, Wilma and John Martin's homely B&B is within walking distance of restaurants, Eden Court Theatre and the riverside. The white-painted Victorian villa stands in a pretty garden on a quiet residential street; inside, 'comfortable', individually styled bedrooms are supplied with bathrobes, toiletries, a clock radio and a hospitality tray. 'Good' Scottish breakfasts include eggs from the garden hens. Sitting room, dining room. ½-acre garden. Free Wi-Fi, in-room TV. No background music. Parking. Children welcomed (high chair, cot, extra bed). 6 bedrooms (1 family room). Per room B&B £73–£110. Closed Christmas.

TRAFFORD BANK GUEST HOUSE,

96 Fairfield Road, IV3 5LL. Tel 01463 241414, www.traffordbankguesthouse. co.uk. 'So much thought' has gone into Lorraine Pun's 'beautifully decorated' B&B, say guests this year. Convenient for the town, the bay-windowed, sandstone Victorian house is filled with polished wood, bold colours and squashy sofas. In the garden, find a surprise round every corner: interesting sculptures dot the grounds. Each of the large, bright bedrooms is well equipped with a mini-fridge, espresso machine and useful amenities (iPod dock, ironing board, hairdryer, hair straightener). Served in the conservatory overlooking the lovely garden, a 'great' breakfast (ordered the evening before) includes home-made scones and oatcakes. Joggers, bring your running shoes: excellent paths unfurl along the nearby Caledonian Canal. 2 lounges, conservatory breakfast room. Free Wi-Fi, in-room TV (Freeview). No background music. ½-acre garden. Children over 5 welcomed. 10 mins' walk from the centre. 5 bedrooms. Per room B&B £94–£140. Closed 21 Nov–10 Jan.

KILMARTIN Argyll and Bute
Map 5:D1

DUNCHRAIGAIG HOUSE, nr Lochgilphead, PA31 8RG. Tel 01546 510396, www.dunchraigaig.co.uk. Standing stones, chambered cairns and impressive henges pepper the prehistoric landscape that surrounds this good-value B&B, itself set opposite an ancient stone circle. 'A delightful couple', Cameron Bruce and Lynn Jones, the owners, are a fount of knowledge on the area, including the best picnic and nature spots. 'Relaxing' bedrooms (with a 'sparkling' bathroom) are traditionally decorated; from rear, woodland-facing rooms, look out for visiting deer and pine martens. Breakfast includes home-made marmalade, jam from garden fruit, and eggs from the resident hens; muffins or rolls are baked daily. Lounge (books, games, information), dining room. Free Wi-Fi, in-room TV (Freeview). No background music. ½-acre garden. Packed lunches £5. Parking. Children over 12 welcomed. 1 mile S of village, 7 miles N of Lochgilphead. 5 bedrooms (1 room accessed via external stairs). Per person B&B £37.50–£50. Closed Dec–Feb. Credit cards not accepted.
25% DISCOUNT VOUCHERS

KIPPEN Stirlingshire
Map 5:D2

THE CROSS KEYS, Main Street, FK8 3DN. Tel 01786 870293, www. kippencrosskeys.com. One of Scotland's oldest, Debby McGregor and Brian Horsburgh's unpretentious inn, tucked between the Gargunnock and Fintry hills, has served as a gateway to the far north for 300 years. Craig Fraser is the manager. The bar is snug, rustic and full of character – just the thing for the lively gathering of locals, walkers, families and dogs who regularly drop by. Choose from a wide selection of whiskies and real ales under the low lintels; log fires keep things toasty in winter. Simple, modern bedrooms have crisp white linen, a television and a small selection of DVDs; underfloor heating in the bathroom. Award-winning Scottish fare – refined pub grub – is cooked by chef Liam Davies using local lamb, and sausages, haggis and black pudding from the butcher across the road. In balmy weather, eat alfresco on the terrace or in the spacious enclosed garden. Bar, dining areas, private dining room. Free Wi-Fi, in-room TV (Freeview). Background music. Civil wedding licence. Beer garden, terrace. Children (extra bed £10 per night) and dogs (£10 per night) welcomed. 10 miles W of Stirling. 3 bedrooms. Per room B&B £55–£90. Dinner £25. Closed Christmas Day, New Year's Day.

LOCHRANZA Ayrshire
Map 5:D1

APPLE LODGE, Isle of Arran, KA27 8HJ. Tel 01770 830229, www.applelodgearran.co.uk. Don't forget the binoculars: Jeannie and John Boyd's welcoming B&B is set in countryside on the Isle of Arran, where red deer and eagles are often spotted. The white-painted Edwardian manse has traditionally furnished bedrooms, each supplied with a hot drinks tray, books and plenty of local information; a self-contained suite with a sitting room and kitchen has French doors opening on to the garden. Breakfast is served at table. On a small sea loch, the village

has a castle and a whisky distillery with a visitor centre. Set out on good walks from the door. The Kintyre ferry docks at the pier 1 mile away. Lounge, dining room. Free Wi-Fi, in-room TV (Freeview). No background music. ¼-acre mature garden. Parking. 4 bedrooms (1 on ground floor). Children over 12 welcomed. Per person B&B £39–£45. 3-night min. stay. Closed mid-Dec–mid-Jan.

MELROSE Scottish Borders
Map 5:E3

BURT'S, Market Square, TD6 9PL. Tel 01896 822285, www.burtshotel. co.uk. An abundance of fish and game are within a stone's throw (a fly cast, or an arrow sling) of the Henderson family's 'excellent', well-established hotel in a lovely Borders town. Floral displays and Scottish-flavoured accents bedeck the listed, white-painted 18th-century building near the banks of the River Tweed. In the 'immaculate', traditionally furnished bedrooms (some small), find jazzy splashes of colour against an understated background. Each room is supplied with a radio alarm clock, tea- and coffee-making facilities, Scottish toiletries. At dinner, head to the busy restaurant for chef Trevor Williams's modern Scottish dishes; lunches and casual suppers may be taken in the bar, over a whisky from the menu of more than 90 single malts. The Hendersons also own The Townhouse, across the square (see next entry). 2 lounges, bistro bar, restaurant (closed for lunch Mon–Sat), private dining room. Free Wi-Fi, in-room TV (Freeview). Background music. Weddings, functions. ½-acre garden. Parking. Children (no under-8s in restaurant) and dogs (in some rooms) welcomed. 20 bedrooms. Per room B&B single from £75, double from £140, D,B&B single from £99, double from £188. Dinner £28. Closed 24–26 Dec.

THE TOWNHOUSE, Market Square, TD6 9PQ. Tel 01896 822645, www.thetownhousemelrose.co.uk. In the centre of town, the Henderson family's smart, modern hotel is liked for its 'excellent' food and 'extremely pleasant, helpful staff'. Sister hotel Burt's (see previous entry) is across the market square. Inviting, individually styled bedrooms vary in size – spacious superior rooms have a comfortable seating area – but all are well supplied with a tea and coffee tray, and complimentary Scottish-made toiletries. Chef Johnny Millar cooks informal meals in the brasserie; the elegant restaurant has chef's specials and tasting menus (plus a sticky toffee pudding 'to die for'). Breakfast is 'just lovely'. 'Good walking nearby.' Bar/brasserie, restaurant (background music); conservatory, patio/decked area. Free Wi-Fi, in-room TV (Freeview). Weddings/functions. Parking. Children welcomed (special menu; family rooms). 11 bedrooms (1 on ground floor). Per room B&B single from £97, double from £134, D,B&B single from £120, double from £186. Dinner £35.50. Closed Christmas Day, Boxing Day.

MOFFAT Dumfries and Galloway
Map 5:E2
HARTFELL HOUSE & THE LIMETREE RESTAURANT, Hartfell Crescent, DG10 9AL. Tel 01683 220153, www.hartfellhouse.co.uk. Robert and Mhairi Ash run their 'good-value' guest house in a 'pleasant' town close to the scenic Southern Upland Way. Traditionally decorated public rooms in the listed stone-built Victorian house retain ornate cornices and woodwork; the 'nice' sitting room upstairs has wide views of the countryside. Bedrooms have Scottish biscuits, fine toiletries, a bed with a memory foam mattress; family rooms are available. 'It's easy to see why the restaurant is so popular with locals': Matt Seddon's modern Scottish dishes (the chef promises 'big flavour and no fuss') are 'excellent'. Wake to a 'good' breakfast: freshly ground coffee, home-baked bread, home-made preserves. Easy access to the M74; a good stop for travellers to and from the Western Isles. Lounge, restaurant (classical background music; closed Sun, Mon). Free Wi-Fi, in-room TV (Freeview). Garden. Bicycle storage, parking. Cooking classes. Children welcomed (high chair, cot). 5 mins' walk from the town centre. 7 bedrooms (plus self-catering cottage in the grounds). Per room B&B £75. Closed Christmas.

NAIRN Highland
Map 5:C2
SUNNY BRAE, Marine Road, IV12 4EA. Tel 01667 452309, www.sunnybraehotel.com. John Bochel and Rachel Philipsen's 'good-value' small hotel is a short walk from the beach. Overlooking the green and the promenade, its glass-fronted lounge faces 'the panorama of the sea'. On a fine day, spend the afternoon in the suntrap hedged garden, surrounded by flowerbeds. Well-equipped bedrooms are traditionally decorated in 'light, cheerful' colours; four have views over the Moray Firth. At dinner, John Bochel's 'homely, competently prepared'

Scottish dishes have a European twist; a 'good choice of wine' and more than 100 malt whiskies provide liquid accompaniment. Good variety at breakfast. Lounge, dining room ('easy listening' background music). Free Wi-Fi, in-room TV (Freeview). ½-acre garden, terrace. Parking. Children welcomed (cot). 8 bedrooms (1 suitable for disabled). Per room B&B £80–£170. Dinner £35. Closed Nov–mid-Feb.
25% DISCOUNT VOUCHERS

OBAN Argyll and Bute
Map 5:D1
GREYSTONES, 1 Dalriach Road, PA34 5EQ. Tel 01631 358653, www.greystonesoban.co.uk. A gem in a stunning setting, Mark and Suzanne McPhillips's modern B&B inhabits the former home of a Scottish diamond mine owner. The historically fascinating Scottish baronial mansion (later a hospital) rears grandly on a short, steep slope to overlook the bay, yet is within easy walking distance of the town centre, harbour and seafood restaurants. Inside, period features such as stained-glass windows, moulded ceilings and a fine wooden staircase are paired with understated furnishings and contemporary art. Fresh and bright, chic bedrooms are minimalist, with a spacious bathroom; most have sea views. Breakfast on porridge with apricots or a cheesy spinach frittata, watching the activity on the bay below. Fancy a day out? The obliging hosts are pleased to share itineraries for favourite trips around the Inner Hebrides. Sitting room, dining room. Free Wi-Fi, in-room TV (Freeview). No background music. ½-acre garden. Parking. 5 bedrooms. Per room B&B £120–£170. Closed Dec–Jan.

PEEBLES Scottish Borders
Map 5:E2
THE HORSESHOE RESTAURANT, Eddleston, EH45 8QP. Tel 01721 730225, www.horseshoeinn.co.uk. Less is more at David Downie's sophisticated restaurant-with-rooms, where the overriding philosophy is to 'keep it small and do it well'. It is in a tiny village a few miles north of Peebles; Mark Slaney is the manager. The well-regarded restaurant occupies a former inn: mingle with fellow guests over a pre-dinner drink in the snug, flagstone-floored lounge; in the elegant dining room, chef Alistair Craig's modern British menus showcase Scottish produce (Stornoway scallops, Eyemouth crab, Shetland fish, Scottish lamb), and vegetables and herbs from the kitchen garden. Eat well, then head across the rear courtyard to one of the 'modest' bedrooms ('small', some guests comment) in a converted Victorian schoolhouse. Each is well equipped with bathrobes and organic toiletries; a hospitality tray holds fruit, home-made cake and fresh milk. Breakfast has local honey and home-made jams and marmalade. Excellent walks from the front door. Lounge, restaurant. Private dining room. Small kitchen garden. Free Wi-Fi, in-room TV (Freeview). Background music, occasionally live jazz. Parking. Children (no under-5s in restaurant) and well-behaved dogs (in some rooms; £10 per night) welcomed. 8 bedrooms. Per room B&B £140–£165. Dinner £30–£50, tasting menu £60. Closed Mon, Tues; 2 weeks Jan, 2 weeks July.

PERTH Perth and Kinross
Map 5:D2
PARKLANDS, 2 St Leonard's Bank, PH2 8EB. Tel 01738 622451, www.theparklandshotel.com. In terraced gardens overlooking South Inch

Park, Penny and Scott Edwards have refurbished their bright, modern hotel with an assured touch. Colourful and contemporary, bedrooms in the Victorian stone-built house have a smart TV and digital radio; tea- and coffee-making facilities are provided. A triple room can accommodate a small family. There's a choice of eating places: fine-dining 63@Parklands has modern Scottish menus; informal No. 1 The Bank Bistro has à la carte and grill dishes. Guests this year thought the hotel 'great' for visitors with dogs: 'the big, open park right outside is ideal for dog walking'. A short walk from the town centre, train and bus stations. Lounge, bar, 2 restaurants. Private dining room. Free Wi-Fi, in-room TV. Background music. Weddings, functions. ½-acre garden leading to park; terrace (alfresco dining). Parking. Children and dogs welcomed. 15 bedrooms (4 on ground floor; 1 family room). Per person B&B from £59.50, D,B&B from £75. Closed Christmas–5 Jan.

SUNBANK HOUSE, 50 Dundee Road, PH2 7BA. Tel 01738 624882, www. sunbankhouse.com. Vibrant Perth nightlife and lively café culture along the River Tay are all within walking distance of Remigio and Georgina Zane's unpretentious, traditionally furnished Victorian house on the outskirts of town. Bedrooms, including family rooms, are spacious and comfortable; those at the back are quietest. Mingle over drinks in the fire-lit lounge, then dine on 'Remo' Zane's uncomplicated, Italian-inflected dinners (booking advised). Out on the trot? Sandwiches and snacks are

served until late in the lounge. Plentiful breakfasts have lots of choice (special diets catered for); packed lunches and picnics are available on request. The hosts have heaps of local information for guests eager to explore the surrounding area. Lounge/bar, restaurant (light background music). Free Wi-Fi, in-room TV (Freeview). Weddings, functions. ½-acre garden, terrace. Parking. Children and dogs (£15 charge) welcomed. Parking. ½ mile NE of town centre. 10 bedrooms (some on ground floor; 2 suitable for disabled; 2 family rooms). Per person B&B from £50, D,B&B from £65.

PITLOCHRY Perth and Kinross Map 5:D2
EAST HAUGH HOUSE, by Pitlochry, PH16 5TE. Tel 01796 473121, www. easthaugh.co.uk. Swap the rat race for riverside rambles and woodland walks: the McGown family's friendly country hotel, in a 17th-century turreted house, is surrounded by large grounds not far from the rivers Tummel and Tay. Sophie McGown is the manager. Tartan and toile de Jouy adorn the cheering, comfortable bedrooms, each thoughtfully supplied with home-baked shortbread and fresh milk. All the rooms are different: one has a peat fire, another a four-poster bed; some are snug, others have a spa bath in a spacious bathroom. In the restaurant, chef Krys Krerowicz focuses on seasonal seafood and game. Outdoorsy guests will find plenty of diversion. Anglers have use of the fishing lodge, with barbecue and cooking facilities, on the River Tay; for stalkers and shooters, days out on nearby estates are regularly arranged. Lounge, bar, restaurant

(background music); patio. Free Wi-Fi, in-room TV (Freeview). Civil wedding licence, function facilities. 3-acre grounds; river beat. Parking. Children and dogs (by arrangement, 3 ground-floor rooms have a pooch porch; £10 per night) welcomed. 1½ miles S of town centre. 12 bedrooms (1 suitable for disabled; 5 in a converted 'bothy' adjacent to the hotel), plus 2 self-catering cottages. Per room B&B from £110, D,B&B from £160. Closed 1 week over Christmas, open New Year.
25% DISCOUNT VOUCHERS

PINE TREES, Strathview Terrace, PH16 5QR. Tel 01796 472121, www.pinetreeshotel.co.uk. Keep an eye out for roe deer and red squirrels in the extensive grounds of Valerie and Robert Kerr's 'warm and welcoming, friendly and quiet' hotel. The 'beautiful' Victorian mansion is set into hillside dotted with pine trees; within, find cosy public areas, 'very comfortable', traditionally decorated bedrooms, and a host of single malt whiskies. Scottish-influenced dishes cooked by new chef Eric Toralba are served in the restaurant overlooking the garden. Fishing breaks may be organised; theatre packages raise the curtain on the town's cultural scene. 3 lounges (log fire), bar, restaurant. Free Wi-Fi (in lounge), in-room TV (Freeview). Soft background music in the evenings. 7-acre grounds. Parking. Children (in Coach House; special menu; cot; extra bed charged) and well-behaved dogs (£7.50 per night) welcomed. ¼ mile N of town. 29 bedrooms (3 in annexe, 6 in Coach House; 7 on ground floor). Per person B&B from £54, D,B&B from £74.

PORT APPIN Argyll and Bute
Map 5:D1

THE PIERHOUSE, PA38 4DE. Tel 01631 730302, www.pierhousehotel.co.uk. 'We were entranced by the ever-changing scenery.' Journey down a single-track road to find Nick and Nikki Horne's 'pretty little hotel' and restaurant in a 'beautiful' setting beside Loch Linnhe. The 19th-century piermaster's house has spectacular views to the Isle of Lismore: peer through huge picture windows at the daily catch being landed, then feast on chef Laura Milne's 'excellent' seafood, including loch-sourced mussels and langoustines, and lobsters and crabs caught at the end of the pier. A small selection of vegetarian, meat and wild game dishes is also available. Breezy, simply decorated bedrooms facing sea or hillside are in a separate wing; the best, looking towards the islands of Lismore and Shuna, have a seating area. 'We could hear the gentle lap of the waves just outside the window.' A terrace leads directly to the shore. Lounge, Ferry bar, snug (books, wood-burning stove), restaurant. Private dining room. Terrace. Free Wi-Fi, in-room TV (Freeview). Celtic and 'easy listening' background music. Civil wedding licence. Sauna, treatments available. Parking. Yacht moorings. Mountain bike hire. Children (special menu; high chair, rollaway bed; 2–12s £30 per night) and dogs (in some rooms; £15 per night) welcomed. 20 miles N of Oban. 12 bedrooms (3 family rooms). Per room B&B from £90. Dinner £35–£40. Closed 24–26 Dec.

ST ANDREWS Fife
Map 5:D3

RUFFLETS, Strathkinness Low Road, KY16 9TX. Tel 01334 472594, www.rufflets.co.uk. A turreted 1920s mansion, built for the widow of a Dundee jute baron, now houses this 'extremely welcoming', family-owned hotel. It is managed by Stephen Owen, with 'excellent' staff. There's an elegant country house feel to the place, from the 'beautiful', award-winning gardens to the smart public rooms – find a spot for dancin' and romancin' along streams, on bridges and around the mature trees in the extensive grounds. Individually styled bedrooms are spread across the main building, and the lodge and gatehouse in the gardens. Each has its own charm, though all are supplied with bathrobes, top-end toiletries and home-made shortbread; a hot-water bottle is tucked under the covers on cool nights. Ask for a turret room, with extra seating and good views. In the Terrace restaurant overlooking the formal gardens, dine on a modern Scottish menu – home-grown fruit and vegetables are used, in season. Drawing room (open fire), library, bar, Terrace restaurant (background music). Free Wi-Fi, in-room TV. Civil wedding licence, function facilities. 10-acre grounds. Children (£20) and dogs (in some rooms, by arrangement; £10 per night) welcomed. 1½ miles W of town. 24 bedrooms (5, on ground floor, in gatehouse and lodge; 2 family rooms; 1 suitable for disabled), plus 3 self-catering cottages in gardens. Per room B&B £120–£430. Dinner £35.

SANQUHAR Dumfries and Galloway
Map 5:E2

BLACKADDIE HOUSE, Blackaddie Road, DG4 6JJ. Tel 01659 50270, www.blackaddiehotel.co.uk. 'Lovely, warm and welcoming', Ian and Jane McAndrew's restaurant-with-rooms,

in a 'beautiful' 16th-century stone-built manse, is 'well worth a detour for the food alone'. The chef/patron has received a Michelin star for his past cooking; guests this year confirm that his fine-dining and eight-course tasting menus, using much local produce, are still 'a culinary triumph'. (Breakfast is 'just as good'.) Bedrooms (some undergoing refurbishment as the Guide went to press) have views over the garden and the River Nith, or towards the hills of Dumfries and Galloway; each is supplied with tea- and coffee-making facilities, home-made shortbread, Scottish tablet and bottled water. Adjacent to the hotel, the River Suite ('very peaceful and private') has its own patio, with a magnificent view of the river. Bring young gourmands: 'The kids were made as welcome as we were.' Bar, restaurant, breakfast/function room, library, conservatory. Free Wi-Fi (can be limited), in-room TV (Freeview). 'Easy listening' background music. Weddings, functions. 2-acre grounds. Good riverbank walks, cycling. Cookery school. Fishing, shooting, photography breaks. Parking. Children (extra bed; over-5s £20 per night) and dogs (in some rooms; £10 per night) welcomed. 7 bedrooms (1 suite), plus two 2-bedroom self-catering cottages. Per room B&B from £120. Dinner £55, tasting menu £75.
25% DISCOUNT VOUCHERS

SLEAT Highland
Map 5:C1

DUISDALE HOUSE, Isle of Skye, IV43 8QW. Tel 01471 833202, www.duisdale.com. Transformed from a Victorian hunting lodge, Anne Gracie and Ken Gunn's friendly hotel on the

Isle of Skye updates Highland heritage with a stylish touch. Overlooking the gardens, the Highlands or the Sound of Sleat, modern bedrooms are decorated with bold colours and sumptuous fabrics. Take afternoon tea by the log fire in the lounge or outside on the south-facing deck; pick a pre-dinner tipple among the wines, whiskies and gins to sip in the Chart Room. In the restaurant, sample chef Brian Ross's daily-changing modern Scottish menus, which use seasonal produce from the island and Highlands. From April to September, take to the high seas: book the hotel's luxury yacht for a day, with lunch and champagne included (whales, dolphins, seals and seabirds optional). The Gunns also own Toravaig House nearby (see main entry). Lounge, bar, restaurant, conservatory. Free Wi-Fi, in-room TV (Sky). Background music. Weddings. 35-acre grounds (10-person garden hot tub). Parking. Children (over-4s £65) welcomed. 7 miles from Broadford. 18 bedrooms (2 family rooms; 1 garden suite in annexe, suitable for disabled). Per person B&B £84–£174, D,B&B £133–£223.

SPEAN BRIDGE Highland
Map 5:C2
SMIDDY HOUSE, Roy Bridge Road, nr Fort William, PH34 4EU. Tel 01397 712335, www.smiddyhouse.com. 'It gets better and better.' Robert Bryson and Glen Russell extend 'the warmest of welcomes' at their restaurant-with-rooms on the scenic West Highland rail route. Arrive to a light afternoon tea in the garden room, or show up in the evening, in time for sherry and home-made shortbread. 'Beautifully decorated' in calming shades, bedrooms

are 'very comfortable', with bottled water, tea- and coffee-making facilities, lots of toiletries; a spacious suite sleeps four. Award-winning Russell's restaurant uses shellfish from the sea and organic salads from the Isle of Skye; 'excellent' vegetarian options are available. Good variety at breakfast. The hosts have plenty of information on walking, fishing, stalking, cycling and golf. Garden room, restaurant (booking essential; restricted opening Nov–Mar). Free Wi-Fi, in-room TV (Freeview). Classical background music. Parking. Golf, mountain bike trails nearby. 9 miles N of Fort William. 4 bedrooms (plus self-catering accommodation in adjacent building). Per room B&B £120–£150 (suite £165–£210). Closed Christmas and New Year.
25% DISCOUNT VOUCHERS

STIRLING Stirlingshire
Map 5:D2
POWIS HOUSE, FK9 5PS. Tel 01786 460231, www.powishouse.co.uk. Beneath the Ochil hills, nine acres of woodland set Jane and Colin Kilgour's listed Georgian mansion well away from crowds and light pollution. (Astronomers-in-training, stargazers and campfire enthusiasts, look no further for dark skies and the celestial wash.) Choose among rustic, spic-and-span bedrooms in the carefully restored and well-documented home (it was built in 1746): retaining original features such as a Georgian fireplace and polished flooring, they're made homely and welcoming with handmade Harris Tweed curtains and bed throws, and a bowl of fresh fruit. For a quirkier option, ask about the gypsy caravans in the grounds: in a secluded tree-lined

glade, with views of the oak field and the resident sheep, each comes supplied with top-quality bedding, and tea- and coffee-making facilities. Ample breakfasts, served in the sun-drenched dining room, include eggs from the Kilgours' hens. Lounge (open fire, board games, DVDs), dining room. Free Wi-Fi, in-room TV (Freeview). No background music. Terrace, garden (ha-ha; listed shafted stone sundial). Parking. Grazing sheep. Children welcomed (cots, extra beds; over-2s £10 per night). 3 miles E of town. 3 bedrooms (plus 3 gypsy caravans). Per room B&B £100. Closed Christmas–Feb.

VICTORIA SQUARE, 12 Victoria Square, FK8 2QZ. Tel 01786 473920, www.victoriasquareguesthouse.com. In the peaceful, tree-lined King's Park conservation area – 'quite a smart part of town' – Kari and Phillip Couser's guest house occupies a 'lovely' double-fronted Victorian building on a stately square. Inside, there are claw-footed baths, graceful bay window seats, and just enough thistle and tartan. Over welcome refreshments, take in the view through huge windows, and the notable decorative ceiling in the lounge. Follow the ironwork balustrades up to most of the elegant, individually decorated bedrooms, each with a seating area; they are well supplied with bathrobes, Scottish toiletries, tea- and coffee-making equipment and bottled water. Mornings, find juices, fruit, yogurt and pastries on the breakfast buffet; cooked dishes include pancakes with home-made fruit compote, and poached eggs with haggis. Lounge, breakfast room. Free Wi-Fi, in-room smart TV (Freeview). No background music. Garden. Parking. Children over

12 welcomed. ½ mile to city centre and Stirling Castle. 7 bedrooms (1 on ground floor). Per room B&B from £99. Closed Christmas.

STRACHUR Argyll and Bute
Map 5:D1

THE CREGGANS INN, PA27 8BX. Tel 01369 860279, www.creggans-inn.co.uk. 'A very attractive hotel in a glorious location.' On the shores of Loch Fyne, Gill and Archie MacLellan's 'welcoming' white-painted inn sits comfortably on the shoreline. A team of 'attentive, friendly' staff welcomes visitors. The pretty bedrooms are bright and light; many have 'breathtaking' views. 'Our standard room was large, with a huge bed, an enormous bath, and stunning views across the loch.' An upstairs lounge also overlooks the water, its vista 'especially fine at sunset'. The popular bistro and restaurant serve the cream of Argyll's crops (though regular Guide readers in 2016 thought the cooking needed sharpening up). Good choices at breakfast include hot chocolate; apricots poached in honey and spices; traditional Scottish porridge with cream 'and perhaps a wee dram'. Two moorings are available to guests arriving by boat. 2 lounges, Macphunn's bar/bistro (background music), restaurant. Free Wi-Fi, in-room TV (Freeview). Weddings/functions. 1-acre grounds; pebble beach. Fishing rods to borrow. Resident dogs, Hector and Boo. 1 hour from Glasgow. 14 bedrooms. Per person B&B from £95. Dinner £30. Closed Christmas.

SWINTON Scottish Borders
Map 5:E3

THE WHEATSHEAF, Main Street, TD11 3JJ. Tel 01890 860257, www.wheatsheaf-swinton.co.uk. Low-key

hospitality and high warmth of feeling make this roadside destination popular with locals and visitors alike. Opposite the village green, the cosy, rough-hewn inn has comfortable, country-style accommodation and an award-winning restaurant. Bright, traditionally furnished bedrooms have pleasing splashes of colour in linen and wool, and a bath or shower room; home-made shortbread is provided. In cool weather, sit by the open fire in the tartan-walled lounge/bar; when the sun's out, find one of the picnic tables in the beer garden. Fresh fish and seafood from nearby Eyemouth dominate the menu. Extensive wine cellar; large collection of single malt whiskies. Lounge/bar, 3 dining areas. Free Wi-Fi, in-room TV (Freeview). 'Easy listening' background music. Functions. Small beer garden. Children (cot; extra bed £20 per night) and dogs (in 2 rooms and Myrtle Cottage) welcomed. 12 bedrooms (1 cottage room, 20 yds from main house; 1 suitable for disabled). Per person B&B from £59.50, D,B&B from £80. Closed 22–26 Dec.
25% DISCOUNT VOUCHERS

TARBERT Argyll and Bute
Map 5:D1

WEST LOCH HOTEL, Campbeltown Road (A83), PA29 6YF. Tel 01880 820283, www.westlochhotel.com. Andrew and Rosaline Ryan's small hotel at the top of the Kintyre peninsula overlooks the loch from which it takes its name. 'A home away from home' – if home has a similarly impressive collection of rare and limited-batch whiskies – it is liked for its 'warm and welcoming' atmosphere. 'They know how to look after you here,'

say regular visitors in 2016. Many of the simply furnished bedrooms in the white-painted 18th-century coaching inn have restful views across the water. In the rustic restaurant, chef Ross Payne serves 'divine' seasonal Scottish menus. 'The fish is especially good, as it comes straight from the sea and on to your plate.' Close to the ferries for Islay, Arran and Gigha. 2 lounges, bar (log fire), restaurant. Function room. Free Wi-Fi, in-room TV (Freeview). Background jazz. Parking. Children and dogs (not in restaurant; £4.50 per night) welcomed. 1 mile from village. 8 bedrooms. Per room B&B single from £49.50, double from £89.50. Dinner £24.

TARLAND Aberdeenshire
Map 5:C3

DOUNESIDE HOUSE, nr Aboyne, AB34 4UL. Tel 013398 81230, www.dounesidehouse.co.uk. On the MacRobert estate in the heart of Royal Deeside, this crenellated country house with turrets and a tower reopened as a luxury hotel and leisure club following extensive renovation in 2016. Choose one of the newly appointed bedrooms, apartments or cottages. Rooms in the main house are characterful, with antiques and artwork; in the grounds, four cottages have their own patio, and a wood-burning stove in the sitting room. Families or large groups might consider one of the modern, architect-designed apartments next to the main building. There's plenty to explore, from the restored tennis court to the state-of-the-art gym, pool and sauna, to the open, fire-warmed library. The extensive grounds include immaculate terraced gardens. Come dinnertime, sit down to modern Scottish dishes using garden-fresh produce whenever possible. Cairngorms national park is on the doorstep. The building is the ancestral home of the three MacRobert brothers killed in flying incidents (two while on active duty during World War II); in honour of their memory, the house is reserved for military guests over six weeks in summer and during the Christmas period. Bar, parlour, library, bistro/restaurant (background music), conservatory. Free Wi-Fi, in-room smart TV (Freeview). Background music. 7-acre grounds, gardens. Tennis court, croquet lawn, putting green. Health centre (indoor pool, spa, steam room; gym, fitness studio; games room). Children (playpark; high tea) and dogs (in cottages only; £20) welcomed. 23 bedrooms (9 in cottages in the grounds), plus 4 apartments in Casa Memoria. Per room B&B from £130, D,B&B from £180.

25% DISCOUNT VOUCHERS

TAYNUILT Argyll and Bute
Map 5:D1

ROINEABHAL COUNTRY HOUSE, Kilchrenan, PA35 1HD. Tel 01866 833207, www.roineabhal.com. Anglers, birders, stargazers, point your rods, binoculars and telescopes towards Roger and Maria Soep's rustic hideaway in the wild glens of Argyll. Their country guest house, beside a tumbling stream, is surrounded by beautiful, peaceful gardens, and little else for miles. Individually styled bedrooms, all with good views, have fresh flowers and shortbread. Breakfast includes locally smoked kippers, porridge and home-made bread. For the evening, book a supper platter of smoked fish, venison, cheese and oatcakes, salads, home-made conserves and desserts (£25). The knowledgeable hosts have plenty of information for planning day trips to Inveraray, Glencoe, Fort William and Kintyre; ferries from the nearby port of Oban offer transport to Skye, Mull, Iona and the outer islands. Lounge, dining room; covered veranda. Free Wi-Fi, in-room TV (Freeview). No background music. 1½-acre garden. Children (over-3s half price) and well-behaved dogs (must have own bedding) welcomed. Resident dog. 18 miles E of Oban. 3 bedrooms (1 on ground floor, suitable for disabled). Per room B&B single from £85, double from £110. 2-night min. stay preferred. Closed Dec–Mar.

TONGUE Highland
Map 5:B2

THE TONGUE HOTEL, IV27 4XD. Tel 01847 611206, www.tonguehotel.co.uk. 'Homely and characterful', Lorraine and David Hook's 'wonderfully remote' small hotel occupies a former Victorian sporting lodge in a sleepy coastal village at the end of a 37-mile single-track road. It is in 'a spectacular area', with abundant opportunities for bird- and otter-watching, hill climbing, fishing and stalking. Cosy tweed and tartan fabrics and dark polished furniture create a warm atmosphere. Staff are 'friendly and helpful'. Each of the traditionally decorated bedrooms has a nostalgic air, with an original fireplace here, a marble washstand there; all are supplied with fruit, sweets and sherry. From each bedroom, too, take in astounding views of the ruin of Castle Varrich or down towards the village at the foot of Ben Loyal, 'the Queen of Scottish Mountains'. Simple Scottish fare is served in the restaurant, beside a warming fire. Breakfast, ordered the night before, has home-made compotes, granola and muesli, and porridge with cream and heather honey – livened up, perhaps, with a glug of whisky. Lounge, 2 bars, restaurant (closed Mon, Oct–Mar). Therapy room. Free Wi-Fi (in public areas), in-room TV (Freeview). Background music. Civil wedding licence. Small garden. Children welcomed (cots, extra beds; 6–13s £20). 19 bedrooms. Per person B&B £45–£65, D,B&B £82–£92.

ULLAPOOL Highland
Map 5:B2
THE SHEILING, Garve Road, IV26 2SX. Tel 01854 612947, www.thesheilingullapool.co.uk. Guests praise the 'superior' accommodation and 'stunning' views at Iain and Lesley MacDonald's comfortable, modest B&B beside Loch Broom. The lovely gardens have a 'spectacular' outlook over the bay and the mountains beyond. Bedrooms are supplied with sherry and sweets; two rooms have views of the loch. Play board games in the lounge or curl up before the open fire with a book or magazine off the shelves. Ordered the night before, a 'superlative' Highland breakfast might include smoked fish or oatmeal porridge with cream, the lot served in a bright, split-level room overlooking the loch. Sitting room, dining room. Sportsman's Lodge (guest laundry, drying room; sauna, shower). Free Wi-Fi, in-room TV (Freeview). No background music. 1-acre garden, lochside patio. Parking. Bicycle store. Fishing permits. Children (cot with bedding £10 per night) and dogs (by prior arrangement, in downstairs rooms; £10 per night) welcomed. 10 mins' walk

to town centre; 5 mins' walk to ferry for the Hebrides. 6 bedrooms (2 on ground floor). Per room B&B £70–£87.50. Closed Nov–Easter.

WALES

ABERGELE Conwy
Map 3:A3
THE KINMEL ARMS, St George, The Village, LL22 9BP. Tel 01745 832207, www.thekinmelarms.co.uk. Birdsong announces the day at this 'delightful, relaxed hideaway' in a secluded hamlet in the Elwy valley. Here, Lynn Cunnah-Watson and Tim Watson have handsomely refurbished their sandstone inn with a modern interior 'finished to a high standard'; Tim Watson's artwork decorates the walls. In the vast, 'beautifully appointed' bedrooms, find high, wood-framed windows, caramel-wood furniture; perhaps a huge slipper bath, a decked balcony or patio. Afternoons, nip down to the new tea rooms to sample a host of home-baked cakes and loose-leaf tea, all of it served on an eclectic collection of fine bone china. Cheery knick-knacks and jars of olives adorn the popular bar, liked by locals for its real ales, Welsh ciders and large choice of wines by the glass. In the conservatory restaurant, chef Chad Hughes champions seasonal produce and local fish and meat, in his brasserie-style lunches and dinners. All the accoutrements of a generous continental breakfast – home-baked bread, pastries, meats, cheeses, yogurt, fruit compote – are delivered by the 'Room Fairy' in the evening. Good walks; golf nearby. Bar (wood-burning stove), restaurant (closed Sun, Mon). Deli/shop. Tea rooms. Free Wi-Fi, in-room TV (Freeview).

No background music. Small rear garden; seating area at front. Parking. 4 bedrooms (2 on ground floor). Per room B&B £135–£175, D,B&B from £195. Closed Christmas, New Year.

AMROTH Pembrokeshire
Map 3:D2
MELLIEHA GUEST HOUSE, SA67 8NA. Tel 01834 811581, www.mellieha.co.uk. In a wooded valley close to the sea, Julia and Stuart Adams run a peaceful B&B in their ranch-style house. It's an ideal base for walkers: the Pembrokeshire Coastal Path provides a clear tramp through coastal towns as far as Saundersfoot. 'Friendly and professional', the hosts offer tea and a 'generous' portion of home-made cake to arriving guests. Most of the neat, bright bedrooms (one has a balcony, another a private terrace) have views over the garden to the sea; each is equipped with thoughtful extras such as bathrobes and a torch (needed in the dark nights). A comfortable lounge has a log-burning stove. 'Properly cooked' breakfasts include a full Welsh with laver bread and cockles. Easy access to the beach; pubs, restaurants and shops nearby. Lounge, dining room. Free Wi-Fi, in-room TV. No background music. 1-acre garden with pond. Parking. Children over 10 welcomed. 2 miles E of Saundersfoot. 5 bedrooms. Per room B&B £80–£98. Closed 18 Dec–3 Jan.
25% DISCOUNT VOUCHERS

CAERNARFON Gwynedd
Map 3:A2
PLAS DINAS COUNTRY HOUSE, Bontnewydd, LL54 7YF. Tel 01286 830214, www.plasdinas.co.uk. Delve into history at this gentlemanly Georgian house, set between the Snowdonia mountains and the Irish sea. Once the country home of the Armstrong-Jones family, it is today a sumptuous B&B run by 'hands-on' owners Neil and Marco Soares-Baines. A mix-and-match of vintage and modern pieces styles the individual bedrooms; the 'delightful' hosts ensure 'all the things you might have forgotten to pack' are within arm's reach. Take drinks in front of a log fire in the drawing room brimming with antiques, portraits and memorabilia, or head out to the terrace in warm weather. Most evenings, Marco Soares-Baines's daily-changing set menus are promptly served at 7 pm in the dining room. 'Breakfast was great.' Drawing room, dining room (closed Sun, Mon). Private dining room. Free Wi-Fi, in-room TV (Freeview). Background music. Civil wedding licence. 15-acre grounds. Parking. No children under 14. Small, well-behaved dogs (2 rooms, by arrangement; £10 per night charge) welcomed. Resident dogs, Malta and Blue. 2 miles from Caernarfon. 10 bedrooms (1 on ground floor). Per room B&B £99–£249 (2-night min. stay at weekends). Dinner £35. Closed Christmas.
25% DISCOUNT VOUCHERS

CARDIFF
Map 3:E4
CATHEDRAL 73, 73 Cathedral Road, CF11 9HE. Tel 02920 235005, cathedral73.com. Old-school cosseting gets a chic upgrade at Nigel John's stylishly converted Victorian town house, a short walk to the castle. Pick one of the smart, superbly equipped bedrooms or a sleek, modern apartment with a fully equipped kitchen (ideal for

the self-sufficient) – whatever the choice, guests may also opt for butler service, a personal chef and the use of a chauffeur-driven vintage chrome-and-yellow Rolls-Royce. Take light lunches and afternoon tea with home-made cakes in the elegant Tea at 73; evenings from Thursday to Saturday, it transforms into a wine bar with live piano music. Sitting room, bar/tea room; terrace. Free Wi-Fi, in-room TV (Freeview). Background music. Limited parking. Civil wedding licence. Children and dogs (in ground-floor room) welcomed. ½ mile from city centre. 12 bedrooms (3 serviced apartment suites; 2-bed coach house behind the hotel; 1 on ground floor, suitable for disabled). Per room B&B from £150. No breakfast, minimum housekeeping on Christmas Day, Boxing Day, New Year's Day.
25% DISCOUNT VOUCHERS

JOLYON'S AT NO. 10, 10 Cathedral Road, CF11 9LJ. Tel 029 2009 1900, www.jolyons10.com. Backing on to Bute Park, Jolyon Joseph's relaxed hotel occupies a Victorian villa in the leafy Pontcanna area; the city centre is a ten-minute walk away, past the cathedral. An eclectic approach to design fills the bedrooms (some compact) with gold-painted armchairs, crystal chandeliers, swathes of leopard print, perhaps a grand walnut wardrobe or tasselled four-poster bed. There are nice extras, too – hot chocolate, cafetière coffee, ethically produced toiletries. Food is served all day in the restaurant: find plush seating, a grand bar and a Welsh-inflected menu. Lounge/bar, restaurant; terrace. Private meeting rooms. Lift. Free Wi-Fi, in-room TV (Freeview). No background music. Limited parking

(pre-booking required). A back gate leads into the park. Children welcomed (cots). 21 bedrooms. Per room B&B from £79, D,B&B from £99. 2-night min. stay preferred.
25% DISCOUNT VOUCHERS

COLWYN BAY Conwy
Map 3:A3
ELLINGHAM HOUSE, 1 Woodland Park West, LL29 7DR. Tel 01492 533345, www.ellinghamhouse.com. In a leafy conservation area near the seafront, Ian Davies and Chris Jennings run their personable B&B in a sensitively refurbished late-Victorian villa. Spacious bedrooms (traditionally decorated, with a modern bathroom) are supplied with bathrobes, biscuits and fruit; the lounge has a TV and a selection of DVDs. Freshly cooked by Ian Davies, breakfast is taken in an elegant room with period features. Well located for Conwy and Llandudno. Lounge, dining room. Free Wi-Fi, in-room TV (Freeview). No background music. Lawned garden with seating. Parking. Children welcomed (high chair, cot £5 per night, extra bed £20 per night); dogs by arrangement (£8 on first night, £5 each additional night). 5 bedrooms. Per room B&B single £69–£90, double £82–£110. Closed Dec–Feb.

CONWY Conwy
Map 3:A3
CASTLE HOTEL, High Street, LL32 8DB. Tel 01492 582800, www.castlewales.co.uk. History infuses the rooms – and sets the floors gently creaking – at the Lavin family's atmospheric hotel and restaurant in the centre of this walled World Heritage town. The

15th-century coaching inn stands on the site of a Cistercian abbey; visits, through the years, from an all-star cast including Charlotte Brontë and Samuel Johnson add to its story. Public rooms are furnished with antiques, and hung with art by John Dawson Watson (who once paid for his board with paintings); nooks and crannies demand exploration. Individually designed bedrooms vary in size – some have castle views, one has a 16th-century, carved-oak four-poster bed. In the restaurant, chef Andrew Nelson showcases Welsh produce – with a list of local ales on the side. Dawson's bar/snug, restaurant; courtyard garden (alfresco dining). Treatment room. Free Wi-Fi, in-room TV (Freeview). Background music. Parking (narrow entrance). Five mins' walk to Conwy Castle. Children (special meals, extra bed; 6–13s £20 per night) and medium-sized dogs (bed 'and other bits' provided; £10 per night) welcomed. 27 bedrooms (some on ground floor). Per person B&B single £89–£102, double £69–£140. Dinner £30. Closed 24–26 Dec.

COWBRIDGE Vale of Glamorgan
Map 3:E3

THE BEAR, 63 High Street, CF71 7AF. Tel 01446 774814, www.bearhotel. com. Once a stopover for mail coaches between Swansea and Cardiff, this lively, well-located hotel in the Vale of Glamorgan is well liked for its friendly atmosphere and community-hub feel. Join locals who come for light lunches, gastropub dinners and all manner of snacks and drinks in between. There's a good selection of real ales at the bar; if Welsh weather allows, the courtyard calls for alfresco entertaining.

Individually styled bedrooms, including suites with a four-poster bed, vary in size and style (from traditional to modern); tea- and coffee-making facilities are provided. Buffet breakfasts. Lounge, restaurant, grill/bar; courtyard (alfresco dining). Free Wi-Fi, in-room TV. Wedding, conference facilities. Parking. Children welcomed. 33 bedrooms (some in annexe), plus 1- and 2-bedroom self-catering apartments a short way away. Per room B&B £100–£155. Dinner £25.

CWMBACH Powys
Map 3:C3

THE DRAWING ROOM, nr Builth Wells, LD2 3RT. Tel 01982 552493, www. the-drawing-room.co.uk. Intimate and elegant, Melanie and Colin Dawson's restaurant-with-rooms charms with its fresh flower-filled drawing rooms, restful bedrooms and fine seasonal menus. The Georgian stone-built house stands on a quiet country road in the scenic Elan valley; inside, find cosy sofas and a hospitable atmosphere. In the open-plan kitchen, the Dawsons use fruit and vegetables from the kitchen garden, along with prime Welsh Black beef, venison and lamb from local farms; breads are home baked. Snug bedrooms are tastefully furnished; bathrooms (one with a large freestanding bath) have underfloor heating. There's no tea- or coffee-making kit in the room, but hot drinks are delivered on request. At breakfast, find fresh fruit, home-made muesli, scrambled eggs with home-cured salmon. Lounge, restaurant (background music; open to non-residents). Free Wi-Fi, in-room TV (Freeview). Exclusive-use cookery weekends. Small garden. Children over 12 welcomed. 3 bedrooms. Per room D,B&B £205–£230. 3 miles N of Builth Wells, on the old A470. Closed Christmas, New Year. 2-night min. stay preferred.

DOLGELLAU Gwynedd
Map 3:B3

FFYNNON, Love Lane, LL40 1RR. Tel 01341 421774, www.ffynnontownhouse. com. A touch of romance in a Gothic setting, this handsomely refurbished Victorian rectory stands at the foot of Cadair Idris within the Snowdonia national park. Owner Debra Harris has added indulgent comforts and a warm palette to period features at her luxury B&B, managed by Angela Lanz. Curl up with a good book from the library or play the piano in the sunny lounge; take a drink from the honesty bar (an old gramophone chest holds local beers and snacks). On a fine day, soak in the outdoor hot tub overlooking the surrounding valley. Well-equipped bedrooms have modern touches; bathrooms have a walk-in drench shower and a deep bathtub or spa bath. In-room spa treatments are available. Freshly cooked breakfasts include plenty of local produce. In the evening, a new restaurant showcases contemporary Welsh dishes, paired with wines from small specialist producers. Lounge (contemporary background music), dining room, study, butler's pantry. Free Wi-Fi, in-room TV (Freeview). Small functions. Drying room. ½-acre garden, patio. Parking. Children welcomed (baby pack; high chair, cot, extra bed; special menu; DVD library; 2–16s £25 per night). Narrow approach. 3 mins' walk to town. 6 bedrooms. Per room

B&B £150–£210. 2-night min. stay at weekends. Closed Christmas.
25% DISCOUNT VOUCHERS

HAY-ON-WYE Powys
Map 3:D4

THE BEAR, 2 Bear Street, HR3 5AN. Tel 01497 821302, www.thebearhay.com. Steps away from the world-renowned bookshops and galleries of this small border town, David Gibbon has turned a rough-hewn 16th-century coaching inn into an urbane, bookish retreat. Bedrooms are styled with eclectic minimalism – quirky artwork and modern accessories offset old beams and vintage furniture. Home-made biscuits add a sweet touch. Well supplied with books, the sitting room is just right for catching up on reading, with its huge, squashy sofa in front of the wood-fired stove. Praiseworthy breakfasts include home-made fruit salads and compotes, and locally baked bread. Sitting/dining room; walled patio. Free Wi-Fi, in-room smart TV (Freeview). No background music. Small car park. Walking, canoeing, fishing nearby. 3 bedrooms. Per room B&B £80–£100 (£25 additional charge during the festival). Closed Christmas, New Year. Credit cards not accepted.

LLANDUDNO Conwy
Map 3:A3

ESCAPE, 48 Church Walks, LL30 2HL. Tel 01492 877776, www.escapebandb. co.uk. Fresh and fashionable, Sam Nayar and Gaenor Loftus's design-savvy B&B is in a serene, white-stucco Victorian villa whose traditional facade gives no hint of the copper baths, cocktail chairs and crystal-encrusted wallpaper that lie within. Come in to a

cool, urban space, where contemporary and vintage furnishings and fabrics contrast with oak panelling, stained glass and period fireplaces. Each bedroom is as different as one might imagine; the Loft, set over three levels, has a wall-mounted fireplace and a body-dryer in the shower room. Choose coastal stripes or a whimsical air; in every room, find fancy toiletries and up-to-date technology. Hole up with DVDs from the library, luxuriate under granny-square crocheted blankets made chic. Welsh breakfasts are praised. The beach and promenade are minutes away. Lounge, breakfast room; honesty bar. Free Wi-Fi, in-room TV. No background music. Garden. Limited parking. Children over 10 welcomed. 9 bedrooms. Per room B&B £95–£149. Closed Christmas.
25% DISCOUNT VOUCHERS

LLANDYRNOG Denbighshire
Map 3:A4
PENTRE MAWR, nr Denbigh, LL16 4LA. Tel 01824 790732, www.pentremawrcountryhouse.co.uk. From cosseting mod cons to quirky glamping, Bre and Graham Carrington-Sykes have every angle covered at their 'excellent' 400-year-old farmstead below Offa's Dyke. Partake of tasty refreshments offered on arrival, then settle in to spacious, country-style bedrooms in the old farmhouse, a modern cottage suite next door, or a canvas safari lodge in the grounds ('Shetland ponies provide the call of the wild'). A hot tub or large spa bath is found in each. On Friday and Saturday evenings, tuck in to a 'great' five-course, home-cooked dinner; bread, cakes and other treats are baked daily. Welsh breakfasts. The village

and pubs are close by. 2 sitting rooms, dining room, conservatory. Gallery for parties/functions. 6-acre grounds, walled garden. Free Wi-Fi (in main house), in-room TV (Freeview). Organ background music. Small, solar-heated saltwater swimming pool, hot tub. Tennis, croquet. Shetland ponies, husky experience; falconry demonstrations are 'highly recommended'. Golf buggy lifts for the mobility impaired. Weddings. Children over 10 and dogs welcomed. Resident dogs. 12 bedrooms (3 suites in cottage, 6 safari lodges). 3 miles from Denbigh. Per person B&B £90–£120, D,B&B £110–£140. Closed Christmas, New Year.

LLANGAFFO Isle of Anglesey
Map 3:A2
THE OUTBUILDINGS, Bodowyr Farmhouse, LL60 6NH. Tel 01248 430132, www.theoutbuildings.co.uk. Quirky and 'very different', this good-humoured restaurant-with-rooms is 'much enjoyed' for its lively, inclusive atmosphere. The converted stone-built barn and granary stand in tranquil farmland with glorious views to Snowdonia. Jack Matthews and Millie Mantle manage for Judith 'Bun' Matthews. Bedrooms (with names like Pink Spotty Jug and Button's Room) are rustic, with a sense of fun, but each is seriously well equipped with tea- and coffee-making facilities, home-made cake or biscuits and a quality music system. For something entirely different, book a stay in the Pink Hut, a cosy shepherd's hut in the grounds, which is fitted with a small wood-burning stove and 'full mod cons'. Light lunches may be served on the patio in good weather; evenings, chef

François Bernier cooks 'excellent' set menus, using local produce and foraged wild ingredients. (Menus are discussed with guests in the morning; 'if anyone wants local crab or lobster, they just have to ask!') Breakfast is a communal affair. 2 sitting rooms, restaurant with sitting area (open to non-residents). Private dining. Free Wi-Fi, in-room TV (Freeview). Background music ('but we're happy to turn it off if required'). Civil wedding licence, function facilities. Holistic treatments. Garden, with seating. Barbecue shed. Tennis court (racquets and balls provided). Parking. Babes-in-arms, children over 12 (extra bed £40) and small, well-behaved dogs (1 room; surrounding farmland has livestock) welcomed. Resident dog. 10 mins' drive from the bridge to Anglesey; 25 mins' drive to the ferry terminal at Holyhead; Llanddwyn beach is close by. 5 bedrooms (1 on ground floor; 1 in garden). Per room B&B £90; Pink Hut £75. Dinner £30–£35.

25% DISCOUNT VOUCHERS

LLANGOLLEN Denbighshire
Map 3:B4

GALES, 18 Bridge Street, LL20 8PF. Tel 01978 860089, www.galesofllangollen. co.uk. On one of the oldest streets of the town, a 17th-century hostelry once again provides good wine and comfortable accommodation to travellers in north Wales. Richard Gale opened his wine bar in 1977; the family-run enterprise now includes rooms, a restaurant and a wine and gift shop. Pip Gale is the manager. Traditionally furnished bedrooms (with a walnut wood or metal-framed bed) are in the main Georgian town house and an older, timber-framed building opposite;

some have Georgian sash windows and exposed beams; some are large enough to accommodate a family. In the informal, wood-panelled restaurant, chef Jack Hartley cooks a succinct, unpretentious menu. The extensive list has many wines available by the glass. Take a tipple home with you – the shop in reception sells all the wines from the bar, alongside unusual selections from around the world. Bar, restaurant (closed Sun). Wine shop. Patio. Free Wi-Fi, in-room TV (Freeview). Background music. Conferences. Parking. Children welcomed (6–15s £10 per night). 15 bedrooms (1 suitable for disabled; 8 in adjoining building, plus a cottage). Per room B&B (continental) £65–£100. Cooked breakfast £10; dinner £25. Closed 25–30 Dec.

LLANWRTYD WELLS Powys
Map 3:D3

LASSWADE COUNTRY HOUSE, Station Road, LD5 4RW. Tel 01591 610515, www.lasswadehotel.co.uk. In a semi-rural patch of the Brecon Beacons, on the edge of the smallest town in the UK, Roger and Emma Stevens's welcoming restaurant-with-rooms is pleasantly cut off from the urban world. Let the sound of traffic and the ring of telephones become distant memories; borrow a book from the collection in the large sitting room, and settle in (a log fire burns in cool weather). The 'superb' views from the traditionally furnished bedrooms stretch for miles: gaze out over a drink from the well-equipped hospitality tray. In the restaurant, Roger Stevens cooks 'exceptional' daily-changing menus with a Mediterranean influence; vegetarian, vegan and gluten-free dishes are happily prepared, by arrangement. Hearty breakfasts are served in the conservatory. The Stevenses are helpful hosts who can advise on walking, pony trekking, lost (and found) gardens and ruined castles with equal expertise. Think green: incentives are offered to guests who arrive by public transport. Drawing room, restaurant (booking essential), conservatory. Function room. Free Wi-Fi, in-room TV (Freeview). No background music. Small garden; patio. Parking. Children (high teas on request; no under-8s in restaurant) and dogs (by arrangement) welcomed. 8 bedrooms. Per room B&B £90–£120, D,B&B £160–£190, except during Royal Welsh Show week. Closed Christmas Day.

MONTGOMERY Powys
Map 3:C4

THE CHECKERS, Broad Street, SY15 6PN. Tel 01686 669822, www.checkerswales. co.uk. A historic coaching inn is today this 'charming' restaurant-with-rooms, overlooking the town square of an unspoilt border town. It is owned and run by sisters Kathryn and Sarah Francis, and Sarah's husband, Stéphane Borie, who has a Michelin star for his classic French cooking. His five- and eight-course tasting menus, served to all diners at a set time, are enjoyed in a setting that's all elegant, rustic simplicity (look out for low doorways and sloping floors); vegetarian and pescatarian menus are 'no problem at all'. 'Tastefully updated', the chic, modern bedrooms are cosy, with a large bed, home-made biscuits and the latest gadgetry; some bathrooms have a freestanding bath. In the morning, there's more feasting to be done: home-made brioche toast, fresh fruit, yogurts, a full cooked plate with local sausages and bacon. Lounge/bar (wood-burning stove), restaurant (closed Sun, Mon); small terrace. Free Wi-Fi (signal variable), in-room TV. No background music. Cooking masterclasses. Children (by arrangement; no under-8s in restaurant in the evening) welcomed. 1 mile from Offa's Dyke; 'epic' walks from the front door. 5 bedrooms (1, in annexe, accessed via roof terrace). Per room D,B&B from £315. 5-course tasting menu (Tues–Fri) £55; 8-course tasting menu (Tues–Sat) £75. Closed Christmas, 2 weeks Jan, 1 week in late summer.

MUMBLES Swansea
Map 3:E3

PATRICKS WITH ROOMS, 638 Mumbles Road, SA3 4EA. Tel 01792 360199, www.patrickswithrooms.com. Run with a generous spirit, this long-established, family-friendly restaurant-with-rooms on the seafront is owned by two husband-and-wife teams, Sally and Dean Fuller and Catherine and Patrick Walsh. Welsh produce and garden-fresh fare, perhaps even freshly foraged sloe berries, dictate the 'excellent' monthly-changing menu in the popular restaurant. (Young gourmets are welcomed, too, by 'accommodating' staff.) In a converted pub and boathouse, individually decorated bedrooms (some interconnecting) are homely and 'comfortable'; all have views of the sea. Cooked to order, breakfast has interesting choices: kedgeree, mushroom frittata, a full Welsh with cockles and laver bread. Lounge/bar, restaurant. Meeting room. Lift. Free Wi-Fi, in-room TV. Background music. Civil wedding licence. Gym. On-street parking (can be difficult at peak times). Children welcomed (high chair, cot, baby monitors, DVDs; playground across the road). 16 bedrooms (1 suitable for disabled; 6 in converted boathouse). Per room B&B £120–£175. Dinner £30.

NARBERTH Pembrokeshire
Map 3:D2

CANASTON OAKS, Canaston Bridge, SA67 8DE. Tel 01437 541254, www.canastonoaks.co.uk. River walks, woodland stalks, in-depth talks – enjoy all this and more at Eleanor and David Lewis's 'very good' countryside B&B. Converted barns, designed and built by Pembrokeshire craftspeople, house homely bedrooms, each with its own front door. They are equipped with thoughtful extras: dressing gowns and slippers, a fridge with milk and water, up-to-date gadgetry, candles, a hair straightener. A family suite of interconnecting rooms has a bathroom and a walk-in wet room, and access to a terrace overlooking vast countryside. For stunning views down to the lake, ask for one of three first-floor rooms in the newly constructed lodge. Attentive and friendly, the hosts provide generous breakfasts with plenty of choice. Lounge, dining rooms. Free Wi-Fi, in-room TV (Freeview). No background music. Parking. Children welcomed (cot, high chair, extra bed, £20 per night). 2 miles W of Narberth. 10 bedrooms (7, on ground floor, in courtyard; 3 in Lodge; 2 suitable for disabled; 1 family room; plus a 1-bed self-catering apartment). Per room B&B £95–£170.

NEWTOWN Powys
Map 3:C4

THE FOREST COUNTRY GUEST HOUSE, Gilfach Lane, Kerry, SY16 4DW. Tel 01686 621821, www.bedandbreakfastnewtown.co.uk. Well located for exploring the Marches area of Mid Wales, Paul and Michelle Martin's restored Victorian country house is run as a family-friendly, eco-aware B&B. Undulating countryside surrounds; inside, find books, maps, magazines, games, an antique Bechstein grand piano – and a suit of armour, complete with a sword that children are allowed to brandish. A kitchenette is available for DIY meals and snacks. Sweetly traditional bedrooms (just the right side of old fashioned) are up the 19th-century oak staircase; each looks over the great floral displays in the large garden. Organic breakfasts include eggs from the Martins' free-range hens. Tuck in, then step outside to visit the small flock of rare-breed sheep. Drawing room, dining room. Kitchenette. Games room (toy box). Free Wi-Fi, in-room TV (Freeview). 4-acre garden, play area (swings, house, timber fort). Tennis court. Parking. Secure bicycle storage. Children welcomed (cot, high chair, extra beds; over-2s £15). Resident cat (Sooty) and dog (Libby), chickens, sheep. 1 mile from Kerry village; 3 miles SE of Newtown. 5 bedrooms (plus 4 holiday cottages in outbuildings). Per room B&B £80–£115. Closed Christmas, New Year (except cottages).

ST DAVID'S Pembrokeshire
Map 3:D1

CRUG-GLAS, Abereiddy, Haverfordwest, SA62 6XX. Tel 01348 831302, www.crug-glas.co.uk. Homespun and hospitable, this rustic restaurant-with-rooms has a laid-back, unpretentious ambience. Janet and Perkin Evans, the 'hard-working' hosts, have deep roots in the area; the Georgian house, at the heart of their 600-acre working farm, is a family home, filled with photographs and inherited china. (A handsome Welsh dresser that has been used for generations now houses a well-stocked honesty bar.) Bedrooms are in the main building, a converted milk parlour and a coach house. Each room is different in size and style; all are 'charming' in their own way. Come dinnertime, take a seat in the former family dining room, where Janet Evans's home cooking (perhaps including 'the best steak') wins praise. Breakfast is 'excellent', with a 'nicely laid out' buffet and a 'superb' selection of cooked dishes. A separate building is a venue for events and weddings. Well situated for St David's and the Pembrokeshire coast. Drawing room, dining room. Free Wi-Fi, in-room TV (Freeview). Classical background music. Civil wedding licence. 1-acre garden on 600-acre farm. Children over 12 welcomed. 3½ miles NE of St David's. 7 bedrooms (2 in outbuildings; 1 on ground floor). Per room B&B £150–£190. Dinner £35. Closed 24–26 Dec.

25% DISCOUNT VOUCHERS

SAUNDERSFOOT Pembrokeshire
Map 3:D2
ST BRIDES SPA HOTEL, St Brides Hill, SA69 9NH. Tel 01834 812 304, www. stbridesspahotel.com. 'After lunch overlooking the beach, we were smitten.' Laid-back, minimalist and very cool, Andrew and Lindsey Evans's chic clifftop hotel has 'great views' of Carmarthen Bay and the wide, sandy shore. There is plenty to see inside, too: the hotel's dedicated gallery of contemporary Welsh art invites a wander. Light, breezy bedrooms (Good, Better, Best) have 'a real nautical feel';

most have sea views, a balcony. Food is served all day in the Gallery bar, or alfresco on a large decked terrace ('it has the wow factor'). In the evening, book a table for an 'excellent' dinner in the Cliff restaurant. Still hungering for choice? Sister eateries, the Mermaid and the Marina, are down by the harbour. The Pembrokeshire Coastal Path is on the doorstep, but for those who prefer to stay in and be lazy, the newly refurbished spa, with its infinity pool taking in the coastal panorama, is an attraction. Lounge, bar, restaurant, Gallery dining area; terraces. Meeting/function rooms. Lift. Free Wi-Fi, in-room TV (Sky). Background music. Civil wedding licence. Art gallery. Spa (steam room, salt room, rock sauna, ice fountain, marine infinity hydro pool with sea views). Parking. Children (special menu) and dogs (some ground-floor apartments; beds, bowls supplied) welcomed. 3 mins' walk into village. 34 bedrooms (1 suitable for disabled), plus six 2-bedroom apartments in grounds (pets allowed in some); village apartments. Per room B&B £130–£310; apartments from £260. Dinner £35.

CHANNEL ISLANDS

ST BRELADE Jersey
Map 1: inset E6
LA HAULE MANOR, La Neuve Route, JE3 8BS. Tel 01534 741426, www. lahaulemanor.com. Stroll along the seafront to reach the village of St Aubin, from the well-maintained gardens of this extended Georgian manor house. Ola Przyjemska is the much-praised manager. A period French air fills the high-ceilinged sitting room (chandeliers, ornate furnishing); well-equipped

bedrooms have tea- and coffee-making facilities, bathrobes and slippers, quality toiletries, a fridge. Plenty of extras – maps, umbrellas, binoculars – are provided on request. Guests are welcomed with a complimentary glass of champagne – all the better to celebrate the expansive vista from the sitting room and the sea-facing bedrooms. No dinner is served, but restaurants, pubs and cafés are easily reached; free transport is provided to the restaurant at sister hotel La Place, barely a mile away. Sitting room, bar, TV room, breakfast room; terrace. Free Wi-Fi, in-room TV (Freeview). Garden. 15-metre outdoor swimming pool (heated Apr–Oct); hot tub. Parking. 10 mins' drive from the airport; complimentary transfers from airport and harbour; twice weekly coastal tours. Children welcomed (over-3s £30 per night). 16 bedrooms (some on ground floor; plus 2 self-catering apartments). Per room B&B £94–£207.

ST MARTIN Guernsey
Map 1: inset E5
BELLA LUCE HOTEL, La Fosse, GY4 6EB. Tel 01481 238764, www. bellalucehotel.com. The Wheadon family's handsomely restored, extended manor house (Small Luxury Hotels of the World) stands in lush walled gardens above Moulin Huet Bay, a tranquil spot much favoured by Renoir in his Guernsey paintings. Ricardo Freitas is the manager. Understated and elegant, the bedrooms are stocked with magazines, bathrobes and slippers; some have a modern four-poster bed. Splurge on one of the spacious loft or garden suites in the oldest part of the building – they have a large bed and a

lounge area; one has a freestanding roll-top bath in the room. Overlooking the courtyard garden, the award-winning candlelit restaurant (chef Sebastian Orzechowski's modern European menu uses much fresh seafood) has a log fire in chilly weather; on fine days, French windows open to a sunny terrace for alfresco meals under the shade of a tulip tree. (Opt for 'uncomplicated' food in the intimate bar.) When an evening chill creeps in, head to the atmospheric vaulted cellar lounge, all vintage armchairs, leather sofas, board games and newspapers: here, copper stills distil the house's small-batch gins, ideal for lingering over. Snug, bar, Bella Bistro restaurant, cellar lounge (tasting room); courtyard. Free Wi-Fi, in-room TV (Freeview). Background music. Civil wedding licence; function facilities. 2-acre garden. Outdoor swimming pool (loungers, sofas), spa. 2 miles from St Peter Port and airport; rock beach 5 mins' walk. Victor Hugo's house is nearby. Trips to Herm and Sark can be arranged. Parking. Children welcomed (special menu). 23 bedrooms (2 on ground floor; some family rooms). Per room B&B from £120, D,B&B from £170. Closed Jan.

ST PETER PORT Guernsey
Map 1: inset E5
LA COLLINETTE HOTEL, St Jacques, GY1 1SN. Tel 01481 710331, www. lacollinette.com. There's a friendly atmosphere at this white-painted, flower-fronted Georgian mansion which has been run by the Chambers family for more than 50 years. Cyril Fortier is the long-serving manager. Most of the bedrooms overlook the grounds and gardens; each is supplied with tea- and

coffee-making facilities and biscuits. Children are made very welcome, with a teddy bear gift as greeting. Newly refurbished in 2016, the relaxed, modern restaurant has a straightforward menu with good seafood options (perhaps Guernsey crab or scallops). Stay by the pool all day, or head out to explore – a stroll through Candie Gardens, nearby, leads to the harbour and shops. Spend the day at the beach, lose yourself down cobbled side streets, or island-hop from the pretty harbour to Sark and Herm. Lounge, bar, restaurant. Free Wi-Fi, in-room TV (Sky, Freeview). 1-acre garden. Background music. Heated outdoor swimming pool. Gym, massages. Children welcomed (baby-listening, high chair, cots, extra bed; children's menu; children's pool; play area). 1 mile W of town centre. 22 bedrooms (plus 15 self-catering cottages and apartments). Per person B&B £50–£82 (suites £78–£120). Dinner £22. **25% DISCOUNT VOUCHERS**

THE DUKE OF RICHMOND, Cambridge Park, GY1 1UY. Tel 01481 726221, www.dukeofrichmond.com. The vista from this refined hotel (part of the Red Carnation Hotel Collection) stretches all the way over the town to the neighbouring islands of Herm and Sark – ask for a room with a sea view, and don't forget the binoculars. Each bedroom is immaculately styled, no matter its outlook. Some are modern, others elegantly traditional; all have tea- and coffee-making facilities, bottled water and a daily newspaper. Beds are turned down in the evening. Public spaces are chic, with a touch of glamour: the black and white lounge has a brass fireplace and a fine collection of antiques; the Leopard bar and restaurant takes its name to heart, with a mix of graphics and animal prints. Let the children be fussed over: there are games, a toy basket, DVDs, bathtime treats, robes and slippers; young guests may even decorate their own cupcake with the chef. The heated outdoor swimming pool and terrace look over Candie Gardens; the town centre and harbour are an easy downhill stroll away. Lukas Laubscher is the manager. Lounge, bar, restaurant; terrace. Free Wi-Fi, in-room TV. Background music. Room service. Swimming pool. Wedding/function facilities. Children and dogs (in 2 rooms; not in restaurant) welcomed. 73 bedrooms (1 penthouse suite). Per room B&B £121–£415, D,B&B £156–£450.

IRELAND

ARDMORE Co. Waterford
Map 6:D5

THE CLIFF HOUSE, Middle Road. Tel 353 024 87 800, www.thecliffhousehotel. com. As striking inside as out, this modern, glass-and-slate hotel (Relais & Châteaux) has a dramatic clifftop position affording every bedroom uninterrupted views over Ardmore Bay. Owner Barry O'Callaghan also owns The Cliff Townhouse, Dublin (see Shortlist entry); Adriaan Bartels is the manager. Bright, cheery bedrooms have a mid-century-modern aesthetic and an original work by an Irish artist; spot dolphins and minke whales from the best rooms, which have a private balcony or terrace. In House restaurant, sample chef Martijn Kajuiter's Michelin-starred modern Irish cooking; the stylish bar has lighter meals (alfresco eating in summer). Great walks and rock fishing nearby (fishing equipment available to borrow); hit eco-friendly golf balls (made of fish food) to a floating green from a tee box in the garden. Library, bar, restaurant (closed Sun, Mon except bank holidays); terraces. Private dining room. Lift. Free Wi-Fi, in-room TV (Sky, Freeview). Background music. Wedding facilities. Spa (sauna, steam room; treatments, therapies). 18-metre indoor infinity pool, gym. Table tennis. Natural rock pool. 1-acre garden. Parking. 2 moorings for yachts. Children (welcome pack, playroom, children's menu) and dogs (heated kennels) welcomed. On edge of village. 39 bedrooms (2 suitable for disabled; plus self-catering cottage). Per room B&B €195–€350, D,B&B from €275. Closed Christmas.

BALLINTOY Co. Antrim
Map 6:A6

WHITEPARK HOUSE, 150 Whitepark Road, nr Ballycastle, BT54 6NH. Tel 028 2073 1482, www.whiteparkhouse. com. Along the undiscovered coast of Whitepark Bay, above the sandy beach, stands Bob and Siobhan Isles's 'exemplary' small B&B. Art, artefacts and souvenirs from the owners' adventures around the world fill their crenellated 18th-century house – an intriguing backdrop for afternoon tea, with home-baked biscuits, in the 'delightful' lounge. Comfortable bedrooms ('ours was more like a suite') have lots of much-appreciated details: fluffy bathrobes, a hot-water bottle, 'facecloths tied with a red ribbon'; lovely views of the garden or sea. Warm and welcoming, the hosts are happy to advise on restaurants and places to visit. Full

Irish breakfasts (vegetarians catered for). 'We were entertained royally.' Sitting room (peat fire), conservatory. 1-acre garden. Free Wi-Fi. No background music. Children over 10 welcomed (in their own room, charged at full rate). 5 miles E of Bushmills. 4 bedrooms. Per room B&B single £80, double £120.

BALLYGALLY Co. Antrim
Map 6:B6

BALLYGALLY CASTLE, Coast Road, BT40 2QZ. Tel 028 2858 1066, www. hastingshotels.com/ballygally-castle. What to do next is the hardest decision you might face at this expanded 17th-century castle (Hastings Hotels) overlooking the beach. It is 'excellently located' for living out fantasies of all kinds: follow the footsteps of giants along the Causeway coastal route; tour nearby Bushmills distillery; trace each moment of the TV series Game of Thrones, which was filmed nearby. Norman McBride manages. Some of the well-appointed modern bedrooms have wide views all the way to the Scottish coastline; others have wooden rafters or are shaped by the castle's original architecture. All rooms have an iPod dock, a radio, tea- and coffee-making facilities. 'Our large, charming corner room under the eaves had a view of the coast in both directions – a bonus.' Feeling brave? Ask about the 'ghost room' in the tower. Classic Irish dishes are given a contemporary twist in the Garden restaurant; an 'excellent' breakfast (with 'proper pats of butter') is taken in a 'pretty, well-lit' room with a view of the grounds. 'Before we left, we went for a stroll in the well-kept grounds – a fitting end to a pleasant experience.' Lounge, bar area, restaurant. Free Wi-Fi, in-room TV (Freeview). 'Easy listening' background music. Wedding/function facilities. 1½-acre walled gardens with stream. Children welcomed (charge for over-4s). 10 mins' drive from the Larne ferry terminal. 54 bedrooms (some suitable for disabled). Per person B&B from £50, D,B&B from £75.

BELFAST
Map 6:B6

THE OLD RECTORY, 148 Malone Road, BT9 5LH. Tel 028 9066 7882, www. anoldrectory.co.uk. Substantial gardens and substantial breakfasts make Mary Callan's homely guest house, all high ceilings, stained glass and striking tiled fireplaces, a good-value base for the city centre and university nearby. Comfortable bedrooms in the Victorian villa are thoughtfully supplied with books, magazines and biscuits. Play games and browse the library of Irish history, architecture and culture books in the drawing room; in cooler months, warm up with a complimentary hot whiskey. Award-winning breakfasts (with vegetarian and gluten-free options) have lots of choice, including a full Ulster, a veggie fry-up, porridge with cream, honey and Irish Mist liqueur. Raspberry jam, whiskey marmalade, soda and wheaten breads are all home made. A small supper menu is available Mon–Fri (£20). Drawing room, dining room ('soft' background music). Free Wi-Fi, in-room TV. Garden. Parking. Children welcomed. 1¾ miles to city centre. 10 mins' walk to Lagan Meadows (river walks). 6 bedrooms (1 on ground floor, 1 family room). Per person B&B £46–£50. 2-night min. stay May–Sept. Closed Christmas, New Year, 2 weeks mid-July. Credit cards not accepted.

RAVENHILL HOUSE, 690 Ravenhill Road, BT6 0BZ. Tel 028 9020 7444, www. ravenhillhouse.com. Olive and Roger Nicholson's welcoming B&B is in a restored Victorian house two miles from the centre, close to pubs and restaurants, independent shops and a park. Arrive to hot drinks and home-made shortbread, before settling in to one of the bedrooms upstairs, each made homely with rustic floral wallpaper and a vintage Hacker radio. (Help is offered with luggage.) Breakfast, served till 10 am on the weekend, is taken seriously: a generous buffet might hold home-made marmalade, lemon curd or apple jelly; stewed fruit or a spiced fruit compote; freshly baked Irish wheaten bread or banana bread. Hot dishes, cooked to order, include Ardglass kippers; good vegetarian options. Sitting room (extensive library of local interest books and maps), dining room. Free Wi-Fi, in-room TV (Freeview). Radio 3 at breakfast. Small garden. Parking. 2 miles S of city. Children welcomed (high chair, cot). 7 bedrooms (1 on ground floor). Per room B&B £60–£110. Closed mid-Dec–end Jan. 2-night min. stay preferred on busy weekends.

BUSHMILLS Co. Antrim
Map 6:A6

BUSHMILLS INN, 9 Dunluce Road, BT57 8QG. Tel 028 2073 3000, www. bushmillsinn.com. On the Causeway Coastal Route, this higgledy-piggledy old coaching inn and adjoining mill house has a grand staircase, a 'secret' library and a web of interconnecting snugs with peat fires, oil lamps and ancient wooden booths. Alan Walls manages friendly staff. Many of the spacious bedrooms have views over the

River Bush; split-level suites have a large lounge and shower room downstairs, a sleeping area and separate bathroom above. Tap your toes to traditional Irish music in the Gas bar (lit by the original gas lights); have a glass from the hotel's private cask. The restaurant overlooking the garden courtyard serves Irish cuisine with a modern twist. Running out of ideas? Smartly thought-out top-10 lists ('10 things to do when it's raining', '…without a car', '…as a family', etc) have plenty of suggestions. Drawing room, restaurant, gallery, oak-beamed loft; patio. Lift. Free Wi-Fi, in-room TV. Background music. Conferences; 30-seat cinema; treatment room. 2-acre garden. Parking. Children welcomed (family rooms; cots). 2 miles from the Giant's Causeway. 41 bedrooms (some on ground floor; spacious ones in mill house, smaller ones in inn; some suitable for disabled). Per room B&B £120–£400. Dinner £37.50. Closed for accommodation at Christmas.

CALLAN Co. Kilkenny
Map 6:D5
BALLAGHTOBIN COUNTRY HOUSE, Ballaghtobin. Tel 00 353 56 772 5227, www.ballaghtobin.com. Experience a slice of living history at Catherine and Mickey Gabbett's easy-going B&B in the 18th-century ancestral home where 14 generations of the Gabbett family have lived. It is a real escape into rural Kilkenny, standing in informal gardens within a 500-acre farm that produces cereals, blackcurrants and Christmas trees. (Wood chips power the boiler for heating and hot water.) Decorated in country style, bedrooms are comfortably furnished with paintings and antiques gathered over generations; the Barrack Room ('where drunken visitors were once sent to sleep') accommodates four. In the morning, wake to a generous breakfast served at a large table in the dining room. Drawing room, dining room, study, conservatory. Free Wi-Fi. No background music. Tennis, croquet, clock golf. Children (50% reduction) and dogs welcomed. Parking. 4 km E of Callan; 30 mins' drive to Kilkenny. 3 bedrooms. Per person B&B €50 (based on 2 people sharing). Closed Nov–Feb. Credit cards not accepted.

COBH Co. Cork
Map 6:D5
KNOCKEVEN HOUSE, Rushbrooke. Tel 00 353 21 481 1778, www.knockevenhouse.com. Splendidly traditional, Pam Mulhaire's welcoming B&B is in a double-fronted Victorian house just outside the historic seaport town. (Splendid, too, are the springtime displays of magnolias, azaleas and camellias in the garden.) The gracious hostess welcomes guests with hot drinks and home-made scones in the comfortable drawing room. High-ceilinged bedrooms, each richly furnished in period style, have terry cloth robes, high-end toiletries and space to sit; large windows overlook the grounds. Generous breakfasts, with seasonal fruits, preserves and home-baked breads, are taken at a large mahogany table. Drawing room, dining room. 2-acre grounds. Free Wi-Fi. Background music. Children welcomed. 1 mile W of town; 3 mins' drive from Rushbrooke railway station. Titanic Trail and Museum, Cobh Heritage Centre, Lusitania Monument close by. 4 bedrooms. Per person B&B from €85. Closed Christmas.

DONEGAL TOWN Co. Donegal
Map 6:B5

HARVEY'S POINT, Lough Eske. Tel 00 353 74 972 2208, www.harveyspoint.com. In a magical setting between Lough Eske and the foothills of the Blue Stack mountains, this traditional, family-run hotel is just right for adventure walks, leisure strolls, loughside picnics and a taste from a range of rare Irish whiskeys. Owners Marc Gysling and Deirdre McGlone lead a professional, friendly team. Choose among spacious bedrooms with views of the surrounding landscape; lakeshore suites (with a separate entrance) have an individual terrace overlooking the water. Fresh milk, fruit and biscuits are replenished daily in the bedrooms. Good-value, compact accommodation for parties and large groups has been created in a newly refurbished lodge on a hill behind the hotel. A turf fire burns in the cosy bar; in the restaurant overlooking the lake, chef Chris McMenamin serves a four-course menu with amuse-bouche. Activity breaks (fishing, canoeing, golf, walks, archery) available. Drawing room, bar, restaurant (closed Mon, Tues in Nov–Mar), ballroom (resident pianist; Irish/classical background music). Lift. Free Wi-Fi, in-room TV (Sky). Summertime cabaret dinners Jun–Oct. Beauty treatments, massage. Wedding, conference facilities. 20-acre grounds. Children (babysitting, early supper; 4–10s €30, 11–14s €50), dogs (in Lakeshore suites) and horses (stabling, grazing) welcomed. 4 miles from town. 64 bedrooms and suites (some suitable for disabled), plus 13 bedrooms in the Lodge for group bookings. Per room B&B from €138, D,B&B from €238. 2-night min. stay at weekends. Set dinner €55.

DUBLIN
Map 6:C6

ARIEL HOUSE, 50–54 Lansdowne Road, Ballsbridge. Tel 00 353 1 668 5512, www.ariel-house.net. The McKeown family's B&B occupies three splendidly refurbished Victorian town houses in the leafy Ballsbridge suburb, close to the centre. Individually designed bedrooms with garden views are spread across the main house and a newer wing. They vary considerably in size and style, from more modern standard rooms in the annexe to superior rooms in the main house furnished with an antique or two. Impressive junior suites, light spilling through their large windows, have crystal chandeliers and a seating area. Arrive to a complimentary afternoon tea in the 'comfortable' lounge, where Victorian-inspired wallpaper and fabrics blend with original stained glass, fireplaces and bay windows. At breakfast, find 'imaginative' choices, perhaps 'excellent' herby poached eggs with smoked salmon. Drawing room, dining room (background music). Free Wi-Fi, in-room TV. Front and back garden. Limited parking. Children welcomed (50% discount). 2 km from the city centre; convenient for the Aviva Stadium. 37 bedrooms (8 in mews). Per room B&B from €150. Closed 22 Dec–4 Jan.

THE CLIFF TOWNHOUSE, 22 St Stephen's Green. Tel 00 353 1 638 3939, www.theclifftownhouse.com. Dapper and discreet, this stylish Georgian town house hotel, opposite St Stephen's Green, was once home to one of the oldest private members' clubs in Ireland. It is owned by Barry O'Callaghan, who also owns The Cliff House, Ardmore (see Shortlist entry); Siobhan Ryan is the manager. Playful, if muted, opulence emanates from the heritage hues, decadent silks and brocades, and finely considered mix of antique and modern furnishing – a snazzy backdrop against which to indulge at the oyster and champagne bar. On the upper floors, some bedrooms have a high ceiling and original fireplace; all have reproduction prints and tweedy blankets. Even the marble bathrooms are classy, with vintage fittings or a quirky hip bath. In the popular restaurant, chef Sean Smith specialises in hearty salads and locally sourced seafood, including native lobster; good vegetarian options. Bar, restaurant (pre- and post-theatre service). Private dining room. Free Wi-Fi, in-room TV (Freeview). No background music. Wedding, function facilities. Reduced rates at St Stephen's Green car park, nearby. Children welcomed. 9 bedrooms. Per room B&B from €179. Closed 24–28 Dec.

THE MERRION, 21–24 Upper Merrion Street. Tel 353 1 603 0600, www. merrionhotel.com. In an excellent location 'both for business and for sightseeing', this large luxury hotel is in four extensively restored Georgian town houses opposite Government Buildings. Peter MacCann manages 'pleasant, keen' staff. Opulent public rooms display an important private collection of 19th- and 20th-century Irish and European art – ask for a guided tour. Airy bedrooms, decked in creamy hues, have squashy armchairs, a writing desk, a 'good' minibar; the best have views over the hotel's 18th-century classical gardens. There are plenty of places to eat and drink: choose between the stylish Restaurant Patrick Guilbaud (Michelin-starred fine dining), the Cellar restaurant (modern Irish dishes) and, in the building's original wine vaults, the Cellar bar (informal gastropub classics). A finely furnished drawing room, its log fire crackling in cool weather, is ideal for afternoon tea. 'Generous' breakfasts. 2 bars, 2 restaurants, drawing room; terrace (alfresco meals). Free Wi-Fi, in-room TV. No background music. ¾-acre grounds. Spa (steam room, treatment rooms, 16-metre indoor swimming pool). Gym. Valet parking (€20 per night). Wedding, function facilities. Children welcomed (cot, extra bed; babysitting; room service menu). 142 rooms (some in garden wing; some suitable for disabled). Room from €375; suite from €580. Breakfast from €29. Dinner (in Cellar restaurant) from €32.

WATERLOO HOUSE, 8–10 Waterloo Road, Ballsbridge. Tel 00 353 1 660 1888, www.waterloohouse.ie. Evelyn Corcoran's hospitable, 'very central' B&B, in 'an attractive couple of elegant houses put together', is 'a useful address', say Guide readers this year. 'The helpful, high-profile hostess gave us good suggestions for nearby restaurants, and made available a courtesy computer.' Traditionally furnished bedrooms (some compact) have a large bed and huge windows; they contain 'everything one might require'. 'Although my room faced the street, noise was not a problem.' An 'extensive' breakfast is served in the dining room or adjoining conservatory: fresh fruit, yogurt, hams, cheeses; omelettes, a full Irish breakfast or 'catch of the day'; home-made muesli and Irish soda bread. St Stephen's

Green is a stroll away. Lounge, dining room, conservatory. Lift. Free Wi-Fi, in-room TV. Background music. Garden. Parking. Children welcomed. 1 mile from city centre. 19 bedrooms (some family rooms; some suitable for disabled). Per room B&B €149–€199.

DUNFANAGHY Co. Donegal
Map 6:A5

THE MILL, Figart. Tel 00 353 74 913 6985, www.themillrestaurant.com. Modern menus and local craft beers cheerily pair with rustic, homely bedrooms at Susan and Derek Alcorn's friendly restaurant-with-rooms. The converted 19th-century flax mill stands on the outskirts of a small resort town along the Wild Atlantic Way; many of the unpretentious rooms overlook the 'lovely' lake. Dinner orders are taken in the conservatory or the drawing room (where an open fire burns on cool evenings). In the popular split-level restaurant, Derek Alcorn serves seasonal menus with an emphasis on local seafood. Enlivened by fresh flowers and well-chosen antiques, bedrooms are well equipped with tea- and coffee-making facilities, bottled water, wine and home-made oatmeal cookies. A new room was added in 2016: the former studio of the painter Frank Egginton (Susan Alcorn's grandfather), which has been artfully refurbished into a spacious, handsomely styled bedroom with a four-poster bed and an in-room roll-top bath. 'Excellent' breakfasts have smoked fish, award-winning sausages, home-made potato bread, a veggie fry-up. Drawing room, restaurant (dinner served 7 pm–9 pm, Tues–Sun; booking advisable), conservatory. Free Wi-Fi, in-room TV. Background music. Garden.

Children welcomed. ½ mile W of town. 7 bedrooms. Per person B&B €50–€75. Dinner €42.50. Closed Jan–mid-Mar.

GALWAY Co. Galway
Map 6:C5

THE G HOTEL, Wellpark. Tel 00 353 91 865200, www.theghotel.ie. Hats off to this glamorous, modern hotel (Edward Hotels), designed by Philip Treacy, milliner extraordinaire. Vibrantly decorated public rooms have a mix of antique and contemporary furniture, original prints and ceramics: find a mirrored wall here, a dramatic light installation there. Bedrooms, styled in calmer shades, overlook the city or the Zen garden; some are roomy enough for a family. The clubby restaurant has European-inspired dishes and Irish steaks; lighter menus and afternoon tea are taken in the lounges. The city centre and airport are within easy reach. 3 lounges, cocktail bar, Gigi's restaurant. Lift. Free Wi-Fi, in-room TV. Background music. Wedding, function facilities. Spa (indoor swimming pool, sauna, steam room, treatments). Gym. Bamboo 'Zen' garden. Parking. Children welcomed (milk and cookies on arrival, DVDs, games library; babysitting). 101 rooms (some suitable for disabled). Per room B&B €133–€500. Dinner €29.50–€48.

GLASHABEG Co. Kerry
Map 6:D4

GORMAN'S CLIFFTOP HOUSE. Tel 00 353 66 915 5162, www.gormans-clifftophouse.com. 'Everything is calm and relaxing here.' The seventh generation to live, fish and farm in this corner of the Dingle peninsula, Síle and Vincent Ó Gormáin have opened their home as a 'flexible, unstuffy' guest house and restaurant. Find a spot to settle into, on squashy seats in the lounge or library (books and board games supplied); on cool days, the hosts provide a warming pot of tea by a turf fire. 'Enormous' bedrooms have magnificent views of the sea or mountains. They are well supplied with 'a good selection of books', a DVD-player and a hospitality tray (tea, coffee, water, wine). 'Two upholstered barrel chairs in our spacious, first-floor room were conveniently placed by one of the windows, so we could sip wine while looking at the sea.' Food is served from midday in the new Borradh na Mara ('Atlantic Wave') bistro, where 'two walls are almost totally glass, so every table has a view'. From scenic lunches to sunset dinners, Vincent Ó Gormáin uses fresh fish, garden-fresh organic vegetables, herbs, salads and fruit in his 'excellent, interesting' dishes ('great vegetarian choices'). Breakfast ('a wide selection including cakes') has home-baked bread, organic compotes, yogurt; home-made muesli, granola, jams; a good variety of hot dishes. Lounge, library, restaurant (closed Sun; light meals available for residents). Free Wi-Fi, in-room TV. 'Very quiet' background music. Children welcomed (50% reduction; no charge for babies and toddlers). 'Friendly, gentle' resident dog, Molly. 12.5 km W of Dingle. 8 bedrooms (1 family room). Per room B&B €120–€165. Closed Nov–Feb. **25% DISCOUNT VOUCHERS**

INIS MEÁIN Co. Galway
Map 6:C4
INIS MEÁIN RESTAURANT AND SUITES. Tel 00 353 86 826 6026, www.inismeain. com. Ruairí and Marie-Thérèse de Blacam's 'stunning' stone-and-glass restaurant-with-suites blends into the landscape, allowing majestic views to Galway Bay and the Connemara mountains. On the most remote of the Aran Islands (a stronghold of Irish culture), the enterprise is deeply rooted in sustainable practice. Ruairí de Blacam cooks four-course dinners based on a philosophy of elemental eating, using hyper-local ingredients, including currach-caught lobster and crab from the bay and garden-fresh vegetables. Minimalist suites have a Scandinavian feel: muted colours, wooden floors, hand-designed furnishings; each has a large bed, living space, vast floor-to-ceiling windows, an outdoor seating area. Escape: island explorers are provided with a hotpot lunch, maps and nature guides, bicycles, fishing rods, walking sticks and swimming towels. A breakfast box is delivered to the suite. This is as far from sliced supermarket toast as it gets: expect freshly baked breads, Irish yogurt, cured meat and fish, boiled eggs, soft cheese, and a sweet for elevenses. Restaurant/lounge (dinner served at 8 pm; closed Sun nights). Free Wi-Fi. No background music. 3-acre grounds. Children accepted, by arrangement. 45-min. ferry from Ros a' Mhíl; 7-min. flight from Connemara airport. 5 suites. Per suite B&B from €240. Dinner €55. 2-night min. stay. Closed Oct–Mar.

KANTURK Co. Cork
Map 6:D5
GLENLOHANE HOUSE. Tel 00 353 29 50014, www.glenlohane.com. Stay 'as if with friends' at this informal, yet discreet, 18th-century country house surrounded by acres of landscaped gardens, meadows and fields. The

house, which has belonged to the Sharp Bolster family for seven generations, is filled with heirlooms, family memorabilia and lots of history. Open fires in winter make it a cocooning place to be. Take refuge from the outside world in the deep-red library, its shelves lined with books; take tea in the large, light drawing room. Traditionally furnished bedrooms have lots of space for lounging. There are plenty of pubs and restaurants in town, but guests may choose to dine with the family (by prior arrangement). The Sharp Bolsters are motorcycle enthusiasts; week-long tours in classic cars, motorcycles and high-performance BMW motorcycles can be arranged. Drawing room, library, dining room. Free Wi-Fi. No background music. 250-acre gardens and parkland (chickens, fantail pigeons, sheep, horses). Resident cat and dogs. 1½ miles E of town; plenty of pubs and restaurants. 3 bedrooms (plus 2-bedroom self-catering cottage nearby, suitable for disabled). Per room B&B single €120–€135, double €220–€235. Dinner €50.

KENMARE Co. Kerry
Map 6:D4
SHEEN FALLS LODGE. Tel 00 353 64 664 1600, www.sheenfallslodge.ie. Fall for the views, over Kenmare Bay and the Sheen waterfalls, at this much refurbished 17th-century fishing lodge (Relais & Châteaux) across the suspension bridge from the heritage town. Part of the Palladian Hotels group, it is a luxury set-up with spacious, modern bedrooms, a collection of charming thatched cottages and villas, a fine restaurant and a serene, stylish spa. Seamus Crotty is the manager. Choose among tastefully decorated bedrooms varying in size; some have

enough space, including a lounge area, to accommodate a family. Take tea and light snacks in the sun lounge; sip from an array of Irish whiskeys in the cocktail bar. In the elegant, well-regarded restaurant, chef Philip Brazil serves modern Irish dishes, including home-smoked salmon. Children are 'happily catered for'. There's much activity outdoors as well: salmon fishing, horse riding, kayaking, falconry, clay pigeon shooting – and gentle strolls through woodland or by the riverside. 2 lounges, drawing room, library, study, cocktail bar, restaurant; terrace (alfresco dining). Private dining room. Free Wi-Fi, in-room TV (Sky). Live piano/traditional Irish folk background music. Wedding, function facilities. Spa (sauna, steam room, beauty/holistic therapies), indoor heated pool. Wine cellar (tours by arrangement). 300-acre grounds (woodlands, 19th-century plantation, private stretch of river). Bicycles available to borrow. Children (cots) and dogs (heated stables, £25) welcomed. 66 rooms (1 suitable for disabled; 11 suites), plus 5 villas available for self catering. Per room B&B from €180, D,B&B from €290. Closed Jan (except New Year).

KILKENNY Co. Kilkenny
Map 6:D5
ROSQUIL HOUSE, Castlecomer Road. Tel 00 353 56 772 1419, www.rosquilhouse. com. A short walk from the 'interesting' medieval town, Phil and Rhoda Nolan's 'pleasing' B&B is liked for its good-value bedrooms and praiseworthy breakfasts. Simply furnished bedrooms are equipped with a tea tray and thoughtful extras (hairdryer, iron); the lounge has books and plump sofas. Spoil yourself at breakfast: there are fruit compotes,

organic yogurt, granola, hams and local cheeses; bread, cakes and scones are all home made. Welcoming hosts, the Nolans have ready recommendations of restaurants and day-trips. Lounge; smoking patio. Free Wi-Fi, in-room TV. No background music. Small garden. Close to Kilkenny Golf Club. Children and dogs welcomed. Resident dog. 7 bedrooms (1 suitable for disabled), plus a self-catering apartment. Per person B&B from €35.

KILLARNEY Co. Kerry
Map 6:D4
THE BREHON, Muckross Road. Tel 00 353 64 663 0700, www.thebrehon.com. Soothe the senses at the O'Donahue family's large spa hotel, surrounded by a spectacular mountain landscape. Brian Bowler is the manager. Understated, modern bedrooms are supplied with tea- and coffee-making facilities, bottled water, bathrobes and slippers; take in views of Killarney national park from wall-to-wall windows or a private balcony. Interconnecting rooms and open-plan suites comfortably accommodate a family. In Danú restaurant, chef Chad Byrne serves traditional dishes with a modern twist; informal meals and snacks may be taken in the bar. Children are warmly welcomed with a host of jolly activities, from a secret fairy trail and a junior afternoon tea to the many family-friendly options (swimming pool, pitch-and-putt course, play centre) at sister hotel The Gleneagle, next door. Lounge, bar, restaurant (pre- and post-show menus). Private dining room. Lift. Free Wi-Fi, in-room TV. Background music. Wedding, function facilities. Playroom. Angsana Spa (12-metre indoor Vitality pool, steam room, herb sauna, tropical showers, ice fountain, kubel dusche, spa bath; fitness centre; massage, treatments). Parking. Children welcomed. ½ mile from town centre; INEC is close by. 125 bedrooms (some suitable for disabled; family suites). Per room B&B from €199. Dinner €42.

KINSALE Co. Cork
Map 6:D5
THE OLD PRESBYTERY, 43 Cork Street. Tel 00 353 21 477 2027, www.oldpres.com. Once the residence of the parish priests, Philip and Noreen McEvoy's rambling, 200-year-old B&B stands on a quiet street in the centre of this historic port and fishing town. Filled with memorabilia and antiques, the house retains a characterful air while incorporating the latest technology, including solar-powered heating. Each of the traditionally decorated bedrooms is different: two rooms have a balcony, another has a sunroom and a roof garden with views over the town. Obliging hosts, the McEvoys provide complimentary hot drinks and snacks, and cheese and wine in the afternoon. In the morning, wake to a substantial organic breakfast cooked by the host, a professional chef. Interesting options (perhaps a crab Benedict or hot, fruit-filled crepe) include good vegetarian and vegan options. Sea and river fishing, water sports and golf can be arranged. Sitting room, dining room; patio. Free Wi-Fi, in-room TV (Freeview). Classical/Irish background music. Parking. Children welcomed. Unsuitable for disabled. 9 bedrooms (3 suites in annexe; 2 self-catering; family rooms). Per room B&B €115–€250. Closed Nov–Feb.

LAHINCH Co. Clare
Map 6:C4
MOY HOUSE. Tel 00 353 65 708 2800, www.moyhouse.com. Walk straight into the spectacular scene of Lahinch Bay from Antoin O'Looney's handsome, white-painted mid-19th-century house: a path leads from the lawns through woodland and on to a stony beach. The small hotel has been sympathetically restored: its candlelit conservatory restaurant overlooks the sea; the drawing room is a welcoming spot, with its blazing fire and honesty bar. Most of the bedrooms are charmingly, individually decorated in traditional style – perhaps with a canopy bed, a turf fireplace or a bay-windowed seating nook – but go for the smart, modern suite, which has a freestanding bathtub in the bathroom, and its own spacious conservatory with views of the ocean. At dinner, Matthew Strefford serves a daily-changing tasting menu using home-grown produce and locally landed seafood. Praiseworthy breakfasts include home-made bread and granola. Caroline Enright is the manager. Drawing room, library, restaurant (background music; closed Sun, Mon in low season). Free Wi-Fi, computer provided, in-room TV (Sky). Drying room. 15-acre grounds. 2 miles outside Lahinch; golf course nearby. Children welcomed. 9 bedrooms (4 on ground floor). Per room B&B from €145, D,B&B from €175. Closed Nov–Mar.

MAGHERAFELT Co. Londonderry
Map 6:B6
LAUREL VILLA TOWNHOUSE, 60 Church Street, BT45 6AW. Tel 028 7930 1459, www.laurel-villa.com. Poets may revel in the rich collection of Seamus Heaney books, poems and memorabilia on display at Eugene and Gerardine Kielt's elegant B&B. The poetry of the late laureate is steeped in the surrounding area, now known as 'Heaney country'; Eugene Kielt, a Blue Badge guide, arranges poetry readings and tours to Heaney landmarks. (Almost as legendary are the hostess's afternoon teas, with home-baked cakes and scones.) Named after great Ulster poets, traditionally furnished bedrooms have pictures, paintings and poems. The large garden has mature trees and a poetry trail. Come morning, a breakfast of fresh fruit salad and an Ulster fry-up is served in the panelled dining room. The Kielts also provide an ancestry-tracing service to help guests trace their Northern Irish roots; their large collection of local genealogical and historical materials is fascinating stuff. 2 lounges, dining room; patio. Free Wi-Fi, in-room TV. No background music. Parking. Children welcomed. In the town centre. 4 bedrooms. Per person B&B single £60, double £80–£90. Closed Christmas, New Year.

MOYARD Co. Galway
Map 6:C4
CROCNARAW COUNTRY HOUSE. Tel 00 353 95 41068, www.crocnaraw.ie. Time slows to a gentle pace between Connemara national park and Ballinakill Bay, where Lucy Fretwell runs her genteel Georgian guest house in acres of gardens and rugged meadowland. 'A terrific hostess', she serves afternoon tea with Aga-fresh scones and strawberry jam by a peat fire in the drawing room. Public spaces have a homely, lived-in feel, with flowers, pictures and ornaments; light-filled

bedrooms are traditionally furnished (one has a claw-footed bath in the bathroom). In the morning, tuck in to a generous breakfast – there's home-made soda bread, and produce from the kitchen garden and orchard. Fully licensed. Private parties with a chef can be arranged. Fishing, angling, pony trekking, golf nearby. Dining room, drawing room, snug. Free Wi-Fi. No background music. Gardens (donkeys), orchard. Children welcomed (special rates; under 6 months, by arrangement). 2 miles from Letterfrack. 4 bedrooms. Per person B&B €35–€58. Closed Nov–Apr.
25% DISCOUNT VOUCHERS

NEWPORT Co. Mayo
Map 6:B4

NEWPORT HOUSE. Tel 00 353 98 41222, www.newporthouse.ie. Experience traditional country house hospitality at Kieran Thompson's grand Georgian mansion overlooking the estuary and quay. Catherine Flynn is the long-serving manager. Intricate mouldings, oil paintings and bronzes fill the traditionally decorated public rooms; the high-ceilinged drawing rooms have stuffed bookcases, 'lived-in' sofas and an open fire. In sight of the gardens and river, chef John Gavin's French-influenced five-course menus include produce from the fishery, garden and farm, home-smoked salmon and 'delicious' home-baked bread. Fly fishers, pack your waders: the house's extensive fishing rights allow lines to be cast along both banks of the Newport river and beside Lough Beltra for spring salmon, grilse and sea trout. Drawing room, sitting room, bar, dining room, restaurant. Games rooms. Free Wi-Fi (in public areas and some bedrooms), in-room TV.

No background music. 15-acre grounds, walled garden. Private fishery. Children (cots, high chairs) and dogs (in courtyard bedrooms) welcomed. 7 miles N of Westport. 14 bedrooms (4 in courtyard; 2 on ground floor). Per person B&B €110–€145, D,B&B €175–€210. Closed Nov–mid-Mar.
25% DISCOUNT VOUCHERS

NEWTOWNARDS Co. Down
Map 6:B6

BEECH HILL COUNTRY HOUSE, 23 Ballymoney Road, Craigantlet, BT23 4TG. Tel 028 9042 5892, www.beech-hill.net. Victoria Brann's vividly decorated Georgian-style home has a style all of its own, with beautiful views over the North Down countryside. Painted an earthy red, the stylish entrance hall welcomes visitors with ornate mirrors, a chandelier, huge oil paintings and thick bunches of fresh flowers. Take a seat: the full aspect of meadows spotted with grazing cows, the Holywood Hills beyond, can be seen from the large sofa in the drawing room (where an open fire burns in cool weather). Spacious, traditionally furnished bedrooms, all on the ground floor, are well stocked with a radio, magazines, local reading material, an electric blanket, a tea and coffee tray, and quality toiletries in the bathroom. In the morning, breakfast is taken at the antique dining table. Help yourself from the sideboard heaped with cereals, croissants, fresh fruit salad, a cheese board, ham and yogurt; the Ulster fry, cooked to order, comes with potato and soda breads. Belfast City Airport and the ferries are a 15-minute drive away. Drawing room, dining room, conservatory. Free Wi-Fi, in-room TV

(Freeview). No background music. 1-acre garden. Children over 12 and dogs welcomed. Parking. 4 miles from Holywood. 3 bedrooms (all on ground floor; plus The Colonel's Lodge, available for self-catering). Per person B&B €55.

RAMELTON Co. Donegal
Map 6:B5

FREWIN, Rectory Road. Tel 00 353 74 915 1246, www.frewinhouse.com. Come in time for a fireside tea at Regina Gibson and Thomas Coyle's gracious B&B, in a creeper-covered Victorian rectory on the outskirts of an unspoilt heritage town. An antiques collector and restorer, Thomas Coyle has refurbished the family home 'with flair', returning the stained-glass windows and elegant staircase to their original grandeur, and adding a well-chosen collection of antiques, sink-into-me sofas and real candle chandeliers. Country house-style bedrooms are spacious, with a compact bathroom and views over the wooded grounds; one suite has its own library. Communal breakfasts are praised; candlelit dinners are served by arrangement. Sitting room, library, dining room. Free Wi-Fi. No background music. 2-acre mature wooded garden. Golf, horse-riding, beaches nearby. Resident animals. 3 bedrooms (plus 1-bedroom cottage in the grounds). Per person (sharing) B&B €55–€75. Dinner €45–€50. Closed Nov–Feb (or open by special arrangement).

RATHNEW Co. Wicklow
Map 6:C6

HUNTER'S HOTEL, Newrath Bridge. Tel 00 353 404 40106, www.hunters.ie. In pretty grounds on the banks of the River Vartry – a charming spot for a picnic or an alfresco G&T – this rambling coaching inn retains all the character of a bygone age. Owned by the same family for five generations, it is said to be the longest-running inn in Ireland. Today, brothers Richard and Tom Gelletlie are at the helm. Antiques, old prints and unabashed swathes of chintz are put to good use in the spacious bedrooms (the creaking floorboards add to the charm); many rooms overlook the garden. At lunch and dinner, chef Martin Barry relies on seasonal produce for his traditional menus. Sunday luncheon is a feast. Drawing room, lounge, bar, restaurant. Private dining room. 2-acre garden in 5-acre grounds (river walks). Free Wi-Fi, in-room TV (Freeview). No background music. Children and dogs (by arrangement) welcomed. 2 km SE of Ashford. Golf, tennis, riding, sandy beach, fishing nearby. 16 bedrooms (1 on ground floor). Per person B&B from €65, D,B&B from €95. Closed 24–26 Dec.

25% DISCOUNT VOUCHERS

RECESS Co. Galway
Map 6:C4

LOUGH INAGH LODGE, Inagh Valley. Tel 00 353 95 34706, www. loughinaghlodgehotel.ie. Cast your net in Lough Inagh – land a fishing spot with history. 'Lovely' and 'peaceful', this 19th-century fishing lodge has been owned by the O'Connor family since 1989. Its 'spectacular' position, surrounded by mountain ranges on all sides, is bested only by the river beats – book a day out on one of the hotel's boats, accompanied by an experienced ghillie. Back on land, relax in the sitting room over tea and

a newspaper, surrounded by antiques, old photographs and interesting knick-knacks; open log fires burn in cool weather. At dinner, chef Martina Linnane cooks 'Irish food with French flair', focusing on seafood and Connemara produce; simpler dishes are available in the oak-panelled bar. Retire to one of the traditionally furnished bedrooms afterwards, and wake to morning views of Lough Inagh and the Twelve Bens mountains. Sitting room, bar, library, dining room. Free Wi-Fi, in-room TV (Freeview). No background music. Wedding facilities. 14-acre grounds. Children (cots, high chairs, special menus) and dogs (must be on lead in grounds) welcomed. 13 bedrooms (4 on ground floor). Per room B&B €155–€220, D,B&B €250–€320. Closed Christmas–Feb.
25% DISCOUNT VOUCHERS

STRANGFORD Co. Down
Map 6:B6
THE CUAN, 6–10 The Square, BT30 7ND. Tel 028 4488 1222, www.thecuan. com. Friendly and laid-back, Peter and Caroline McErlean's 200-year-old inn is on the main square of a conservation village on the shores of Strangford Lough. The McErleans have presided for more than 25 years; fans return for the modest but comfortable bedrooms, the popular local pub and the warm, community-hub atmosphere. Traditional roasts in the restaurant are an attraction, too, as is the local seafood, including langoustines freshly caught from the lough. The hosts have put together packages to suit many tastes, from sporty breaks to winning Winterfell experiences inspired by the Game of Thrones TV series. 2 lounges, bar, restaurant (traditional background music). Free Wi-Fi. Wedding/function facilities. Live music events in the summer. Children welcomed. 9 bedrooms (1 suitable for disabled), plus 2-bedroom self-catering cottage. Per person B&B single £57.50–£65, double £42.50–£47.50; D,B&B single £73–£80, double £58–£63.

THOMASTOWN Co. Kilkenny
Map 6:D5
BALLYDUFF HOUSE. Tel 00 353 56 775 8488, www.ballyduffhouse.ie. Come in to oil paintings, fresh flowers, book-lined shelves and open fires – this elegant Georgian country house, amid farmland and gardens, is run as a B&B with 'real style and friendliness'. In a 'fabulous situation' on the banks of the River Nore, Brede Thomas has styled comely country bedrooms (each with lovely, tall windows) with antiques and pretty fabrics; rooms look over river or rolling parkland. 'Delicious' full Irish breakfasts are taken in the elegant dining room; afterwards, the rural life beckons outside: fisherfolk might enjoy a spot of salmon or trout fishing on the Nore; there are country and riverside walks aplenty. Drawing room, library, dining room. Free Wi-Fi. No background music. Fishing, canoeing. Children and pets (by arrangement) welcomed. 1 hour from Dublin. 6 bedrooms. Per person B&B €50.

WATERFORD Co. Waterford
Map 6:D5
FOXMOUNT COUNTRY HOUSE, Passage East Road. Tel 00 353 51 874308, www.foxmountcountryhouse.com. In large, well-kept gardens, Margaret and David Kent's ivy-clad Georgian house

pleases with its country charm. It stands on the Kents' working dairy farm, but this is farmhouse living at its most cosseting, with antiques, family photographs and a grand marble fireplace just right for sitting beside at afternoon tea. (Fancy something stronger? Guests are welcome to bring their own wine and aperitifs.) Homely, traditionally furnished bedrooms have high windows overlooking the garden; a spacious room is suitable for a family. In the morning, breakfast on a wide selection of home-baked breads, eggs from the farm, compotes and preserves made from home-grown fruit; fresh flowers are a cheery addition to the table. Dining room, drawing room. Free Wi-Fi. No background music. 4-acre grounds. Children welcomed; dogs stay in kennels in the grounds. 3 miles SW of the city. 4 bedrooms. Per person B&B €55. Closed Oct–Feb.

WATERVILLE Co. Kerry
Map 6:D4
BUTLER ARMS. Tel 00 353 66 947 4144, www.butlerarms.com. Gazing across the ocean, this welcoming hotel is in a little village on the Wild Atlantic Way. A 'well-run' place, it has been owned by the 'hands-on' Huggard family since 1915. Many of the 'simple, clean and unfussy' bedrooms have stunning views towards Ballinskelligs Bay; some garden rooms have a sitting area with a fireplace, and large doors opening on to the garden. There's a choice of eating and drinking spots: mingle with the locals over light meals, sharing platters and a pint of the family's Huggard pale ale in the 'lively' Fishermen's Bar, or take a seat in the Chaplin conservatory lounge for relaxed lunches and dinners. In the evening, Charlie's restaurant serves 'excellent' Irish cuisine, featuring plenty of local seafood. Lounge, bar, Charlie's restaurant, coffee shop. Free Wi-Fi, in-room TV (Sky). No background music. Wedding, function facilities. Garden. Parking. Golf nearby. Children (family rooms) and dogs welcomed. 36 bedrooms (10 on ground floor). Per room B&B €120–€180, D,B&B €180–€240. Closed Dec–Feb.

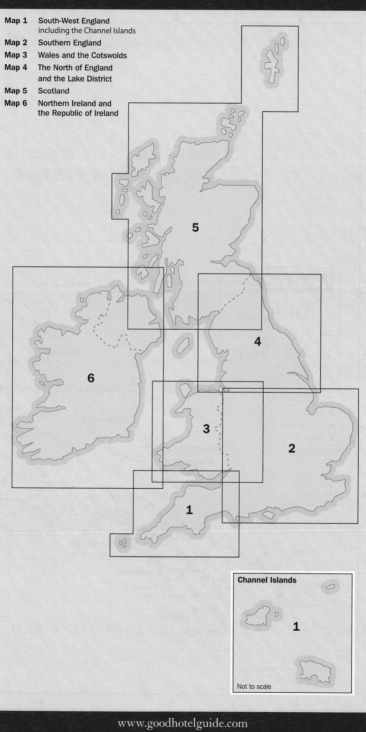

BRITISH ISLES MAPS

Map 1   South-West England
                 including the Channel Islands

Map 2   Southern England

Map 3   Wales and the Cotswolds

Map 4   The North of England
                 and the Lake District

Map 5   Scotland

Map 6   Northern Ireland and
                 the Republic of Ireland

Channel Islands

1

Not to scale

MAP 1 • SOUTH-WEST ENGLAND

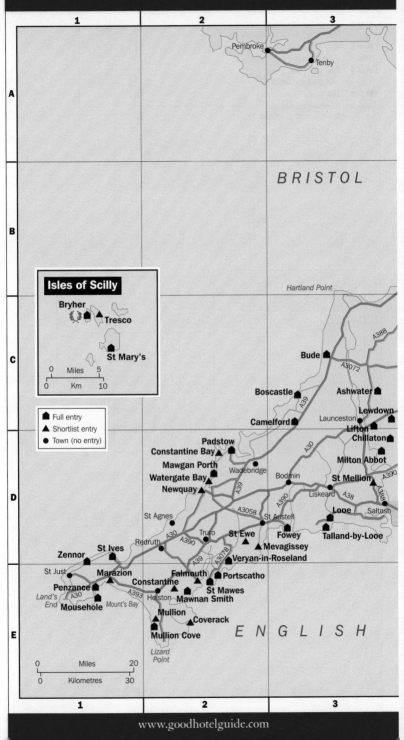

Isles of Scilly

Bryher
Tresco
St Mary's

0   Miles   5
0   Km   10

■ Full entry
▲ Shortlist entry
● Town (no entry)

Pembroke
Tenby

BRISTOL

Hartland Point

A388

Bude
A3072

Boscastle
Ashwater
Lewdown
Camelford
Launceston
Lifton
Chillaton
A39
A30
Milton Abbot

Padstow
Constantine Bay
Mawgan Porth
Watergate Bay
Newquay
Wadebridge
Bodmin
St Mellion
A390
A38
Looe
Liskeard
Saltash
St Agnes
A3058
St Austell
St Ewe
Fowey
Talland-by-Looe
Truro
Mevagissey
Redruth
A30
A390
Veryan-in-Roseland
St Ives
Zennor
St Just
Marazion
Constantine
Falmouth
Portscatho
Penzance
St Mawes
Helston
Mawnan Smith
Land's
End
A30
A393
Mount's Bay
Mousehole
Mullion
Coverack
ENGLISH
Mullion Cove
Lizard
Point

0   Miles   20
0   Kilometres   30

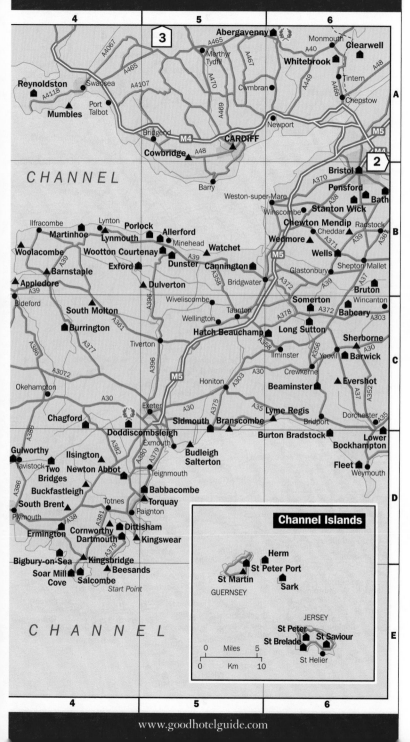

MAP 2 • SOUTHERN ENGLAND

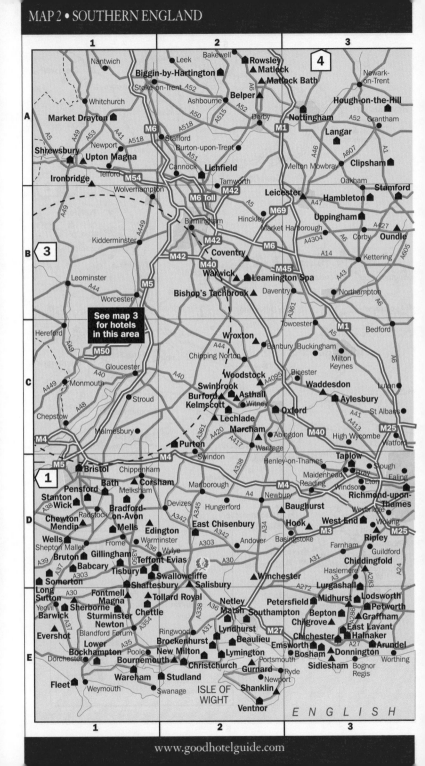

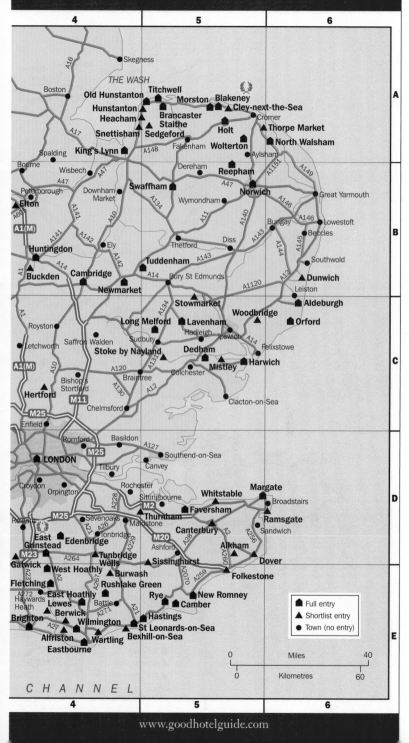

4 **5** **6**

Skegness

Boston

THE WASH

Old Hunstanton **Titchwell** **Morston** **Blakeney**
Hunstanton **Cley-next-the-Sea**
Heacham Cromer
Brancaster
Staithe **Thorpe Market**
Snettisham **Sedgeford** **Holt** **North Walsham**
Fakenham **Wolterton**
King's Lynn Aylsham

Spalding

Bourne
Wisbech **Reepham**
Peterborough Dereham
Elton Downham **Swaffham** **Norwich** Great Yarmouth
Market Wymondham
Ely **Bungay** Lowestoft
Huntingdon Thetford Diss **Beccles**
Buckden Southwold
Cambridge **Tuddenham** Bury St Edmunds **Dunwich**
Newmarket Leiston
Stowmarket **Aldeburgh**
Royston **Long Melford** **Lavenham** **Woodbridge** **Orford**
Letchworth Saffron Walden Hadleigh Ipswich
Stoke by Nayland Sudbury **Dedham** Felixstowe
Hertford Braintree **Mistley** **Harwich**
Bishop's Colchester
Stortford
Chelmsford Clacton-on-Sea
Enfield

Romford
LONDON Basildon
Southend-on-Sea
Tilbury Canvey
Croydon Rochester **Margate**
Orpington Sittingbourne **Whitstable** Broadstairs
Reigate Sevenoaks **Faversham** **Ramsgate**
East **Edenbridge** **Thurnham** Sandwich
Grinstead Maidstone **Canterbury**
Gatwick Tonbridge Ashford **Alkham**
Fletching **Tunbridge** **Sissinghurst** **Dover**
West Hoathly **Wells** **Folkestone**
Burwash
East Hoathly **Rushlake Green** **New Romney**
Haywards **Lewes** **Rye**
Heath Battle **Camber**
Brighton **Berwick** **Hastings**
Wilmington **St Leonards-on-Sea**
Alfriston **Wartling** **Bexhill-on-Sea**
Eastbourne

▲ Full entry
▲ Shortlist entry
● Town (no entry)

0 Miles 40

0 Kilometres 60

C H A N N E L

4 **5** **6**

MAP 3 • WALES AND THE COTSWOLDS

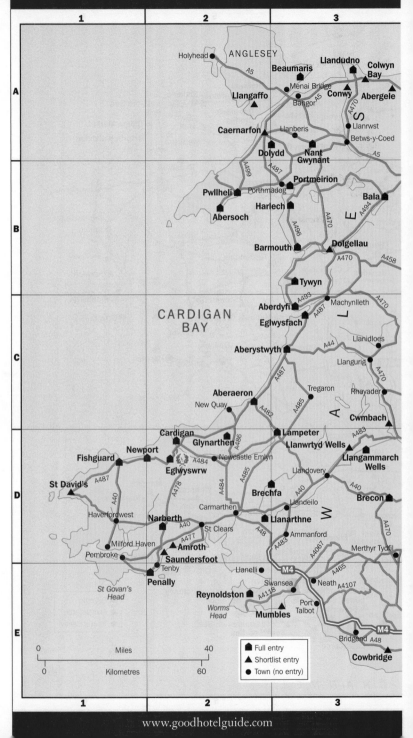

1   **2**   **3**

ANGLESEY

Holyhead

A5

Beaumaris

Llandudno

Colwyn Bay

Menai Bridge

Llangaffo

Bangor *A5*

Conwy

Abergele

A

Llanberis

Llanrwst

Caernarfon

Betws-y-Coed

A5

Dolydd

Nant Gwynant

A499

A487

Portmeirion

Pwllheli

Porthmadog

Bala

A494

Harlech

Abersoch

A496

A470

Dolgellau

B

Barmouth

A470

A458

Tywyn

A493

Aberdyfi

Machynlleth

A470

CARDIGAN BAY

Eglwysfach

A487

Llanidloes

Aberystwyth

A44

Llangurig

A470

C

A487

Rhayader

Aberaeron

Tregaron

New Quay

A485

Cwmbach

A482

Cardigan

Lampeter

A483

Glynarthen

A486

Llanwrtyd Wells

Newport

Newcastle Emlyn

Llangammarch Wells

Fishguard

A484

Eglwyswrw

Llandovery

St David's

A487

A485

Brechfa

A40

Brecon

D

A478

A484

Llandeilo

Haverfordwest

Carmarthen

Llanarthne

A40

Narberth

St Clears

Ammanford

A40

Milford Haven

A477

Amroth

A48

A483

Merthyr Tydfil

Pembroke

Saundersfoot

A4067

Tenby

Llanelli

A465

Penally

M4

Neath *A4107*

St Govan's Head

Reynoldston

Swansea

Port Talbot

A4118

Worms Head

Mumbles

Bridgend *A48*

M4

E

	Miles		40
0			
0	Kilometres		60

Cowbridge

- 🏠 Full entry
- ▲ Shortlist entry
- ● Town (no entry)

1   **2**   **3**

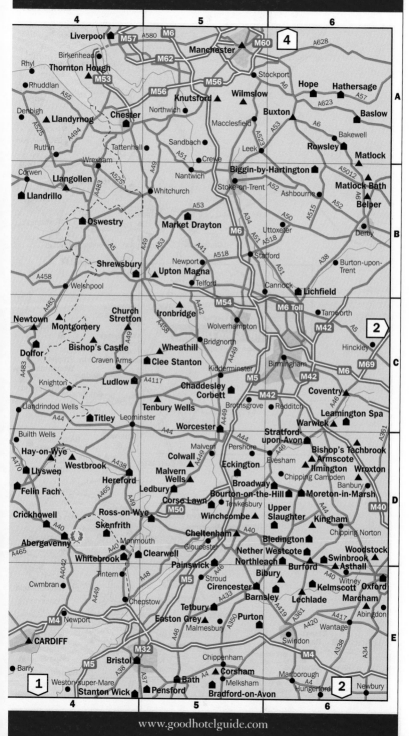

MAP 4 • THE NORTH OF ENGLAND AND THE LAKE DISTRICT

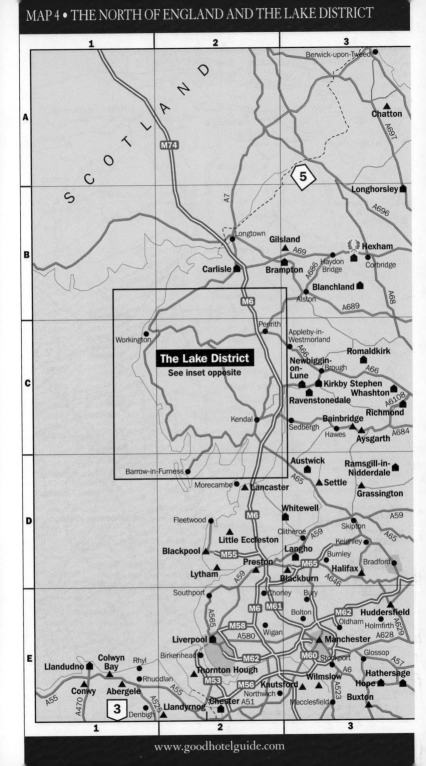

SCOTLAND

Berwick-upon-Tweed

Chatton

M74

5

Longhorsley

A7

A697

A696

Longtown

Gilsland

Hexham

A69

Corbridge

Carlisle

Brampton

Haydon Bridge

A686

Blanchland

A68

M6

Alston

A689

Penrith

Workington

Appleby-in-Westmorland

Romaldkirk

The Lake District

See inset opposite

Newbiggin-on-Lune

A66

Brough

A66

Kirkby Stephen

Whashton

A6108

Ravenstonedale

Richmond

Kendal

Bainbridge

Sedbergh

Hawes

A684

Aysgarth

Barrow-in-Furness

Austwick

Ramsgill-in-Nidderdale

A65

Settle

Grassington

Morecambe

Lancaster

Whitewell

A59

M6

Skipton

A59

Fleetwood

Clitheroe

A59

Keighley

A65

Little Eccleston

Langho

Burnley

Bradford

Blackpool

M55

Preston

M65

Halifax

A646

Lytham

A59

Blackburn

Southport

Chorley

Bury

M62

Huddersfield

A565

M6

M61

Bolton

Oldham

Holmfirth

A629

M58

Wigan

A628

Liverpool

A580

Manchester

Birkenhead

M62

M60

Stockport

Glossop

A57

Llandudno

Colwyn Bay

Rhyl

Rhuddlan

Thornton Hough

M53

M56

Knutsford

Wilmslow

A6

Hathersage

Conwy

Abergele

A55

Northwich

A523

Hope

A470

A525

Llandyrnog

Chester A51

Macclesfield

Buxton

3

Denbigh

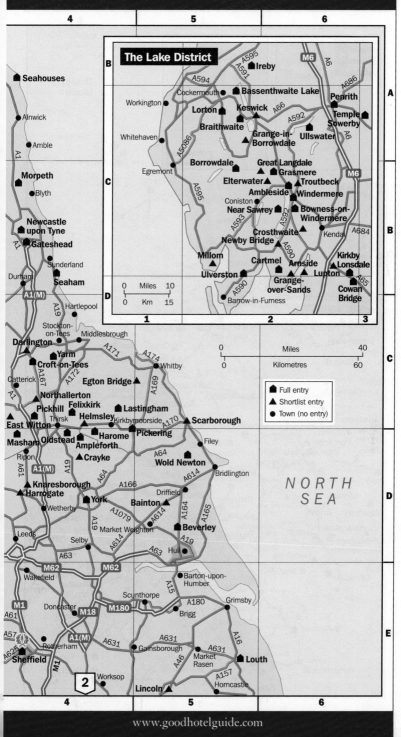

The Lake District

Ireby
A595
A591
A594
M6
A6
A686

Cockermouth
Bassenthwaite Lake
Workington
Penrith
Lorton
Keswick
A66
A592
Temple Sowerby
Braithwaite
Whitehaven
Grange-in-Borrowdale
Ullswater
A5086
Egremont
Borrowdale
Great Langdale
Grasmere
M6
A595
Elterwater
Troutbeck
Ambleside
Windermere
Coniston
Near Sawrey
Bowness-on-Windermere
A593
A592
Crosthwaite
Kendal
A684
Newby Bridge
A590
Millom
Cartmel
Arnside
Kirkby Lonsdale
Ulverston
Grange-over-Sands
Lupton
A65
A590
Cowan Bridge
Barrow-in-Furness

0 Miles 10
0 Km 15

Seahouses
Alnwick
Amble
A1
Morpeth
Blyth
Newcastle upon Tyne
Gateshead
Sunderland
A1
Durham
Seaham
A1(M)
Hartlepool
A19
Stockton-on-Tees
Middlesbrough
Darlington
A171
Whitby
Yarm
A174
Croft-on-Tees
A172
Egton Bridge
A169
Catterick
A167
Northallerton
Felixkirk
Lastingham
Pickhill
Helmsley
A170
Scarborough
Thirsk
Kirkbymoorside
East Witton
Harome
Pickering
Masham
Oldstead
Filey
Ampleforth
A64
Ripon
Crayke
Wold Newton
A61
A1(M)
A19
Bridlington
A64
Knaresborough
A166
Driffield
Harrogate
York
Bainton
A164
A165
Wetherby
A1079
A614
Beverley
Leeds
A19
Market Weighton
Hull
Selby
A614
A63
A19
M62
M62
Wakefield
Barton-upon-Humber
A15
Scunthorpe
M1
Doncaster
M18
M180
A180
Grimsby
A61
Brigg
A57
A625
Rotherham
A631
Gainsborough
A631
A16
Sheffield
M1
A46
Market Rasen
Louth
Worksop
A631
Lincoln
A157
Horncastle

NORTH SEA

Miles 40
Kilometres 60

■ Full entry
▲ Shortlist entry
● Town (no entry)

2

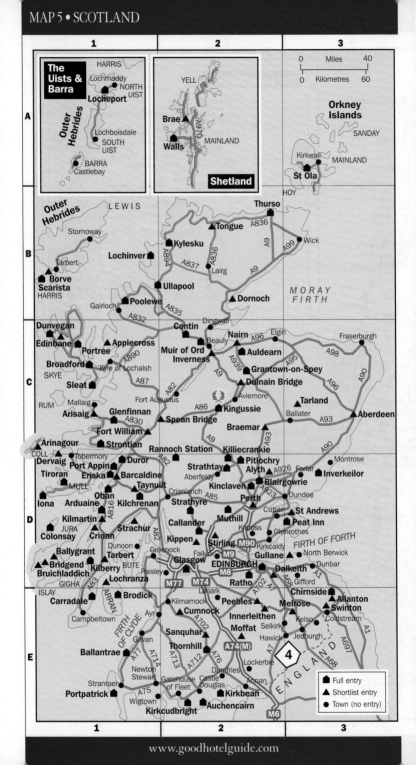

MAP 5 • SCOTLAND

The Uists & Barra

HARRIS
Lochmaddy
NORTH UIST
Locheport
Outer Hebrides
Lochboisdale
SOUTH UIST
BARRA
Castlebay

YELL
Brae
Walls
MAINLAND
A970
Shetland

0 — Miles — 40
0 — Kilometres — 60

Orkney Islands
SANDAY
Kirkwall
MAINLAND
St Ola
HOY

Outer Hebrides
LEWIS
Stornoway
Tarbert
Borve
Scarista
HARRIS

Lochinver
Kylesku
A894
A837
A837
A836
Lairg
Tongue
A836
A9
A99
Wick

Ullapool
Dornoch
MORAY FIRTH

Gairloch
Poolewe
A832
A835

Dunvegan
Edinbane
Portree
Applecross
Broadford
SKYE
Kyle of Lochalsh
A890
Sleat
A87
RUM
Mallaig
Contin
Dingwall
Beauly
Muir of Ord
Inverness
A862
A96
Nairn
Elgin
Auldearn
A939
A9
Grantown-on-Spey
A95
A96
A98
Fraserburgh
A90

Arisaig
Glenfinnan
A830
Fort William
Spean Bridge
Fort Augustus
A86
A82
Aviemore
Kingussie
Ballater
Dulnain Bridge
Tarland
A93
Aberdeen

Arinagour
COLL
Dervaig
Tobermory
Tiroran
MULL
Strontian
Port Appin
Duror
Eriska
Barcaldine
Taynuilt
Rannoch Station
A82
Strathtay
Aberfeldy
A9
Killiecrankie
Pitlochry
Alyth
A926
Forfar
Montrose
Inverkeilor
A90

Iona
Oban
Arduaine
Kilchrenan
A819
Strathyre
Crianlarich
A85
Kinclaven
Blairgowrie
A923
Dundee
Perth
Cupar
St Andrews
Peat Inn
Kilmartin
JURA
Strachur
A82
Muthill
Kinross
Glenrothes
Colonsay
Crinan
Dunoon
Callander
Kippen
Stirling
M90
Kirkcaldy
FIRTH OF FORTH
Ballygrant
Tarbert
Greenock
Falkirk
M9
Gullane
North Berwick
Bridgend
Kilberry
BUTE
Glasgow
EDINBURGH
Dalkeith
Dunbar
Bruichladdich
Lochranza
Paisley
M8
Ratho
A702
A7
Gifford
GIGHA
M77
M74
A1
ISLAY
Carradale
Brodick
ARRAN
Lanark
Peebles
Melrose
Chirnside
Allanton
Cumnock
Kilmarnock
Innerleithen
Swinton
Kelso
Coldstream
A1
Campbeltown
FIRTH OF CLYDE
Ayr
Moffat
Selkirk
Sanquhar
A702
Hawick
Jedburgh
A697
A68
Ballantrae
Thornhill
A74(M)
4
A77
A714
A76
Lockerbie
Newton Stewart
A712
Castle Douglas
Stranraer
Girvan
A713
Dumfries
Annan
ENGLAND
Portpatrick
A75
Gatehouse of Fleet
Wigtown
Kirkbean
M6
Kirkcudbright
Auchencairn

Full entry
Shortlist entry
Town (no entry)

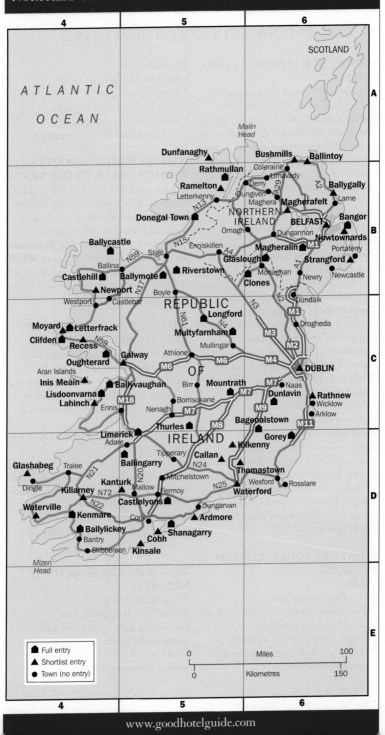

SCOTLAND

ATLANTIC

OCEAN

Malin
Head

Dunfanaghy   **Bushmills**   **Ballintoy**

Rathmullan   Coleraine
                   Limavady

Ramelton   Derry   A29   **Ballygally**
Letterkenny   Dungiven   Larne
                   Maghera   **Magherafelt**

Donegal Town   NORTHERN   **Bangor**
                   IRELAND   **Newtownards**
                   Omagh   **BELFAST** M1   Portaferry
Enniskillen   Dungannon
Ballycastle   A4   **Magheralin**   **Strangford**
            Sligo   **Glaslough**
Castlehill **Ballymote** **Riverstown** Monaghan   Newry   Newcastle
            N59   **Clones**   A1
Ballina   N2   Dundalk
Newport   Boyle   M1
Westport   Castlebar   Drogheda
                   REPUBLIC
Moyard **Letterfrack**   **Longford**   M3
Clifden **Recess**   **Multyfarnham**   N4   M2
            N59   M3
Oughterard   Athlone   Mullingar
Aran Islands   **Galway**   M6   M6   M4   **DUBLIN**
Inis Meáin   **OF**
Lisdoonvarna **Ballyvaughan** Birr **Mountrath** M7 Naas **Rathnew**
Lahinch   M18   Borrisokane   **Dunlavin** Wicklow
         Ennis   Nenagh   M7   M9   Arklow
         Thurles   M8   **Bagenalstown** M11
Limerick   **IRELAND**   **Gorey**
         Adare   **Kilkenny**
Glashabeg Tralee Tipperary **Callan** **Thomastown**
Dingle   **Ballingarry** N24   Wexford Rosslare
Kanturk   N20 Mitchelstown   N25 **Waterford**
Killarney N72 Mallow Fermoy
Waterville N22 **Castlelyons** Dungarvan
Kenmare   Cork   **Ardmore**
Ballylickey   **Shanagarry**
Bantry   **Cobh**
Skibbereen   **Kinsale**
Mizen
Head

Legend:
- ■ Full entry
- ▲ Shortlist entry
- ● Town (no entry)

Miles   0 ———————— 100
Kilometres 0 ———————— 150

FREQUENTLY ASKED QUESTIONS

HOW DO YOU CHOOSE A GOOD HOTEL?

The hotels we like are relaxed, unstuffy and personally run. We do not have a specific template: our choices vary greatly in style and size. Most of the hotels in the Guide are family owned and family run. These are places where the needs and comfort of the guest are put ahead of the convenience of the management.

YOU ARE A HOTEL GUIDE – WHY DO YOU INCLUDE SO MANY PUBS AND B&BS?

Attitudes and expectations have changed considerably since the Guide was founded in the 1970s. Today's guests expect more informality, less deference. There has been a noticeable rise in the standards of food and accommodation in pubs and restaurants. This is demonstrated by the number of such places suggested to us by our readers. While pubs may have a more relaxed attitude than some traditional hotels, we ensure that only those that maintain high standards of service are included in our selections. The best B&Bs have always combined a high standard of accommodation with excellent value for money. Expect the bedrooms in a pub or B&B listed in the Guide to be well equipped, with thoughtful extras. B&B owners invariably know how to serve a good breakfast.

WHAT ARE YOUR LIKES AND DISLIKES?

We like
* Flexible times for meals.
* Two decent armchairs in the bedroom.
* Good bedside lighting.
* Proper hangers in the wardrobe.
* Fresh milk with the tea tray in the room.

We dislike
* Intrusive background music.
* Stuffy dress codes.
* Bossy notices and house rules.
* Hidden service charges.
* Packaged fruit juices at breakfast.

WHY DO YOU DROP HOTELS FROM ONE YEAR TO THE NEXT?

Readers are quick to tell us if they think standards have slipped at a hotel. If the evidence is overwhelming, we drop the hotel from the Guide or perhaps downgrade it to the Shortlist. Sometimes we send inspectors just to be sure. When a hotel is sold, we look for reports since the new owners took over, otherwise we inspect or omit it.

WHY DO YOU ASK FOR 'MORE REPORTS, PLEASE'?

When we have not heard about a hotel for several years, we ask readers for more reports. Sometimes readers returning to a favourite hotel may not send a fresh report. Readers often respond to our request.

WHAT SHOULD I TELL YOU IN A REPORT?

How you enjoyed your stay. We welcome reports of any length. We want to know what you think about the welcome, the service, the building and the facilities. Even a short report can tell us a great deal about the owners, the staff and the atmosphere.

HOW SHOULD I SEND YOU A REPORT?

You can email us at editor@goodhotelguide.com. Or you can write to us at the address given on the report form opposite, or send a report via the GHG's website: www.goodhotelguide.com.

Please send your reports to:

The Good Hotel Guide, 50 Addison Avenue, London W11 4QP, England, and stamped normally.

Unless asked not to, we assume that we may publish your name. If you would like more report forms please tick ☐ Alternatively, you can either photostat this form or submit a review on our website: www.goodhotelguide.com

NAME OF HOTEL: _____

ADDRESS: _____

_____

Date of most recent visit: _____ Duration of stay: _____

☐ New recommendation   ☐ Comment on existing entry

Report:

Please continue overleaf

I am not connected directly or indirectly with the management or proprietors

Signed: _____

Name: (CAPITALS PLEASE) _____

Address: _____

_____

Email address: _____

INDEX OF HOTELS BY COUNTY
(S) indicates a Shortlist entry

ALPHABETICAL LIST OF HOTELS

(S) indicates a Shortlist entry